DATE DUE

DATE		ISSUED

D1304679

DISCARD

Chicago Public Library

REFERENCE

Form 178 rev. 11-00

Microsoft®

Microsoft® Windows® 2000 Performance Tuning Technical Reference

John Paul Mueller and
Irfan Chaudhry

IT Professional

PUBLISHED BY
Microsoft Press
A Division of Microsoft Corporation
One Microsoft Way
Redmond, Washington 98052-6399

Library of Congress Cataloging-in-Publication Data
Mueller, John, 1958-
    Microsoft Windows 2000 Performance Tuning Technical Reference / John Paul Mueller,
Irfan A. Chaudhry.
       p. cm.
    Includes index.
    ISBN 0-7356-0633-1
    1. Microsoft Windows (Computer file)   2. Operating systems (Computers)   I. Chaudhry,
Irfan A., 1972- II. Title.
    QA76.76.O63 M82   2000
    005.4'4769--dc21   00-029219

Printed and bound in the United States of America.

1 2 3 4 5 6 7 8 9   WCWC   5 4 3 2 1 0

Distributed in Canada by Penguin Books Canada Limited.

A CIP catalogue record for this book is available from the British Library.

Microsoft Press books are available through booksellers and distributors worldwide. For further information about international editions, contact your local Microsoft Corporation office or contact Microsoft Press International directly at fax (425) 936-7329. Visit our Web site at mspress.microsoft.com. Send comments to *mspinput@microsoft.com*.

Acquisitions Editor: David Clark
Project Editor: Lynn Finnel
Technical Editors: Jack Beaudry, Robert Lyon, Lynn Lunik

Contents

Part III Tuning the Network

14   Microsoft Windows 2000 and the Internet   405

PART V Special Tuning Tools

Tables

Dedication

This book is dedicated to our wives, Rebecca Mueller and Noreen Chaudhry, who have given up many hours of comfort for the reader's illumination.

Acknowledgments

Thanks to Rebecca Mueller for helping to complete this book. She researched and compiled some of the information that appears in this book (especially the Glossary). She also did a fine job of proofreading the first draft and page proofing the final result. Lynn Lunik, Robert Lyon, and Jack Beaudry deserve thanks for their technical edit of this book. They greatly added to the accuracy and depth of the material you see here. In addition, they worked very hard in researching some additions for the book. Matt Wagner, our agent, deserves credit for helping us get the contract in the first place and taking care of all the details that most authors don't really think about. We really appreciate the thoughtful and kind way that he dealt with some of the problems we had while writing this book. Certainly, he made our jobs much easier than they could have been under the circumstances.

The technical support staff at Microsoft deserves credit for answering the questions that helped fill in the blanks, especially when it came to finding some of the product features we talk about in this book. The vendor support staffs listed in Chapter 16 were also quite helpful. Likewise, we'd like to thank the people on the various Internet newsgroups we visited.

Finally, we would like to thank David Clark, Tracy Thomsic, Lynn Finnel, and the rest of the production staff for their assistance in bringing this book to print. It was a real joy working with all of them and both of us look forward to working with them on future projects.

Introduction

Everywhere you look in the trade press today, someone's talking about performance issues. It doesn't matter if the article is about local area networks (LANs), wide area networks (WANs), metro area networks (MANs), the Internet, an individual server, or even a single component within that server. Everyone wants to get the performance they paid for, and, if possible, get better performance than they expected. That's why performance tuning and optimization (PTO) is so important. Time is money, and everyone wants to reduce costs by reducing the time required to perform tasks on their network.

Okay, so management is thrilled that it takes half the time today to get a report out than it did yesterday. What's in PTO for you? If an administrator can tune a server to provide even a modicum of performance improvement, management is certain to take notice because of the savings in new equipment and user efficiency. In addition, users react favorably when they see that network tasks are completed in record time. In short, the techniques in this book will reduce your workload, enhance how management views your capabilities, and make you popular with the people using the network.

What You Learn

What can you expect to learn by reading this book? This book concentrates on PTO problems that occur in a variety of places. We begin by looking at the server (both hardware and software), and then move to the network, special devices like storage area networks (SANs), and even the user. Obviously, we mention relevant infrastructure problems that could cause poor Windows 2000 performance, but that isn't the main focus of the book. We also cover generic tuning topics like application performance and tuning.

Besides generic tuning topics, we look at some of the more important Windows 2000 Server-specific topics like Active Directory optimization. The book addresses issues regarding replication of Active Directory services across enterprise networks, multiple domains, and single domains in LAN or WAN networks. Since Active Directory services is a new technology, many administrators aren't certain how to proceed when it comes to tuning this essential part of Windows 2000. Armed with the knowledge in this book, you'll be able to deal with most of the Active Directory PTO problems that can occur on a system.

Any book that wants to truly address the needs of today's administrator needs some material on working with the Internet. The Internet introduces a wealth of difficult-to-find, yet frustratingly widespread, tuning problems. The fact that network bandwidth of the Internet is at a premium doesn't help matters much. As part of the Internet coverage, we review Internet-specific applications. In addition to this, we explain new features that Windows 2000 has that allow the administrator to fine tune the operating system when hosting Web sites on the server.

Windows 2000 Server is an operating system that requires in-depth knowledge in order to gain the most from the product. This book helps you understand how to approach PTO for a Windows 2000 Server. You get a lot of hands-on techniques and pointers to other places where you can find additional information. This book contains both theoretical and real-world information about PTO in the world of Windows 2000 Server.

Who Should Use This Book?

Anyone who wants to know more about the benefits of Windows 2000 Server PTO is a potential candidate for reading this book. We tried very hard to make every procedure clear, every bit of theory easy to understand, and every real-world experience as simple as we could. However, there are limits to what authors can cover in one book. *Microsoft Windows 2000 Performance Tuning Technical Reference* targets the experienced Microsoft Windows NT or Windows 2000 administrator. If you're a novice who's never worked with Windows before, you're definitely going to have trouble figuring out the contents of this book.

There are certain assumptions that we make about your current capabilities and knowledge level. For example, we assume you're already familiar with the Windows 2000 operating system and don't need additional information to complete common tasks that administrators should be familiar with. We also expect you to have some knowledge of common computer terms, although the Glossary in the back of the book should help with any terms you're unfamiliar with. This isn't a book that helps novice readers discover how to work with Windows 2000, nor does it assist intermediate readers with the vagaries of security or application installation.

What You Won't Find Here

It's important you understand that this is a book about PTO. We definitely cover just about everything you can think of when it comes to the issue of performance and how to correct performance problems through the use of tuning and optimization. However, this isn't the book you want to buy to learn to set up your system. We assume you already have a server in place and have spent some time working with it. You should have some ideas on what performance problems your server has when you pick this book up. We make every effort to point out other pitfalls you need to know about.

This book also has very little in the way of troubleshooting information. If you can't figure out why your network interface card (NIC) no longer communicates with the network, this book isn't going to help you find an answer. We're assuming your hardware works, for the most part, and all you really need to do is tune it to get optimum performance.

Finally, you won't find specific answers for your particular piece of equipment. This book is generalized PTO. What this means to you, as a reader, is that you find lots of suggestions on how to fix a problem, but that you probably have to perform some amount of research to find the specific solution that works for your equipment. Consider this book a flashlight that casts light on the topic of PTO. Even though we can shine a light for you, you still need to interpret what the light makes visible.

How This Book Is Structured

This book is packed with a lot of useful information about PTO. The following paragraphs summarize the book's structure and help you understand how the book can help you. Each description provides an overview of the chapter in question, which means you can gain a better appreciation of what the book can do to help you by reading these few paragraphs.

Chapter 1 Introduction to Performance Tuning and Optimization

This chapter contains information you need to understand the importance of PTO and how it can affect the performance of the server. The main purpose of this chapter is to provide you with a good reason to optimize your system, other than the fact that the boss has asked you to do it. Any task becomes easier if you have a personal reason to care and the knowledge to understand why the task is important.

Chapter 2 The Microsoft Windows 2000 Kernel

Even though the subject of the operating system kernel can be found in books that cover Windows 2000 Server, we feel it's absolutely necessary for this particular text because you need to understand the architecture behind the processes that take place under Windows 2000 Server. Also, changes that have taken place at the kernel level of the Windows 2000 operating system should be discussed and described so you understand how those changes might help with PTO. We take a look at a variety of kernel topics in this chapter, including an in-depth look at the hardware abstraction layer (HAL), Windows 2000 subsystems, Windows 2000 managers, and Windows 2000 applications.

Chapter 3 Processes and Threads and Memory Management

This chapter goes into detail about the theory behind processes, threads, multiprocessing, and memory management under Windows 2000. We explore both symmetric multiprocessing (SMP), which is the most common type of multiprocessing in use today, and asymmetric multiprocessing (AMP).

The purpose of this chapter is to explain how the multiprocessing capabilities of Windows 2000 can help improve the efficiency of the server. However, the chapter's purpose isn't just to define these terms, but to explain how features such as single-threaded processes, multithreaded processes, and thread priorities can affect performance of the server. You need this information to understand how multiprocessing and multithreading can have a negative effect on the server if not correctly tuned or configured.

Part of understanding processes and threads is learning how to view and work with them. This chapter will show you how to use various tools to view, monitor, and tune the performance of processes and threads. We'll look at both common and developer tools as part of the discussion. This part of the chapter represents the most direct use of process and thread theory that you can achieve.

This is one of those chapters that will seem long on theory and short on practical use. However, theory is very important when it comes to PTO. We also use this information in later chapters. For example, in Chapter 5 we use the information in this chapter to help you understand how to avoid processor bottlenecks.

Chapter 4 Performance Monitoring in Microsoft Windows 2000

This chapter provides a detailed look at the built-in System Monitor tool in Windows 2000. (This tool is actually part of the Performance MMC snap-in, all of which we cover in this chapter.) System Monitor is a tool Windows 2000 administrators must understand if they're looking to do any form of performance optimization. You also have an opportunity to review changes made to the Performance Monitor tool under Windows 2000. The chapter goes into detail on how to monitor the hundreds of counters available to administrators for performance analysis, but more importantly, it explains how to record data so they have results that are truly useful when analyzing PTO issues.

Chapter 5 Diagnosing Processor Bottlenecks

Processor-bound applications—those that rely heavily on the processor to perform their task—are quite common on Windows 2000 Server because of Microsoft's COM focus. This chapter begins by telling you how to detect and diagnose processor bottlenecks. Once you know how to recognize processor bottleneck problems, we review ways of correcting this problem. In addition to looking at current processor technology, this chapter also explores upcoming processor technologies that will reduce or eliminate common processor bottlenecks.

Chapter 6 Diagnosing Memory Bottlenecks

Understanding the causes of memory bottlenecks in your system is critical to diagnosing many kinds of Windows 2000 Server performance issues. For example, memory fragmentation—the way applications are placed within memory—can reduce the efficiency of Windows 2000. Memory bottlenecks don't just affect the operating system.

Poorly written applications can cause a myriad of problems, including inefficient use of memory by processes or threads. You might find that an application won't run because the server lacks enough memory to do so, yet the application will report an unrelated error to the user. In addition, application memory leaks cause a slow degradation of the server over time.

Of course, there are hardware-related problems that affect the Windows 2000 Server as well. For example, using error-correcting code (ECC) memory can improve server reliability, but often at the expense of server performance.

This chapter provides a multistep process for you to check for various types of memory problems. You learn to determine if a memory bottleneck exists; whether the cause of the bottleneck is the operating system, application, or hardware; and how to correct the problem.

Chapter 7 Diagnosing Disk Bottlenecks

This chapter helps you understand the causes of and cures for disk activity-related bottlenecks on your server. While Component Object Model (COM) or a spreadsheet application loads the processor, database applications load the disk drive. In short, it pays to know what type of application the server will run so you can predict which part of the server architecture will become the bottleneck.

We begin by helping you learn what you need to do to detect disk bottleneck problems under Windows 2000. We then look at how an administrator can correct those problems using built-in tools found in Windows 2000.

Of course, there are some unique areas of discussion for disk drives. We explore disk technologies such as RAID-5, mirroring, and duplexing, and how these technologies can help increase the performance of the server—for example, how RAID-5 can affect read/write performance of the server. Finally, since the enterprise server is moving toward external disk units, we cover performance issues related to technologies like SANs.

Chapter 8 Network Problems

The whole reason to install a server is to share resources of all types on a network. That's why network tuning is such an important issue for this book. Of course, given the complexity of network setups, it pays to look at sources of problems on the individual server first, and then look at network tuning issues. That's why this important chapter appears after the individual server-tuning chapters in the book—we're looking at a progression of simple to complex.

As in the past two chapters, this chapter begins with the sources of network bottlenecks. This means looking at features such as network topologies since different topologies have different problems.

Once you know the problem is network-related, you can utilize the tools available to you such as System Monitor and Network Monitor to analyze the network problem. System Monitor is packed with several network-related counters. The chapter explains the differences between these counters and what counters are the most commonly used when detecting network problems.

The chapter then goes into changes you can make at the Windows 2000 Server to correct these network-related problems. For example, there are several TCP/IP settings you can adjust. Another approach is to modify registry settings to increase server response time, in particular when running an Internet-based application. In addition to operating system-specific solutions, we also look at the other environmental factors that affect server performance like the hardware used to create the network and the kinds of tasks users typically perform on the network.

Chapter 9 Microsoft Active Directory Services and Tuning

In this chapter, we explore issues relating to replication of Active Directory services. Since Active Directory services is a new feature of Windows 2000, this chapter does spend a little time explaining how Active Directory services affects you, especially when it comes to performance. We then look at how the administrator can optimize Windows 2000 to increase performance of Active Directory services. The chapter covers items the administrator should watch for like slow network connections. A large part of the discussion centers on methods that can help decrease the time it takes for Active Directory replication.

Chapter 10 New Tuning Features in Microsoft Windows 2000

Windows 2000 has several new features that increase the performance of applications running on a Windows 2000 Server. This chapter explores how you can use each one to performance tune Windows 2000. For example, we look at what you can do to make your Web site react faster, yet more consistently, to user requests through the user of CPU and bandwidth throttling. We review how you can use process accounting to verify the amount of resources that each process is using on your Web site. Finally, we explain the latest method to use less bandwidth—HTTP compression.

This chapter doesn't stop with new Internet features. Microsoft has improved multiprocessor support in Windows 2000, so we review how this affects PTO. There are also some new technologies covered in this chapter like quality of service (QoS), Resource Reservation Protocol (RSVP), and Network Load Balancing (NLB).

Chapter 11 Capacity Planning

Most people have a basic understanding of what capacity is about—it relates to the server's ability to handle a specific load level. If the server had the same load every day, it would be easy to predict the capacity required to support more users or another application. However, real networks have shifting loads of various types. One application might load the server, while another could load the disk.

This chapter covers the topic of capacity planning and what exactly it is. We touch on how the administrator can use methods and tools already covered in the book to develop a plan that predicts capacity requirements in the future. This means explaining how the administrator can use these tools to analyze trends in server usage today and use historical context as a basis for predicting future needs. One of the more important, real-world topics in this chapter is the issue of what the vendor tells the administrator versus what the product actually supports.

In addition to these topics, we'll discuss some issues you may not have thought to add to your capacity planning strategy like the importance of planning for a reliable system, as well as one that can handle a larger load.

Chapter 12 Microsoft Windows 2000 and Its Versions

If Windows 2000 came in just one size, one set of tuning types could potentially cover many of the issues that administrators face, at least at a generic level. However, there are multiple versions of Windows 2000 to deal with and Microsoft has slated each one to cover a particular kind of environment, which means tuning tips for one version of Windows 2000 don't necessarily work for the other versions. Windows 2000 Server is offered in three versions:

- Standard Edition
- Advanced Server
- Datacenter Server

This chapter covers the key differences between each of these versions and when you want to deploy one over the other to help with PTO issues. This chapter explores how switching from one version to the other can be part of an organization's capacity planning. Finally, we take a real-world look at some of the tuning technique differences between one server version and another.

Chapter 13 Microsoft Windows 2000 and Clustering

One way to increase the performance of applications and file/print services on a Windows 2000 Server is to implement clustering. This chapter covers the new clustering features found in Advanced and Datacenter versions of Windows 2000. The chapter also reviews the Windows 2000 cluster technology and how you can install and deploy the service. Also covered is the topic of cluster designs and what each solution has to offer in terms of performance, scalability, and redundancy.

Chapter 14 Microsoft Windows 2000 and the Internet

Many environments have deployed or will deploy Windows 2000 Server as their Internet server of choice. This leads to issues regarding performance of the server under the constant and heavy traffic over the Internet. Windows 2000 technologies such as Processor Quotas and Accounting are covered in detail in this chapter. The ability to assign quotas is new to Windows 2000 and specifically Web sites running on a Windows 2000 Server. The chapter has examples on how to set these quotas and then monitor them. The chapter also explores available Web technologies such as Active Server Pages (ASP) and how selecting the right technology can contribute to your performance-tuning needs.

Chapter 15 Microsoft Windows 2000 Resource Kit Performance Tools

This chapter provides an overview of performance monitoring and enhancing tools in the Windows 2000 Resource Kit. We definitely don't cover the whole resource kit since doing so would require a book in and of itself. Microsoft normally includes a wealth of tools in the resource kit that help the administrator locate problem areas on the server. These tools can also point out areas where the server needs to be tuned, which is how we approach the topic in this chapter.

You'll be surprised at the number of new tools found in this version of the Windows 2000 Resource Kit. We don't cover all the new tools, but we look at some new tuning options that you might not have known existed in the past. For example, we review the Clear Memory utility, which is designed to clear the server memory for you and prevent certain types of memory fragmentation problems. We also look at the Page Fault Monitor, a tool designed to help you see when a particular application uses excessive amounts of memory or to determine when it's time to perform a memory upgrade on your server.

Chapter 16 Third-Party Tuning Tools

This chapter provides you with an overview of third-party tuning tools. The intent of this chapter is to give you some idea of what's available out there and where to find it. Third-party tuning tools can help reduce the time required to perform certain types of server tuning or eliminate the need for manual tuning in the first place.

This chapter is divided into four software categories. The main category is shareware tools. Shareware is a relatively inexpensive way to experiment to see what tool features you need. Some shareware is of such high quality that it exceeds what you find in shrink-wrapped software in both performance and functionality.

We also look at three kinds of shrink-wrapped software. This chapter provides some ideas on the types of general administration, hardware-oriented, and network-specific tools available to you. As previously mentioned, however, there are a lot of tools out there and only a little space in which to cover them. This chapter is designed to provide you with ideas of what you might want to look for to complete your tuning toolbox.

Conventions Used in This Book

This book uses special icons to help you find information that you need faster or to highlight its importance. You'll also find that some icons are used to tell you about special operating system requirements or to warn you about dangers of using specific techniques. The following list tells you about each of these icons and how you should interpret them.

Note Notes tell you about interesting facts that don't necessarily affect your ability to use the other information in the book. We use Note boxes to give you bits of information that we've picked up while using Microsoft Windows 2000 or products like Microsoft Visual Studio.

Tip Everyone likes tips, because they tell you new ways of doing things that you might not have thought about before. Tip boxes also provide an alternative way of doing something that you might like better than the first approach we provided.

Caution This means watch out! Cautions almost always tell you about some kind of system or data damage that occurs if you perform a certain action (or fail to perform others). Make sure you understand a Caution thoroughly before you follow any instructions that come after it.

More Info The Internet contains a wealth of information, but finding it can be difficult, to say the least. The More Info boxes help you find new sources of information on the Internet that you can use to improve the way you manage your network or learn new techniques. You'll also find newsgroup More Info boxes that tell where you can find other people to talk with about Windows 2000. Finally, More Info boxes help you find utility programs that make working with Windows 2000 faster and easier than before.

Planning This is a special box that helps you understand the requirements you need to satisfy before you start to use a procedure or technique within the book. For example, if you want to install a new product on your server, you might need to perform some preinstallation steps first. In some cases, the preparation has nothing to do with the server. Perhaps you need to set up some paperwork before you perform a technique to ensure that all the results are properly recorded.

Real World

Sometimes you need to separate theory from practice. A technique might appear to work all the time in theory. Only when you spend some time performing the technique do you see the rather large pothole in the road. The Real World box is intended to help you see the pothole before you use a particular technique. It's intended to relate experiential knowledge based on someone else's experience.

Part I
An Overview of Performance Tuning and Optimization

Chapter 1
Introduction to Performance Tuning and Optimization

Performance tuning and optimization or PTO—sounds like one of those mundane courses you take in college or something you do because the boss tells you to. Because you're reading this, you must be at least a little interested in the subject, but perhaps it's for the wrong reason. When you talk about performance, tuning, and optimization, think race cars—think excitement! The main purpose of this book is to show you how to get the most out of your network with the least amount of effort. We're also hoping, however, that we can turn this rather mundane task into something that's both fun and interesting.

Every day, you do PTO without necessarily realizing it. When you adjust the tracking on your VCR, change the temperature in your bedroom, or play around with the graphic equalizer on your stereo, you are fine tuning and optimizing the performance of your equipment.

In the computer world, PTO is as necessary as any other administrative task that you perform. This is one of the few administrative tasks, however, that the user really notices. Imagine sitting in the coffee break room after you tune the system and hearing someone remark about how fast the network is running today. What will that do for you? PTO ensures your Microsoft Windows 2000 Server is running as efficiently as possible. It's also a task you do for yourself. A network that's running well draws fewer complaints and allows you to get more interesting tasks completed.

Performance tuning Microsoft Windows 2000 involves more than just adjusting a few operating system parameters. When you have either responsiveness or stability problems with your Windows 2000 Server, you need to take many considerations into account. The situation could be caused by a poorly written application, a weak network topology design, or a hardware failure. There are a lot of places to look for performance problems, many types of fixes you can implement to tune the system, and various types of optimization you can use depending on your goal.

In this book, you examine the most common issues behind Windows 2000 Server performance problems. You explore how to detect these problems and then how to resolve them. You also delve into other aspects of PTO, including capacity planning. Of course, the real reason you'll want to read this book is to look good for the boss and your coworkers! Performance tuning and optimization is all about making your current equipment do more. How many bosses do you know who hate to save a buck? Obviously, making the network faster and more error free will go over well with your coworkers too. We're willing to bet you'll be a hit with both your coworkers and the boss, and end up with fewer network problems by the time you finish this book.

Capacity planning goes hand in hand with PTO—a well-thought-out strategy for the future of your enterprise network helps to avoid many of the performance issues you may face with Windows 2000. The book also focuses on running Windows 2000 Server for Internet purposes. With more and more people using Windows 2000 as the platform on which their Web sites run, you need to understand how the latest improvements to the operating system let you gain the highest performance for your sites.

Why Is PTO Important?

The benefits you gain from a properly tuned server go beyond a box that is humming along. If your Windows 2000 Server is correctly tuned, it has a positive effect on every aspect of your network, from the equipment itself to the users attaching to the server. The following paragraphs describe a few of the benefits of having a well-tuned server running on your network.

Lower Equipment Costs

Performance problems hit every network—and every network administrator has to deal with them—so don't feel alone when performance becomes a problem for your network. Some misinformed network administrators attempt to throw hardware at the problem—they increase RAM, add an additional hard drive or two, and may even unnecessarily replace a questionable server. All this is done in an attempt to fix a performance problem that might better be addressed by simply replacing an old application. Hardware solutions like this may correct the problem in the short term, but they seldom offer the best solution in a situation where the exact cause of poor performance is still an unknown.

If these administrators instead tried tuning a server using the data collected on the network, they may have found a solution to the problem without having to throw money at replacement hardware. Many problems that seem to be caused by a lack of hardware are actually caused by the software. Often, software problems can be corrected with an updated version of the software or a patch.

One company noticed that its Web site was not responding as quickly as it did when it was first created. After much troubleshooting, the company found a message transfer agent (MTA) service running on one of the servers that was taxing the CPU. Because of the pressure the network administrator was feeling from management to get the site to respond the way it used to, he decided to run the MTA service on a dedicated server. Unfortunately for the network administrator, this did not correct the problem; in fact, it only added to the problem because he now had an additional server on the network for which there was no use.

It is usually best to explain to management the benefits of troubleshooting the problem using PTO—how it can save not only time and money, but how it can also help avoid future problems. Remember, there is no one else more willing to listen to methods on how to save money than management. Keeping the total cost of ownership (TCO) for equipment as low as possible helps keep their accounts balanced and everyone happy.

Increased User Productivity

A poorly tuned Windows 2000 Server can result in system downtime. System downtime equates to expense in the corporate world. When you have an entire department unable to access server resources or work, or—in the worst-case scenario—an entire company down, a corporation can lose millions of dollars in a single day. A server that is showing system degradation can result in a decrease of user productivity. To meet your goal of increased productivity, it is imperative that you first establish a strategy. Even organizations with high system performance demands can benefit from a PTO-based strategy.

When running any kind of customer service department, you need to expect and address the shortcomings in system performance brought on by high system demand. A sales department unable to input customer orders because of system downtime is obviously not good for business. In some cases, high system demand may only be resolved through additional servers. This is where the importance of capacity planning is critical. Capacity planning accurately predicts the needs of your environment before you need them. In Chapter 11, "Capacity Planning," you learn about the subject, not only from a server point of view, but also from the application, network, and client perspective.

Improved User Attitude

A slow-responding server or a server continually offline or requiring regular rebooting can result in frustrated end users. Persistent problems such as the earlier scenario of sales people who can't keep up with customer orders because of downtime eventually result in reduced productivity because of the frustration caused by constant interruptions in their work. System users should be able to concentrate on work assignments without worrying that services available through the network or individual servers may fail at any moment. A reduction in the frequency of critical services going offline improves user attitude. As the system administrator, you have the ability to affect user attitude through planning and ongoing PTO.

Greater Reliability Due to Lower Equipment Stress

Each of us feels stress at some point in the day. But does equipment feel stress? Actually, equipment stress can result from over utilization or from improper tuning of a server. An example of equipment stress is a disk bottleneck that affects the hard disks of your system. If your computer becomes bottlenecked, this means that the operating system is constantly accessing the hard drives; this may result in the decreased reliability of the drives. Drive reliability may be challenged if disks experience prolonged or improper use due to necessary manual shutdowns with the operating system in an inaccessible state. Typically, repeated "dirty" restarts cause hard disk stress. It's true—stress is stress whether man or machine!

Reduced Application Errors

Your server may suffer from a processor bottleneck, disk bottleneck, or some other performance-tuning issue, but you may not be in what all system administrators fear—a "system down" situation. End users may describe the "network" as running a little slow, but they can still get their work done. Productivity comes to a complete halt as a result of application errors. The operating system may be running, and users able to connect to server resources, but the one application they are trying to reach is inaccessible. This type of application nonavailability leads to frustration on the part of the end user and may be referred to incorrectly as a server problem.

Application errors may be the result of an incorrectly installed application, a bug in the application software, incorrect tuning of the application itself, a performance-tuning issue with the server, or any combination of these. Since it is our goal to approach PTO from the operating system level, it is necessary to quickly identify opportunities to performance tune variables within our control: namely, to coordinate application-specific problems such as incorrect installation or an application bug to the responsible party while addressing server performance tuning and, in some instances, performance tuning of applications. Our approach to participate in the reduction of application errors begins with understanding operating system elements within our control.

Applications that have made performance counters available to the Windows 2000 Performance console allow you to monitor application-specific performance. In addition to application-specific performance counters, you can combine monitoring application and operating system performance through operating system-specific performance counters. The comparison of application-specific performance counters combined with operating system-specific performance counters yields results as the valuable analytical tool the Performance console was designed to be. We provide an overview of the Performance console as part of our discussion of PTO in the section entitled "Overview of the Performance Console." It's accurate to state that understanding tuning requirements for applications occurs through use of the Performance console. Reducing the number of application errors results from identifying the source of the issue, which may be possible through review of application-specific performance counters.

Reduced Administrator Troubleshooting Time

We've all been there; spending hours, days, and nights in front of an administrator's console pulling our hair out in an attempt to get a server running the way it did or the way we know it can. Then, having gone through gallons of coffee and repeated calls to our spouses promising we'll be home soon, we realize that the problem was remedied by a simple patch available from the Internet.

You can avoid such problems with consistent PTO. By paying attention to how the server is performing, you may detect problems more easily, which allows you to make corrections. Accurate corrections benefit both you and your end users. In addition, understanding how to diagnose performance issues helps reduce the time spent remedying them.

An example would be experiencing hard disk thrashing and not immediately diagnosing the processor as the problem, when instead the problem is likely due to low memory. Correlating a cause (disk thrashing) with an effect (low memory) is a benefit gained by understanding the Performance console and the System Monitor and Performance Logs and Alerts applications.

Overview of the Performance Console

In Windows 2000, the primary tool for monitoring system performance is the Performance console. The Performance console helps a system administrator accurately pinpoint many performance problems that occur in Windows 2000. Identification of performance issues occurs by monitoring system hardware and software through counters. A counter is an object designed by either the operating system designer or the application designer as a measurable indicator of function for the respective object. Counters can be as simple as the number of packets transmitted or as complex as the number of instances of an object class. Counters can be roughly categorized as either hardware counters or software counters.

Hardware counters monitor the number of visits to the device. The physical disk device, for example, keeps a count of disk transfers made, expressed as transfers/sec. Figure 1-1 illustrates the processor and memory hardware counters being monitored.

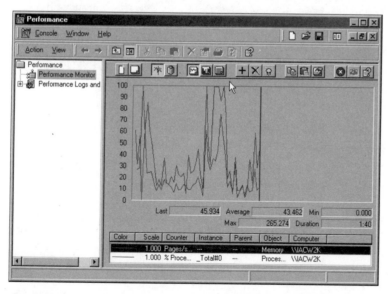

Figure 1-1.   *At first glance, the information displayed by the Performance console may not be decipherable. Can you tell if a bottleneck exists?*

Software counters monitor activity related to application software running on a server. Microsoft SQL Server 7.0 is an example of application software with counters available to the Performance console. A widely reviewed application counter for SQL Server is the User Connections counter. This counter accurately monitors the number of users connected to SQL Server database application. As part of troubleshooting issues related to the number of users and performance of SQL Server with increased user connections, you can review the User Connections counter by monitoring for user connections during a known peak period. Review of statistical information from the Performance console simplifies the troubleshooting process.

The Performance console is an extremely user-friendly application. With a few clicks of the mouse, you begin to monitor your system and can even log data. The available modes to display data in the Performance console using the System Monitor snap-in include chart, histogram, or report views. (See Figure 1-2 for an example of the histogram view.)

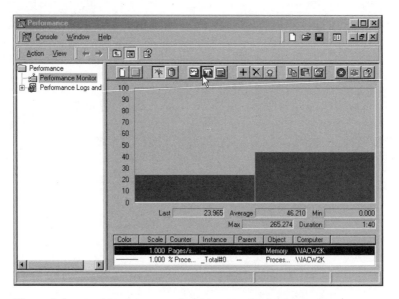

Figure 1-2. *Performance console histogram display.*

In the chapters covering bottlenecks and other performance issues, you learn to interpret the Performance console results for successful diagnoses and resolution of performance-tuning issues. Chapter 7, "Diagnosing Disk Bottlenecks," for example, defines some performance counters to track in pursuing disk bottlenecks.

What Is a Bottleneck?

The next time you drink from a 16-ounce bottle of your favorite beverage, notice how the neck helps to restrict the flow of liquid out of the bottle. In this case, the neck is there for a good reason—to prevent people from pouring the soda all over themselves. The neck can be considered a bottleneck as it is restricting the flow of the soda. The literal definition of bottleneck!

Similarly, bottlenecks in the computer world pertain to the part of the computer that is restricting the flow of data. Although the analogy is a little rough, our goal as system administrators is to reduce bottlenecks as much as possible. Our familiarity with the System Monitor in the Performance console is a good starting point. As you will discover, it is possible to use the Performance console to address bottlenecks of various forms: processor, memory, disk, and so on. Let's examine processor bottlenecks first.

Processor Bottlenecks

The simplest form of processor bottleneck is one where the processor is utilized to its maximum. Processor bottlenecks can exist with lower utilization levels, however, and that's when it may become more difficult to diagnose and correct such problems. Chapter 5, "Diagnosing Processor Bottlenecks," covers processor-bound applications. Knowing which applications tend to be processor hogs allows you to be prepared for potential problems with your system. Remember, you can avoid most performance issues by staging and configuring the server right the first time. So, if you know that a certain application requires a dual processor environment, attempt to deal with it now, if possible, rather than later. In Chapter 5, you also review current processor technologies available to Windows 2000, allowing you to determine which processor platform is right for your environment.

Memory Bottlenecks

Memory bottlenecks may result from a shortage of RAM, which can then lead to reduced performance of the overall system. In Chapter 6, "Diagnosing Memory Bottlenecks," you learn the signs your machine exhibits if a memory bottleneck plagues your system. You also learn methods to correct the problem, including software configuration and related hardware solutions.

Disk Bottlenecks

Hard disks store programs and the data that programs process. A minor pause while working in an application that is disk intensive may indicate the hard disk is a bottleneck. Additionally, if memory is tight the disk begins chattering, typically as a result of swapping data to the virtual memory. A memory-driven problem such as this is common in many environments. One configuration parameter that we as system administrators tend to underestimate when outlining the specifications for the server is memory. When memory problems do begin we should not be surprised. Over time the number of user connections may increase as the number of software applications running on the server increases. Part of good PTO is keeping track of such information, allowing you to better estimate how much memory is needed in the server. Even though increasing the memory in a server is a viable solution to some disk bottlenecks, it isn't necessarily right for every disk issue. In Chapter 7, "Diagnosing Disk Bottlenecks," you explore other methods to circumvent this problem through new disk technologies, such as storage area networks (SANS).

Network Bottlenecks

In our quest to address network bottlenecks, we address a complex problem. There are so many parts to a network, how can we possibly find a single bottleneck? Or is more than one device causing the bottleneck? One of the complexities of designing networks is keeping all the individual parts working together. So, to say that network bottlenecks may be the most difficult to detect out of all the bottlenecks covered in this book may in fact be an understatement. Since networks are composed of routers, switches, backup devices, workstations, servers, links, and an array of protocols, we must make an attempt to broadly categorize the areas listed above. It goes without saying that the server is not always the cause of the problem! Chapter 8, "Network Problems," covers many of the reasons behind network bottlenecks, including network topology limitations. Your network's topology is the foundation of your environment, and, like any structure, its strength and reliability depends on how solid the foundation is.

What Is Capacity Planning?

Capacity planning is not limited to those in an enterprise network environment or large organization. Capacity planning is imperative for any environment, especially if you want to avoid performance-tuning problems. Capacity planning involves keeping records of performance data for your server and network environment, which you can use when considering future upgrades or expansion. Performance data records help you analyze trends that may be occurring on a server or servers. You may find higher process utilization over time, or even a decrease. Either way, you can make better decisions when determining what hardware or software resources you need.

PTO and the Internet

At one point, having a simple Web page meant a company had a presence on the Internet. This Web site's purpose was to serve as a marketing tool; it contained basic company facts, e-mail addresses, or contact information. Now, the needs of customers have changed. A phone number and a contact person no longer suffice. Customers have more sophisticated demands that require the creation of customer-focused Web sites. In response, companies now have to create Web sites that not only are more elaborate, but that also require greater hardware resources, software resources, and bandwidth.

How does all this fit into the subject of PTO and the Internet? The increase in demand on system resources leads to systems requiring a higher level of performance tuning and optimization. Running an application that is accessible over the Internet is not the same as running one over your local area network (LAN) and wide area network (WAN).

When you release applications over the Internet, there is one factor you cannot account for and that is the traffic your Web site may generate. A corporate Web site can have hundreds of thousands of hits per day and, in some cases, per hour. As the system administrator of such a site, you need to be ready for performance-tuning issues. These issues may call for increasing the amount of hardware in the Web servers, adding more Web servers to an existing cluster (you review performance optimization through clustering in Chapter 13, "Microsoft Windows 2000 and Clustering") or tuning the application.

Windows 2000 encompasses many new improvements to the operating system that allow for more detailed tuning of the server when running on the Internet. In Chapter 14, "Microsoft Windows 2000 and the Internet," you explore new features and other aspects of hosting your Web site on a Windows 2000 Server. This includes information on how to handle seasonal Web site traffic, dealing with performance inhibitors that you can't stop, and the performance benefits you can gain from multiple providers.

Summary

This chapter gives you many reasons to performance tune your Windows 2000 Server. Which one of these really convinces you to go ahead and reevaluate the situation with your server is unique to your environment, which differs from the next person's. What you should keep in mind is that the end result will be the same. Most important, network performance will be faster, and you'll be spending less time chasing down ongoing problems with the system and more time working on new and exciting projects. We reviewed some of the more common performance issues you will face with Windows 2000 Server, such as processor bottlenecks, disk bottlenecks, and memory bottlenecks. We have dedicated entire chapters to each of these problems and others not mentioned in the chapter, including Active Directory replication. In these chapters, we'll explain how to detect, correct, and avoid these problems.

PTO requires a thorough understanding of the technology behind the problem. For example, chasing down a network bottleneck requires that you understand how traffic is sent from the back of a server, down a wire (or fiber), and across your network. Only then can you understand the logic behind the provided solution. For this reason, each chapter that discusses a performance problem at hand introduces enough background material to give you all the information you need to tackle the problem head on.

Chapter 2
The Microsoft Windows 2000 Kernel

The central part of the Windows 2000 operating system is the kernel—you can't do anything without it. The kernel is the very core, the essence, of what makes Windows 2000 unique. As a result, any performance monitoring, tuning, and optimization efforts you do involve the kernel.

Of course, that begs the question of what precisely the kernel is. Obviously, it's a very important part of the operating system, but that doesn't tell you where this rather mysterious object resides. Physically, the kernel is in the %SystemDrive%\System32 directory of your hard drive. It's made up of a multitude of dynamic-link libraries (.dll) and executable files (both .exe and .com) files. From a processor perspective, it's the part of the operating system that executes in protected mode. In short, the kernel is the engine; you don't see it, but it makes the whole operating system run.

Surrounding the kernel (protecting it might be a better way to think of it) is the executive. The executive is the part of the operating system core that applications will access and it provides the operating system's personality. An application will never access the kernel directly; it will always access the kernel through the executive. So, it's very common to view the kernel and the executive as a single entity—one part can't do anything without the help of the other. When we're talking about the executive in the chapter, we'll actually be talking about the interface to the kernel. Some documentation doesn't make a distinction between the two, so it's helpful to know that the kernel and the executive are closely related and virtually inseparable on the Windows platform.

Note This chapter isn't meant as the end-all of Windows 2000 low-level operating system feature discussions. To do that, you need an entire book, or perhaps even more than one book. The point of this chapter is to acquaint you with the kernel and its associated components from a theoretical and a performance perspective. What you should walk away with is a better understanding of how this engine that makes Microsoft Windows run also affects Windows' performance as a whole. View this as an introductory discussion. We'll look at many of these issues again in later chapters in much greater depth.

We'll begin the tour of Windows 2000 with the "Executive Service" section. It helps to think of the Windows 2000 executive as the person sitting in the corner office of a company. This person takes the grand view of everything happening within the company, but leaves the details to others. That's how the Windows 2000 executive views things. It's at the top of the Windows 2000 operating system organization, but the actual labor required to make the operating system work is handled by others in the organization.

In the "Hardware Abstraction Layer (HAL)" section of the chapter, we'll move from the very top of the operating system to the very bottom. The HAL is what allows Windows 2000 to communicate with the hardware of your system. Since Windows NT and Windows 2000 were originally written to work on more than one machine type (platform), the HAL allows all platform versions to use the same application and kernel code. In theory, the only thing that changes when you move to a different machine is the HAL. In practice, you're going to need new device drivers and other platform sensitive components to move from one platform to another.

We've now looked at the very top of the Windows 2000 operating system and the very bottom. The portions in between these two extremes consist of subsystems (major divisions of operating system labor) and managers (portions of the operating system that are responsible for completing a specific task). We'll look at the Windows 2000 subsystems first in the "Windows 2000 Subsystems" section. This section will pay special attention to subsystems that you can easily optimize, and a little less time on subsystems that you need to know about but can't really tune easily. Next, we'll look at the managers in the "Windows 2000 Managers" section. While the managers will get some mention in other sections, this is where you'll look for detailed information.

Riding on top of everything is the application. We're not talking about standard applications in this case—these applications help the operating system provide certain levels of compatibility with other operating systems. In short, you won't see anything about Word in the "Windows 2000 Applications" section of the chapter. You will, however, learn about how Windows 2000 provides Win32, Win16, and POSIX support for the applications that you'll use.

Executive Service

As previously mentioned, you can think of the Windows 2000 executive service as the person sitting in the corner office. This person takes the grand view of everything happening within the company but leaves the details to others. Let's talk a little bit about what that means in operating system terms. The executive is the part of the operating system that a client (an application, for example) interacts with, just as clients interact with some level of executive in most companies. As a result, you can look at the executive as something that finds work to do and then distributes it to other parts of Windows 2000 to perform.

Tip You can find most of the Windows 2000 executive in the NTOSKRNL.EXE file in the %SystemDrive%\System32 directory. This file also contains part of the actual kernel. There are a few significant facts to remember about NTOSKRNL.EXE from a performance perspective. For one thing, the version of this file that you use depends on your machine model. When you install multiprocessor support on a Windows 2000 machine, one of the files you change is NTOSKRNL.EXE. In fact, this is the file that reflects the machine's personality from a user-application level and, therefore, affects performance to a great degree.

User Mode versus Kernel Mode

Before we go much further, this is a concept that you need to know about when working with the lower-level portions of Windows (any version). There are two kinds of security in your machine: one is software-based and controlled by the operating system; the second is hardware-based and controlled by the processor. The 80286, Intel processor architecture includes four rings of protection for the software running on the machine. The inner ring is surrounded by a layer, which is surrounded by a layer, with this process continuing until a total of four rings (layers) envelope the processor core. You can look at these rings as hardware-based security—or walls around a castle. To pass through each ring, you need to know the secret password and tell it to the guard at the gate.

Ring 0 is where the operating system resides. This ring is fully protected from any access by any application in any other ring. Ring 3, on the other hand, is where application programs reside and it's not protected much at all. Microsoft has designated these two rings as kernel mode (Ring 0) and user mode (Ring 3). So, when you hear these terms, you know that kernel mode is fully protected, while user mode isn't protected much at all.

Understanding the Executive Exported Functions

Now that we've discussed the difference between user and kernel mode, let's look at what the executive does for you. The executive deals with five kinds of tasks (or functions in programming terms). These functions appear in Table 2-1. Each function operates in either user mode and addresses user needs, or kernel mode and addresses operating system needs.

Table 2-1.   Executive Exported Functions

Function Type	Mode	Description
API (Application Programming Interface) Calls	User	These functions allow applications to perform various tasks on the computer. For example, an application calls one of these functions to read or write data on the hard disk. You find the actual interface for these functions in NTDLL.DLL. Most developers now use libraries and other methods to access the API functions without having to resort to using low-level calls.

(continued)

Table 2-1. *(continued)*

Function Type	Mode	Description
Internal System	User	An application could theoretically call these functions, but they're designed for use by operating system applications instead. These calls allow an operating system application to create a paging file on disk or to perform a local procedure call (LPC). They also allow an application to ask the operating system about low-level information like the security ID (SID) of an object. In many cases, this last type of information is available through higher-level calls in a more usable format.
Driver	Kernel	Drivers operate in kernel mode because they need to access the operating system directly and often require low-level access to system resources. Most developers use the Windows 2000 driver development kit (DDK) to access these kinds of functions.
Internal System Component	Kernel	Even though various operating system managers have areas of specialty that they take care of, there's also a need for these managers to communicate. For example, the I/O manager may need to send data to the graphics subsystem for display on screen.
Internal Component	Either	Components, those COM entities that have taken over the Windows 2000 operating system, often require special access to the operating system. For example, a Microsoft Management Console (MMC) snap-in may require special knowledge about the processes currently executing on the system in order to provide the user with the proper feedback. Components, depending on what they're designed to do, can operate in either kernel or user mode, but not both.

The overview of executive functions in Table 2-1 provides just a hint of what the executive provides in the way of support. Figure 2-1 shows a view of NTOSKRNL.EXE using a Windows 2000 Support Tool called the Dependency Walker. Dependency Walker also ships with Microsoft Visual Studio (the example uses the copy in the 6.0 version, but you can find Depends in other versions of Visual Studio and the separate Microsoft programming products) and allows you to see how one .dll or .exe depends on other files. Highlighted in the middle right pane is one of the many functions that NTOSKRNL.EXE exports. There are, in fact, 1,209 exported functions in this one executable file, which gives you some idea of its importance just from an application interface perspective.

Tip Microsoft provides Depends and other utilities as part of the Windows 2000 CD, but the Setup program doesn't install them automatically. You'll find the Windows 2000 Support Tool setup in the \Support\Tools directory of the Windows 2000 CD. Double-click the Setup icon in the folder to start the installation process. What you'll get is a wealth of tools that will allow you to perform a wide variety of tasks on your system, including PTO.

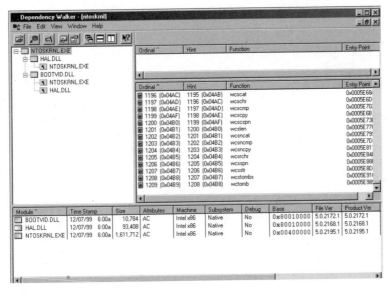

Figure 2-1.   *The Dependency Walker utility provided with Visual Studio can be a helpful tool in learning about Windows 2000 from a low-level perspective.*

An Overview of Executive Components

The executive does more than wait in the background and provide exported functions for applications of various types to use. It also contains several of the managers that we'll discuss in detail later. These managers fall into two categories: (1) they answer needs outside the executive, referred to in Table 2-2 as "External," or (2) they provide internal support for other managers, referred to in Table 2-2 as "Internal." Refer to Table 2-2 for a specific overview of these managers and their areas of responsibility. We'll discuss these managers in more detail in the section entitled "Windows 2000 Managers."

Table 2-2.   Overview of Managers Associated with the Executive

Name	Responsibility	Description
Cache Manager	External	The cache described here is the one that places recently accessed data from the hard drive into memory. This allows the I/O subsystem (which includes the I/O manager, device drivers, and other components) to access the data faster during subsequent requests. Of course, you can also cache writes to the hard disk to accept data more efficiently.
I/O Subsystem	External	The purpose of this manager is to accept application requests for various types of device access and present those requests to the device drivers in a device-independent manner. The I/O subsystem doesn't actually perform the device interaction.

(continued)

Table 2-2. *(continued)*

Name	Responsibility	Description
Local Procedure Call (LPC) Facility	Internal	There always have to be rules for passing data between processes. The LPC facility passes data between clients and servers on the local machine. It's actually an optimized version of the remote procedure call (RPC) facility used by other data passing technologies like the Distributed Component Object Model (DCOM).
Object Manager	Internal	Allows the operating system to create, manage, and delete objects. This includes abstract data types that represent operating system objects like threads, processes, and synchronization objects.
Process and Thread Manager	External	Even though the kernel manages the processes and threads for Windows 2000, it doesn't provide an interface for requesting this service. The executive provides functions that allow applications to create and terminate both processes and threads.
Run-Time Library	Internal	You can call this the miscellaneous category. An operating system does more than just pass data back and forth; it massages the data in some way. The run-time library provides the arithmetic, string, data type conversion, and structure processing functions of the operating system.
Security Reference Monitor	External	This manager enforces security on the local computer. Obviously, this means ensuring that any access to operating system resources is authorized. The security reference monitor also provides run-time object protection and audits all types of access when requested to do so.
Support Routines	Internal	These routines are linked directly to the executive. They allow the executive to allocate system memory (both paged and nonpaged) and interlock memory access. Finally, these routines allow the operating system to create two special kinds of synchronization: resource and fast mutex.
Virtual Memory Manager (VMM)	External	Virtual memory is an essential part of Windows 2000, so it's not surprising that there's a special manager for it. The VMM provides a large, private address space for each application, protects private memory from access by other applications, and provides the underlying support for the cache manager.

More Info Windows 2000 provides expanded memory capabilities that large applications, such as database managers, can use to perform their job faster. Unlike Windows NT Server 4.0 Enterprise Edition, Windows 2000 makes 3 GB of RAM available for large application use. However, even this vast amount of memory may not be enough in some cases, so you can further expand the memory available to large applications using Windows 2000 DataCenter Server. You can find out more about the memory capabilities of this version of Windows 2000 at *http://www.microsoft.com/HWDEV/ntdrivers/awe.htm*.

Working with Executive Objects

The executive is the core of the operating system when it comes to the operating system interface. It provides the absolute view of the operating system as it really is. It's important to realize, however, that the interface provided by the operating system isn't necessarily the one that an application for a given environment expects. Consider, for a moment, the difference between working with a POSIX (Portable Operating System Interface for Computing Environments) and a Win32 application when it comes to file access. The methods used by POSIX are completely different when it comes to file access than Windows 32. In short, they both need their own environment.

Since the executive can't provide the resources for each environment to do things its own way, there has to be some type of translation between the application environment and the executive. What happens, in this case, is that there are Windows 2000 applications that act as environments for other applications (we'll discuss these applications in the Windows 2000 Applications section of the chapter). An application calls the functions in this operating environment. The operating environment, in turn, calls executive objects—essentially primitives that allow the operating environment to produce a result similar to what the application normally expects.

Due to the method that Windows 2000 uses to create an operating environment for applications, the application isn't necessarily expecting the same features that Windows 2000 has to offer. An operating environment can provide a set of objects for applications that it supports that's either greater or lesser than the number of objects found in the Windows 2000 executive. In fact, given the nature of the objects found in the Windows 2000 executive, you're probably going to find that most operating environments offer more objects that are combinations of the simple objects provided by the executive. So, what are the executive objects? The following list provides a brief description of each object type:

- **Object directory**   A container that's used to hold other objects. For example, the object directory can be used to create the hierarchical directory you see in the Windows Explorer application available on all Windows platforms. It's also the basis of containers in applications like Microsoft Word.

- **Symbolic link**   An object pointer. You use it to reference another object indirectly. If you think about this object as you do the shortcuts in Windows, you'll have the right idea.

- **Process**   An application. The process contains a set of thread objects, each of which can perform a series of preprogrammed instructions. The process also contains virtual address space and control information.

- **Thread**   One element of execution within a process. This is the only execution unit within Windows. Every process contains at least one thread, but every process has the potential of containing more than one thread.

- **Section**   Memory that's shared by more than one thread or process. This region of memory is referred to as a file-mapping object in Win32. So, one of the purposes that this type of object is used for is file caching. The region of memory used to store information normally found on disk is shared by every application that needs to access that part of the hard drive.

- **File** One of the few universal objects. Every operating system and operating environment includes some kind of object that allows you to work with data on the hard disk.

- **Port** An object that's used to pass messages between processes.

- **Access token** A security element. It determines what rights an object has to access resources held by another object. An access token normally includes the security ID (SID) of the requestor, along with any group rights that the object may have, and any restrictions on the rights that the requestor claims to have.

- **Event** A special object that has a persistent state and is used to notify other objects about a system occurrence or to synchronize the activities of two objects. An event can be signaled or nonsignaled.

- **Semaphore** A guard object. It contains a counter that increments each time an object requests access to another object. The counter is decremented each time an object indicates it no longer needs access to another object. The semaphore restricts access to the protected object once some access count level is reached.

- **Mutex** An object. Some books refer to it as a mutant. The purpose of this synchronization object is to serialize access to some resource.

- **Timer** Simply an alarm clock for threads. When the time elapses, the timer object notifies the thread that created it.

- **Queue** Essentially, a waiting line. Objects go into the queue at one end, and come out the other. In this case, the queue is used to notify threads about completed I/O operations.

- **Key** The familiar registry object. A key holds data that defines the properties for a resource or object in Windows 2000. The key itself contains zero or more values, each of which defines one object or resource property.

- **Profile** Measures the execution time of a process within a given address range.

The translation of object representations between the executive and the operating environments that Windows 2000 supports yields a performance loss in some respect. Any time you perform a translation, you add another layer of software, which slows the movement of data on the server. In this case, however, the performance loss is something you have to live with because each kind of application requires a specific environment (unless you want to try to convince every application developer out there to rewrite their code).

Synchronization Issues

There's one additional problem that the objects in the executive have to handle that you may not have considered at first. Windows 2000 is a multitasking, multiprocessing operating system. This means that more than one application can attempt to access part of the executive's memory at the same time through the requisite operating environment. The application doesn't even realize that this access is taking place because it occurs at such a low level—even the application developer is unlikely to be aware of it. For example, whenever an application requires access to memory, requests more memory, or frees memory, the memory manager has to access the page frame database. Unfortunately, there's only one such database for the operating system. If two applications perform some memory-related task at the same time, it's possible that the page frame database would get accessed simultaneously, which would obviously cause problems.

Note   The page frame database is used to keep track of the page frames. For example, it shows whether a page frame is in use by a certain application and whether the page frame is currently in memory. The combination of a page frame, page table, and page directory allow Windows 2000 to translate a memory address into a physical memory location. Translation begins with the page directory, which is the first 10 bits of a 32-bit address. Once a page directory is selected, Windows 2000 uses the next 10 bits of the 32-bit address to find a specific page table. Finally, the last 12 bits are used to find the page frame.

The operating system gets around this problem by synchronizing access to various system resources, especially resources like the page frame database. The act of synchronization ensures that memory is accessed without incident. Of course, it also exacts another performance penalty, since one or more applications are waiting in a queue to access the resource they need. In short, one way to optimize system resource usage is to ensure that applications spend the least amount of time possible accessing a synchronized resource.

No matter what you do, the executive has times when synchronized access to a resource is required. One way to handle the problem is to use what's known as a spinlock. Unfortunately, the spinlock literally locks the processor and gives the requesting process sole access to the system resource. There are some pretty severe limitations on using this method. For one thing, you need to access the protected resource quickly (for obvious reasons) and without any complex interactions with other code, because the other code is going to be locked out anyway. A second limitation is that the critical code section (the code that created the spinlock) can't be paged out of memory, make any references to paged data, call any external procedures (including system services), and generate any exceptions or interrupts. In short, a spinlock is for something very short and very specific to the current process.

Another synchronization method involves the use of dispatcher objects. These are synchronization objects the kernel provides to the executive. They're user mode-viewable, which means they can be used in either user or kernel mode. An application developer recognizes these objects as the ones that get returned by Win32 API calls like WaitForSingleObject() and WaitForMultipleObjects(). An application thread can use dispatcher objects to synchronize with a process, thread, event, semaphore, mutex, waitable timer, I/O completion port, or file object. In addition, there are many ways in which a thread can become synchronized with other Windows objects. The point is that there are synchronization techniques that developers can use to ensure system resources are available for application use, and not in use by other applications.

Drivers and other kernel mode applications have another synchronization method open to them called executive resources. None of these resources are available as part of the Win32 API; and even if they were, user mode applications can't use them. Executive resources include both exclusive access and shared read access to objects. An example of an exclusive access executive resource operates like a mutex. You use it when a driver makes changes to the hardware configuration or performs some other task that doesn't work well with multiple application read access. An example of shared read access occurs when more than one kernel mode application requires access to a security structure. Since the content of the structure can't be changed by any of the participants, there isn't any concern about all participants reading the structure at the same time.

Executive resources aren't actually objects. They're specialized data structures that determine how the executive reacts to requests from kernel mode applications like a device driver. The executive resource data structures are allocated from the nonpaged memory pool, which means they can't be offloaded to the hard disk if memory becomes an issue on the server. The inability to page this memory means that the requesting application should use the resource and release it as soon as possible to prevent performance problems. Executive resources use their own special services to initialize, lock, release, query, and wait on requests that an application makes of them. Of the three types of synchronization used by the executive, this type of synchronization provides the most flexible access, but also has the greatest potential to cause performance problems when used incorrectly.

Hardware Abstraction Layer (HAL)

Windows NT and Windows 2000 were originally designed to work on more than one type of machine and even across processor versions. This means that the operating system can't assume anything about the hardware it's working with. It has to function with whatever hardware the server has to offer, at least within reason.

Normally, an operating system works directly with the device drivers, which then talk directly to the system hardware. This arrangement means that the entire operating system has to be written in the native language of the machine's processor and that each driver has to include support for both the operating system and the device the driver accesses. In short, older versions of operating systems were impossible to move from system to system without a total rewrite.

The hardware abstraction layer (HAL) is a key part of the answer to the question of portability. The operating system uses the HAL to access the devices that the server can provide, including the processor. You'll find the HAL within HAL.DLL in the

\%SystemDrive%\System32 directory. This is a replaceable file. Every hardware platform has a different HAL, which makes it possible for Windows 2000 to operate on just about any platform with a minimal level of rewrites. The operating system communicates to the device driver, which communicates to the HAL, which talks to the hardware. Since the HAL always has the same interface, the operating system doesn't really care where you place it as long as the correct HAL for the current platform is installed. Of course, the operating system still needs device drivers that know how to interact with the installed hardware. So, even though the HAL takes care of issues like the processor, I/O interfaces, and interrupt controllers, you need new device drivers to access things like the hard disk and display adapter.

Tip If you want to find out more about the HAL from a low-level perspective, the Windows 2000 DDK (Driver Development Kit) provides complete HAL documentation. A device driver developer needs this information to interact with devices other than the one that the device driver accesses. In addition, designers of custom machines need this information. Even if Windows 2000 doesn't include support for your particular machine, a vendor can supply a disk with a HAL on it that does. As previously mentioned, this is a fully replaceable part of the operating system that gives Windows 2000 a lot of flexibility when it comes to supporting other machine types.

In theory, the use of a consistent API and the HAL allows most applications to run on every platform that supports Windows or a Windows emulator, like the one found on the Apple Macintosh. To a certain extent, this is true. But you'll find that in the real world, incompatibilities still creep in, making it impossible to simply move software from one platform to another and expect it to work. The use of these technologies, however, reduces the amount of code that requires rewrite in order to move the application from one platform to the other.

More Info For those of you who want to know even the smallest detail about the HAL, you can download the Microsoft Windows HAL Development Kit and read the documentation it contains. You'll find this kit at *http://www.microsoft.com/DDK/ halkit/default.htm*. Some of the techniques we'll talk about in this section of the chapter require special implementation procedures. For example, you'll need to perform some special procedures to install an alternative version of the HAL, if your hardware vendor provides one to you. Although vendors should supply installation procedures, there are times when they don't. Fortunately, Microsoft provides generic procedures that work with most hardware. You'll find these procedures (along with a lot of other great information) on the Server Operating Systems Newsflash Web page at *http://support.microsoft.com/servicedesks/ productflashes/serveros/ntfl0549.htm*.

How the HAL Affects Performance

So, what are the performance problems of using the HAL? For one thing, you're adding several additional layers of abstraction to the operating system, which means it takes longer to move a request from the client application software to the intended device. In short, you're losing a little performance to gain an advantage in platform independence.

Of course, there's the question of just how much performance you'll lose. In some cases, vendors do provide customized versions of the HAL that you can use to optimize the performance of Windows 2000. While this particular component is rare, it's always a good idea to check with the vendor for possible support. Using the custom HAL definitely speeds your server up at a system level. Every hardware access goes through the HAL, which means that every part of the entire Windows environment realizes a performance benefit, even if the gain from using a custom HAL is small.

Let's talk a little more about device drivers and the HAL. There are actually four kinds of device drivers: (1) hardware, (2) file system, (3) filter, and (4) network redirectors and servers. Of these four driver types, only the hardware driver, the one that directly accesses a physical device, uses the HAL consistently. Obviously, the other three driver types need to use the HAL on occasion, but the driver with the most to gain from an efficient HAL is the hardware device driver.

It was previously mentioned that using the HAL added layers to the path between the client application and the hardware. One of the problems you'll encounter is just how well the hardware device drivers that you get with a piece of hardware access the HAL. In some cases, a vendor might be tempted to try to bypass the HAL to gain better access to the device and gain a marginal performance benefit. Of course, there are problems with this approach, most notably problems in portability. So, part of the performance problem with the HAL is the way that hardware device drivers are written to either interact with the HAL, or attempt to circumvent it altogether.

Understanding the I/O Hierarchy

The HAL isn't the only consideration when it comes to addressing I/O. It's important to understand that Windows 2000 is built on a multitude of layers of software—each layer performs a different task. Some of these layers can be tuned, but all of them affect the performance of your server. Windows 2000 actually provides six major components in the I/O stream, in addition to the hardware itself and your application. The following list describes these six levels of I/O support.

- **Operating environment API** For most of the applications you use, this is the Win32 API. The Win32 API calls one or more internal executive routines to perform specific tasks on the calling application's behalf. Applications can also call on the services provided by custom DLLs. The custom DLLs will access the internal executive routines directly.

- **I/O subsystem API**   The internal executive routines that are exposed to application through the Win32 API or other operating environment interfaces. This set of API functions includes calls like NtReadFile and NtWriteFile. Although applications require an additional layer of API support, DLLs call this API directly.

- **I/O manager**   Drives the processing of I/O requests. The I/O manager has two important tasks. First, it directs I/O requests to the proper kernel mode driver (there's one driver for each device type). Second, it maintains status information for each of the I/O requests. DLLs can access the I/O manager through calls like IoAttachDevice and IoAllocatedErrorLogEntry.

- **Kernel mode device drivers**   Translates the client requests into commands that the hardware can understand. Theoretically, there isn't any reason for a DLL to call a kernel mode device driver directly, so they usually don't provide any type of interface except the calls required by the I/O manager. It's important to remember that the hardware commands output by these drivers aren't ready for the device; they're transmitted to the HAL first. The kernel mode device driver actually relies on a series of predefined driver support routines to accomplish a task.

More Info   Windows 2000 uses a new type of device driver—one that will also be compatible with newer versions of Microsoft Windows 9x. This new device driver uses a technology known as the Windows Driver Model (WDM). This is a real plus for network administrators, because it means you no longer have to worry about getting several versions of the same driver; a single WDM driver does the job. You can find out more about the WDM drivers at *http://www.microsoft.com/DDK/ ddkdocs/win2k/01intro_3prb.htm*.

- **Driver support routines**   A set of HAL calls that are designed to allow a device driver to accomplish a given set of tasks in a nonhardware-specific manner. Most of these calls begin with Io, Ex, Ke, Mm, Hal, or FsRtl (there are others that aren't used quite as often).

- **HAL I/O access routines**   Acts as the insulating layer that accepts input from the kernel mode device driver and translates the routines into platform-specific hardware commands that devices on the machine understand. Even though each HAL provides the same set of input calls through the driver support routines, the HAL itself is unique for a given platform and is the one piece of the operating system that can't be ported from one machine to another.

Understanding the I/O Manager and Kernel Mode Device Drivers

There are a few additional facts you need to know about the I/O manager. This is the part of Windows that creates an orderly framework for responding to I/O requests. The I/O manager is packet-driven, much as any network is. These packets are referred to as I/O Request Packets (IRPs). IRP is actually a data structure containing the name of the affected kernel mode device driver and the operation that the driver should perform (like reading or writing), as a minimum. In some cases, IRP also contains the data that the requesting application wants sent to the device, or a pointer to a buffer that receives the data from the device. A single IRP can affect more than one device. For example, the requestor may want the current status of all devices on the system. So, if a single kernel mode device driver can't satisfy the entire request, IRP gets passed to the next kernel mode device driver in line. In some cases, the kernel mode device driver performs some of the work, and then passes IRP back to the I/O manager for completion.

By now, you should have some idea of why some kernel mode device drivers cause system conflicts. A driver that doesn't handle IRP correctly (as an example, it might not pass IRP to the next device driver when necessary) causes system conflicts. However, because IRP is relatively well documented, most device vendors who write their own kernel mode device drivers can get this particular issue corrected with a small amount of planned testing.

From a performance perspective, a custom kernel mode device driver always provides better access to device features and better performance than the generic kernel mode device drivers provided with Windows do. Of course, one of the biggest problems is getting a driver for your particular device in a timely manner from the device vendor. In many cases, it's best to begin looking for device drivers during the operating system beta process. This is the time that you should start asking the vendor about support for a new version of Windows.

One of the facts you need to realize about the I/O manager is that it also contains a lot of generic code. This code is used to answer I/O requests of a generic nature. For example, the I/O manager manages the buffers used to hold various types of data returned by the kernel mode device drivers. It also keeps track of all the device drivers loaded on the system and performs tasks for the device drivers, like providing time-out support. By placing all of this generic code in the I/O manager, Windows reduced the complexity of writing custom device drivers for individual devices. In addition, this generic code can be hand-tuned for a particular version of Windows, which normally enhances system performance.

The I/O manager is also the part of the operating system that's responsible for coordinating the operating environment specific requests. For example, it knows when to send a request for a Win32 version of a kernel mode device driver or a POSIX version of the same driver. The I/O manager also provides a level of synchronization support for requests from different operating environments.

Windows 2000 Subsystems

As you now know, the Windows 2000 architecture contains two major layers: user mode and kernel mode. Earlier in the chapter in "User Mode versus Kernel Mode," you learned the major differences between these two layers of the Windows 2000 architecture. You can see from the architecture layout that not only does it consist of layers, but also components within each mode of operation. In this section, you examine the two components of user mode—the environment subsystems and the integral subsystems. See Figure 2-2 for an illustration of where these subsystems reside in relation to each other and the executive.

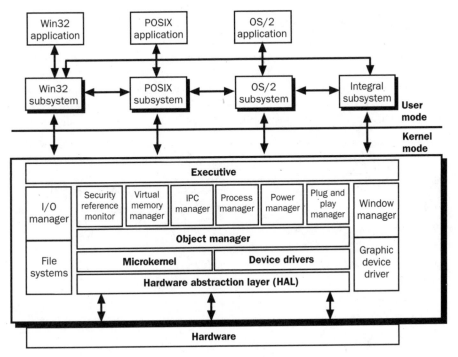

Figure 2-2.   *The Windows 2000 architecture is based on a layered model; the design also provides a modular architecture.*

In Figure 2-2, you can see the separation between the subsystems and the HAL. Interaction between these two layers takes place strictly through the executive. Also note how the integral subsystem and the Win32 subsystem have direct interaction with each other. As you'll read later, the integral subsystem consists of other components, including security components that control access to the local machine and the resources defined on the server.

Environment Subsystems

The designers of Windows NT had several goals in mind when developing the operating system that would eventually evolve into Windows 2000 Server. This includes making Windows 2000 the most reliable and robust operating system available on the market. In addition, they wanted to create a product that allowed the user maximum scalability and extensibility.

The Windows NT architecture enabled applications to run safely in their own assigned address space, protecting the operating system from any potential damage caused by the application. In fact, the design also protected applications from each other, a problem that was all too common under the 16-bit Windows 3.*x* environment.

In addition to creating a robust, reliable, scalable and extensible operating system, the Windows NT team wanted to create a truly interoperable operating system; an operating system that would allow a user to run software from their MS-DOS or Win16 software library. Actually, for many businesses that couldn't afford to simply toss away software, the compatibility provided through Windows NT was a saving grace. Some of these MS-DOS or Win16 applications were critical to their daily business operation; in some cases, there was no alternative application available. Businesses could turn to Windows NT knowing it would provide their applications with a robust, protected environment in which to run the applications within.

These design goals have been carried over into the Windows 2000 product. Windows 2000, like its predecessor Windows NT, has been designed to be even more reliable and scalable than its predecessor. Through new features found in the kernel such as Scatter Gather I/O, improved sorting, and Extended Memory Architecture, the Windows 2000 operating system is capable of offering users a stable and robust operating system.

Many of the features of Windows 2000 that improve upon Windows NT are referred to in this book. These features have been designed to take advantage of the architecture of the operating system. They work together to produce maximum operating system efficiency.

Earlier in this chapter, we covered two major layers of the Windows 2000 architecture, the Executive Services and the HAL. In this section of the chapter, we'll discuss the components that make up the Executive Services and how each one relates to one another. We'll then cover the topic of the Windows 2000 subsystems. The subsystems are what enable Windows 2000 to be the interoperable operating system that it is. We'll also discuss the Integral subsystem, the backbone of the security architecture of the Windows 2000.

Windows 2000 is capable of running applications designed for other operating systems (including those written for MS-DOS, IBM OS/2 1.*x*, Windows 3.*x*, and POSIX). Through the environment subsystems (Win32 subsystem, OS/2 subsystem, and POSIX subsystem), Windows 2000 provides users with a method of emulating multiple operating systems, and running applications within each subsystem without causing instability with the main operating system.

Emulation of the operating system and applications occurs by the environment subsystems converting the actual API call so that Windows 2000 can interpret those calls.

An API consists of a set of functions that allow you to work with an operating system, application, or component. The API allows programmers to hook into that operating system or application using any one of the popular development tools, such as C++, Microsoft Visual Basic, and Microsoft Visual J++. You can write APIs for use with

Windows 3.*x*, Microsoft Windows 95 and 98, UNIX, and the Novell NetWare operating systems. Of course, many APIs are now available so developers can take advantage of the extensibility of features of Windows 2000, such as the Active Directory Services Interface (ADSI).

Windows 2000, through this emulation process, enables you to run applications written for 32-bit operating systems, such as Windows NT 3.*x* and 4.0 and Windows 95 and 98. You can also run applications written for the POSIX and OS/2 platforms.

When you run a non-Win32 application on the Windows 2000 platform, you're running the platform-specific application and the operating system that is being emulated within its designated Windows 2000 subsystem. Because Windows 2000 must emulate the environment for these non-Win32 applications, there are limitations for each type of environment Windows 2000 must emulate. These limitations are covered in "Windows 2000 Applications," later in this chapter.

Limitations with operating systems you may be emulating aren't the only hurdle you'll face. Performance is one other factor that suffers through this process of converting API calls in order to complete the emulation process. This conversion process adds yet another layer of code in the processing of commands running within these pseudo operating system environments (or Windows 2000 subsystems). This, in turn, has a direct effect on the performance of applications and the operating system being emulated. With certain applications, you may find that a process within a Win16 application is executed faster on your original Windows 3.*x* desktop than it is on your Windows 2000 system.

However, for the slight performance hit you may suffer by running these applications on Windows 2000, you gain as much from the overall reliability of the operating system. Under the Windows 3.*x* environment, you always ran the risk of having an application crash, taking the operating system with it. As you read on, you see how each application running within a Windows 2000 subsystem runs in its own address space. This increases the overall stableness of the system, and also helps you avoid system crashes, such as those caused by General Protection Faults (GPF).

Limitations of Environment Subsystems

The environment subsystems are capable of emulating various operating systems. In addition to running the actual operating system, you also have the ability to run the applications designed for them. Here are a few limitations that the environment subsystems and the applications that run within them face.

Run at a Lower Priority Level than the Kernel-Mode Processes

As applications running within the environment subsystems are technically running within user mode, the application's processes are running at a lower-priority level than their counterparts running in kernel mode. When a process is running a lower-level priority, it means the process has less access to the processor or processors if running in a multiprocessor system. Windows 2000 does allow you to increase or decrease the priority level of a process running within user mode; however, you're limited to adjusting the priority level ranging from 15 (high) through 32 (low).

Can't Access Hardware Directly

When the environment subsystems and applications running within each subsystem need to call on hardware, they're restricted from accessing the hardware device directly. This limitation is brought about by the actual API call for the application having to be converted to a format that Windows 2000 can understand. Once these conversions have taken place, the subsystem passes the converted API to the executive for processing; therefore, the actual process doesn't have the ability to access the hardware device it might be calling.

Don't Have Direct Access to Device Drivers

Device drivers are what allow applications to talk with hardware devices. In the case of Windows 2000, hardware devices communicate with the operating system via device drivers. The scanner attached to your Windows 2000 machine has a driver written specially for it; this way, the application and the operating system know exactly what can and can't be done with this particular hardware device. In the case of an operating system or application running within the subsystem, they can't access the device driver directly. The device driver has to route its request to the I/O manager instead, which then passes it to the HAL (for more information on HAL, see "Hardware Abstraction Layer," earlier in this chapter).

Environment Subsystems and Applications Limited to Assigned Address Space

This shouldn't be considered a limitation, even though it's under the section stating so. The reason it shouldn't be considered a hindrance is that it brings stability to the operating system. When you're emulating other operating systems under Windows 2000, the environment created by Windows 2000 is almost as it is under the native OS itself. This means that applications running under these other operating systems behave much the same way as they did in their native environment. This includes many of the limiting features of either the application or operating system that caused you to abandon the emulated platform in the first place.

For example, if you run a 16-bit application on your Windows 2000 Server and allow it address space where the operating system kernel resides, the entire operating system can be affected as soon as the application locked up for one reason or the other.

That's why each application and environment subsystem runs within its own assigned address space. The keyword here is assigned—no other applications or subsystems know of the other's address space, thus, no intrusion by one system into the other's space. This way Windows 2000 protects itself from instability by a misbehaving application.

Win32 Subsystem

The Win32 subsystem is responsible for controlling Win32-based applications. In addition to running 32-bit applications, it's also responsible for the input and output of all keyboard and mouse commands. The Win32 subsystem was designated to control all I/O between input devices (the keyboard and mouse, for example) and output devices (a video monitor, for example) because it provides a consistent look and feel regardless of the application the user may be running. This subsystem has been designed to provide preemptive multitasking, thus increasing overall performance for 32-bit applications that run within this subsystem. The Win32 subsystem is also responsible for providing an environment in which Win16 and MS-DOS applications operate. For more information regarding how Win32, Win16, and MS-DOS applications run within the Win32 subsystem, see "Win32" in the applications part of this chapter.

OS/2 Subsystem

The OS/2 subsystem provides a set of APIs that enable Windows 2000 to run OS/2 1.*x* 16-bit applications and character-based applications. When you launch an OS/2 application, the subsystem begins to use Windows 2000 resources; even after exiting the application, those resources are still in use. The only way you can free the resource is to quit the OS2SRV process that's spawned once the OS/2 subsystem is put to use. Otherwise, as long as you don't run OS/2 applications, the subsystem does not use any resources.

Tip   To kill the OS2SRV process or any other process running under Windows 2000, go to the Task Manager by pressing the Ctrl+Alt+Del keys simultaneously. A dialog box appears; using your left mouse button, click Task Manager. Task Manager presents you with a graph illustrating current CPU usage. Click the Processes tab to view individual processes running on the server. Select OS2SRV from the list and click End Task to kill the task. If the program is hung, the task may not end immediately. In that case, you'll be prompted to force an end to the task by clicking End Task one last time. See Chapter 3, "Processes and Threads and Memory Management," for more information on how to view and manage processes using Task Manager.

POSIX Subsystem

POSIX is a standard that was designed and put into place by the Institute of Electrical and Electronic Engineers (IEEE). This standard defines certain criteria an operating system must meet to be considered as a POSIX-compliant operating system. These standards include programming interface, networking, security, and the graphical interface for the operating system. This standard is known as POSIX.1. The POSIX subsystem enables you to run POSIX applications that meet the POSIX.1 requirements.

Integral Subsystems

You have explored three of the four environment subsystems—Win32, OS/2, and the POSIX subsystem. Now you examine the fourth, the integral subsystem. The integral subsystem isn't a subsystem in which applications run, or a subsystem that emulates other platforms for the operating system. The integral subsystem is responsible for multitude of other tasks, including the overall security of the local computer.

The term integral subsystems is used in a broad sense, mainly because the integral subsystems perform a variety of operating system functions and not just one task, as is the case with the environment subsystems. The functions of the integral subsystems include the server service, workstation service, and security subsystem.

Server Service

The server service is essential to Windows 2000 Server because it's the component that enables the operating system to provide network resources, such as sharing a directory. The server service accomplishes this by providing the system with an API to access the network server of the operating system.

Depending on the number of applications and types of applications you have installed on your Windows 2000 Server, you may find that multiple services depend on the server service. For example, if you've installed Message Queuing, the service does not start unless the server service has been launched. If you're running an application whose performance depends heavily on the message queuing service, make sure to have the server service launch automatically rather than manually. This way, in case the server is rebooted, you won't be scratching your head wondering why the application exchanging information with your legacy mainframe can no longer do so because the message queuing service isn't doing its job.

Workstation Service

The workstation service does the opposite of what the server service is designed to do. Workstation service is what allows a Windows 2000 Server to access the network and attach to those resources shared by other machines. In the case of the workstation service, it provides the system with an API so the network redirector can be accessed.

Security Subsystem

The security subsystem consists of a number of security components. These subcomponents enable the security subsystem to control access to the Windows 2000 Server and the resources defined on the server. The security subcomponents are logon processes, local security authority (LSA) and security reference monitor.

Table 2-3 provides an overview of the functions the security subsystem is responsible for, and the security subcomponents that enable it to accomplish those tasks.

Table 2-3. Functions of the Security Subsystem and Components Behind Each Function

Function	Subcomponent
Accepts logon requests from users (either locally or from a remote logon)	Logon Processes
Keeps track of which system resources need to be audited	Local Security Authority
Keeps track of rights and permissions associated with user accounts	Security Reference Monitor
Responsible for initial logon authentication	Logon Processes

Windows 2000 Managers

As you now know, the executive is the layer of the Windows 2000 architecture that oversees what occurs at the kernel level. You also reviewed how the executive contains the Windows 2000 kernel-mode components and that each of these components is either responsible for an internal service or external service, also known as a system service. The difference between the two is in what components of the architecture they serve. A manager that provides system services is available in both user mode and kernel mode. For example, when the Win32 subsystem needs to pass a call to the file system, the I/O manager intervenes and passes on the request. The Win32 subsystem does not have direct contact with the file system itself. Components that service only internal routines are only available to components within the kernel. Next, you take a look at these components, also known as managers (see Table 2-2 for a listing of each component of the executive).

I/O Manager

The I/O manager is the part of the Windows 2000 executive that takes care of all input and output to the operating system. Part of an operating systems input/output occurs between the operating system and external hardware devices. The I/O manager was covered in some detail earlier in the chapter in "Understanding the I/O Manager and Kernel Mode Device Drivers." Here you learn about the three components that make up the I/O manager—file systems, device drivers, and cache manager.

File Systems

The file system component of the I/O manager accepts I/O requests and conforms these requests into calls that the physical device recognizes. The I/O manager, which is also responsible for network requests, treats the network redirector and network server as file system drivers.

Device Drivers

Drivers, in particular device drivers, are the means of communication between the operating system and hardware devices. However, not all parts of the operating system can talk directly with hardware devices; this is where the I/O manager factors in. When referring to the I/O manager, you can see drivers from two perspectives: high-level and low-level. High-level drivers are those that don't communicate with hardware devices directly because they know nothing about the physical device. Low-level drivers, also known as device drivers, communicate with hardware devices directly. Higher-level drivers rely on the I/O manager to pass logical I/O requests down to device drivers so that requests to the physical device occur.

Cache Manager

The cache manager is a critical component of the I/O manager and a critical piece for a well-performing system. That's because it provides caching services to the servers' file systems. Just to refresh—the cache is designated location on a hard disk allocated to store frequently used data. A simple algorithm defines what is frequently used. The cache manager has the single responsibility of handling cache for the entire I/O system in order to increase overall system performance. The basic principle behind caching is to store frequently accessed data in a temporary location to decrease the burden placed on the device where the data is originally being read. If you take a look at your server, you find that cache storage of some sort exists at the processor, disk controller, and even video level. In the case of the cache manager, it provides caching services to all file systems and network components that are part of the I/O manager.

An example of the cache manager at work in your system is when a disk I/O transaction occurs. If you have a Windows 2000 Server staged for the purposes of file services, you're bound to have a multitude of disk I/O transactions occur. Say, for instance, that a document resides on the server that's being accessed continuously by users on the network. Each time a user opens that document, a disk I/O transaction occurs. The cache manager monitors this activity and, because of the continuous access of the document, retains it in RAM to decrease the overall disk access. Now when users access the document, not only do they find the response of the server faster, but they also find it helps increase the performance of the file system.

Not everything read from the file system is placed in cache. For that reason, when you monitor cache manager activity via Performance console using the System Monitor snap-in, you find that activity fluctuates for the counter. That's because not all documents are read continuously, but rather sequentially, and those documents aren't placed in cache. So, at any time, you may have more or less cache activity occurring at the server.

Cache manager also improves overall performance for file system activity through the methods of lazy write and lazy commit. A lazy write (available only with FAT file systems) is when cache manager records changes in the file structure cache rather than disk, because writing to cache is quicker than physical disk. Cache manager then writes these changes to disk when it finds that the processor utilization is at a low point.

A lazy commit (available only with NTFS file systems) works the same way as a lazy write; however, committed information isn't marked as successfully completed. A lazy commit caches committed information and then writes to the file system as a background process. From a performance perspective, you want to have as many file system requests of the server cached. The more cache the better, as long as it's managed well.

Note It isn't possible for you to change or set what the cache manager chooses to cache. So, if you find that you'd like to have particular data cached, you have to rely on the cache manager logic to actually place it in cache.

LPC Facility

The local procedure call (LPC) facility is designed to facilitate calls made between applications and Windows 2000 subsystems. When you make a remote connection to a server from your workstation, you're initiating a remote procedure call (RPC) in the background.

The RPC establishes communication between your machine and the server, providing a shared resource. An LPC is established only when the client (application) and server (subsystem) reside on the same computer. So, when your application requests the services of the I/O manager, the stub in the application process packages the parameters for the call. After the actual call has been packaged, it's sent to the executive via the LPC.

Object Manager

Whenever an application launches, a process is started with which a thread(s) and other operating system resources, such as a data structure, may be spawned. The object manager is responsible for deleting these processes, threads, and other objects created to represent an operating system resource. In addition to deleting these objects, the object manager is also responsible for retention, naming, and security of objects.

Security Reference Manager

The security reference manager enforces security policies on the local computer at both the kernel mode and user mode levels. This way not only are users restricted from accessing data or an object that they're not supposed to access, but they are also restricted from processes running in kernel mode. The security reference manager checks with the LSA to see if a user has the needed permissions to an object he or she may be attempting to access. If a request to audit access to a resource has been established, the security reference manager generates an audit message. The message is passed to the LSA, which then logs the audit message.

Virtual Memory Manager

In Chapter 3, "Processes and Threads and Memory Management," you learn the actual mechanics of how virtual memory works in the Windows 2000 Server environment. In this section, you explore the process of virtual memory and the role the virtual memory manager (VMM) plays in this process.

No matter which operating system you're talking about, assignment of virtual memory is the method by which the operating system can see more RAM than the system physically has. Assigning virtual memory allocates a unique virtual address space for each process that's created on the computer in RAM. The process's threads can then use this set of addresses. Virtual address space that's created for the purposes of virtual memory is divided into equal blocks known as pages (this is where the term page swapping derives from). Every process is allocated its own virtual address space, which causes the process to think it has more memory than is physically in the machine.

As you learn in Chapter 3, a process of demand paging occurs when using virtual memory. Demand paging involves swapping data between physical RAM and a temporary paging file created on a hard disk called a swap file. The actual swapping of data between physical RAM and the swap file (hard disk) is managed by VMM. Each time a process requests data, a page swap occurs where data is sent back to physical RAM storage from the temporary swap file on the hard disk. VMM determines which data to move out of

RAM by keeping track of what data has been in physical memory the longest. It's that data which is first removed when things start to become tight with physical RAM. In one sense, it acts much like a traffic light: It signals when it's okay for certain data to be swapped into physical RAM, and when others should wait in line.

When page swapping, VMM maps the virtual addresses in the process's address space to physical pages in the computer's memory. By mapping the virtual addresses, VMM hides the actual physical makeup of memory from the process's thread. This process is essential to keeping a stable environment running, without which you'll never have a well-tuned server. Thus, when a process requests data, the thread can access the memory allocated to its respective process. This way, there's no chance the thread will attempt to access the address space of another process, potentially causing instability of the operating system and an unreliable operating environment.

From a performance perspective, the faster VMM can swap out memory (from RAM to disk and vice versa) the better. Not only are data requests serviced faster, but also space within memory is freed quicker so the process can continue. Basically, VMM can prevent a "traffic jam" from occurring when too many processes are lined up so data can be swapped out from disk to RAM.

Windows 2000 Applications

In "Windows 2000 Subsystems," earlier in this chapter, you examined the subsystems that allow Windows 2000 to emulate other operating systems. As part of this emulation, it also allows the operating system to emulate the applications that run within these subsystems. Here, you review how these applications actually run under the Windows 2000 operating systems.

Win32 Application

When running a Win32 application on Windows 2000, you gain multiple benefits. For starters, Windows 2000 has been designed to run Win32 applications; unlike the OS/2 or Win16 applications, it creates emulators for or runs in virtual machines. One example of Windows 2000 facilitating Win32 applications is in the desynchronized input model Win32 applications run under. This is compared to a synchronized input model for Win16 applications. A desynchronized input model consists of the Win32 subsystem storing all requests for Win32 applications in a separate input queue for each Win32 application. This way, no one Win32 application can delay another Win32 application from retrieving information from the queue. A synchronized input model causes all requests to be stored in a single queue, allowing an application to hold up requests that may be waiting for other applications running on the server. The Win32 subsystem stores all messages headed for the input queue in a single queue for all Win16-bit applications.

As mentioned, in addition to running traditional 32-bit applications designed for Windows 2000 and Windows NT, the Win32 subsystem also runs MS-DOS and 16-bit based applications. It does so by creating a virtual DOS machine (VDM). A VDM is basically a Win32 application that creates a complete computer running within that single process. This enables an MS-DOS or Win16 application to run in its own address space, which also protects the operating system from any hectic behavior by the VDMs running on the server.

POSIX Application

As mentioned earlier in "POSIX Subsystem," POSIX is a standard that defined certain criteria an operating system must meet in order to be considered a POSIX-compliant operating system. These standards include programming interface, networking, security, and the graphical interface for the operating system. This standard is known as POSIX.1. The POSIX subsystem enables you to run POSIX applications that meet the POSIX.1 requirements. Windows 2000 meets POSIX.1 compliance, which includes many of the features that the operating system allows, such as case-sensitive file naming and files that have more than one name.

Limitations do exist with the POSIX subsystem; you can't run more than one POSIX session at a single time. Unlike the OS/2 and Win32 subsystems that allow for multiple sessions to run within their own address space, the Windows 2000 operating system does not allow you to launch a second POSIX application. Performance-wise, this can become a significant hurdle because you're limited to the number of POSIX tasks a single Windows 2000 machine can execute at a single time.

POSIX applications can't call any Win32 APIs; neither do they have access to DDE (dynamic data exchange), OLE (object linking and embedding), memory-mapped files, window sockets, or other Win32 features. This limits you to the types of applications you can develop and the performance enhancements you could possibly gain by utilizing Win32 APIs.

Lastly, POSIX applications aren't considered network-aware. They can access files over the network, but your clients are not able to attach to your Windows 2000 Server for the purposes of sharing access to POSIX.

OS/2 Application

Compatibility of OS/2 applications running on Windows 2000 Server is limited. You can only run OS/2 2.1x 16-bit applications or character-based applications on x86 computers. Running OS/2 applications on a RISC-based computer isn't supported unless you're running OS/2 real-mode applications in the MS-DOS environment on the RISC computer. Other limitations include not being able to run applications that access hardware memory or I/O port at Ring 2 or below. The OS/2 application subsystem was included with the Windows NT Server for the purposes of compatibility of what was then a target audience of OS/2 users. As the market for OS/2 has diminished over the years, Microsoft didn't improve this particular subsystem in relation to other subsystems.

Summary

This chapter focused on the Windows 2000 kernel. You learned that the kernel is actually a complex set of interrelated applications and not a single entity on the hard disk. In fact, the kernel itself is actually just a small part of what most people associate with the kernel.

We've talked about several pieces of Windows 2000 that are normally associated with the kernel. For example, in the first section of the chapter we looked at the Windows 2000 executive, the part of Windows that provides the kernel with an interface that both kernel mode and user mode application can access. You explored the HAL, a piece of software engineering that allows Windows 2000 to communicate with the hardware without actually knowing what hardware it's installed on. The HAL is a completely replaceable part of the operating system and the Windows 2000 Setup routine normally checks your hardware before it installs a particular HAL as part of the installation process.

In the chapter, you also reviewed the subsystems and managers that make up the Windows 2000 architecture. You saw how each subsystem enables Windows 2000 to create a virtual machine for the operating system it emulates. This ability of Windows 2000 to run multiple operating systems from a single desktop makes it a truly interoperable operating system. The environment subsystems allow Windows 2000 to do this, while keeping the Windows 2000 operating system environment stable from any disruptions as a result of the individual subsystems. You also learned how the integral subsystem of Windows 2000 architecture is key to the Windows 2000 security model.

Chapter 3 is going to help you better understand how all the components in Windows 2000 work together to help you run an application. You learn about processes and threads in the beginning of this chapter. Remember that a process is essentially a container that includes at least one thread, some memory, and some control settings. Threads are the executable code that makes the application run.

Chapter 3 will also talk about memory management. Because memory is used for everything from disk caches to application code storage to data store, it's essential that Windows 2000 manage this resource. Unfortunately, the operating system can only guess how you want to use the server. So, it might end up using too much memory for the disk cache and not enough for application data. The point is that memory is one of those areas that you should consider managing too. This chapter gives you the knowledge required to make changes in the operating setup and get the most out of the resources that your server has to offer.

Chapter 3
Processes and Threads and Memory Management

When all's said and done, your server's main purpose in life is to run the applications you need to run your business. Everything about your server is designed for this task. The fact that even a service ultimately enables a business application to run means that every part of the server is dedicated to the task of running the business application.

If applications are central to the operation of your server, they are also central to the performance, tuning, and optimization of the server. This chapter looks at three basic elements of every application: processes, threads, and memory. These elements affect how an application works in the operating system environment. Every application has processes and threads. The very existence of these processes and threads means that the application also uses memory. Any application on your server will use these three elements, no matter how simple or complex.

"Understanding Processes and Threads" examines these first two building blocks of all applications. We'll look at how a process defines the starting characteristics of an application, and how it's used as a container for the threads that perform the work you request. This section also looks at the kinds of threads applications use. It may surprise you to know that application performance characteristics are often based as much on the kinds and number of threads they use, as they are on the way the application manages resources. It's important to understand that not all applications are created equal—they have different characteristics even at a low level of the application hierarchy.

Obviously, you can't just look at an application to determine how processes and threads are used. These application elements are normally hidden from view because the user doesn't need to know they exist. Developers do need to know about processes and threads, however, so there are tools available to view them. In "Ways to View Processes and Threads," you explore some tools used to see these application elements. We'll not only discuss the types of analysis tools, but also the information the tools provide as an end result, in addition to seeing a list of threads within a specific process.

By this time, you have some idea of what processes and threads are all about, but don't know how to use them in a practical sense. In "Prioritizing Processes and Threads," you explore some tuning tips for these application elements. The reason I specified tuning, rather than optimization, is that Microsoft Windows 2000 is very self-optimizing in this area. It automatically changes process and thread priorities to give each application an equal share of resources, like processing time. Tuning implies that the system may not be optimized when you finish, but that a particular application runs within the constraints that you need it to run to accomplish a certain task. In short, tuning application processes and threads normally means your system runs less efficiently. The trade-off may be that you're giving up some efficiency to complete a specific task faster.

One of the methods you have for optimizing performance, once you tune it, is to add more processors to a server. Even though Windows 2000 is a multitasking operating system, the reality is that it only works on one task at a time—it appears it's performing more than one task at a time because of the way it switches between tasks. Adding more processors allows Windows 2000 to perform true multitasking—the simultaneous execution of more than one application at a time. "Multiprocessing and Performance" covers this issue and helps you understand how using more than one processor can often be more effective than doubling the speed of a single processor on the same machine.

Processes and threads use memory. The mere act of loading an application requires memory. Once the application is loaded, it requires even more memory for items like variables and other application features. In short, knowing how to manage memory will affect every application on your machine. The simple act of conserving memory when possible allows all applications on your server to work faster and, often, more efficiently. We'll take an initial look at memory management in "Microsoft Windows 2000 Memory Model." This is where you'll learn how Windows 2000 automatically conserves memory for you and what you can do when the automatic methods fail.

The last section of this chapter, "Virtual Memory Management," looks at a topic that has probably evoked more discussion than any other—at least when viewed across a wide range of platform types. Using hard disk space to emulate memory means you're losing some system performance in order to simulate something that all applications require in relatively large quantities. So, how does using hard disk space for memory make Windows 2000 faster? That's the question we'll answer in this section.

Understanding Processes and Threads

A lot of people have heard the terms *process* and *thread*, but many people have no idea of what these terms mean in regard to application development or performance. In fact, some developers may have a hard time explaining the roles of processes and threads when it comes to the way applications behave under Windows 2000. Unless you're writing relatively complex applications, using multiple threads doesn't even enter into the picture.

Note   This section of the chapter is fairly technical and includes some programmer jargon. Processes and threads are constructs that most users never see, much less care about. A discussion of these two application elements requires the use of some technical language. All programming terms, especially jargon, are explained within the text, and again within the Glossary at the end of the book.

The following three sections explore the roles of processes and threads in the Windows 2000 environment. The first thing we'll do is look at what tasks these two entities perform and how they affect the structure of an application. There are separate sections for processes and threads because these two entities perform completely different tasks under Windows 2000. The third section examines a special thread issue. Unlike processes, there's more than one type of thread. It helps to know about these thread types because they affect the performance characteristics of your application. We'll look at the way the various thread types work and how they affect your application's performance. You can't do much about the thread structure of off-the-shelf applications since you don't have access to the source code, but knowing about threads can help you understand the issues developers of custom applications for your company and others face.

Note   Although the term *application* is used to refer to user applications in most cases, user applications form only a small part of all the classes of applications that run on your server. Services, drivers, components, and other operating system features can also be called applications in the true sense of the word. Keep this definition in mind as you read the following sections. Application is used in the broadest sense of the term in these sections. The information can apply equally to user applications and those used by the operating system, unless specifically noted within the text.

Processes Define the Application

Every application running on your server has one, and only one, process. The process is the application container and is used to hold the threads that do the actual work that the application is designed to perform. From a user's perspective, the process is the one element that you can view without any special tools (as we'll see in "Ways to View Processes and Threads," later in the chapter). Because the process is the only element that's readily seen, most users tend to view the process and the application as synonymous. Programmers know there's more lurking under the surface, however, and that's the point of this section.

Viewing a process and an application as one and the same is an error of perception. The process is simply a container used to hold something else. It's akin to the milk container in your refrigerator—you need the container to hold the milk, but the milk itself is the main event. Yet, when you look in the refrigerator, you see the container (the milk is only visible in clear containers). Someone who doesn't know to open the milk container may assume the carton is all that milk consisted of. Likewise, because a user can't normally see inside a process, there's a tendency to view the process (the container) as the entire application.

The process acts as a container for other application elements. It holds the virtual memory space, data, and system resources, along with application settings. Although a thread can allocate, reallocate, and deallocate memory, it's the process that receives the initial allocation of memory and distributes it to all the threads that require memory. Likewise, data is originally created as part of the process, and then funneled to the various threads that require access to it. System resources can include a variety of objects, like file handles (a pointer to the data structure that defines the file object), semaphores (an object used to synchronize application actions), and dynamically allocated memory.

The presence of a process on a machine indicates there's at least one thread present as well. However, the presence of a process doesn't indicate that any work is taking place. A process merely indicates the allocation of resources to perform work. If the threads within the process are low priority, the process may simply consume resources without performing any work. An application does useful work when the system scheduler gives it execution control. The scheduler uses the thread's priority to determine when the thread runs. The process determines the initial priority of a thread when the application gets loaded into memory. As time passes, the system scheduler increases the priority of a thread until it's sufficiently high to allow the thread to execute. The thread's priority is then reset to its original (load time) setting.

Threads Are Application Laborers

A thread is a single path of execution contained within a process that shares all the process's resources. It also includes a stack (variables and other data stored in memory), CPU register state information (so the thread can restore its environment), and an entry within the system scheduler's execution list. Every thread defines some kind of work the application needs to do to accomplish a given task.

Processes can hold more than one thread. For example, a word processor may use one thread to allow the user to enter data, and a separate thread to print a document in the background. The process always knows about the threads it contains. On the other hand, threads don't necessarily know about the existence of other threads within the same process. In fact, a thread requires special programming to keep informed about other threads in the same process. Threads that work together need some type of synchronization to reduce the chance of collisions—for example, two threads might try to change the same variable at the same time. Most multithreaded applications avoid using synchronized threads because of the problems they can cause in a case such as addressing the same variable above.

Threads can get quite complex and there isn't room in this book to cover every detail. However, there are many facts you can learn about threads to help you do a better job when tuning and optimizing your server. For example, there are times when an application allows you to modify the number of threads it executes in the background. Changing the number of threads could affect performance in the right situation. Even if you can't change how an application uses threads, you can use your newfound knowledge to do a better job of performance monitoring an application, which may help you build a case for either upgrading or getting rid of an application that uses threads inefficiently. The following sections provide you with additional information about how threads affect the performance of your server.

Understanding Thread Uses

Theoretically, you can use multiple threads of execution in any kind of application, including something as small as an ActiveX component. Threads don't need to be large or complex to make an application more efficient and responsive to user needs. In fact, you can use threads to perform small maintenance tasks in the background at regular intervals—something you may not want to interrupt your main application thread to do. A thread can also replace timer-related tasks in some cases. In other words, threads aren't limited to performing any particular task. Threads are the executable unit within an application and are fully configurable (at least at an application programming level) for any task you need them to do.

> **Tip**   There's a simple rule of thumb that you can follow when working with multithreaded applications. More threads often equate to better user response times. However, threads use up resources, which means that more threads often add up to lower overall system efficiency and throughput. Adding threads also increases application complexity, which often equates to lower application reliability (based on more points of failure).

There are some factors a developer needs to consider before he or she starts using threads for every small task that an application may need to perform. Some of these factors affect application development time, some affect performance, while others affect the application's reliability. In short, adding threads to enhance application response time or the application's ability to get a task done in the background during "user think" time usually means a trade-off in some other area of application execution. The following list provides you with some guidelines on what developers commonly think about before using threads.

- **Debugging**   The biggest consideration, from a developer perspective, is that threads greatly increase the difficulty of debugging an application. A thread can actually hide bugs, or at least make them more difficult to find, because the developer now has to watch more than one thread of execution at a time. What this means to you is that multiple threads reduce application response time at the cost of increased development time and reduced application reliability.

- **Development**   Most developers are used to thinking about application programming in a fairly linear fashion. In other words, given a specific event, the application performs a series of steps to handle it. The use of multiple threads forces the developer to think about the application processes in parallel, rather than in a linear fashion. Any time people do something new in a way that's unfamiliar, they're more likely to make mistakes. From a performance perspective, multiple threads could mean applications that spend more time waiting for something to happen and less time working. A good development strategy includes improving efficiency, sometimes through the use of multiple threads and parallel processes.

- **True efficiency**   While it's true that placing some tasks into background threads can make use of idle time in the application, there are situations when there isn't any idle time to exploit. In this situation, the application is actually less efficient than before because there's a certain amount of overhead and housekeeping associated with using multiple threads. In other words, developers of a custom application should only use threads in situations where they anticipate there will be some amount of idle time to exploit. When working with off-the-shelf applications, you need to decide whether you can configure the application to use more or less threads. For example, a word processor can probably make use of idle time to check spelling and grammar in the background, so this is a good use of multiple threads.

- **Reliability**   Multiple threads of execution don't necessarily make an application failure-prone, but there are more failure points to consider. Any time you add more failure points to anything, it becomes less reliable. There's a greater probability the application will break simply because there are more things that can go wrong with it. Obviously, an unreliable application affects performance by not allowing the application to run at all.

- **Unexpected side effects**   No matter how carefully a developer crafts a multithreaded application, there are going to be side effects that he or she has to deal with, especially if the threads in the application interact. Even if the developer makes the application thread-safe and uses critical sections (these principles are covered in "Understanding Thread Synchronization," later in the chapter), there's a chance two threads may try to access the same variable at the same time in an unanticipated way. Not only do these unexpected side effects increase development and debugging time, but they also make it more likely a user will face a problem that the developer can't duplicate with his or her test setup. In other words, multithreaded applications are more likely to increase application support costs.

Now that you have a fairly good overview of the way in which threads can be used in general, let's look at some specific multithreaded usage types. The following sections explore the three most common ways multiple threads are used: end-user applications, dynamic-link libraries (DLLs), and system services. Each of these areas represents a major application type.

Applications

We've already explored this topic to some extent. Any time an application can perform a task in the background, like monitoring your spelling as you type, or sending a document to the printer, using a thread is a natural choice. Applications can benefit from multiple threads of execution in a number of ways. The only requirement to realize a performance gain using threads is the availability of idle time on the server. In fact, some of those ways seem quite natural from a programming perspective because the tasks in question can be broken from the main thread of execution quite easily. The following list gives you some ideas on how developers can use multiple threads with applications.

- **Printing**   This is the one major task that can always benefit from multiple threads in any application. Queuing a print job takes time, which means the user is left staring at the screen, doing nothing. In fact, some print jobs could take so much time that the user gives up trying to use the computer and does something else while waiting. Printing in the background in a separate thread is always an efficient way to handle this task.

Tip   There are probably a few tasks a developer won't add to background threads, simply because it's not feasible to do so. The one rule of thumb most developers use is whether the user needs to interact directly with the thread. In many cases, any task that requires direct user interaction on a constant basis should be handled as part of the main thread. On the other hand, anything the user can set once, and then allow the computer to complete, is a good candidate for a separate thread. The point is that some developers use threads for everything, which really isn't a smart way to program. Developers should make sure the application realizes an efficiency gain, and the user gains increased responsiveness, any time they create a thread.

- **As the user types**   There are a lot of tasks that fall into this category, but the two most common are spelling and grammar checks. Many applications offer the ability to check the user's spelling and grammar as she types, which reduces the need to check the whole document later. Of course, there are a lot of less common tasks that fall into this category as well. For example, you can check the validity of an equation as the user types it or make sure a database entry is correct. For that matter, you can even suggest (as some applications do) a completed entry for the user based on past input.

- **Repetition**   Repagination and other repetitive tasks can always occur as background threads. There isn't any need to take up the foreground task's time with duties like updating the application clock. You can relegate most repetitive, continuous tasks to a background thread.

- **Data saves**   Most applications now include an automatic-save feature simply because many users are very poor at saving data themselves. It's not hard to figure out why—users are engrossed in getting their document completed and simply forget to perform the data save. An automatic data-saving feature can allow the user to complete a document without worrying about power failures or other computer glitches that can cause data to disappear.

- **Updates** As users rely more and more on remote computing, the need to provide them with updates in the field increases. Updates, in this case, aren't necessarily limited to data. For example, a user might check in with the company each morning for updated pricing schedules. System administrators could use this habit to their advantage by also including a background thread that downloads any system updates the user may require. In other words, the user receives both a data update and an application update at the same time. Of course, automatic data updates are a nice feature as well. The application could update pricing tables or other forms of application-specific information in the background at regular intervals, provided the machine has the capability of creating a remote connection to the company.

Tip There are other ways you can combine multiple threads and system updates. For example, you might want to include a virus-checking thread that runs in the background and checks all incoming data before it gets placed on the client machine. Another use of background threads includes running diagnostics in the background, as the user works, to ensure the machine is fully functional. An alarm tells users that their machine requires service and that they should save any data before it's too late. As you can see, there are a lot of ways you can use threads to protect users, their data, and the client machine from damage.

- **Calculations** Math operations are notorious for consuming vast amounts of processor cycles. In some cases, you have to accept the heavy penalty of a calculation because the user requires an answer immediately. However, there are other situations where the calculation could be completed just as easily in the background as a separate thread. In fact, many spreadsheet and graphics applications use this technique now to make foreground features more responsive to user input. However, custom applications can benefit as well. Consider an order entry system. The calculations required to complete the order can take place in a background task as the user types entries in the foreground. The result is the application can correctly total the order immediately, and the user can provide the customer with interim order totals.

Dynamic-Link Libraries

Dynamic-link libraries (DLLs) have been around since Microsoft Windows was first created. In fact, DLLs are actually the descendants of the libraries used by MS-DOS applications. For the most part, DLLs allow for the same uses of threads as applications do. The main difference is that you want to place common thread types in DLLs—threads that perform work that you may need to do in more than one application. However, there are some thread categories that do get placed in DLLs simply because they're major components of an application that the developer may not want to recompile every time the application is updated.

DLLs are also used for other, nonapplication tasks on a server. One of the unique uses of threads within DLLs is to allow the DLL to answer multiple queries from the same client. Each thread answers one query and allows the application to receive answers as quickly as they become available.

One of the problems in figuring out how DLLs use threads is to establish whether they use them at all. In some cases, a single-threaded DLL appears to be multithreaded because of the way Windows handles it. This is the case with server-side components for the most part. For example, all the new COM+ applications are DLLs created for a special purpose. Every time a user makes a request, the single-threaded DLL is called on to create an object. The user application interacts with this server object in order to perform a given task. To the untrained eye, it could appear that a single multithreaded DLL is executing, when in reality, special features in Windows 2000 allow multiple instances of a single object—one for each application request to the server.

System Services

For the most part, users never interact with system services. System services wait in the background and perform tasks such as enabling a machine's hardware to operate or creating network connections. As a result, there are some fairly specialized uses for threads within a system service. The following list provides you with a few ideas.

- **Service priority upgrade**   Some system services are low-priority background tasks to begin with. You normally don't want them to consume valuable processor cycles unless the machine is idle or there's some type of priority task to perform. It's when you use a service in this second capacity that high-priority threads come into play. Rather than change the priority of the entire service, you can simply launch a single thread to perform the high-priority task.

- **Discovery**   Most system services are low-level applications that need to discover a great deal about the system to ensure it's working properly. This discovery phase can occur once during service initialization in some cases; in other cases, it's an ongoing process. Consider the network driver that has to keep track of the current system configuration, including the status of remote resources. A good use of threads, in this case, is to allow the service to perform multiple levels of discovery at the same time, without reducing its availability to the system as a whole.

Understanding Thread Synchronization

Until now, we've looked at the issue of single-threaded applications versus multithreaded applications from the outside. We've looked at the advantages, disadvantages, and performance parameters of both application types. There's one issue for multithreaded applications that we haven't really talked about, the issue of thread synchronization. As stated earlier, synchronization can incur a performance penalty by forcing one thread to remain idle while it waits for resources in use by another thread. We're not going to get into programming practice in the following sections, but understanding thread synchronization when analyzing processes and applications for efficiency helps you to understand what the issues are and how programmers normally deal with them. Consider the following sections a very brief overview of a very complex topic.

Understanding Thread-Safe DLLs

One of the benefits of using DLLs is code reuse. Once the code is written and tested, a developer can place it in a DLL and forget about it. The functionality that a developer requires for a particular application is available without a lot of additional work. There are other tangible benefits to using DLLs, such as reduced development time. A developer can also spend more time optimizing the code within a DLL that will be used by a number of applications, which enhances overall server performance—at least if the optimization takes place.

Unfortunately, the black-box functionality of DLLs can be a double-edged sword for both the developer and network administrator. One of the biggest problems you face when using DLLs with threads is that the DLL isn't necessarily thread-safe. In other words, if two threads attempt to access the same object or function at the same time, there could be a collision, resulting in a frozen application, lost data, or other unanticipated results. Unless the developer has hand-coded a DLL, there's no assurance that the developer who wrote the original code used thread-safe practices. A DLL can be a time bomb waiting to go off.

Fortunately, a developer can protect applications that use DLLs in a number of ways. One method is to use some form of thread synchronization to ensure that just one thread can access a resource at any given time. For example, a developer can use critical sections as needed to ensure that a sequence of events takes place without interruption. (Critical sections are addressed in the text that follows.) A second way is to allocate variables and objects on the stack. The stack is a unique memory structure that contains all the information passed to a single instance of a DLL. By passing variables and objects on the stack, the developer ensures that only that instance of the DLL has access to the variables and that they're safe from other threads.

Most applications that require some level of thread-safe operation will use thread synchronization. There are three kinds of thread synchronization currently in use: semaphores, mutexes, and critical sections. It's important to understand that each of these techniques has a particular use, but you really don't need to get mired in the details of how they're implemented. For the most part, all you need to know is whether the DLLs you use with an application are thread-safe.

Understanding Semaphores

As the term implies, a semaphore acts as a flag. It signals when a specific resource is overloaded and can't accept any more thread access. A semaphore maintains a count of the number of threads that are accessing the object. When the number is too high, it rejects any more requests for access and places the requesting thread in a queue to wait its turn to use the resource. The threads accessing the resource don't have to be in the same process, which means a semaphore works with shared resources.

From a performance perspective, the use of semaphores incurs the least amount of penalty. It allows an application to control access to a resource, without creating a bottleneck in many cases. A semaphore is a good method of synchronizing access to a resource, where updates by more than one thread aren't an issue, or the resource is opened for read-only access.

Understanding Mutexes

The term *mutex* stands for mutually exclusive. A mutex is like a semaphore in that it controls access to a resource. However, only one thread is allowed to access the resource at any given time. The resource is actually locked and no other thread can access it in any way. Consider a mutex the ultimate in resource protection.

The problem with using a mutex is that it only provides access to one thread. This can create performance bottlenecks and slow an application to a crawl. Imagine what would happen if a developer were to use a mutex in a place where a semaphore would work? The application would run slower without any appreciable change in application safety. On the other hand, consider the effect of using a semaphore where a mutex is really required. The application might work, but your data won't remain safe for very long. (I'm obviously oversimplifying a more complex set of issues, but explaining what's going on beneath the surface shows you how these issues ultimately affect your server's performance.)

Understanding Critical Sections

A critical section is a piece of code that can only be accessed by one thread of an application at one time. In addition, some forms of critical section ensure that the code sequence gets completed without interruption. There are a lot of reasons a developer may want to create a critical section, the most important of which is data integrity. An application changes the contents of variables and the status of objects to meet the needs of a particular user. If another user suddenly decides to execute the same code, the contents of those variables and objects would be ruined for both parties.

While the semaphore and mutex directly manage resources, the critical section manages resource access indirectly. Just how much a critical section affects application performance depends on how the developer designed the rest of the application. If there are other tasks a thread can do while waiting for access to the resource controlled by a critical section, an application could provide both completely secure data access and high performance.

Understanding Thread Types

As far as Windows is concerned, there are threads and the processes that contain them and nothing else. However, from a developer perspective, there are actually two kinds of threads: worker and UI (user interface). Both thread types can perform a single sequence of execution within the application. The difference comes in the way these two kinds of threads are implemented and used. The following sections talk about these two thread types and how they're used.

Worker Threads

Worker threads are normally used for background tasks that require either minimal or no user interaction. A process or another thread creates a worker thread and then forgets about it. The worker thread performs whatever work is requested and then exits. In short, this kind of thread is normally reserved for tasks like printing a document in the background. An application gets all the information needed to print a document, starts the worker thread and feeds it the configuration information, and then allows the user to continue some other task in the foreground. The only time the user would know the printout is complete is if the print-spooling software is set up to provide a completed printout notification, or if the printer itself experiences some type of error. Both of these notifications happen in other threads, so the worker thread can perform its work without any user interaction at all.

Worker threads are called as functions; they aren't created as objects. This means some of the utilities used to spot UI threads don't work with worker threads. (The following section covers UI threads in detail.) However, from a developer's perspective, worker threads are extremely easy to code and implement within an application. This is the low-cost entry into the world of threads for many developers.

Of the two thread types the worker thread is the most efficient. It requires fewer resources than a UI thread and operates at whatever speed the operating system thinks best. In other words, the operating system can optimize the performance of this thread type without any thought about the effect of the thread's priority on the user. As far as the user is concerned, the printout completes at some time, but there isn't any specific time required or even considered.

The only disadvantage of using a worker thread is that it provides no interface. Since the user is unaware of the thread's status and the application doesn't have to track it, a worker thread could fail in some way and no one would know about it immediately. In fact, when a worker thread terminates, it doesn't provide any feedback to the initiating thread. In short, when using worker threads, a developer has to take a proactive approach to check the actual results of the worker thread's error status. The application also has to ensure that the worker thread is terminated if it hasn't completed its task when the user wants to end the application. Finally, if the worker thread does need to communicate, it can't do so. The developer needs to add code to the main thread that will communicate any problems that the worker thread encountered to the user.

UI Threads

As the name suggests, UI threads are normally created to provide some type of user interface functionality within an application. A developer uses this kind of thread when an application can still do other work in the background while the new thread takes care of the user's needs in the foreground. For example, a spell checker likely uses a UI thread because performing a spell check on a document requires some level of user participation.

A UI thread is actually an object that's created using the *CWinThread* class instead of using a function, as with the worker thread. Obviously, this means that implementing a UI thread is more complex than a worker thread, but the developer also gets more flexibility. For example, since a worker thread is created in a "fire and forget" manner, the application doesn't have any access to it once it starts. Yes, the application can terminate the thread, but it doesn't have control over it. A UI thread object, on the other hand, allows the initiating thread to do all kinds of performance enhancements, such as changing the UI thread's priority as needed to ensure prompt responses for the user. The initiating thread can also suspend and terminate UI threads.

UI threads aren't as efficient as worker threads for a number of reasons. The most important reason is that the UI thread has more resource requirements, like a window with which to interact with the user. Obviously, there isn't a one-size-fits-all solution to application development, so the developer needs these two kinds of threads. As long as the threads are used properly, an application can achieve both a high level of performance and high user responsiveness.

Ways to View Processes and Threads

There are a lot of ways to view processes and threads under Windows 2000, many of which are right at your fingertips. The following sections provide a very brief overview of many of these tools. We'll focus on how you can use these tools to monitor the performance of your server, even though some of the tools have additional purposes. The main purpose of this section is to acquaint you with ways of reducing the complex task of monitoring your applications into more manageable pieces. In this case, we're looking at the physical separation of an application into threads of execution, each of which can be monitored for potential performance problems.

Task Manager

The easiest way to see which threads are running is the Task Manager. Right-click the taskbar, choose Task Manager from the Context menu, and then click Processes to see a display similar to the one shown in Figure 3-1. As you can see, this view provides a list of the process names, the process identification (PID) number, the amount of CPU time it's used, and the amount of memory in use. To see which of these processes is part of a main application, right-click one of the names of applications on the Applications tab and then click Go To Process, which takes you directly to that application's process on the Processes tab.

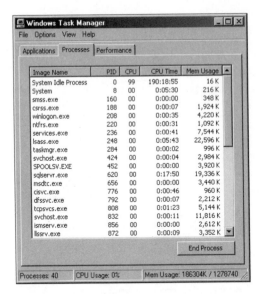

Figure 3-1. *The Windows Task Manager is one of the easiest ways to see which processes are running on your server.*

Tip Highlighting a process in the Windows Task Manager dialog box and then clicking End Process stops that process from running. This is a useful feature to know about. You can use it to stop errant processes that don't provide any form of user interface or other means of stopping. Remember that you can stop services using the Services Microsoft Management Console (MMC) snap-in, so don't use the End Process feature with services unless you've tried other methods of stopping the service first. Likewise, you can stop applications by clicking End Task on the Applications tab of the Windows Task Manager dialog box. In short, use End Process as your last-ditch method of stopping the process because it stops the process immediately, without allowing the process to perform any required cleanup. In many cases, using this feature restores the server's functionality, but leaves some resources in limbo. The server isn't able to use these resources because it thinks they're still in use by the process that you stopped. It's normally a good idea to reboot the server to free resources as soon as it's feasible to do so after using the End Process feature of Task Manager.

It's important to note that the Windows Task Manager dialog box shown in Figure 3-1 shows only the default view. You can obtain additional information about the processes on your server by using Task Manager and selecting the Processes tab, then select View/ Select Columns command to display the Select Columns dialog box shown in Figure 3-2. Notice that there's a lot of additional information you can display about the processes running on your server without using any other tool. We'll cover many of these statistics as part of the discussions in Chapters 4 through 8, so I won't cover them here. The important fact to think about now is that you can easily view the processes running on the server, and garner performance information about them, using just the Task Manager and nothing else.

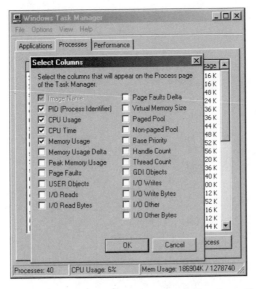

Figure 3-2.   *The Select Columns dialog box allows you to choose which process statistics you want to track with Task Manager.*

Tip   You're going to see the System Idle Process in quite a few of the process monitoring tools provided by Windows 2000. This is a special process that runs when the server isn't doing anything else. You can't stop the System Idle Process and there isn't a good reason to do so since it doesn't use any system resources when they're needed by other processes. However, you can use the System Idle Process as a quick check of server health (albeit a very cursory check). The CPU statistic for the System Idle Process can tell you quite a bit about how much of a load the server carries. A high System Idle Process CPU statistic usually indicates that the server isn't heavily loaded—at least not at the time you check Task Manager.

System Monitor

The main problem in using Task Manager is that you don't get to see any of the threads. Task Manager is designed to look at an application as a whole from the process level. You can't tell if the entire application is running slowly or if a particular thread is monopolizing system resources. So, how do you monitor threads? System Monitor is the main method most network administrators use. We'll cover this MMC snap-in in detail in Chapter 4, so only the process and thread monitoring capabilities of this utility are covered now.

You start System Monitor by selecting Performance from Start/Programs/Administrative Tools. Figure 3-3 shows what the Performance window looks like. Notice that Performance includes two MMC snap-ins: System Monitor and Performance Logs and Alerts. Figure 3-3 shows the right-pane display you see when System Monitor is selected. This particular display shows the chart view; there are also histogram and report views that we'll discuss in Chapter 4.

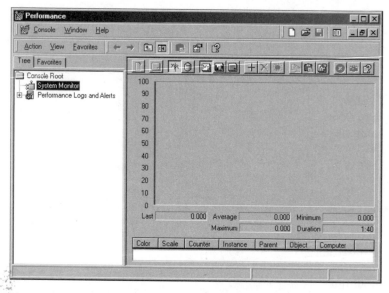

Figure 3-3. *System Monitor allows you to obtain performance data for your server.*

At this point, you need to select some counters to monitor. (A counter is a performance indicator for a specific Windows 2000 object statistic, like the amount of processor time a specific thread requires.) Click the Add button (looks like a plus sign in Figure 3-3) and you see an Add Counters dialog box. The first thing that you need to select is the Performance object you want to monitor. There are entries in the Performance Object drop-down list box for both Process and Thread objects. We already had a quick look at the Process objects on the server, so let's look at the Thread object. Figure 3-4 shows a typical list of counters.

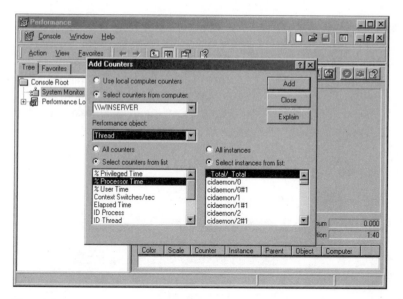

Figure 3-4. *The Add Counters dialog box allows you to choose which objects to monitor.*

Tip If you're unsure about the meaning of a particular counter, click Explain in the Add Counters dialog box. System Monitor displays an additional Explain Text dialog box that provides a brief description of the selected counter. Just highlight the counter you want explained to see an explanation of it in the Explain Text dialog box.

The bottom half of the Add Counters dialog box has two list boxes. The left list box allows you to choose a counter for the performance object that you selected. Figure 3-4 shows that you're looking at the % Processor Time counter of the Thread object. The right list box allows you to choose a specific instance of a counter. Figure 3-4 shows that the Total/Total instance is highlighted. This is a special instance that allows you to monitor all instances using a single entry on the graph, histogram, or report. Below this is a series of entries for cidaemon.

There are actually three parts to each specific instance entry in Figure 3-4. The first part is always the process name, cidaemon in this case. The second part is the number of the thread for that process. As you can see, cidaemon has at least three threads running (0, 1, and 2). The number following the pound sign (#) is the number of the processor. This is a dual processor machine. If you don't see a processor number, the instance refers to the first processor in the machine. In other words, there's an instance for each thread and for each processor that the thread can run on. We'll examine the specifics of counters in more detail in Chapter 4. However, this explanation should give you enough information to understand how threads are viewed using System Monitor.

Computer Management

Up to this point, we've looked at ways of monitoring the performance of a specific process or thread. There are other ways to monitor the processes on your server that provide information to help you locate potential performance problems. Open the Start/Programs/Administrative Tools/Computer Management utility. Choose the System Information MMC snap-in, and then the Software Environment/Running Tasks folder. You'll see a Computer Management window similar to the one shown in Figure 3-5. As you can see, this window presents a list of the running processes, just like you saw in Task Manager. The difference is that instead of seeing performance information, you see the path to the file associated with the process on the hard disk, along with the version number, size, and date of that file.

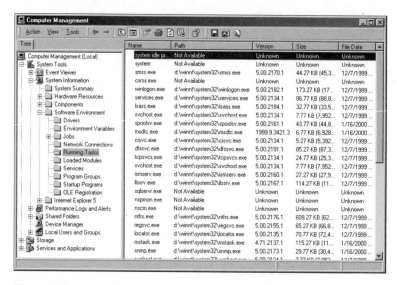

Figure 3-5. *Looking at the contents of the Running Tasks folder can help you find old files on your server that could affect server performance.*

Note Figure 3-5 shows the contents of the Running Tasks folder—that is, the .exe files currently running on the server. You'll need to look in the Loaded Modules folder for a list of currently running .dll files. The Drivers folder shows which drivers are loaded for the server and whether they're currently running. Finally, look in the Services folder to see which services are currently running on the server.

Let's look at one way you can use this information. What happens if you test process performance and find it lacking? What can you do to ensure you're using the most current version of the .exe or .dll file? A wealth of problems can occur if the server isn't running the correct version of an .exe or .dll. The problem can be quite subtle. For example, consider what happens if you have two versions of the same .dll used by several applications on the server, one of which appears in the %SystemRoot%\System32 directory and another that appears in just one application's directory. If the application-specific version of the.dll gets loaded first, other applications that rely on the .dll might not work. You could trace this problem using the Running Tasks feature of the System Information MMC snap-in.

Tip   The vast majority of Windows 2000-specific .exe and .dll files have a version number starting with 5.00 for the initial release of Windows 2000. Files with other version numbers are usually provided by third-party or supplemental products and may not be written to work under Windows 2000. You'll want to check with the vendors of these products to ensure that their product is written to use the performance-enhancing features for Windows 2000. In many cases, you'll find that vendors will provide upgrades for Windows 2000 and it pays to go to their Web site to download new versions of these files.

Developer Tools

Not every tool that you can use to monitor the processes and threads running on your server is installed as part of Windows 2000. There are a few developer tools you can use to learn how the applications on your server are set up in order to get a better idea of how processes and threads work together. All these tools are part of Microsoft Visual Studio (I'm using Visual Studio 6.0 SP3 for this book). The following sections provide a brief overview of each tool. Note that we're taking the user's view of these tools, not the programmer's view.

Tip   One of the utilities we won't talk about in this book (because it has nothing to do with performance tuning or optimization) is Error Lookup. In some cases, a developer fails to translate a rather ambiguous error number generated within an application into human-readable form. What you see when an application error occurs is a dialog box that contains strange numbers that you'll never figure out. The Error Lookup utility can help you translate those error numbers into something you can understand, at least in some cases. You have to be careful using this utility because the error number generated by the application might be a custom error code and not one of the universal codes recognized by Windows.

Process Viewer

Process Viewer is one of the easier ways to look at threads and processes. Figure 3-6 shows what this tool looks like. As you can see, Process Viewer allows you to view processes on other machines, not just the current machine. All you need to do is provide a universal naming convention (UNC) computer name (such as \\winserver) in the Computer field, and then click Connect.

> **Note**   You can find at least some of the tools discussed in this chapter in Windows 2000 Support Tools or Windows 2000 Resource Kit. Windows 2000 Support Tools come as part of Windows 2000, but aren't installed for you automatically. The Windows Installer file for the support tools is located in the %CDROM%\SUPPORT\TOOLS\ directory. Just right-click on 2000RKST.MSI and choose Install from the context menu. The Windows 2000 Resource Kit is discussed in greater detail in Chapter 15.

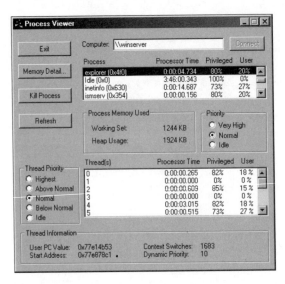

Figure 3-6.   *The Process Viewer allows you to see processes and threads in one easy step.*

The top half of Process Viewer is devoted to the process. The Process list contains all the processes executing on the computer that you've selected (the local computer if you haven't made any other selection). The statistics include the amount of processor time, and the amount of time spent in user mode versus kernel (privileged) mode. Directly below the Process list are statistics for the currently highlighted process that include the amount of memory used and the process's priority. The priority is important because it tells you how this process is given various resources compared to other processes running on the same server. The default setting for user applications is Normal. Some system services, such as Session Manager, receive a priority of Very High, while others, such as Task Scheduler, run at a Normal priority. Background tasks, such as System Idle Process, run at an Idle priority.

The lower half of Process Viewer is devoted to threads associated with the process currently highlighted in the Process list. Like the Process list, the Thread(s) list tells you how much processing time the thread has gotten and how it's spent that time. To the left of the Thread(s) list is the current thread priority. A thread normally inherits the priority of its process, but this isn't a hard-and-fast rule. The higher the priority of the thread, the more processing time it gets.

The Thread Priority setting only indicates the thread's base (or starting) priority. The current thread priority appears in the Thread Information block in the Dynamic Priority field. This value changes as the thread executes. If a thread isn't getting any runtime, the operating system bumps its dynamic priority up. Likewise, if the system detects that a thread is wasting system resources, the dynamic priority level is decreased. We'll see in later chapters how dynamic priority comes into play when tuning your system. For example, in Chapter 10, we'll see how you can use CPU Throttling to adjust the priority of Internet Information Server (IIS) threads to keep one Web site from dominating your server.

There's one additional Process Viewer feature that you may want to look at. Click Memory Detail and you see the Memory Details dialog box shown in Figure 3-7. As you can see, this dialog box contains very detailed information about precisely how a process is using memory. In fact, the level of detail provided by this dialog box is overkill for most network administrators, so I plan to cover it only briefly. However, you'll see in a few moments why this particular dialog box could come in handy.

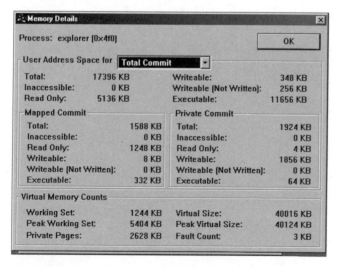

Figure 3-7.   *The Memory Details dialog box from the Process Viewer application provides extremely detailed information about how a particular process is using memory.*

The User Address Space field of the Memory Details dialog box contains the name of the address space that you're viewing. The Total Commit value means you're looking at the memory used by the entire process. If you click the arrow next to the combo box, you see a list of all the .dlls and .exes used by this application. Select one of these entries and you see the memory used just by that piece of the application.

There are two things you should look for in this dialog box. First, look for a number in the Inaccessible field. Any value other than 0 in this field tells you the process has some type of memory problem. The second item is the Total memory field for the User Address Space. Compare this value for the Total Mapped Commit entry to the Total memory field value for the User Address Space or the Private Commit. If you see that one .dll is using a substantial amount of memory and the others some small amount of memory, you need to ask why this one .dll is responding in this particular way. In many cases, you'll find nothing wrong, but there are a few situations when a buggy .dll will keep grabbing memory until it begins to impinge on the resources available to other applications.

Microsoft Spy++

Just in case you don't have enough ways to view threads yet, there's one other utility that you should look at called Microsoft Spy++. As the name implies, Spy++ allows you to spy on what the server is doing. For the most part, Spy++ provides you with more information than you need to optimize a server, but this very detailed look at your system has advantages, especially when it comes to identifying a particular thread.

When you start Spy++, it opens with a Window view that doesn't help you very much. What you need is the Process view. Close the Window view, and then click Processes on the toolbar to see a Process view similar to the one shown in Figure 3-8.

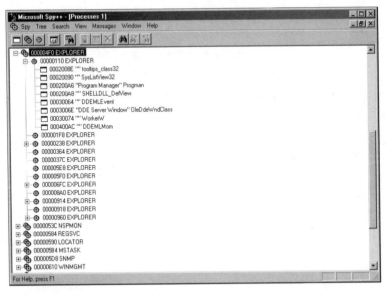

Figure 3-8. *Spy++ provides yet another way to view processes and threads on your server.*

Notice that I've located the Explorer process, in this case, and opened it up so that you can see the various threads and the resources that one thread is using. The first thing you should notice is that some threads have a plus sign next to them, while others don't. The threads with plus signs are all UI threads; the threads without are worker threads.

Let's take a closer look at the UI thread that I opened in Figure 3-8. If you spend enough time looking at the various entries, you can figure most of them out, even if you're not a developer with programming skills. For example, you can see from the first entry that this thread supports tooltips (those little balloons that appear when you place the mouse cursor over a button or other object on an application). Tooltips are the resources that allow you to identify a particular thread. Right-click the entries one at a time, and then choose Properties from the Context menu. Any window, dialog box, control, or other physical feature of an application that has some kind of identifying mark on it provides a Window Caption, as shown in the Window Properties dialog box in Figure 3-9. You can use this information to identify this thread for the purpose of monitoring its performance.

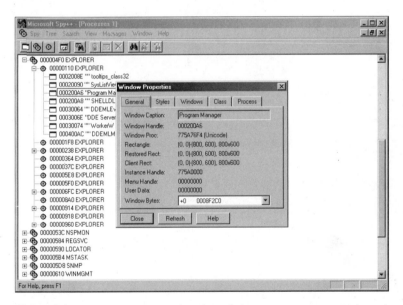

Figure 3-9.   *Spy++ properties of UI threads have one or more windows that make it easy to identify the thread's purpose within the application.*

Prioritizing Processes and Threads

There are a few issues we haven't covered yet with regard to processes and threads. One of the more important issues is the matter of setting the process priority. If you look at Figure 3-6 again, you see that Process Viewer allows you to see the current process and thread priorities, but it doesn't allow you to change them. You can, however, use this utility to see the effects of any changes you do make.

Fortunately, changing the priority of a process is relatively easy. All you need to do is display the Processes tab of the Windows Task Manager dialog box, right-click the process you want to change, and then use the options on the Set Priority menu, shown in Figure 3-10, to adjust the priority of the process.

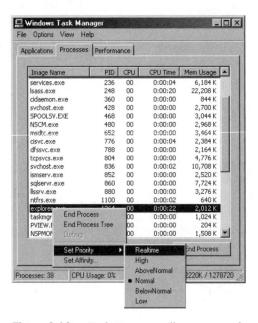

Figure 3-10. *Task Manager allows you to change the priority of processes on your server.*

As an experiment (if you have Process Viewer installed on your machine), start a second instance of Microsoft Windows Explorer and in Task Manager set its priority to High. Windows 2000 displays a cautionary message you should read, and then click OK. Open Process Viewer and you see a display similar to the one shown in Figure 3-11. Compare this figure to Figure 3-6 and you notice that the priority of the process has indeed changed, but that the priority of the thread (at least the thread we have highlighted) hasn't.

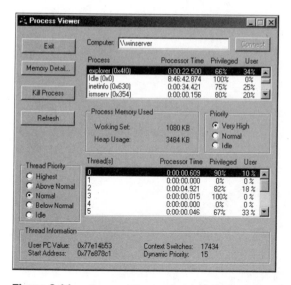

Figure 3-11.   *Process Viewer shows that changing the priority of a process makes an instant change in Process Viewer as well.*

Thread priorities follow those of the process, but only as the operating system services the thread. In short, although you don't have direct control over thread priorities, you can affect them by changing the process priority. If you exercise Windows Explorer at this point, you'll see that the priorities of one or more of the threads will get upgraded. You may notice a performance difference as well, depending on what task you're performing and how long it takes. Once you've spent some time testing out the priority-changing mechanism, make sure you reset Windows Explorer to its original priority level.

Affinity is another setting that affects the way threads get executed by the operating system. The affinity setting is actually a mask that's part of the application settings within the process. This setting determines which processors can execute the application. You use this setting if you want to control an application's use of resources. Perhaps this is a low-priority background task that you only want to execute on the second processor to keep the first processor free for more important tasks. (The affinity setting doesn't appear on single processor machines. Having only one processor means that every process and thread must use that specific processor and the affinity setting has no meaning in that environment.)

Setting the processor affinity is easy. Right-click the process you want to change, and then choose Set Affinity from the Context menu. You see the Processor Affinity dialog box shown in Figure 3-12. Windows 2000 defaults to allowing every application to execute on any processor. Checking the box next to a CPU option allows the application to execute on that processor.

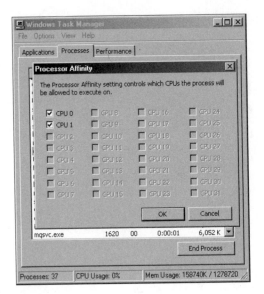

Figure 3-12. *The Processor Affinity dialog box is where you determine which processors an application can use.*

So, how does the operating system determine which processor to use if you select multiple processors for an application? The operating system looks for a processor that isn't doing anything first. Since that seldom happens on any server, Windows 2000 looks at the processor's load next. It chooses the processor queue that has the least amount of activity scheduled at the time the task is scheduled.

Multiprocessing and Performance

It doesn't take very long to realize that there are going to be situations where a single processor can't handle the processing load you place on it. Many, if not most, servers today, come with more than one processor because people expect servers to do more. Multimedia, voice over Internet protocol (VOIP), video conferencing, and other processing needs on today's networks require immense amounts of processing power. Of course, the question most network administrators need to answer is just how much power a second processor (or more) adds to the capacity of a server.

Once an administrator has a second processor in place, the question of how to optimize the server to make the best use of this processor comes into play. It's not safe to assume that a single optimization methodology is going to work for all application types. Processor-intensive applications often require different handling in a multiprocessor environment than disk-intensive applications will. Obviously, this means that a network administrator needs to do some research on processor usage as part of preparing to install the server. He or she will need to learn what kinds of applications a server will run, the level of response the user requires to complete tasks in a timely manner, and the amount of throughput the company needs to service all the users on the network.

We're going to look at these and other questions in an overview format in the sections that follow. You'll find more detailed information about processor performance tuning in Chapter 5. "Improved Multiprocessor Support" in Chapter 10 answers the question of what kind of multiprocessor support Windows 2000 provides. You'll find that it's a vast improvement over what you may have experienced in the past. Finally, we'll look at what you need to do in order to prepare for future processing needs in Chapter 11. This chapter looks at capacity planning from a number of angles, including what's best for the user, the company, and the network, and the applications available through the network.

Two Processors Don't Equal Twice the Performance

In a simple world, you could add a second processor to a server and expect it to provide you with twice the performance. There are a number of influences that affect processor throughput (as we'll discover in Chapter 5). For example, a processor that gets tied up with disk activity doesn't spend as much time performing computationally intensive tasks like invoice calculations. The simple fact is that two processors seldom equate to twice the computing performance in any server because of the way applications are normally handled by the operating system.

In addition to application problems, servers with two processors often lose some performance because of operating system housekeeping tasks. It takes more operating system time to manage two processors. For one thing, the operating system attempts to balance the processor load, which means it spends more time monitoring applications.

Finally, there are architectural problems that keep your server from performing at twice its normal speed with two processors. For one thing, two processors tax whatever bus system the vendor provides for getting data from memory to the processor. Even though local cache goes a long way in making processors work more efficiently, the fact remains that the local cache is only so large and can do only so much to mitigate the effects of a slow bus. In short, until vendors find a way of making the bus larger and faster, main memory continues to lag behind the processor, and the processor ends up waiting for the data it needs.

Symmetric versus Asymmetric Multiprocessing

There are two kinds of multiprocessing that you need to know about, only one of which Windows 2000 directly supports. The first kind of multiprocessing is called asymmetric multiprocessing, which can use two or more different kinds of processors to improve system throughput (although this isn't necessarily a requirement). An asymmetric multiprocessing system normally incorporates the idea of a master processor as well. In most cases, the master processor is used only for operating system processing (including protected mode access of devices), which means the operating system gets dedicated processor support. The advantage of using this method is that each processor can be specially designed to perform one task really well. This means each processor can contribute to the whole, but that none of the processors are burdened with a task that they're ill equipped to perform. While this setup works very well for a workstation, it doesn't provide much of a boost for a server. In most cases, servers perform a lot of iterations of the same mundane tasks, which means the potential for performing specialty tasks is greatly reduced.

Real World

A few years ago, I had the pleasure of using a workstation that included an 80486 and an i860 processor. The two processors shared memory and other resources, but they performed entirely different tasks. The 80486 was used exclusively for disk and computational tasks. Meanwhile, the i860 handled all graphics tasks, including rendering data for output to a printer. The speed of this workstation was absolutely amazing for its day. When used in a workstation environment, a true asymmetric processing setup can enhance performance to a much greater degree than symmetric multiprocessing does, but only if you have the required drivers and operating system support.

Symmetric multiprocessing, the type supported directly by Windows 2000, relies on multiple copies of the same processor to work together. There isn't a master processor; an application can execute on any available processor. The advantage of this methodology is that every processor works the same—there isn't any special coding required. In addition, every processor can perform every task. This is the best setup for a server based on how servers handle tasks. Servers aren't normally called on to perform advanced graphics rendering or other specialty tasks that lend themselves to an asymmetric processor setup.

These two situations that I've just talked about are pure processing scenarios. I only considered the main processor. The reality is that today's computer often has a little asymmetric processing bundled in with the symmetric processing a server needs. For example, very few graphics adapters ship without a processor today because of the intense graphics requirements of many workstation applications. Do you need a high graphics processor for your server? Probably not, but you may find one in the box anyway.

One place where you can garner tremendous benefits using asymmetric processing in a server is with the disk drive host adapter. That's the card you place in one of the server's slots before attaching the hard drive cables. Many host adapters don't provide any logic onboard as a means to keep server costs down. Those that do provide onboard logic are a lot more expensive, but can offload part of the processing load from the main processor. In fact, these "smart" adapters can often perform data transfers between peripherals in the background without the main processor's help.

Understanding Application Multiprocessing Requirements

One of the misconceptions that people have about multiprocessing scenarios is that they'll automatically get a boost out of every application they run. That's not the case with many applications. If you have an application that's single-threaded, it works at the same speed in a multiprocessing scenario as it does with a single processor. You may see a small performance gain, but that's because the operating system is able to give the application more processing cycles in a given timeframe, not because the application is working any faster.

Applications that routinely use background tasks run a little faster in a multiprocessing scenario, but only while the background task is in operation. For example, I noticed a slight performance gain using Microsoft Word in a multiprocessing scenario because Word uses a separate thread for the spelling and grammar checker that runs in the background. The foreground performance was improved because the background task was moved to another processor. Since Word is always using the spelling and grammar checker while you type, the performance gain was more or less constant. However, if you use this same scenario for an application that uses a background thread for printing, the only operation that actually works faster is printing—the application itself plods along at the same speed as before.

There's a third group of applications that makes extensive use of threads for a variety of tasks. For example, a database manager will often create one thread of execution for every client that makes a request. Some multimedia applications will create multiple threads of execution in order to service each data stream (often associated with a specific instrument) as a separate entity. Depending on how the developer puts the application together, you can see a significant performance gain in this case. Unfortunately, some developers use too many threads, which actually kills part of the performance gain that the server might otherwise experience. Using too many threads won't make the application run faster, but it does increase the number of housekeeping chores the operating system has to perform. More operating system time means less time to execute application code.

Microsoft Windows 2000 Memory Model

Memory—it seems today's operating systems eat it for breakfast, and then need a snack immediately afterward. As applications and the operating system are called on to do more work, the requirement for memory also increases. Memory holds data and code, and acts as a scratch pad for various pieces of hardware. In short, you can't get by without memory when running Windows 2000. In fact, Microsoft specifies a minimum limit of 128 MB of RAM for Windows 2000 Server and recommends that you have a minimum of 256 MB installed. Windows 2000 requires more memory because it can do more things for you.

Windows 2000 uses a flat 32-bit memory model. This means you're limited to using 4 GB of physical memory with Windows 2000. When an application makes the right settings, 3 GB of this memory can be reserved for application use. Normally, however, applications are limited to using 2 GB of memory. Windows uses the remaining 1 or 2 GB of memory for operating system use. This assumes that your server actually has 4 GB of RAM installed; many servers don't. In that case, Windows 2000 uses the memory your server does have as efficiently as possible. There are also certain "tricks" Windows 2000 can use to make it appear that you have more memory available.

Besides the physical memory that you install on your system, Windows 2000 also uses virtual memory. This is memory that actually resides on the hard drive, but Windows makes it appear to applications that it's installed on your machine. When some piece of application memory hasn't been used for a while, Windows 2000 copies it to disk. Likewise, when the application requests access to that piece of memory, Windows 2000 copies some other piece of memory to disk and places the requested memory back into physical memory. The size of these memory pieces is a consistent 4 KB. In other words, every time an application makes a request for memory, the memory is allocated within a 4-KB page. The process of swapping the contents of physical memory to and from the hard drive is called paging. The file on disk that emulates memory is called the paging file. We'll look at the various techniques you can use to optimize this file in Chapter 6.

Applications obviously don't ask for memory in 4-KB pages. Sometimes developers need a few bytes, other times a few MB. If a memory request is smaller than 4 KB, Windows allocates a single page. It keeps honoring memory requests from that page until it's used up, at which time it allocates another page of memory. If a memory request is larger than a single page can handle, Windows allocates enough pages to fulfill the request. Applications can't share memory pages. This means that no matter how little memory an application requires, it always uses a minimum of 4 KB of RAM.

Virtual Memory Management

The Virtual Memory Manager (VMM) is an operating system component that manages virtual memory on your machine. All memory access goes through VMM. This means that whenever the operating system needs to page memory to disk, it makes the request of VMM.

VMM is also responsible for translating memory locations. The physical layout of memory bears little resemblance to the virtual layout of memory, which is what an application uses. An application is given memory locations to use that can be on the hard drive or anywhere in physical memory. It doesn't matter to the application where the memory is physically located; all it knows is that it has access to a given virtual memory address.

As with other services, VMM provides other services to the operating system. These services include support for memory-mapped files, copy-on-write memory, and application support for large, sparse memory address spaces. As you might expect, VMM also provides a set of services that allow applications to allocate and free memory, and share memory between processes. The operating environments also require support that allows them to flush memory to disk, retrieve information about a range of virtual pages, and to either secure or release the virtual memory pages as needed.

There's a hierarchy of virtual memory management that you need to be aware of as well. When a parent process creates a child process, the parent is allowed to work with the child's memory, but the child is excluded from modifying any memory held by the parent. The parent can allocate, reallocate, deallocate, read, or write memory on behalf of the child process using a variety of virtual memory services, and passing a memory handle to the child process as an argument. This technique is typically used in situations when the parent has to maintain control of the child process. For example, this is how the debugger for most programming languages works.

The final way in which VMM affects the system is to provide services to the operating system itself. VMM allows the operating system to allocate and deallocate physical memory (in contrast to the virtual memory used by everything else), lock and unlock physical memory, and perform tasks like direct memory access (DMA) data transfers. DMA transfers normally occur in the background between two peripheral devices without the aid of the main processor. A DMA transfer allows the data to move quickly and reduces the load on the processor, enhancing system performance.

Summary

This chapter has presented you with an in-depth look at memory, processes, and threads. We've looked at how these three elements can affect the performance of your server and how you can monitor them. It's important to understand that much of this theory is put into real-world terms in later chapters. For now, you should leave this chapter with a better idea of what threads, processes, and memory mean when it comes to the overall performance of a single server.

The first part of the chapter concentrated on processes and threads. We defined how processes and threads differ. It's important to remember that processes are actually application containers. They hold threads, application settings, resources, and memory. Threads, on the other hand, contain executable code and form the only method that the operating system has for performing tasks. There are two kinds of threads: worker and UI. The essential difference between the two is that the UI thread has a window and can interact with the user, while the worker thread performs its task in the background.

This chapter also touched on the tools you can use to view the threads, processes, and even memory. We've looked at a variety of tools because there isn't any one tool that works in every situation. A network administrator needs to have more than one tool to do the best job of looking for potential system performance problems.

Part of getting the best performance out of your server is realizing the importance of multiprocessing in today's computing environment. We briefly touched on the topic of multiprocessing and how it can speed application execution. This topic is touched on again in other chapters.

Finally, we looked at memory. Windows sports two kinds—the real memory that you install in the server and the artificial kind that gets created from a paging file on the hard disk. Understanding both real memory and virtual memory is essential if you want to see how some of the tuning techniques presented throughout the book work.

The next chapter provides you with an in-depth look at the main monitoring tool in your arsenal. System Monitor is an essential first stop, in many cases, because it's the only way you can get a historical view of your system in operation. Not only does System Monitor help you find the source of performance problems, but it can also help you determine the effectiveness of any remedial steps you take. Performance isn't a clear-cut science where you have a precise cure for the disease of system inefficiency; sometimes you need to use the trial-and-error method to find the precise answer. System Monitor is the tool you need to ensure that the steps you take work today and in the future.

Chapter 4
Performance Monitoring in Microsoft Windows 2000

The activity of performance tuning and optimization (PTO) isn't limited to the world of workstations and servers. Engineers and scientists constantly have to performance-tune systems to ensure the equipment performs up to par. A system that isn't accurately tuned can result in inaccurate data being output by the system, and the consequences of that can be drastic. If the computer that reports the altitude and attitude aboard an aircraft is off by the smallest percent, for instance, the result can be disastrous.

No matter what the system, it can't be tuned unless it can be measured. However, measuring the system is just half the battle; you must also understand what to look for when measuring the system. Simply watching a few dials and meters isn't going to get the job done if you don't know how to interpret the data.

A good example of how important it is to know how to interpret data accurately is what a doctor must do when diagnosing a patient. When people feel ill, they know that their body requires some form of tuning so they can get back on their feet. They go to the doctor so she can measure how their body is doing, diagnose their problem, and prescribe the right medication to correct the situation.

When the doctor checks your body's performance, she does so using various types of equipment. She measures your blood pressure with a sphygmomanometer, listens to your heartbeat with a stethoscope, and takes your temperature with a thermometer. Each one of these tests allows the doctor to measure your body's performance and make a comparison to predefined acceptable threshold limits. If your body is performing within those limits, there's nothing for her to do; however, if they're beyond those limits, she uses her expertise and more specialized equipment, if necessary, to form a diagnosis.

Once in a while, your Microsoft Windows 2000 Server, like your body, requires tuning. This may consist of resolving a memory issue through a simple upgrade, or doing detailed analysis of the server when hunting down a runaway process. No matter what the reason, when the server falls out of tune you need to know how to diagnose it quickly. You need accurate information before you can make a decision on what's causing the problem and how to correct it.

There are several facts you need before diagnosing any problem with your server. What hardware device or software application is the bottleneck in your system? Is the server really to blame? Can it simply be a case of impatient users? You need a way of comparing current server performance to a predefined baseline. This will help you determine if a problem exists and what type of a problem it may be. If you find that your server isn't responding the way it used to and nothing has changed on the server, for example, you can make a strong argument that the server needs further looking into. You can then decide what part of the server is causing the problem.

In this chapter, you explore the performance-monitoring application of Windows 2000 Server called the Performance console (formerly known as Performance Monitor under Microsoft Windows NT). The Performance console consists of System Monitor and Performance Logs and Alerts, which are both Microsoft Management Console (MMC) snap-ins, meaning they can be added to any management control panel you may have created.

Keep in mind that measuring the system is just the first step in PTO; knowing what to do from the data you collected is the second. In this chapter, you learn how to collect data using System Monitor and Performance Logs and Alerts. You also review how to use the tools available to you in the Performance console for PTO of your Windows 2000 Server. Understanding the material in this chapter is essential if you want to use many of the methods of PTO discussed in the chapters ahead.

Using the Microsoft Management Console

New under Windows 2000 is the MMC. Unlike Windows NT, where you have individual administration programs for each task (such as Dynamic Host Configuration Protocol (DHCP) Manager, Windows Internet Naming Service (WINS) Manager, User Manager and User Manager for Domains, and Performance Monitor), Windows 2000 allows you to configure an MMC so you have a choice of administrative tools from a single console. This way, you can launch and view System Monitor and manage DHCP servers and Microsoft SQL Server 7.0 from the same management console.

By default, the Performance console is configured with System Monitor and Performance Logs and Alerts as the administrative applications in the console. You can get to the Performance console by clicking Start/Programs/Administrative Tools/Performance. MMC opens, showing System Monitor and Performance Logs and Alerts (see Figure 4-1); from here, you can view current activity on the server and select information to be collected for analysis. To learn more about the MMC and other new features of Windows 2000, see the online help.

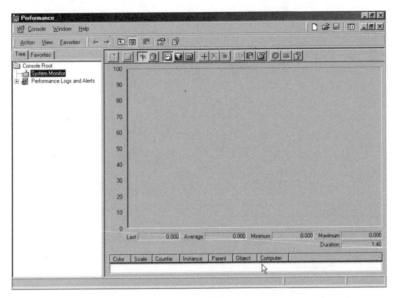

Figure 4-1. *The Microsoft Management Console (MMC) provides the capability to perform many administrative functions simultaneously using MMC snap-ins. A single configurable console offers both system monitoring and administration.*

System Monitor allows you to measure the performance of your own computer and the performance of remote computers on your network.

View Real-Time Performance Data from the Comfort of Your Computer Screen

When running System Monitor to collect data from a local or remote computer you're able to view performance information in real-time. Real-time performance analysis is particularly useful when you can't wait for data to be collected in logs or reports.

Using the chart view or report view under System Monitor, you're able to monitor the performance of your Windows 2000 Server and the applications running on the server. So, seeing a spike occur with processor utilization when a particular application or process is running on the server may point you in the right direction when diagnosing the problem. Figure 4-2 illustrates a case where System Monitor is reporting continuous spikes with processor utilization.

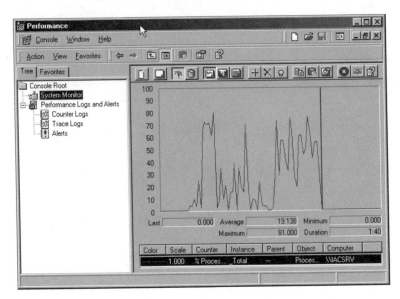

Figure 4-2. *Can you determine why spikes are occurring with processor utilization with just a quick look at the chart?*

Now that you have this data in front of you, what do you do? What do these spikes tell you about server performance and processor utilization? Are you able to determine the cause of the problem from the chart alone? The answer to this last question is no. You need more information than this. In the case of a processor that's spiking as shown in Figure 4-2, one possible step in diagnosing the problem is to see what processes were running when these spikes occurred. For more information on diagnosing problems with processor bottlenecks, see Chapter 5, "Diagnosing Processor Bottlenecks."

Analyze Data Collected Either Currently or Previously in a Counter Log

As the network administrator for a Windows 2000 Server, you will have times when problems occur with the system that can't be easily diagnosed with a real-time snapshot of system performance. You may need to collect data over time—from a single hour, to a day, to several days. You can view counter data collected by Performance Logs and Alerts during collection as well as after collection has stopped. See the "Performance Logs and Alerts Views" section later in this chapter for additional detail on analyzing collected data.

Ability to View Collected Data in Various Views

In the same section, "Performance Logs and Alerts Views," you explore the possible views available to you under System Monitor to display collected data. Interpretation and analysis of System Monitor data depends heavily on how the data is presented to you. You may find, when monitoring multiple counters, that the chart view, with many possible counters to monitor, is too difficult to read, while the report view is more readable. Figure 4-3 illustrates what the chart view looks like when collecting data from multiple counters.

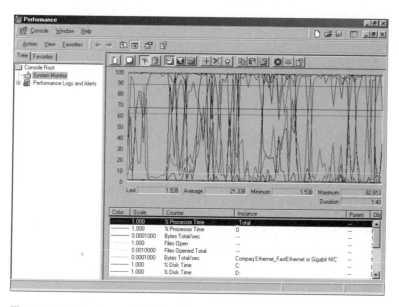

Figure 4-3. *The System Monitor MMC snap-in chart view can become chaotic at times; you may find the report or alert views more readable depending on the type of information required.*

Understanding Performance Counters, Objects, and Instances

The ability to measure a system must exist before you can begin to performance tune that system. Measuring a system not only allows you to set expectations for the system, but also allows you to compare the system to baseline values collected as part of proactive network administration. Later in the chapter, in the section titled "Performance Logs and Alert View," you discover the methods to collect baseline data for analysis.

When you begin hearing complaints from users that the server or network is slow, how can you confirm this? Sitting in front of a workstation and running a few applications may confirm that fact; however, you may be as impatient as your users, and everything seems slow. By what standard can you determine if the server is truly unresponsive? If you have no yardstick to measure your Windows 2000 Server performance against, you have no way to manage it for proper tuning and optimization. This is where performance counters come in. In this chapter in the section titled "Commonly Used Objects under Windows 2000 Performance," we review important server objects for System Monitor. Prior to this you review the relevance of objects and instances as part of the System Monitor MMC

Snap-in. Now you learn about the counters that report the actual performance of these objects.

Counters under System Monitor and Performance Logs and Alerts are what allow you to measure your Windows 2000 performance. Counters allow you to measure performances of both hardware devices and software applications configured on your Windows 2000 Server. For example, when measuring activity of hardware devices, some counters count the visits made to the device by the operating system. Other counters that are part of software applications running on the server measure utilization of server resources by the applications themselves and also report on application performance. A specific example is the Current Files Cached counter (part of the Internet Information Services Global performance object), which allows you to measure the number of files cached for WWW or FTP services. See Figure 4-4.

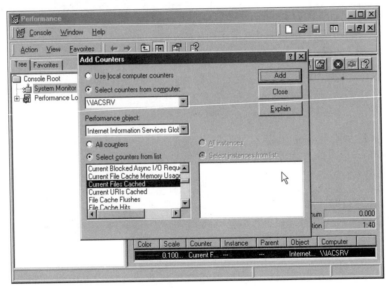

Figure 4-4. *The Current Files Cached counter for the Internet Information Services Global performance object is selected.*

Objects and Instances

When you add counters to System Monitor or Performance Logs and Alerts, you'll notice the amount of counters available for you to track. (You'll see how to add counters later in this chapter.) Because there are so many counters and because determining their purpose can be dizzying, the counters have been organized into a logical hierarchy defined by the structure of the (measurable) hardware equipment and (measurable) software elements.

At the top of the counter hierarchy is the computer. Each computer has distinct elements called objects. Objects are available for hardware devices such as physical disk, memory, processors, and network adapters. Other objects include those for measuring individual processes, paging file performance, and Microsoft BackOffice applications such as SQL Server 7.0.

The naming scheme in System Monitor follows the logical order of object:counter:instance. For example, the naming convention for the processor object is Processor (object)\Utilization (counter)\ 0 (instance — for a single processor identified as processor 0). In this case, the counter measures the total utilization of the processor. Because multiple processors may exist in any one system, objects can have multiple instances that you measure. So, in the case of a server that was configured with dual processors, you have two instances of processor to select from. For example, the first processor instance is 0, while the second processor instance is 1. You can choose to monitor only one processor at a time, or both. Similarly, you'll see multiple instances of network cards or hard disks, each one being assigned an instance number by System Monitor beginning at 0.

Selecting Objects to Monitor

The System Monitor is intuitive when adding counters for monitoring. You can add counters by starting a Performance console by selecting Start/Programs/Administrative Tools/Performance. Once the Performance console opens, select the System Monitor Snap-in in the left console pane. With System Monitor open, click the plus sign to open the Add Counters dialog box. When the Add Counters dialog box appears, the processor is the default performance object, presumably because the processor object is one of the most commonly selected objects. From the dialog box, you can select objects to add for data collection. (See Figure 4-4 for an example of a software performance object.) Scroll down the list to see what other objects are available for you to monitor. The list varies according to the hardware and software installed on your server.

Selecting which objects to use for measuring system performance can be hard if you don't have a specific problem you're chasing down. Even though System Monitor may make many more objects available, there are some commonly used groups of objects you can use to begin monitoring your system that can help point to some common problems with Windows 2000 Server. These objects are discussed in the following section.

Note   If you've installed Microsoft Internet Information Services or a BackOffice application such as Microsoft SQL Server 7.0, you'll find additional System Monitor objects to select. These objects are known as extended objects. An example of one of the SQL Server extended objects is the *SQL Server Cache* object. This measures the activity of the cache under SQL Server. If you want to view Windows 2000 operating system cache performance, select the cache object.

Overview of Important Performance Objects

Table 4-1 lists commonly used objects under Windows 2000 Server and what each object may tell you about your server. Use this list as the starting point for diagnosing system problems. Although other counters help you narrow your search, these objects provide you with the best overall view of your server's performance.

Table 4-1. Commonly Used Objects under the Windows 2000 Performance Console

Object Name	Description
Cache	The file system cache is used to buffer physical device data. A high cache object counter indicates good performance output from the system because data is being retrieved from a cache rather than a physical disk. You can also tell a lot about the care with which an application was written using the data flush counters. These counters indicate how often an application forces Microsoft Windows to flush the cache to disk. A high number of disk flushes may indicate that the developer didn't understand the performance benefits of using the cache. On the other hand, too few disk flushes may indicate that the application is too reliant on cache and is a candidate for data loss if the system fails unexpectedly.
Memory	Random access memory (RAM) is used by the operating system and applications running on Windows 2000 Server. The rule is the more RAM, the faster the system. However, RAM is not the "end all and be all" for your system configuration. For a truly efficient server, all aspects of your hard ware must be configured to coincide with the amount of memory in the machine. A high count of page reads indicates you are running low on RAM and the system is having to resort to reading/writing to the page file. Because reading or writing to RAM is much faster than disk, your system shows signs of low-system performance if the page file is overused.
Objects	System software objects include events, mutexes, processes, sections, semaphores, and threads. By measuring the threads counter for the object's performance object, you are able to monitor the number of threads in the computer at that moment. A high thread count and low processes count can point to an application that is resource-intense just by the number of threads it requires to run.
Paging File	The paging file is used by a server to read and write certain data objects to virtual memory. Monitoring page-file activity is critical if you want to see how the memory resources on your server are doing. A continuous high usage count of the paging file points to low-memory resources.
PhysicalDisk	Physical disk includes single hard disk drives and a redundant array of independent disks (RAID) device you may have configured in your server. Disk bottlenecks are common causes of server lag time. You should be in the habit of monitoring the activity of your hard disks, particularly if you have disk I/O intense applications, such as database applications that call for mass inserts or deletes to the database.

(continued)

Table 4-1. *(continued)*

Object Name	Description
Process	When you launch a program, the process is the object created when a program is run. Each program is considered an instance of the process performance object. A second copy of a program is shown with a pound sign (#) and number designating its instance number. If you suspect an application is misbehaving by not giving up processor time, select the process performance object so you can monitor the application.
Processor	The processor is one piece of hardware you don't want to see causing a bottleneck. Processor bottlenecks can take a server that was running at breakneck speeds to a mere crawl. Processor bottlenecks can also be the most difficult to track down. For example, you may run across a case where you are unsure whether the application(s) or operating system is causing the high usage of the processor. The processor performance object offers you the *%Privileged Time* counter that illustrates how processes running in privileged mode are using processor time. Privileged mode is a processing mode designed for operating system components and hardware-manipulating drivers. To see how applications are using processor time, monitor *%User Time*, which tracks how processes running in user mode are doing. User mode is a restricted processing mode designed for applications, environment subsystems, and integral subsystems.
Redirector	The redirector is the file system that diverts file requests to network servers. High redirector traffic can cause a network bottleneck. A server acting as a file server may show a higher *Bytes Total/sec* counter than a server restricted to a limited amount of users.
System	The system performance object has a list of counters that apply to all system hardware and software. The system performance object paints an overall picture of your server. You can monitor operating system level operations such as the *Context Switches/sec* counter.
Thread	A thread is the basic executable entity that can execute instructions in a processor. Similar to using the system performance object, you can monitor operating system level activity with it. The thread object also has a *Context Switches/sec* counter, but in this case, it's the rate at which switches are made from one thread to another. This counter gives you the ability to monitor how the operating system is affecting application activity.

Selecting Instances to Monitor

We reviewed in the prior section that it's common to find multiple instances of an object when more than one occurrence of the object type exists. When selecting performance counters for an object with multiple instances, you should be aware that each instance has its own private copy of those counters so you can observe their behavior individually. So, when monitoring the PhysicalDisk object and selecting to monitor the *%Idle Time* counter, you must also select an instance to monitor. A private copy of the counter for each object can also help isolate the problem to a single instance of hardware. If you suspect a particular hard drive is the bottleneck, just monitor the instance for that hard drive.

In some cases, summary counters exist for an object. An example of this is the System object *%Processor Time* counter, which is an average of the Processor object *%Processor Time* counter for all processor instances on a multiprocessor system.

> **Tip** When you plan on monitoring the performance of applications running under Windows 2000, open System Monitor and add common performance counters such as memory, processor, and disk performance counters. You should then start the application. This way upon startup, you can see what resources the application immediately uses. You may find a particular application allocating a chunk of memory as you double-click its application executable file.

As you review an object and the related counter there may be multiple instances of the counter active. An example of multiple instances appearing is when the Processor object:*%Processor Time* counter provides multiple instances of any number of instance objects. Some instances exist that have a parent instance to help identify which object they belong to. No matter what object you're tracking, if multiple instances exist for it, they are listed in either alphabetical or numerical order. An instance at the top of the list doesn't have significance over an instance at the bottom. When you want to select more than one instance to monitor, or multiple instances, you do so in the same manner as when selecting multiple process counters. If you highlight the top instance, hold down the Shift key and highlight the bottom instance, all the instances for that object are selected. You can also select the All Instances option to monitor all the instances for that particular object. To select noncontiguous instances, hold down the Ctrl key and click each instance with your left mouse button to select it.

When processor and memory was limited, you were restricted to a single copy of a program; however, times have changed. Launching more than one copy of Microsoft Internet Explorer is not only done on a regular basis, but in some cases is necessary to review information from the Web, for example. If you want to monitor one of the copies of Internet Explorer you've launched, how can you distinguish one copy from the other? System Monitor denotes each copy with the nomenclature of *Instance#(number),* where Instance represents the name of the program and the number after the pound sign the number for that program. So, the IEXPLORE instance is the first copy of Internet Explorer you launched and the IEXPLORE#1 instance is the second copy. Under older versions of Windows NT, Performance Monitor was unable to distinguish between multiple copies of the same program.

You've already explored parent instances and what they stand for under the Performance console. There's one other type of instance you should also be aware of, and that's the mortal instance. Mortal instances are so named because they're born, and then die, within the same moment of system operation. For example, Windows 2000 Server may launch a thread for some routine task; you see the instance for this thread appear and then disappear from the Instance list. If you begin to monitor a mortal instance, System Monitor doesn't wipe it from the list as soon as it dies; rather, the counter value for that instance drops to zero. System Monitor continues to look for that instance with each snapshot.

> **Note** A snapshot is an instance when the Performance console measures the system for the counters selected for that particular session. A snapshot is taken according to the interval selected. For example, setting an interval of 10 seconds has System Monitor taking a snapshot of the system every 10 seconds. For more information on intervals, see the "Setting How Often to Monitor," section in this chapter.

If you need to capture all instances of the data no matter how short the duration, you can choose to log performance data. By logging data, rather than charting it or capturing it in report view, you can review the log for an occurrence of a particular instance for every snapshot in that System Monitor session.

Selecting Counters to Monitor

You can select counters to measure from the Add Counters dialog box. Launch System Monitor and click the plus sign from the tool bar. The Add Counters dialog box opens. You must first specify a performance object to monitor; each performance object has a unique set of performance counters. You may find performance counters with the same name for different performance objects. For example, the Server performance object has a *Bytes Total/sec* performance counter. In the case of the Server performance object, the *Bytes Total/sec* counter relates the number of bytes the server has sent and received from the network. The NBT Connection performance object also has a *Bytes Total/sec* performance counter. However, its counter is the rate at which bytes are sent or received by the local computer over a NetBIOS over TCP/IP (NBT) connection to some remote computer.

Looking at the list of counters available for analysis can be overwhelming. How do you know exactly which ones to measure? (You can see particular counters you should understand discussed in the following section titled, "Overview of Important Performance Counters.") In some cases, you may find that selecting the default counter for any given object tells you the most about that object's activity. When monitoring the PhysicalDisk object, for example, the *%Disk Time* counter is the default performance counter selected. This particular counter immediately tells you how busy the disk drive has been kept servicing read and write requests. This number alone tells you whether your system's disk I/O is being taxed. From that point on, you can decide whether to begin monitoring application activity more closely to determine whether your applications are to blame for the high disk I/O or some other operation running on the server.

When selecting the counters to measure, you must be aware of what each one actually does for you. The name of the performance counter may not be enough of a description. If you are reviewing the counter object for the first time or need a refresher on what information the objects provide, you can click the Explain button to see a detailed description for each counter (see Figure 4-5). As long as the Explain Text dialog box is open, you can get an explanation for each counter by simply selecting it.

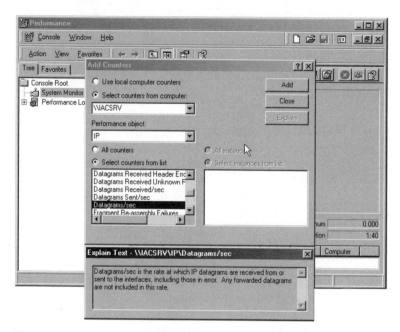

Figure 4-5. *By clicking the Explain button you can see the definition for what the Datagrams/Sec counter measures for the IP object.*

When you are monitoring server performance, particular problems with the server may call for selecting all the counters for an object. However, this isn't a wise move under chart view. Monitoring multiple counters on a real-time chart can make your head spin when you try to decipher what's going on with the system. If you want to track multiple counters, do so under the report view. Report view is text-based and easier to read when monitoring multiple counters (see Figure 4-6). More times than not, changing the view under System Monitor can help shed some light on what is causing the problem. Later in this chapter, in the section titled "Exploring System Monitor Views," you learn about the multiple views of System Monitor and how each may offer a distinct advantage over the other when diagnosing problems.

To select all or more than one counter at a time, highlight the top counter, hold down the Shift key and highlight the bottom counter in the list. You can also click the All Counters option to select all the counters for that particular object. If you want to select noncontiguous counters, hold down the Ctrl key and click the counter name with the left mouse button.

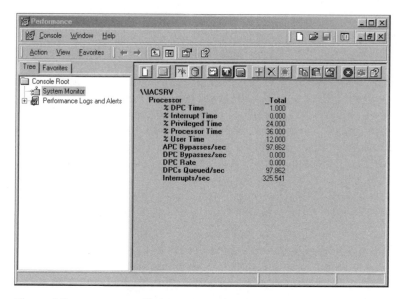

Figure 4-6. *Monitoring all the counters for the Processor object under the report view.*

Overview of Important Performance Counters

With a basic installation of Windows 2000, you have available multiple performance objects for monitoring. Each object can then have several counters to assist in analysis of your Windows 2000 server. This combination of objects and counters gives you literally thousands of performance counters to choose from for PTO of your system.

The ability to monitor multiple objects and several counters per object is truly a strength of the Performance applications because it allows an administrator great flexibility in the performance data you gather from a server. However, this ability to track so much information can also work against you. If you're unclear which one of the objects and counters gives you the answers you're looking for, having all these counters available may work against you by confusing the matter even more.

In this section of the chapter, you explore specific performance counters you'll find extremely useful when fighting the most common types of performance issues under Windows 2000 Server. By understanding what counters tell you or what you're looking for, you're bound to diagnose the problem more quickly. In doing so, you save yourself time and get the job done more quickly, allowing you to get to the projects you want to instead of camping out in front of a System Monitor session.

A proper understanding of the Performance console is critical for quick diagnoses of common problems. That's why knowing which counters to turn to for answers is something you can't overlook.

Let's take a look at an example that shows the importance of knowing what counter relates the information you're looking for. You find, over time, that your Windows 2000 Server's performance is degrading. You realize that the problem began to occur after you loaded a third-party application being used by the accounting department. As part of your troubleshooting process, you visit the software company's Web site and find a tech note in the Support section related to a possible memory leak with the application. Now what? How can you verify that a memory leak is causing the problem in this situation? What counter do you turn to? Even if the problem turns out not to be caused by a memory leak, you can at least cross it off your list of possible causes and move on to investigate other possible causes of the problem.

In Table 4-2, specifics regarding common counters that you'd turn to in situations such as the possible memory leak example are listed. However, only the basics are included about each counter. Detailed information regarding counters and the problems they detect are discussed in the chapters covering detecting bottlenecks, such as Chapter 6, "Diagnosing Memory Bottlenecks."

Table 4-2. Helpful Performance Counters for Common Performance Issues

Problem	Counter	Description
Processor Bottleneck	System*Processor Queue Length* (all instances) Processor\Interrupts/sec System\Context Switches/sec	Processor bottlenecks can be caused by a multitude of factors. However, the first step is to confirm if a processor bottleneck exists, and you can do that only by monitoring the appropriate counters.
Processor Usage	Processor*%Processor Time* (all instances)	Many administrators monitor only the Processor*%Processor Time* when determining if a processor bottleneck exists. This object and counter is really only a good indicator of processor usage.
Disk Bottleneck	PhysicalDisk*Avg. Disk Queue Length* (all instances)	With applications becoming increasingly data-intensive, disk I/O utilization is hit harder than ever. If you see a high percentage for PhysicalDisk*Avg. or Disk Queue Length*, and the processor and memory utilization is low, a strong possibility exists that the bottleneck is the disk. The PhysicalDisk*Avg. and Disk Queue Length* counters are found with the disk performance object.
Disk Usage	PhysicalDisk*Disk Reads/sec* PhysicalDisk*Disk Writes/sec*	Monitor disk usage as a preemptive measure against disk bottlenecks. If you find utilization is increasing steadily, you can begin to take steps earlier rather then later.

(continued)

Table 4-2. *(continued)*

Problem	Counter	Description
Memory Bottleneck or Leaks	Memory\ *Pages/sec* Memory\ *Page Reads/sec* Memory\ *TransactionFaults/sec* Memory\ *Pool Paged Bytes* Memory\ *Pool Nonpaged Bytes*	A memory leak is a problem that occurs after a period of time, unlike a memory bottleneck, and for this reason, memory leaks can be difficult to diagnose.
Memory Usage	Memory\ *Available Bytes* Memory\ *Cache Bytes*	Along the same lines as disk usage and processor usage, monitoring memory usage is more of a preemptive measure. When you detect increased memory usage, measure additional counters to help determine if a process gone wrong or a natural occurrence such as increased user load causes the problem.
Network Throughput	Protocol Transmission counters (varies with networking protocol); for TCP/IP; Network Interface\ *Bytes Total/sec* Network Interface\ *Packets/sec* Server\ *Bytes Total/sec* or Server\ *Bytes Transmitted/sec* and Server*Bytes Received/sec*	Consider this set of counters your indicator of network efficiency. Just how well is the network using the resources at its disposal? In addition, the counters associated with the network throughput object can help you detect network-related problems. For example, if you're seeing a lot of resent packets, you know there is a reason. The reason might be a bad network adapter, a faulty cable, or a poorly written application. The fact that you know the problem exists is the first step in finding it.
Network Usage	Network Segment\ *% Net Utilization* As you will be measuring traffic on your network and not just the local computer, the Network Monitor driver must be installed for this counter to work.	Like network throughput, network usage is an object that helps you monitor your network's performance. However, in this case, you're looking at capacity. How much of your available network resources are in use? You can use this information to plan upgrades to your server. When you begin to see the *% Net Utilization* counter go up, you know that more of the network's bandwidth is in use and it's time to look at adding additional bandwidth to the system to support future requirements.

The counters listed in the table are ones you'll find yourself turning to the most because the problems they track are some of the most common that infect Windows 2000. These counters also monitor the most basic resources utilized on the server, no matter what role that server is playing. Keep in mind that because each server is unique, you must monitor counters in addition to these that best describe the role of your server.

Consider saving a System Monitor configuration that monitors your server for the critical services running on the box. For example, if you've deployed a Windows 2000 Server as an enterprise database server, monitoring the above-listed counters alone doesn't help much when the database engine continues to crash. Enterprise databases running on Windows 2000 Server may have counters you can monitor for such functions as database activity, user connections, or transactions per second. The configuration you save consists of the counters listed in Table 4-1, plus those counters unique to your database application. On the other hand, if your server is providing SMTP mail services, keeping a list of common counters to monitor these services makes sense.

Note One method of keeping a "list" of counters ready is to have multiple MMC sessions saved, with each one having System Monitor configured to track that list of counters. This way, you can have an MMC to track SQL Server activity with another to track key indicators of Microsoft Exchange server activity (see Figure 4-13).

Tip As long as system resources permit it, it is recommended that you run System Monitor in the background so it collects data on counters you feel will best help track your server's activity. For long-term analysis of System Monitor data, collecting data under chart view may not be the way to go. Instead, using logging data is more appropriate. This chapter covers the performance views, including chart and report view along with logging options under Performance Logs and Alerts in the section entitled "Exploring System Monitor Views."

To illustrate the flexibility and power of the Performance console as a tool to monitor specialty services running on your server, this section finishes with a discussion of three counters you'll find if you're using your server as a telephony server. A telephony server is any remote access server (RAS) or a server that's being used as a small private branch exchange (PBX) or telephone switch. You can monitor the three counters to help point you in the right direction when the system's not acting as it should.

Note The counters listed below will not be listed unless you are running the appropriate telephony services on your machine.

- **Telephony*Incoming Calls/sec*** This counter measures the rate at which calls are answered by the server. If you find it to be a lower number than usual, you may be experiencing an interruption in service. A low number can also be an indicator of low-user activity. As you can see, counters usually cause more questions before you can make a determination regarding server performance.

- **Telephony*Outgoing Calls/sec*** This counter measures the outgoing calls made by the computer. If you find a high *Outgoing Calls/sec* counter, this may mean your users are dialing into your RAS server and requesting the server to call back.

- **Telephony*Total number of calls*** This counter represents the total amount of calls for both incoming and outgoing. You can use it in any number of ways to help trace a variety of problems, such as tracking down total activity for a RAS server or a PBX switch.

Monitoring Legacy Programs

You've briefly looked at the Performance console and the capabilities in monitoring applications, mainly those that come with BackOffice applications or those that have been written by a third party or on your own. It's been assumed that these applications are all 32-bit apps, which is not a bad assumption because it's hard to find developers who continue to write 16-bit applications for new platforms such as Windows NT or Windows 2000. However, there are times when the need to support 16-bit applications still exists—environments still run Windows 3.11 and even MS-DOS! When environments running these older operating systems have to transition to a 32-bit operating system, they have to convert their applications from a 16-bit platform to a more robust 32-bit environment.

With any application that runs under Windows 2000 also comes a need to monitor the application, and if you plan on running MS-DOS or 16-bit applications under Windows 2000 Server, you must understand the context in which they run before you can begin to monitor them.

In Windows 2000, 16-bit Windows-based programs run as separate threads in a multithreaded process called a Windows NT Virtual DOS Machine (NTVDM). The NTVDM process simulates a 16-bit Windows environment. An MS-DOS-based program runs in its own NTVDM process.

When you need to monitor a 16-bit program or an MS-DOS program, you must do so by monitoring the Process*%Processor Time*\\ntvdm instance (see Figure 4-7). When monitoring the instance, you can use processor utilization, memory utilization, or any of the counters available for process instances. Figure 4-8 illustrates System Monitor monitoring a 16-bit application for processor utilization.

Note If you launch an MS-DOS or 16-bit application, it only appears under System Monitor as an ntvdm process. Launching the command prompt does not spawn off another ntvdm process. For that you must be running a native MS-DOS or 16-bit application such as Windows 3.1 application.

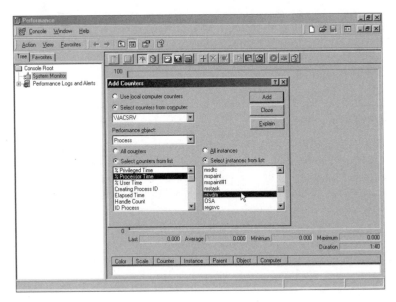

Figure 4-7. *If you're running an MS-DOS or 16-bit application on your server, you have to select the ntvdm instance.*

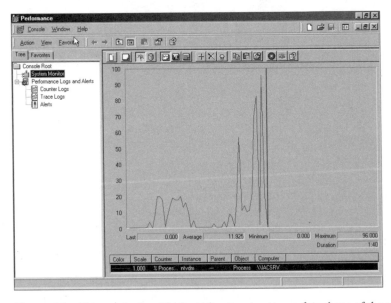

Figure 4-8. *This particular 16-bit application is using a fair share of the processor.*

Monitoring Other Computers

When you first launch System Monitor, it's configured to measure your local computer by default; however, you have the ability to select remote computers and begin to monitor performance for each computer you select. Performance console data is sensitive, as is any data residing on a computer; for this reason, only people with rights to *Access this computer from the network* are allowed to remotely monitor any computer on your network.

To assign the appropriate rights to a user, follow these steps.

1. From the Administrative Tools folder, launch the Local Security Policy program.

2. Under Security Settings, double-click the Local Policies folder to expand it.

3. Select the User Rights Assignment folder; the list of currently defined User Rights is displayed in the detail pane. See Figure 4-9.

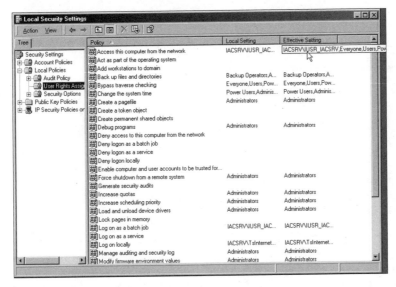

Figure 4-9. *You can view currently defined User Rights for the server from the Local Security Settings console.*

4. The User Rights are listed in alphabetical order; *Access this computer from the network* is somewhere at the top. Select the policy setting and edit the settings by right-clicking and selecting Security.

5. The Local Security Policy Setting dialog box appears. See Figure 4-10.

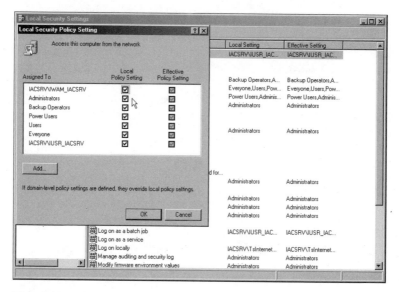

Figure 4-10. *The users currently assigned to the policy are listed in the Local Security Policy Setting dialog box.*

6. To assign additional users to the policy, click the Add button. A list of users and groups appears in the Select Users Or Groups dialog box; select the users or groups of users you want to assign to the policy and click the Add button. Click OK to exit the Select Users Or Groups dialog box.

System Monitor allows you to remotely monitor Windows NT (3.*x* and 4.0) Workstations and Servers, Microsoft Windows 2000 Professional, and Windows 2000 Server (standard, Advanced, and Datacenter).

The ability to monitor the performance of computers remotely can help reduce the overall time spent administering your network. If you're managing an enterprise network with Windows 2000 Servers sprawled across a campus-wide network, for example, you have to run between the various buildings to get to the servers. This is all avoided by tracking the system remotely using System Monitor. You can gather all sorts of data from the other workstations while remaining at a single workstation, providing you with a better picture of what's going on with your network.

When collecting performance data from remote computers, you must take the speed at which you connect into consideration. If your remote computers are located in another building, city, state, or country, you're limited to the methods of data collection for that machine. The faster the speed, the greater the choice in how you can monitor the machine; the slower the speed, the more you're limited in how data is gathered.

In the case of a company that has a T1 running between buildings, for example, the administrator can choose to view data in graphical, report, log, or alert mode. However, when a slow connection, such as dial-up with a 56K modem, is the only method of connecting, it's time to reconsider what views and intervals you want to run System Monitor or Performance Logs and Alerts under.

When you connect to the remote machine over a slow connection, the delay caused by the media speed only frustrates matters more. Using chart view in graph mode can be very resource-intensive. Despite this fact, graph mode provides a large amount of data in a relatively short time. Running the report view may decrease the time in screen refresh, but you still need to deal with slow response when monitoring data over a small interval. Gathering data at a one-second interval doesn't happen over a slow connection because the delay in communication causes a delay in how quickly results are displayed at your end.

When something does go wrong with your remote servers, you don't have time to wait for screen updates of System Monitor data. You need that information now. Therefore, you have to configure the server so it's continuously gathering data. Then, when something goes wrong, all you need to do is collect that data over a single transmission. Configuring the server so it's collecting performance data via logs allows you to eventually export these logs for report generation; you can even present data from the logs in graphs or histograms using System Monitor. Log files can have up-to-the-minute data, saving you the irritation of delayed screen updates or interruptions in data gathering. Views and logs are covered in more detail later in this chapter in the section titled "Exploring System Monitor Views."

To begin monitoring other computers, launch the Performance console that includes the System Monitor snap-in. Select Start/Programs/Administrative Tools/Performance. Once the Performance console is open, select the System Monitor snap-in. From the toolbar, click the plus sign as if you were adding a counter to the chart. The Add Counters dialog box appears (see Figure 4-11).

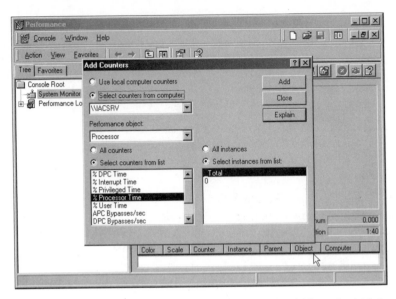

Figure 4-11. *You can select to monitor computers remotely from the Add Counters dialog box.*

From the Add Counters dialog box you have two choices: collect data from the local computer only, or, select to monitor counters of another computer. By default, the Use Local Computer Counters option is selected. Click the Select Counters From Computer option and choose a remote computer from the drop-down list (see Figure 4-12).

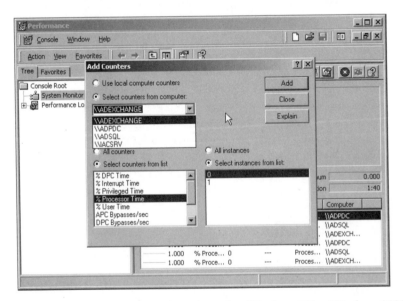

Figure 4-12. *From the drop-down list, select Windows NT or Windows 2000 remote machines you want to monitor.*

Note   If the computer you want to monitor isn't listed, type its name in the drop-down list box. Use the UNC path such as \\servername and then select the counter(s) you want to monitor. Click Add when done.

Selecting to monitor counters from other computers still allows you to monitor your local computer's counters. In fact, System Monitor allows you to monitor counters from remote computers or your local computer. This can be particularly useful when comparing the performance of systems to each other. If you select multiple computers, objects, and counters to monitor, save your current selections; this way, you don't waste time going through the selection process again.

To save your settings, take the following steps.

1.   Open the Performance console.

2.   Configure the System Monitor snap-in with the computers, objects, or counters you want.

3.   From the Console menu, click Save As. You can type the name you want for this console (see Figure 4-13). Remember to name the console something that helps to describe what this console is monitoring. Having to open up and view console files trying to determine what data is being collected can be a painstaking task.

4.   Click Save when done.

If a computer is shut down while you're monitoring it, System Monitor receives a time-out while attempting to access that computer. System Monitor stops data collection until the computer is up and running.

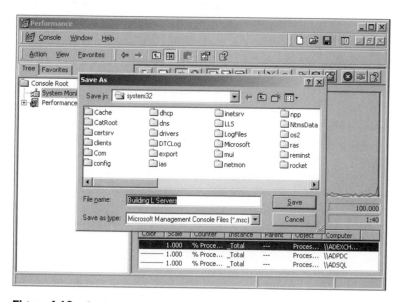

Figure 4-13. *Saving current console settings allows System Monitor to remember what data collection settings you've chosen.*

Reducing Overhead

When collecting data from multiple computers at the same time, you run the risk of clogging your computer or network with measurement data. Even though you're not limited to the number of computers you can monitor at a single time, hardware constraints have you thinking twice about whether you want to monitor more than one computer from a single PC. Overhead is generated by the visits the Performance console makes to the remote computer to capture the data. These visits are called snapshots; the more snapshots, the more overhead increase the local computer experiences.

If you do find your computer or network coming to a crawl, consider employing the following tactics to reduce unnecessary overhead:

- **Reduce the frequency of data collection**   The Performance console allows you to control the interval at which data is collected. The amount of overhead on the system is directly affected by the interval you choose to set. The lower the interval, the higher the number of snapshots taken, which then increases the overall overhead. Many administrators set the interval at 10 seconds or even lower without taking overhead into consideration; this low-interval rate taxes the system, especially if you're monitoring multiple systems. Try increasing this interval to a higher value, high enough where the system isn't clogged and you're still able to retrieve data for good analysis.

Note   When remotely measuring a computer, there's a certain amount of overhead. Performance allows you to measure this overhead, thus giving you the ability to see whether you can create a performance issue with your local computer or your network. By measuring the network protocol objects, you can determine the number of bytes being transferred across the network and the processor overhead on each machine.

- **Reduce the number of objects monitored**   Another factor that affects overhead on a system being monitored is the number of objects you select. Similar to the interval factor, a relationship exists between the number of objects and system overhead. The more objects you select to monitor, the higher the overhead on the system. As a rule, be logical and systematic when adding and removing objects from System Monitor. Adding objects randomly only confuses you even more, and creates a chaotic scene painted across your System Monitor chart.

- **Select different views to help reduce overhead**   The system resources needed to graph Performance console data are much greater than any other view under the Performance console. The alert view requires no graphing of data, resulting in a reduction of system resources used. If you find that an application is crashing and you suspect the processor is being overutilized, for example, rather than tracking processor performance and having a pretty picture painted for you, you can set an alert to trigger each time the processor utilization crosses a threshold you set. In the section titled "Performance Logs and Alerts Views," you discover ways to establish alert thresholds for important events.

Note   Even though the above hints are geared to users monitoring multiple computers from a single PC, they can also be used when monitoring the local computer itself. Keep in mind that the Performance console is like any other application you run under Windows 2000; it requires resources, and the more you ask of System Monitor, the more it requires from your system.

Interpreting Performance Data

Now that you've covered the methods to select objects and counters, you can begin gathering performance data on your Windows 2000 Server or other remote computers. Before you do this, consider what you're going to do with that data once you have it and how you will decipher it.

When collecting performance data under Windows 2000, there's a great deal of flexibility in how you collect that data and how it's displayed. How you display data affects how you interpret it, and interpreting performance data may well be the most difficult part of performance tuning Windows 2000. Failure to interpret performance data correctly leads to delays in correcting the current problem at hand, and can very well lead to further problems.

One example is a network administrator who is hearing complaints that the database server running under Windows 2000 is showing significant lag time when responding to queries. More significantly, this lag time seems to occur after a period of time and not immediately. The network administrator decides to run System Monitor and track a few counters including user load, cache activity, processor utilization, and memory. After configuring System Monitor with the counters he wants to track, he sets the interval to five-second increments. He monitors performance data using the chart view, but fails to see anything that could be causing the problem. As complaints from the user community grow louder, he decides to try anything and increases the amount of memory in the server. For a short period, everything's better and query results are almost instantaneous; and then the problem reappears. At this point, the network administrator finds that he needs to run a performance analysis once more.

A better approach to this problem is to log data, rather than view it in real-time, because the problem only seems to crop up after the server has been running for a significant amount of time. If the network administrator logs data for a day or two and sets the interval to a longer period of five minutes, he may find data more fit for analysis. Because the network administrator is unsure of what is causing the problem, he can easily add the counters listed in Table 4-2 to gain an overall picture of his system. If the processor or network is the bottleneck, he sees that from the data collected.

In this case, by tracking the various counters to monitor memory for bottlenecks, leaks, and usage (refer back to Table 4-2), the network administrator discovers that memory resources are slowly depleting over time, a strong indication that a memory leak exists. Memory leaks are caused by applications or the operating system not releasing memory that has been allocated to it. Adding more RAM doesn't solve the problem; in one sense, it only feeds it.

This example illustrates that selecting the right counters under System Monitor isn't the only determining factor for proper diagnoses of performance problems; the choices you make regarding the interval, scale, and views for data collection also play an important role.

Setting How Often to Monitor

The interval settings determine how often you want to monitor the machines listed in the Add Counters dialog box. The interval value determines how often a snapshot is taken of your system to gather performance data. The lower the interval, the more snapshots; the higher the interval, the fewer snapshots. If you're monitoring a large number of objects and counters at a low interval, you generate large amounts of data and consume disk space. Try to keep the interval at a level at which enough data is collected so you can analyze it thoroughly, but yet not go overboard.

> **Tip** Always try to control the number of counters and objects you're monitoring at a single time. If you don't, not only do you collect useless data, but you also consume system resources. Data collection doesn't mean you need a pile of paper sitting on your desk for analysis. Good data collection involves collecting only the amount of data that gives you the answers you need to solve the problem as quickly as possible.

When determining how often to monitor, there are a few basic rules you can go by.

- **Are there specific problems you're monitoring?** Not all problems occur at fixed times, and neither are they apparent as soon as you launch System Monitor. For problems that manifest themselves slowly, such as a memory leak, you want to increase the interval time. Setting the interval to a shorter period, such as 10 seconds or 30 seconds, means you have to go through a mountain of data before seeing the trend in memory utilization that memory leaks tend to show. If you're monitoring activity of a specific process at a set time, set the interval so it's updating more frequently.

- **How long do you expect to monitor the system for?** Updating data collection so it takes a snapshot every 15 seconds is reasonable if you are monitoring the system for fewer than four hours. If you need to monitor the system for longer than that, consider setting the interval to a number greater than 300 seconds.

- **What view will you be monitoring with?** There are several views you can choose from when monitoring your system, including chart, report, alert, and log. Each view has a purpose; for example, graphs are useful for short-term and real-time monitoring. So, if you're monitoring the system for processor spikes that occur every five seconds, keep the interval below five seconds so you can capture all the activity leading up to spikes. Graphing such activity allows for quick analysis of data. On the other hand, if you're monitoring data over an extended period of time, generate a log.

Note After a Performance log has been generated, you can choose to view data from any particular time range you wish. This means that you won't miss any data that could lead you to the cause of the bottleneck or performance problem you are experiencing at that time. For more information on data collection using logs, see "Performance Logs and Alerts Views," later in the chapter.

These rules are actually guidelines. Each situation you encounter when performance tuning your server calls for a different approach when attacking the problem. Simply be aware of the consequences of running intervals that can hinder data analysis and use up system resources unnecessarily.

Exploring System Monitor Views

You've just reviewed intervals and how you can adjust the interval setting for better data analysis. Now you explore System Monitor views, and what each offers when monitoring the performance of your system.

The System Monitor snap-in supports three basic views of real-time data: graph, histogram, and report. Graph and histogram are graphical, while the report view is strictly text-based. This difference alone is a good reason you use one view over the other. We'll go into that in more detail when each view is covered later in this section.

Changing views under System Monitor can shed a new light on the data you're collecting—so much so that you may even interpret the data differently. In this next example, you see how a network administrator was able to interpret performance data completely differently simply by switching from one view to another. This administrator's problem stemmed from the Web server hanging up every half-hour to an hour. The only thing the administrator could do was reboot the server. As part of troubleshooting the problem, she launched System Monitor to track common objects/counters such as Processor, Memory, and Network performance. In addition to these counters, she also tracked Web server specific objects/counters including *Server Connections/Sec* counter, an extended counter written by the company whose Web server software her company was running on its server. This is important to note, as you'll see shortly. After only a minute of collecting data, the administrator found a trend with the data that was hard to believe. According to the chart view of System Monitor, spikes were occurring with the number of *Server Connections/Sec*. The spike occurred every 10 seconds, and, according to the data, the *Server Connections/Sec* jumped to 1000. In fact, no matter how high the administrator set the vertical scale, the *Server Connections/Sec* peaked beyond whatever vertical scale she set.

The data the administrator was seeing was hard to believe for more than one reason. First, the company never experienced more than 100 users at a single time on its Web site, mainly because the server was restricted to clients of the company. Second, there were only 200 client logins defined for the server. As soon as she restarted the Web server, the *Server Connections/Sec* shot up to 1000 or more.

To clarify the issue, the administrator changed the view from chart to report. The report view allowed her to view the actual number for *Server Connections/Sec*, and this showed a more believable result. The data under the report view showed that no spikes were occurring with the *Server Connections/Sec*. In fact, the counter reported data that made sense. However, the administrator wanted a second opinion to verify what she was seeing so she set up an alert under System Monitor that triggered an event each time the *Server Connections/Sec* crossed a threshold that she set.

Before you go into the various System Monitor views in more detail, review the System Monitor's toolbar in the sidebar titled, "System Monitor Toolbar." You will also want to go through the System Monitor Properties dialog box in the section titled "Graph Mode" found under the "Chart View" section. These are two parts of System Monitor to familiarize yourself with because you need them to adjust property settings that affect how data is reported and displayed under the chart and report views.

System Monitor Toolbar

As with other applications launched from an MMC, there are many ways to accomplish the same task. You can right-click while in the MMC to bring up a quick menu, launch items from a file menu, or use a toolbar. Here you take a quick look at the toolbar under System Monitor and how you can use it to speed up execution of the most common operations. In the sections to come, you'll learn about other methods of executing these common operations, such as using hot keys.

The System Monitor toolbar is directly above the chart or report being displayed. You can get a brief explanation of what each icon does by placing your mouse over the icon to display the tooltip. The command options available to you (starting from left to right) are shown in Table 4-3.

Table 4-3. System Monitor Toolbar Command Options

New Counter Set	Clears the current display so you can begin to add a new list of counters.
Clear Display	Clears the display, but keeps the current list of counters and immediately restarts monitoring the listed counters.
View Current Activity	If in log view, you can switch back to monitoring data in real-time or at the interval you set.
View Log File Data	If data is being logged, you can switch from the current activity view to log file data.
View Chart	Switches to chart view from the current display mode.
View Histogram	Switches to histogram view from the current display mode.
View Report	Switches to report view from the current display mode.
Add	To begin adding counters to a new or existing chart or report, click the Add icon to open the Add Counters dialog box.
Delete	Too many counters on the screen at one time? Clicking Delete deletes the currently selected counter.
Highlight	Finding it hard to track a particular counter? Click the highlight button so the currently selected counter stands out from the rest.
Copy Properties	Allows you to reuse the current settings for a new System Monitor session.
Paste Counter List	Allows you to paste the counters used in a previous chart or report view, saving you from having to re-add them to the counters' list.
Properties	Opens the System Monitor Properties dialog box.
Freeze Display	See something of interest? Clicking this icon freezes the display; data continues to be logged in the background.
Update Data	If you're monitoring data and have set a manual update, click the icon to update the chart or report.
Help	If all else fails, you can launch the online help for System Monitor.

Chart View

Each view under System Monitor has a unique feature that helps distinguish it from the other. This distinction is the reason you decide to monitor data under that view, or choose to go with some other view. In the case of chart view, it is a graphical view under System Monitor. The chart view is comprised of the graph and histogram modes. The other views, report, alert, and log, are all generate text-based output either in real-time format or appended to a specific log file. In this section, you learn how you can begin collecting data.

The chart view offers you the ability to collect data in real-time in either graph or histogram modes. If you're looking to analyze performance factors over time, view the data in graph mode. If you need to monitor multiple instances of a given counter at the same time, select histogram mode. In the following sections, you explore in detail how to monitor data under both graph and histogram modes.

Graph Mode

When you first begin monitoring performance with System Monitor, you are presented with a blank chart that's providing a chart view in graph mode. No matter if you're in graph or histogram mode, between 0 and 100 data points are displayed for each counter shown. To begin monitoring a counter under graph mode, click the plus symbol on the toolbar. Add the default counter Processor\ *%Processor Time* to chart it. As the counter begins to monitor the system, notice the vertical line in the middle of the chart. This is the time line. The time line is always red and one space beyond the last observed value. The time line moves to the right when the display is updated according to the interval you set for the chart. The time line wraps to the left edge of the chart once it has plotted the 100th data point on the chart.

To change the time interval, take the following steps.

1. Right-click within the chart and select Properties (or click the Properties button on the toolbar).

2. The System Monitor Properties dialog box opens.

3. Under the General tab, select to *Update automatically*, and then enter a time value for the interval. If *Update automatically* isn't selected, you have to manually update the chart or report.

From the System Monitor Properties dialog box, you can choose to add or remove the legend at the bottom of the chart by selecting or deselecting the check box in the Display Elements section. This legend includes the following information:

- **Color of the counter** Adjust the color of counters so it becomes easier to distinguish between counters. (You'll find out how to do this shortly.)

- **Scale of the counter** All counters aren't created the same; neither do they measure in the same units. You explore the scale factor later in this section.

- **Counter Name**   Useful, for example, when having to keep track of several counters that start with the term "Processor."
- **Instance Name**   If you have more than one instance of a particular counter, this clarifies which one is which.
- **Parent Instance Name**   The parent for that particular instance.
- **Object Name**   The performance object that particular counter is associated with.
- **Computer Name**   The name of the computer that counter is monitoring.

In addition to the legend, you can have the Value bar displayed or not displayed. The Value bar shows the numerical statistics for the currently highlighted counter and is a quick and easy way to get status information on the activity for that counter up to that point. The Value bar displays the last value the counter reached, the average value for the counter, the minimum and maximum values, and duration. The duration value indicates the total elapsed time displayed in the graph based on the update interval. You also have the option of not displaying the toolbar above the chart or report. Turning off all options in Display Element and maximizing the System Monitor screen allows the chart view (and even the report view as you will discover in the next section) to be displayed to its fullest size.

Part of viewing data under chart view is the ability to change the appearance of how data is presented to you. Under the General tab, you can select the graph to be either 3D or flat by choosing the appropriate option from the Appearance drop-down list. You can also have a fixed single border displayed by selecting it from the Border drop-down list. Selecting the Source tab will allow you to select where data being charted should be retrieved from: Current Activity or a previously logged file. Apart from the General tab another option for changing how data is displayed is under the Data tab. You can add additional counters to the chart or report and select the color, scale, width, and style for each counter to be displayed under graph or histogram modes. You'll find when monitoring multiple counters or multiple instances of the same counter, the default colors and line settings selected may not suffice in helping distinguish each counter. If you're adding a lot of counters at once, the color selection wraps and colors are reused. Each time the colors wrap, the line width increases automatically; this may add to the confusion. Therefore, changing the color or width to your own choice helps you track the counters without struggling while staring at the screen.

Tip   If you need to zero in on a particular counter, try using the highlight option. Click the Highlight button on the toolbar and the current counter you're monitoring is displayed so it's distinguishable from all other counters. Another way to turn on the highlight feature is to hit the Ctrl+H keys together.

The next three tabs—Graph, Colors, and Fonts—allow you to spruce up your graph or histogram. From the Graph tab, you can add a title to the chart as well as add text describing the vertical axis. You can also choose to display vertical and horizontal grids. Adding vertical grids is extremely helpful, particularly when you need to determine the time period a particular value for a counter falls under. From the same tab, you can turn off the option to display vertical scale numbers. If you're tracking counters in real-time, keep the option to display vertical scale numbers turned on; otherwise, it is difficult to determine what range these numbers are falling under.

The vertical scale to the left of the chart is displayed by default. To adjust the vertical scale, enter a maximum and minimum number. You can adjust the vertical value so it ranges between 0 points (minimum) and 100000000 points (maximum).

Adjusting the vertical scale is particularly useful if you want to track the true value for a counter instead of a scaled value. If the vertical scale is set to the default values of 0–100, counters set to a scale of 1.0 max out at 100. In the case of a counter with a scale set to something other than 1.0, System Monitor multiplies the scale factor times the counter value, and charts that value instead of the original counter value. This applies to both graph and histograms. Each counter has a preset scale, one that reflects the numbers that counter tends to produce. With percentage-based counters, such as *%Utilization* counters, the scale always has a default value of 1.0. On the other hand, counters that can reach 100,000 have a scale factor of .001 or smaller. If they were set to 1.0, you'd be unable to read counters displaying numbers in the 30s, 40s, or 50s. You can change the scale factor for a counter from the Data tab.

Histogram Mode

The histogram is the other method of displaying counters graphically. To switch to histogram mode, click the Histogram icon on the toolbar or select Histogram under the General tab of the System Monitor Properties dialog box. Viewing data in the histogram mode is beneficial if you're monitoring many instances of a given counter at one time. Monitoring the performance of processors installed in a server under the histogram view allows you to see real-time, head-to-head performance. If your fear that the hardware on a dual processor server is being underutilized, you can confirm those fears by monitoring both processors' activity simultaneously. Under the graph mode, you don't get such a definitive answer, particularly when monitoring real-time data.

In Figure 4-14, you see the *% Processor Time* counter of many processes. This view allows you to see what processes currently running on your server are taking up the most processor time. The definitive picture that the histogram mode paints helps clarify the results. Under the histogram mode, there is no question as to which process is utilizing the most processor time. Viewing the same data under graph mode takes some squinting, particularly if you have numerous counters being monitored at the same time. The display options covered in the previous section also apply to the histogram mode.

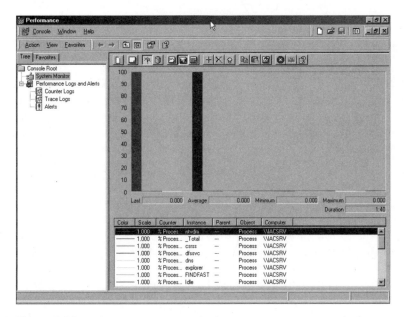

Figure 4-14. *When monitoring multiple counters at one time, the histogram view will help interpret results more easily.*

Report View

As mentioned earlier, each view under System Monitor offers some advantage over the other, and the report view is no different. You just saw how the graph and histogram modes under chart view can help "visualize" a problem. Rather than having to decipher between obscure numbers, you can see a trend occur with these resources. There are times, such as when you have to monitor multiple counters, however, that graphical views tend to work against you and not for you—for example, if you're monitoring 11 counters that are not only extremely active, but are also operating on different scales.

Under report view, there's no scale factor because you can always observe the entire value. When monitoring multiple counters under graph or histogram modes, you find yourself having to watch each counter individually, rather than glancing at the chart and seeing an obvious trend or problem.

To open System Monitor in report view, click View Report from the toolbar or select Report under the General tab in the System Monitor Properties dialog box. You can begin to add counters to the report much the same way as you do under chart view. As you add objects and counters, they're added to the bottom of the report. After a while, you have to scroll down to view counters that extend beyond the window. This can be a real drawback of the report view, especially if you want to view performance in real-time. You may be better off collecting performance data to a log, or exporting the data to an external application such as Microsoft Excel. In the following section, "Performance Logs and Alerts Views," you see how to collect log data, while the section, "Exporting Performance Data" provides insight into methods to export specific data elements.

Under report view you don't have the multiple options available to you under graph or histogram. In fact, the only option in report view is for the time interval. Setting an interval is optional. You still have the option of manually collecting data by deselecting the *Update automatically* option in System Monitor Properties and clicking Update Data from the toolbar.

When you first begin to collect data under report view, you see a delay before the first counter values appear. During that delay, you see minus signs, indicating that data is missing. The data itself is grouped according to the computer it belongs to. Objects for that computer are listed in the order you select them. Counters for each object are listed top to bottom according to the order you selected them in. You may have the urge to add more than one counter for a single object all at once. If that's the case, the counters are displayed in alphabetical order. Instances follow the same rule objects and counters live by. When added to report view, they're displayed in the order added, or alphabetically if added at the same time.

Deleting counters from a report is accomplished the same way as under chart view. Select the counter you want to delete and either hit the Delete key or select Delete from the toolbar. If you want to delete all the counters belonging to an object, select the object and hit Delete. That way, you don't have to delete counter after counter. Selecting New Counter Set from the toolbar erases all collected data on the report and gives you a clean slate. The Clear Display option isn't applicable under report view.

If you're a numbers person, reports are great for you. However, your boss may not be. In that case, you can export reports to either an .htm file or a .tsv (tab delimited) file. You can then take these exported files and import them to a favorite application for further massaging of the data. Exporting data is covered in more detail later in the section "Exporting Performance Data."

Performance Logs and Alerts Views

Performance Logs and Alerts under the Performance console are two views available to you that may be the most powerful of any of the views you've learned about. This isn't to say these particular views should be used all the time and no other views can compare to them. As with chart and report views, log and alert views are put to best use when used in the correct situation. The only way to understand which situation is correct for the implementation of these tools is to fully understand their capabilities and limitations.

Performance Logs and Alerts allow you to collect data from local or remote computers. *So what?* you ask yourself. Well, to begin with, the log view allows you to collect this data over an extended period, something neither chart nor report can do for you. Second, you can view this logged data in *any* view under System Monitor. This means you're not giving up the comfort of a graphical view, such as the histogram, if that's what you want. You can then take this logged data and export to an external source for analysis and report generation.

Performance Logs and Alerts are designed for serious data collection and for those times when you can't immediately detect the problem under chart or report view. When you need to collect server performance data over days, weeks, or even months, logging is the only way to go. Otherwise, trying to collect data over long periods leaves you with charts that take up precious server resources and are cumbersome to analyze.

There are two types of logs that you can generate under Performance Logs and Alerts: counter and trace. You create a counter log by adding counters to the log, much like you do to any of the other views, setting a time interval and starting the log. The log file consists of counter data taken for each counter you specified, at the time interval you set. Trace logs record data of certain activities such as a disk I/O operation or network TCP/IP. When such an event occurs, the provider sends the data to Performance Logs and Alerts.

Performance Logs and Alerts then allow you to view this collected data while it's being collected or after collection has completed. Viewing the data during collection doesn't mean data stops being logged. The service continues to write to the log file so you don't miss any critical trends that may occur at the server.

The two log types and how to create counter and trace logs under Performance Logs and Alerts are covered next.

Counter Logs

The Performance Log provides a sample counter log called System Overview. This counter log consists of counters that give you an overview of your server. Right-click the log file and select Properties. This launches the System Overview Properties dialog box. Notice that under Counters on the General tab, the counters listed are part of this particular log file. To add additional counters, click Add and the Select Counters dialog box appears. From here, you can add counters to the log file the same way you did under chart or report view. To remove counters from the log, click Remove from the System Overview Properties dialog box.

Note   If you try to modify the sample System Overview counter log a warning box appears telling you this isn't possible. Neither can you delete these default logs. You have to recreate a separate log file with the settings you want, and then run the log.

To create a new counter log, take the following steps.

1. Right-click anywhere in the details pane of Counter Logs and select New Log Settings.

2. In the New Log Settings dialog box, type the name for the new counter log and click OK.

3. The property dialog box appears. Click Add to begin adding counters to the log file.

4. After you add the desired counters, set an update interval.

5. Clicking the Log Files tab allows you to change the name for the log file by typing a new name in the File Name text box. You can also have the file name end with a particular connotation. The options include yyyymm (four-digit year and two-digit month). Having the files end with a date or time stamp can help you further distinguish log files from each other.

6. You can select what type of log file to create—binary, text .csv file, text .tsv file, or binary circular file. Use a binary file if you want to be able to record data instances that are intermittent; that is, stopping and resuming after the log has begun running. A binary circular file continues to write to the same log file, overwriting previously created records. You can type a comment for the file, yet another way to describe and distinguish the file.

7. Select a log file size if you want to limit the size of the file to a particular amount of KB. Remember, the more counters you select, the shorter the update interval; the more data you record, the larger log files are. If you're limited on disk space, limit the size of the file. Click the Schedule tab to set a stop and start time.

8. The Schedule tab allows you to specify a start time, or you can manually choose to start the log file using the shortcut menu. You can stop data collection at a particular time or when the log is full. You can also stop data collection after an interval of time has passed such as an hour, day, or second. After the log file closes, you can choose to start a new log file, or run a command, such as a command to copy the log file to a separate location. Click OK when you're done.

If you choose to manually start data collection, you can right-click on the log file and click Start from the shortcut menu; otherwise, the log file begins data collection as soon as you close the properties window.

Counter logs are extremely useful if you want to collect data for a specified counter, particularly if you don't know which counter is the one causing the most problems. Creating a counter log can also be useful for capacity planning. If you have extensive logs you can reflect back on, you can more accurately predict your environment's needs. For example, when sizing a new server, you have some real data to analyze.

Trace Logs

As mentioned earlier, trace logs record to the log file when a provider sends data to the Performance Logs and Alerts service.

Trace logs are created in the exact manner as counter logs; however, there are some differences you must note at the property screen for the trace log. First, you have to specify the event to be logged by the system provider. Second, the type of file you can create is an .etl file. A parsing tool is required to interpret the trace log output. You can also specify the amount of memory you want to allocate so the log service can temporarily save trace log data to memory buffers before transferring the data to the log file.

Viewing Data from a Specified Time Range

Performance allows you to manipulate time ranges within logs, so you can view data fluctuations that occur between update intervals you specify.

To view data from a specified time range, take the following steps.

1. Open the Performance console.
2. Right-click the System Monitor details pane and click Properties.
3. Click the Source tab.
4. Under Data Source, specify the location for the log file you want to use.
5. Click Time Range. Drag the left or right side of the bar to shorten the time period you want to view. Click OK when done.
6. You must now add the counters that have been monitored to your chart or report to view the output. You have the choice of only adding a single counter from the log or all of them. Change views to help get a different perspective on the data.

Note   When viewing logged data in report view, you only see the average value for each counter.

Alert View

Up to this point, you've reviewed several methods of collecting and monitoring data using System Monitor or Performance Logs. Each method has a distinct advantage over the other. The alert view, like the other views, allows you to monitor counters for multiple objects from a local or remote computer. But the alert view has a few unique attributes. Alert view requires you to specify a threshold value for each counter you want to monitor. With a threshold value specified, the alert view can then send you an alert when the counter approaches that threshold value. An alert can be triggered before the counter approaches the threshold, or after it passes the threshold.

Rather than having to pay attention to several counters at a single time, you can sit comfortably, knowing you'll be notified when a counter behaves a certain way. For a majority of counters, you want to be alerted if the counter becomes greater than some value. For others, you want to be alerted if the value falls below a certain value. Examples of these counters are Logical Disk*%Free Space*, or Memory*Available Bytes*.

You add counters to the alert view much as you would to a chart or report, by taking the following steps.

1. Open the Performance console.

2. Double-click Performance Alerts and Logs and right-click Alerts.

3. From the drop-down menu, select New Alert Settings.

4. Type a name for the alert and click OK.

5. In the properties dialog box for the alert, type a comment describing the alert and begin to add counters to be monitored. If you want the alert to trigger when the counter value is over the threshold value, select Over from the Alert When The Value Is drop-down box. Otherwise, select Under to have the alert trigger when the value drops below a threshold value. See Figure 4-15 for an example.

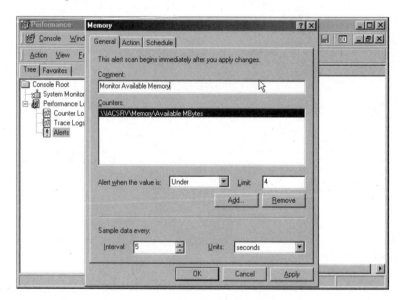

Figure 4-15. *Creating an alert to trigger when available memory falls below 4 MB.*

6. To specify an update interval, select an interval that best suits the counters you may be monitoring. If you set a period that's too long, you may miss activity that you're setting the alert to track.

7. Click the Action tab to specify what action the Performance service should take when an alert is triggered. This tab is the "meat and potatoes" of the alert view; it's here you have the alert view do the work for you.

There are four possible actions the Performance console can take. They are:

- **Log an entry in the application event log** The Performance console writes to the Windows 2000 Event View Application log. A sample log entry consists of the counter that triggered the event, the value for the counter when it triggered the event, and the threshold it crossed (see Figure 4-16).

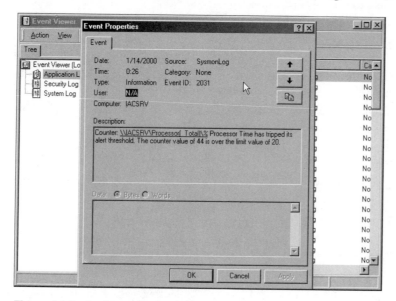

Figure 4-16. *In this example, an entry is written to the Application Event Log as the processor time crossed a limit of 20 percent.*

- **Send a network message to** You can type the name of a computer on your network where the alert message should be sent. Usually, the network administrator or administrator for a particular computer is notified. Users are notified via a message that pops up on their screen using the Windows 2000 Messenger Service.

> **Note** Be careful whom you choose alerts to go to and how the actual alerts are configured. You don't want to flood users' desktops with alert after alert; not only can these messages become network hogs, but they also can be extremely annoying to a user. Choose to send a network message when the alert triggered is critical to network operations.

- **Start performance data log** You can have the system start to write to a predefined log when an alert is triggered. If you have a log created that measures counters you feel are being affected, or affect this particular event to trigger, the log reflects what activity was occurring at the time the event triggered.

- **Run this program** Selecting this option allows you to run a program on the server; you are also able to pass arguments to the program that's run in response to the alert. The possible arguments you can pass at the time the application is launched are:

  - **Single argument string** Specifies whether to pass the arguments as a single argument wrapped with double quotes or as multiple arguments.

  - **Date/time** Specifies whether the date and time should be included as an argument passed to the program.

  - **Measured value** Passes the actual measured value for the counter as an argument passed to the program.

  - **Alert name** Passes the name of the alert as an argument in the command line.

  - **Counter name** Passes the name of the counter that triggered the alert as an argument in the command line.

  - **Limit Value** Passes the value of the threshold as an argument in the command line.

  - **Text message** Includes a text message to be part of the command line.

The last tab is the Schedule tab. From here, specify the start and stop time for the alert. Refer to "Counter Logs" for specific detail on setting values in the Schedule tab. After applying the property settings you want, click OK to continue.

If the alert was created to start scanning immediately, the icon representing the alert turns from red to green, symbolizing that the alert is running. If the alert was set to run manually, or at a later time, it is red. You can kick on an alert view to begin monitoring by right-clicking its icon and selecting Start from the shortcut menu. From the same shortcut menu, you can select to stop the alert or to delete the alert. You're also able to save the alert's property settings to an .htm file, which can then be viewed or imported back in to be used by other alerts or views under System Monitor.

The alert view can be a powerful ally if configured correctly. You don't want to create alerts for each event that occurs on your server. Alerts are most useful when they monitor tasks or events that are likely to hinder operations; or, in some cases, help track down a performance issue that may be occurring at the server.

Exporting Performance Data

System Monitor allows you to export your data so it can be massaged and manipulated by popular programs such as Excel, Microsoft Notepad, or any application that can import either tab-delimited or comma-delimited ASCII files. System Monitor also allows you to export data collected under chart or report view to an .htm file. Using your browser, you view the exported data in either graph, histogram, or report view (see Figure 4-17). When you open the .htm file in the browser, the System Monitor toolbar is displayed at the top of the screen. Using the toolbar, you can add additional counters for monitoring, change System Monitor properties, or change views under which you monitor the data.

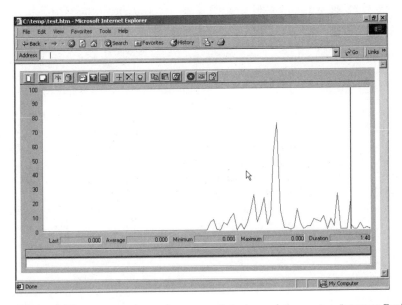

Figure 4-17. *Monitoring performance data in real-time using Internet Explorer.*

If the traditional views under System Monitor lack the flexibility you require, you can always import a file you exported as a tab-delimited file into a spreadsheet or database report writer application. You can then create the graphs or charts you need for your presentation or further data analysis.

To export data from either chart or report view, take the following steps.

1. Right-click anywhere on the chart or report and select Save As.

2. The file is saved as an .htm file by default; you can change this to .tsv format by selecting Report from the Save As drop-down list.

3. Once you select the file format you require, type a name for the file and click Save.

Summary

At the start of this chapter, it was mentioned that you can't tune a system unless you can measure it. A few examples were given of real-world systems and the instruments used to measure these systems. In this chapter, you learned about the one tool that comes with your Windows 2000 Server that was designed to monitor the hardware and software components on a production server. The Performance console is an application that allows you to begin monitoring the most critical components of your server in seconds. However, no matter how quickly you can get a basic chart up, you are not able to tap into the full potential of the Performance console unless you understand how to use it. Second, the data it reports doesn't do you any good unless you understand what it is telling you. In this chapter we reviewed the features that comprise the Performance console. These features include the System Monitor Snap-in and the Performance Logs and Alerts application. Reviewing the System Monitor Snap-in you learned about the types of real-time reporting available through the chart, histogram, and report views. Your review of the Performance Logs and Alerts application showed the counter logs, trace logs, and alert views available through this improved logging application for Windows 2000.

The Performance console is a powerful application and has a lot to offer you in terms of system monitoring. However, it shouldn't be your only performance tool of choice. A better approach is to use the Performance console with other performance monitoring and system tuning applications available to you. A few of these applications are covered later in the book. It's strongly recommended that you become familiar with Chapter 15, "Windows 2000 Resource Kit Performance Tools," and Chapter 16, "Third Party Tuning Tools," for additional resources to augment the Performance console. A combination of these applications along with the strengths of the Performance console can create the optimal set of tools for monitoring your Windows 2000 Server.

Part II
Battle of the Bulge: Handling Bottlenecks

Chapter 5
Diagnosing Processor Bottlenecks

Processors are at the heart of every computer system. They perform a variety of tasks that include everything from acting as a traffic cop to performing mathematical computations. Every application makes some use of the processor, even those that work mainly with other system hardware such as the hard disk. In short, no matter what application you run, you need a good (fast) processor with which to execute it.

Since every application running on your server needs processor support, processor availability is a major concern. If one or two applications consume all the available processor cycles, there aren't any processor cycles left to service other application needs. The subject of processor availability brings us to the first topic of this chapter—the definition of a processor bottleneck. In days gone by, the definition of what makes the processor a bottleneck in overall system performance was easy. Any time the rest of the system was idle while the processor churned away on some task, the application was said to be processor-bound. Today, processors and the systems they support are more complex, and the number of areas that can cause a bottleneck more numerous; all of which spells increased complexity in defining what a processor bottleneck consists of.

The processor does affect every part of the operating system environment; however, it's the applications running on the operating system that most people are concerned about when it comes to performance. The next section of the chapter examines the various kinds of applications that use the processor more than any other resource on your machine. Understanding the needs of these applications can greatly enhance your ability to tune the system for peak performance. You can also use your knowledge of how the application works to optimize the application itself, reducing the number of processor cycles required when performing a given task. One way to painlessly tune a system, for instance, is to turn off product features that run in the background and that perform tasks that you're really not concerned about. (A good example of a background application task is the spell checker in Microsoft Word, which automatically checks your spelling as you type.)

Finding solutions to the processor bottleneck problem is the topic of the next section of the chapter. Some people feel that the only way to fix this problem is to add new hardware. In fact, because of the nature of processor-bound applications, many people discard totally usable machines to buy new models with higher speed processors. Obviously, this is the most expensive way to fix the problem, and the fix normally doesn't last very long. In short, this is the solution of last recourse, not the first avenue you should try.

> **Note** The main focus of this chapter is the Microsoft Windows 2000 Server operating system. To give you a better idea of how the processor fits into the overall computing picture, we'll also cover some hardware-specific issues. The hardware-specific information won't make you a system hardware engineer, but it will make you better able to understand why two "identical" machines with 733 MHz Intel Pentium III processors don't seem to act the same.

The final two sections of the chapter deal with the issues of current and future processing technology. The processor market is ripe for a major shakeup, or at least the appearance of major new technologies. New processors are based on copper, rather than aluminum. In addition, Intel is being challenged on every side by competitors—some of whom have superior products (at least from a raw processing perspective). We'll visit these and other processor issues in the last two sections of the chapter titled "Current Processor Technology Overview" and "Future Directions in Processor Technology."

What Is a Processor Bottleneck?

The concept of a processor bottleneck isn't difficult to understand. The easiest way of looking at this performance inhibitor is to say that the rest of the machine is waiting on the processor to do its work. In other words, other subsystems like the hard disk are idle while they wait for the processor to perform some given set of tasks. Processor bottlenecks are normally viewed as problems that affect the entire system because the processor is needed to perform just about every task. In short, a processor bottleneck is an all-encompassing performance inhibitor that affects every application to some extent.

You might think, at this point, that processor bottlenecks are the worst thing that can happen to your machine and that you need to do everything to stop them. In part, this view is true. Processor bottlenecks do tend to cause network administrators the greatest amount of grief from angry users who want to do something as simple as log in or issue a database query but can't. However, saying that a processor bottleneck completely stops the server from operating isn't accurate because this overlooks quite a few factors that influence processor bottlenecks. Some disk drives, for example, can perform direct memory access (DMA) transfers in the background without any processor help. Depending on your server setup, you can be guaranteed some level of system activity despite a processor bottleneck. It's just the level of activity you get that's in question.

The following sections look at some of the issues that define a processor bottleneck. In the first section, "Quantifying a Processor Bottleneck," we'll talk about how you can quantify a processor bottleneck. You look at what makes a processor bottleneck a continuing problem, rather than a blip on the scope of server performance. The next section, "Testing for Processor Bottlenecks" shows you how to test for processor bottlenecks. A single-user machine is fairly easy to test; in contrast, servers run in very complex environments that defy easy testing.

Quantifying a Processor Bottleneck

Of course, the first problem is quantifying a processor bottleneck versus an application that uses processor resources a lot. On a single-user machine, you're able to detect a processor bottleneck in part by the amount of delay you experience in system response. On a server, response time may not be a true indicator of server processor load. Outside influences like the availability of network bandwidth can give an administrator a false impression, even if the administrator is using the server console to perform a given set of tasks.

There are other operating system problems to consider when it comes to a processor bottleneck. For one thing, Microsoft Windows 2000 includes new features like object pooling. A COM+ component requires considerably more time to invoke the first time than it does for subsequent invocations. Part of the reason is that the resources required to create the object aren't destroyed after the first client gets done using the object—the object is marked as unused for some interval and placed in a pool of available objects.

The first time people invoke the component, they see a delay that can be interpreted as server overload. In reality, the first invocation reflects the true time required for loading the component from disk and making the required resources available for use. Even a lightly loaded server requires some time to invoke a component the first time—and there's disk activity and other factors to consider.

The next invocation of the component appears simultaneously, if there's an object already in the object pool, because the server doesn't have to load the component code from disk or allocate any resources. The user sees a much quicker application response because the resources are already available and the component constructed; the component is merely marked as unused. In short, even if the server is more heavily loaded during the second component invocation, the user is likely to get the false impression that the server has a lighter load. What this means to the administrator is that a server with many components can appear to be processor-bound after downtime or a weekend without use. The moral is that when looking for a server processor bottleneck, you have to consider the kind of application that the server is running at the time, before you assume there's a problem at all.

If there are so many factors that can make it appear that you have a processor bottleneck, when in fact you don't, how do you determine that a processor bottleneck exists at all? In the next section, "Testing for Processor Bottlenecks," we'll talk about some specific methods you can use to test your server for bottlenecks such as indicators in Task Manager; but testing your machine all the time isn't an answer either. Most network administrators learn enough about how their network operates that they can eventually "feel" when things aren't right. The solution is to quantify these internal rules of thumb so that you can at least gauge network performance when the operating system environment isn't quite as comfortable. You may be using Windows 2000 for the first time and that usually means using new hardware as well. With this in mind, let's look at a list of rules you can use to gauge your network performance.

- **Consistency** Unlike a workstation, where the running application lists constantly change, servers normally deal with the same application consistently. A network administrator can detect true processor bottlenecks by looking for consistent slow-processing problems. For example, you may batch process weekly statistics every Friday. If you see a consistent server-processing problem on Friday, it may be an indication that your server has a processing bottleneck. Obviously, you'll want to verify that the application you're running is of the type that causes processor bottlenecks. We'll look at this issue in "Processor-Bound Application Types," later in the chapter.

- **Application-specific** It pays to track which applications are running when users report problems with server processing speed. In many cases, you'll see a problem application. Of course, you need to determine whether the application is faulty (for example, it might have poor resource management), the application is overloaded by too many users, or if you really do have a processor bottleneck. The application vendor can usually provide you with specifications and guidelines for the application that make this determination easier.

- **Task-specific** Component technology allows a single application to execute on more than one machine. COM+ extends this idea by allowing a single application to execute on more than one server. You now have the potential of not being able to identify a specific application, or the machines that the application is working on, without a lot of work. You can often get around this problem, at least on a moderately sized network, by observing user tasks' patterns. A specific group of tasks may rely on a component on a single server to complete. An understanding of how the users are completing the tasks, the components used in the affected applications, and the locations of those components on servers can help you find a processor bottleneck problem.

- **External indicators**   There's a whole class of performance clues that you can term "external indicators." These are the nagging pointers to something going wrong on your network. For example, you might have an application that normally works fine but suddenly starts having problems after you install a new server or upgrade another application. Changes in patterns, both positive and negative, are indicators of something going on in the background that you need to be aware of.

- **Feature-oriented**   A processor bottleneck may not show up immediately after you install an application or make a change to the network configuration. In many cases, just one or two of the application features can cause performance problems that significantly alter the way the network runs. To give you some idea of how this works in a real-world situation, consider what happens after you install a complex application on the network. The users of the application probably begin by working with the simpler features. However, once those users gain some experience, and perhaps some training, with that application, they use some of the more complex features. It's at this point that you may start seeing a slowdown of the network as a whole.

Testing for Processing Bottlenecks

Once you have some idea that a particular server is having a performance problem, you need to test for a specific type of problem. A component-based application that performs a lot of calculations is a good candidate for processing bottleneck problems. However, you still have no idea of how severe the problem really is or how to tune the server to better respond to user needs. All you know is that this server is the most likely candidate and you have a good idea that a particular application is causing the problem.

Using Task Manager to Ferret Out Problems

The first thing you want to do, at this point, is to verify that the server is actually having a performance problem. Remember that there are a lot of false indicators in the world of performance tuning. Starting out with a simple look at current processing levels can tell you a lot about the server as a whole, especially for component-based applications and servers with more than one processor. The first tool to use is also the easiest to find. Right-click the taskbar, and then choose Task Manager from the Context menu. Click the Performance tab and you see the Windows Task Manager dialog box shown in Figure 5-1.

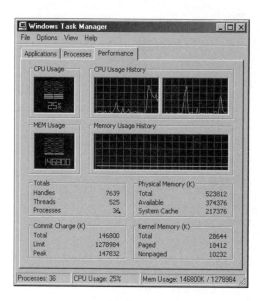

Figure 5-1. *The Performance tab of the Windows Task Manager can provide a quick view of current server performance.*

There are five windows on this dialog (including the two CPU Usage History windows that are separated from each other by a thin gray bar). The CPU Usage window gives you some idea of overall CPU usage at the current time. The two CPU Usage History windows in Figure 5-1 show CPU usage over time for the two processors installed on this server. This display also provides two memory windows. The first, MEM Usage, shows the current memory usage, while the second, Memory Usage History, shows you memory usage over the same interval as the processor history.

Tip You can configure the Windows Task Manager Performance tab using the View menu options. For example, there's an object to display individual CPU usage histories, or to combine them into a single view. You can also change the speed of the history graph updates and perform a view refresh to capture the current statistics.

Keeping track of the various statistics is important. If your server is starved for memory (as shown by the two memory graphs), the processor is working harder just to manage the memory, not to mention application requests. This display can help you determine if a problem really is processor-related, or if it's due to a lack of machine resources. The CPU Usage History graph helps you see the processor-usage picture over time. Remember that a consistently high processor-usage level over a long time indicates a processor-bound application problem. Spikes in processor usage like the ones in Figure 5-1 are very normal—you don't need to worry about them at all.

If you do decide you have some type of a processor problem, you need to take another step with this dialog box. Click the Processes tab. You'll see a list of processes running on the current machine. Now, click the CPU column and you'll see a display similar to the one shown in Figure 5-2.

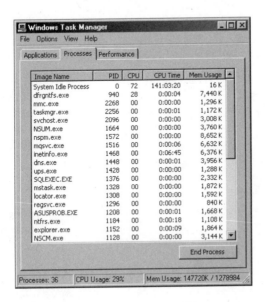

Figure 5-2. *The Processes tab of the Windows Task Manager dialog allows you to determine which process is using the greatest number of processor cycles.*

Notice that the processes that are using the highest number of processor cycles float to the top of this display. Using this setup allows you to quickly see which applications are using the most processor cycles. Notice that the top application in Figure 5-2 is something called the System Idle Process. This is a special "do nothing" process that executes while the processor is waiting for something else to do. As you can see, this system isn't heavily loaded at this moment. The System Idle Process is consuming most of the processor cycles.

There are several other columns of information on this display. The process identification number (PID) column tells you the identification number for that specific process. Every process gets a unique number, which allows you to track that process on the system. If you have the skills, you can use a program such as Microsoft Spy++ to see how the application is using memory and processor cycles. For the moment, though, let's keep things simple and assume that we won't need to use the PID.

The CPU Time column show how much time the application has used since the server was last booted. This is another good indicator of processor loading. Click the button at the top of this column and you'll sort the currently loaded processes by CPU time. On a normally loaded system, the System Idle Process probably has more CPU time than any other process. The reason is simple: The System Idle Process is the only process that's always running on the server. A high number here tells you that the machine does have time to idle—to sit and wait for something to do. If the System Idle Process time is low, the server isn't just busy right now—it's busy all the time.

Finally, look at the Mem Usage column. This column tells you how much memory each process is using. Again, processes that require large amounts of memory may be wasting system resources. However, here's another place you can look for potential optimization. If a particular process uses a lot of memory, yet very little processor time, you need to ask whether it's important to run this particular process all the time. Perhaps you can optimize your system by running the process on an as-needed basis.

Using System Monitor to Check Specifics

At this point, you've either determined that there's a processor-bound application running on your server and that it's causing some type of system degradation, or you've ruled out the processor entirely. If you still think there's a problem with overuse of processor resources, you need to track the exact cause of the problem using System Monitor MMC snap-in (which is part of the Performance console). We've already discussed the general operation of this Microsoft Management Console (MMC) snap-in in Chapter 4, in "System Monitor." However, we're now looking for a specific piece of information about a particular process.

Note   Make sure the application process that you want to monitor is actually running before you start the System Monitor snap-in. Otherwise, the process doesn't appear in the list of processes that you can monitor.

You can track everything a particular process is doing by setting up some counters for that task. Figure 5-3 shows the Add Counters dialog box of the System Monitor snap-in. Notice that the Process option in the Performance Object list is selected. The right list contains all the processes currently executing on the machine, while the left list tells you the kinds of things you can monitor.

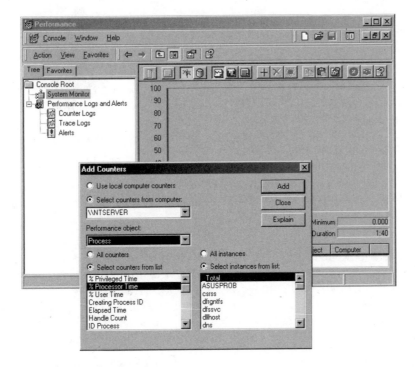

Figure 5-3. *System Monitor allows you to monitor individual processes using the Process performance object.*

Many of the items on this list won't help you very much, but there are a few items you'll definitely want to check out. Scroll through the *Select counters from list* field and you'll notice there are a series of I/O (input/output)-related counters. This is one of the items you'll want to check. Determining whether the application is really processor-bound, or simply an I/O-bound application masking itself as a processor-bound application, is important. An I/O-bound application requires a different set of optimization techniques than a processor-bound application does.

You can also use these counters to look for application problems. For example, the Thread Count counter can help you locate applications that create worker or UI threads unnecessarily. Threads are normally used to perform tasks like printing in the background, or to allow the application to update multiple displays simultaneously. Applications that create too many threads, however, often waste processor cycles in ways you can't afford on a server. In some cases, you can optimize the application to use fewer threads and save processor cycles as a result, and still get all the services you need from the application.

Processor-Bound Application Types

Some applications tend to require more processor time than others. A very common illustration of this situation is a spreadsheet application (which is normally processor-bound) versus a database manager (which is normally considered disk-bound). The spreadsheet application will always use a lot of processing cycles because it performs a lot of calculations. Most people use spreadsheets to perform complex analyses. The fact that spreadsheets are normally used for graphing as well only increases the potential for this application to become processor-bound. Graphics of any kind rely heavily on calculations, which means they rely heavily on the processor. A spreadsheet is also used to compare data—one value against another. While performing a comparison consumes fewer processor cycles than most complex calculations, it's still considered a processor-intensive task.

Database applications are normally disk-bound because they're used to manage data. Most of the application's time is spent moving data to and from the hard disk. If you're using a database to store the company's contact list, it very easily fits into this stereotypical view. Appearances can be deceiving, however. Consider the case of a database manager that's used to store financial data. A lot of databases are used for this very purpose, so the idea of a database-oriented financial program is very realistic. In this case, the database program becomes balanced—it likely uses an even mix of processor and disk resources.

Let's add another wrinkle to this scenario. What if your financial program is component-based and relies on Microsoft's Distributed interNetwork Architecture (DNA) model? Figure 5-4 shows an example of this model. Notice that in this block diagram I've separated the business logic from the database management system (DBMS). In reality, you can use any number of servers, but you're likely to begin with one or two during development. It's important to remember that you could gain access to any number of DBMSs through an application of this type, but that the component technology tends to hide the complexity of these connections from the user. As the network administrator, however, you must know where the data is located, what components are being used, and which servers the components are installed on. In sum, you need a diagram of the application when working in complex DNA environments.

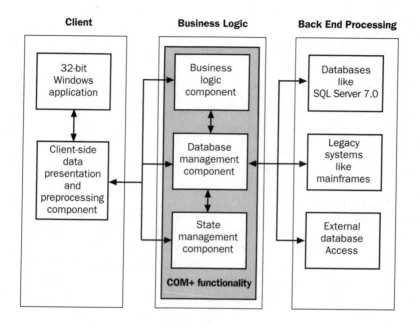

Figure 5-4. *Microsoft's DNA model makes it easier to create scalable applications, but also increases tuning and optimization complexity.*

As you can see from Figure 5-4, it's very possible that your application will reside on two or more servers. One server might hold the business object components used to perform the analysis on the data stored on another server. The server that contains the business object components might be processor-bound, while the second server might be disk-bound. As you can see, the more complex your application setup and your network, the harder it is to determine exactly what might happen using theory alone. That's why monitoring of suspect applications is important.

Deciding whether an application is processor-bound can be difficult in many cases; but in some cases, it comes down to a simple analysis. The following steps help you analyze most applications, no matter how complex the application and network models get.

1. Break the application down into its component parts.

2. Determine the task that each component performs. For example, a business object will most likely perform calculations. Understanding how the user works with the application helps you understand the roles of the various components. Make sure you spend time with the developer as well—a good programmer should be able to help you understand the application at the overview (block diagram) level.

3. Determine the location of each component part.

4. Decide whether the tasks performed by a set of components on a specific server are more likely to be processor-, memory-, or disk-bound. Processor-bound tasks are normally calculation-intensive. Any component that performs data analysis, works with graphics, or manipulates data in memory is processor-intensive.

5. Verify your assumptions by tracking the performance characteristics of the components using System Monitor.

6. Track application performance over a period of time to look for usage patterns.

Tip Keep records of how your application works after initial installation and after the application has been in place for a few months. These benchmarks help you see changes in usage patterns that may help you prevent the processor-bound application scenario. If you can detect an increase in application load early, you can add servers to support the additional user requirements before those requirements become critical. We'll look at the topic of capacity planning in Chapter 11, "Capacity Planning."

Potential Solutions for Processor Bottlenecks

If you've gotten to this point in this chapter, it means that you've determined there's a problem on your server with a processor-bound application. Needless to say, the kind of application you're working with determines what you do next. In some cases, you may have to take the ultimate step of adding a new server to your network—but first, let's look at a few things you can try to fix the problem.

Check for Simple Problems First

The first thing to always check on your server is some simple settings that can make a very big difference in server performance. Right-click My Computer and choose Properties from the Context menu. You see the System Properties dialog box. Click the Advanced tab, and then the Performance Options command button and you see a Performance Options dialog box like the one shown in Figure 5-5.

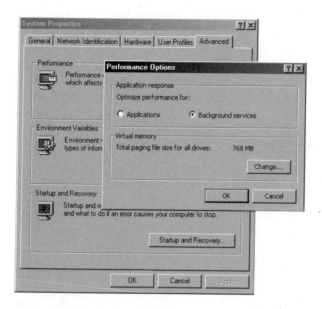

Figure 5-5. *The Performance Options dialog box is the first place to look for processor-bound application problems.*

Notice that the Background Services option is selected in Figure 5-5. Unless you're using your server as a workstation, there isn't any reason to select the Applications option. The Applications option always results in better foreground task performance, but poorer background task performance. Since most server applications are run as background tasks, you'll want to keep the Background Services option checked.

Remove Unneeded Services

Look again at the Processes tab of the Windows Task Manager dialog box shown in Figure 5-2. This is a list of all the tasks currently running on your machine. You need to check each of these tasks to see if they're active and if they're essential. For example, it's common practice to install various types of monitoring software on the server. Normally, this software provides you with feedback on the current state of the server's hardware and environment. If you have two or more pieces of monitor software installed with overlapping functionality, however, it pays to get rid of one of them—especially if this software is consuming a lot of processor cycles. Obviously, you'll want to monitor the application to ensure it's processor-bound. You'll also need to be very careful when uninstalling software.

There's an alternative to removing the software completely if it relies on services rather than running as a foreground task. Open the Services MMC snap-in and you see a list of all the services installed on the server, like the one shown in Figure 5-6. Not all these services are running and not all the running services are processor-bound. Look in the Status column to determine if the service is loaded and running. Those services marked Started are running.

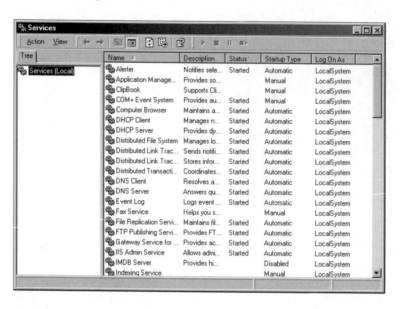

Figure 5-6. *The Services snap-in allows you to manually stop services to test their effect on server performance.*

You can stop a service by right-clicking its entry in the Services snap-in and selecting Stop from the Context menu. Make sure you understand what the service is doing before you stop it. The Description column of the Services snap-in gives you some information about the service, but don't assume anything about a service that you haven't worked with in the past. Always check the vendor documentation to ensure you understand the effect of stopping the service.

Tip The Services snap-in allows you to restart a service instead of stopping and then starting it as two separate steps. Restarting a service can help you find services with memory leaks and other resource-usage problems with a minimum of service interruption.

You'll also want to check the service for dependencies—a list of services that depend on this one to operate. Stopping this service also stops any services that depend on it. Right-click the service, choose Properties from the Context menu, and then click the Dependencies tab to see a list of dependencies. Figure 5-7 shows the dependencies of the Microsoft Distributed Transaction Coordinator (DTC). DTC depends on remote procedure call (RPC) and Security Account Manager (SAM) services to run—these services have to be running before you start DTC. On the other hand, you must start DTC before you can start message queuing. Stopping DTC also stops message queuing, so you don't want to stop this service without ensuring you can stop message queuing as well.

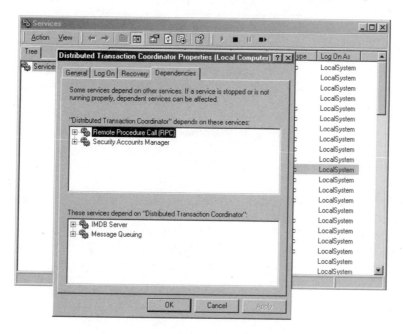

Figure 5-7. *Always check dependencies before you stop a service to ensure you won't stop a service you do need on the server.*

So, what makes a good candidate for server optimization? It depends a great deal on your server setup. Look at Figure 5-6 again and you'll notice that one of the services listed is the FTP Publishing Service. If your company isn't using the FTP server, you could probably stop this service and no one would notice any loss of functionality. The point of this kind of server optimization isn't to force people to get by with less functionality—it's to remove services that no one is using to provide the other services the resources they need to work well.

Perform Task Scheduling

Sometimes an optimization technique requires the use of an existing technology in a new way. Most versions of Microsoft Windows now come with a task scheduler that you can use to run tasks at a more convenient time. You can monitor server operation as a whole to determine when the processor is the least busy. It might be midnight or 1 A.M., but that's the time you need to run processor-bound tasks that don't require any user interaction. Batch processing of orders falls into this category, as do a wide variety of maintenance tasks.

Current Processor Technology Overview

It seems that every day brings yet another processor on the scene. At times, the number of processors seems to exceed the number of purposes to which they can be employed. Some processors, like the Intel Celeron, are purposely created to reduce system purchase prices at the expense of raw computing power. Other processors, like the Intel Pentium Overdrive with Multi-Media eXtensions (MMX), are optimized to provide significant performance boosts in a specific area. Still other processors, like the recent Intel Pentium III offerings, are more balanced—they're designed to provide good overall performance, yet provide all the features a user is likely to need.

Note As new processors come out, features that were at one time unique become standard parts of the processor. For example, at one time MMX technology was a unique feature of some Pentium processors. Today, MMX is a standard feature. In most cases, you can count on successful processor additions becoming part of the standard processor—at least until something better comes along.

Processor performance is further influenced by a number of factors both within and outside the process. For example, the amount of level two (L2) cache that a processor provides can greatly increase performance. The L2 cache helps memory keep up with the processing speed of the processor—making it less likely that the processor burns processing cycles waiting for memory to do something. When you compare this to processors that are equal in every other way, the one with the larger L2 cache normally performs better when working with processor-intensive tasks.

Tip One of the least explored but most helpful hardware-specific, processor-tuning techniques is to add more external processor cache. (Don't confuse this with main memory—the external processor cache is usually a separate set of memory modules on the motherboard.) Many computers ship without any external processor cache—those that do are often populated with less memory than the motherboard could support. Processor cache is often created from relatively expensive static random access memory (SRAM) or other exotic technologies, which is why vendors are reluctant to add very much (doing so would increase system cost). The external processor cache is designed to be very fast to keep up with the processor as much as possible. An increase in external cache size can dramatically improve processing speed for processor-bound tasks that rely heavily on memory access for computations. A graphics application is a perfect example of this type of processing. It's processor-bound because the calculations are required to draw the image on a virtual screen, yet it requires large quantities of memory to store and manipulate the image components.

There are other performance factors to consider as well. For example, the chipset used to control processor activity can make a great deal of difference. A single processor can normally work with several different chipsets. The Pentium III processor, for instance, can work with the 840, 820, 810e, 440GX, and 400BX chipsets as a minimum. The chipset affects the bus speed used to access peripheral devices, the speed of the memory bus, and some of the features you'll get with a system such as the level of graphics processor support. The motherboard you purchase normally has the chipset soldered in place, making an upgrade impossible. With careful purchasing, however, you can often buy a new motherboard for a relatively low cost and move your existing memory, peripherals, and processor. The result is higher performance and extended features, all at a very low cost.

Your choice of processors isn't limited to Intel either. Advanced Micro Devices, Inc. (AMD) has recently come out with a new processor called the Athlon that (at the time of this writing at least) outperforms the Intel offerings when it comes to raw processing capability. Of course, this is where those external factors come into play. Even though the Athlon provides a lot more raw processing power than the Intel offerings, Intel has come out with the new 820 and 840 chipsets that make things a bit more even in the real performance department. In short, when it comes to processor optimization, you need to look at a variety of internal and external influences.

More Info Both AMD and Intel make it easy for you to find a fast processor with relative ease. You'll find links to the Intel processor specifications at *http://www.intel.com/intel/product/*. The AMD processor specification links appear at *http://www.amd.com/products/products.html*. Obviously, there are other vendors out there, but these are the two major PC processor vendors at the time of this writing. You also need to consider factors like price when making your purchasing decision. These Web sites help you obtain the information you need to make a good purchasing decision.

The universal nature of the processor also makes it one of the first targets of optimization—people understand that the processor is one area they can enhance with relative ease through a simple upgrade. It's also the one area where tuning can affect the system as a whole and every application that the system is running. However, making the processor faster doesn't tune or optimize your operating system to use the processor more efficiently—it simply hides the problem. There are times when a processor upgrade is required; but you should first try tuning your applications, removing unneeded services, and scheduling tasks.

When a processor upgrade is inevitable, check with your motherboard vendor first for downloadable motherboard upgrades. For example, ASUSTek Computer Inc. (ASUS) (a motherboard vendor) recently produced a BIOS upgrade that allows its motherboard customers to use Intel's newer processors on older motherboard products. What this means to ASUS users is that they can now get faster processing speeds at a lower upgrade cost than buying an entirely new machine.

As you can see, PTO from the processor perspective involves a lot more than just application and operating system tuning—it begins when you decide on which machine to purchase. A good processor for one task may not be the right choice in another situation.

Future Directions in Processor Technology

To say that processors are evolving at a high rate of speed is an understatement. It seems that the new machine you buy today is outdated before it leaves the manufacturer's loading dock, much less the store. State of the art today often means you're using yesterday's technology when it comes to the processor within the machine.

The processor characteristic that most people focus on when it comes to processor evolution is speed. Only recently has anyone even questioned whether we need a newer, faster processor to run word processing applications. When it comes to servers, however, no one has yet questioned the need for additional speed. If anything, the introduction of new operating systems like Windows 2000 has only served to whet the appetite of network administrators. Speed will continue to be a factor in server development for quite some time to come.

Speed comes in several different forms. The two most common forms are the processor's clock speed and the processor's data processing width. Obviously, clock speed improvements are the most common method of improving overall processor speed today. Intel and other vendors will eventually introduce 64-bit chips (which increases the data processing width of the chip), but these evolutionary moves are relatively slow and predictable.

More Info   Some network administrators discount the usefulness of BIOS upgrades when tuning their servers. This is a mistake from several different perspectives, the most important of which is the ability to use higher speed processors. For example, a BIOS upgrade may allow you to run a higher speed processor. So, for the cost of a new processor and the time required to download the update for your server's BIOS, you could gain a relatively large performance improvement. Even if the gain doesn't directly affect performance, it can affect the efficiency of your machine. A new addition to many BIOS updates includes the ability to use the Advanced Configuration and Power Interface (ACPI). ACPI allows your company to become more efficient at using a variety of resources. You can find out more about ACPI at *http://www.teleport.com/~acpi/*. This site includes a link to the ACPI specification, as well as overview information. There's a PDF formatted version of the ACPI specification available at *http://www.edtn.com/scribe/reference/appnotes/md0052a7.htm*. If you'd like to find out how ACPI affects new hardware initiatives like Wired for Management, look at the Intel site at *http://www.intel.com/ial/WfM/design/pmdt/acpidesc.htm*.

Internal processor modifications are also common today. For example, many processors include extended special purpose instruction sets that may be considered a wasted investment for servers. Intel introduced processors with MMX instruction set to help with the home market, especially in the presentation of graphics and sound for games. Unless your server is performing some type of multimedia processing, this type of processor enhancement is probably wasted on your server.

Fortunately, other processor enhancements, like pipelining, can help your server run more efficiently. (Pipelining affects the way that the processor queues instructions for execution, making the execution process much more efficient.) The problem is that many of these new features require special programming. This is what happened when the Pentium III originally came out on the market. People tested it and concluded it didn't perform much better than the Pentium II. The reason is simple: The software they used for the test wasn't optimized for the Pentium III. So, how does this relate to PTO? Custom application can be written to take advantage of the capabilities provided by advanced processors. As a result, you can partially optimize your system by requesting custom application updates as needed.

Custom application optimization can go even further with processors like the Pentium III. For example, the Pentium III includes a true random number generator in hardware. Not only does this hardware-based random number generator work orders of magnitude faster than those created in software, but it's also more secure. In short, many of the most exciting processor updates make some types of tuning unnecessary in the future.

Speed and interesting new features that make applications run faster are good processor additions, but how will the processor of the future help you out when it comes to operating system-specific features? Windows 2000 represents a major leap in the way Microsoft views the operating system. This version of Windows contains many new scalability features and it's obvious Microsoft is doing everything possible to provide you with an optimized operating system right out of the box. It's likely this trend is going to continue. As processor vendors such as Intel develop new technologies like the true random number generator found in the Pentium III, Microsoft will add features to Windows that will allow you to use them. In fact, it wouldn't be surprising to find a patch, service release, or hot fix that addresses this very Pentium III feature sometime in the near future.

Summary

We've covered a lot of ground when it comes to processor technology in this chapter. One of the most important facts that you can remember is that not every hardware performance problem means getting a new server. There are always performance indicators that you can check to determine whether a performance problem is hardware related. Even if the problem is hardware related, replacing an individual server component is often more cost effective and faster than replacing the server as a whole. Replacing an old processor with a new one is relatively simple and often requires nothing more than a BIOS upgrade to support new processor features.

Of course, the problem for the network administrator is figuring out just what kind of performance upgrade to perform. The place to start is to analyze the kinds of applications running on the server. Computationally intense applications like graphics and financial programs always require a lot of processing power. If you're running an application like a database manager, then the problem is more likely hard disk, rather than processor, oriented. Once you've determined what kind of problem you have, you need to determine how to tune your server. In many cases, you can simply change application settings to get the performance boost you need. In those few situations where application tuning won't work, tuning the hardware might do the job. The option of last result is to replace the processor or even the server as a whole.

Our journey into hardware tuning has just begun. Chapter 6 continues the journey by looking at memory bottlenecks. We'll look at the ways memory affects server performance. In fact, we'll look closely at the memory itself. This chapter also answers questions like which kind of memory is best for a given server and application type.

Chapter 6
Diagnosing Memory Bottlenecks

Memory, as everyone knows, is volatile data storage. Remove the power from your computer and the contents of memory disappear. It's a temporary place to put data that the computer is working on or the instructions required to perform the data manipulation. Our topic of discussion is almost absurdly simple from a conceptual perspective. Most people, including complete novices, understand the concept of computer memory.

Although memory begins as a simple concept, it doesn't stay that way for very long. Most computers today are filled with a variety of seemingly contradictory types of memory. Memory comes in a wide enough variety of acronyms to confuse the typical Rhodes scholar, and more types appear on the market every day. If the physical distinctions between various kinds of memory aren't enough, the same kind of memory can be used for a number of purposes. In fact, those purposes are often interchangeable and can change during the computing session. The first section of the chapter, "Understanding and Using Memory," helps clear up some of the confusion behind the types of memory. By the time you finish this first section, you'll have a better understanding of why synchronous dynamic random access memory (SDRAM) is being replaced by Direct Rambus dynamic random access memory (DRDRAM), and why you need static random access memory (SRAM) for the processor's external cache.

The volatile nature of memory raises some reliability concerns. What happens if power gets removed from your server before the data in memory is placed in permanent storage (normally a hard drive)? This question has plagued network administrators since the days of mainframes and we'll explore it again in the "Reliability Considerations for Memory" section of this chapter. However, we'll be looking at the question from a performance perspective. We'll also look at the question of how we can ensure the reliability of data, yet maintain the performance benefits of using RAM.

Memory is a storage device. It doesn't perform processing tasks like the processor does— you can't rely on memory to produce a result. However, memory still needs to perform work in managing the storage of data. It can therefore become a bottleneck in the processing stream. If the processor is spending time waiting for memory to complete a task, the user is going to notice a delay in the processing of requests. The "Detecting Memory Bottlenecks" section of the chapter looks at the question of memory as a bottleneck to performance.

Once you decide your server has a memory bottleneck, you have to figure out how to fix the problem. There are two paths you can take to clear a memory bottleneck. The first is to reconfigure Microsoft Windows 2000 to operate more efficiently, while the second is to add more memory to the server. Unlike the processor solutions that we talked about in Chapter 5, however, adding more hardware can also clear memory bottlenecks. There are times when you need additional memory to complete a given task and no other solution will work. The "Configuration Solutions for Memory Bottlenecks" section of the chapter will cover these two fixes to the memory bottleneck problem. We'll talk about configuration changes first, since that's the least expensive way to handle the problem.

Understanding and Using Memory

Memory comes in a lot of sizes and styles. Part of the reason for all this diversity is historical. The first PC I worked with used individual dual in-line package (DIP) chips on the motherboard. There weren't any memory modules, and memory on that particular system was limited to 64 KB. While this solution to memory worked fine in the early days of computing, you probably wouldn't want to use it now. Memory modules are a lot more convenient to install and use.

The following sections help you discover today's memory and answer the question of why things are the way they are. The first section covers the various kinds of memory that you'll find on a system. We'll talk about the various acronyms vendors have come up with to describe memory and what they really mean to you.

The second section looks at how Windows 2000 uses memory. Not surprisingly, there are some rather archaic memory uses within the operating system that are steeped in history. Other memory uses are as new as Windows 2000 itself. It pays to know how the operating system uses memory. The first step in optimizing the system is to understand how the system works.

Memory and Its Acronyms

Memory is known by a lot of acronyms, each of which defines a different method of storing data that part of the computer is working on in some temporary form. Let's start off very simply. You've probably seen the terms *dynamic random access memory* (DRAM) and *static random access memory* (SRAM) in many forms over the years, but what do these terms really mean?

The following sections describe many of the terms used for memory in history and today. What you should take away after reading this information is a better understanding of why memory is designed a certain way and why certain designs have better performance characteristics. It's important to understand what you'll gain from a memory upgrade, especially when you have to make a choice between two types of memory like SDRAM and DRDRAM when buying a motherboard.

DRAM and SRAM

DRAM was originally composed of an electronic component known as a capacitor (there are other parts included in DRAM today, which is part of the reason for all the strange acronyms). Think of the capacitor as a little battery that loses energy at a fairly constant rate as long as the circuit load remains the same. DRAM is relatively easy to make and, because there are very few components involved, you can place a lot of memory on a single chip. The problem with DRAM is that it loses its charge over time. As a result, DRAM has to go through a periodic time-consuming refresh cycle. The operating system can't access the memory during a refresh cycle, so system performance is affected.

SRAM was originally composed of four or more transistors in a circuit called a flip-flop. Each flip-flop represents a single data bit. The flip-flop, as its name suggests, is set to a state and stays there until some external force changes it. As a result, SRAM requires no performance-inhibiting refresh cycle, which results in faster and more consistent access by the processor. However, because SRAM requires more components to create (a minimum of four transistors compared to one capacitor), it also takes more space and power. SRAM also costs more because you can't pack as much memory on a single chip. SRAM is therefore a good choice where you need high speed, but it isn't a good choice for system memory.

VRAM

One of the problems with using DRAM for video memory is that monitors use fairly complex timing, which means the monitor output circuitry has some fairly tight constraints when it comes to drawing on the screen. In addition, an application can't draw to video memory at the same time that the monitor output circuitry is using it for display refresh purposes. As a result, developers used to have all kinds of very strange algorithms for getting data to video memory fast enough and at the right time so it wouldn't affect drawing (displaying) the contents of memory on screen.

Someone at Texas Instruments thought there had to be a better way to work with memory than using all these complex coding methods. The result is video RAM (VRAM). VRAM is also known as double-buffered memory because both the input and the output have special holding areas known as buffers.

VRAM set a precedent that's still in use in some ways today. A VRAM module is actually DRAM, with a serial input buffer and a parallel output buffer. The two buffers are actually a set of flip-flops used to hold one memory entry (usually one byte or 8 bits). The use of double buffering accomplishes three things. First, VRAM allows the monitor output circuitry to read memory a lot faster. Second, because both the input and output are buffered, the DRAM refresh cycle has less of an effect on system performance. Third, because both the output and input are buffered, an application can write to VRAM without checking the state of the monitor output circuitry first.

VRAM is relatively expensive because of the extra buffering circuitry, so you only find it on high-end graphics cards today. However, some of the principles that VRAM espoused made their way to other memory architectures. It's important to keep the speed advantages that VRAM demonstrated in mind as you look at other types of memory.

EDO DRAM

Other memory vendors were quick to mimic the technology introduced by VRAM. Instead of double buffering the data like VRAM does, Extended Data Out (EDO) DRAM buffers the address data and the output data. This change represents a major reduction in circuitry and still enhances performance. EDO DRAM works by loading the column address data in a buffer. The entire page of RAM is read into a buffer, the correct column selected, and the data is then output while the next incoming address is buffered. Unfortunately, EDO DRAM operates at 40 MHz, which is better than the 28.5 MHz of standard DRAM, but far below the 66 MHz bus speed present at the time of its introduction. Needless to say, the situation is even more critical today with 100 MHz and 133 MHz bus speeds.

Developers originally assumed application developers would want to access memory one bit at a time. This was true in the days of DOS, but is no longer true with operating systems like Windows 2000. Processor-bound applications tend to access memory in short bursts of at least 4 bits. Direct memory access (DMA) transfers to and from disk tend to happen in medium-sized streams of 32 bits minimum. Graphics access tends to occur in long data streams that reflect the size of the video buffer currently in use. In short, accessing memory one bit at a time is part of the past.

SDRAM and BEDO DRAM

It wasn't long before someone decided DRAM didn't have to be truly random anymore. Sure, you still have to access individual data segments randomly, but once you've done this, the application more than likely needs to sequentially access the memory. That's where synchronous DRAM (SDRAM) and Burst EDO (BEDO) DRAM come into play. The designers of these two memory types didn't assume anyone needed to access a single bit of data—they assumed the application needed a minimum of 4 bits or 8 bits of data at a time. The secret to the speed of this DRAM is that the RAM itself provides the address of the next bit of data to retrieve. In other words, the RAM delivers data in bursts. The processor programs a burst length and burst type into the SDRAM or BEDO DRAM, and then allows the RAM itself to deliver the requested data as quickly as possible. In most cases, the new memory architecture allows a burst-mode operation of 100 MHz. Note, however, that SDRAM and BEDO DRAM still have latency (data search) times similar to DRAM. In short, it takes just as long as it did before to find the data, but once the data is found, memory can deliver it much faster.

Tip   You may have spent time looking at the bus timing numbers found in many PC BIOSs today without really understanding what they mean. When looking at memory bus timing numbers, you'll normally see something like 5/1/1/1. These four numbers represent the number of bus clock cycles for each bit transmitted on the bus. The first bit you get from memory typically takes five clock cycles for SDRAM. After that, each bit requires only a single clock cycle. In some cases, you can get a slight performance boost by modifying this timing. For example, if you're using high quality SDRAM, you may be able to change the timing to 4/1/1/1. However, there are always reliability concerns when you do this. It's important to maintain the reliability of your server and still get the best performance from it. With this in mind, always perform tuning of this nature before you place the server in production and be prepared to change the settings back to their original state if memory appears less than stable.

SDRAM provides two additional features that previous DRAM memory types don't. The first is the ability to open two pages of memory within the chip at one time. This allows the chip to deliver sequential data faster. One page of memory is delivered, while the chip looks up the second page. The process of using alternate memory pages is called interleaving—SDRAM is interleaved to produce an apparent doubling of access speed internally. Some motherboards also support external interleaving in either two or four bank access schemes.

SDRAM is different in another way as well. Unlike previous memory configurations, which sent data out as quickly as possible, SDRAM is clocked to synchronize its operation with that of the processor. That's why it's called SDRAM. The use of synchronization improves bus efficiency, further improving the ability of SDRAM to deliver data quickly. Since everything is synchronized, there aren't any delays due to mismatches in data delivery and acceptance timing.

One feature that appeared in SDRAM and has appeared in most memory chips since is Serial Presence Detect (SPD). The SPD tells the motherboard what type of memory you have installed on your system and how to configure itself to use that memory. The SPD always provides the system with the vendor's suggested memory configuration, rather than the maximum performance configuration you might be able to use. Most BIOS configuration programs in use today provide an SPD position in the memory configuration area so you don't need to worry about the vagaries of memory-timing parameters. The SPD setting represents the safest way to configure your system's memory if the motherboard and memory you purchase both support this feature.

An early problem with SDRAM was the proliferation of different specifications by different vendors. In other words, you might buy SDRAM for your machine only to find it won't work as anticipated because of the lack of standardization. In short, early SDRAM adopters had to work directly with the motherboard vendor when making a memory purchase to ensure the memory worked as anticipated. That particular problem went away when Intel came out with its PC100 specification. PC100 SDRAM is standardized and works in every machine that supports it. Part of the PC100 specification is that the memory needs to provide 8 ns (125 MHz) memory, rather than the 10 ns (100 MHz) memory actually required for a 100 MHz bus. This speed differential is the engineering "fudge factor" mentioned previously and can allow you to tune your system to use a higher bus speed or different timing characteristics. Reconfiguring your system for higher performance, however, always comes with risks.

More Info There's a lot more to SDRAM than covered here—only the highlights are provided so you can see why SDRAM is such an important part of the memory performance picture. You can learn more about SDRAM in general and even obtain specification sheets for the IBM version of this product at *http://www.chips.ibm.com/products/memory/sdramart/sdramart.html.* If you would like to learn more about PC100 specification memory, look on the Intel site at *http://developer.intel.com/design/chipsets/memory/pcsdram/pcsdram.htm.* Texas Instruments has information about a wide range of memory products, including both VRAM and SDRAM, at *http://www.ti.com/sc/docs/schome.htm.*

DRDRAM

That brings us to Direct Rambus DRAM (DRDRAM), the latest technology on the memory horizon. It seems SDRAM is starting to fall behind in its ability to keep up with today's modern processors. Until just recently, the bus speed of most motherboards was 100 MHz. That speed has increased to 133 MHz, and will most likely increase even further. SDRAM is able to keep up with current bus speeds, but just barely at the 100 MHz level it was designed to work at. SDRAM may be out of the picture when 133 MHz memory bus speeds become popular—it'll definitely be out of the picture once the memory bus gets up to the 200 MHz level that many industry pundits expect in the next year or two.

DRDRAM gets around the bus speed problem by using a different approach to moving data around. For one thing, it uses a special bus known as the Direct Rambus Channel, a 400-MHz, 16-bit bus. It may seem counterproductive at first to reduce the width of the data bus (current machine architectures are at 64 bits and moving toward 128 bits), but the reduction in width allows the higher bus clock speed. DRDRAM transfers data on both the up and down stroke of the clock, effectively doubling the transfer rate. Theoretically, DRDRAM should be able to move data at 1.6 GB/s.

There are several conventional methods used to increase the speed of DRAM. For one thing, you can make the individual components smaller, which reduces the space between them, allowing the electrons to move faster. Another method is to use performance-enhancing access schemes such as interleaving. DRDRAM takes the third of the more conventional approaches—a different construction method. In this case, we're talking about the same methods used to create complementary metal-oxide semiconductor (CMOS) chips. These are the same chips used to store computer configuration information. The use of this low component count construction technique allows DRDRAM to provide higher performance than SDRAM at a lower level of power consumption.

Tip There's a lot of concern over licensing issues for DRDRAM right now. Many vendors are leery of using the new technology because they don't want to pay licensing fees. Even though Intel is going ahead with its plans to support DRDRAM, other licensed buses (like the Micro Channel Architecture or MCA bus) of the past haven't made it in the marketplace. If you do decide to use DRDRAM for your next server, you may want to wait to see how the licensing issues turn out first. Otherwise, you could end up with a server that has memory no one supports. The competing technologies in this section, DDR SDRAM and SLDRAM, are likely to be better choices because the specifications for these memory architectures are in the public domain.

DDR SDRAM and SLDRAM

There's a contender for the current memory king crown. Some vendors have begun using Double Data Rate (DDR) SDRAM. DDR SDRAM is effectively the same technology as SDRAM—the only difference is that this type of RAM transfers data on both the up and the down clock. In essence, it transfers data at twice the speed because it transfers data twice per clock cycle. This is the same kind of technology currently being used to speed the Accelerated Graphics Port (AGP) and Peripheral Component Interconnect (PCI) buses, so it should come as no surprise.

More Info There are a lot of places to look for more information about both DDR SDRAM and DRDRAM. The best DRDRAM information is at the Rambus Web site at *http://www.rambus.com/*. Other memory chip vendors you'll want to check out include Intel (*http://www.intel.com/*), Hyundai Electronics America (*http://www.hea.com/*), Fujitsu Microelectronics (*http://www.fujitsu.com/*), Hitachi Semiconductor America (*http://www.hitachi.com/semiconductor/*), IBM (*http://www.ibm.com*), and Enhanced Memory Systems (*http://www.edram.com/*). All these Web sites can provide different takes on precisely how DRDRAM and DDR SDRAM can help you get the most out of your machine.

Another contender for the memory crown is Synchronous Link DRAM (SLDRAM). A consortium of about 20 major manufacturers is creating this particular standard. Unlike DRDRAM, SLDRAM builds on current SDRAM technology. It uses a higher speed 200-MHz, 64-bit bus. As with many newer memory technologies, SLDRAM performs two data transfers per clock cycle for a theoretical 3.2 GB/s transfer rate.

More Info   You can find out more about the SLDRAM standard by looking at the SLDRAM Consortium Web site at *http://www.sldram.com.*

If you're starting to see a pattern here, you can be sure it'll continue for as long as vendors come up with new ways to improve memory performance. This particular speed battle has been at the forefront since the PC was invented, for good reason. Main memory, RAM, has a very large effect on system performance. The kind and speed of memory you get for your server will always matter because memory is always going to be one of the best ways to make your system run faster with very little effort.

How Microsoft Windows 2000 Uses Memory

Windows 2000 uses memory in all the ways that Microsoft Windows installations of the past use memory. There are caches for the icons on your system as well as the fonts. Windows 2000 also requires some memory for internal use, as well as application-generated requests for operating system services. In short, every device driver, every dynamic-link library (DLL), every thread of every process requires some type of memory. You can get a good idea of how much memory is being used in your system by right-clicking the taskbar and choosing Task Manager from the Context menu. Choose the Performance tab and you see a memory display similar to the one shown in Figure 6-1.

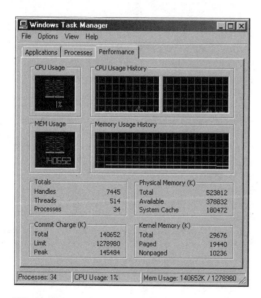

Figure 6-1.   *The Performance tab of the Windows Task Manager tells you about system-wide memory usage.*

You can also view the memory used by some but not all of the processes running on your server, using the Windows Task Manager. There are some cases when a process may not show up in the list. However, these occasions are rare. Click the Processes tab and you'll see a list of processes currently running on your machine, as shown in Figure 6-2. The Mem Usage column contains the total amount of memory used by each of these processes.

Image Name	PID	CPU	CPU Time	Mem Usage
System Idle Process	0	99	132:25:44	16 K
System	8	00	0:00:46	220 K
smss.exe	160	00	0:00:00	348 K
csrss.exe	188	00	0:00:03	1,832 K
winlogon.exe	208	00	0:00:53	8,876 K
services.exe	236	00	0:00:24	7,436 K
lsass.exe	248	00	0:04:09	20,688 K
ntfrs.exe	276	00	0:00:19	712 K
svchost.exe	444	00	0:00:01	3,560 K
NSPMON.exe	484	00	0:00:00	1,528 K
msdtc.exe	632	00	0:00:00	4,824 K
dfssvc.exe	756	00	0:00:04	2,196 K
tcpsvcs.exe	776	00	0:00:36	5,328 K
svchost.exe	800	00	0:00:01	5,872 K
ismserv.exe	816	00	0:00:00	2,776 K
lssrv.exe	832	00	0:00:08	3,668 K
SQLSERVR.EXE	920	00	0:01:03	6,872 K
explorer.exe	1132	00	0:00:09	2,528 K
NSCM.exe	1172	00	0:00:00	3,144 K

Processes: 34   CPU Usage: 0%   Mem Usage: 140936K / 1278980

Figure 6-2. *The Processes tab allows you to see the amount of memory used by exposed processes.*

Tip   You can use the System Monitor MMC snap-in, which was discussed in Chapter 4, to check the memory usage of each process running on the system in detail. For example, you can determine how much private memory the process uses. Private memory can't be shared by other applications, so this is a good indicator of the memory each running instance of the application requires. System Monitor's forte is providing you with a historical view of process memory usage, which is an important part of tuning your system over the long run. Windows 2000 also comes with Process Viewer utility (PVIEWER.EXE). This utility is a part of the Windows 2000 Support Tools, which is located on the Windows 2000 CD in the Support directory. Process Viewer is great for giving you a very detailed look at the various processes currently running on your server. (It doesn't give you a historical view of the various processes.)

When working with a server, you also have to consider the role it performs within the company. For example, a database server allocates memory in pieces that match the size of the records in the various tables. A multimedia server allocates large pieces of contiguous memory for use as a buffer for transmitting data to clients. A communication server requires small buffers that correspond to each client session currently supported by the server. The list of role-oriented memory uses goes on.

It's important to understand that Windows 2000 Server uses memory for both console uses and client requests. This makes the memory-usage patterns for this operating system different from those of a client operation system such as Microsoft Windows 2000 Professional, yet some administrators attempt to use the same memory management techniques in both environments. Reducing the needs of the system console won't influence server performance that much because servers are normally used to service client needs. In other words, there's an entire class of workstation-specific aids that provides a marginal level of performance gains, but it's much better to concentrate on the memory used for the server's role-based tasks.

Keeping the server orientation of this book in mind, the following sections help you better understand how Windows 2000 uses memory from both a console and server perspective. The first three sections look at the main areas of Windows 2000 Server-oriented memory uses—those uses required for the local console. The next four sections look at the various role-based memory uses. When looking at the needs of your server, you need to combine the console and the server requirements for your particular situation. In addition, it's important to consider some of the factors that we really don't look at in this section like unique hardware requirements. For example, if your server is used for data acquisition, you may have some memory requirements that I won't address here.

Internal Data Structures

Windows 2000 relies on a wealth of internal data structures to perform its work. Some of these data structures are easy to see. For example, the registry is a data structure used to hold various kinds of configuration information that Windows 2000 requires for starting services, interacting with hardware, ensuring resources are available, and answering user requests.

There are various kinds of caches that allow Windows 2000 to do tasks faster. For example, there are separate cache files for both fonts and icons. Using cache files allows Windows 2000 to access these resources faster, providing a significant performance boost for the user. You'll normally find these cache files in the main system folder (usually \WINNT) or in the \System32 folder. The ShellIconCache file is an example of disk cache storage that gets loaded into memory.

Windows 2000 also depends on a lot of hidden data structures that you can't see very easily. Many of the Windows 2000 API calls depend on data structures to pass information from applications or services to the operating system and back again. There are also data structures that get passed around as part of Windows 2000 event and messaging systems. Finally, data structures are used for interprocess communication. Two processes can communicate using techniques like named pipes and even mail messages. In short, data structures allow Windows to communicate. The more communication that takes place, the greater the memory set aside for the purpose. Processing all these communications require processing cycles that could be used for other tasks. As a result, most programmers try to keep the amount of communication performed by the applications to a minimum. (There are also gabby programs that communicate at every opportunity.)

Normally, these data structures are well maintained and you don't need to think about them very much. In some cases, however, the data structures can become like overstuffed filing cabinets. For example, if network administrators remove ActiveX controls from the server without deregistering them first, the registry can become filled with control entries that are no longer valid. As the registry gets larger, it consumes more memory and takes longer to search. Obviously, this is a performance inhibitor you can easily do without.

Drivers and Low-Level System DLLs

Device drivers are just about the first components that get loaded as part of the operating system start sequence. After all, even the operating system needs access to the hardware. Unlike many other parts of the operating system, device drivers are almost Spartan in their use of memory. Because device drivers are required to perform so many operations for the server, they're written with speed in mind. In addition, because these components lack any form of user interface, the device driver has little need for anything other than configuration information. In short, device drivers are the least of your worries when it comes to any kind of memory management and they aren't good candidates for any kind of optimization in most cases (unless you want to remove them from the system).

Low-level system DLLs provide various types of services required by the operating system. Applications never access these DLLs directly since they operate at a higher security level than the rest of the system. Like the device driver, low-level system DLLs are written to provide the very best in speed. In many cases, they're written in hand coded C—in a few cases, you'll find them written in hand-coded assembly language. As you can probably tell, the memory used by these DLLs isn't up for negotiation—you can't remove them without degrading system functionality in some way. It's usually best to avoid any optimization tricks on the low-level system DLLs.

Services

You'll find an entire list of operating system services in the Services MMC snap-in such as the ones shown in Figure 6-3. Services are the one operation system element that you run by choice. If you want to use a particular operating system feature, you need to start the service for that feature. Installing a service, but not running it, uses hard drive space. The only time you also allocate memory and processing cycles for services is when you start the service.

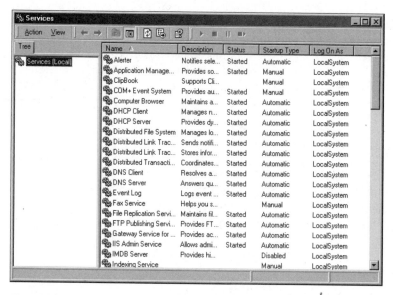

Figure 6-3. *Services are the backbone of Windows 2000 functionality.*

We talked about the processor impact of running services in Chapter 5. The "Turning Off Unneeded Services" section in this chapter examines the memory impact of using services. For the most part, you should consider turning off any services that users aren't working with, as long as turning the service off doesn't affect other areas of the server.

Data, I/O, and Resource Buffers

Applications use a lot of memory to interact with the outside world. Users need applications to allow them to manipulate data in various ways, and then see the results of those manipulations. Applications use a variety of interface elements to provide the user with feedback in a way that's best suited for the task at hand.

Most of the memory used by an application has something to do with data. The application creates temporary variables to hold the data, provides buffers in which another application can store data, or creates variables for other data needs. Application variables used for data access needs are also the most commonly abused memory element. In many cases, data variables are responsible for various kinds of memory leaks and their misuse can result in a lot of different kinds of application reliability problems. (Memory leaks occur when an application allocates memory, then doesn't release the memory before it terminates. Windows doesn't know if the memory is still in use so it isn't available for use by other applications.) In short, this is the kind of memory problem you'll have to deal with most often. Since data variables also hold your company's future, this is also the kind of memory problem you need to deal with quickly.

I/O represents the second class of buffer storage requirement in an application. You won't deal with this kind of memory usage very often within a server environment because the client-side application normally deals with vagaries of displaying the results of data manipulations. Server-side applications normally use I/O to store data on disk, create log entries, print data on the user's behalf, or perform some type of data streaming like the multimedia presentations provided by Web sites.

Tip   The problems of application I/O extend to more than just moving bits from the server to the printer or the client. The configuration of the motherboard, memory, and the system bus all affect a server's I/O performance. Currently, there's a movement away from the special memory setups that we've been talking about for the hard drive, display adapter, and processor to a combined memory setup called the Unified Memory Architecture (UMA). AGP is actually a form of UMA because it allows the display adapter to use main system memory to store certain graphics features like textures. A complete UMA solution most definitely decreases system costs because you're using main memory for everything. Many analysts, however, say UMA also decreases system performance by an order of magnitude because current memory architectures depend on sequential memory access to overcome the problems of DRAM latency. A UMA system completely randomizes memory access because main memory is now being used for a variety of purposes. Before you purchase a UMA system for use on a server, be sure the vendor has compensated in some way for the performance penalties of true random access. In most cases, you'll find that the cost savings of UMA aren't worth the performance penalties when it comes to a server.

Resource buffers normally contain pointers (or handles) to other parts of Windows or to objects used by the application. For example, various display elements like icons normally fall into the resource buffer category. A resource buffer can also include a handle to a resource held by another application. Many of the common icons, dialog boxes, and other display elements used by applications fall into this category. In this case, the resource buffer holds a 32-bit value instead of the resource itself.

Objects of Various Types

Windows and the applications running under it use objects to better model the application after the real world. An object is a combination of data and code. The data can include various kinds of resources like icons or bitmaps. The code gives the object a personality. An object has methods to allow the application to request services, properties to adjust the characteristics of the object, and events to alert the application to a specific occurrence.

Using objects allows a developer to create complex applications from simple components. For example, every command button within an application is considered a separate object. A dialog box can contain several command buttons, edit boxes, static text boxes, and the like. Figure 6-4 shows a very simple application I created using a dialog box, edit boxes, command buttons, and static text boxes. As you can see, there isn't anything very complex about this program. Figure 6-5 shows the Microsoft Spy++ display for that example program. (Spy++ is a programmer utility, included with Microsoft Visual Studio, designed to make it easier to track the various parts of an application during testing.) As you can see, this display tells you everything about the contents of the Catalog Table Test application shown in Figure 6-4, including all the objects used to create the dialog box.

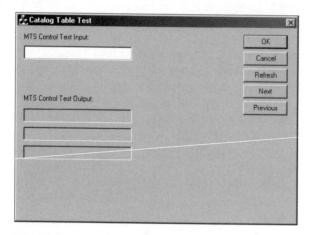

Figure 6-4. *A simple dialog-based test application that uses a variety of display objects.*

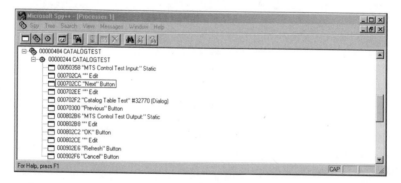

Figure 6-5. *Spy++ is a handy utility because it allows you to look at the component parts of an application.*

This application is representative of most applications out there. It consists of a process with an ID of 00000484 and a single thread with an ID of 00000244. The numbers next to each of the objects under the thread are the handles for those objects. Double-click the thread and you can see how it's using processor time, as shown in Figure 6-6. For tuning purposes, you need to know that CPU Time is the total time the processor has spent servicing this thread, User Time is the amount of user-specific service time, and Privileged Time is the amount of processor time used for system services. As you can see, there are utilities available to help you diagnose precisely how an application is put together and assess how it's using memory.

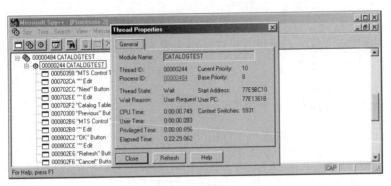

Figure 6-6.   *Clicking the various objects within Spy++ allows you to assess the memory and processor load they represent.*

Data Streams

Another component of application memory usage is data streams. Normally, data streams are associated with multimedia. For example, a client who visits your Web site may want to download streaming data in the form of audio or video presentations. Some types of objects also use data streams, rather than deliver data all in one piece.

Whatever the use, data streams require buffers at both the server and client end. These buffers are normally allocated right before the application sends data to the client, and then deallocated. Streaming allows the server to transfer data efficiently with a minimum use of memory, as long as the developer allocates and deallocates memory as needed. Unfortunately, this kind of memory use can greatly accelerate memory fragmentation (because the application is constantly changing its memory footprint) and could cause application errors in low-memory situations.

Application Code

The final application memory component is the code required to perform tasks. Unlike device drivers and other low-level system components, the application code footprint grows and shrinks as the application is called on to perform certain tasks. Part of the reason for the change in memory footprint is that the application may store the code required to perform a given task on disk until needed. A word processor, for instance, doesn't load its spelling module until the user actually asks to do a spelling check.

Some applications also use a technique where the code is compressed until needed. This means the application's code takes less space on disk and loads faster. This technique does require additional startup processor cycles for code decompression and it means you can't count on the application having a certain footprint in memory. However, this is a useful technique for applications with a lot of different modules, some of which may not be used by the client.

Reliability Considerations for Memory

There are a lot of ways to look at the question of reliability. However, the one constant in any definition is that reliability always includes data integrity. The moment a system begins to lock up for no apparent reason or data starts getting corrupted, users look at the system as unreliable. Since few of us enjoy the side effects of an unreliable system, it stands to reason that any tuning or optimization must maintain current reliability levels or, in the best-case scenario, improve reliability.

As previously mentioned, there are ways to increase the reliability of your system. PC100 SDRAM, for example, comes in two types. One is less expensive and provides just the memory. The second, while more expensive, provides error-correcting code (ECC) benefits. The ECC SDRAM is more reliable because it's more likely to detect and repair memory faults before they become a problem. In fact, this is such an important feature that most motherboards include special BIOS settings to ensure that the ECC feature gets handled properly.

So, if ECC SDRAM isn't going to make your system run any faster, how does using it help system performance? Part of the performance problems with today's systems is user confidence. Users who aren't confident about system reliability tend to do updates more often. They may save their word-processed file four or five times as often as someone who's confident about system reliability. In short, system reliability affects user confidence and usage patterns. Users who save too often or request constant updates waste system resources and make the system appear to run slower than it should.

Tip Some ill-informed network administrators turn off the ECC features of their server with the idea that ECC support uses processor cycles that could be used for some other purpose. ECC support, on the contrary, has no effect at all on the raw processing power of your system. It does, however, affect reliability.

The reliability of the server's memory is also affected by other environmental factors. For example, as previously mentioned, you can set the bus timing on most systems. If you change the memory timing, however, what you're really doing is betting that the memory used in your server is higher quality than the vendor will admit. It's true that engineers often add extra capacity to ensure their products work as advertised, and that you can use this capacity to enhance server performance. However, when taking a gamble of this type, you also have to test system integrity extensively before placing the server in production use, and a system tuned in this way requires additional testing during use. The performance gains you get from tuning a server to make use of every available cycle can end up being wasted by additional administration time.

Heat and dust affect memory more than any other component. If you want to run your system at maximum capacity, you need to ensure it is in a cool location and that you clean it from time to time. This is another situation where good maintenance habits can affect the performance of your system and allow you to tune it in ways you ordinarily can't. In fact, the problem of heat has become so important in today's systems that you'll often see a monitor like the one shown in Figure 6-7, running on the server. This particular monitor can send an alert to the network administrator if the temperature of the system gets too high, the fans stop running, or the power supply voltages waiver.

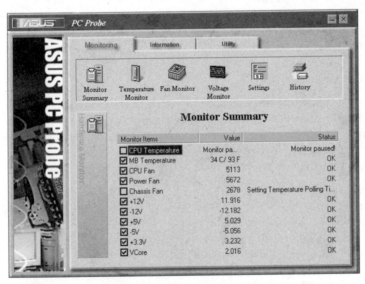

Figure 6-7. *Memory is greatly affected by heat and dust, which makes monitors like these an important addition to your server.*

Memory can become fragmented. How does this affect reliability? When memory gets fragmented, applications experience problems allocating memory in large enough pieces to perform the tasks the user has requested. This, in turn, causes the operating system to swap data between memory and the pagefile (swap file) more often. The disk begins to thrash (experience a very high level of activity) and Windows begins to complain about its inability to allocate enough memory to perform a given task. Yes, this analysis is a tad extreme, but it serves to point out how memory could be affected by constant use.

In the past, I restarted my server weekly. The main purpose for doing this little jig was to prevent memory fragmentation from becoming a problem. The server performed better because it allocated memory in the size needed without relying on the pagefile. In addition, because the applications and operating system didn't have to work so hard moving things around, the system was more reliable.

So far, preliminary testing shows you won't have to restart Windows 2000 nearly as often as its predecessor. In fact, Microsoft is going to great lengths to reduce the number and types of reboots you have to perform in order to achieve the 7/24 operating times many companies are looking for. Still, it pays to keep the reboot system trick in mind if you suspect your memory reliability problems are nothing more than fragmentation rearing its ugly head.

Detecting Memory Bottlenecks

Memory bottlenecks are notoriously difficult to detect under Windows because of all the ways memory gets used. Some memory is used for system calls, while other memory is used by the application itself. Memory might not be attached to a single process—it might actually be shared with several processes. If you get down to the thread level, a requirement for detecting some types of memory problems in applications, deciding how memory is being used gets even harder.

Despite the relative difficulty in figuring out which process is using memory and for what purpose, the fact remains that a system-wide shortage of memory is hard to miss. Applications that leak memory, memory fragmentation, processes that don't clear (free) memory when they're finished, and services that gobble all memory in sight all have a very distinct and easily discerned effect on system performance.

The following sections show you the three most common ways to find the memory bottlenecks in your server. We've already looked at one of these methods (the Task Manager) from an overview perspective, but we'll take a closer look in this section. The important fact to remember is that your system can't run without memory—it's like a car without gas. Sure, the engine works fine, but if there isn't any fuel, you can't go anywhere.

Using Task Manager to Monitor Processes

We've already talked about the role Task Manager plays in showing you the memory used on your machine as a whole and by individual processes. You can see these two uses for Task Manager in Figures 6-1 and 6-2. What we'll do in this section is take a little closer look at what the various numbers mean.

There are three windows dedicated to memory use on the Performance tab of the Windows Task Manager: Commit Charge (K), Physical Memory (K), and Kernel Memory (K). Each of these windows tells you about a different aspect of Windows memory management.

The Commit Charge (K) window contains three statistics that tell you about virtual memory. The Total statistic is the total amount of virtual memory currently in use by both applications and the operating system. The Limit statistic tells you how much virtual memory is available for use on the server. Finally, the Peak statistic tells you the most amount of memory used during the current session (since the machine was last booted). The two statistics you really need to watch are Limit and Peak. When the Peak value begins to reach the Limit value, your server is in trouble and needs some type of memory infusion. You either need to add more physical memory, enlarge the page file (and hope that it works), reduce the number of services running, reduce the number of applications running, or place some of the clients that rely on this server on another machine.

The Physical Memory window contains three statistics that tell you about the current state of physical memory on your machine—the RAM installed on your system. These statistics don't reference the page file at all, so they're a good indicator of when a page file increase won't work. The Total statistic tells you how much memory Windows has detected for your server. If this number doesn't match the amount of RAM you have installed on your machine, you need to check for faulty or incorrectly installed memory. The Available statistic tells you how much memory is available for use by processes. This statistic doesn't include memory available to applications through paging. However, every application requires some amount of physical memory to run—you can't use paged memory entirely. The System Cache statistic tells you how much memory is available in the system cache. This is the amount of physical memory left after the operating system has taken the memory it needs to run.

The Kernel Memory window tells you about the needs of the operating system components running at the highest privilege level. These components normally deal with low-level services like directly accessing the hard drive. In short, these statistics show you what the core operating system services require to run. The Total statistic tells you how much virtual memory the operating system requires. The Paged statistic tells you how much of the total memory used by the operating system comes from the page file on disk. The Nonpaged statistic tells you how much physical memory the operating system is using. Remember that these statistics are for privileged services and not for all operating system services as a whole. The vast majority of operating system components operate as applications. For the most part, the Kernel Memory statistics should remain the same from session to session unless you do something that affects core operating system services like adding a new device. Monitoring kernel memory statistics can tell you about the health of the operating system as a whole—a big change here normally signals some type of problem that may affect performance in the disguise of a memory bottleneck.

Monitoring Memory Problems with System Monitor

Sometimes you don't get enough information to determine the source of a memory bottleneck using just the Windows Task Manager. As with the processor tuning technique we discussed in Chapter 5, memory bottlenecks often require long-term monitoring using System Monitor. We've already discussed the general operation of this MMC snap-in in Chapter 4, so I won't cover the basics again here.

There are actually two levels of monitoring that you can perform: system-wide and individual application. Both levels are available using the Add Counters dialog box shown in Figure 6-8. In this case, I've chosen the Memory performance object. Notice that there aren't any entries in the Select Instances From List field. That's because this performance object monitors system memory as a whole. Yes, you can detect a particular element of system memory like the number of pages read from or written to disk per second, but this performance object only works with the system as a whole. You'll use this level of monitoring to look for faults on a system level—places where performance has been adversely affected by one or more applications. This is the start of your search for memory bottlenecks.

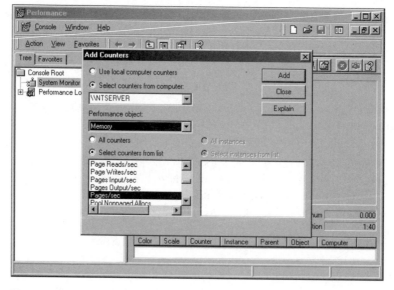

Figure 6-8.   *The Add Counters dialog box allows you to choose which performance object to monitor.*

Once you have an area of memory to examine, you need to determine which process is affecting it. That's when the Process performance object comes into play. This performance object also includes a number of memory-related counters. In this case, however, you can also specify which instance you want to look at, the process you want to examine for memory problems.

Creating Memory-Related Alerts

Memory problems can become your worst nightmare as a network administrator. If your server runs low on processing power, it still runs, but at a reduced rate of speed. Running out of memory means more than just performance problems—you can face application errors and lost data. That's why alerts are so important—they allow you to react to a low-memory problem before it wreaks havoc on your system. Not only does this allow you to detect memory problems with greater ease, but it also allows you to tune the system faster and give the server what it needs, memory.

Alerts allow you to react in one of four ways to an impending emergency. You can send an e-mail to the network administrator, run an application, make an event log entry, or start a performance data log. We looked at what you need to do to create an alert in Chapter 4. You have access to the same performance objects and counters that we discussed in the previous section. Just choose the appropriate performance object and counter, choose a trigger level for the alert, and then tell System Monitor what you want to do if the limit is reached.

Configuration Solutions for Memory Bottlenecks

Once you understand the source of a memory bottleneck, and perhaps why the bottleneck occurs, you'll need to do something about it. Getting rid of application features you aren't ever going to use is one way to control memory consumption. Configuring services and applications to use smaller buffers may be another alternative. However, remember that while using a smaller buffer allows you to run more tasks simultaneously, it also reduces the speed at which data gets transferred from the server to the client in most cases. The following sections provide you with the best ways to control memory consumption once you get past the application level.

Efficient Use of Virtual Memory

Virtual memory can really help or hinder server performance. Provide the server with too little virtual memory and you'll choke your applications for memory. Give the server too much virtual memory and there's a chance you'll choke your system for hard drive space, not to mention processor cycles (the operating system incurs a certain amount of overhead for processing virtual memory that increases as the size of the page file increases). Getting just the right amount of virtual memory isn't tricky, but it's important that you do this bit of tuning because Windows doesn't do it for you.

The first thing you need to know is how to get to the virtual memory settings. Right-click My Computer, and then choose Properties from the context menu. You'll see a System Properties dialog box. Select the Advanced tab, and then click Performance Options. You'll see a Performance Options dialog box like the one shown in Figure 6-9. Notice that this dialog box allows you to choose the type of application response that the server provides and the total virtual memory for the server.

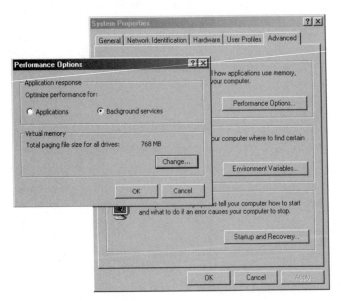

Figure 6-9. *The Performance Options dialog box shows how much virtual memory you have allocated on your machine.*

Click Change and you'll see a Virtual Memory dialog box like the one shown in Figure 6-10. Notice that Windows has set the virtual memory pagefile size to start at 768 MB and end at 1,536 MB. Normally, this is too much memory for a standard server setup because the applications running on the server exhaust physical memory before the page file gets close to this size.

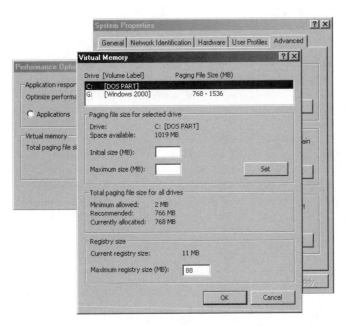

Figure 6-10. *The Virtual Memory dialog box allows you to change the size and location of the pagefile for your server.*

There are several approaches you can take to setting the virtual memory size of your computer. The first approach, and the one that I normally follow, is to set the paging file to the same size as physical memory with no room for growth (which means you set the values in both the Initial size and Maximum size fields the same). For example, if you have a server with 512 MB of RAM, then you would set the Initial size and Maximum size fields to 512 MB. This method works very well for servers running a mix of application types including components. Using the no-growth approach maximizes efficiency because the pagefile doesn't change size. A pagefile that changes size incurs a performance penalty over time because the hard drive gets fragmented and the pagefile with it. (See "Disk Optimization, A Hidden Performance Boost" later in the chapter for details.)

Another approach you can use is for Web servers. In this case, you'll set the pagefile about half the size of physical memory. The reason is simple: Web applications are disk-intensive and normally don't run long enough to get paged to the hard drive. You'll probably want to allow the pagefile to grow to at least the size of physical memory, in this case, to adjust for changing conditions.

The third approach is for servers that work with databases or other pooled, long-term applications. In this case, users may start a session with the server at the beginning of the day and not end it until they go home at night. Database applications tend to have lots of opportunity to build the size of the page file on disk and use virtual memory with great efficiency. In most cases, though, you'll want to err on the side of too much virtual memory at the outset, rather than allow the server to change the size of the pagefile while the application is running (the fragmentation problem is pretty severe in this case). A good starting setting, in this case, is to make the page file twice the size of installed memory. However, you'll definitely want to monitor the server and adjust the size of the page file as required. Since database applications rely heavily on the drive, any drive space you can save can only increase hard drive performance.

Turning Off Unneeded Services

As with the processor tuning tips in Chapter 5, you can monitor Windows 2000 for unneeded services. Unlike the processor, however, a service that's just sitting there doing nothing still uses up memory. You don't get any kind of a break while the service isn't running. For this reason, it's even more important to get rid of unneeded services from a memory bottleneck perspective than it is for processor bottleneck reasons. Since we've already covered this method in the "Remove Unneeded Services" section in Chapter 5, I won't cover it again here.

Disk Optimization, A Hidden Performance Boost

Microsoft Windows NT, the predecessor to Windows 2000, didn't come with any way to optimize the hard drive. As a result, fragmentation eventually occurred. This means the server wasted processing cycles waiting for the hard drive to find a specific piece of data. The problem of fragmentation affects virtual memory as well, especially if you allow Windows to manage the size of the virtual memory pagefile on disk. As the pagefile grows and shrinks, the problem of fragmentation becomes worse. At some point, you'll notice a definite degradation in performance, especially in applications that require large blocks of memory like graphics applications.

Now that Windows 2000 provides the Disk Defragmenter utility, you can remove the performance-robbing effects of disk fragmentation. We'll discuss the hard drive side of the picture in Chapter 7. For now, let's talk about how defragmenting a hard drive can help in the area of memory.

The first aspect you need to consider is how the pagefile fits into the memory performance picture. The operating system automatically uses the pagefile for some of its tasks, which means the pagefile is always used from something even if you have plenty of the real thing. When the server does begin to run low on memory or if you have an application that remains idle for a relatively long time, some of the contents of memory are swapped out to the hard drive. If a client or application requests access to data that the operating system swapped to disk, a page fault occurs and the operating system transfers the request data from the hard drive to memory.

Obviously, accessing data located on the hard drive is considerably slower than accessing it in memory. Your application could spend quite a bit of time waiting if the amount of data request is large. Now, consider what happens if the data needed for the client request appears in more than one location on the hard drive due to fragmentation. Moving the hard drive head is a lot slower than looking for a particular cluster in the same cylinder. As the distance between data locations grows, so does the time required to access the data. Given that the data is already going to take longer to access because of the slower access speed of the hard drive combined with the natural latency of mechanical devices, you could have a real problem on your hands.

It gets worse. Multiply the delays that a single application could see by hundreds of clients accessing the server. You can see how the use of virtual memory could become a real hindrance to system performance. However, the use of the Disk Defragmenter and a little manipulation of virtual memory can make a great deal of difference in system performance.

Note   Changing the pagefile location or size on your server requires a reboot of the server. You need to ensure that no one is using the server at the time of the configuration change. In fact, it's a very good idea to defragment the hard drive when no one is using it because the Disk Defragmenter utility isn't able to move files that are opened, reducing the effectiveness of this procedure.

If you have a two- (or more) drive system, the first task you'll want to perform is to move the virtual memory pagefile to one of the drives you're not using at the moment. Right-click My Computer, and then choose Properties from the Context menu. You'll see a System Properties dialog box. Select the Advanced tab, and then click Performance Options. You'll see a Performance Options dialog box like the one shown in Figure 6-9.

Click Change and you see a Virtual Memory dialog box like the one shown in Figure 6-10. Notice that this system contains two drives (actually two separate partitions on the same hard drive). You can temporarily move the pagefile to the C drive from the G drive to defragment the G drive. All you need to do is highlight a drive, type the initial and maximize pagefile sizes, and then click Set. To remove a pagefile from the drive, set both the initial and maximum values to 0.

At this point, you can defragment your main Windows 2000 Server hard drive, and then move the pagefile back to its original location. The whole purpose of this exercise is to reduce both drive and pagefile fragmentation. You'll find that the results on a badly fragmented hard drive are dramatic.

Summary

Memory is the one resource that your server needs to perform any work. Consider memory the gasoline for your server's engine. When you run out of memory, you run out of capability to perform work as well.

This chapter has looked at several areas of memory management. Of course, you must first determine whether you have an application that wastes a lot of memory or whether the use of that memory is legitimate. Administrators regularly add memory because applications are getting larger. One constant in the world of computing is that applications will always grow to consume the amount of memory provided on the server.

We also looked at several tuning issues. The two most important tuning issues are the size of the pagefile you use and the use of disk defragmentation to make accessing the pagefile as fast as possible. However, there are many other areas to tune, including the removal of services and applications that you no longer require.

Chapter 7 is going to continue our saga of hardware tuning. We'll look at what you need to do to make the hard drive work as efficiently as possible. Of course, this is the meat and potatoes tuning area for database and other disk-bound applications.

Chapter 7
Diagnosing Disk Bottlenecks

The disk drive is the only mechanical device that affects the overall speed of your server to any great degree. Since the disk drive is a mechanical device that relies on computer circuitry to access memory and the processor, there are a lot of ways in which you can optimize its performance from a pure design perspective. There's also a wealth of standards that govern the construction of disk drives, and new technologies on the horizon that will supposedly make sense of the wide range of offerings from vendors who often can't decide on the best technology to use themselves. In short, although the choice of a disk drive should be relatively easy to make, most network administrators must rely on an Ouija board to make their final decision.

More Info   There aren't any "best" places to find information about disk drives since the technology is a moving target and this particular part of the server is more dependent on the kinds of applications you run than any other part. There are, however, good places to at least research your hardware needs. One of the first places to look is Tom's Hardware Guide at *http://sysdoc.pair.com/*. This site contains a wealth of information presented in a relatively unbiased manner. (Any review you read is going to reflect the bias and life experience of the reviewer.) If you're having trouble with all the new terms vendors throw your way, spend some time with the Webopedia at *http://webopedia.internet.com/*. As the site name suggests, this Web site provides you with encyclopedic coverage of all the latest computer terms. Not only that, but you'll also find this site provides relevant links to other Web sites that contain additional information, all within the context of the current term.

The proliferation of hard-disk technologies that are guaranteed to make your life easier doesn't help either. A few years ago, a vendor assured me that the days of the mechanical hard drive were numbered. Supposedly, we were all going to purchase solid state hard drives because these drives are faster and more reliable than their mechanical counterpart. The vendor was wrong and it's not too difficult to figure out why. Solid state drives have their place, but they're still very expensive when compared to the relatively cheap mechanical drive. (A solid state drive uses battery-backed memory in place of physical components; we'll discuss these drives in further detail later in the chapter in "Working with Solid State Drives.")

In another case, I was looking for a device with the speed and storage capacity of a hard drive, but with the replacement convenience of a floppy disk. SyQuest was producing a drive at the time that apparently met my needs—too bad that drive isn't around today. SyQuest had a good product, but they didn't keep up with technology advances and lost customers as a result. If you want floppy disk convenience today, you need to look at an Iomega Zip or Jaz drive, which may or may not be around tomorrow. The point of these two examples is that new technology is great, but you can't count on a particular technology to answer every need or even to stay around long enough for you to realize a benefit from it.

> **Tip** It used to be that Zip drives, at 100-MB capacity, were really only good enough for large file transport. Today, the Zip drive provides a 250-MB capacity, which may be good enough for a variety of other purposes. Jaz drives are even better because they hold up to 2 GB of data—more than enough to back up critical data for quick restores later. (A server still relies on tape for backups of the entire system, or at least a major portion of the system.)

As you can probably tell by now, this chapter examines the various methods you can use to speed hard-drive performance. Unlike the processor and memory techniques in Chapters 5 and 6, however, divining the precise cause of hard-drive performance problems isn't always a precise science. Given the number of factors that affect hard-drive performance, an enhancement that helps one server setup may not do very much for someone else. In fact, there are times when tuning the drive system the wrong way or at the wrong time can actually cause performance degradation.

The first section, "What Is a Disk Bottleneck?," looks at the question of how disk bottlenecks typically occur. There are some very definite system-related problems that always incur a performance penalty. We also look at a few of the more esoteric causes of when disk bottlenecks occur, especially when it's the result of a tuning problem within the operating system.

"Detecting Disk Bottlenecks" helps you understand some of the methods you can use to find disk-related problems with your server. The troubleshooting phase is especially important, in this case, because disk problems can masquerade as other problems, or not be apparent at all. That's right—you can have a disk bottleneck on your server right now and not be aware it exists. Disk bottlenecks have a habit of sneaking up on you so slowly that you don't notice them until they become a significant problem (or you begin to have network users beating down your door and asking why they can't get their work done).

There are some applications that rely more heavily on the disk drive than others do. "Disk-Bound Application Types" looks at this issue in detail. Some of the problem applications are obvious. For example, everyone expects a database application will make heavy use of the disk drive. However, depending on the amount of memory and processing power on your system, even a graphics application could become a problem. The reason is simple: Large memory allocations require use of the swap file (or paging file), which resides on the hard drive. A disk-thrashing problem could be related to something as simple as a fragmented hard drive. (We briefly looked at the issue of defragmenting in Chapter 6 in "Efficient Use of Virtual Memory"; this chapter looks at it in greater depth.)

The next section, "Potential Solutions for Disk Bottlenecks," helps you understand what you can do from an operating system level to make your drives run more efficiently. (Get any idea out of your head right now of making the drive run faster—it can't.) We'll obviously look at some of the system settings you can change to make the drive faster, along with some maintenance tasks you could perform. This section also looks at some of the more esoteric things you can do, such as rearranging your current drive setup for maximum performance. You may find that two medium-sized drive partitions actually work better than one large partition for your particular server setup.

As mentioned earlier, drive vendors are always introducing new and improved methods of moving data from one point to another. "Using New Disk Technologies" helps you separate the gimmicks and gizmos from the truly useful server technologies. Of course, the information in this section is only current as of the time of writing. By the time you read this section, I'm sure the vendors will have something newer and more improved still.

There's one disk organization technique that requires some special thought because you can't easily undo it later. The way you format your drive greatly affects the kind of performance you can expect from your sever. Of course, once you have the operating system and application installed, it's too late to change your mind and decide that you should have gone a different route. This section helps you decide which partitioning and formatting technique to use before you set your server up. We look at some of the more popular methodologies, including disk mirroring, disk duplexing, drive striping, and redundant array of inexpensive disks (RAID). Of course, you want to combine the information in this section with the new technology material covered in "Using New Disk Technologies" to come up with the best solution.

Planning Requirements for Disk Drives

Unlike many other areas in the book where you can take a "try it and see" approach to tuning your server, disk drives require a certain level of pre-planning as well as post-installation maintenance. Because of this planning requirement, you need to spend some time before you read this chapter gathering information about your server, the performance goals that you're required to meet, and the limitations of your company's budget.

It's important to know which applications you plan to run on this server. Make a list of them, along with the vendor's list of requirements for using the product. Consider the vendor-specified requirements a bare minimum to run the application—I usually triple the disk requirements because vendors very seldom allow for the amount of data that companies actually use. Obviously, the amount of data you need to plan for is directly related to the number of users the server will support, the kind of data being stored, how often you plan on archiving old data, and the setup of the application itself.

Performance goals are difficult to quantify unless you spend time performing some level of testing. You need to answer a number of questions, for instance, "How long are users willing to wait before they get frustrated and do something terrible to your application?" Most of the studies I've read say that a user starts getting frustrated at around 10 seconds, but will wait up to a full minute before doing something truly strange with an application in an effort to get a response. In short, you need to answer the question of how productive your company expects the users of your application to be.

You can keep adding hardware to your server in an effort to get maximum performance. Unlike many other areas of your system, disk drives don't have too many limits (unless you're trying to store a terabyte database on an 8088 processor machine). The problem is that all that hardware gets expensive, so you need to set some limits on how much you're willing to spend to get a specific level of performance.

What Is a Disk Bottleneck?

Have you ever watched the drive light on your server flicker on, and then stay on for what seemed like hours? Perhaps you could hear the drive being ground to dust as the operating system hit it over and over again. Eventually, if the drive system doesn't get a rest, the drive will fail—it's a mechanical device after all and can only withstand so much abuse. Long before the drive turns to dust or fails due to abuse, however, the users of your network will begin to complain about slow processing times and even longer waits for applications such as database management systems. You might even see the server freeze because it runs out of the one resource it must have to operate—disk space.

These are all symptoms of a disk bottleneck—an extreme disk bottleneck in most cases. Even small disk bottlenecks can cause devastating consequences on a network server. You might see anything from strange glitches to unexplained data loss to the more benign slow application response. Of course, the first question you need to answer is what causes a disk bottleneck to happen.

A simple definition of a disk bottleneck is that the data you need to write to disk overwhelms some part of the disk circuitry. If the drive can't react fast enough, the Small Computer System Interface (SCSI) host adapter is too slow or provides too narrow a data path, the cabling is wrong, or the server itself gets overwhelmed, you experience the effects of a disk bottleneck.

Real World

Disk bottlenecks are never simple. Consider the company that installed a new server containing the latest in SCSI host adapter technology. The disk drive was likewise a new technology solution and the server itself had both a fast processor and a large amount of memory. In short, this server should have produced better than average results for the people using it.

Company IT staff, test workers, and managers overseeing the project were a little surprised, therefore, when they started the system for the first time and it choked on a mere five users. A check of the performance characteristics of the server showed that the hard disk drive was the source of the problem. After due consideration, the company promptly replaced the hard disk drive, then the cable, and finally the SCSI host adapter. To the surprise of all, the machine started working as they originally anticipated as soon as the company replaced the host adapter with a new one.

Sometimes truth is stranger than fiction. There was absolutely nothing wrong with the SCSI host adapter—it tested perfectly when returned to the vendor. The problem was one of configuration. In this case, the host adapter was incorrectly set to use a slower speed than it needed to with the hard disk drive. It's problems of this type that make disk bottlenecks hard to find in some cases. The company could have saved a lot of time by creating a checklist that told the administrator to check the SCSI host adapter settings.

For those of you who haven't worked much with SCSI drives, the configuration utility for this type of host adapter is separate from the system BIOS or the operating system. A short message usually gets displayed during the boot process that allows you to enter this special configuration utility. If you don't know that this utility exists, it's very easy to overlook this potential source of problems. In some cases, tuning and optimization does't involve making strange setting changes to the operating system or using exotic hardware; it means making sure the machine is configured to perform its best.

Disk bottlenecks don't occur in the vacuum of a single server either. Consider a COM+ application where one server relies on the services of a second server. If the second server has some type of disk bottleneck problem, the user will likely blame the application as a whole. The problem for the network administrator is finding out which server in the group that services that application has the problem, and whether the problem actually has something to do with the storage subsystem.

Let's make the situation a little more complex (as if it weren't complex enough already!) What if the COM+ servers are operating in a cluster? If the application uses Component Load Balancing (CLB), the network administrator can get truly lost in finding which server has a problem. CLB gives a COM+ component request to the server best able to service it at that time. Unless the network administrator is watching the servers every moment of every day, the choice of server may as well be random. There just isn't a good way for the network administrator to identify the problem as a disk bottleneck, much less identify the particular server that's responsible for the problem.

As you can see, disk bottlenecks can potentially cover a lot of ground. They include everything within the disk subsystem: the host adapter, cabling, and disk drive. A disk bottleneck can also include certain types of network problems—getting data from permanent storage to memory is technically the responsibility of the disk subsystem. Transferring data from one server to another in a way that's transparent to the end user is difficult, to say the least, when one of the servers isn't operating at peak capacity. Finally, disk bottlenecks could involve the interaction of multiple machines in some applications. Consider the fact that a data transfer is incomplete until all the data that the client requested is in memory and available to the application. This means that if the data stored on another server becomes unavailable, the problem could show itself as a disk bottleneck.

Detecting Disk Bottlenecks

Disk bottlenecks are hard to pin down, in part because they can be masked as so many other kinds of problems. There aren't any easy answers when it comes to detecting a disk bottleneck. You're not going to open the Task Manager, look at the performance indicators it contains, and instantly know that the problem you're seeing is something disk-related—it just doesn't work that way. Finding a disk bottleneck requires a great deal of detective work on your part.

Using Disk Defragmenter as an Analysis Tool

The obvious place to start is System Monitor MMC snap-in in Performance, but it's not the first tool I turn to in this case. I look at the drive light. If the drive light stays on nearly all the time, I know that the system is accessing the hard drive a lot for some reason. The drive light doesn't tell you why; all it tells you is how much. A drive light that stays on all the time is abnormal, no matter how heavily the server is loaded at the time. The light should either stay off for relatively long intervals with short levels of activity (optimum), or flash on and off at a regular interval (more likely to happen).

At this point, try to figure out if the problem is processor-related by using the techniques in Chapter 5, "Diagnosing Processor Bottlenecks." If it isn't processor-related, check for memory causes as discussed in Chapter 6, "Diagnosing Memory Bottlenecks." The reason you need to look for these two sources of problems first is that the drive activity light is affected by both processor and memory bottlenecks. If your server is heavily loaded and short of memory, it's going to access the swap file on disk a lot more often and that could cause you to think you have a disk bottleneck.

Once you determine a problem is very likely disk-related, you can use the Disk Defragmenter snap-in shown in Figure 7-1 to figure out if the problem is fragmentation-related. (You can find the Disk Defragmenter snap-in in the Programs/Accessories/System Tools folder of the Start Menu or under the Storage folder of Computer Management.) Drive fragmentation is a very serious problem for a lot of reasons. A file that's fragmented in several places causes the hard drive head to move more often. Moving the head is expensive in terms of performance because the drive head moves relatively slowly compared to the rest of the computer. It's much faster to access data if the entire file is located on one track of the hard drive because the hard drive head doesn't need to move.

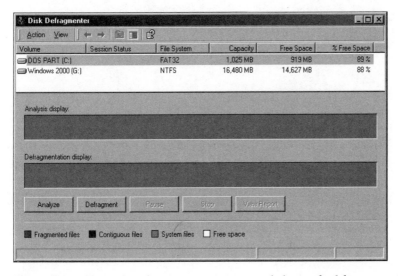

Figure 7-1. *The Disk Defragmenter snap-in can help you find fragmentation problems on your hard drive.*

Disk fragmentation causes problems in several other ways as well. For example, if your hard drive has a lot of little open places to write data, but no large places, the operating system is forced to perform writes in more than one place to store large files. As with the read operation, writing across multiple drive areas means moving the head, which means a loss of time. As you can see, the effects of disk fragmentation can become quite noticeable.

Checking disk fragmentation is almost too easy. Click Analyze. After some amount of time, Disk Defragmenter displays a dialog box similar to the one shown in Figure 7-2 if your drive doesn't require defragmentation. However, this message box doesn't tell you the whole story. The operating system might think the drive is just fine when some critical file is very fragmented.

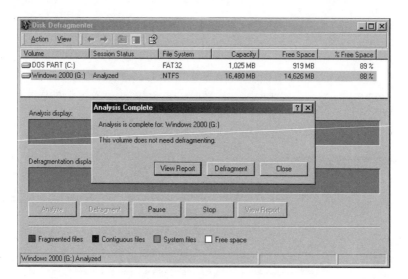

Figure 7-2. *The Analysis Complete dialog box only provides an overall fragmentation status report.*

Click View Report and you see an Analysis Report dialog box similar to the one shown in Figure 7-3. Notice that this display has two windows of statistics. The top window provides you with general statistics about the drive itself. You can find out information such as the amount of free space on the drive and the actual amount of fragmentation. This window provides valuable information, but still, it doesn't really tell you about the status of your drive. If you have a very large drive, the amount of fragmentation overall might be small, but the fragmentation of critical files might be high. In this case, you still want to defragment the drive to make it perform better.

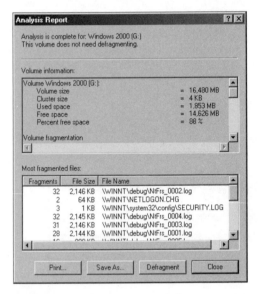

Figure 7-3. *The Analysis Report dialog box provides you with detailed information about the fragmentation status of your hard drive.*

The Most Fragmented Files window is the one you need to look at. It contains a list of the files that are most fragmented on your drive (not necessarily in order of fragmentation level either). Click the Fragments column to move the most fragmented files to the top and start going through the list of files. In a lot of cases, you can tell if a critical file (such as the swap file) is fragmented simply by looking at the filenames in the list. If you see that a critical file is heavily fragmented, defragment the drive even if the Disk Defragmenter snap-in doesn't recommend that you do so.

There are some facts you need to consider before you defragment the drive, however. The Disk Defragmenter snap-in won't touch any file that's open or connected with normal operation of the system for some reason. It's normally a good idea to perform this kind of maintenance when the system isn't in use by other people or when the amount of activity is minimal. Stop any services that the system doesn't absolutely require to ensure that the Disk Defragmenter can work with as many of the files as possible. It's also important to move the swap file from the current drive to another drive, if possible, since the utility won't touch this file at all. Moving the swap file to another drive, and then moving it back, allows you to defragment the swap file. I've already covered the process for defragmenting the drive in Chapter 6, "Disk Optimization, A Hidden Performance Boost," so it's not covered here in detail again.

Closing the Analysis Report dialog shows you a display like the one shown in Figure 7-4. Notice that the Analysis Display window now contains a graphic display of the fragmentation status of your hard drive. You want to look at the red areas (Fragmented files in the legend) of the display. A lot of red areas also indicate a fragmentation problem.

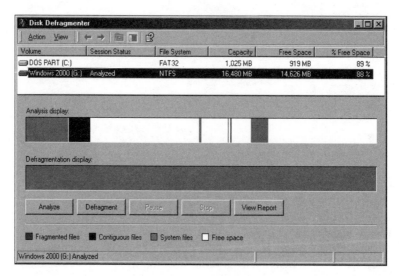

Figure 7-4. *The Analysis Display window of the Disk Defragmenter snap-in allows you to see a graphic presentation of the fragmentation status of your drive.*

Tip   Large networks require a lot more in the way of disk defragmentation than the Disk Defragmenter can provide. Even though Microsoft doesn't provide a utility that uses it, there's an application-programming interface (API) that allows defragmentation of the drive before the operating system starts. This means you can defragment all the files on a drive without worrying whether the operating system is using them. In most cases, you want to get a third-party defragmenter if complete defragmentation is desired. While it's true a third-party addition complicates the network administrator's job, there just isn't any other way to get the job done in some cases. Third-party solutions are covered in Chapter 16.

Checking Your Hardware

When it comes to the processor or memory, you can get a pretty good idea of what your system contains just by looking at the indicators that the operating system provides. You don't need to open the box to know that you have a 733 MHz Pentium III processor installed. The system tells you this information during the boot process in most cases, and you can easily find it out from Microsoft Windows 2000 as well using the System Information MMC snap-in in Computer Management.

Disk drives aren't nearly as easy to check. Microsoft Windows tells you about the drive itself—at least the drive's name—but it doesn't tell you about the characteristics of that drive (in some cases, it doesn't get the drive name correct either). The only way you can check the configuration of the server and be absolutely certain that you know what the server case contains is to open it and check.

Note   Some people use the term *box* in place of *server case*. This term also appears in some magazines and the trade press. I use the term *server case* throughout the book because it's less ambiguous.

The important things to check are the operating characteristics of the hardware. You need to ensure that the system has the proper hard drive, cable, and host adapter installed to obtain the level of performance that you're expecting from the server. You want to check the condition of that hardware as well—it's not unknown for a cable to develop a performance-robbing kink when the server case gets closed incorrectly.

If you have a drive system that requires external configuration, like a SCSI host adapter does, it's important to check this configuration as part of your hardware inspection. Make sure the SCSI adapter is correctly configured for the kind of disk drive you're using. It's especially important to set features such as the drive negotiation parameters and the bus speed.

There are some special considerations for Windows 2000. For one thing, you need to make sure all the host adapters in your machine actually show up in the Device Manager. (You can access the Device Manager by right-clicking My Computer, choosing Properties from the Context menu, selecting Hardware on the System Properties dialog box, and then clicking Device Manager.) Figure 7-5 shows a typical Device Manager display that includes two host adapters. This machine originally had a resource conflict that prevented both host adapters from appearing. A simple configuration change allowed both host adapters to work and gave full access to the drives.

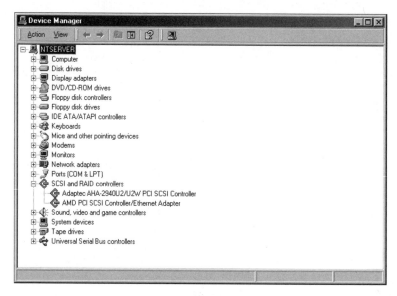

Figure 7-5. *Always check to ensure that Windows 2000 sees the host adapters and drives for your system.*

While you're in Device Manager, you can check several other important configuration options. Right-click the drive, choose Properties from the Context menu, and then look at each tab on the drive properties dialog box. Figure 7-6 shows a typical example of a configuration setting for a CD-ROM drive. Checking the Digital CD Playback option provides better performance, but can result in unstable CD-ROM operation. Figure 7-7 shows a setting for a SCSI hard drive. In this case, checking the box improves performance, but could result in lost data if power is suddenly removed from the server. Unfortunately, these options vary by vendor, drive type, configuration, and driver features, so I can't provide you with precise tuning in this case. Check the vendor documentation for details.

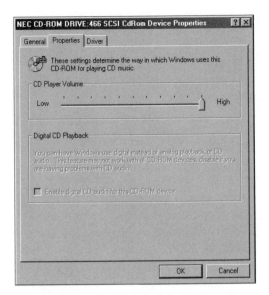

Figure 7-6.   *CD-ROM drives usually provide some form of optimization in the method of playback or data caching.*

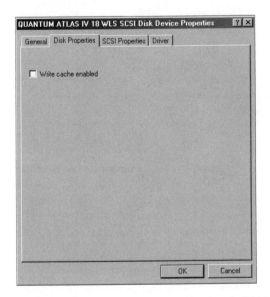

Figure 7-7.   *Hard drives normally provide DMA support, write cache support, and other features that enhance performance.*

Using System Monitor to Find Disk Problems

Unlike with other kinds of bottlenecks, System Monitor should be the last tool you use to find a disk bottleneck. The reason is simple. There are a lot of different operating system elements that affect the performance of the disk drive. If you make System Monitor the first stop on your voyage of discovery, you're likely to conclude (wrongly in most cases) that there's some kind of disk bottleneck in your system. It's important to eliminate other potential sources of problems, such as processor and memory bottlenecks, before you take this step. When looking for disk bottlenecks, use the other techniques we've talked about in the chapter first, then use System Monitor to refine your search once you've determined there is a disk bottleneck.

Once you do get to the point of using System Monitor, you need to decide what kind of problem you want to look for first. The disk subsystem has more counters in Windows 2000 than just about any other component of the operating system. There are so many counters, in fact, that finding a disk bottleneck becomes more a problem of eliminating sources that aren't affecting performance, than looking for the needle in the proverbial haystack that is.

To give you an example of a problem that looked like a disk bottleneck but wasn't directly related to the disk subsystem, consider the company that recently installed Windows 2000 on its network. Erratic performance caused all kinds of testing problems and the network administrator was about to pull the cord on what he considered a very bad experiment. It was then he noticed that there was a pattern to the disk bottleneck problem. Further investigation showed that the Indexing Service was causing the hard drive to work harder during periods of lower user activity. Turning the Indexing Service off during normal work hours (until the index was completely built) allowed the system to operate normally. Once the indexing process was complete, the network administrator was able to turn the indexing service on full time without any ill effects on system performance.

There are two Performance objects that directly affect the drive. The first is the Cache Performance object. It contains counters that allow you to check the performance of the system cache in answering requests from memory, rather than going to the disk drive. The larger the cache you have on your system, the better the performance of this particular element. The way to tune this particular element is to tune the memory in your server—Windows 2000 automatically allocates more cache memory if it's not using very much for other purposes.

The second Performance object is Physical Disk. You can use the counters provided by this object to detect disk usage patterns. The drive light tells you there's disk activity— nothing more. These counters tell you what kind of disk activity is taking place. By knowing what kind of disk activity the system is experiencing, you might be able to find an application tuning problem or decide whether to use one of the riskier drive configuration options.

The Physical Disk Performance object is useful for another type of disk bottleneck detection. The kind of remediation you perform is often based on the kind of disk activity taking place. For example, if you find out that users are reading from the drive a lot more than they're writing to the drive, it might be that they're searching for information. That knowledge might lead you to a database application that users need to enter orders for the company. Asking the developer to create a memory-based database for some of the static data, such as abbreviations for states or ZIP codes for certain areas of the country, might make a big difference in performance. Creating a special index of that area of the drive using the Indexing Service might yield an increase in performance as well.

A Quick Overview of NTFS5 versus NTFS4

Windows 2000 ships with a new version of NTFS that includes some interesting features to help you optimize your drive setup and make it easier for you to manage the drives as well. NTFS5 also adds new capabilities that enhance the operating system's ability to provide services to the user.

One of the features that affects the storage efficiency of Windows 2000 is the support NTFS5 provides for FAT32. FAT32 is the file system that originally appeared in the OSR2 version of Microsoft Windows 95 and is now in all versions of Microsoft Windows 98, as well as Windows 2000. (You can't format a partition to use both NTFS5 and FAT32. Windows 2000 supports use of either formatting method, and you can use them on the same machine on two separate partitions.) This means you can use the more efficient FAT32 file system for dual-boot machines. Many network administrators maintain a DOS partition on their server to hold diagnostic and hardware monitoring software. In times past, this partition used space inefficiently—you no longer have this problem with NTFS5.

NTFS5 also supports the Universal Disk Format (UDF), which is based on ISO-13346. This file system replaces the older Compact Disc File System (CDFS), which is based on ISO-9660. There are a lot of low-level differences between these two standards. From a user perspective, however, the difference is very easy to understand. UDF supports both CD-ROM drives and DVD-ROM drives. This additional support allows you to gain the advantages that DVDs provide when it comes to choice of media and density of data storage.

Although FAT32 and UDF support is interesting, there are a lot of other changes you should know about that affect NTFS5 directly. For one thing, NTFS5 supports reparse points. Essentially, this is a change in the way NTFS handles file paths. Each step of the directory path is individually parsed and, if necessary, redirected to another location. For example, if you had a path of C:\Windows\README.TXT, the path gets parsed once for C: and again for Windows. This capability will eventually allow for multiple drive links into one, so you can connect to any drive on your machine using a single drive letter. This feature is also extensible. A developer can create customized reparse filters that adjust the way the file path gets parsed.

Another feature of NTFS5 is per-disk and per-user quotas. The use of quotas keeps one person from consuming all the space on a server hard drive. Of course, this applies equally well to processes or any other object as well. Before the use of quotas, an errant application could fill an entire hard drive with log file entries, for example, and the administrator might not realize there was a problem before it was too late to do something about it. Once your machine runs completely out of hard drive space, it's susceptible to a crash from several different sources, including the inability to increase the size of the swap file and registry. Quotas are based on the security identifier (SID) of the owner—whoever created the file is responsible for the space it consumes.

More Info This chapter doesn't cover all the intricacies of reparse points—at least not from a programmer level. However, Microsoft makes available detailed information about reparse points and other NTFS5 features as part of the Installable File System (IFS) kit. The IFS kit is available at *http://www.microsoft.com/hwdev/ntifskit/*. This Web site also provides access to a mailing list that will keep you up-to-date on the latest IFS developments.

NTFS5 also supports native property sets. The default property sets appear on the Summary tab of a file's Properties dialog box, like the one shown in Figure 7-8. This feature is like the property pages you attach to a COM object. They allow you to define attributes for a file. For example, you can attach a description of a graphics image to a graphic file using this technique. One of the perks of using this new feature is that Microsoft Index Server is set up to use property sets. Anything you attach to a file is used to index it, which makes searches much easier for the user.

Tracking all the changes that occur to the file system is another NTFS5 feature. You can record file creation, deletion, and modification, as well as changes to properties, security, encryption, and compression. In short, you can now actually track how the file system gets used.

You'll really like the new sparse file support in Windows 2000. When you're creating a normal file, the file size reflects every byte you actually use. A sparse file, on the other hand, allocates a certain number of bytes but doesn't actually have to use them. This is known as allocation on demand. It allows you to create a file that provides enough space for what you need to eventually store, rather than allocate bytes as you use them. Fortunately, the system only "charges" you for the bytes that are actually in use. For example, say you allocate a 1GB file. When users click that file, they see a 1GB file. However, if you only placed 64KB of data in that file, the quota system sees that you only used 64KB of your allocated space on the drive.

Figure 7-8.   *Native property sets make it easier to define the precise use of a file, and then find it later using Index Server.*

The sparse file support feature can have an interesting effect on the results you get back from the Disk Defragmenter. You might see a relatively small file listed in the report that has an absurdly large number of fragments. In most cases, this is the result of using the sparse file support feature. Unfortunately, no amount of effort reduces the number of fragments for this kind of file since the file isn't actually consuming very much space on the hard drive. This is one case when you need to know how Windows 2000 works to understand the results you get from a disk maintenance utility.

Disk-Bound Application Types

Every application uses the disk to a certain extent, but unlike other kinds of resource usage on a machine, disk bottlenecks are normally associated with only certain kinds of applications. In other words, you won't find a spreadsheet application that provides too much of a challenge for the disk subsystem. About the only time a spreadsheet application even uses the disk subsystem is when you start the application, and again for each file you need to open.

Planning   No one runs out and buys a shiny new server without having some idea of what they want to do with it. After all, most server costs begin under $10,000 and may range into the $100,000 plus mark today. Unfortunately, some people do get the server without considering the resources that various applications use once installed. Now that you have a better idea of what constitutes a disk-bound application, you may want to look again at the application inventory that you created at the beginning of the chapter. Be prepared to allow extra space for disk-bound applications to move. You don't want to lose server performance by choking a disk-bound application.

The effect of applications on the disk subsystem is also different than the effect you see for memory or processor usage. The kind of applications you run normally determines how fast the disk bottleneck occurs and the severity of the disk bottleneck. If a system is short on disk space, the disk subsystem isn't configured properly, or if the server is short on memory, a disk bottleneck is going to occur. The current disk load determines when and how often it happens, not whether it will happen.

So, what application type taxes the capability of the disk subsystem the most? You'll find that the database application, the most common application out there, is also the most disk-bound. A database requires constant disk access to locate and read data records. It also edits or writes records as the user makes changes. Unlike streaming applications, database applications usually write information in short, choppy blocks that makes performance tuning difficult, to say the least. Even if reads are done using a query (so that the application retrieves an entire recordset), user actions may cause reads to occur in short blocks as well. This constant activity by a myriad of users looking for different records in different places on the drive tends to make the cache less efficient. In short, adding memory isn't quite as good a solution for bottlenecks caused by database applications as a good hard drive and host adapter are.

Multimedia is another disk-intensive application. In this case, however, disk access occurs in much longer segments. A multimedia application tends to read data in long streams from sequential sectors of the disk. Cache, especially the read ahead buffer, is very important with this kind of application because the operating system can predict with relatively high accuracy what data the user needs next. When working with a multimedia application, you need to add memory to get better performance, although a good disk drive and host adapter are still very helpful.

Word processing can be a disk-intensive activity, but only in certain cases. A small document probably fits in memory. In this case, the word processor acts much like a spreadsheet as far as the disk subsystem is concerned. However, what happens if the document won't fit in memory? In this case, the word processor normally reads a few pages before and after the current cursor position. If the user is reading rather than writing the document, the process of scrolling forces the word processor to discard some pages in memory while it reads new ones in. The word processor acts much like the database manager—it reads short, choppy blocks of information. The similarity isn't precise, however, because the word processor reads those blocks sequentially, making the cache slightly more effective than with the database application. Finally, if the word-processed document contains other elements such as graphics or a spreadsheet, the reads tend to get longer but may occur in multiple drive locations. As you can see, a word processor's disk usage pattern is difficult to predict.

Another application that can prove difficult to track is the graphics application. Some graphic images are small enough to fit in memory, which means a graphics application doesn't need to access the hard drive except when it opens, saves, or closes the file. However, what happens if the image is actually a large computer-aided design (CAD) file? Does the graphics application read the entire file into memory? The answer is that it depends on the graphics application vendor. The way the application is designed, in this case, helps determine how large files affect the drive.

Potential Solutions for Disk Bottlenecks

So far, we've looked at many different causes of disk bottlenecks and explored what these various sources can do to the disk subsystem as a whole. By now, you know that disk bottlenecks can be caused from a variety of things, sometimes even from a combination of things. For example, a common disk bottleneck scenario is one where the network administrator has installed a SCSI host adapter with less than stellar performance characteristics, hasn't optimized the drive for quite some time, and then packs the server with more database users than it can possibly handle. To get rid of the disk bottleneck, in this case, you have to fix more than one item. You need to begin by replacing the antiquated host adapter with something that can keep up with user needs. Disk optimization comes next. If you still don't get the performance you need, you have to take a final step of moving users to another server. As you can see, disk bottlenecks might require multiple remediation steps.

Over the years, operating system vendors have tried a number of ways to make it appear that the drive subsystem is actually faster than you think it should be. Let's face it—the disk drive is a mechanical device that provides the poorest performance of any system component. Through the use of memory in the form of a cache, however, the operating system vendor has figuratively pulled a rabbit out of the hat and produced better than average disk performance.

The only problem with using a cache is that you can't be sure just how much of a disk bottleneck problem is the result of the mechanical portion of the disk drive and how much is due to the cache. In some cases, no amount of additional disk drive configuration nets you an increase in system performance. The hard drive is moving data as fast as it can and that's all there is to it. By adding extra memory, however, you can make it appear that the disk drive is moving faster. The cache makes up the difference between what the disk drive can actually do and what you expect it to do in the way of performance. So, one of the more common fixes to a disk bottleneck problem is to add memory to the server to allow for a larger drive cache.

If you have a lot of memory, and a correctly configured disk drive of good quality, there may be another solution to your disk bottleneck problem. The way you set the disk drives up in the first place can affect performance. For example, if you use drive mirroring, Windows 2000 can write to one drive while it reads from the other. Both drives contain the same information, so the user won't notice that the operating system is using this trick. However, the user will see that the system is faster because you now have two disk drives to access. Using drive mirroring isn't the end of the line. You can use disk duplexing to increase the performance of your system even further. In this case, not only does the operating system have two disk drives with the same information at its disposal, but also two host adapters (two channels) to use for moving the information around. This topic is covered in more detail in "Comparing Disk, Formatting Technologies" later in the chapter.

At this point, we've done everything possible to the server to make it run faster. If you need still more speed, it's time to look at two other sources of disk speed problems. The first is the application itself. Microsoft provides a very large number of ways to access data, some of them less efficient than others. When working with developers, ensure that they use recordsets, rather than individual record queries, within an application. Make sure the application uses the proper buffering and that requests don't get made more than once. You can also look at some of the features that Microsoft has made available for components under Windows 2000. For example, technologies such as object pooling can reduce the load a database application places on the system during loading and component instantiation.

You also want to explore how the applications on your server conduct business. For example, one developer recently used transactions for every database activity in the application he created. This normally isn't considered a problem, but even the ZIP code and state abbreviations were handled as transacted queries. Since the ZIP code and state information can be checked with ease for errors and since this information is relatively impervious to change, placing these queries in a transaction wasted more than just disk resources.

User usage patterns also make a difference in how a server performs. Imagine the effect of every user moving back and forth between two records in a database during a phone call. If you can't imagine someone actually doing this, watch what people do during phone calls. You'll find ample evidence that doing something mindless such as doodling or playing with the controls on the computer is common while users are engaged in other activities such as talking on the phone. In some cases, a simple note is all it takes to get at least a few users to minimize their activity on the server to what they actually need to get their work done.

Using New Disk Technologies

Remember those new disk technologies we talked about earlier? It turns out that some of them do require at least some level of consideration when it comes time to design your network. For example, a SAN (storage area network) can reduce the amount of time it takes a network administrator to maintain your network, increase uptime, reduce repair time to nearly zero, and still allow you to make optimal use of system resources.

This section looks at several new disk technologies. We also look at a few established disk technologies that fall outside the range of the normal disk drive you place in your server. The goal of this section is to look at technologies that might be useful in certain situations.

I emphasize the point that the technologies might help, and only in specific situations. There are very few perfect solutions to any problem on the market today, and disk drives fall into the category of being more difficult than average to figure out. We look at the specific situations where these technologies can help turn your Windows 2000 Server into a speed demon in the race to develop the optimum server setup.

Planning Now might be a good time to consider alternate storage strategies for your company. You may find that external data storage in the form of a SAN is the method that best suits your company's data storage needs. The use of removable storage is becoming widespread as well. The use of cartridges to make the storage of completed project data easier is becoming one of the more accepted techniques for ensuring data longevity and easy access.

Working with Storage Area Networks (SANs)

A SAN is one of the more interesting network solutions today because it offers several distinct advantages over the normal methods of storing data. Think of a SAN as a special form of local area network (LAN). It's a high-speed subnetwork that consists exclusively of storage devices. The goal is to take the hard disk drive out of the individual server, create a new entity out of the existing peripheral device, and make it accessible to multiple servers on the same network.

SANs are part old technology and part new technology. The concept has been around in mainframe systems for quite some time. The original mainframe version relies on a bus technology known as Enterprise System Connection (ESCON). ESCON allows the mainframe to dynamically connect to a variety of peripheral devices, including drive arrays and clusters. In fact, the DEC VMS network environment is based on a combination of

SANs and clustered servers. Unfortunately, the original mainframe setup is too expensive for the typical PC network—it was only through the introduction of newer technologies that SANs are able to move from the glass house to the place where most of us live.

Something else that makes SANs a technology to watch is the fact that lower costs (it still isn't cheap) and high reliability are making it the technology of choice for larger companies. No longer do large organizations that rely on LANs need to worry about a failed server—SANs make it possible to gain mainframe reliability without the cost of buying a mainframe. If you're part of a large company and have a lot of database applications, SANs represent one of the safest, most efficient, and reliable methods of reducing disk bottlenecks in your organization today. Obviously, there are a lot of "ifs" to this equation that you need to work out as part of your company's upgrade strategy.

Note Some network administrators might think a SAN obviates the need for any bus-attached data storage for a server, but this isn't true. A SAN, or any external storage, is really designed for client needs. It's the method of choice for storing the data your company needs to operate, not necessarily the best storage area for your server software and server-specific files such as the swap file. In most cases, the server still requires local storage for its own needs. However, this local storage is now inaccessible to the user and less likely to get used for nonserver needs. In short, by moving to external data storage, you can also remove one of the more common causes of server failure—running out of disk space for server operating system needs.

SAN Advantages

Using a SAN means a downed server no longer spells data loss or inaccessible data. The sever acts as a path to the data, not as the data storage platform itself. As long as you have one server that can access the SAN, the users of your network have access to their data. This means you can take a server offline for maintenance or repair and not have it affect the network. It also means your network comes closer to that 24/7 ideal that more companies are striving to achieve today.

Another good reason to use SANs is that they allow better access to the hard disk drives. If one drive fails, the SAN vendor normally provides a solution that allows you to drop a new hard disk drive in and allow the rest of the system get the hard disk drive up to speed. In most cases, SANs provide some level of RAID support to accomplish this task. In short, a lost hard disk drive no longer means lost data.

More Info SANs are a relatively new technology, which means you'll find it hard to get good information about them. The best place to find out about the latest standardization efforts for SANs is the Storage Networking Industry Association Web site at *http://www.snia.org/*. Since SANs are designed to work with Fibre Channel networks, in most cases, you'll also want to check on the efforts of the Fibre Channel Industry Association at *http://www.fibrechannel.com/* or *http://www.fccommunity.org/*.

Unlike many data storage solutions where you're tied to one operating system, a SAN can work with multiple server types. For example, there are companies that are currently marketing solutions that work with Windows NT, Windows 2000, DEC VMS, UNIX, and Novell NetWare. Depending on the network configuration you use, one storage methodology can service the needs of multiple server types and provide your company with an efficient single storage solution rather than multiple incompatible storage systems.

More Info   One of the companies currently offering more than one SAN solution is StorageTek. You find a variety of SAN and associated technology solutions on its Web site at *http://www.network.com/*. This Web site provides some interesting information about SANs that you may not have considered. For example, if you're using a SAN as a 24/7 solution, you need a different method for backing up the data that it manages. StorageTek can introduce you to the wonders of dynamic backup and recovery.

Theoretically, SANs should reduce total cost of ownership (TCO) for servers by allowing all servers to use the same storage. Instead of replacing the server and the storage when it becomes obvious the server no longer has the required processing power, a company can now replace just the server case containing the processing components. Since you no longer have islands of data storage but a central repository of data, the cost of buying storage can be amortized across the entire company. Finally, the human factor of TCO is also reduced. Network administrators spend less time working with a centralized network than they do running around to individual machines. Reducing the TCO of your network while increasing overall processing speed is a winner for everyone—particularly, you.

Distance isn't much of a factor with SANs either. You can separate SAN from the servers they support by up to 10,000 meters (as defined by the current capability of multimode fiber to transmit a light signal) or 300 times the distance that SCSI supports. Although a server can't be in another country and expect support from a SAN, you can theoretically allow a server in another building on the same lot to get serviced by SAN. No, it's not a perfect solution, but it provides a lot more flexibility than other high-speed drive solutions.

SAN Disadvantages

As with many new technologies, SANs aren't for everybody. You don't get this improvement in network performance for free. For one thing, the vast majority of SAN solutions are built around high-speed Fibre Channel networks. Alternatives to Fibre Channel include Small Computer System Interface (SCSI), High-Performance Parallel Interface (HIPPI), ESCON, and Serial Storage Architecture (SSA), all of which suffer from distance limitations. If your company isn't already wired with Fibre Channel, you can find yourself spending a lot of money to implement a SAN storage solution.

Tip You aren't always required to implement a full-fledged SAN to get the benefits of a SAN for a medium-sized network. For example, Microsoft's Cluster Server allows you to implement most of the features of a SAN using relatively inexpensive SCSI host adapters and special software. This technology shares a drive array between two servers and is well suited for companies on a budget. We discuss this particular technology in detail in Chapter 13, "Microsoft Windows 2000 and Clustering."

SANs are also designed with large enterprise networks in mind. In other words, you need a setup where there are many servers located in one place to use a SAN efficiently. Although you can use a SAN with a network that has a large distribution, remember the cost factor for the network involved in implementing such a solution. The current cost of the combination of Fibre Channel and the SAN hardware keeps it tied to applications that require a lot of bandwidth such as video or graphics processing. Some data mining solutions are also being built with SANs in mind, but they're for large-scale processing needs of a Fortune 500 company.

Although the network administrator gains a high-speed disk solution that guarantees maximum server performance for disk-bound applications, a SAN does introduce some negative factors into the equation as well. One of the most critical network administrator problems is that a SAN setup is more complex than the standard network. Not only do you have all the servers to worry about, but you also have the SAN hardware now as well. A network administrator requires additional training to use a SAN solution in most cases.

Reliability is also a factor. Consider for a moment that a SAN will likely enable your network to meet the 24/7 criteria that most companies are looking for today, yet it's more complex than other solutions you used in the past. Yes, the network as a whole will likely remain operational, but the probability of individual components breaking will increase. The user will see increased reliability, but the network administrator will spend more time servicing individual components on the network.

Understanding Network Attached Storage (NAS) and SAN Attached Storage (SAS)

There are three methods currently in use for attaching disk drives to a server. The method most people are familiar with is known as a bus-attached drive. The storage mechanism, reliability, and availability are limited to what the server can provide. The type of host adapter used (SCSI or Integrated Device Electronics (IDE), in most cases) determines, in part, what type of performance you can expect from the drive. In at least some situations, the fact that the server is already overloaded servicing the needs of processor-bound applications can adversely affect the performance of the disk drives.

Network Attached Storage (NAS) is the next rung on the performance ladder. A NAS attaches directly to the LAN through an Ethernet or other common network connection. The storage array or cluster is installed within a case in a SAN configuration. The case also includes all the features of a server, but in embedded form in most cases. Using embedded components allows the NAS to handle disk requests very efficiently. In other words, other servers access the drive array operating system, not the clients.

Since the operating system for NAS is optimized for disk access and there isn't any overhead for application processing or client requests, NAS gains a very large performance boost over the bus-attached drive. You do pay a little more for this setup, but the cost is substantially less than SAN Attached Storage (SAS). SANs aren't directly attached to the host servers in this case—NAS acts as an intercessory, so there's a little overhead that you pay for in the way of reduced performance. In addition, because you're using the same network bus that the clients are, there's a performance penalty every time NAS needs to use the network and it's busy.

SAS is the ultimate (for right now) in performance. The SAN is directly attached to all the servers through a special bus. This bus is totally separate from the Ethernet or other common network bus used by the clients, so SAS doesn't experience the performance penalties of NAS. However, the addition of a special high-speed network does make the cost of a SAS quite a bit higher than a NAS.

A SAS consists of three major components: SAN interfaces, SAN interconnects, and SAN fabric. These three elements may appear as separate elements, but are normally combined in some way. In all cases, data travels from the interface, to the interconnect, to the fabric, back to the interconnect, and finally back to the interface. There are separate drive-side and server-side interfaces and interconnects.

The SAN interface is the method of connection between the physical device and the special network. PC networks normally use Fibre Channel Arbitrated Loop (FC-AL) host adapters. However, there are other options available such as SCSI, HIPPI, ESCON, and SSA. In some cases, a single device has multiple interface channels to increase both reliability and performance.

SAN interconnects make the physical connection between the externalized drive access and the SAN fabric (or network cabling). A SAN can use any of a number of devices to create an interconnect. Some of the more common choices include extenders, multiplexors, hubs, routers, gateways, switches, and directors.

A lot of people hear the term "fabric" and think of something more complex than simple cabling. However, in the case of a SAN, the fabric is really nothing more than redundant network cabling—the same cabling you use to create most high-speed networks. There isn't anything mysterious here. The most common SAN fabric components are Switched-SCSI, Fibre Channel Switched (FC-S), and Switched-SSA.

SAN Uses

A SAN definitely benefits any kind of disk-bound application. Any time you widen the data path (through the addition of another bus in this case), you can increase the throughput of the server and application processing speed. There are, however, six ways in which a SAN makes your networking experience better from a pure management perspective. The following list provides an overview of all six uses.

- **Clustering**   A SAN is going to make your network more reliable. You gain the ability to react to server and disk drive failures automatically. Clustering also improves network performance and allows your disk-bound applications to execute much faster without affecting server performance nearly as much.

- **Data protection**   SANs support all the methods of data protection currently available on the market, but do it in a way that allows the data to remain accessible. You still have all the good features of RAID, disk mirroring, automated backups, and journaling that bus-attached drives provide.

- **Data vaulting**   Most SANs support some type of offline data storage, usually through the use of tape media. When the SAN software detects that data hasn't been accessed for a while, the data is moved to offline storage, which is a lot less expensive than the drives in your SAN. When a user requests the data, it's automatically moved from offline storage to the drive again. The user never knows that the data was archived (except for the longer than average access time).

- **Data interchange**   Networks are typically made up of different machines, some of which may use operating systems other than Windows 2000. Moving data from one operating system to another used to present problems because you typically couldn't get the servers to talk to each other directly. A SAN can act as an intermediary, allowing data to flow between systems with little effort and at high speed.

- **Disaster recovery**   Theoretically, you can use the data-vaulting capability of a SAN to move data off-site. You can move copies of the data to another building in your company or even to a data vault. Since this activity happens automatically, you aren't exposed to the risks of human intervention in your data recovery plan. The storage of data in a safe place happens automatically, which means it's available when you need it.

- **Network architecture**   The use of SANs promotes the externalization of data storage and all the benefits that such externalization provides. We've talked about this issue in this chapter, so it's not covered again here. It's, however, important to note that SANs represent just another use of the network to provide superior data handling, reliability, and performance for the user.

Working with Zip and Jaz Drives

Removable drives of various types have made appearances over the last few years—most of them have disappeared a few months later. Iomega seems to have escaped the removable media drive extinction because its drives are well designed and easy to use. The two drives that we're most interested in are the Zip and Jaz drives because these are the two drives in common use within businesses today.

Zip and Jaz drives can both have a place on your network as a tuning or optimization solution. Both of these drives provide replaceable media akin to floppy disks, but with the speed of a hard disk drive. The Zip drive provides either 100-MB or 250-MB capacity, which is large enough for diagnostic software or something of that nature, but not large enough for most corporate uses. The Jaz drive is a better choice at 1-GB and 2-GB capacities. A Jaz drive allows you to store long video segments, large graphics files, or all the files for a specific project.

More Info   You can find out more about both Zip and Jaz drives in a variety of places. Of course, the first place to look is the Iomega Web site at *http://www.iomega.com/*. There are also a lot of third-party Web sites to help you out. For example, The Unofficial Iomega Page at *http://www.juip.com/* contains news to keep you up-to-date on the latest Zip and Jaz developments. This Web site provides links to other sites that contain drivers, reviews, usage tips, and other helpful information. Interestingly enough, you'll also find newsgroups to help learn about both types of drive, the most popular of which appears to be *alt.iomega.zip.jaz*.

As you can see, there are a lot of different ways you can use Jaz drives on your server, but most networks seem to use them right now for project-oriented uses. At 2GB, a Jaz drive provides a perfect place to store all the files for a project. Windows 2000 allows you to use the same security measures on a Jaz drive that you can on a standard hard disk drive. Given the size of the Jaz drive, you can create folders and set the project up just as you do on a standard hard disk drive. Your users won't notice the difference when it comes time to work on the project. When the project is complete, you can remove the cartridge from the drive and put it someplace safe for future reference.

Tip   The Jaz drive is perfect for sensitive project data. Simply remove the cartridge and lock it in a safe before you leave for the day. The added physical security provides you with peace of mind—a rare commodity in a world that seems less secure all the time.

Iomega states that the Jaz drive is on par with many hard drives. It's actually on par with many workstation hard drives with a 10ms read and 12ms write-seek time, 7.4 MB/s average transfer rate (20 MB/s burst), and 16 ms access time. For a small hit in performance, however, you get a great deal of flexibility in your system configuration. In addition, using Jaz drives for your projects definitely makes the network administrator more productive. Cleanup after a project is completed and takes a matter of seconds, rather than days.

A Jaz drive is a poor choice for a company (or organizational unit) that doesn't work on projects. Yes, you can store large files on a Jaz drive, and it does come in handy for both data exchange and hard-disk data backup needs. However, using a Jaz drive for these purposes on a server might prove counterproductive, especially if your company keeps the server locked up in a closet somewhere. In most cases, tape is still the best option for server backup, and data exchange is best accomplished through a network connection. If you really do need to exchange data with another company, the Jaz drive might be a good solution, but have it installed in an easily accessible workstation, not a hard to access server (most servers are stored in locked closets to keep them secure). In short, a Jaz drive is a good solution, but only in certain situations.

Working with Solid State Drives (SSDs)

Everyone knows that accessing memory is much faster than a disk drive. If you can create a server with sufficient memory, and then find some way to keep that memory intact when the power is turned off, you have a superior solution to the mechanical hard drives we've been using. Several companies have done just that—they've created solid state drives (SSDs) that contain no mechanical parts, work faster than any mechanical hard drive can imagine, and use a battery backup to ensure the data remains intact.

> **More Info** We can't talk about every aspect of SSDs in this chapter—there are too many different types of drives to cover and configurations to consider. However, you can find out more about the basic principles of the SSD at the Compass Polaris Web site at *http://www.compass-corp.com/solidstate.htm*. SSDs are so popular in the embedded world that many vendors concentrate on this particular area alone. For example, Scale-Tron (*http://www.scaletron.com/code/edisk.htm*) makes the EDisk, an SSD for smaller applications. SSDs even come in a form that's usable as a SAN. Bit Microsystems makes such a device and you can learn about it at *http://www.bitmicro.com/index.htm*.

Unfortunately, this kind of drive has one problem—cost. Memory is a lot more expensive than a standard hard disk drive and most forms of optical media storage like DVD-RAM drives—it's just not cost-effective to use solid state drives in a server. In fact, the memory used for an SSD costs even more than the memory used for main memory in your machine—a 1-GB SSD can cost you as much as $40,000. Part of the cost for this drive is the extra circuitry required to make it look like a standard hard drive and the battery backup circuits.

> **Tip** It's theoretically possible to create an SSD from flash ROM. Using flash ROM has the advantage of eliminating the need for battery backup. This makes the drive less likely to lose data and improves the SSD's reliability. The downside of using flash ROM is that it has a longer write time than standard memory. In other words, you gain only part of the performance benefit that's possible when using an SSD. However, even with a slower write time, using flash ROM is still much faster than using a mechanical hard drive. One place to look for flash ROM SSDs is M-Systems. You'll find its Web site at *http://www.m-sys.com/*.

Since an SSD isn't a good candidate for main permanent storage, what can you use it for? Any temporary file that the user is going to access often during a session, but not need when the session is over, is a good candidate for SSD storage.

Another good use of this technology is storing small databases that contain information users need to access often. For example, a database containing state acronyms or ZIP codes is a good candidate. The contents of these tables are static, which means a failure of the battery backup for the SSD doesn't cause problems, yet people need to access these tables for every order they enter in a database. You don't want to place tables that contain a lot of volatile information on an SSD because of the reliability factor—losing an essential database in the name of performance just isn't a good option.

SSDs are a good place to store transactional data or the message queues for disconnected applications. This kind of data is transitive. The server only needs to hold onto it long enough to ensure that the transaction is complete or the message has been answered. In fact, using an SSD mitigates some of the performance problems of using logging with Queued Components (QC).

Comparing Disk-Formatting Technologies

We still haven't reached the end of the line when it comes to tuning the drive subsystem on your server. You can configure the disk drive correctly, get the very best hardware, and even go to the expense of working with experimental hardware and still not get the maximum performance from your system. The way you configure and format your disk drives can have a very big effect on performance, especially on a server.

This section explores four different drive configuration and formatting techniques that can help improve the performance of your server. We start with the least complicated solution (and the one that provides the least performance boost) and move up to the most complex solution. In most cases, these tried-and-true enhancements make your system more reliable while they increase performance, which is the reason so many network administrators use them.

Note   All fault tolerance options under Windows 2000 require the use of dynamic disks (covered in the next section). This means that a fault tolerant drive can't contain any partitions other than the one used by Windows 2000. You also can't use the drive for MS-DOS access. All these limitations are straightforward and make sense when you think about them. However, the use of dynamic disks is an important consideration and you need to keep it in mind as you read through the sections that follow.

Understanding Dynamic Disks

Dynamic disks are a new Windows 2000 feature that allows you to perform some types of disk administration tasks without shutting the machine down or interrupting users. For example, you can create, extend, or mirror a dynamic disk volume without restarting the machine afterward. The same holds true for the process of adding a new disk—you can add a disk without restarting the machine afterward, a real boon for those times when you need to replace a server disk drive quickly without affecting the user. Most of the changes you make to a dynamic disk take place immediately.

There are a few facts you need to know about dynamic disks. For one, dynamic disks can contain only dynamic volumes. A dynamic volume must be created using the Disk Manager shown in Figure 7-9. It can't contain partitions, like the drive shown in Figure 7-9. In addition, you can't access a dynamic volume from MS-DOS. In short, dynamic volumes are a Windows 2000-only proposition.

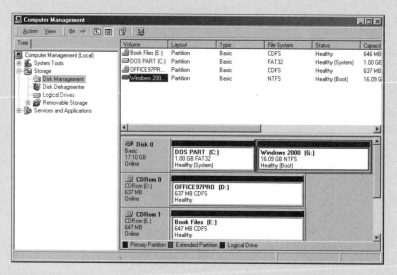

Figure 7-9. *You use the Disk Manager to create dynamic volumes, which in turn are used to create dynamic disks.*

Converting a normal volume to a dynamic volume is also a one-way process. You can't reverse the change once you make it without reformatting the drive. What this means is that you need to evaluate the use of dynamic volumes and dynamic disks carefully before you make the change. Given the amount of time that this feature can save for the administrator, however, the decision to convert the drive shouldn't be hard to make.

Disk Mirroring

Disk mirroring (or a mirrored volume in Windows 2000 parlance) represents one of the easiest ways to build fault tolerance into your server. The principle is simple. All you need to do is add two hard disk drives with exactly the same characteristics and size to your system. When you restart the server, Disk Management allows you to mirror them. Both drives contain precisely the same information. If one drive fails, the other takes over immediately, which means the user doesn't see the failure. All you need to do to fix the problem is install a new drive of the same size and remirror.

Disk mirroring also provides a performance benefit. Since there are two drives with precisely the same information, Windows 2000 can read from or write to either disk. In most cases, you find that mirrored volumes have faster write performance than redundant array of independent disks (RAID) level 5 setups (configurations) because Windows 2000 can write to both drives simultaneously. Read performance is faster than a single drive, but slower than RAID-5 because Windows 2000 only reads from one disk at a time.

One of the reasons many companies have started using RAID-5 over disk mirroring is cost. Yes, it costs more to start a RAID-5 setup, but then you get full use of your hard-disk drive investment. When working with mirrored drives, you discover that half of the capacity of the combined total is used for fault tolerance. In other words, the cost per MB of hard-disk drive space is double when using mirrored drives.

Disk mirroring works best for small- to medium-sized networks with relatively small storage requirements. The fact that you get better write performance is a plus with certain types of applications, such as order entry systems where the users are likely to write more data than they read. As the size of the server's storage increases, the cost benefits of RAID-5 become more apparent. So, you may want to start with disk mirroring, and then switch to RAID-5 as your network grows.

Disk Duplexing

Disk duplexing is disk mirroring with a kick. Instead of connecting two identical hard disk drives to the same host adapter, you use two host adapters and two hard disk drives. Windows 2000 doesn't require you to do anything differently to use this solution than you need to do when working with mirrored volumes. So, from an administrative point of view, both solutions are the same.

There are some very important differences between the two solutions, however. The most important difference is that the fault tolerance of your system is enhanced. Not only are you protected from drive failures, but you're also protected from host adapter failures.

Depending on your system setup, the use of disk duplexing can improve performance as well. Now you have two completely separate data channels in the machine, which means there isn't any chance of data from one drive being delayed as Windows 2000 works with the other drive. Read performance of a duplexed drive is still slower than RAID-5, but it is an improvement over disk mirroring. Write performance likely improves as well, but only in small increments.

Obviously, disk duplexing adds to the cost of your server. Not only do you lose half of the capacity of the hard disk drives, but you also need two host adapters. Considering the performance and fault tolerance of disk duplexing, the added cost might be worthwhile if you need maximum performance or the data you're working with is especially critical. In most cases, you'll want to consider a SAN for larger networks in place of disk duplexing because you get many of the benefits of disk duplexing with a lower per MB cost once the initial cost of the system is paid back.

Drive Striping

Drive striping (creating a striped volume in Windows 2000 parlance) allows you to combine two or more hard disk drives of the same size into a single volume. Windows 2000 alternates the data between the two hard disk drives in stripes. Unlike mirrored drives, where half of the capacity of the two-drive setup is wasted, drive striping allows you to use the full capacity of both drives.

Unfortunately, drive striping offers no fault tolerance. This means that if you lose one hard disk drive of a striped set, the data on both hard disk drives is lost (or at least useless). So, although this drive setup is extremely efficient and does provide a performance boost, it doesn't allow you to recover from faults. You don't want to use this setup in an environment where the user is writing critical data to the drive.

From a performance perspective, drive striping offers several advantages over the other options in this section. For one thing, you can use it to combine up to 32 hard disk drives with no loss of capacity. This means you can create huge volumes from relatively small and inexpensive disks. Read performance is on par or a little faster than RAID-5 because Windows 2000 can read across all hard disk drives simultaneously and there isn't any parity bit to consider. Write performance is still slightly slower than the performance you get with drive mirroring, but faster than what you get with RAID-5. Again, the performance boost comes from lack of a parity bit.

RAID-5

Windows 2000 offers the redundant array of independent disks (RAID) level 5 solution. This is the best offering in both performance and fault tolerance for large networks with lots of disk storage. Using RAID-5 requires a minimum of three hard disk drives.

The setup is similar to drive striping. However, instead of just alternating data between two hard disk drives, a third drive with a parity bit is added to the picture. The data is written in round robin fashion so all three drives contain parity bits. Using this methodology means that one hard disk drive can fail and the other two still allow the system to recover using the parity bits. Unlike disk duplexing/mirroring, a RAID-5 setup can recover automatically—you don't need to remirror the drives to regain fault tolerance.

RAID-5 is more efficient than disk duplexing/mirroring because in the worst-case scenario, only one-third of the drive capacity is lost. If you have three 10-GB hard disk drives, the user sees 20 GB of capacity. Of course, increasing the number of disks also reduces the amount of space taken for fault tolerance. For example, moving to five 10-GB drives allows the user to see 40 GB of capacity or a loss of only one-fifth of the drive capacity.

Normally, RAID-5 provides better read performance than disk duplexing/mirroring because data is read across all drives at once. This means the maximum potential transfer rate of the host adapter is available. If one drive fails, however, the read performance degrades because Windows 2000 has to construct the data on the missing hard disk drive from the parity bits on the other hard disk drives. There isn't any degradation when you lose a hard disk drive with disk duplexing/mirroring.

Summary

There are a lot of performance problems that can look like a disk bottleneck because of the way they affect the disk subsystem. For example, a low-memory situation can look like a disk bottleneck because the server makes greater use of the swap file on disk to compensate for the lack of memory. Because of the way disk bottlenecks appear on a server, you need to spend the time required to troubleshoot other problems first, and then concentrate on the disk bottleneck when it become apparent the disk subsystem is at fault.

Disk bottlenecks are seldom caused by a single problem under Windows 2000. A disk bottleneck is more likely the combination of two or three problems that all work together to make the bottleneck apparent. What this means to you as an administrator is that you can't stop looking for problems when you find the first disk bottleneck. It's important to verify there aren't any other problems that contributed to the disk bottleneck.

Tuning and optimization in the world of the disk drive isn't always straightforward. Sometimes a tweak at the operating system level works; other times you need to change the configuration of the drive at the BIOS level. In some cases, no amount of tweaking produces the desired results. When this happens, you need to look at alternative hardware solutions such as SAN and removable storage media that we talked about in this chapter. When working with mechanical devices like the disk drive, it's important to keep your options in mind.

In Chapter 8, "Network Problems," we look at what you need to do to interact with the network. This is a more complex problem than dealing with a single server because you have the interactions of all the other machines on the network to consider. Chapter 8 concentrates on the physical network. In the chapter that follows it, we also look at the role Active Directory services plays in making the network run smoothly. In short, the next two chapters help you understand how to tune your network for optimum performance.

Part III
Tuning the Network

Chapter 8
Network Problems

The network presents more challenges when it comes to performance monitoring than any other part of your system. The reason's simple: You can't monitor the network's performance if the amount of traffic isn't at normal levels. Yet, having the traffic at normal levels means you have to consider the interactions of multiple machines when monitoring performance. In addition, the monitoring you perform today only remains valid as long as the network configuration remains unchanged. So, the difficult process of monitoring a network for specific problems occurs on a regular basis.

Although network monitoring is difficult, optimizing network performance is even harder. Any change you make to one machine normally changes the performance characteristics of the network as a whole and of each machine on the network. For example, adding a higher performance network interface card (NIC) to one workstation may adversely affect the performance of other machines on the network that have lower performance NICs installed. Even something as simple as a cable change can affect network performance because cable length affects network timing and, therefore, the rate at which data moves on the cable.

In short, the network is the most difficult part of the tuning process. You not only have the operating system and the local hardware to worry about, but there are also other machines to consider. That's why this chapter is so important to the optimization of your system as a whole. The ability to communicate with other users is what makes the network popular, while the interactions and complexity of the network environment is the stuff of nightmares for the network administrator. This chapter seeks to reduce the complexity of the network performance monitoring and optimization equation.

The first section of the chapter, "Overview of Network Bottleneck Sources," summarizes some of the most important network problems that you encounter. We'll divide this conversation into four major components: the operating system, the local machine, remote machines, and other sources. These four major sources of network bottlenecks are the first place to look for performance problems on the network.

One of the most difficult problems to assess is the effect of network topology on network performance. This topic is the center of discussion of the second section, "Overview of Network Topology Limitations." You can tune the local machine's hardware and use every operating system performance trick in the book, and still not obtain your network performance goals if the network topology is incapable of producing the desired results. For example, anyone who thinks they get the full 10 Mb/s of bandwidth from an Ethernet network is in for a surprise. There are a host of factors that make it impossible to realize the full performance benefits from any network topology. In fact, this is such a significant problem that we'll spend time talking about the very problem of theoretical vs. real world topology performance potential.

The third section, "Understanding Network Component Interactions," looks at how various network elements can work together to improve performance, or conflict to degrade network performance. The whole idea of interactions causes some network administrators to dismiss this area of tuning as too difficult to manage, especially on large networks. However, the gains or losses a network can encounter due to interactions tend to dwarf other areas of network optimization. You can't afford to ignore interactions—they must be managed to optimize data throughput. Fortunately, there are ways to make the interaction picture easier to see and, more importantly, manage.

In the fourth section, "User-Oriented Network Bottleneck Solutions," we look at how the user affects network performance. This is one of those areas where you can't predict the results because user-oriented solutions depend on the cooperation of the user to work. For example, what happens to network performance if you have 50 people using a word processor all day and they unconsciously hit the Save button every few seconds? What you end up with is a lot of unnecessary network traffic because of a "nervous twitch" that can be avoided. The problem from the network administrator's perspective is finding out the source of this nervous twitch, and then finding a remedy for the situation that the user is willing to try. A solution for this kind of problem can be as easy as setting the word processor to automatically save at given intervals, and then demonstrating that the feature does indeed work.

The user isn't the only source of potential network performance enhancements. Given the state of the art, you'll find that hardware is the most common solution to network performance problems. That's the topic of the fifth section, "Hardware-Oriented Network Bottleneck Solutions." You may find that your network is suffering from too many users on one network segment. Perhaps the answer to a network performance problem isn't in the operating system or the user, but in creating a new network segment so the users have the additional bandwidth required to get their work done. There are also other issues to consider, such as the quality of the hardware you use, the kind of drivers, and the way the hardware and drivers are configured. All these items impact the way the network performs.

The sixth, and final, section, "Software-Oriented Network Bottleneck Solutions," contains a discussion of the software elements you need to consider when it comes to network performance. This section looks at two major areas of the network: the local operating system and the applications designed to use the network. Both areas require tuning at some level. In some cases, tuning takes the form of software options. In other cases, wise use of network resources is the answer to performance problems.

Overview of Network Bottleneck Sources

The purpose of a network is to allow users to share both data and peripheral devices. In short, the use of a network is supposed to make users more efficient while reducing the cost of performing the work. Like most things in life, however, the benefits of using a network don't come free. Users constantly seek new ways to get the benefits of networks without sharing the data they create with others. Network bottlenecks cause performance reductions until a company purchases more hardware, which, in turn, reduces the cost savings of using the network. In short, for every benefit you can gain from a network, there are potential problems that reduce or even eliminate the effect of using the network in the first place.

Real World

Data sharing on a network is important from several performance perspectives. Consider what happens when a user hides data in order to maintain control of it. If other users also follow this practice, server performance can suffer because users will make redundant data requests from different areas of the server hard disk drive. The first performance problem that will occur is due to the loss of hard disk drive space that could be used for temporary files and virtual memory. The second performance problem is that the hard disk drive cache won't work as it normally would to enhance server performance. When users make shared data requests, the first request moves the data from the hard drive to server memory. Subsequent requests use the cached copy of the data, which results in a performance gain on the server because reading from memory is faster than reading from the hard drive. In addition, caching multiple copies of the same data from different locations on the hard drive wastes server memory. The third performance penalty is on the network. Every time a data modification occurs, network traffic increases because every user has to modify his or her copy of the data separately, rather than make one change to a single master document. In short, both network and server performance suffer when users fail to share data and treat the network drive as an extension of their local drive.

There isn't much you can do about certain network performance inhibitors, so we don't even discuss them in this chapter. Users adamantly protect their right to hide data—no amount of training changes that stance. Topology limitations in effect today are unlikely to disappear tomorrow, no matter how much you'd like to get rid of them. However, other network performance inhibitors are actually very easy to remedy and result in massive savings of both time and effort for the network administrator. Not only does the administrator benefit, but also the user. A network that performs well can make users feel as if they're accessing local resources, when, in fact, those resources reside on another machine and can be physically located in another building.

The following four sections don't provide an in-depth view of network bottlenecks, but they do give you an overview of the kinds of problems you'll run into. Sometimes classifying a network bottleneck is the most difficult problem of all because the problem looks like it can be part of several major subsystems. These sections help you reduce the complexity of the problem by breaking it down to one of four major network areas: operating system, local machine (both hardware and software), remote machine (both hardware and software), and other (like users). The purpose of this section is to make network problems easier to resolve by making them easier to see. (You can't easily fix what you can't see or at least understand.)

Operating System Sources

The first aspect you need to understand about Microsoft Windows 2000 is that there are several layers of network-specific software. An application doesn't send data directly to the NIC, and then through the NIC to another machine. The data goes through several transformation layers before it becomes the packet that eventually gets transferred to another node on the network. Once the data arrives at the other node (possibly another machine or a peripheral device similar to a printer), there are several additional layers that interpret the packet and make it suitable for use on the remote node. The actual number of layers the data encounters depends on the protocol used to transmit the data and various operating system options such as data encryption.

Tip The best way to view a protocol is as a set of rules. Think of a diplomatic situation between two countries. Two diplomats (the operating system) interact in a specific way based on a treaty (the protocol). These diplomats represent the countries (the physical machine) and their interests (the application software). In short, you can view a protocol as the rules of engagement and the language used to communicate between two machines.

So, where does the operating system itself come into play? The operating system implements the various layers that are mandated by various networking standards. For example, the TCP protocol has requirements that an operating system must meet to ensure interoperability with other operating systems that also implement TCP. The same holds true with IP and other protocols you may use in setting up network communications. The idea is that all the layers contribute toward one goal—network communication—but that each layer requires separate handling by the operating system to ensure modularity.

Since each layer in the networking model is independent, you can mix and match protocols that are compatible within a networking model. In fact, you'll find that Windows 2000 doesn't always use the familiar TCP/IP protocol pair to communicate across the network. Sometimes it uses UDP/IP instead. The protocols used to communicate between nodes must be agreed on in advance and are often dictated by the application in use at the time.

The independence of each network layer means you can tune each layer within the confines of the protocol specification. The interdependence of each layer, however, means a change at one layer, of necessity, affects all the other layers in the network model. In short, you need to consider how a performance change in one layer will affect the other layers around it. As you can see, the question of tuning a network model that's implemented by Windows 2000 isn't an easy issue to discuss. You need to consider each layer not only individually, but also as part of the greater whole.

The following sections help you better understand how this layering works. First, we look at the network layers from a conceptual point of view. We talk about how the layers fit together from a very generic, standards-orientedF08wpt01.eps perspective. The second section covers a specific network model implementation. We actually tear a network packet (the envelope used to transfer data from one node to another) apart to see what makes it tick. As a result of reading these two sections, you should walk away with a better idea of how the layering of protocols to create a specific kind of network model works and how you can use this information to better tune your system.

Understanding Operating System Layers

Let's look at the various operating system layers using the Open Systems Interconnection (OSI) reference model for comparison. Figure 8-1 shows the OSI model and a typical Internet model side-by-side. It helps to look at how the operating system eventually transfers data from one point to another using these various layers to encapsulate the data in a package. Think of the data as a letter, and the various layers as the envelope used to ensure prompt delivery. Just as the envelope has specific physical characteristics and requires certain information, a network packet needs to help the system identify the sender and receiver of the information you ask it to transmit.

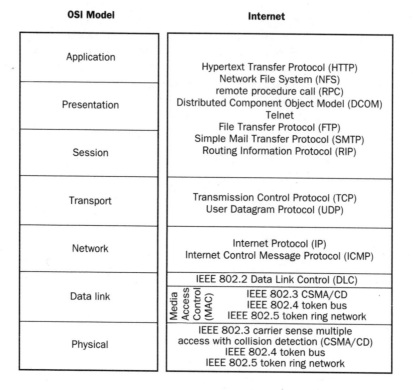

OSI Model   **Internet**

OSI Model	Internet
Application	Hypertext Transfer Protocol (HTTP) Network File System (NFS) remote procedure call (RPC) Distributed Component Object Model (DCOM) Telnet File Transfer Protocol (FTP) Simple Mail Transfer Protocol (SMTP) Routing Information Protocol (RIP)
Presentation	
Session	
Transport	Transmission Control Protocol (TCP) User Datagram Protocol (UDP)
Network	Internet Protocol (IP) Internet Control Message Protocol (ICMP)
Data link	IEEE 802.2 Data Link Control (DLC) Media Access Control (MAC): IEEE 802.3 CSMA/CD IEEE 802.4 token bus IEEE 802.5 token ring network
Physical	IEEE 802.3 carrier sense multiple access with collision detection (CSMA/CD) IEEE 802.4 token bus IEEE 802.5 token ring network

Figure 8-1. *The OSI reference model provides an ideal data-packaging scheme, although the Internet model reflects the reality of data transfer.*

Let's talk about the OSI reference model first. Originally, it was supposed to be the next big thing in networking, but the original promise of the model fell through as vendors argued for their particular wants or needs in a networking model. In short, no one could agree on the appearance of a consolidated network model. The OSI reference model, however, accurately portrays everything that needs to go on in a data transfer, so many people now use it as a teaching aid. The following list provides a very brief overview of the seven layers of the OSI reference model.

- **Application** The functions of this layer can be performed by the application, but normally get performed by the operating system. It includes identifying the parties in a communication, defining the anticipated level of service, and specifying any security requirements such as user authentication and any special requirements such as data syntax.

- **Presentation** This is the layer that defines how the data is presented to the user. In many cases, the data must be converted in some way. For example, the operating system may have to convert a text stream into meaningful entries in a dialog box.

- **Session**   Every operating system provides some type of session that defines the connection between two entities. The session layer begins and ends the transaction, as well as coordinating the resources of the two parties to keep this conversation from interfering with other conversations that the entity may engage in. It's the session layer that defines the two parties in the conversation and ensures that their conversation remains unique.

- **Transport**   This layer ensures that the data gets transferred as requested. This means it checks the packets for errors and requests copies of packets that get lost in transit.

- **Network**   The operating system uses the network layer to route the data across the network. In other words, it ensures that the data gets from one physical location to the other. When the network layer receives a packet that belongs to another party, it forwards the packet to the requested destination.

- **Data link**   This is another error control and synchronization layer. It takes care of the needs of the physical layer, however, rather than the application.

- **Physical**   Anything you can physically touch belongs in this layer. It includes the NIC that converts the data for transmission and the cable that allows actual transfer of data from one machine to the next.

More Info   You can find out more about the general nature of the OSI reference model at *http://whatis.com/osi.htm*. This Web site provides a very good overview of the reference model and links to other locations where you can find out more. If you want to see a detailed pictorial view of the OSI reference model, check out the Web site at *http://whatis.com/osifig.htm*. Although this chapter provides a good overview of what OSI is all about, this Web site provides detailed information about which technologies work together to create a complete OSI implementation. (Clicking on a picture element displays another window containing a description of that element.) Finally, if you like slide shows, you'll find a slide show presentation of the OSI reference model at *http://etcom.uccb.ns.ca/Networking/osi/index.htm*. Currently, the OSI reference model is sponsored by the International Standards Organization. Its home page is at *http://www.iso.ch/*. The OSI reference model is also part of the International Telecommunication Union's (ITU) X.200 standard. (The ITU was formerly known as the Consultative Committee for International Telegraph and Telephony or CCITT.) You can find out more about the ITU at *http://www.itu.int/*.

Now that you have a better understanding of the OSI layers, let's look at the corresponding TCP/IP layers in Figure 8-1. Notice that the layers don't match up precisely; but, by comparing the two, you can get some idea of what each layer in the Internet protocol stack does. (All the protocol layers of a network communication scheme are referred to as a protocol stack.)

More Info There are many Institute of Electrical and Electronics Engineers (IEEE) standards that control the configuration of networks and how they transfer data from one location to another. For example, there are several standards that appear in Figure 8-1 that control the transmission of data on Internet networks. You can find out more about these standards at *http://standards.ieee.org/index.html*.

There are a lot of acronyms for the Internet model in Figure 8-1, but the vast majority of them should mean something to you if you've been working with computers any length of time. You need to select one protocol from each layer to build up a protocol stack. For example, intranet browser users commonly have a protocol stack that consists of HTTP for the browser data, TCP/IP for data transfer, and carrier sense multiple access with collision detection (CSMA/CD) (one implementation of which is better known as Ethernet) for the physical connection.

It doesn't take long to figure out that all these data translation layers don't exist in a vacuum. If a Web server does a poor job of creating Web pages for a browser, it's certain your network sees additional packets to transfer the additional data. Likewise, responses from the browser to the Web server require some sort of data translation, and then transmission. All the layers perform some type of work on every piece of data that gets transferred from one machine to another, which means all these layers affect the performance of your system in some way. The efficiency with which all these layers do their work makes a difference in the overall performance of your network and affects what the user sees in the way of response time.

You also shouldn't be too surprised to find out that each of these layers may require some type of tuning. For example, at the physical layer, most NICs provide some type of enhanced options (the most common of which is direct memory access (DMA) data transfers) that improve system performance. We cover the various hardware and software enhancements that you can make to the various layers in the appropriate sections of the chapter. For now, all you really need to understand is that the layers exist and that many of them can be optimized.

Understanding Packet Configuration

The previous section helped you understand what the various operating system layers are all about. However, knowing that the operating system processes the network connection in layers doesn't tell you the whole story. When you get to the bottom of whatever network model you're using, you end up with a data packet that contains a lot of information about how the data should be transferred from one point to another. You can see this data using various utilities, including Microsoft's Network Monitor. Before we delve into these monitoring utilities, however, it's a good idea to know what a packet actually looks like as it travels along the cable from one machine to the next. Figure 8-2 shows a network packet for a TCP/IP data transfer. I've tried to use relatively standard values, but the values you actually see using a network monitoring utility or hardware (such as a sniffer) depend entirely on your network configuration.

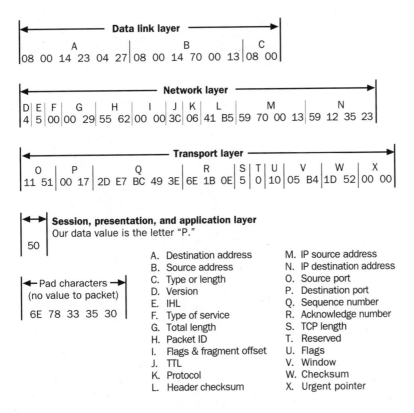

Figure 8-2. *Packets include a lot of information about how the data should get transferred and to where it should get transferred.*

There are two rows of identification information and one row of data shown in Figure 8-2. The first rows of identification information tell where the data fits within the OSI model (for example, in the data link layer). This helps you correlate the existence of certain data with its purpose in the overall scheme of network data transfer. The second row tells the purpose of a specific piece of data (for example, the destination address). Table 8-1 contains a listing of the various data elements (in the order they appear in the figure) along with a description of their purpose.

More Info You can find the specifications for TCP/IP in two separate documents: one for TCP and a second for IP. The TCP specification appears in RFC 793 at *http://www.faqs.org/rfcs/rfc793.html*. The IP specification appears in RFC 791 at *http://www.faqs.org/rfcs/rfc791.html*.

Table 8-1. **TCP/IP Data Packet Elements**

Element	OSI Level	Description
Destination Address	Data Link Layer	The unique address of the destination machine's NIC.
Source Address	Data Link Layer	The unique address of the source machine's NIC.
Type or Length	Data Link Layer	This packet element can contain one of two values. It either contains the length of the remainder of the packet, or more commonly, the packet type. In this case, we're looking at the packet type, which is 0800 for an Ethernet II packet.
Version	Network	The version of the software used to create the packet. In this case, we're looking at a version 4 packet.
IP Header Length (IHL)	Network	The length of the IP header in DWORDs. One DWORD equals 4 bytes, so the IP header is 20 bytes long in this case. This value includes both the Version and IHL elements, so you start counting the 20 bytes at the end of the data link layer.
Type of Service	Network	Prioritizing packets on the network is very important. This field prioritizes the packet as a whole and helps network components such as routers deliver the packets according to their importance to the network as a whole.
Total Length	Network	The length of the entire datagram. The datagram begins at the very end of the data link layer and ends at the end of any data included within the packet. The datagram doesn't include the data link layer or any padding characters used to flesh out the packet to a given transfer size. In this case, the datagram is 29 hexadecimal bytes, or 41 decimal bytes. According to the TCP specification mentioned earlier, the datagram requires 5 bytes of padding to meet the minimum requirement of 46 bytes.
Packet ID	Network	An identification number that makes this packet unique. The packet ID is used to ensure that all the packets arrive at the destination and that the packets don't end up in another session. Each session uses a unique packet ID.
Flags and Fragmentation Offsets	Network	There are actually three fields in this packet element. Bit 15, the last bit in the word, is unused. Bit 14 contains the Don't Fragment flag. This flag tells any routers in the path that you don't want to break the packet into smaller pieces for faster transport. Bit 13 contains the More Fragments flag. This flag tells the recipient there are more packets on the way. Bits 0 through 12 contain the fragment offset. This tells where this packet gets placed within the completed data transfer. We don't need to fragment the data, in this case, so the word contains zeros.
Time to Live (TTL)	Network	Tells the network how long this packet has to live. If the network can't find the destination address in the time allotted, the packet is declared dead and deleted. The sending machine then receives an error message saying the destination address doesn't exist.

(continued)

Table 8-1.   *(continued)*

Element	OSI Level	Description
Protocol	Network	Determines which protocol receives the packet when it gets transferred from the network to transport layer. In this case, the value of 06h tells Windows 2000 that this is a TCP packet. A UDP packet has a value of 11h.
Header Checksum	Network	Allows the network layer to check the integrity of the packet once it arrives at the destination machine.
IP Source Address	Network	Contains the IP address of the source machine. Don't confuse this with the physical address of the NIC that we looked at earlier.
IP Destination Address	Network	Contains the IP address of the destination machine.
Source Port	Transport	Determines the source port used to transfer data. The port, in this case, is the TCP/IP port used by the application to transfer data to the client.
Destination Port	Transport	Determines the software port on the receiver that's responsible for accessing the data. The destination port often tells you which application is in use on the client machine. The example shows a value of 17h (23 decimal), which equates to Telnet. If the client were using HTTP (a browser), the port number would be 80 decimal in most cases.
Sequence Number	Transport	Identifies a specific packet within a group of packets. The sequence number doesn't start at any particular value. All that must happen is that the source and destination need to increment the number at the same interval. Essentially, it tells the destination if it missed a packet.
Acknowledge Number	Transport	Tells the source that the destination received a certain number of bytes of data.
TCP Length (Data Offset)	Transport	Defines the length of the TCP header in DWORDs (4 bytes). The example shows a length of 20 bytes, which includes the transport layer, but nothing else.
Reserved	Transport	This element isn't used for anything.
Flags	Transport	The first two bits of this element aren't used—at least in the example. The remaining six bits represent the following flags: urgent, acknowledgment, push, reset, synchronize, and finish. The urgent flag tells the recipient that the content of the urgent field is valid. The acknowledgment flag indicates that the acknowledgment field is valid. The push flag tells the sending TCP to rush the delivery of data through the rest of the layers. The reset flag initializes the connection to a known state after an error occurs. The synchronize flag helps two nodes to synchronize their transmissions. The finish flag indicates that this is the last packet of data.
Window	Transport	Determines the rate at which two nodes can transfer data. Of course, this depends on a lot of factors including the load on each node.

(continued)

Table 8-1. *(continued)*

Element	OSI Level	Description
Checksum	Transport	Allows the transport layer to check the integrity of the TCP header. If the checksum of the package doesn't match this field, the packet is corrupt.
Urgent Pointer	Transport	The receiver counts this number of bytes from the beginning of the sequence number field to the point in the data stream where urgent data exists.
Data	Session, Presentation, and Application	The information that an application on one node needed to transfer to an application on a second node. In this case, we're transferring one byte of data, the letter P. How the source and destination nodes handle the data depends on what kind of application is creating and receiving the information. For example, a browser normally deals with the data at the application level.

Local Machine Sources

The local machine is the one the user uses to gain access to the resources the network can provide. This means working with both operating system-specific applications such as Windows Explorer and user-oriented applications such as Microsoft Office. The methods that these applications employ to gain access to network resources on the user's behalf determine a number of network performance factors, such as the amount of bandwidth used to service the call.

There are four sources of potential network bottlenecks on the local machine. The first is the application that isn't designed for network use and is hostile to any attempt to use it with the network. Fortunately, there are few of these applications in use anymore and the vast majority of them are custom applications designed to perform a specific task. Network hostile applications usually require special handling by the operating system because they don't provide any resources of their own. These applications take resources away from other applications when they do require access to the network.

The second type of bottleneck comes from database applications. A database application is always designed with network use in mind because the database is normally held on a central machine for everyone's access. However, databases deal with small bits of data in the form of records. If the database application is designed without any form of buffering, it likely accesses the database server constantly, which means it generates a lot of network traffic. All this traffic eats up network bandwidth and can quickly become a problem if many users are accessing the database at one time.

A third source of network bottlenecks for the local machine is the network agent that operates in the background. Agents are really helpful applications in many cases. For example, an agent can detect potential hardware problems long before the user realizes they exist and allows the network administrator to fix the errant hardware before it becomes a problem. Agents are also used to back up local data. However, agents that run constantly, yet provide only a modicum of information once a week (or even as often as once a day), use network resources without providing much in return. In some cases, you find that agents become more of a network bottleneck and performance inhibitor than a help in making the network run smoothly.

The fourth major source of network bottlenecks for the local machine is the application or hardware that's experiencing some sort of problem. For example, Ethernet NICs can experience a problem where they continuously generate packets even if there isn't any data to transfer to another node. An application that can't find a desired node may simply keep generating request packets, rather than acknowledge that a problem exists and reporting it to the user. Both of these errors create bottlenecks on the network that can easily be fixed once the network administrator can identify their source.

Tip   A sniffer or other form of network packet reader is an indispensable tool in finding errant hardware and software on the network. You can use the packet-sniffing capabilities of these devices to locate the source of packet streams that don't appear to have any use other than to use up network bandwidth. Once the source of a packet stream is identified, you can usually troubleshoot the local machine and find the source of the problem rather quickly.

Remote Node Sources

Network bottlenecks come in different forms when you look at things from a server perspective. The first factor you need to consider is the kind of server that's in use at the time. Many modern printers can act as servers, but the kind of services they offer are limited to rendering a document in printed form. A printer offers fewer potential sources of network bottlenecks than a database server does.

There's one constant when it comes to the server, however, and that's the fact that an overwhelmed server creates a backlog of requests, which in turn creates a network bottleneck. The reason is simple: Many applications repeat requests for service if an initial request isn't handled within a given amount of time. Even if the application doesn't repeat the request, the user that's working with the application most certainly does. These repeated requests only increase the server's backlog and create a self-perpetuating problem.

The method used to handle requests can affect the request backlog. For example, using threads allows the server to handle more requests in a more graceful manner than using single threaded server-side components. The down side is that creating multi threaded components takes more time, requires better error handling, and places certain constraints on the developer. In short, there's no free lunch, but there are options that can make it easier to deal with some of the bottlenecks on your network.

For most network administrators, finding a way to handle server request backlogs isn't a problem. There is, however, a wealth of other network bottleneck sources from the server perspective. Consider, for a moment, the problem of keep-alive messages that a server might generate. Keep-alive messages are generated for most distributed computing situations such as the Distributed Component Object Model (DCOM) and Web services. On the one hand, the server needs to know that the client is still connected so resources the client is using aren't wasted. In other words, the keep-alive messages are necessary because a server can end up with lots of dead sessions where the client didn't inform the server of its intent to disconnect. On the other hand, a server that broadcasts keep-alive messages too often wastes local processing cycles generating requests, network bandwidth creating an excessive number of request packets, and client machine resources responding to the keep-alive message requests. There has to be a balance between the server's need to maintain control over essential resources and the use of resources in the name of management requirements.

More Info There are always ways to increase the performance of your system, especially when it comes to the network. The Pure Performance Web site at *http://www.pureperformance.com/* contains a wealth of tips for all the Windows platforms. Although many of these tips are more useful for a workstation than a server, you find some of each kind of tip. Many of the tips require you to download software of some type—in many cases, the software is simply Microsoft updates that you should know about. The author is also concerned enough about your ability to use this Web site that user input is solicited almost constantly. In short, this is a top-notch place to go for the information you need in a format that's easy to use and understand.

Many servers provide what is termed a browser function as well. They scan the network, determine which nodes are available, what these nodes have to offer, and vital statistics about the node such as the node's human readable name. When a machine requests access to network resources, the browser feature of the server provides a list of the resources it's scanned. Without a browser, every machine has to scan the network itself to make a determination of what resources are available. As you can see, using a browser is an essential way to optimize network performance. Although this is an extremely important feature, some network administrators fail to realize that a network only needs a single machine to perform the browsing function. As a result, more than one server ends up scanning the network for resources, which generates an inordinate amount of network traffic and doesn't really provide any additional functionality for the other nodes on the network.

In some cases, a server also advertises the services it offers, making it easier for a client to find the services it needs. In most cases, the need to advertise services isn't required. If a user has to find a specific service on the network, the browser provides a list of available resources the user can access without the need to first advertise the service. As a result, although service advertising was once a necessary service, it isn't required any longer in today's computing environment. If a server offers service advertising, it's often easier to turn the service off and gain the network bandwidth that a lack of service advertising can provide. Before you turn off service advertising, consider the configuration of your network because older clients (such as Microsoft Windows 3.*x*) may require the service advertising feature to work properly.

Servers also exchange information for backup and propagation reasons. Depending on how and when the information gets exchanged, the server conversations can become a source of bottlenecks. Again, this is a configuration issue where you must consider the network as a whole. If the servers do need to exchange the information, then it's up to the network administrator to tune the servers in such a way that the exchange of information occurs at times of lower than average network activity.

Security has a role to play as well in the network bottleneck picture. For example, a DCOM application can select from several levels of security check, and the level chosen depends a great deal on the security requirements of the application. You also need to understand the performance ramifications of using a specific level of security. Adding more security to an application normally means the application runs slower and that network traffic increases. Consider the cost of moving from a Connect level of authentication to a Call level of authentication. In the first case, the user's identity is only checked once for each server connection. In the second case, the user's identity is checked every time the client application makes a call to the server. Obviously, the second method produces a lot more network traffic than the first method. The second method is also much more secure, however, which means you're making a choice between performance and security when you look at the Authentication Level setting. We'll discuss security settings more later in this chapter in "Understanding Authentication Choices in DCOM."

Other Sources

So far, we spent a lot of time exploring mechanical (non-human) sources of network bottlenecks—we looked at the sources of operating system, local machine, and remote node bottlenecks. All these bottlenecks have one thing in common: The network administrator either has total control over the source of the bottleneck, or the bottleneck is the result of an engineering decision and no one can change it.

There are network bottlenecks that fall outside the mechanical realm that we've talked about so far. One of these other kinds of bottlenecks is the network user, the person whom the network is designed to serve. The way a user interacts with the network can affect performance more than many other network factors. For example, a user who nervously saves a document every two seconds is going to use a lot more network bandwidth than a user who allows the application to automatically save the user's data at specific intervals. Another example of a usage problem is the user who keeps all the applications he or she will ever use open constantly and without regard to actual use at the time. Network-aware applications typically use some amount of network bandwidth even when the user isn't interacting with them.

Tip   Here's an example of an unused network-aware application problem. Many power users keep a copy of Windows Explorer open all the time with the idea that they'll use it to search for data on the network. I was able to garner a 3- to 5-percent performance increase simply by keeping Windows Explorer closed unless I needed it to look for a file or other resource on the network. It turns out that Windows Explorer does perform some work in the background on the user's behalf. Keeping a shortcut on the taskbar allows me to open Windows Explorer very quickly and still retain the performance benefits of not running the application unless needed.

The problems of the network user, however, go well beyond unfortunate habits that use network bandwidth needlessly. Some users inappropriately use gizmo software that relies heavily on network resources. For example, NetMeeting is an excellent product for conducting meetings over the network, but its use can tax network resources. A network administrator or company trainer can also use it as a training tool to help other people understand how the software on their machine works. Unfortunately, this software can also be abused by allowing two employees to conduct their own talk-a-thon over the network during business hours, hopefully without getting noticed. Since NetMeeting consumes vast amounts of network resources, everyone definitely notices the effects of such abuse. In short, the user can become a potential source of network bottlenecks through the inappropriate use of network-intensive applications.

More Info   Do you feel as though you have a problem that can't be solved without a little help from another human? The Computing.Net Web site allows you to start conversations with other professionals that can help you solve problems with your server setup. This site bills itself as the original technical support site, and the quality of the help does seem quite good. There are special sections for most versions of Windows, including Windows 2000. The Windows 2000-specific area is at *http://computing.net/windows2000/wwwboard/wwwboard.html*. Just scroll down to the bottom of the list of current message threads and start a new thread if you don't see what you need. If you do want to get in on a current thread, open the thread, read the responses, and then reply using the form that appears at the bottom of the page. Not only does this site cater to Windows, but you also find areas for DOS, Novell NetWare, UNIX, IBM OS/2, and the Apple Macintosh as well.

Besides the user, a network administrator has to contend with acts of nature (or things that look like acts of nature). It normally doesn't matter whether these events are manmade or the real event—acts of nature do produce performance-robbing effects on networks. For example, unless you fully protect a network from all outside influences, a simple thunderstorm can introduce enough noise on the network through the cabling to perceptibly reduce network performance. The reduction isn't enough to bring work to a crawl, but it is enough that users notice and probably complain about delays. In many cases, simply ensuring you use the proper cable, ground the network, and use isolation devices such as an uninterruptible power supply (UPS) can reduce the effects of these "acts of nature" to an acceptable level (or potentially get rid of them completely).

One final source of network bottlenecks is what many people place into the glitch category. Some combination of events conspires to cause the network to slow down for some unknown reason. In some cases, the effect of the bottleneck is localized to a single machine. Perhaps a packet gets corrupted and causes a single user's workstation to slow for a moment. In other cases, the bottleneck affects the network as a whole. For example, a poison message in Message Queing can slow all the workstations that rely on that queue for data communications. Unless the application developer included some form of automated handling for errant messages, the problem can require network administrator intervention to fix.

Note Message Queuing is a message queuing and routing system. In previous versions, Message Queuing was called Microsoft Message Queuing Server or MSMQ 1.0. Message Queuing refers to the routing system used in Windows 2000, and MSMQ refers to the routing system used in Windows NT 4.0, Windows 95, and Windows 98. Since Message Queuing is based on MSMQ 1.0, components and other elements still use the term MSMQ.

Overview of Network Topology Limitations

A network's topology defines the combination of hardware and software required when making connections between the various nodes of the network. In a very real sense, the network topology is the network; the nodes merely serve as endpoints that give the network a purpose. It's important to understand how the network topology affects network performance because the network topology allows very little in the way of tuning potential. In short, the network topology reflects the upper limits of the performance curve that you can hope to achieve. Any further increase in performance requires you to change the network topology at a basic level.

The configuration of a network determines certain physical characteristics that you can't alter with any ease. A 10 Mb/s Ethernet network doesn't suddenly provide 11 Mb/s worth of bandwidth after tuning—there's a physical limitation of the topology that prevents any performance in excess of the topology limit. In fact, you find that the specified topology limits rarely reflect real-world performance. You're very lucky to get the full 10 Mb/s out of the Ethernet network because there are other factors you have to take into account. In fact, it's these other factors that we cover in the section that follows entitled "Theoretical vs. Real-World Performance."

Many of you are probably wondering why I've wasted precious book space talking about old 10 Mb/s Ethernet technology. The truth of the matter is that many companies continue to use this older technology because it provides acceptable performance given the task the company needs to perform on the network. Of course, not every company is using older technology. That's why this chapter looks at something much newer—fiber optics—in the section "Understanding Fiber-Optic Performance Characteristics." The reason this technology is in a special section is that fiber optics impose special restraints on network topology—these restraints are seldom mentioned outside the circles of electronics specialists, so you may not even be aware they exist.

The final section, "Performance and Aging," covers one topic that many of you have probably faced more than one time in your careers—cabling problems that occur due to environmental conditions. It's important to consider the fact that a new network has new cables, connectors, and electronics. These new components provide the very best performance that you can hope to achieve once they're tuned for your company's needs. As the equipment ages, however, you notice a drop-off in performance. It's not because the equipment is broken—the loss of performance simply reflects the vagaries of aging. You have to consider this particular network bottleneck during your design and setup phase because it's unavoidable unless you want to continually change your equipment. Since no one realistically replaces network components until they're either broken or so out-of-date as to be unusable, you have to plan for some drop in performance due to aging as part of your design.

Theoretical versus Real-World Performance

When you look at the specifications for a network, you need to remember that these are the theoretical performance parameters of the network topology. Let's talk about a real-world example. When you read on the NIC package that the device is capable of transferring data at a rate of 10 Mb/s, that's the theoretical delivery speed. In the real world, collisions, noise, and other performance inhibitors lower the amount of data that actually gets transferred across the wire. In fact, you may be surprised to learn that in a normal network setup, the 10 Mb/s that you're supposed to get actually translates into 6 Mb/s real-world rates.

Note The example in this section is just that—an example. Any network topology is going to be affected by enough outside influences that a precise calculation of network bandwidth requires on-site measurements. In addition, any change to the network changes the performance characteristics of that network. For example, if you add a node to a network, the performance characteristics of that network change due to insertion losses, increased collisions, and various media losses such as the increased resistance of a copper network.

The point of this example is that there are certain realities in the world of networks, one of which is that there are factors outside the realm of the operating system that affect perceived operating system performance. A user who experiences slow network performance more than likely blames a slow server because it's the easiest part of the network to see and understand. The reality is that you may need 10 Mb/s of network bandwidth when only 6 Mb/s worth of network bandwidth is available. The user sees a slow network not because of a faulty server, but because of the physical limitations of the network topology.

Of course, the network bandwidth is just one source of theoretical vs. real-world performance problems. Consider for a moment the length limitations of most network topologies. Many network administrators take the specifications at face value and extend their network within the limitations of the topology-specified length criteria. However, these specifications assume a network in perfect environmental conditions, which is rarely the case. For example, as the noise around the network increases, the length that you can make the network cabling decreases in proportion to the noise level. Many network administrators don't account for this problem and pay with decreased network bandwidth.

The situation becomes even worse when a network administrator tries to extend the network the extra five feet needed to connect one more workstation. In this case, you not only have signal strength and noise problems to deal with, but you also have timing problems to contend with. In short, even the specifications for a network topology have to be read with a grain of salt. These specifications always assume your network is operating under perfect conditions because the engineers who create the specification can't anticipate every network problem. They assume the on-site network administrator takes noise and other environmental hazards into consideration during the network design process and acts accordingly.

Real-world performance is also based on the load that the unique combinations of your company's applications provide. Theoretical performance values are usually created using test suites of applications that your company may not use. Someone writing a specification very likely tries to achieve a generic application load—one that can reflect the load that a majority of companies place on the network. Unfortunately, there isn't any such thing as the generic company or the generic load. As a result, the performance you actually see when you design a network varies from the theoretical norm.

Let's consider the problem of application load for a moment on the theoretical vs. real-world network throughput. If your company uses applications that place large continuous loads on the network such as a graphics application, you can expect that the network provides maximum throughput, but that the applications can appear to run slowly because of their ravenous appetites for network bandwidth. On the other hand, a database application creates small, record-sized packets that may require padding. The use of padding characters wastes network bandwidth, so the efficiency of the network decreases. However, because of the kind of load the database places on the network, you might see very little in the way of a performance drop on a fully loaded network. There are other applications that place other kinds of load on the network—depending on how they create a load, you may see a loss of either performance or efficiency, or, in some cases, both.

There's one final real-world consideration to make. When the theoretical limits of a network topology are created, the engineers use lab-type equipment in a lab setting. This equipment is specially designed to help the engineers make the required measurements. In short, even if everything else is equal, the hardware you use to create a network isn't equal to the hardware used for testing. There just isn't any way you achieve the highest performance that's possible with a network because no one buys lab equipment for general office use.

Understanding Fiber-Optic Performance Characteristics

The emergence of fiber-optic cabling as the media of choice for networks is easy to understand. Companies need to move more data, faster than ever before. It doesn't matter what application you work with—there isn't a single environment today that can't benefit from some sort of performance boost. Of course, there are copper solutions that get almost the same level of performance as a modern fiber-optic network achieves and with a lot less hassle. Recent technology advances in the production of fiber-optic cable and the components required to make it work have made fiber-optic cable a viable choice for most companies. Not only does fiber-optic cable lack some of the potential security risks of copper, but it's also achieved cost parity with copper as well, making fiber-optic networks a very attractive choice. In short, fiber-optic networks have earned a place in many companies because of their performance, cost, and security characteristics.

As we've discussed throughout this section, tuning in the general sense can go only so far in making a network run faster. At some point, you're going to run up against the wall of the network topology. No matter what you do, at some point, no amount of tuning changes the performance characteristics of your network. So, the alternative is to change the network topology, and that's precisely what many companies are doing today. The move from copper to fiber-optic alternatives means network administrators have to learn new skills when it comes to diagnosing and fixing network performance problems. Don't make the mistake of thinking that all network cabling is the same—fiber optics are completely different from copper when it comes to performance characteristics and problem areas.

Fiber-optic cabling started out as a single wavelength, single-mode telephony system. Unfortunately, it wasn't long before the market reached the limits of this technology. Today, fiber-optic cabling normally means using dense wavelength, division multiplexed (DWDM) broadband systems. These systems include high-quality components such as splitters, couplers, and optical amplifiers.

Unfortunately, as you increase the complexity of a network topology, you also increase the number of factors that can inhibit performance. As a result of the added complexity of today's systems, fiber-optic networks require more advanced testing and performance-monitoring equipment. You can't use the simple equipment found in early fiber-optic networks simply because it can't handle the multiple wavelengths of data that these new configurations can work with. The following list provides you with some ideas about the performance inhibitors that affect fiber-optic networks as a whole.

- **Connectors**   Unlike copper, fiber-optic cabling is affected by a number of problems at the connector. For example, the way the end is cut can make or break the connection. Fiber-optic networks require absolutely straight cuts that can only be achieved by special equipment. In addition, there are reflection losses from the end of the cable and insertion losses.

- **Fiber-optic cabling**   Like copper, fiber-optic cabling suffers from span losses—a degradation of signal strength as the length of the cable increases. Fiber-optic cabling also suffers from chromatic loss (the refraction of some light into other wavelengths), polarization dependent loss (PDL), and polarization modal dispersion (PMD). Polarization is the effect you get from sunglasses. It reduces glare by changing the characteristics of the light in one direction. Unfortunately, because you're trying to maintain a consistent light condition on a fiber-optic network, polarization is an undesired side effect of using glass for the cable.

- **Dispersion compensating devices**   These devices collimate (make all of the individual light beams parallel) the laser light that moves through the fiber-optic cable. You have to perform this step to keep the light from dispersing so much that the signal becomes gibberish at the receiving node. Even these devices, however, suffer from various losses that include insertion loss, PDL, and delay ripple (moving the signal through the dispersion-compensating device incurs a delay that degrades the signal). Insertion loss occurs every time you add another device to the cable. The insertion of the device causes some of the light to reflect back toward the source, reducing signal strength in the process.

- **Transmitter**   Every fiber-optic transmission begins at the transmitter. The accuracy with which the transmitter creates the laser light at a given wavelength determines the starting signal strength. Obviously, some transmitters do a better job than others at creating the required light at the proper frequency. In addition, the transmitter quality can affect the output power, spectral width (the width of the light in terms of frequency), long-term output stability, and side mode suppression.

- **Receiver**   The biggest factor here is how sensitive the receiver is. A sensitive receiver picks up a smaller signal. In addition to sensitivity, the power range, signal degradation, and loss of signal threshold experienced by the receiver affects the overall throughput that you get from the network.

- **Dense multiplexers and demultiplexers**   DWDM requires multiplexing prior to transmission, and then demultiplexing once the signal is received. Remember that we're actually sending more than one signal across the fiber at the same time. The process of multiplexing and demultiplexing incurs loss in the form of bandwidth, insertion loss, delay ripple of each passband, and the differential loss between channels.

- **Optical amplifiers**   Increasing the signal strength of the transmitted data incurs a loss of wavelength in most cases, which means the signal is louder, but distorted. There are also various types of noise that an amplifier adds to the signal, which means the quality of the signal is degraded. Finally, there's only so much amplification that can occur before the amplifier produces a flat response and begins to add signal harmonics. As with any other fiber-optic device, there's also a certain amount of insertion loss.

- **Overall link**   When viewed as a whole, the fiber-optic network experiences end-to-end losses in the form of signal dispersion and other light refraction problems. A certain amount of the light returns the source because the devices inserted in the line and the walls of the fiber-optic cable itself reflect it. This is called the optical return loss (ORL). Finally, the fiber-optic link as a whole experiences a PMD loss.

More Info   This section of the chapter has provided you with a very brief overview of the kinds of losses you incur using fiber-optic cabling. Obviously, this is a very complex and a very new technology. The Rifocs Web site at *http://www.rifocs.com/* provides press releases, white papers, a glossary, demos, and other resources that make understanding this topic a little less difficult. In addition, this site contains descriptions of the test equipment you need to work with fiber-optic networks, along with some of the components these networks require to run efficiently.

Performance and Aging

Everything on your network ages. Cables get older, as do connectors and the electronics that support the network. Unfortunately, this is a part of the network picture that few people plan for and most people don't know how to anticipate, even if they did intend on accounting for it.

Consider the lowly cable. Your network can't operate without some type of cabling unless you're using a wireless technology. If you look at the end of a coaxial cable connector, you notice that part of the cable sticks out—the center conductor—and makes contact with the NIC. This conductor can corrode over time, with the corrosion affecting the electrical characteristics of the cable. Not only can corrosion cause reduced signal strength, but also problems such as intermittent contact with the NIC (corrupting packets as a result). Other cable-aging problems include brittleness—a cable breaks easier as it gets older. You find that there are other vagaries of aging as well, all of which affect the performance of your network in a way that you can't compensate for.

Connectors and plugs rely on metal with a certain amount of spring. Just look at any RJ plug and you see four or more connection fingers that are configured as springs. The act of pushing the connector into the plug creates a connection, due in part to the spring action of these fingers. Every time the plug is removed from the connector, the little fingers move back out—flexing the metal again. Eventually, the metal fatigues and you don't get the same level of connectivity you once got. The connector doesn't fail; it simply doesn't perform as well as it can.

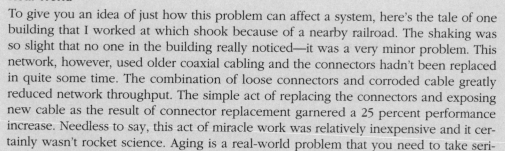

Real World

To give you an idea of just how this problem can affect a system, here's the tale of one building that I worked at which shook because of a nearby railroad. The shaking was so slight that no one in the building really noticed—it was a very minor problem. This network, however, used older coaxial cabling and the connectors hadn't been replaced in quite some time. The combination of loose connectors and corroded cable greatly reduced network throughput. The simple act of replacing the connectors and exposing new cable as the result of connector replacement garnered a 25 percent performance increase. Needless to say, this act of miracle work was relatively inexpensive and it certainly wasn't rocket science. Aging is a real-world problem that you need to take seriously as you design and maintain a network.

Aging definitely affects any mechanical component within your network. For example, some devices on the network may use relays. A relay is a physical device with springs, contacts, and other mechanical features that can wear out. Likewise, some devices use hard drives for internal storage purposes. Like any spinning device with bearings, the bearings eventually wear out and you have to replace the device. Of course, it's not too difficult to figure out that the physical devices will fail. However, what happens during the time the device hasn't failed, but it's also too worn out to perform its job completely? That's the point where you see certain types of performance degradation on your network. Since these devices often appear within hubs or other non-user related peripherals, finding the source of the degradation can be very difficult.

The effects of aging certainly aren't limited to the parts of your network that encounter physical stress. You find that aging affects every part of the network to some extent, even with regard to electronic components. For example, it's not at all uncommon for the characteristics of an amplifier to change over time. Most amplifiers today contain some type of compensating circuitry that helps with the aging process, but the fact remains that even compensating circuitry doesn't keep the amplifier performing at peak performance forever. At some point, the amplification capability of the circuit falls below desirable levels, even if the device itself hasn't failed.

Understanding Network Component Interactions

A network is a system of devices that work together toward the same goal of promoting communication between nodes. Each device is individual, and to a certain extent, you can treat the device as an individual device. There are limits to what you can assume about any device on the network, however, because all these devices are connected together, forming a cohesive whole. As a result, a change on an individual device affects the performance of the network in some way.

Consider the following scenario. A network administrator installs the vendor-supplied device driver for a NIC on one machine on the network, but uses the generic Microsoft Windows driver on another. At this point, the first machine, the one with the vendor-supplied driver, likely performs a little faster than the second machine, but not too much faster. What happens, though, if the user of the first machine decides to use the settings for the vendor-supplied drivers to increase the performance of the NIC on the first machine? What might seem like a sensible course of action can backfire. The first machine definitely sees an increase of network performance. However, because of the increased network traffic, the second machine may actually experience a decrease in performance if there isn't enough network bandwidth to support the first machine's increase in activity. As you can see, an interaction has occurred between the two machines, making one machine faster and the other slower. Although one change was anticipated and even expected, the second change certainly wasn't anticipated or even wanted.

It doesn't take the network administrator very long to find the culprit in this case. However, real-world networks contain more than two machines and more than just two configurations of the same hardware. If the same problem occurs on a network with 100 machines, it definitely takes longer to find the problem—if the network administrator can identify the source of the problem at all.

Some problems aren't nearly so obvious as that one. For example, it might seem like a good idea to change the setting for Application Response on the Performance Options dialog box shown in Figure 8-3 from Applications to Background Services. This change, however, can have the unanticipated side effect of reducing overall server performance, especially if the server is used to run components, more than act as a file server.

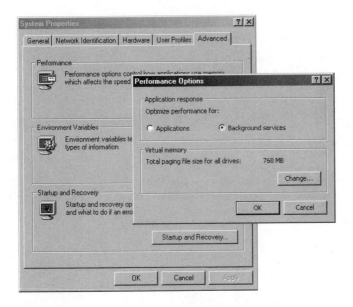

Figure 8-3.   *Some changes to a server's configuration can make a big difference in network performance.*

Interactions between network components can become even more entangled when you start adding more than one server to the picture. The servers need to communicate to keep each other up-to-date. Trying to time the updates so that each server gets what it needs without interrupting the other servers at a busy time can quickly turn into a logistical nightmare. Consider the simple matter of replicating Active Directory information. You may find that some times of the day are better than others for performing this task. Open the Active Directory Sites And Services MMC snap-in and you find a hierarchical list of the sites that work with Active Directory.

Let's look at one of the scheduling options for a typical setup. Click on the first site in the list (named Default-First-Site-Name during setup) and you see a minimum of three entries in the right pane. One of these entries should be NTDS Site Settings. Right-click this icon, and then choose Properties from the Context menu. You see the NTDS Site Settings Properties dialog box. The Site Settings tab of this dialog box contains a Change Schedule button. Click this button and you see a Schedule For NTDS Site Settings dialog box like the one shown in Figure 8-4. This is where you set up the schedule for replicating Active Directory information across the network. Notice that the current schedule performs the replication once an hour every day of the week.

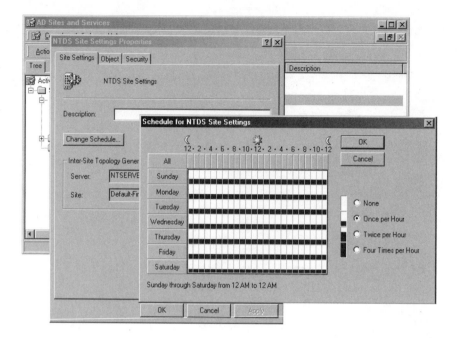

Figure 8-4. *You need to set up a reasonable schedule for Active Directory replication.*

All of this seems pretty simple, but it isn't. Consider the time that the information in Active Directory changes the most. It's going to be the time when users are most active on the network because users make most of the Active Directory changes as part of their daily work. So, now you have an interaction problem. Active Directory should get updated more often when a large number of changes are being made, yet replicating the data consumes valuable network bandwidth that users may require to get work completed. One answer to this problem is to replicate the data right after peaks in usage occur. For example, you might turn Active Directory replication off while users are logging in, and then allow one update per hour during the first half of the day, and increase the replication rate to four times an hour during lunch. The rate can go back down again during the rest of the work day and increase again sometime during the night while nothing else is going on to ensure that all the sites are up-to-date for the next day. The point is that a change here is going to affect the network as a whole, so you need to make any decisions carefully.

Interactions can take place in the network setup itself. There are actually a lot of network-tuning features that you can use, depending on the protocols installed on your machine, but let's take a look at just one area—file and printer sharing. Right-click My Network Places, and then choose Properties from the Context menu. You see a Network And Dial-up Connections dialog box. Right-click Local Area Connection, and then choose Properties from the Context menu. You see a Local Area Connection Properties dialog box. One of the entries in the Components Checked Are Used By This Connection list is File

And Printer Sharing For Microsoft Networks (at least if you installed the default level of file and printer sharing support). Highlight this option, and then click Properties. You should see the File And Printer Sharing For Microsoft Network Properties dialog box shown in Figure 8-5.

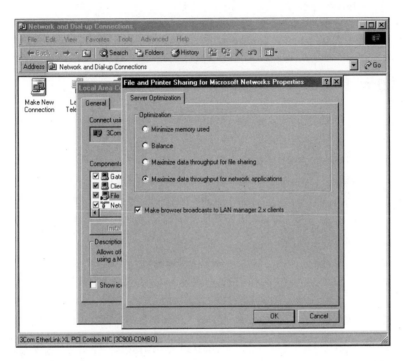

Figure 8-5.   *Choosing the right file and printer sharing settings can affect network performance as a whole.*

Notice that this dialog box offers you several choices on how to configure your server. The problem is that the choices look more like all-or-nothing options than anything else. What these settings really affect is the amount of memory used for caching purposes. A server that's short on memory (128 MB or less) always needs to use the Minimize Memory Used setting. If you're running a lot of COM applications on this server or it's the domain controller, you probably want to choose the Balance option. If you have a server with lots of memory (more than 128 MB, preferably in the 256-MB or greater range) and it's used mainly for file sharing, choose the Maximize Data Throughput For File Sharing option. Finally, if your server is mainly used to serve up applications and you have lots of memory (in this case, a minimum of 256 MB, depending on the number and type of applications being run), use the Maximize Data Throughput For Network Applications option.

Tip There's a little checkbox on the Server Optimization tab of the File And Printer Sharing for Microsoft Networks Properties dialog box that doesn't seem to do much. All that the help file says is that it allows LAN Manager 2.1 clients to use the services offered by the server. Checking this box does allocate some system memory for the purpose of working with LAN Manager 2.1 clients. You can get a little more performance out of your server by unchecking this option, unless you really do need it.

User-Oriented Network Bottleneck Solutions

Users represent the most frustrating part of performance monitoring, tuning, or optimizing your network. Let's look at the question of performance monitoring first.

Monitoring Network Performance

A consultant can take several approaches to monitoring the network's performance, one of which is to tell everyone that performance monitoring is taking place. This has the advantage of warning users that there may be small glitches with the network and not to worry about them. However, it also seems to have the effect of changing everyone's behavior. Unless you schedule enough time to do the monitoring, what you get is a skewed view of the network's performance because most users subconsciously change their behavior. They feel as though they're being watched and therefore don't do some of the performance-inhibiting things they normally may do.

Another approach to the performance-monitoring problem is telling the network administrator and management about the event, but keeping silent around the users. Unfortunately, even a single glitch can end up costing the company money because the users are unprepared for the event. In addition, you find that the user cooperation level greatly decreases because they associate you with "big brother"—a definite problem when it comes time to make changes to the users' network usage habits.

Training Network Users

Monitoring problems aside, once you do come up with a picture of the network's performance, you have to decide what action to take. The hardware and software solutions aren't hard to implement because you have full control over this part of the network. Retraining the users to do something differently, on the other hand, might be problematic to say the least. People tend to reject change, especially if they perceive the change as threatening or inconvenient.

Of course, tuning the way people interact with the network is only part of the process. You have to optimize any new procedures later. This leads to the confusion syndrome. Some users end up using the old method, some use one of the failed methods, and still others use the optimized method you created.

By now, you may be thinking that any change in a user's behavior, no matter how attractive from a performance perspective, just isn't worth the work. Unfortunately, that kind of an attitude backfires as well. Now the users perceive that you don't think they're worth the effort of training to do the job better. In short, you're going to have to face the fact that performance monitoring, tuning, and optimization from the user perspective is going to be an error-prone, time-consuming process that few enjoy (especially the consultant doing the work).

Now that you're perfectly terrified about the prospects of doing anything with the users of a network, it's important to understand one fact. A network is designed to serve the needs of the user, and as a result, the user has the greatest impact on network performance. Users who aren't completely sure how to use the network waste precious network bandwidth trying to figure out the best way to get their work done. In addition, poorly trained users don't know that the network can perform certain tasks for them automatically, which means they waste time doing things in some convoluted manual fashion. So, the first user-oriented network bottleneck solution is to ensure that everyone is actually trained to use the network.

Setting Network Security

No matter what you do, some users insist on at least attempting to abuse network resources. With this in mind, part of your user-oriented network bottleneck solution is to check network security. Ensure that users can only reach the applications they actually need to use. In some cases, you may need to perform the additional work required to secure high bandwidth applications, such as NetMeeting, until the user actually needs them to do work. A good network usage policy (and requisite enforcement) should keep this kind of micromanagement to a minimum.

Monitoring Network Application Performance

At some point, your users are trained to use the network, and are aware of all the security and application usage policies for the company. Even with these two goals met, you may still find that network performance lags. That's where certain types of monitoring come into play. You don't want to become "big brother" because that kills user productivity and can cause your company to lose valuable employees. What you do want to do is look for application-usage problems, especially with custom applications. In some cases, you may find that a change in the design of the application interface nets improved network performance; in others, you may find that more user training on specific procedures is mandated. Whichever route you go, it's important to understand what kind of problem the user is facing before you assume that a network performance-inhibiting usage habit is all the user's fault.

Other User-Oriented Network Influences

Finally, there are user-oriented network bottlenecks that fall into the truly weird category. Consider the user who unplugged his or her computer from the network every day to avoid being bothered by e-mail. Once the user completed a task, the computer would get plugged back into the network, e-mail would get checked, and then the computer would get unplugged again. The network administrator of this network was plagued by calls of intermittent network errors and slow network performance. It was months before the network administrator finally figured out what was happening and straightened the problem out. No, these kinds of problems don't happen every day, and they're always unexpected when they do; but, as a network administrator, you have to be prepared for any eventuality when it comes to tuning your network for optimum performance.

Real World

User-initiated network bottlenecks can occur with the most common applications. Consider how e-mail can affect network performance. If a user sends a large document to a long list of recipients, the load on the network can become quite difficult to manage. For example, a 1 MB document sent to 100 users would place a 100 MB load on the network for a single user. That's an incredible load for something that could be handled in a better way. The network administrator could simply enforce a rule that says all e-mail must use links rather than attachments. One way to do this is to place limits on message size as well as on the size of the mailbox given to each user. In most cases, sending links instead of attachments lowers the load on the network because not every recipient wants to look at the attachment. In addition, not every recipient looks at the document at the same time, which means the load gets spread out over a longer time.

Applications like e-mail can also produce unanticipated loads. For example, a user might send a message to a group of people instead of the single recipient originally intended. Many of these unintentional recipients will respond with messages saying they don't want to receive this type of e-mail any more, further increasing network load. Unfortunately, the only way to avoid this kind of problem is to provide user training and hope that the user takes time to view the message recipients before sending it.

Hardware-Oriented Network Bottleneck Solutions

Hardware upgrades or complete replacements are the basis of many network bottleneck solutions today. The idea is a simple one. Make the data pipe bigger and faster so it can handle all the data that today's applications generate. In addition, better hardware can route data faster and perform some functions, such as certain types of security checking, faster than software. Obviously, any time you increase the size of the data pipe, modify routing, or change security techniques, a lot of interrelated hardware is affected. At a minimum, the NICs, cabling, and hubs require change to allow for a larger pipe. However, there's a lot more to ensuring your hardware is prepared for optimum performance than simply plugging in new hardware. The following sections help you understand the full scope of the hardware-oriented network bottleneck solutions at your disposal.

Ensuring It Works

Most people think that looking for hardware solutions for your network speed problems is a matter of deciding what new devices to add. Although this is certainly a part of the solution that we visit later, the first real step is to ensure that the current network hardware is fully operational, installed correctly, and configured for maximum throughput. Perhaps the plumbing for your network is simply clogged, rather than unable to handle the amount of data that you want to put through it.

Let's consider the aspect of equipment repair first. It's possible for a network cable to become partially bad. Standing waves (a kind of signal that acts in opposition to the originating signal) generated by such a cable use up part of the network bandwidth, making it appear that the network is having performance problems, when in reality, a single cable replacement can fix the problem. (The presence of standing waves reduces signal strength and increases the number of packet retries a network experiences.) There are a lot of ways to detect this kind of a problem, most notably checking suspect cables after a significant performance loss. A time-domain reflectometer (TDR) helps you find cables that are open, shorted, and performing below specifications. Most cable-checking devices even help you locate the approximate position of a crimp or other malformation.

Grounding is another common network problem. Noise generated on the network cable often causes signals to experience corruption of various types. A packet that has errors must be resent, using up precious network bandwidth that can be used for other purposes. Ensuring that your cables and hubs are grounded properly often results in a slight, but very definite increase in network performance.

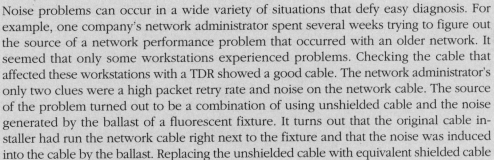

Real World

Noise problems can occur in a wide variety of situations that defy easy diagnosis. For example, one company's network administrator spent several weeks trying to figure out the source of a network performance problem that occurred with an older network. It seemed that only some workstations experienced problems. Checking the cable that affected these workstations with a TDR showed a good cable. The network administrator's only two clues were a high packet retry rate and noise on the network cable. The source of the problem turned out to be a combination of using unshielded cable and the noise generated by the ballast of a fluorescent fixture. It turns out that the original cable installer had run the network cable right next to the fixture and that the noise was induced into the cable by the ballast. Replacing the unshielded cable with equivalent shielded cable resulted in a significant performance boost for the network.

Sometimes a configuration problem hides as a performance problem. It can be as easy as switching on a particular performance-enhancing feature. In some cases, the vendor assumes you don't want to use the feature by default to ensure maximum compatibility. You look for these special device settings in a variety of places, depending on the device in question. When working with a NIC, you normally look at the Properties dialog box for that NIC in the Device Manager. Figure 8-6 shows a typical example of special settings on the Advanced tab of the Properties dialog box.

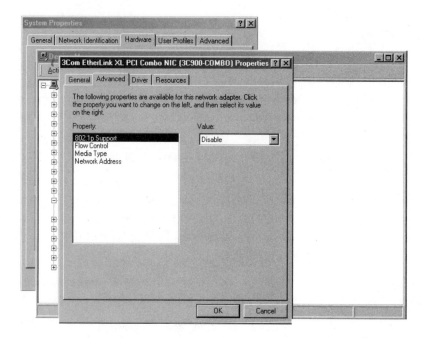

Figure 8-6. *The Properties dialog box for a device shown in Device Manager often contains special settings that can speed performance.*

Unfortunately, there isn't any standardization when it comes to most of the hardware out there. The settings you find in the device's Properties dialog box reflect the capabilities of that particular device and the accessibility to those features provided by the driver. Consult the vendor documentation before you turn on any hardware features you're unsure about. In some cases, a setting change might actually reduce performance, especially if the rest of the server hardware isn't designed to support the feature.

Using Vendor-Supplied Drivers

Microsoft provides drivers for a lot of the hardware that Windows supports, which is a nice feature in most cases. However, many of those drivers are generic—they're intended to provide minimal functionality and work across a wide range of hardware solutions with approximately the same characteristics. Vendor-supplied drivers, when available, normally make use of all the features the hardware has to offer. There's a good reason for this seeming dichotomy in support. The vendor is motivated to show you all the features of your current hardware in the hope you'll buy more hardware later. On the other hand, Microsoft needs to make the operating system as compatible with as much hardware as possible. Although it's in Microsoft's best interest to provide at least minimal functionality for your hardware, there really isn't a good reason for them to expend the time and energy required to fully exploit the hardware's capabilities.

Does this mean you should use only vendor-supplied drivers? The answer is fairly easy to figure out. First, you need to ask whether the vendor-supplied drivers are up-to-date. Many vendors don't have Windows 2000-compatible drivers right now, which makes the generic choice the only one you have. Being up-to-date, however, means more than just supplying a driver. A driver that doesn't support current Windows 2000 features is unlikely to deliver all the performance it can, which means you need to look at the performance it does provide. If the features the driver provides surpasses those of the native Windows 2000 environment, you probably want to use the vendor driver even if it isn't quite up-to-date with current Windows technology.

Vendor-supplied drivers normally provide a configuration program. For example, 3Com provides an application that not only configures your NIC, but also allows you to test it as well. Figure 8-7 shows what the Configuration tab looks like. Notice that there are options that determine how memory and processor cycles are used to support the NIC, as well as settings for the NIC itself such as half or full duplex operation.

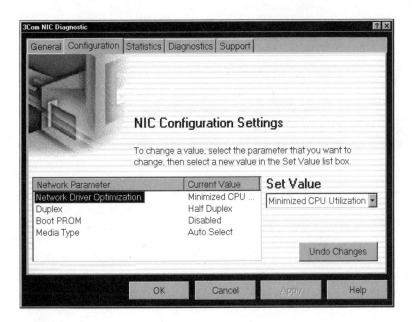

Figure 8-7.   *Most vendor-specific drivers come with configuration aids that allow you to maximize hardware feature use.*

From a network administrator perspective, the Statistics tab (shown in Figure 8-8) offers more in the way of performance monitoring. Notice that this NIC has had some transmit deferrals, along with both single and multiple collisions. Since this is an Ethernet network, all three conditions are expected to occur. However, it's important to monitor the percentage of completed transfers to those that are stopped for some reason. A sudden increase in any of the three statistics might point to a hardware failure of some kind, either locally or on the network. In most cases, you have nothing to worry about if all three percentages remain below 5 or 6 percent.

Figure 8-8. *Vendor-supplied monitoring software can help you trace the source of problems with your network hardware.*

A final benefit of using vendor-supplied drivers and monitoring software is the inclusion of diagnostics. Figure 8-9 shows the diagnostic aids that came with a 3Com card on my network. Notice that you can test the NIC's ability to communicate with another workstation, as well as perform an internal test. This particular NIC doesn't include the Remote Wake-up feature, so that test is disabled.

Figure 8-9. _Diagnostic aids help you check local hardware for problems, as well as test communication lines._

Widening the Pipe

We've talked about this particular issue several times in the chapter. The bottom line is that you need to consider the limits of the topology of your current network. The data pipe created by a certain network topology can't be modified without changing the topology itself. Sure, you can make the pipe more efficient and reduce the number of losses within the pipe, but the pipe itself is a fixed size.

Changing a network's topology is an expensive proposition. Not only do you have to change the cabling, but you also need to change hubs, routers, NICs, and just about every other piece of network hardware you own. Some network hardware is designed to support multiple speeds, which means you can make the transition from one sized pipe to another slowly instead of all at once. The fact remains, however, that you eventually need to change all your hardware to derive the maximum benefit from any topology change.

Quality Does Make a Difference

Some people view all hardware as being essentially equal given equal specifications. The trade presses shout that we're in a commodity market and hardware prices tend to justify that assumption. To some extent, however, there are still quality differences between various makes of hardware. Perhaps the cost between a really good NIC and a bottom of the barrel NIC is only $10, but that extra expenditure now can save you a lot of problems later.

Getting high quality network hardware is especially important for a number of reasons, the most important of which is longevity. Since a problem with any given piece of network hardware can bring the entire network to its knees, you want to keep failure to a minimum. No one wants to explain why the network is down due to the loss of one hub or a single NIC.

Hardware quality is usually coupled with driver, management software, and level of support as well. A good device driver can usually provide a substantial increase in network performance. In addition, you need a vendor-specific driver if you want to make use of any special hardware features. The management software you get can help you create the optimum configuration for a given server, test the server's ability to communicate with others on the network, and provide you with valuable statistics about the operation of the hardware. The need for good technical support is obvious. No matter how much you learn about the hardware on your network, the vendor always knows more.

Software-Oriented Network Bottleneck Solutions

The software portion of the network-tuning process is relatively straightforward and easy to understand. Essentially, you follow the process of tuning network software that you do for any other software. Make a change, look for the right results, and then look for any negative consequences. As with hardware changes, any change you make in the software is going to interact with every other piece of software on the network, at least in some small way.

It helps to understand what piece of software you're changing. An operating system change is going to affect all the applications on that server, as well as any clients that access the server, and potentially other servers as well. A change to a single application has a much smaller effect on the operation of the network as a whole, but affects individual users and parts of the network to a greater degree. We look at this question in more detail in "Operating System vs. Application Problems," the section that follows.

Another problem is one of authentication. You need to answer the question of how much and what level of user authentication is required to ensure the security of the network. It can be a difficult question to answer because some applications handle data that's more sensitive than others. In addition, you'll find that the level of authentication required is determined by the accessibility of the data. For example, data transferred over the Internet requires more authentication than data that arrives on a LAN connection. We look at a specific application in this case, DCOM, in "Understanding Authentication Choices in DCOM."

The final two sections, "A Look at Bindings" and "A Look at Providers," are designed to help you understand the whole layering effect of the operating system's support for a specific network model. These are the two sections where you put what you learned earlier in the book into practice.

Operating System versus Application Problems

Some software-oriented network bottlenecks are easy to figure out. If every application on a server is having problems communicating with users over the Internet, but not over the LAN, it's a good bet that some operating system setting is wrong. Those are the easy problems, however, and you don't run into them very often. Configuration problems of this sort normally happen one or two times during initial server setup—it's a rare occurrence in a production environment.

A more common problem is that users are having problems accessing the contents of a database, no matter what form of connection they use, during a certain part of the day. Is the problem on the database server? Perhaps the application server is close to being overloaded and more users request data from the database during this time of the day. A memory leak or other application problem can cause this to happen as well. In short, you need to determine where the problem is happening before you can fix it.

Sometimes, you need to take a deep breath and patiently analyze the situation. For example, an operating system problem, as previously stated, normally affects all applications on a given server. So, one of the first steps in diagnosing and fixing a software problem is to see how many applications and how many users are affected. In most cases, a single user or a single application problem is related to that user or application, not to the operating system as a whole.

A lot of problems defy such easy analysis, however, and you need to do more in-depth research. One of the best tools you can use to find and diagnose software problems is System Monitor, which was discussed in Chapter 4. One of the checks you can make is to use the Processor object. Two of the counters, % Privileged Time and % User Time, can help you differentiate between an operating system and an application problem. The one that's hitting the processor more often is a likely candidate for further checks. Of course, this is a very crude check of system performance.

You'll want to correlate any findings you make with the network itself. This means using the Network Interface object to check the amount of data going through the NIC. One of the more interesting counters here is Packets Received Unknown. You use this counter to determine how many packets the operating system is discarding because it doesn't recognize the protocol. Of course, the question is whether the problem is of an operating system nature or application-oriented. A check of the packets reveals what protocol isn't recognized. The fix here can be something as simple as choosing a different protocol for a particular application to use in communicating with the server.

If you suspect a particular network protocol is involved with a problem, you can choose that object in the Add Counters dialog box. For example, most of your Internet communication takes place using IP. You may want to monitor the various counters for this protocol to determine if there's excess network activity.

You'll want to refine your search using the various other tools that Windows 2000 provides; and, in some cases, third-party tools as well. Network Monitor allows you to check traffic between two nodes on the network and detect how the packets are sent—at least to an extent. (You can install Network Monitor using the Add/Remove Programs applet in the Control Panel.) If you have a large network, with lots of nodes, Network Monitor really isn't the tool of choice. Get a third-party sniffer to intercept and read packets that flow between specific clients and the server. The use of these tools helps ensure you can differentiate between operating system and application-specific sources of problems.

Understanding Authentication Choices in DCOM

The Distributed Component Object Model (DCOM) is Microsoft's first true distributed computing environment technology. As a result, DCOM is a good choice for showing the effects of authentication on network performance. DCOM relies on network connections to create remote connections and, as part of the remote connection strategy, provides various levels of user authentication. When you move from the local machine to a distributed application environment, authentication becomes essential to ensure all data transactions take place in a secure environment.

You access the DCOM settings for components on a server using the DCOMCnfg utility. Just use the Run command on the Start menu to display the Distributed COM Configuration Properties dialog box shown in Figure 8-10.

There are two ways to set the authentication level for your component: at the DCOM or individual component level. You find the DCOM level of authentication on the Default Properties tab of the Distributed COM Configuration Properties dialog box shown in Figure 8-11. The default authentication level is Connect. For a component, the authentication level property is found on the General tab of the component's Properties dialog box as shown in Figure 8-12. The default setting, in this case, is Default. Both authentication level settings determine the minimum security requirements for the client and server to gain access to each other's resources. In other words, this setting determines how the client and server exchange security information during a session.

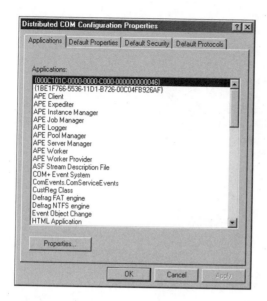

Figure 8-10.   *The Distributed COM Configuration Properties dialog box allows you to set various DCOM communication parameters.*

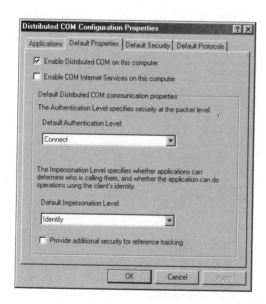

Figure 8-11.   *You find the overall authentication settings for DCOM on the Default Properties tab of the Distributed COM Configuration Properties dialog box.*

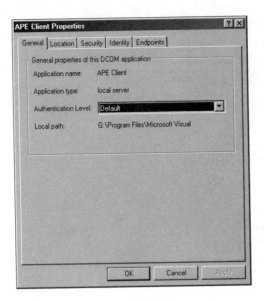

Figure 8-12. *DCOM provides the means for setting the authentication level of individual components as well.*

These two default DCOM authentication settings (overall and individual component) represent a minimalist approach to DCOM security. There are other settings that may provide you with better security. Table 8-2 describes each of the Default Authentication Level settings.

Table 8-2. DCOM Default Authentication Level Settings

Setting	Description	When to Use
None	The client and server don't authenticate each other at all.	You must use this setting when creating anonymous connections. However, this setting also comes in handy working in a small workgroup network situation where physical security is high and there aren't any connections to the outside world. This setting reduces overall network traffic to the lowest possible level, but also represents the greatest security risk.
Call	Authentication occurs for every call while a connection is maintained.	This is a moderately high security level that ensures the client and server verify each other's identity for each method call in the application, which may involve several packets. You may notice a slight increase in network traffic when using this level of authentication and there's no guarantee of complete security from third-party intrusion.

(continued)

Table 8-2.   *(continued)*

Setting	Description	When to Use
Connect	One-time authentication takes place during object creation.	The client and server verify each other's identity during this initial request. There's a good chance a third party can break network security when using this mode because the client and server don't have any way to verify either packets or requests. The advantage to this method is that initial authentication places limits on what the user can do, and network traffic is kept to a minimum.
Default	Standard setting used by DCOM.	At the individual component level, this setting means the component uses the general DCOM setting. At the DCOM level, this setting means that DCOM as a whole uses whatever security the authentication method uses in general. For example, the default Windows 2000 security services uses Connect level authentication. The results of using this setting vary according to the authentication method used.
Packet	A minimal level of secure protection that encrypts the user's identity.	This is the first of three levels of truly secure DCOM communication settings. The sender's identity is encrypted and packaged with the packet. This means the receiver can verify the authenticity of the sender with every packet and greatly reduce the probability of third-party intrusion. This method also bloats the size of the packet, however, and can greatly increase DCOM-related network traffic. This setting represents the most reasonable level of protection for a network that allows outside access.
Packet Integrity	The sender's identity and a packet signature are encrypted as part of the packet.	Using these two forms of authentication ensures that the sender is authorized and that the packet hasn't been modified in any way. This method doesn't ensure that a third party hasn't read the packet, however, and it does increase network traffic over packet authentication. You only need to use this setting when the integrity of the data is absolutely essential, but you don't care who reads the packet.
Packet Privacy	Paranoid security for extreme situations.	In most cases, this is the paranoid level of security. Not only does the packet contain the sender's identity and a packet signature, but the packet itself is also encrypted to ensure a third party can't read it. This level of authentication greatly increases network traffic and can actually slow communications to a crawl when used on slower traffic media such as a dial-up connection. However, this is the level of authentication you need to ensure safe financial transactions and the transmittal of critical confidential information from one site to another.

A Look at Bindings

One of several things to look at for an easy performance boost on any network is the number and type of bindings in use. A binding is simply a connection between the operating system and the device driver that makes the protocol supported by the device driver active. Each binding in use by the server consumes processing cycles and generates network traffic. Avoid unused bindings because they use both processing cycles and network bandwidth without producing any benefit for the end user.

Finding out which bindings are in use on your server is easy. Right-click My Network Places, and then choose Properties. You see the Network And Dial-up Connections dialog box. Select Advanced Settings from the Advanced menu. You should see the Adapters And Bindings tab on the Advanced Settings dialog box shown in Figure 8-13.

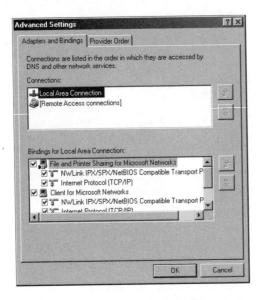

Figure 8-13. *The Adapters And Bindings tab of the Advanced Settings dialog box allows you to determine which bindings are in use and for what purpose.*

Notice that there are three things to look at on the Adapters And Bindings tab: the connection, the list of services, and the bindings. The connection you select determines which bindings are shown because the bindings are connection-dependent. Look in the Bindings For Local Area Connection list shown in Figure 8-13 and you see there are several services in this list. Each service requires one or more bindings to communicate with the client in a specific way. For example, Figure 8-13 shows that a client can use TCP/IP to access the File And Printer Sharing for Microsoft Networks service.

Let's assume, for the sake of argument, that all your clients have TCP/IP installed on them. In the case of the example shown in Figure 8-13, you save both network bandwidth and processing cycles by unchecking the IPX/SPX/NetBIOS option.

Another way to enhance performance using the features on the Adapters and Bindings tab is to change the order of the bindings. You may find that clients use TCP/IP to access the network more often than NetBIOS. Giving the prevalent protocol higher priority also boosts network performance for that protocol slightly because it has a higher priority for the server. You can reposition the protocols in the list by highlighting it, and then using the up and down arrows on the right side of the dialog box to move it up or down.

A Look at Providers

A provider allows one machine to access resources residing on another machine. There's one provider for each kind of network installed on your server. The order in which a machine accesses providers determines how fast it finds a given resource. You normally want to place the provider that the server needs to access most often at the top of the list of providers to search. This way the server is more likely to find what it needs with one search, rather than many. It takes some time to figure out the most commonly used provider—something you can get done using System Monitor.

Setting up the provider order is relatively easy. Right-click My Network Places, and then choose Properties. You see the Network And Dial-up Connections dialog box. Select Advanced Settings from the Advanced menu, and then click the Provider Order tab to display the dialog box shown in Figure 8-14. From the Provider Order tab, you can use the up and down arrows to reposition the providers.

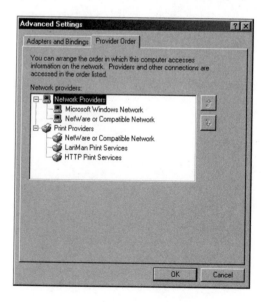

Figure 8-14. *The Provider Order tab determines the order in which Windows 2000 accesses resources on the network.*

Summary

Network bottlenecks can be one of the most complex areas of your network to tune and optimize. Not only do you have a host of interactions to worry about when locating the source of a potential performance problem, but you also need to worry about interactions during the tuning process. Since the entire network is connected and works as a single entity, the number and complexity of interactions that you need to deal with is no surprise.

For the most part, you find that network bottlenecks occur in three distinct places: the user, the hardware, and the network software. The user contributes to network bottlenecks by employing less than efficient methods of working and by using bandwidth-hungry software. The hardware you use contributes to network bandwidth problems in two ways. First, the hardware may not be tuned for optimum efficiency. Second, the hardware may not be of the highest quality or use the best drivers for support. Part of the hardware problem relates to the network topology you use because the topology places limits on the maximum performance that you can expect from the network as a whole. Finally, software contributes to the network bottleneck problem in two areas: application and operating system. Just trying to figure out which component is at fault can be a major problem. As a general rule, operating system problems tend to affect all applications running on the server, while application problems tend to greatly affect a small group of users for a single application.

The previous three chapters looked at specific areas of tuning on a large scale. Chapter 9 explores a part of the operating system that affects everything you do, but works at a much deeper level, Active Directory. We specifically look at how replication works and what you can do to make the process of replication faster. Every server on the network requires access to a current copy of Active Directory services, so tuning this element of Windows 2000 can mean big improvements in overall system performance.

Chapter 9
Microsoft Active Directory Services and Tuning

One of the challenges faced by network administrators of Microsoft Windows NT environments was the lack of an enterprise-class directory service. Finding resources wasn't very difficult under the Windows NT directory service in a small environment, such as a local area network (LAN)—the Network Neighborhood on a user's desktop did a sufficient job of locating folders, files, servers and even printers. The task of managing users and domains in these smaller environments was easy enough through User Manager for Domains. As the network grew, however, so did the challenge of managing these resources and the complex domain relationships that formed as part of the growth.

With the release of Microsoft Windows 2000 Server and Microsoft Active Directory services, administrators finally have a directory service that can handle the needs of an enterprise network, yet be scalable enough so network administrators with smaller networks can also take advantage of its powerful features. Deploying Active Directory services, however, can come at a cost. As you will see in our discovery of the rich features of Windows 2000, running a server as a domain controller and the overhead of replication traffic taxes both server and network resources.

In this chapter, we explore what you should be aware of when deploying Active Directory services. Because each installation and environment is different, we review performance issues you may be dealing with in a network scenario. For instance, network administrators of LANs don't face the same challenges that administrators of wide area networks (WANs) with multiple sites and numerous domains do, challenges such as the management of additional network devices (such as routers, dedicated lines, or firewalls) or Active Directory design issues, including global catalog server placement, replication and resource access.

Because Active Directory technology is new, I feel it's important that the first portion of the chapter cover Active Directory basics, such as terminology, structure, installation, and configuration. This gives you an opportunity to review not only your Active Directory knowledge, but also performance issues that may lie at the core of the directory service. For example, we discuss performance issues you encounter when upgrading from Windows NT directory service to Active Directory services, issues such as the need to run more robust servers to help accommodate the needs of Active Directory services. In the last few sections of the chapter, we review actual methods of performance tuning Active Directory services.

Active Directory Terminology and Structure

In this section of the chapter, we explore the terminology used to describe the objects that make up the directory service. We also review the structure of the directory tree. Understanding the terminology and structure of the directory service is imperative for anyone who wants to performance tune Active Directory services. If you were expected to diagnose a problem with your car, it is helpful for you to understand not only the fuel injection system, spark plugs and distributor cap, but also where each one is located in the car and how they're related to each other.

No matter what directory service you may be dealing with, there's a certain amount of complexity you face when contemplating the structure of the directory tree alone. The structure of a directory service is referred to as a *directory tree* because of the tree-like structure it eventually takes on once built. If you were to view the Active Directory architecture within a namespace, you would find that the directory tree has roots, branches, and leaves. The directory tree, along with other factors that we discuss later in the chapter, contributes to how well the directory service performs on your network. Once you understand the structure and terminology behind Active Directory services, you understand how each piece of the directory service fits in and how tuning each part affects the overall performance of Active Directory services.

Schema

When working with any type of directory service, you find a formal definition of the directory's information model and structure in the *schema*. The Active Directory schema contains definitions for the types of objects that can be stored in the directory service, all the attributes that are defined for these objects, and relationships between these objects. In addition to this, the schema also holds information regarding rules that control how hierarchical naming can take place within Active Directory services. When you install Active Directory services, it is populated with a default schema, which you can edit using the Active Directory Schema Manager snap-in for Manager Microsoft Management Console (MMC).

Object

An *object* consists of attributes that help describe a resource or entity created in the directory service. An application can be represented by an object, for example, and that object can have attributes that help describe the object. In the case of an object that describes a user, the attributes can include the user's first and last name, login ID, and office extension.

Scope

When dealing with directory services, you often hear the term *scope*. Scope refers to how large a particular directory service can grow in size. From the scope, you can tell how many and what types of objects you can potentially create within the directory.

Within a single directory, you can create objects that represent commonly used resources in a network. For example, you can create users, printers, files, file servers, and one or more domains. Active Directory services scales up to 1 million objects, a number that can easily accommodate the needs of most enterprise networks.

Namespace

Another term associated with directory services is *namespace*. All directory services are a namespace, as is Active Directory services. A namespace refers to a space within which you can resolve a name. A telephone book is a good example of how a namespace works. Say you need to look up the phone number for John Fortune. All you have to do is turn to the white pages and look up the last name Fortune, and then the first name, John; you eventually find the telephone number (as long as it's publicly listed). In the case of Active Directory services, the namespace resolves the name of an object to the object itself. In other words, when you search the directory for the file server FS1, the name resolves to the file server object FS1.

Real World

When searching for objects in Active Directory services, you're essentially asking the directory service to find the object and resolve the name of the object. This is where Active Directory performance really counts. When your users have to query (search) Active Directory services, they expect quick results. If users are looking for the file server resource named FS1, for instance, it doesn't do them any good if they have to watch an hourglass while the directory service is doing the search. Impression is everything for your users; if the network is slow, that points directly back to you. When developing an Active Directory design for your organization, take into account searches, additions, and deletions. Between a well-thought-out Active Directory design and other performance tuning done in the environment, it all adds up to a well-performing directory service. We cover ways to avoid lag time for directory services throughout the chapter.

Object Attributes within Active Directory Services

Unlike the objects that exist within the Windows NT directory service, Active Directory objects can contain detailed attributes about the object. The preceding example in the section discussing objects showed what the user object's attributes may contain. Part of Active Directory services' extensibility is the ability it gives you to create additional attributes for the objects available within the directory service. For example, you can create an attribute for the user object that stores the date a user started with the company. When you begin to partition your directory tree, you have to consider using global catalog to help speed up the searching of information located across multiple partitions. Along with this, you have to determine what attributes of each object are also to be stored as part of the global catalog. Therefore, you should create attributes that make the most sense when users need to search for an object using its attributes. If your directory service has objects with numerous additional attributes, these additional attributes affect overall performance of Active Directory services. The more attributes you have for objects, for example, the bigger the Active Directory database grows. The size of the database affects how long replication takes, and the performance of searches run against the directory service. The Active Directory database is a file called NTDS.DIT located in the %SYSTEMROOT%\winnt\ntds folder.

Container

A container is similar to an object in that it resides in the Active Directory tree and contains attributes. However, a container doesn't represent a single entity the way an object does. The container can contain groups of objects and other containers. Containers are a good way to group common objects together. For example, you can create a container that stores departmental printers.

Tree

The tree is the blueprint for the directory service. The tree describes the hierarchy of objects and containers of the directory service. The tree also illustrates where nodes and endpoints exist in the tree's structure. An object is considered an endpoint, while a container is a node.

Name

The term *name*, when used in the context of Active Directory services, simply refers to the name by which an object is identified in the directory tree. An object can have two kinds of names: distinguished and relative distinguished.

Distinguished Name

The distinguished name is used to identify the object, the domain it belongs to, and its exact location in the hierarchy. The following is a typical example that illustrates the distinguished name for a user.

/O=Internet/DC=com/DC=Microsoft/CN=Users/CN=John Fortune

The breakdown is as follows:

O=Internet Organization that the distinguished name belongs to is the Internet.

DC=Domain Component=com A distinguished name that's part of the Internet can have a domain component such as net, org, gov, edu, or the very popular com.

DC=Microsoft A distinguished name that can have multiple domain components. For example, because there are many divisions within the Microsoft Corporation, the user can be part of the domain component Microsoft and then part of the domain component Marketing. In that case, the distinguished name is:

/O=Internet/DC=com/DC=Microsoft/DC=Marketing/CN=Users/CN=John Fortune

CN=Users Most objects in the directory tree have a CN (common name). In the case of the preceding example, Users is the common name for this container.

CN=John Fortune The actual user object is identified as a common name.

Relative Distinguished Name

If you don't want to hassle with the distinguished name, an object in the directory tree can be identified by the relative distinguished name. In the preceding example, the relative distinguished name is CN=John Fortune. The limitation you face with the relative distinguished name is not knowing the context in which the object belongs. Within a container, two objects can't have the same relative distinguished name. For example, if a user is created in the Users container, you can't have two users identified by CN=John Fortune.

User Principal Name

When an administrator creates an object in Active Directory services, the directory service identifies the object by its distinguished name. However, this can be extremely cumbersome for users to work with. Having to memorize the fully distinguished name for your own user object and for the color printer located in human resources is difficult. For this reason, Active Directory services allows administrators to identify users by a principal name. The principal name for John Fortune can be *jo.fort@microsoft.com*. To simplify matters, a user can log in with the principal name instead of having to enter the distinguished name. All of us who've had to deal with sending electronic messages using X.400 addressing can appreciate the concept of user principal names. Besides, I don't think they make business cards that have enough space for a distinguished name!

Contiguous Name

If you look at the actual structure for Active Directory services, you see a structure that looks like a tree, branches and all. For this reason, the structure is referred to as a directory tree. Expand the entire directory and you see how the containers, and the objects that reside within those containers, tend to branch off in different directions. Individual branches consist of objects and containers that are combined hierarchically. By isolating any one of these branches, you can form what's known as a contiguous name, for example, marketing.microsoft.com.

Domain Tree

When designing your Active Directory environment, it is still necessary to create multiple domains within your organization. When you do so, you create what's known as a domain tree. The first thought that may cross your mind is establishing trust relationships between these multiple domains—trust relationships that you were hoping went away with Windows NT. Well, you can calm your fears. Although the concept of domains didn't vanish, the difficult part of administrating the trust relationships did.

When you create a domain tree, you create an environment where all the domains share a common schema: configuration and global catalog. The domain tree also forms a contiguous namespace. If the root of the tree is .com, for example, marketing.microsoft.com is the child domain of microsoft.com. Domains within a domain tree also form a trust relationship via transitive and bidirectional trust relationships. This translates to a user being able to be authenticated by any domain within the domain forest, which we'll explain in the next section. No longer does the need exist for an administrator to create an individual username for the user in each domain.

Note Although a trust relationship is established implicitly between two domains, it doesn't mean the user has rights to all the domains within the forest. Rights must be granted to the user by the administrator for each domain the user needs access to.

Forest

A forest is a set of domain trees that *do not* form a contiguous name (see Figure 9-1). All trees that make up a forest share some commonalties including schema, configuration, and global catalog. When you merge domains into a domain tree (see previous section "Domain Tree" for more information), the administrative overhead that comes with merging the domains goes away as a transitive trust relationship is formed between the domain trees.

Domain Forest

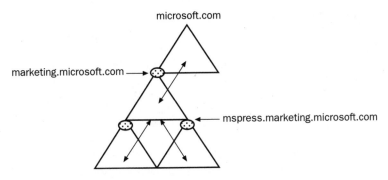

Figure 9-1. *Domain trees within a domain forest do not form a contiguous namespace.*

Site

For users who have administered Microsoft Exchange servers in the past, the term *site* isn't new to their vocabulary. In the case of Exchange, the site refers to a group of one or more Exchange servers that are all on the same LAN. In the world of Active Directory services, *site* is used in a similar sense. The site is one or more well-connected TCP/IP subnets (with *well-connected* meaning transferring data at 10 Mb/s or faster). When you isolate servers to be located within the same subnet, locating information in the directory service is quicker since machines in the same site are close to each other in network terms. Communication among machines in the site is reliable, fast, and efficient. Determining the local site at login time is easy because the user's workstation already knows what TCP/IP subnet it is on, and subnets translate directly to Active Directory sites. A well-thought-out Active Directory site can go a long way in reducing the amount of unnecessary traffic on the LAN and across WANs.

Partition

A partition is that portion of the directory tree that extends from the beginning point of a branch to the bottom of the tree, or to the edges of the new partition. Once a partition is created, replication occurs along partition lines. If you find that the current size of the directory tree is too large to manage, consider creating a partition to help ease administration of the Active Directory services. Creating a partition will decrease the number of objects you are managing at a single time.

Global Catalog

We briefly covered the scope of Active Directory services and how the scope directly relates to the number of objects that can be stored within the entire directory service. We also touched on the subject of partitions and how they help to further manage the directory service. It's simply impractical and extremely difficult for an administrator to manage a directory service that has objects in the hundreds of thousands if they're all residing within the same partition.

As soon as you create a partition, however, the issue of replicating directory service data between two partitions becomes a performance issue. Even though you created the partitions to help decrease the overall management of the tree, reduce the size of an individual Active Directory database, and cut the time it takes to replicate data, replication of information between the two partitions still needs to occur. In instances such as this where access to objects residing in one partition is needed by users residing in another partition, and the only method to share these objects is by replicating information, Active Directory services creates global catalogs as part of the replication process.

Global catalogs are populated with directory service data from two or more partitions. A global catalog helps reduce the time it takes users to look for objects in the directory tree by storing key attributes for each object. The default attributes for objects stored in the global catalog are defined by Microsoft, but are fully modifiable using the Active Directory Schema Manager snap-in. Therefore, administrators have the ability to select which attributes are actually stored in the global catalog. We have just completed reviewing the actual parts of the Active Directory services, and we will now discuss how you deploy the directory services for the Windows 2000 operating system.

Active Directory Deployment

No matter what part of your system you're performance tuning, extensive knowledge of how that portion of the system operates is a must. Up to this point, we reviewed various performance issues that you may face with Windows 2000 Server. These performance issues ranged from processor bottlenecks to file system caching. We covered performance topics that you can correct by tuning the operating system, and problems that are external to the OS, such as poor network cabling running through your building. In each case, time has been taken to introduce the topic and background information regarding the subject matter. Following the precedent of giving background material to the performance topic at hand, we now explore how Active Directory services is installed, configured, and managed. This gives you greater insight into the new directory service of Windows 2000.

Note Even if you're already familiar with installing Active Directory services, don't skip this section. Performance tuning and optimization topics are mentioned here because they relate to the installation and upgrade to Active Directory services.

Active Directory Installation

There are a few performance issues that you must take into account before installing Active Directory services. First, you have to determine how many domain controllers you need to configure for your environment. Remember, servers running as domain controllers are running the various domain controller services at a cost. Processor and disk are two resources that Active Directory services depends heavily on. So, configuring each server as a domain controller is out of the question and also an unnecessary overhead. On the other hand, having only a single domain controller leads to poor performance when users are querying the directory service for a particular resource. It can also lead to lag time when they're logging in, and poses a risk because you have no additional servers providing any form of fault tolerance specific to domain controller services.

Planning   There are two schools of thought on planning how many domain controllers to include in your environment. One is to always pick a conservative number when choosing how many domain controllers are to be part of your network. You can always choose a low number at first; then, if you find latency in Active Directory response time, you have the flexibility of making an existing server a domain controller. Once that server is configured as a domain controller, however, it can't be converted back to a stand-alone server. Another school of thought is to purposely plan extra from the onset. This provides the quickest end-user response time and provides capacity for growth.

Those of you coming from the world of Windows NT can appreciate the need for a balanced number of domain controllers. Windows NT directory services required a minimum of a Primary Domain Controller (PDC). For redundancy and performance, however, a Backup Domain Controller (BDC) was always recommended.

Note   Under Windows 2000 and Active Directory services, BDCs no longer exist. The domain consists of domain controllers, each domain controller is a peer to each other, thus forming the multi-master relationship under Active Directory services.

There's no number written in stone that states how many domain controllers you should have in proportion to the number of clients and servers. Each site, each environment is different. In one case, you may have clients who are continuously querying the directory service. In another, you may have clients who log in early in the mornings, open a few documents, and stay that way for the rest of the day. Another factor to consider is the number of applications that rely on Active Directory services. Each application can possibly query Active Directory services, or add, remove, change, or delete object information in the tree. Keep all these factors in mind when configuring the number of domain controllers on your network.

Another point to remember is your current network infrastructure and whether it has the ability to support Active Directory functions such as replication, directory searches, and integration of your applications with Active Directory services. In the section of this chapter called "Active Directory Performance Issues," we cover in some detail what Active Directory services requires of your network and some of the things you can do to optimize your infrastructure to support Active Directory services.

> **Note** Windows 2000 Servers can coexist in a Windows NT 3.x or 4.0 domain. You can configure a Windows 2000 Server to be either a PDC, BDC, or standalone server in a Windows NT domain. The same rule applies when configuring any server for the role of PDC or BDC. Take into consideration the amount of RAM installed in the server, disk space, and network interface card. All these factors contribute to the performance of the server in the role it plays in the domain. These configuration parameters are especially important if you're going to fully migrate from the Windows NT domain directory service to Active Directory services. Active Directory services requires a greater amount of RAM and a faster processor because the directory service plays a heavier role in your environment. For example, Active Directory services can replace existing Lightweight Directory Access Protocol (LDAP) directory services already configured on your network, thus increasing the size of the database. In addition, you have the flexibility of adding additional attributes and objects that never existed in the Windows NT world. Whenever upgrading an existing Windows NT 3.x or 4.0 server to Windows 2000 you should always review the Hardware Compatibility List to assure your existing hardware will be compatible with Windows 2000.

Upgrade Issues

If you're installing Active Directory services to an existing Windows NT 3.51 or 4.0 server domain controller, you need to select the upgrade path. Upgrading the server keeps your existing users and group information by converting the Security Account Manager (SAM) to the format needed by Active Directory services. When upgrading an existing server, keep in mind the disk space needed by the upgrade process because information from the Windows NT domain and Active Directory services is temporarily stored on the server.

It's also recommended that you don't upgrade directly from Windows 3.51 to Windows 2000 and Active Directory services. Limitations exist with Windows 3.51 that are corrected through the combination of Windows NT 4.0 and Windows NT 4.0 service packs. Administrators should first upgrade their servers to Windows NT 4.0 and the latest service pack, and then proceed with the actual upgrade process to Windows 2000 Server and Active Directory services. You should also note the current hardware configuration of your Windows NT 3.51 server because hardware requirements to run NT 3.51 and Windows 2000 Server have changed greatly. Always check the Hardware Compatibility List for Windows 2000 Server to assure your current hardware is compatible with Windows 2000 Server.

The Installation Process

Many important considerations must be addressed during the installation of Active Directory services. Since the installation process includes various steps, and since our focus is on performance tuning and optimization, it is important to refer to the various resources with additional details on installation. An abbreviated resource list for learning about the installation process includes Online Help, Microsoft Windows 2000 Server Resource Kit, the Microsoft Web site, and various other Web-based resources through third parties. If you've never installed Active Directory services, consult these resources in addition to the following steps to fully understand the installation process. Making a mistake during the process can be irreversible, and the only choice left is to reinstall Windows 2000 Server.

Installation During or After Setup?

Installation of Active Directory services can take place either during the Windows 2000 Server setup or after Windows 2000 Server has been installed and is up and running. If you have all the necessary information needed to configure Active Directory services before installing the operating system, you can easily install Active Directory services during the setup process. The information you need includes:

- The name of the domain the server is to join or the domain you create.
- The static IP address of the server.

Note   Windows 2000 setup attempts to assign an IP address to the server by "sniffing" what IP addresses it detects on the network. The setup program can also configure the server with a DHCP-assigned IP address. However, it's recommended that you configure servers with a static IP address for increased availability. If you configured a server for Web services, for example, you face problems when a new IP address is assigned to the server and the Domain Name System (DNS) server is unable to dynamically update its information.

- Either the information for the DNS server already configured on your network or configuration information if you plan on running DNS services along with Active Directory services on the same server.
- Network adapter type for the server in case Windows 2000 Server's plug and play feature fails to detect it.
- WINS Server's IP address. If you need to communicate with Windows NT servers that are not part of the domain and are not using DNS, you will need the addresses of valid WINS servers on the network.

We now go over the installation steps for installing and configuring Active Directory services through the Configure Your Server program. On new Windows 2000 Server installations, the Windows 2000 Configure Your Server program automatically launches upon logging in.

The first step in the Active Directory installation is to log in to the server with a user ID that has administrator privileges for the server and the domain. After this, the Configure Your Server program should appear on your desktop. If it fails to appear upon login, you can find it in the Administrative Tools program folder. Once the program is up and running, click the Active Directory icon located in the left pane of the dialog box (see Figure 9-2).

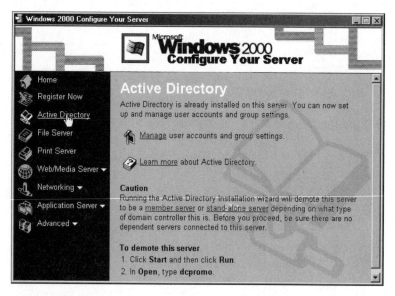

Figure 9-2. *The Configure Your Server program provides one method of installing Active Directory services on a server currently running Windows 2000.*

From the Configure Your Server program you can choose to install Active Directory services on any Windows 2000 Server. When installing Active Directory services, you have the option of either setting up the server as the first domain controller on your network or adding the server as an additional domain controller. Apart from adding the server as an additional controller, you also have the option of selecting:

- **A new child domain** If you plan to create a subdomain of a preexisting domain, select to create a new child domain. For example, the subdomain for microsoft.com can be marketing.microsoft.com.

- **Domain tree** Select this option to set up the domain as a member of a domain forest that was created earlier. The domain doesn't become a child domain, as is the case when you select Child Domain.

- **Domain forest**   If you want to create a new domain forest instead of joining one, select this option. The new domain that is created at the end of the process is the first domain tree in that forest.

At this point, you can begin the installation of Active Directory services by taking the following steps.

1. From the Configure Your Server program, click the Start The Active Directory wizard at the bottom of the window.

2. The Active Directory Installation wizard appears. Click Next.

3. At the next screen, select whether the server will be a domain controller for a new domain or an existing domain. For the purpose of this example, click Domain Controller For A New Domain. Click Next.

4. We want to create a new domain tree in the next selection. Click the option to do so and click Next.

5. You can select either to create or join a forest of domain trees. If you joined an existing forest, users in your domain can gain access to resources in other domain trees in the forest. Click Create A New Forest Of Domain Trees and click Next.

6. In the next screen, specify your full DNS name for the domain. An example of a full DNS name is microsoft.com. This would give you the user principal name of *jo.fort@microsoft.com*. Click Next.

7. Because Active Directory services are backward-compatible, it makes a NetBIOS name available to users running pre-Windows 2000 versions of the server or workstation. It is possible to change the default NetBIOS name generated by the Active Directory Installation wizard at this point. Click Next.

Note   Microsoft Windows 95, Windows 98, and Windows NT workstation clients work as Active Directory clients as long as you have the appropriate client services installed and configured on the machine. If not, they log in to the domain as if they were Windows NT directory services clients. Logging in as Windows NT directory services clients doesn't enable them to use the new Kerberos authentication protocol. The Kerberos authentication protocol is a more robust and secure network authentication protocol than Windows NT LAN Manager (NTLM) authentication protocol. The Kerberos protocol can also outperform NTLM because the application server no longer needs to connect to a domain controller for authentication. Plus, because of the transitive properties of domains created under Active Directory services, users can be authenticated by a domain controller in the domain, domain tree, or forest.

8. The next screen asks where the Active Directory database and log files should be stored. Make sure you select a location that has enough storage for a database that can easily grow into the hundreds of megabytes and beyond. Specify the location and click Next.

More Info You can find the installation files for Directory Services Client on the source CD-ROM for Windows 2000 Server. The files are located in the \Clients folder.

9. The advice for disk storage in the preceding More Info note applies to the location where the Sysvol folder is stored. The Sysvol folder is where copies of the domain's public files are stored. These files are shared by other controllers in the domain. The exact location for the Sysvol folder is %SYSTEMROOT%\SYSVOL.

10. If you have a properly configured DNS server specified in your TCP/IP settings, Active Directory services continue with the installation. Otherwise, you need to have Active Directory services install and configure DNS services for you, or you can choose to install it yourself. Select Yes to configure and install the DNS services. Click Next.

11. This next screen is critical if you want to ensure full compatibility with pre-Windows 2000 servers that may become part of this domain. If you have pre-Windows 2000 servers in this domain, click Permissions Compatible With Pre-Windows 2000 Servers. Otherwise, if you know that only Windows 2000 servers are to be part of this domain, click Permissions Compatible Only With Windows 2000 Servers. Click Next.

12. Specify the password you'll use for Active Directory restore mode and click Next.

13. A summary of your requested configuration settings is shown in the next screen. Review the settings and click Next. Click Back if you want to change something.

14. Active Directory services now begins to write these configuration settings to the server (see Figure 9-3). This can take a while. After Active Directory services is installed and configured, the setup completes the DNS portion of the installation.

15. Click Finish to complete Active Directory services installation and select to restart the computer.

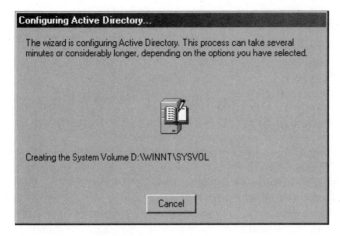

Figure 9-3.   *Active Directory Installation Wizard configuring the directory service.*

Active Directory Management

In the Windows NT world, the User Manager for Domains administration tool was the primary method for administrating users and groups under Windows NT. Even if you were administrating multiple trusted domains, User Manager was still your primary interface for domain management.

In Chapter 4, "Performance Monitoring in Microsoft Windows 2000," you learned of the various administrative tasks available using the Performance console with the System Monitor MMC snap-in. System Monitor is a good example of using a snap-in and its associated program. Remember, two of the benefits of the MMC are the capability to administer multiple services at the same time and to create custom MMCs for ease of administration. Active Directory services provides three snap-ins, each designed to administer one particular aspect of Active Directory services. This split in administrative tasks to individual snap-ins allows for a logical and structured approach to administrating Active Directory services. In the following sections, you learn about the MMC snap-ins that provide many administrative functions for a Windows 2000 network. These MMC snap-ins include Active Directory Users And Computers, Active Directory Sites And Services, and Active Directory Domains And Trusts.

Active Directory Users and Computers

For day-to-day administration of Active Directory services, this is where you find yourself most often. Through the Active Directory Users and Computers snap-in, you can manage objects such as users, groups, computers, and containers. You can modify the access control lists and group policies for objects and containers as well.

Active Directory Sites and Services

This snap-in plays an important role in administrating replication through the domain, domain tree, and forest. Replication contents may include the schema, configuration, and domain partitions. Through the Active Directory Sites and Services snap-in, you provide Active Directory services physical information about your network by creating sites. Active Directory then uses this information to determine how to replicate directory service data throughout the network. In addition to creating sites, servers, and subnets, you can also designate site links and site link bridges (see Figure 9-4).

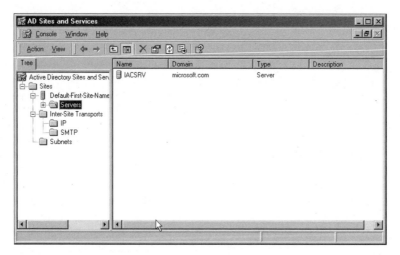

Figure 9-4. *The Active Directory Sites and Services MMC snap-in is an essential tool for managing Active Directory replication.*

Active Directory Domains and Trusts

For those of you who thought domain trust relationships went away with the addition of Active Directory services, I have some news for you—they didn't. However, there's some very good news. Creating and maintaining domain trust relationships are no longer the mammoth tasks they once were for two reasons. First is the transitive trust relationships that are established between two or more domains that are part of the same tree structure in Windows 2000. Second, through the use of trust relationships configured using the Active Directory Domains And Trusts snap-in, administrators can view any domain in the console tree and any child domain created as part of it. They can then easily establish, remove, or maintain trust relationships between each domain. The interface helps illustrate complex domain relationships in a logical and systematic way.

ADSI (Active Directory Service Interfaces)

We just covered the snap-ins for administering Active Directory services. These tools are the primary method through which you can add, delete, or modify information in the directory service using a graphical user interface. We also reviewed the user, domain, and site level administration possible through these snap-ins.

Windows 2000 provides many useful administrative tools in the various MMC snap-ins for Active Directory configuration. To reduce the number of repetitive administrative tasks in our lives, we can automate some of them. When we automate specific tasks, we are optimizing how we perform as administrators. Some administrators prefer to optimize all facets of the network, including individual administration. They not only want to optimize their environment, but also optimize how they get their work done. When adding a user to the domain, for example, there's more involved than just adding a user ID to the directory tree. Administrators must add the user to a group, create a home directory and computer account, and specify profile settings.

In this section, we explore the Active Directory Service Interfaces (ADSI). ADSI enables applications to interact with Active Directory services. For example, you can write an application that retrieves information from the directory service and, after further manipulation, adds that information to a Microsoft SQL Server 7.0 database. You can also write a script using VBScript to automate the task of making a global change to users' attributes in the directory tree.

Active Directory services isn't the only directory service that ADSI enables interaction with. Using ADSI, these same applications can interact with other directory services such as Netscape's Suitespot, NetWare NDS (Novell Directory Service), Windows NT 4.0, and many more.

Using the new ADSI API, developers can have their applications integrate with the Windows 2000 Server directory services, making this a much simpler task than it was with the Windows NT directory services. The following snippet of Microsoft Visual Basic code adds access control entry (ACE) permission to an object:

```
' Note: you must have the credentials to create objects.
Dim TheObject As IADs
Dim SecDes As IADsSecurityDescriptor
Dim SecDes As New SecurityDescriptor
Dim Dacl As New AccessControlList
Dim Ace As New AccessControlEntry
```

```
' Create an access control entry (ACE).
Ace.AccessMask = 0
Ace.AceType = 1
Ace.AceFlags = 1
Ace.Trustee = "cn=Groups,o=Microsoft"

' Add the ACE to the access control list (ACL).
Dacl.AceCount = 1
Dacl.AclRevision = 4
Dacl.AddAce Ace

' Set the ACL as the discretionary ACL (DACL) for the Security
' Descriptor object and use the DACL instead of the default.
SecDes.Revision = 1
SecDes.OwnerDefaulted = True
SecDes.GroupDefaulted = True
SecDes.DaclDefaulted = False
SecDes.SaclDefaulted = True
SecDes.DiscretionaryAcl = Dacl

' Attach the security descriptor to the ADSI object.
TheObject.Put "ntSecurityDescriptor", SecDes

' Commit the changes to the directory service.
TheObject.SetInfo

' Read the properties back in to the property cache.
TheObject.GetInfo

' Retrieve the SecurityDescriptor object.
Set SecDesc = TheObject.Get("ntSecurityDescriptor")
```

In addition to the ADSI API, developers can utilize the LDAP C API; however, it's only available for use with the C/C++ programming language. For backward-compatibility, Active Directory services also supports the Messaging Application Programming Interface (MAPI). You may be wondering why I mention Active Directory APIs in a book dealing with Windows 2000 performance tuning. Remember, performance tuning isn't just adjusting settings in the operating system or adding more memory to the server. Accomplishing tasks more efficiently or using the operating system's features, such as APIs, to their fullest is all part of performance tuning. The preceding code example uses the ADSI API to apply permission to an object. This task normally requires an administrator to first launch the program, find the user, and then shuffle through the permission settings. Using applications, you can search through and manipulate Active Directory services faster than it would take single person to do so. You can then take information extracted by the application and put it to use. You can take user's data, for example, and add it to a database you're building with the names of all employees who are up for a review. Each person can then be e-mailed when their review is scheduled. You just cut down on the time it takes a human to search through the directory service for this user and type the information into the database. Imagine having to do that for 1,000, 5,000, or even 10,000 users.

Active Directory Performance Issues

When dealing with a database server, you can easily notice when the server isn't performing up to par. Queries executed by users suffer increased lag times when responding. Updates to the database take an unnecessarily long time. Performance of the database over a set period may degrade. All these are legitimate performance issues that any DBA (database administrator) can recognize. Similarly, in this section of the chapter, we look at some common performance issues that you come across when deploying Active Directory services. Understanding when you have a true performance issue with Active Directory services can point you in the right direction when the cries come down from the user community that the network is slow!

Replication Issues

Replication issues may be the most prominent performance problem you have to deal with, particularly if you're in a WAN spanning multiple sites and multiple domains. Replication issues can be the most difficult to predict as they're commonly caused by poor network performance and not so much the result of a glitch with the directory service itself. For additional information on replication in the Active Directory environment, see the section entitled "Active Directory Replication" later in the chapter.

If you're replicating Active Directory data across a T1 to a global site, for instance, can you predict when traffic running across that T1 may pick up? Sure, you can schedule updates for a set time at night when you think traffic may have decreased; however, even that can be unpredictable or costly. The worst part about replication issues is that it's the user community that detects the problem first. They don't call the help desk to complain that their site's domain controllers are not being updated. Instead, they complain about what they perceive the problem to be: that they're not seeing a resource that should be there. As the network administrator, you need to be ahead of the game. Anticipating problems with replication by running checks at domain controllers, seeing if they're receiving updates, verifying site links, and making sure traffic is flowing smoothly between sites is part of the job. In the sections to follow, we address the measures you can take to ensure that data is being replicated on time throughout your network. A well-designed network and Active Directory design can help avoid many of these problems.

Directory Roaming

Earlier in the chapter, I mentioned the effect that poorly designed directory trees, domain trees, and domain forests can have on performance when users are searching through the directory. If you have a directory that contains hundreds of thousands of objects, just clicking on a portion of the tree produces lag time if a bottleneck exists in your network. Replication problems eventually become apparent to the user community; however, not as fast as lag time when they're trying to find a resource on the network. Problems such as these are what paint the wrong picture about you and the systems you're responsible for. Several factors can contribute to performance issues when just roaming the directory tree. These include poor network design, poor directory service design, and poor resource availability.

Poor Network Design

We cover this subject in more detail later in "Network Issues." Briefly here, network design is an enormous factor in how your environment responds to users' requests, no matter what system we may be discussing. For instance, a simple file request by a user can result in a slow response if the network is busy with additional traffic. The same issues you face with file and print requests, or lag time in your client/server applications responding, has an effect on how Active Directory services performs. Remember, when you interact with Active Directory services, you're essentially dealing with a database. And, as is the case with any database, response time depends on the design of the database and the network it runs on.

Poor Directory Service Design

I just mentioned how poor database design can affect the response of the directory tree when a user roams (queries) Active Directory. Database administrators understand that creating an index in the right place makes a world of a difference in query response time. They also understand that creating a table or tables without any consideration for how data is to be retrieved is asking for trouble.

One method to improve Active Directory performance specific to accessing objects is to create containers and objects in the most logical places. Creating a container where all printers for the entire company reside isn't the best design. If you know that a printer is only accessed on a departmental basis, and navigating through the tree to reach the single printer's container increases network traffic, you should create the printers in the container for each department. This way, users only need to browse through their own department container and not work their way up or down the tree just to find a printer to connect to.

Poor Resource Availability

At first, poor resource availability may sound a bit confusing. Basically, it points to several factors, including poor replication, as addressed earlier in "Replication Issues." When users roam the directory tree for a file and they don't see that resource the first time, their immediate reaction is to call you. Knowing that the resource is located in a secondary domain and that replication may be causing the problem, you instruct the user to try again later. The user does as you say; however, the resource fails to appear. The numerous attempts by the user not only leads to unnecessary network traffic load on the servers, but also frustration for the user. Combating one problem, such as replication, can lead to better performance for other factors, such as resource availability. As you can see, a number of factors contribute to poor resource availability. These include poor network design and Directory Service design, and may be identified by something as simple as finding a printer or as complex as locating a nearby domain. In any event, take time to carefully plan these various components of your network to improve the overall experience for users working with Active Directory services.

More Info   There are many sources that you can reference on detailed Active Directory design including Active Directory specifics such as domain design, site design, and OU (organizational unit) design. Many of these sources are available through Microsoft Press, online white papers, and third-party materials.

Active Directory Services and Applications

The goal at Microsoft was to create a directory service that not only served the purpose of Windows 2000 users, but also any user on the network. Active Directory Services was designed to be truly interoperable, enabling users from multiple platforms, including NetWare and UNIX, to connect to the directory tree. Based on this goal, it increases the role of Windows 2000 in your environment, and the resources needed at the server. Microsoft also understood the need to have authentication and directory service control at the application level, so it made numerous APIs available to developers, allowing them to create directory-enabled applications, directory-enabled management, and directory-enabled networks.

Increasing Performance of Active Directory-Enabled Applications

We already explored how applications can tie directly into Active Directory services in the section "ADSI (Active Directory Services Interface)." Now we cover what steps you can take to increase the performance of these directory-enabled applications. Before we do this, however, let's first understand what each type of application can do when interacting with Active Directory services.

Common Uses of Directory-Enabled Applications

- Locating user resources in the directory service
- Authenticating users for access to Windows 2000 services
- Creating interfaces for user-directed browsing
- Updating directory service schema with application-specific data definitions

Common Uses of Directory-Enabled Management

- Synchronizing directory service information between applications and Active Directory services

- Editing directory service system information
- Generating reports run against Active Directory services to extract information for further manipulation

Common Uses of Directory-Enabled Networks

- Enabling network resources' access to directory service to determine user privileges
- Publishing information about specific network resources
- Discovering network resources and determining policy directives about each resource

From this list of uses for each type of application, you see a heavy need to search the directory service for user-specific or resource-specific information. When developing applications and wanting to ensure optimal performance of the applications, you can do the following.

- **Search for objects using proprietary attributes**   Developers should recognize the advantage they gain by using Microsoft's proprietary objectCategory attribute for executing searches for an object using its class as the search criteria. The objectCategory attribute is indexed, unlike the objectClass attribute. Information in any database that's indexed helps increase the speed of searches done against the database.

- **Beware of the dialect used**   When working with Active Directory services, use the LDAP dialect, rather than the SQL dialect, unless you're working with applications writing/reading directly to a database such as SQL Server 7.0.

- **Search against indexed attributes whenever possible**   After reading this chapter, you may begin to think you've just read a chapter on performance tuning SQL Server 7.0 because of the number of times indexes have been mentioned. Well, I'm about to mention it once more. When writing queries against Active Directory services, you should write them against indexed attributes, particularly when using the OR term in the query. However, indexing doesn't increase performance if you have wildcards in the middle or beginning of a query string.

- **Use paging to save network resources**   When you write a query against a directory service, the results can possibly saturate the network and overload the client. Therefore, consider paging your results in order to decrease the burden on the network and the client.

- **Use global catalogs and domain directory efficiently**   Global catalogs (GCs) are designed to increase the response of searches made against Active Directory services. Therefore, in your code, don't forget to use GCs whenever appropriate (when the GC has the attribute you're searching for). If the GC doesn't have the attribute you're searching for, you can turn to the domain directory.

- **When searching, use the right names**   Earlier in the chapter, we explored how the CN (common name) is used as a naming attribute for most objects in the Active Directory tree. However, not all objects use this connotation; some objects, such as the OU (organizational unit), or DC (domain component), use different naming attributes. When developing applications to search for an object using the object's name as the search criteria, you should search against the naming attribute used for that object.

Other factors to consider when tuning your applications for increased performance against Active Directory services include setting the search scope, sorting the results of the search, and returning only attribute name parameters. Also, use the GUIDs of an object when referring to the object in the application. This enables the application to keep track of the object, even if it's renamed or moved.

We just reviewed a few of the things you can try to get the most out of your code. Practicing good coding techniques when writing applications against Active Directory services can go a long way to overall enhanced performance of your applications and Windows 2000 Servers.

Active Directory Replication

We already covered the basic architecture and mode of operations of Active Directory services in a Windows 2000 environment. Through the introduction of the Active Directory technology, we reviewed performance issues that you may come across during the installation and configuration process. Now we cover the topic of replication under Active Directory services. Replication plays a major role in directory service response and resource availability.

Windows NT Replication

In the Windows NT world, replication of directory service data could, at times, be a slow process. When you made a change in the NT Domain, you were making it directly to the security database, after which replication would have to occur so BDCs within the same domain were made aware of the changes. This form of replication was coined "master/slave" (see Figure 9-5). The PDC acts as the master and all BDCs are slaves to it. As soon as the master (PDC) gets updated with information, it then replicates this information to each slave (BDC). This approach was fine for smaller networks where all the servers were located within the same building or there was a high-speed connection between buildings. However, as soon as you began dealing with larger networks such as those with 10,000 or more users in a single or multiple master domain, directory service replication became a real issue.

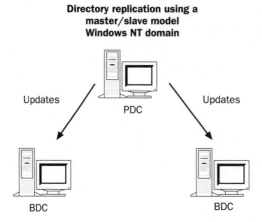

**Directory replication using a
master/slave model
Windows NT domain**

Updates PDC Updates

BDC BDC

Figure 9-5. *Windows NT replication using the master/slave method.*

On enterprise-wide networks, where BDCs can be located across a campus, country, or—in some cases—globally, the replication of data can take a few minutes or even hours depending on the number of servers and transportation media running between the server. There is nothing you can do to change how data is replicated, so administrators find themselves turning to structural changes. For example, if replication is occurring over large distances, such as an update across country, another domain can be created just so BDCs residing in one part of the country don't have to wait for an update from a PDC residing in another part of the country.

Another method of combating this replication problem in Windows NT is to increase the bandwidth between networks. Instead of a 56K line between sites, companies can run T1s, for example. Fortunately, the Windows NT replication model is replaced under Windows 2000 and Active Directory services. Replication still occurs, just in a different form. After all, that's the power of a distributed directory structure.

With Active Directory services, the entire approach of a master/slave replication method is thrown out. Instead, Active Directory services employs a method called multimaster replication.

Directory Replication through Multimaster Replication

As we saw in the case of Windows NT directory replication, the method a directory service uses to replicate information directly determines its usability, performance and, to some extent, its scalability. Network administrators are limited to how they can deploy the directory service, fearing latency in data replication will lead to further problems.

Because of the many problems with the Windows NT approach to directory service replication, Microsoft decided to offer multimaster replication in Active Directory services through Windows 2000. Multimaster replication is a more efficient method of replicating directory services data between domain controllers. When you update information to the Active Directory database, changes are automatically replicated to *all* other copies of the directory. No longer is there a waiting period where domain controllers must rely on a single domain controller to send down the changes to each server. When you add a user to the Active Directory tree, for example, domain controllers begin to get the change as soon as you click the Add button.

Note   Distance still makes a difference. Domain controllers that are physically closest to the domain controller where the actual Active Directory change takes place get updates faster than those domain controllers residing further away. This limitation is caused by how fast data can travel across media, not by a limitation in the replication method. We review replication latency directly related to network issues in greater detail in "Network Issues," later in chapter.

Multimaster replication is the core method of replicating information between domain controllers in an Active Directory environment (see Figure 9-6). However, multimaster replication isn't the only method by which directory service data is replicated. For example, changing passwords for a user is an everyday task all administrators do. Users may change the password themselves, or the administrator may have to do it for them. Either way, under Windows NT, the problem of the change not being replicated immediately was always present. A user could log off and then try logging back into the workstation, only to find that the new password wouldn't work. In fact, it's sporadic. Users can log in with the right password one time and then the next time they log back in, they have to revert to the old password. This all-too-common problem is due to replication under Windows NT. Not all BDCs in the domain received the update; thus, the sporadic behavior with the users' login.

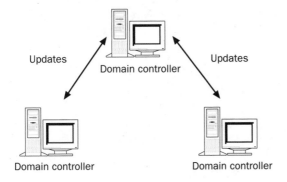

Figure 9-6.   *Replication within the Windows 2000 Active Directory environment.*

With updates that are considered urgent, such as changing a password or restricting someone from logging in, Active Directory services uses push replication instead of multimaster replication to get the changes replicated. The domain controller where the change took place initiates a push replication, causing the changes to be sent to its replication partners (other domain controllers on the network).

Keeping Track of Updates

With possibly hundreds or thousands of replications taking place at any one point in time, the domain controllers need a mechanism and system for keeping track of these updates. In the case of Windows NT, there was a central source for all updates, enabling Windows NT's directory service to use time stamps to keep track of updates. This way BDCs could tell that the latest updates being sent by PDC were the most up-to-date because they had a more recent time stamp than the copy of the database they currently had.

Active Directory services and its multimaster replication model, unlike other methods of replication, do not rely on time stamping as a primary means of tracking updates. Time stamping is notorious for possible discrepancies that can occur when you have more than one domain controller sending updates to the other domain controllers. As you will learn later in this section, time stamps are used only as a last resort for tracking updates.

Active Directory services instead uses an update sequence number (USN) to keep track of updates. Each domain controller stores a unique USN for each object in Active Directory services. Along with the USN, a version number is also stored. Each time a change is made to an object, the version number is incremented. The version number then acts as an indicator to the object that contains the most recent updates. The object also carries a USN and version number for each property. If the property is updated, a new USN is assigned and the version number is incremented.

During the replication process, a domain controller asks for updates from its replication partners (other domain controllers) for changes with a USN greater than what it currently has. The replication partner then searches through its directory for objects that have a USN number greater than what was presented to it by the computer requesting the changes. Even though version numbers are a good method for avoiding collisions during replication, Active Directory services can use the time stamp as a final resort for resolving any form of conflicts that can occur.

Replication between sites can be costly (see Figure 9-7). Depending on your environment's network topology, domain controllers handle replication differently. If you have servers residing within the same site (see the definition of *site* earlier in this chapter), such as a LAN, replication is considered to occur *intrasite*. If, on the other hand, you have servers in different sites, *intersite* replication is occurring. In the next three sections, we explore how replication occurs in each of the two scenarios (intrasite and intersite), and how overall performance of the network is affected by the method of replication adopted by the servers.

Replication between sites

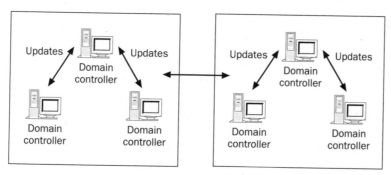

Figure 9-7. *Replication between sites can be costly, particularly over heavily used WAN lines such as a T1.*

Intrasite Replication

Intrasite replication occurs when you have replication between domains or domain controllers located in the same site. A site, in the terms of Active Directory services, is defined as a well-connected segment(s) with plentiful bandwidth. A good example of a site is a domain located within a LAN. The bandwidth between domain controllers is high (10 Mb/s or better). In this case, the controllers use RPC (remote procedure calls) over IP to send information back and forth; and because updates are occurring within the same site, replications occur more frequently. That's because Active Directory services doesn't have to bother with compressing information to make it more efficient when sending it across the network. In turn, this decreases the amount of work the CPU running on a domain controller has to perform.

Intersite Replication

You guessed it: Intersite replication occurs when you have Active Directory data being replicated between two or more sites. Usually, replication traffic between the sites is occurring over slower links, causing Active Directory services to adjust how it handles updates. Unlike intrasite replication, replication is scheduled and compressed. Compressing any replication data increases CPU usage for domain controllers. For this reason alone, you want to increase the processor speed of servers that take part in intersite replication.

Intersite replication occurs on a scheduled pull basis, configurable by the administrator. When a recipient domain controller requests an update, it does so by pulling updates from other domain controllers. Scheduling updates decreases replication traffic to set times. If you know that increased bandwidth is available between midnight and 4 A.M., you can schedule replication to occur only at those times. All replication settings between sites are done through the Active Directory Sites and Services snap-in.

Another way you can tune site replication to help stem traffic so it flows more efficiently is to designate only one domain controller in each site to handle replication traffic. This forces all replication traffic to go through a single server, commonly referred to as a bridgehead server, rather than others configured in the site. You can turn this to your benefit in many ways. For one, you don't have to increase the CPU speed on each domain controller, only the designated bridgehead server.

Global Active Directory Replication (Enterprise Networks)

There are some differences in how replication occurs between intersite replication and replication within an enterprise network. With replication information within an enterprise network, Active Directory services replicate the configuration and schema containers to all controllers. It also replicates the partial domain data to global catalog servers. The replication of configuration and schema information to *all* domain controllers generates additional network traffic on your network. You should anticipate this by preparing your network for the traffic. In the section that follows, we explore network configurations you must consider in order to allow the most efficient replication to take place.

Network Issues

In this chapter, we've seen that replication issues can be attributed to multiple factors, including directory service schema design, server configuration, and actual replication configuration settings. Later in the section "Active Directory Database Sizing and Fragmentation," we discuss one more factor: the Active Directory database size. In this section, we review Active Directory configurations that have a direct impact on the performance of the directory service.

Site Links

Site links in the context of Active Directory services represent an area where similar network connections exist. For example, two sites connected via IP create a WAN link. Site links are important when dealing with replication because they allow you to determine the cost factor for replicating between sites. Table 9-1 illustrates the cost of common site links that you may have. Notice that faster bandwidth connections have a lower cost associated with them.

Table 9-1. Possible Cost Values for Bandwidth Connections Utilized in the Replication Process

Site Link	Cost
Backbone Link	1
T1 to Backbone	200
56K Link (Frame Relay)	500
Branch Office Connection	1000
Continental Link (International Link)	5000

The preceding site links and costs are examples. You can associate the cost factor for each link you create to what you think makes the most sense. In the table, I set the Continental Link to 5000 mainly because I want to keep traffic limited. Having replication traffic cross over my Continental Link interferes with other network data, possibly slowing network performance experienced by my users.

Another method of performance tuning replication traffic between sites is to take advantage of the transitive properties of site links. If you have site A that's connected to site B, which in turn is connected to site C, you can use site B's link to replicate data from site A to site C. This can be done even if site B is lacking a domain controller. This is also illustrated in Figure 9-8. Recognizing site links that you can take advantage of for replicating traffic across your enterprise network can save network and server resources when you have to deploy Active Directory services throughout an enterprise-wide global network.

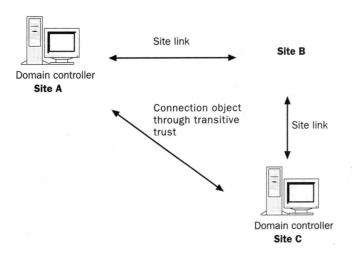

Figure 9-8.   *Active Directory replication and the transitive property of site links.*

Site Link Bridges

Site link bridges are used to connect site links together, and are treated as bridges and routers in a WAN. You create a site link bridge if you want to further control how traffic is replicated through site links. By disabling the transitive property between sites (site links are transitive by default), you can group site links together to form a site link bridge. Active Directory services then determines the most optimal intersite replication topology and schedule using cost values for each site link in the bridge you created.

Network Topology Considerations

When planning for Active Directory services, consider the following when designing your network topology:

- **Map out where sites, site links, and site bridges are to be placed**   Create a detailed map of where your sites exist and where the site links are to be placed. This helps you track possible routes for replication traffic, detect potential bottlenecks just by the routes that are to be configured, or discover if you're missing connections to sites that you should have.

- **Understand the bandwidth you have available to you**   When creating links between sites, or selecting where to route replication traffic through, find out what bandwidth you have available to you. Also take into consideration redundancy that may or may not exist between the sites. If your T1 goes down, do you have an alternate method of replicating traffic to the sites? Knowing the bandwidth you have also allows you to estimate costs for each link.

- **Create low-cost sites running over the highest speed backbones available**   Group your subnets into sites creating pockets of LAN bandwidth. This way, you can have traffic run over these low-cost, high-bandwidth connections. Grouping sites into subnets also allows you to regroup them more easily later.

- **Know when and where to create medium-cost and high-cost site links**   Medium-cost site links should be formed between sites that are connected with a comparable IP transport. These sites should exist between sites that need updates less frequently than low-cost sites (every four hours). High-cost site links should be formed between sites that require daily updates, but nothing more frequent than that. A high-cost site link normally links sites crossing a WAN link. Creating a high-cost site where you need frequent updates reduces the efficiency of your network links.

Active Directory Replication Traffic

We explored ways to reduce the time it takes to replicate Active Directory information between domain controllers. You need to balance your needs when designing your network to handle Active Directory traffic. Your immediate goal may be to increase directory service response and reduce the time it takes for replication to occur between domain controllers. After configuring Active Directory services to replicate data as fast as possible, you may find that you have too much data running across your network. If you find large amounts of data moving across your network, you can do a number of things to ensure efficiency. The first step is to understand how much bandwidth replication consumes. Sometimes, this is a result of an incorrect setting for the replication interval. A modification of the replication interval from the default of every 15 minutes to every 4 hours may remedy some of the bandwidth constraints.

After some analysis of the situation, you may find setting a higher interval between updates doesn't affect the way users get their work done in the way you had thought it would. Replication updates come at a cost, and you need to determine what cost you can live with.

Measuring Replication Traffic

Using the Windows 2000 Performance console or Network Monitor (for more information on installing and configuring Network Monitor see the Windows 2000 online help), you can measure Active Directory replication traffic. Under Performance Monitor, you must select the NTDS object and the following counters:

Note   DRA is the acronym for Directory Replication Agent.

- **DRA Inbound Bytes Total**   Total number of bytes replicated in. This is the sum of the number of uncompressed bytes (never compressed) and the number of compressed bytes (after compression).

- **DRA Inbound Bytes Not Compressed**   Number of bytes replicated that weren't compressed at the source (which typically implies they arrived from another directory system agent (DSA) in the same site).

- **DRA Inbound Bytes Compressed (Before Compression)**   Original size in bytes of inbound compressed replication data (size before compression).

- **DRA Inbound Bytes Compressed (After Compression)**   Compressed size in bytes of inbound compressed replication data (size after compression).

- **DRA Outbound Bytes Total**   Total number of bytes replicated out. This is the sum of the number of uncompressed bytes (never compressed) and the number of compressed bytes (after compression).

- **DRA Outbound Bytes Not Compressed**   Number of bytes replicated out that weren't compressed (which typically implies they were sent to DSAs in the same site, or that fewer than 50,000 bytes of replicated data were sent).

- **DRA Outbound Bytes Compressed (Before Compression)**   Original size in bytes of outbound compressed replication data (size before compression).

- **DRA Outbound Bytes Compressed (After Compression)**   Compressed size in bytes of outbound compressed replication data (size after compression).

To measure replication traffic using Network Monitor, you first have to edit the registry so the IP port used by the replication server is a static value and not dynamic. Run REGEDIT.EXE and navigate to the following location:

```
HKEY_LOCAL_MACHINE\SYSTEM \CurrentControlSet \Services\  NTDS \Parameters
\TCP/IP Port
```

You can edit the TCP/IP Port value to 1349 (decimal) or any other value that's available on your server. Next, you must configure Network Monitor to measure all traffic being sent to and from the port you set.

DNS Services

Active Directory services is tightly integrated with Domain Name Services (DNS). Active Directory services uses DNS as its locator service. A locator service is used to translate a name such as microsoft.com to an IP address such as 10.0.0.0.

> **Note** The question can be asked whether it's better to use Microsoft's DNS services or an alternative DNS product. Is there a compatibility or performance incentive with running Microsoft's DNS services in your environment? Compatibility-wise, there's no issue with running the Microsoft DNS service, because the Microsoft DNS service is an RFC (Request for Comment) and BIND (Berkeley Internet Name Domain) compliant implementation of DNS. The DNS available in Windows 2000 can be used by any platform and device including UNIX. However, there are some administration and performance incentives for using Microsoft's DNS service instead of some other DNS platform. Performance-wise, the Microsoft DNS service cuts down on the time it takes to replicate DNS information between servers. Windows 2000 DNS provides the ability to configure DNS data storage within Active Directory services. This allows DNS data to be replicated via Active Directory replication. This replication process is faster than Zone transfers, the transfer method found with other DNS servers. The DNS server service packaged with Windows 2000 Server supports Dynamic DNS (DDNS). If you have computers using DHCP and DNS for name resolution, administering those records in the DNS server is an extremely cumbersome task because the IP address for each computer can change from one day to the next. A dynamic DNS automatically updates its record information for each DHCP client on your network, cutting out of a lot of administrative overhead on your part. Lastly, Windows 2000 DNS supports Active Directory DNS replication, zone transfers, and many other features, providing the ability to integrate a Windows 2000 DNS into a legacy DNS structure or develop a new DNS structure using the new features in Windows 2000 DNS.

Active Directory Database Sizing and Fragmentation

Chapter 11 covers the topic of capacity planning. As we describe the real capacity planning goes hand in hand with performance tuning and optimization. Many times, network administrators find they can avoid performance problems with their network operating systems or network infrastructure if they go the extra mile and prepare for the natural growth that comes with any environment.

If you walk into your server room today and take a quick survey of the equipment, can you say for sure that you're prepared for the demands that may be asked of you and your environment? For example, management may decide to finally give the nod to a new project that's been awaiting approval for the last six months. This project calls for an entire new location to be brought up, and an additional 20 demanding users hired for the current location. Do you have enough room on your switch to handle the extra 20 people? Is your server configured so it can support users logging in from another location?

Whatever the answer may be, if you plan ahead, you have time to handle what may come your way. Active Directory services require the same attention to detail as your network environment does. It requires that you plan for the future. Simply creating the directory and your basic objects and containers isn't enough. Active Directory services is a powerful directory service; and, as with most powerful applications and tools, it requires well-thought-out planning. In the next section, we explore the Active Directory database and how it can affect the performance of the directory service.

Database Size

The size of the Active Directory database is governed by the number of objects in the database and the values assigned to those objects. If we take two Active Directory databases with the same number of objects created in the database, we find that the database whose objects have a greater number of values also has the larger database. A database with 500,000 users (with only mandatory attributes set) in Active Directory services takes about 1.8 GB. This is quite a large space occupied on your domain controllers and global catalog servers (GCs don't store the entire database). The number of objects and values for each object depends heavily on your needs.

As the network administrator, you need to keep the size of the database under control. Otherwise it has a negative effect on replication of the directory service, searches performed against the directory service, and overall administration. Other than keeping control of objects and the values for those objects, another method of keeping tabs on the size of the Active Directory database is to keep the database defragmented. Planned defragmentation requires a planned service outage, a thorough review of the size and state of the Active Directory services while optimizing its performance.

Database Defragmentation

Anyone who's been around Microsoft Exchange server understands that after a while, the Exchange Information Store requires maintenance, including possible defragmentation. Defragmentation is the process of taking data in the database and rearranging it—data that because of the method it was written to the database, may become fragmented over time.

A database that isn't defragmented causes longer wait times when reads occur against the server. In addition, it takes up additional space on your server's hard disk drives. You have the option of defragmenting the database either online or offline.

Online Defragmentation

Online defragmentation essentially means you can run the defragmentation process while the domain controller is still running the directory server service. Online defragmentation runs automatically through the Extensible Storage Engine (ESE) at a regular interval. While ESE runs the defragmentation process, users can be authenticated against the server. This means users can still use the server to search directory service information, and that the server can still take part in the replication process. However, online defragmentation does have a weak point. Space available for retrieval by running the defragmentation process isn't released to the file system. If disk space recovery is imperative because you're running low at the server, use offline defragmentation.

Offline Defragmentation

Offline defragmentation must be run in Directory Services Restore mode. To put the domain controller in Directory Services Restore mode, reboot the server and press the F8 key. This displays the boot options, one of which is the Directory Services Restore mode. The boot options available to you are:

- Safe Mode
- Safe Mode with Networking
- Safe Mode with Command Prompt
- Enable Boot Logging
- Enable VGA Mode
- Last Known Good Configuration
- Directory Services Restore Mode (Windows 2000 domain controllers only)
- Debugging Mode
- Boot Normally

Note After you select the Directory Services Restore Mode, the server boots into Windows 2000 Server; however, it no longer does domain controller duties until it's rebooted into normal mode. Prior to running in Directory Services Restore mode you should execute a full backup of your Active Directory database in case the repair is unsuccessful. You should also run a test restore to validate the backup before executing the Directory Services repair. Lastly, if you need to restore the database, make sure you restore the database prior to the time period when corruption occurred with the database.

The NTDSUTIL.EXE program, which you can find in the %SYSTEMROOT%\system32 folder, completes the defragmentation option and places the file NTDS.DIT in a separate folder. After the file has been created, you can move the defragmented file into the NTDS folder after archiving the original NTDS.DIT file. You should notice that you have additional free space on your server's hard drive and a database file reduced in size.

Monitoring Active Directory Activity

This chapter has covered the topic of performance tuning Active Directory services. A major portion of this topic has been on the subject of Active Directory replication. We explored factors that can cause directory replication performance to degrade, including

DNS services, network infrastructure, and poor directory services design. We also covered methods to correct replication problems. With any problem that can lead to performance issues, early detection and correction of the problem is always beneficial.

Unfortunately, you may not realize that you're having a problem with Active Directory replication until it's too late. There are no early warning signs that a domain controller is failing to receive directory updates other than the one where users fail to see objects that should be in the directory, or when an object is missing updated information. With any operating system tool that relies on a directory service for authentication, resource advertisement, resource management, and synchronization of the database is critical. We will now review a tool that enables network administrators to monitor the status of replication of the Active Directory services between domain controllers in order to verify each one is synchronized.

Repadmin is a powerful command line interface to Active Directory services. To begin using it, you must install the Windows 2000 Support Tools. You will find the setup file for the support tools on the source CD-ROM for Windows 2000 Server in the \SUPPORT\TOOLS folder. Simply launch the SET.EXE program to begin the installation of the support tools. After installing the tools, you will find the repadmin tool under \PROGRAM FILES\SUPPORT TOOLS.

Typing **repadmin** without any options displays the following:

```
Usage: repadmin <cmd> <args> [/u:{domain\\user}] [/pw:{password|*}]

Supported <cmd>s & args:
        /sync <Naming Context> <Dest DSA> <Source DSA UUID> [/force] [/async]
            [/full] [/addref] [/allsources]
        /syncall <Dest DSA> [<Naming Context>] [<flags>]
        /kcc [DSA] [/async]
        /bind [DSA]
        /propcheck <Naming Context> <Originating DSA Invocation ID>
            <Originating USN> [DSA from which to enumerate host DSAs]
        /getchanges NamingContext [SourceDSA] [/cookie:<file>]
        /getchanges NamingContext [DestDSA] SourceDSAObjectGuid
            [/verbose] [/statistics]

        /showreps [Naming Context] [DSA [Source DSA objectGuid]] [/verbose]
            [/unreplicated] [/nocache]
        /showvector <Naming Context> [DSA] [/nocache]
        /showmeta <Object DN> [DSA] [/nocache]
        /showtime <DS time value>
        /showmsg <Win32 error>
        /showism [<Transport DN>] [/verbose] (must be executed locally)
        /showsig [DSA]
```

```
/showconn [DSA] [Container DN | <DSA guid>] (default is local site)
/showcert [DSA]

/queue [DSA]
/failcache [DSA]
/showctx [DSA] [/nocache]
```

```
Note- <Dest DSA>, <Source DSA>, <DSA> : Names of the appropriate servers
      <Naming Context> is the Distinguished Name of the root of the NC
            Example: DC=My-Domain,DC=Microsoft,DC=Com
```

In this next example, we run the repadmin command against a domain controller to view what replicated values it currently has for the newly created user in the directory service. To troubleshoot replication problems correctly, you need to run this command against each domain controller on your network. The results allow you to compare the replicated values with each domain controller, enabling you to determine whether all domain controllers have the same replicated values that they should.

The user object, in this case, is FortuneJ, so the command line looks as follows:

```
repadmin /showmeta "CN=FortuneJ, OU=Finance, OU=Accounting, DC=EASTCOAST,
DC=microsoft, DC=com" ACC1
```

CN=FortuneJ is the username assigned to the user, OU=Finance is the organizational unit they belong to, and OU=Accounting is part of the hierarchy for the organizational unit. DC=EASTCOAST, DC=microsoft, and DC=com complete the fully qualified domain name for the object. The last part of the command specifies the domain controller against which you're running the command. Executing the above command line displays a result similar to:

Loc.USN	Originating DSA	Org.USN	Org.Date/Time	Ver	Attribute
1639	Luxembourg\EMBY	1639	1999-04-23 15:29.37	1	objectClass
1639	Luxembourg\EMBY	1639	1999-04-23 15:29.37	1	cn
1639	Luxembourg\EMBY	1639	1999-04-23 15:29.37	1	sn
1668	Luxembourg\EMBY	1668	1999-04-23 15:37.12	1	c
1668	Luxembourg\EMBY	1668	1999-04-23 15:37.12	1	l
1668	Luxembourg\EMBY	1668	1999-04-23 15:37.12	1	st
1706	Luxembourg\EMBY	1706	1999-04-23 15:38.39	1	title
1667	Luxembourg\EMBY	1667	1999-04-23 15:37.12	2	description
1668	Luxembourg\EMBY	1668	1999-04-23 15:37.12	1	postalCode
1667	Luxembourg\EMBY	1667	1999-04-23 15:37.12	1	physDevOffName
1667	Luxembourg\EMBY	1667	1999-04-23 15:37.12	1	telephoneNumber
1639	Luxembourg\EMBY	1639	1999-04-23 15:29.37	1	givenName
1639	Luxembourg\EMBY	1639	1999-04-23 15:29.37	1	instanceType
1639	Luxembourg\EMBY	1639	1999-04-23 15:29.37	1	whenCreated
1640	Luxembourg\EMBY	1640	1999-04-23 15:29.37	1	displayName

```
1668      Luxembourg\EMBY    1668  1999-04-23  15:37.12    1  streetAddress
1776      Luxembourg\EMBY    1776  1999-04-23  16:32.44    2  NTSecurityDescriptor
1851      Luxembourg\EMBY    1851  1999-04-23  17:06.09    2  wWWHomePage
1639      Luxembourg\EMBY    1639  1999-04-23  15:29.37    1  name
1649      Luxembourg\EMBY    1649  1999-04-23  15:29.38    3  userAccountControl
1640      Luxembourg\EMBY    1640  1999-04-23  15:29.37    1  codePage
1668      Luxembourg\EMBY    1668  1999-04-23  15:37.12    2  countryCode
1704      Luxembourg\EMBY    1704  1999-04-23  15:38.19    2  homeDirectory
1704      Luxembourg\EMBY    1704  1999-04-23  15:38.19    2  homeDrive
1641      Luxembourg\EMBY    1641  1999-04-23  15:29.37    2  dBCSPwd
1640      Luxembourg\EMBY    1640  1999-04-23  15:29.37    1  scriptPath
1640      Luxembourg\EMBY    1640  1999-04-23  15:29.37    1  logonHours
1640      Luxembourg\EMBY    1640  1999-04-23  15:29.37    1  userWorkstations
1641      Luxembourg\EMBY    1641  1999-04-23  15:29.37    2  unicodePwd
1641      Luxembourg\EMBY    1641  1999-04-23  15:29.37    2  ntPwdHistory
1641      Luxembourg\EMBY    1641  1999-04-23  15:29.37    2  pwdLastSet
1640      Luxembourg\EMBY    1640  1999-04-23  15:29.37    1  primaryGroupID
1643      Luxembourg\EMBY    1643  1999-04-23  15:29.37    1  supplmntlCredentials
1640      Luxembourg\EMBY    1640  1999-04-23  15:29.37    1  userParameters
1669      Luxembourg\EMBY    1669  1999-04-23  15:37.12    2  profilePath
1639      Luxembourg\EMBY    1639  1999-04-23  15:29.37    1  objectSid
1776      Luxembourg\EMBY    1776  1999-04-23  16:32.44    1  adminCount
1640      Luxembourg\EMBY    1640  1999-04-23  15:29.37    1  comment
1640      Luxembourg\EMBY    1640  1999-04-23  15:29.37    1  accountExpires
1641      Luxembourg\EMBY    1641  1999-04-23  15:29.37    2  lmPwdHistory
1639      Luxembourg\EMBY    1639  1999-04-23  15:29.37    1  sAMAccountName
1639      Luxembourg\EMBY    1639  1999-04-23  15:29.37    1  sAMAccountType
1639      Luxembourg\EMBY    1639  1999-04-23  15:29.37    1  userPrincipalName
1704      Luxembourg\EMBY    1704  1999-04-23  15:38.19    1  userSharedFolder
1639      Luxembourg\EMBY    1639  1999-04-23  15:29.37    1  objectCategory
1667      Luxembourg\EMBY    1667  1999-04-23  15:37.12    1  mail
1705      Luxembourg\EMBY    1705  1999-04-23  15:38.39    1  homePhone
```

Earlier in the chapter, I reviewed how Active Directory replication keeps track of what's being replicated via the USN number. As you can see from the preceding output, the USN number is clearly listed for each attribute listed in the far right column. For example, if you were to make a change to the homePhone attribute, the next time you ran the repadmin command, you'd find the USN number has increased by one and the time stamp has changed along with it.

Summary

There are many factors that can affect the performance of your Windows 2000 Server. Throughout this text, we've covered what we believe to be the most prevalent on a Windows 2000 Server and the environment it runs in. Active Directory services is one more factor for you to take into consideration as a cause behind Windows 2000 Server performance issues. In fact, Active Directory services performance should be high on your priority list because it's the one factor among all that we have explored in the book that your users have the most interaction with. The moment they log in to their workstations, they interact with the directory service. When they browse for a resource in the domain or a trusted domain, the response of Active Directory has a direct effect on the user's impression of the network.

In the chapter, we reviewed performance issues with Active Directory services that you must be aware of from the moment you install the directory service on your Windows 2000 Server—issues such as ensuring your server is configured correctly to handle the additional load generated by directory service requests, having the correct topology in your environment, and configuring the right connectors between sites for optimal replication. We also looked at the repadmin tool available for the purposes of monitoring replication between domains and checking to make sure domain controllers are receiving the correct updates on time.

Active Directory services has been designed as a fully extensible directory service, meaning it has a flexible development environment where administrators and developers can now interact with it more than they can with any other directory service. This also means the performance of the directory service does not only affect the experience of users interacting with the directory service at a file and print level, but also at the application level. Developers want to tie the directory service to the applications they write, heavily depending on Active Directory services. Thus, you need to make sure Active Directory services is tuned and optimized; otherwise, not only does overall network interaction suffer, but also the applications' performance.

Part IV
Other Tuning Considerations

Chapter 10
New Tuning Features in Microsoft Windows 2000

As the computing world gets more complex, so do the servers, applications, and operating systems used to create it. Microsoft Windows 2000 is the most complex operating system that the company has created to date. It contains many new security, management, and application support features. Microsoft has also included a wealth of new management products within this release, including some features that are specifically designed to help the network administrator performance tune the entire network.

This chapter takes you on a tour of the new operating system features that Microsoft has added to Windows 2000 that either help you tune the system or help you keep system resources under control. We'll look at how these features can help reduce your workload and the best ways to use them effectively. In many cases, we'll also look at how you can use the tools together in such a way that they augment each other's capabilities. Learning to use the tools, and then using them together, is important if you want to get the maximum potential from everything Microsoft has provided.

The first section of the chapter, "Disk Quotas and Accounting," looks at the newest methods for tracking what resources users request, how much of that resource they use, and finally, when the peak usage times are for individual users and the company as a whole. Tracking resource usage is great; being able to do something about excessive usage is something else. Windows 2000 provides you with a quota system that allows you to reduce the amount of resources that each user can access. This, in turn, should help to reduce resource usage on the network as a whole and hopefully keep you within the new equipment purchase guidelines set by management.

Windows 2000 includes a wealth of new features to make your Web site run more efficiently. First, there's a new job object that we'll explore in the "Web Site Support" section. This feature allows you to determine in advance how much processing time to allocate for certain Web site applications. By reducing the amount of processing power that processor-intensive applications use, you can ensure that all the applications on a Web server get their fair share of processing time. Bandwidth throttling is another feature that ensures that every application gets its fair share of server resources. Although this feature was actually added in Microsoft Windows NT 4 Option Pack, it's been improved for Windows 2000 and you should take another look at it. One of the new Web site monitoring features that we'll look at is process accounting. With process accounting, you can determine how much processing power each Web application is using and tune the applications as needed to allow for proper load balancing. Finally, HTTP compression allows an application to make use of the bandwidth that the server makes available to it. Not only does the application run more efficiently, but the client should also see faster downloads (this assumes the client is using a browser that's compatible for Windows 2000 compression methods such as Microsoft Internet Explorer versions 4 or 5).

It may seem, with the massive increases in computing power in recent years, that a single processor server should be enough for small networks. Microsoft has spent considerable time tuning Windows 2000, which will also net some increase in available computing power. However, Windows 2000 also contains a wealth of new features that require processing cycles so that the gains in processor performance and operating system feature-tuning have been offset by the added requirements of the new features. Any serious network installation will likely require more than one processor in the future. For this reason, Microsoft has also spent a great deal of time tuning the multiprocessor support in Windows 2000. We'll look at this feature in "Improved Multiprocessor Support."

One of the reasons you'll want to have a second processor on the server has to do with a new Windows 2000 feature called Intelligent Input/Output (IO) or I2O. This feature allows the operating system to offload some types of IO to a second processor, freeing the first processor for other processing needs. You definitely want to use I2O support in high-bandwidth applications such as groupware, network video, and certain types of client/server processing. We'll explore this feature in "I2O Support."

Windows 2000 provides you with two features for managing networks including Quality of Service (QoS) and Resource Reservation Protocol (RSVP). QoS ensures that applications receive a minimum level of network resources. In other words, the application may not receive anything more than it absolutely needs to run, but it will receive at least this minimal amount of support. RSVP allows an application to request the resources it needs to run from the server in advance, which ensures that you can manage resource usage and that the operating system can plan ahead for application needs. This is an especially important feature for resource-hungry applications such as multimedia or voice over LAN. We'll review both of these features in "Networking Needs."

Disk Quotas and Accounting

Any network administrator who's spent much time trying to keep resource usage, especially hard-drive usage, under control will appreciate one of the new additions to Windows 2000. The ability to both monitor and assign users hard-drive space quotas is a real plus for any administrator who wants to manage this resource. Of course, the biggest problem is figuring out just how much disk space is too much or too little.

Let's look at the mechanics of the quota system first. Right-click on any NTFS hard drive on your system, choose Properties from the Context menu, and then click the Quota tab. Figure 10-1 shows what the Quota tab looks like when disk quotas are active. Notice that the quota system is only enabled in this case—we haven't chosen to do anything if the quota is breached in any way. Normally, you choose to take some action when the quota is breached. The mildest solution is to create a log entry when users have reached their limit. You can also create a log entry if the user exceeds the warning limit. Of course, a much harsher, but probably more practical solution, is to deny any additional disk space once users have exceeded their limit.

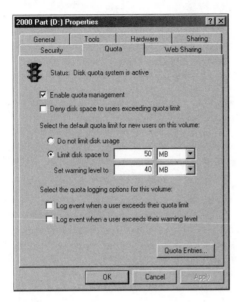

Figure 10-1. *The Quota tab of the disk Properties dialog box allows you to assign quotas to an NTFS hard drive as a whole.*

There are several problems with the quota settings shown in Figure 10-1. For one thing, the Quota tab specifies the default setting. Everyone, including the system, is held to that default, unless you tell the system to use some other limit. The way you specify quotas for users is to click the Quota Entries button. You'll see a Quota Entries window similar to the one shown in Figure 10-2. Notice that there's an Above Limit entry because we haven't accounted for the system's use of disk space.

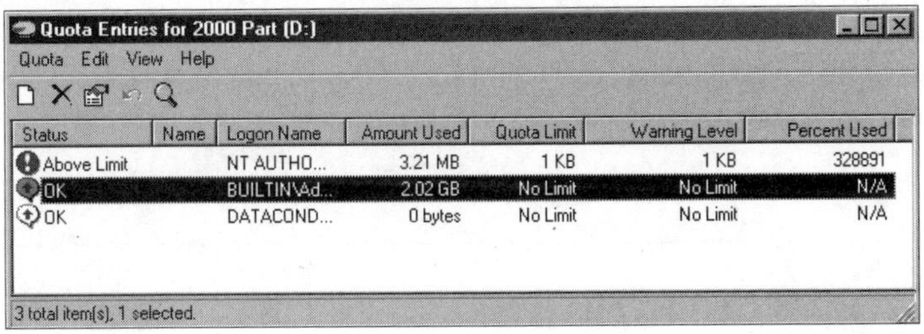

Status	Name	Logon Name	Amount Used	Quota Limit	Warning Level	Percent Used
Above Limit		NT AUTHO...	3.21 MB	1 KB	1 KB	328891
OK		BUILTIN\Ad...	2.02 GB	No Limit	No Limit	N/A
OK		DATACOND...	0 bytes	No Limit	No Limit	N/A

3 total item(s), 1 selected.

Figure 10-2. *The Quota Entries window shows you who has exceeded the limits set by the general quota settings.*

Double-clicking the entry shows that this isn't a normal log entry, but a method for changing the individual quota for this particular entity as shown in Figure 10-3. Since the operating system requires total access to the resources of the system, select the Do Not Limit Disk Usage option.

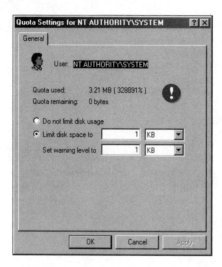

Figure 10-3. *The quota system allows you to create entries that give specific entities the ability to exceed the default disk quota.*

Unfortunately, the quota system is a disk-level-only tuning tool. In other words, although you can set a quota for the entire hard drive, you can't set it for individual directories. Users with a 50-MB quota can use any part of that quota on any part of the hard drive they can access. In short, you can't count on quotas alone to tune hard-drive usage on your server, but it's a very big step in the right direction.

So, how do you provide more complete control over the quota system? Of course, part of the solution is to ensure you check both Log Event When A User Exceeds Their Quota Limit and Log Event When A User Exceeds Their Warning Level check boxes. This means Windows 2000 provides an event log entry every time someone exceeds his or her warning level or quota limit, which allows you to react as appropriate to the situation. You'll also want to control where users spend their quota by ensuring that security is set up properly on the server. Finally, it's important to train users to use their quota wisely. Otherwise, you'll spend a lot of time answering questions about why the quota system is in place at all.

Web Site Support

Just in case you've been living in a cave on a desert island, the Internet has become one of the major development areas for companies today. According to many trade press articles, despite the amount of heavy development taking place, we haven't even begun the main event yet. The Internet will continue to grow at its current insane pace for quite some time to come. Just consider the fact that most of the companies on the Internet today were developed specifically for that environment. This past holiday season saw the first of the "brick and mortar" stores take their initial steps into the Internet pool. Suffice it to say that you're going to hear a lot about the Internet and you need to know how to manage a Web server.

This book isn't about Web servers or the Internet, but it is about tuning your server for optimum performance, which is something that even Web servers need to do. Windows 2000 provides four new Web site support options that help you in your quest for optimum Web server performance. The use of the job object allows you to keep CPU usage under control. Bandwidth throttling is just what you need to keep network resource usage under control. Process accounting allows you to monitor and tune individual applications. Finally, HTTP compression allows you to get more out of the available bandwidth on your system.

> **Note**   Some purists insist on pointing out that bandwidth throttling is part of the Microsoft Internet Information Server (IIS) portion of the Windows NT 4 Option Pack. While it's true this feature is available for Windows NT 4, it's also true it wasn't included as part of the original product and may be new to some of the companies that are upgrading to Windows 2000. Bandwidth throttling is new enough, crucial enough, and improved enough in Windows 2000 that we'll review it as a new feature in "Bandwidth Throttling." However, it's important to realize that this feature is available with your older Windows NT 4 servers if you're not upgrading all the servers in your company to Windows 2000 at once.

Now that you have some idea of how Web servers fit into the performance picture, let's look at these features in more detail. The following sections cover each of the new Web site support features in Windows 2000 in detail. We explore how you can use these features to get more out of your Web server and the network as a whole. In addition, you'll see how these features work equally well for a public Internet site, a local intranet, and a Virtual Private Network (VPN) that just happens to use the Internet as a transport mechanism.

Process Throttling

Process throttling is a long overdue feature for Windows 2000. It allows you to retain control over one of the most precious of server resources, processor cycles. A server can continue to operate, even with an errant, processor-hogging application, as long as it can maintain control over the CPU cycles that application uses. In fact, process throttling is more than just a tuning and optimization feature; it can help your server stay online when it would normally die from a buggy application.

The whole key to process throttling is the job object. Just like any other object under Windows 2000, job objects are designed to perform a specific service. In this case, they're designed to manage all the processes required to do a specific task, such as the backend processing for a Web application. (One typical example is an application that tracks the

CPU usage of a particular Web application.) You can name, secure, and share these objects, just as you do any other Windows 2000 object.

The concept of a job is actually quite old—it's not something Microsoft just dreamed up. Mainframes have used jobs for years to control when certain applications run, how many resources they're allocated, and what they're allowed to do. It's no small wonder that the concept of a job has appeared as part of Windows 2000 as well. Of course, Windows 2000 isn't using mainframe job technology as such; it's using something that's more compatible with the Microsoft Windows environment and the kinds of networks that Windows normally works with.

Creating a job should be familiar to anyone who's used Task Scheduler in the past. All you need to do to create a job is to add a special entry to the Scheduled Tasks folder, which invokes Task Scheduler at the proper time. Jobs use the familiar Windows NT AT command, which was used in the past to run scripts or applications at a specified time. Using a command line interface means job objects can get added to Task Scheduler in a variety of ways, including through Active Server Pages (ASP) and Windows Scripting Host (WSH). (Job objects do have human-readable names, contrary to the numbers that were assigned by the AT command in the past.)

Note Don't confuse job objects with regular scheduled tasks. They're very different kinds of objects and are treated differently by the system. Job objects have the same limits from a security perspective as tasks scheduled with the AT command in Windows NT. The main difference is that job objects are much easier to manage and have extended capabilities that allow you to do more than tasks would. In addition, you can upgrade a job object to a scheduled task by making modifications in the Scheduled Tasks folder. In short, job objects are new, but they're also an extension of existing technology.

Application developers can also add job objects (known in programmer terms as job kernel objects) directly to an application to make it better behaved using one of many new Windows 2000 API calls such as *CreateJobObject*. From a developer perspective, job objects solve another very important problem that has plagued Windows from day one. Suppose you start an application that starts other applications. These other applications are asked to do some quantity of work, and then terminate. The work these outside applications do affects the user's data, but not necessarily the main application.

So, what happens if the user decides about halfway through this whole processing scheme that there's no longer a need to complete the work? Getting the main application to stop isn't a problem because the user has direct control over it. However, there isn't a parent/child relationship between applications in Windows, so getting those ancillary applications to stop can be a problem. Unless the developer has some powerful magic up his or her sleeve, those background applications continue to run, even after the main application has stopped doing any processing or even terminated. That's where job objects come into play—they allow a developer to group applications together so that all the applications required to do a given task can be controlled as a group.

Job objects, no matter how they're created, essentially act as a container for a group of related processes. In other words, these processes are executing within a carefully controlled environment and don't know much about the world outside the container—at least not from certain perspectives. So, just what can a job object control? There are three overall job object areas as listed here.

- **Basic and extended services**   Controls which resources the processes within a job can access and how much of each service that the processes are allowed to use as a whole. If you want to create a special environment for a single process, you need to create a single job just for that process.

- **Basic UI**   Determines how processes within the job can interact with the user. A job can limit the processes it holds to no user interaction at all or allow complete freedom with regard to user interface access. The user interface restrictions also affect tasks that a process can normally do on the user's behalf such as logging off or shutting Windows down.

- **Security**   Allows the job object creator to determine the security restrictions of the processes within the job independently of what the process is normally allowed to do. This means you can create a custom security environment for every user of an application that meets the needs of that specific user. It also means you have very definite control over how processes access the resources on a machine. For example, you may allow registry access, but that access can be limited to a very small subset of keys within the registry.

As you can see, job objects are a very powerful addition to Windows 2000. However, they still have a few limitations you need to know about. For one thing, deleting a job doesn't terminate the processes within the job. All that deleting the job does is prevent the job from accepting any new processes, which means that eventually the job and the processes cease to exist. Fortunately, there are special Windows API calls that allow a developer to terminate all the processes within a job before the job itself is deleted. This means you still have control over process deletion, but this control must be added to the main application as a feature.

Job objects also provide process accounting. Unlike the counters provided by System Monitor, however, a developer can't extend the job object counters. This means that process accounting within a job object is limited to what the job object provides by default and the additional special purpose counters that a developer may add to the process. In short, job objects do allow you to account for the performance of processes without any special programming, but the statistics you can expect are limited to those that the job object collects by default. Table 10-1 shows the kinds of accounting information you can expect from a job object if you request the basic job object statistics. There are other kinds of statistics available for other job object features. You can request I/O statistics for your job object, for example, but it requires special handling to do so. The I/O statistics include information such as the number of bytes read and written by all the processes within the job object.

Tip   As a general rule, you can assume that all job object counters refer to the statistics for all processes within the job as a whole. In other words, the counters reflect the job's performance in most cases; not the performance of individual processes within that job. However, Windows 2000 also tracks the performance of the individual processes within the job.

Table 10-1.   Basic Job Object Accounting Summary

Job Object Statistic	Description
Pages/Sec	Tracks the total number of page faults that all processes within this job have created. This counter is most helpful in tracking the job's memory usage, especially in handling large memory requests.
Process Count - Active	Specifies the total number of active processes within the job. A process must be performing some work (not in an idle state) to count as active. This counter is a basic indicator of the job's ability to use multitasking successfully.
Process Count - Terminated	Reflects the total number of processes that the operating system has killed within the job because the process exceeded any limit value. (It's not certain whether this statistic also reflects the number of processes killed for other reasons, such as the developer issuing a *TerminateJobObject* API call to terminate them.) You should view this counter as an indicator that the job isn't set up correctly or that there are errant processes within the job that require update.
Process Count - Total	Specifies the total number of processes, active or not, within the job. This counter helps you understand how many processes the job will typically generate under a specific set of circumstances.
This Period mSec - Kernel Mode	Tracks the same kind of information as the Total mSec - Kernel Mode counter. However, the developer can reset this particular counter using certain programming calls. In other words, you can use this counter to document the time required to do a certain part of the task, rather than complete the task as a whole. This counter is most useful in helping you track the job's operating services load for a specific portion of the processing cycle.
This Period mSec - Processor	This statistic tracks the same kind of information as the Total mSec - Processor counter. Like the This Period mSec - Kernel Mode counter, this counter can be reset. This counter is most useful in helping you track a job's load on the processor as a whole for a specific portion of the processing cycle.
This Period mSec - User Mode	This statistic tracks the same kind of information as the Total mSec - User Mode counter. Like the This Period mSec - Kernel Mode counter, this counter can be reset. This counter is most useful in helping you track the job's internal processing requirements for a specific portion of the processing cycle.
Total mSec - Kernel Mode	Tells how much user mode time (in milliseconds) that all the processes in a job have used. Kernel mode time is the time spent interacting with the operating system in some way and usually requires operating at the kernel's level of security. This counter is most useful in helping you track the job's operating services load.

(continued)

Table 10-1. *(continued)*

Job Object Statistic	Description
Total mSec - Processor	Tells how much processor time (in milliseconds) that all of the processes within a job have used. This includes both active and terminated processes, along with processes that have completed a given task. This counter is most useful in determining the total processor cost of running a job in a given set of circumstances.
Total mSec - User Mode	Tells how much user mode time (in milliseconds) that all the processes in a job have used. User mode time is the time spent actually performing user-specified tasks at the user's level of security. This counter is most useful in helping you track the job's internal processing requirements.

Job objects also appear in System Monitor using the same counters that you use with any process. The difference is that the processes within the job appear with the job name prepended to the process name, followed by a slash. If you have a job named My Job and it contained Notepad as one of the jobs, for example, the process appears in System Monitor as My Job/Notepad. You can set up counters to track all the processes within the job as a whole, or to track individual processes within the job.

Depending on how the job object is created and what abilities a developer adds to custom applications, a job object can also provide you with notifications. For example, it's possible for a job object to provide you with notification when all the processes within the job have completed their task. You can also get a notification if one or more of the processes in the job exceed their CPU time limit. In many cases, you don't care about the notifications that job objects can provide—a job may fall into the start and forget category. However, it's still nice to know that the capability of tracking the job through notifications exists.

You can also set process throttling at the Web-site level. In other words, because a Web site is really just a process running under Windows, you can encapsulate the Web site within a job and control its use of CPU resources. We'll look at this aspect of process throttling as part of the bandwidth throttling discussion in the following section.

Bandwidth Throttling

One of the network resources Web applications can really chew up is bandwidth. Just think about the amount of bandwidth that streaming audio can consume today or that voice over IP (VOIP) applications will require in the future. (A single pulse code, modulation-encoded VOIP conversation consumes about 64 Kb/s of network bandwidth.) Now, multiply that number by all the people on your network and you can see why bandwidth throttling is an important Windows 2000 feature. A network typically requires enough bandwidth to handle the constant flow of data on the network, plus a little extra bandwidth to handle surges in data.

Note Any statistics in this section are for example purposes only. For instance, it's possible to compress a VOIP signal down to 32 Kb/s if the user is willing to live with some distortion. Some developers have also noted that about 56 percent of all voice conversation is dead time. A future specification may define some way of reducing voice bandwidth requirements by transmitting only the data and leaving out the dead time. These solutions are in the future, however, so we'll concentrate on the actual bandwidth requirements for a telephone quality signal today.

At present, Windows 2000 provides two levels of bandwidth throttling. The first is at the server level, while the second is at the individual sites. You adjust the bandwidth setting using the Microsoft Internet Information Services MMC snap-in shown in Figure 10-4. Notice that this figure shows a typical server with the three default sites you need to worry about (one FTP site and two Web sites). Even though we're using a generic setup for discussion purposes, the information presented applies to any Web site setup.

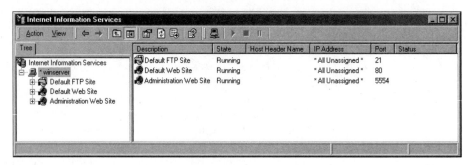

Figure 10-4. *The Internet Information Services MMC snap-in allows you to configure the sites supported by your server, including bandwidth throttling.*

Setting bandwidth throttling at the server level is really a way of ensuring that intranet usage of the Web server doesn't conflict with other local area needs. You don't need this setting for a dedicated Web server with access to the outside world in most cases (unless your ISP requires you to set up some type of bandwidth maximum at the server level). You enable and set bandwidth throttling at the server level by right-clicking the Computer icon, and then choosing Properties from the Context menu. You find bandwidth throttling on the Internet Information Services tab shown in Figure 10-5. Notice that this server has bandwidth throttling enabled and that Internet Information Services (IIS) is limited to 1 Mb/s of network bandwidth as a whole.

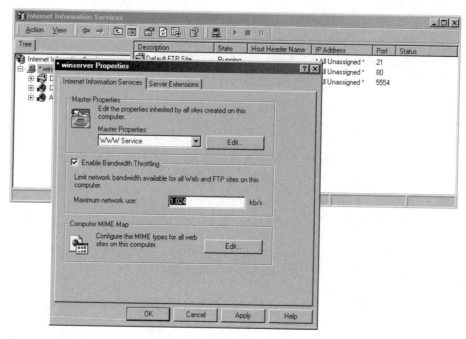

Figure 10-5. *The server level of bandwidth throttling affects all Web and FTP sites supported by that server.*

Although you can certainly limit bandwidth usage at the server level, it's far more common to limit it at the site level. Using site-level bandwidth throttling allows you to control the amount of bandwidth that a particular site uses without limiting the server's bandwidth use as a whole. To set an individual site's bandwidth limitation, right-click the site icon, and then choose Properties from the Context menu. Choose the Performance tab and you'll see a dialog box like the one shown in Figure 10-6. Notice that this dialog box contains options to set both bandwidth and process throttling. (For a discussion of process throttling, see the previous section of the chapter.)

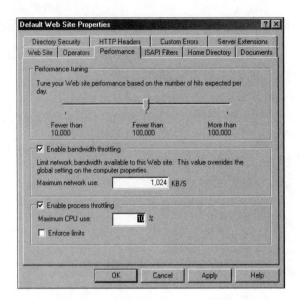

Figure 10-6. *The Performance tab of a Web site's Properties dialog box allows you to set both bandwidth and process throttling.*

The bandwidth throttling setting affects only the Web site in question. You can't set bandwidth throttling for an FTP site. It's also important to note that bandwidth throttling at the site level overrides the server level setting, even if the site-level setting is higher than the server-level setting. So, you can't count on the site-level setting to help you distribute a bandwidth allocation set at the server level.

Let's look at the process throttling setting in a little more detail. Checking this option alone creates an event entry every time the processes for a given Web site exceed the limits you set. If you want Windows 2000 to do something about a process that exceeds the limit, check the Enforce Limits option as well. So, what happens if an application exceeds the limits? There are actually three levels of consequences and the one invoked depends on how far the errant application has exceeded its threshold.

- **Level 1**   The application is allowed to continue running, but IIS places an entry in the event log notifying the network administrator of the problem. If the problem builds slowly enough and the network administrator checks the event log often enough, the network administrator can fix the problem by increasing the site's Maximum CPU use setting, or by stopping and starting the Web site.

- **Level 2**   When the application reaches the 150 percent level, its priority is set to idle. In short, the application isn't allowed to run unless the server is completely idle. IIS also makes another entry in the event log.

- **Level 3**   If the server isn't doing anything, it's possible that an application can reach the 200 percent level of usage. When this happens, the application is stopped and not allowed to run at all. IIS writes another event log entry informing the network administrator about the problem.

So, how do these levels work? CPU usage is based on a 24-hour day. Every 24 hours, every site is given a new piece of the CPU pie. So, if you set the CPU percentage to 10 percent, the site is allowed to use 2.4 hours of CPU time to handle out-of-process applications. When these applications exceed the threshold and are either set to idle or stopped completely, the change only lasts for the remainder of the 24-hour period. As soon as the 24 hours elapse, everything returns to normal and the applications begin to run again. So, if you're having a problem with a particular site, you don't need to do anything but set process throttling. The site automatically receives its fair share of processing time every 24 hours. It's also good to know that Web site operators can't change this setting—this is a network-administrator-only setting.

Tip   If you decide to set process throttling, you'll also want to change the timeout settings for any out-of-process applications. For example, the default timeout value for Common Gateway Interface (CGI) applications is five minutes. If a CGI application fails, IIS waits five minutes before it terminates the thread. The entire time is counted against the application's quota, so it's important to terminate threads as soon as you're certain processing can't proceed. You can change the various timeouts that IIS provides by right-clicking the computer icon in the Internet Information Services snap-in, and then choosing Properties. On the Internet Information Services tab, select WWW Service in the Master Properties drop-down list. Click Edit and you'll see a WWW Service Master Properties dialog box. Click the Home Directory tab. Click Configuration and you'll see an Application Configuration dialog box. The App Options and Process Options tabs of this dialog box allow you to set the various timeout values.

Process Accounting

As Web servers grow in complexity and more companies embrace the Internet as a way of conducting business, it becomes more important to know exactly how the server's resources are being used. We explored methods of ensuring that applications only use a specific amount of processing power in previous sections of the chapter. What happens, however, if you only want a detailed log of how CPU cycles get used? Process accounting is the answer to this question. It's an extension to the current W3C log file format that allows you to monitor CPU resources as well as other Web site statistics such as which user requested what resource. The fact that this new statistic is part of the Web site log means you get fairly intense data about application resource usage that you can use as part of the tuning process. You can also use this information to troubleshoot errant applications and even discover some of the activity of crackers (unusually high resource usage with an application that doesn't normally need it is one indicator that the user wasn't just working with that application).

There are some process-accounting limitations you need to be aware of. Process accounting doesn't track individual applications; only the total CPU usage required to answer a request is tracked. As a result, you see the sum of all applications used to answer a request. In addition, process accounting only monitors out-of-process applications. You see the results of using a CGI script, but not an in-process application such as an ISAPI extension. This feature is only available for Web sites—you can't track CPU usage for your FTP site. Finally, you must use the W3C extended log file format to use this feature.

Tip   One of the ways you can use process accounting is to determine if a Web site requires process throttling. A single Web site that uses a high amount of CPU cycles deprives other Web sites of the resources they require to perform well. Although this may not be a big issue on an intranet, it's going to be an issue for a public Web site, especially if you host more than one Web site from a single server.

Enabling Process Accounting

Now that we've looked at what process accounting can do for you and what you need to do to use it, let's talk about using it. Getting process accounting set up on your server is relatively easy. All you need to do is set up new logging properties for the W3C logging format because this is an extension of that format. The following steps get you started.

Planning   Before you add process accounting to your log file, it's important to determine which counters you'll actually need to monitor. In addition, look at other log entries to ensure that they're actually important to the data you want to collect about a Web site. Remember that we're trying to tune the entire server. Because the log files can get large rather quickly with just the default settings, adding more information makes the situation worse. You'll want to ensure you collect enough information, without needlessly using disk space collecting too much.

1. Right-click the Web site icon you want to add process accounting to, and then choose Properties from the Context menu. (Remember that process accounting is only available on Web sites.) Click the Web Site tab. The Web Site Properties dialog box will be similar to the one shown in Figure 10-7.

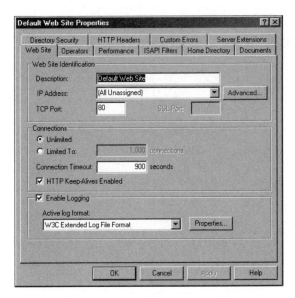

Figure 10-7.   *General logging options on the Web Site tab of the Web Site Properties dialog box.*

2.   Check the Enable Logging option. Choose W3C Extended Log File Format in the Active Log Format drop-down list. At this point, your server is set up to log events in the correct log file format.

3.   Click Properties and then choose the Extended Properties tab. You'll see an Extended Logging Properties dialog box similar to the one shown in Figure 10-8. Notice that there are quite a few counters you can include in the log file that measure various Web application performance issues. Scroll down the list of extended logging options until you see the Process Accounting entry.

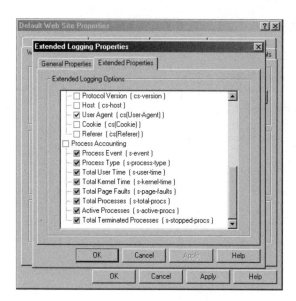

Figure 10-8. *The Extended Logging Properties dialog box allows you to choose which Process Accounting counters you want to include in the log file.*

4. Check the Process Accounting entry, and then check any of the counters you want to include in the log file. Uncheck any counters you don't need in the log file.

5. Click OK twice to make the change permanent.

Understanding the Log Entries

If you enabled process accounting using the procedure just described, your Web server is now generating process accounting information for one or more sites. Although this information is nice to have, it's not very useful if you don't know what it means. Table 10-2 contains a list of the various process accounting-specific log file entries and what they mean.

Table 10-2.   Process Accounting-Specific W3C Log File Entry Definitions

Field Name	Description
Process Event	The Web server can detect and record various types of process events for you. These process events include site starts, stops, and pauses, administrator-defined periodic log entries, reset interval start, reset interval end, reset interval change, logging interval changes, new event log starts, and various types of priority changes.
Process Type	Indicates the kind of process that triggered a log entry. Default process types include CGI, Application, and All.
Total User Time	Shows the total amount of time the process spent in user mode, in seconds. Remember that this setting doesn't show the amount of time spent working with a single process, but with the request as a whole. Most user mode time is spent at the user's security level taking care of user requirements.
Total Kernel Time	Shows the total amount of time the process spent in kernel mode, in seconds. Remember that this setting doesn't show the amount of time spent working with a single process, but with the request as a whole. Kernel mode reflects the amount of time the process spent performing special operating system functions at the kernel's security level (in most cases).
Total Page Faults	Defines the number of memory requests that resulted in a page fault. A page fault occurs every time the required data is on disk, rather than in memory.
Total Processes	Indicates the total number of CGI and other out-of-process applications created during the current interval. (An interval is normally 24 hours.)
Active Processes	Indicates the number of CGI and other out-of-process applications that are currently executing. An active application is one that has resources allocated and uses processor cycles to do some type of work.
Total Terminated Processes	Shows the number of processes that the Web server stopped during the current interval because they exceeded 200 percent of the CPU usage threshold level set by process throttling.

HTTP Compression

The Internet is about speed. Getting data from one place to another as quickly as possible is the main goal. Conserving bandwidth while transmitting the data is just as important, in some cases, as getting the data to the client. IIS provides a feature called HTTP compression. Data is compressed as requested and stored in a temporary compression directory. The client receives requested data faster because the data is compressed so fewer bits need to travel across the wire. Even if you add in the compression and decompression times, the time saved can be substantial. More importantly, bandwidth is conserved.

There are actually two levels of compression supported by IIS. A Web server can compress static files alone, or compress both static files and applications. When IIS receives a request for a certain file, it checks to see if the browser has included the compression-enabled flag within the HTTP request header. If so, IIS looks in the temporary compression directory, sees if the file is already there in compressed format, and sends the file if found. If not, IIS locates the file on disk and compresses it before sending it to the requestor.

IIS also compresses static files with dynamic content. In this case, however, the file isn't stored in the compressed-file directory. Otherwise, the Web server isn't forced to recreate the dynamic data for each requestor. In short, files with dynamic data still benefit from HTTP compression, but not nearly as much as files that are pure static data.

All compressed files are given a date of 1 January 1997 to ensure that they don't get cached anywhere such as proxy servers or the user's machine. The main reason for this restriction is to ensure that browsers that don't support compression don't get a compressed copy of the file. Of course, this limitation also counteracts some of the time savings of HTTP compression because it forces the browser to request the data each time it's needed.

> **Tip** HTTP compression isn't always the answer to Web server performance needs. If your Web site serves a lot of dynamic content, memory is low, and the processor is already overloaded (an average of 80 percent processor time or more), HTTP compression may actually cost more time than it saves. It's also important to consider the percentage of visitors to your Web site that can use the compressed files because the server needs to compress the files whether one site or a million sites request the file. You want to consider this option carefully because the benefits of using it in the right situation are very high, but the costs of using it in the wrong environment are equally high.

There are quite a few factors to consider when using HTTP compression, such as its effect on the processor usage of your server. Before you can make any kind of determination about the effect of this particular feature, however, you need to enable it on the server. The following steps show you how to enable HTTP compression within IIS. Once you complete these steps, you should use a performance monitor on your server to see what effect the option has. You also want to survey users to see what type of performance they're seeing. No matter what you do, the processor needs to work harder, if for no other reason than it is able to respond faster to user requests.

1. Right-click the Computer icon in the Internet Information Services snap-in, and then choose Properties.

2. On the Internet Information Services tab, select WWW Service in the Master Properties drop-down list.

3. Click Edit and you'll see a WWW Service Master Properties dialog box. Choose the Service tab, which looks like Figure 10-9. This is where we choose the kind of compression used for a single Web site. IIS forces you to configure each Web site separately because not every Web site requires the HTTP compression feature.

4. Choose a Web site from the drop-down list box. IIS always starts out with the Default Web Site, but you can choose from any Web site on the server.

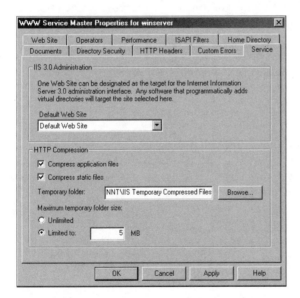

Figure 10-9.   *The Service tab of the WWW Service Master Properties dialog box allows you to set HTTP compression options for a Web site.*

5. Check Compress Application Files if you want to compress the applications you send to the client site. Notice that the application files don't provide a temporary directory because they aren't cached.

6. Check Compress Static Files if you want to compress static content. This option offers the largest potential gain when using HTTP compression on a Web site, so you normally want to check this option. You also need to choose a compressed folder location, although the default location works fine in most cases. (It's always a good idea to place the temporary compressed file folder on your fastest drive to reduce the amount of time required to handle this process.)

7. Select a size for the temporary (compressed file) directory. This is one area where you'll have to spend some time figuring out how much space to allocate. There's also an Unlimited option, but that's an invitation to disaster if you run a Web site with any amount of content.

8. Click OK to complete the process.

Improved Multiprocessor Support

There was a time when you could expect decent performance out of a single-processor server, but that's not really the case any longer (unless you have very low expectations for the load your server will carry). If you only used a server to provide file and printing support, it might be able to cope with today's complex computing environment, but how many servers provide print and file services alone? Even a small company is likely to require the server to provide database and perhaps proxy services beyond the typical print and file services. Servers are required to handle a lot of situations they didn't handle in the past—even the older mundane tasks are becoming more complex. In short, most servers require more than one processor if you want them to handle anything more than a print and file service load.

That's one of the reasons Microsoft has spent considerable time tuning multiprocessor support in Windows 2000. You'll notice within a very short time that tasks get distributed more evenly across both processors, and that the processors share system resources such as memory better. All you need to do to confirm this is to watch a multiprocessor server under a load using System Monitor for a while. You'll notice that while all the processors have busy and slack times that don't necessarily coincide, they all receive about the same level of application load. The ability to balance a load between all the available servers makes Windows 2000 better able to fully use all the resources a server has to provide.

Optimization of the server's processing load is only a first step; Windows 2000 also provides better scalability. Depending on which server product you choose, Windows 2000 supports 1-, 2-, 4-, 16-, and 32-way processing. The additional processors help a single server to scale in situations that would normally require more than one server, which should reduce the operational costs of your network.

The more processors you add, the more users the server can support—within limits. It's important to keep both memory and hard-drive space in mind as you add more processors to a server (one that accepts additional processors at least). Adding more processors to a server generally means you have to add memory as well. (Whether you have to add hard-drive space depends on how much room you have right now.) A server that contains 32 processors isn't going to provide you much in the way of added performance if the server only contains 512 MB of RAM or a 9-GB hard drive. You must match the number of installed processors to the amount of RAM and hard-drive space the system has installed.

Multiprocessing Myths Exposed

There's a misconception when it comes to working with a multiprocessing system. A two-processor system doesn't necessarily work twice as fast as a single-processor system. There are a lot of factors that affect the actual performance that you see. A two-processor system incurs more housekeeping traffic, for instance, which reduces the efficiency of both processors. In addition, you now have two processors fighting over bus bandwidth. When you consider all the tricks vendors currently employ on single-processor systems to help peripherals keep up with the processor, you have to wonder how well that same bus supports two or more processors.

A few people may tell you that the maximum performance boost for a two-processor system is twice the speed of a single processor system. They use simple logic that says that two processors should perform twice as fast as one. In some rare situations, you'll find that a two-processor system can actually exceed twice the speed of a single-processor system. The reason is simple: Because the server can handle requests faster, there's a smaller backlog of requests that the server has to track and maintain a list of. The two-processor system can appear to run more than twice as fast because it gets rid of some of the inefficiencies of a single-processor system. Does this always happen? More than likely it's a rare event that occurs when the single-processor system was overloaded in the first place.

There are some rules you can use when working with multiprocessor systems. From a performance perspective, a two-processor system that has enough memory and hard-drive space should perform at least 1.8 times as fast as a single-processor system. If you're not getting that 1.8-performance boost, you need to ask if there are other bottlenecks that are keeping performance low. Whether you actually get the two times or more performance that some vendors tell you that you'll get depends on what kinds of applications you're running and how the server is configured. A system that chugs away at a few processor-intensive tasks all day long is unlikely to see a two times performance increase. It's more likely that you'll see a performance gain in the 1.5 to 1.8 range.

Reconfiguring Your Server for Multiprocessor Support

There's a chance, however small, that your multiprocessor machine may have been recognized as a single processor machine during setup. One of the easiest ways to check for this problem is to right-click the task bar, and then choose Task Manager from the Context menu. Click the Performance tab, and then select CPU History and then One Graph Per CPU from the View menu to set the view to display a performance graph for each of the CPUs that Windows 2000 recognizes. If you have a two-processor system, you should see two CPU Usage History windows like the ones shown in Figure 10-10. If everything is working correctly, the two graphs show slightly different performance curves—proving there are two CPUs and that both are working.

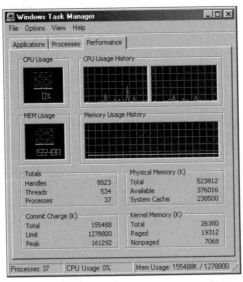

Figure 10-10. *A two-processor machine displays two CPU Usage History windows in Task Manager.*

If you don't get these results, it means something is wrong and you need to determine why multiprocessor support didn't get installed. In many cases, the only problem is one of detection. For whatever reason, the Windows 2000 Setup program didn't recognize the two (or more) processors in your server. Of course, this problem occurs if you install a second processor after Windows 2000 is installed. Unlike other kinds of machine additions, installing another processor requires some manual labor on your part. The following procedure shows you how to add multiprocessor support to your server.

1. Right-click My Computer, and then choose Properties from the Context menu. Select the Hardware tab, which looks like Figure 10-11.

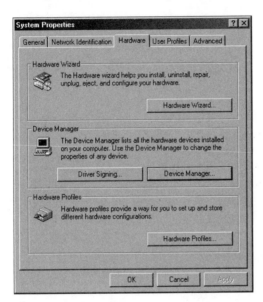

Figure 10-11.   *The Hardware tab of the System Properties dialog box allows you to manage your system's hardware setup.*

2. Click Device Manager. Click the plus (+) sign next to the Computer icon. You'll see a display similar to the one shown in Figure 10-12. Notice that I've highlighted the MPS Multiprocessor PC entry. The example server has this entry because it already has multiprocessor support installed. If your machine doesn't have multiprocessor support installed, you see another entry such as Standard PC or MPS Uniprocessor PC.

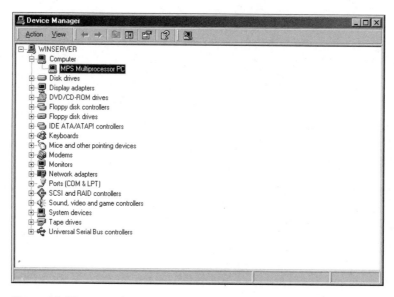

Figure 10-12. *A multiprocessor PC always includes the word* Multiprocessor *in the model name.*

3.   Right-click the computer model object (MPS Multiprocessor PC in Figure 10-12), and then choose Properties from the Context menu. Click the Driver tab as shown in Figure 10-13. Note that Figure 10-13 shows what this dialog box looks like if you already have multiprocessor support installed on the server.

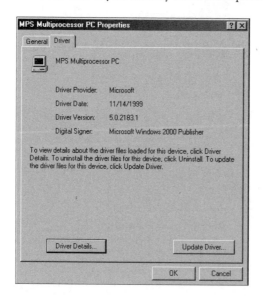

Figure 10-13. *You need to choose the Driver tab to update the multiprocessing support for your server.*

4. Click Update Driver. You'll see an Upgrade Device Driver wizard dialog box.

5. Click Next. You'll see an Install Hardware Device Drivers dialog box.

6. Choose the Display A List Of The Known Drivers For This Device So That I Can Choose A Specific Driver option, and then click Next.

7. Select the Show All Hardware Of This Device Class option. You'll see a Select A Device Driver dialog box like the one shown in Figure 10-14. Notice that there are only two multiprocessor PC options to choose from in this list.

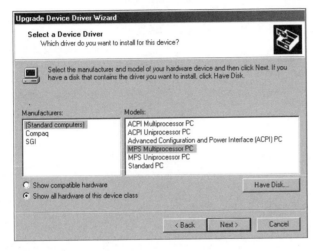

Figure 10-14. *There are only two Microsoft-supplied multiprocessor device drivers supplied for Windows 2000.*

Caution   You must choose the correct multiprocessor device driver for your machine in Step 7. Otherwise, when you reboot your machine to complete the installation process, it may freeze and refuse to work. Even though you can theoretically recover from this problem by reverting to the previously known good hardware configuration during boot, experience shows that this is rarely the case. You literally get one chance to do this step correctly.

Tip   You can also click Have Disk if your motherboard vendor provides a special multiprocessor PC driver for Windows 2000. Many vendors will supply this device driver once Windows 2000 has been on the market for a while. Using a vendor-supplied device driver normally allows you to use more of the motherboard's features and can enhance system performance. Always use a vendor-supplied, Windows 2000-specific, multiprocessor device driver when available. Never use a multiprocessor Windows NT device driver intended for use with Windows 2000—it won't work.

8. Click Next twice, and then click Finish. Windows 2000 installs the support required to support multiple processors on your server. You'll need to restart
your machine to complete the process (Windows 2000 will likely ask you to
perform this step).

I2O Support

Imagine, for a moment, that you have two processors in your server. One of these processors takes care of the client's computational needs, while the second takes care of any
I/O needs. With Windows 2000 you get precisely this kind of support. Intelligent Input/
Output or I2O is all about balancing system requests by allowing each server in a two-
(or more) processor system to handle one part of the client's processing needs. In the
past, Windows placed most of the processing load on a single server. That one server
needed to handle both the computational and I/O needs of the client. Today, the load is
divided, with the second processor handing the I/O requirement. The result is better
application performance in many cases.

Overview of the I2O Standard

The I2O standard is more than a new acronym for Windows 2000, however; it's also a
new I/O standard and processing technology that Intel is championing. Let's talk first about
the standards part of the equation. Today, if an operating system vendor wants to support a piece of hardware, it has to ask the hardware vendor to write a driver for the device.
Once the driver is written, beta testers must test the driver to ensure it works with the
hardware. If not, both the operating system vendor and the hardware vendor must work
together to fix the problems and submit the new version of the driver to the beta testers.
In short, the testing and update of drivers is a time-consuming process that occurs every
time the hardware vendor introduces new equipment or the operating system vendor
updates the operating system.

Life isn't very good for the network administrator either. Even if the operating system
vendor creates generic drivers that work with the majority of hardware using a specific
chipset, as Microsoft does, there's little chance the driver maximizes the potential performance of the hardware. In addition, it's very likely the driver has small interaction
problems with the hardware. If the user waits for the hardware vendor to write a driver,
the deployment of a new version of the operating system may be delayed several months,
giving competitors an edge in the upgrade cycle.

The I2O specification seeks to solve this problem in a manner that looks very much like
the Windows hardware abstraction layer (HAL). Hardware vendors can write a device
driver for their hardware that conforms to the I2O specification. The driver will provide
information in a very specific way and the operating system will be able to rely on its
output. Likewise, the operating system vendor will include I2O support in the operating
system. This means that any I2O device driver will be able to talk to the operating sys-

tem. The device driver is operating-system independent and the operating system vendor gains instant access to a multitude of hardware devices. The benefits for the network administrator are obvious too. Now you can get the full performance benefits of a piece of hardware without having to track which operating system the requisite drivers are written for.

More Info   You can find out more about the I2O bus at Intel's Web site at *http:// www.intel.com/design/iio/i2osig.htm*. There's also an I2O SIG that you can visit for information about the specification at *http://www.i2osig.org/*. Interestingly enough, this Web site also provides a fairly substantial list of vendors who are making or plan to make I2O compatible hardware and software. You can also learn about the top 150 hardware standards that Microsoft supports and which versions of Windows support them at *http://msdn.microsoft.com/standards/top150/ hardware.asp*. This site provides a brief description of the standards and normally tells you where you can go for additional standards information.

Tip   Microsoft has created I2O drivers for Windows NT so you can get the benefits of using I2O in that environment as well. You can download these drivers at *http://www.microsoft.com/NTServer/nts/downloads/other/NTI2O/nti2o_list.asp*.

Overview of the I2O Processor

The I2O standard doesn't stop with device drivers. Intel is also proposing a special processor to address high-performance server I/O needs. Currently, I/O is managed by the main processor, which steals processing cycles away from computing tasks. Even with two processors and Microsoft's new technique for offloading some of the I/O requests to the second processor, you're still giving up at least part of a processor to I/O needs. Intel's I2O processor would allow most I/O requests to take place without any interaction by the main processor.

To get a better idea of how this works, consider how a file server works. With current technology, an I/O request arrives from the client and waits until the processor has time to handle it. Once the processor does have time to handle the I/O request, it must ask the hard drive for the location of the data, and then transfer that data to memory. Once the data is in memory, it's transferred to the NIC, and finally sent back to the client. Offloading this time-consuming task to a specialty processor makes sense because it allows the processor to continue working on processor-intensive tasks without interruption.

There are other ways that I2O affects the computing scene. For example, the main processor uses main memory and the system's bus to transfer data to the client. The I2O processor, on the other hand, has its own internal memory, so data requests never even touch main memory. In addition, because the processor directly interacts with the hardware, the system's main bus is relieved of at least some data traffic (although the actual amount of relief on the main bus is uncertain).

Hard drives would benefit in two other ways from I2O, at least given the right conditions. RAID drives currently require you to install a proprietary controller and require the host processor to service I/O requests. In addition, the processor is responsible for compressing and decompressing data on the RAID drive as the client performs reads and writes. Using an I2O processor allows the RAID drive to maintain a more independent existence. (There are, of course, other solutions to this problem such as the storage area networks (SANs) we talked about in "Working with Storage Area Networks (SANs)" in Chapter 7.) In addition, using an I2O processor allows backups to take place in the background without the help of the main processor. Normally, tape backup is restricted to off-peak hours right now because of the processing requirement. Using an I2O processor means real-time backup can become a reality.

Networking Needs

Our last performance-enhancement topic is the network. The days of the independent PC are long gone; everything is connected today. That means network performance is the one item every administrator can relate to. It doesn't matter what applications you're running and what you plan to do with your system—you have a network of some type today and you want it to run at its top efficiency.

The following sections look at two new Windows 2000 features that make the dream of an efficient network a little closer to reality. In the first section we look at the issue of connection quality. QoS is designed to address the issue of network applications getting enough bandwidth to do a good job the first time, rather than having the user ask for a repeat performance. One of the ways to ensure that your application, especially high-bandwidth applications such as voice, run as anticipated, is to reserve the resources in advance. RSVP allows the application and system to interact in such a way that the application knows in advance whether it can run at the expected performance level, and the operating system can reserve the required resources so other applications don't use them.

Working with Quality of Service (QoS) Settings

For some network administrators the concept of QoS is easy enough to understand, but very hard to put into concrete terms. Think of the network as a pipe filled with water that everyone needs to live. Everyone on this pipeline has a spigot and can open the spigot to get water as needed. Now, if everyone takes only what is needed and doesn't hoard water, the pipeline should be able to provide for everyone's needs.

Unfortunately, as in real life, if something's in limited supply, someone is almost certainly going to hoard. QoS is like the water conservation officer who goes around and turns off the spigots of water hoarders. QoS ensures that everyone gets his or her fair share of network resources. Of course, this is a somewhat simplistic view of a more complex process, but it does provide you with an idea of what to expect.

The following sections explore QoS in a little more detail. We look at issues such as the hardware you require to implement QoS and what you need to do to get it installed.

Hardware Requirements

Implementing QoS isn't free. The first thing you need to consider is if your network's hardware is compatible with QoS. For example, the lowly NIC is an important part of QoS. It has to support the IEEE 802.1p standard. So, how do you determine if your NIC provides this support? Open the Advanced tab of the Properties dialog box for the NIC within Device Manager. As you can see in Figure 10-15, a NIC that supports the 802.1p standard has a special entry for enabling this support on the Advanced tab. There's also a series of IETF standards that your network should support as listed in Table 10-3. (Draft standards haven't reached the request for comment (RFC) stage yet, so these are new standards that your network will very likely need to support in the future.)

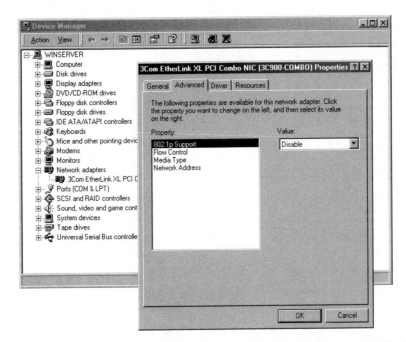

Figure 10-15. *It's easy to determine if your NIC provides the required level of support for QoS.*

Table 10-3.   IETF Standards for QoS and RSVP Support on a Network

RFC Number	Description
Draft	A Framework for Providing Integrated Services Over Shared and Switched IEEE 802 LAN Technologies
Draft	Integrated Service Mappings on IEEE 802 Networks
2689	Providing Integrated Services over Low-Bitrate Links
2208	Resource ReSerVation Protocol (RSVP) Version 1: Applicability Statement: Some Guidelines on Deployment

(continued)

Table 10-3. *(continued)*

RFC Number	Description
2205	Resource ReSerVation Protocol (RSVP) Version 1: Functional Specification
2209	Resource ReSerVation Protocol (RSVP) Version 1: Message Processing Rules
2747	RSVP Cryptographic Authentication
2207	RSVP Extensions for IPSEC Data Flows
2750	RSVP Extensions for Policy Control
2211	Specification of the Controlled-Load Network Ethernet Service
2212	Specification of Guaranteed Quality of Service
Draft	SBM (Subnet Bandwidth Manager): A Protocol for RSVP-based Admission Control over IEEE 802-style networks
2210	The Use of RSVP with IETF Integrated Services

Installing the Software

Windows 2000 doesn't start out with QoS installed and enabled. If it did, you might find yourself with a nonfunctional server before you even had a chance to configure it and the associated network. You'll need to install the QoS Admission Control as the first step of the software installation process. The following steps show you how.

1. Open the Control Panel, and then the Add/Remove Programs applet. Click Add/Remove Windows Components. You'll see the Windows Components wizard dialog box.

2. Highlight Networking Services (don't clear or check the associated check box).

3. Click Details. You see a Networking Services dialog box like the one shown in Figure 10-16. Notice that I've already highlighted the QoS Admission Control Service entry.

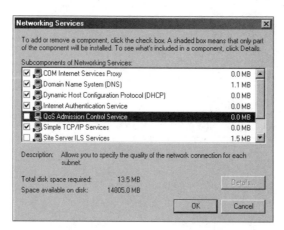

Figure 10-16. *The Networking Services dialog box contains the QoS Admission Control Service entry.*

4.   Check the QoS Admission Control Service entry, and then click OK.

5.   Click Next. Windows 2000 begins the installation process. You may need to provide the installation CD sometime during this process. Once the installation process is complete, you see a Completing the Windows Components wizard dialog box.

6.   Click Finish to complete the process.

Once you have QoS in place, you'll need to install the QoS Packet Scheduler on every machine on the network that may make reservations using the QoS Admission Control. The following procedure shows you how to install the QoS Packet Scheduler.

1.   Open Network And Dial-Up Connections.

2.   Right-click the Local Area Connection icon, and then choose Properties from the Context menu. You'll see a Local Area Connection Properties dialog box like the one shown in Figure 10-17.

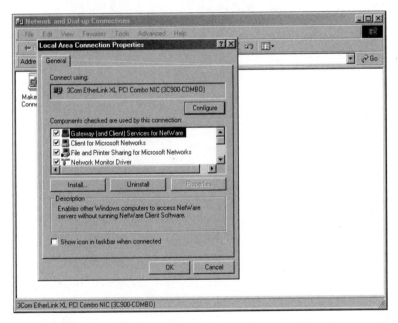

Figure 10-17.   *The Local Area Connection Properties dialog box contains a list of all the currently installed clients, services, and protocols.*

3.   Click Install. You'll see a Select Network Component Type dialog box.

4.   Highlight the Service entry, and then click Add. You'll see a Select Network Service dialog box like the one shown in Figure 10-18. Notice that I've highlighted the QoS Packet Scheduler.

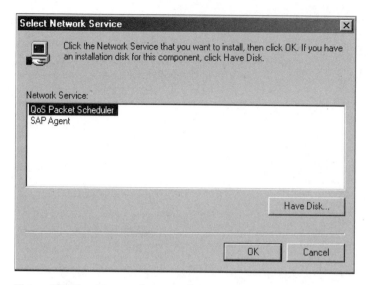

Figure 10-18. *You need to install the QoS Packet Scheduler found in the Select Network Service dialog box.*

5. Highlight the QoS Packet Scheduler entry, and then click OK. After a few moments, the Local Area Connection Properties dialog box appears with the QoS Packet Scheduler service installed.

6. Click Close to complete the process.

Configuring QoS

Once you install the QoS Admission Control, you'll need to configure the various policies that shape network performance, as well as define any subnetworks that these policies affect. You'll use the QoS Admission Control MMC snap-in shown in Figure 10-19 to perform any configuration. Notice that this snap-in provides two folders for configuration purposes. The first is Enterprise Settings, which is where you set policies that affect the use of network resources. The second is Subnetwork Settings, which is where you define which subnetworks are affected by the policies you set.

Tip You must have domain administrative privileges to set up the QoS Admission Control snap-in the first time. Local administrative privileges aren't enough to install this snap-in. If you attempt to install the snap-in without appropriate permission, MMC will exit with an "Access is denied" error message.

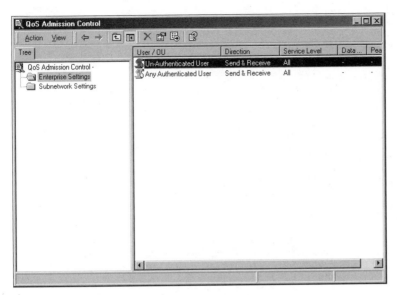

Figure 10-19. *The QoS Admission Control MMC snap-in allows you to set QoS policies and which subnetworks these policies concern.*

The QoS admission policy is a combination of two policies that exist at the time you install QoS support. The first is the Un-Authenticated User policy, which determines how users who haven't logged in are treated. The second is the Any Authenticated User. This second policy defines how authenticated users are treated (those who are logged into the domain in most cases). Any policies you add to these two policies determine exceptions to the rule. For example, you may say that unauthenticated users can't access the network at all, but any authenticated user can use up to 50 percent of the network resources. An obvious exception to this rule is the network administrator who may need more than 50 percent of the network's resources in an emergency.

Configuring any of these processes is relatively easy. All you need to do is right-click the policy, and then choose Properties from the Context menu. Figure 10-20 shows what the General tab of the Un-Authenticated User Properties dialog box looks like. Table 10-4 describes the entries on the various tabs of the dialog box.

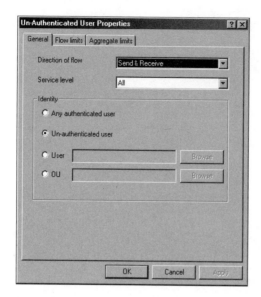

Figure 10-20. *The policy Properties dialog box allows you to configure how you want the policy to work.*

Table 10-4. Policy Properties Dialog Box Configuration Options

Field	Tab	Description
Direction of flow	General	Determines what kind of network traffic the policy changes. You can choose to modify the way a user sends, receives, or sends and receives data.
Service level	General	Determines what level of service the policy affects. The policy defaults to All, which determines the policy for all levels of service. You can also choose Best Effort (no guarantees), Controlled Load (approaches the level of service of an uncongested network), and Guaranteed Service (promises both network resources and a low delay).
Identity	General	A series of four options. The first two are for the default authenticated and unauthenticated user settings. The third option is to assign the policy to a specific user, while the fourth assigns it to a specific organizational unit.
Data Rate	Flow Limits	Defines the normal rate at which data can flow on the network for a single-data stream. There are three options. The first, Resource Limited, allows the entity to send data as fast as the network can transmit it. The second, Use Default Policy Settings, allows the entity to transmit data at the same rate as the authenticated user. The third option allows you to enter a specific flow rate in Kb/s.
Peak Data Rate	Flow Limits	Defines the maximum rate at which data can flow on the network for a single-data stream. This setting uses the same three options as the Data Rate field.

(continued)

Table 10-4.   *(continued)*

Field	Tab	Description
Duration	Flow Limits	Determines the length of time that the flow limits reserved by the policy remain in effect for a single-data stream. There are three options for this setting. The Unlimited option allows the policy to remain in effect until the application no longer requires the reservation. The Use Default Policy Settings option allows the policy to remain in effect for the same time period that the authenticated user policy allows. Finally, the third option allows you to set a specific timeframe in minutes.
Data Rate	Aggregate Limits	Same as Data Rate field on the Flow Limits tab, except this setting determines the flow rate for all data streams.
Peak Data Rate	Aggregate Limits	Same as Peak Data Rate field on the Flow Limits tab, except this setting determines the maximum flow rate for all the data streams.
Number of Flows	Aggregate Limits	Determines how many data streams the application affected by the policy is allowed to create. There are three options. The Unlimited option allows the application to create an unlimited number of flows. The Use Default Policy Settings option allows the application to create the same number of flows as the authenticated user. Finally, the third option allows you to set a specific number of data flows for this policy.

Understanding the Resource Reservation Protocol (RSVP)

It's time to look at the topic of network bandwidth reservations. We saw in the previous section how you can manually change these settings using the QoS Admission Control, but applications need a way to do this task automatically in the background. RSVP is the message protocol used by the QoS Admission Control and its clients to reserve resources, notably bandwidth, on the network. This is a signaling protocol that carries bandwidth information along a predetermined path by the network routing protocol.

RSVP supports both multicast and unicast transmissions, which means a single transmission can be used to make bandwidth reservations at more than one point along the network. In addition, RSVP passes the bandwidth reservation along to every component in the traffic flow path, which means the chance of one component remaining uninformed about the reservation is minimal. It's also the protocol that maintains the reservation at the various components along the traffic flow path. This includes the sending and receiving computers; any servers, hop points such as routers, other computers, and switches; and any other RSVP-aware components on the network.

There's a potential problem you need to know about. Although RSVP does try to inform all routers and switches along the traffic path about the reservation, the information does pass through nonRSVP routers and switches without being recognized. What this means to you, as a network administrator, is that an application can't be guaranteed the resources it requires. To fully guarantee a reservation, every switch and router along the traffic path must be RSVP-aware and grant the application the requested bandwidth. If any network component rejects the request, the application is informed immediately. The application now has the choice of using some other type or level of bandwidth request, or waiting until later to make the request again.

Unlike many of the set-and-forget protocols available today, RSVP is a soft-state protocol. This means it doesn't retain the reservation you make forever. The reservation must get refreshed from time to time or the system will forget about it. This is actually a good feature because it means an application that fails can't hold network bandwidth hostage. The network eventually makes the bandwidth available to other applications, even if the requesting application doesn't clear the reservation.

Summary

This chapter has looked at some of the more important performance-enhancing features that you find in Windows 2000. Knowing how the operating system can help you optimize the server for maximum performance is at least as important as knowing what you can do with it personally. In many cases, automatic-tuning features provided by the operating system do more—at least more on a dynamic basis—than you can do by statically tuning the performance characteristics of individual operating system features.

The first area we looked at was the issue of keeping disk use under control. In times past, an application or user could continue to use hard drive space until there wasn't anything left for anyone else to use. Windows 2000 eliminates this problem and helps you track hard-drive usage as well.

The second area we looked at in the chapter dealt with the Internet. It's important to realize that Windows 2000 is designed to make working with the Internet (or a local intranet) as easy as possible. Many of you will find that these tuning features can help resolve performance issues that occur continually and end up eating most of your time. For example, both bandwidth and processor throttling work automatically and resolve many of the usage (or perhaps a better term is overuse) issues that network administrators face today.

Having more than one processor in a server has become a fact of life today with the proliferation of processor-hungry applications. There's only one thing that's a certainty in the computer world. Applications continue to use processor capacity as fast as that capacity becomes available. In short, a multiprocessing server that can manage all the resources at its disposal, including the processors, is a real benefit. Microsoft has gone to great lengths to load balance and tune Windows 2000 to use processing cycles more efficiently than ever before.

Our next section looked at I2O. Intelligent processing of input/output ranks right up there with multiprocessor support, especially if you run a lot of disk-intensive applications such as database managers. In fact, I2O gives you a real reason to upgrade your server to multiple processors because much of the I/O processing is offloaded to that second processor.

Finally, we looked at how Windows 2000 can meet your networking needs. There are two ways Windows 2000 can help you get more out of your network resources. First, it helps you ensure that high-bandwidth applications have the resources they need through QoS. Second, if an application uses a lot of network resources and you want to ensure that it gets a minimum level of network support, you can use RSVP to reserve those resources.

We're going to delve into a really interesting topic in Chapter 11, capacity planning. Rather than run around trying to find the resource you need after the client load has already increased beyond comprehension, you can use capacity planning to look at future client needs. This means you can get the equipment and software in place long before it actually becomes necessary. In short, you can use this technology today to save yourself resource headaches in the future.

Chapter 11
Capacity Planning

It's that time in the book when we need to bring out the crystal ball and make some predictions about the future. This is the way many network administrators approach the topic of capacity planning. Either the needs of tomorrow aren't planned for at all, or network administrators make a good guess at what they'll need. Of course, in some respects, this viewpoint is correct. There isn't any way you can predict what tomorrow will hold with 100 percent accuracy. So, in a sense, capacity planning is a matter of guessing what you need.

However, there isn't any reason to avoid planning for tomorrow. You can predict, with a reasonable amount of certainty, the planned needs of your company with regard to network capacity. I stress the word *planned* here because there are internal and external factors you can't plan for. All you can do is plan for future capacity based on what you know today. At least, planning in this way will give you some kind of target to shoot at, which is why capacity planning is so important. No, you don't know for sure that you'll need 20 GB of extra disk space; but based on current usage trends and the new technologies you know about, you can say with reasonable certainty that you'll need at least 20 GB of extra disk space within the next year.

This chapter will help you assess your future capacity needs. We'll base our discussion on some of the factors you can reliably track when it comes to your network needs. The first section of this chapter, "Deciding What Level of Performance You Need," combines the elements that we reviewed in the book so far (performance monitoring) and extends that information out to the needs of tomorrow. The first step in planning for additional capacity is to decide what level of performance you can live with as technology advances become available.

Some network administrators plan for added capacity, but fail to improve the network as a whole. The "Adding Reliability to Your Performance Picture" section of the chapter addresses that need. Consider the fact that you spend a certain amount of time today maintaining the network. If the size of your network doubles within the next five years, do you have the extra staff required to perform twice as much troubleshooting? The answer, at least according to many industry experts, is no. There's a real shortage of qualified staff today, which means your support team might actually shrink a little during the next five years instead of grow. Obviously, you have to make your network more reliable so your support staff can keep up with maintenance as the network grows.

The third section of the chapter could be titled *Caveat Emptor* (let the buyer beware). Vendors make all kinds of unsubstantiated claims based on small tests run on small networks with inadequate supervision. Although it isn't right to say they're not telling the truth, the truth can be a matter of perspective. "Understanding Vendor Claims versus Real-World Performance" helps you separate vendor hype from what you can really expect.

Another problem with capacity planning is that some network administrators don't know what they have. If they've conducted an inventory, the information is in a form that isn't very easy to use and certainly difficult to analyze in any meaningful way. The "Creating a Graphical Representation of Your Network" section of the chapter helps you reorganize the inventory of your network into something you can use for future planning.

The final section of the chapter, "Looking for Performance Bottlenecks," revisits one of the topics we covered before. However, rather than use the information for tuning the server, this time we'll use it as an aid to see where you need to go. Capacity planning is a matter of knowing where you are today, and where you need to be in a certain amount of time. You draw a line between the two points in the capacity chart and use it to determine new equipment purchases, software upgrades, user training, and even custom software requirements. In short, capacity planning means looking at what your network needs to perform as it should.

Deciding What Level of Performance You Need

One of the cornerstones of capacity planning is to determine how much capacity you actually need. Some people tend to view capacity and performance as the same thing, but they really aren't. For the purposes of this chapter, we define capacity as the ability to perform work and performance as a measure of the actual amount of work performed by the system. A system usually requires more capacity than it needs to maintain an average level of performance in order to support peaks in load and various types of performance losses.

Performance is usually measured by a system's ability to do a given amount of work in a specific amount of time—which translates to understanding how the system's current capacity is affected by the amount of load you place on it. In fact, you can easily look at the whole picture of performance on a network using this equation: Performance = (Capacity - System Losses) / Load. Increase the system's capacity as a whole and you increase the performance as well (at least if the load has the ability to use the extra capacity). Reduce the system losses by making processes more efficient and you see an increase in performance as well. Increase the load and performance decreases.

The issue of how much more performance you need to meet tomorrow's demands is a complex one because there are a lot of issues to consider. By dividing the question into three main areas, you can reduce complexity and make the question easier to answer. The following sections consider the question of how much performance you really need based on the performance equation. We look at how the three main performance factors—capacity, system losses, and load—all affect the way you should view the question of how much performance you actually need to get the job done today and tomorrow.

Differences Between Performance Needs and the Performance You Want

There's a distinct difference between the performance you need and the performance you want. We'd all like to have a system that responds instantly, has an unlimited amount of memory and disk space, and allows us to keep working without ever upgrading the system. Unfortunately, this kind of system doesn't exist. Application use tends to expand to match any increase of capacity that you provide and systems rarely stay state of the art for more than a few years. By the end of the third year, most PC users are looking for ways to get rid of an old system, in part because their applications have expanded to use all the available system capacity. It's important to differentiate between the measured performance requirements for your system today, what you need tomorrow, and what you'd personally like in the way of system performance.

It's easy to say that most performance issues are a matter of personal preference. Some network administrators think that as long as the system responds at all, performance isn't an issue. However, the level of performance you need isn't necessarily limited to personal desires. An application must respond quickly enough to maintain a minimum level of user productivity and interest. When performance falls below a given level, users make more mistakes and become less productive, which means the company spends more to perform a given task. In addition to current user productivity goals, you must provide some room for tomorrow's needs. The user is often the focal point for the performance issue because it's the user's productivity that becomes an overriding issue.

Real World

Physical and technological constraints often get in the way of getting the performance you want. For example, a friend who normally spends time at heavily used Web sites complained that moving from a dialup connection to a cable modem didn't necessarily mean a corresponding decrease in response time. There was nothing wrong with the equipment; the Web site simply didn't have the ability to use the increased capacity, a problem that happens all too frequently. It doesn't pay to add capacity when the applications or other components can't respond.

From a real-world perspective, the amount of performance you need is the level of performance an application can use to provide a response in a reasonable amount of time. Reasonable here is hard to quantify; but few things are instantaneous, even if you provide the capacity required for making them so. A good rule of thumb is what I call the impatient syndrome. Users wait a certain length of time and then start fidgeting. It's at that point that a process is taking too long and performance is probably lacking. For a Web site, most industry pundits say a download interval between 10 and 30 seconds normally works fine.

Relationship Between Capacity and Performance

Capacity and performance are related, but aren't the same. It helps to understand the relationship between capacity and performance when you're planning for future upgrades. Since we're looking at the capacity part of the picture, you probably want to restructure our equation as Capacity = (Performance * Load) + System Losses. It's relatively easy to measure performance as response time. How long does it take the application to produce a result? That's the question System Monitor answers through the use of counters. Deriving some measure of system capacity from a performance measurement means changing the way you look at the data. You need to consider the capacity (the ability to perform work at a given load) a system needs to accomplish work that the performance statistic documents.

> **Note** Chapter 4 provides an overview of System Monitor that you should review if you need to know more about the counters used by Microsoft Windows 2000 to track performance.

So, what do you need to do to change your way of viewing performance data into something that looks more like a measurement of capacity? When you look at hard-disk usage statistics, what you're really looking at is how long it takes the hard drive to respond to an application's request for data. A high level of activity means the system is using more of the available capacity to respond to application and user requests, which means the performance measurement closely reflects the actual amount of available capacity. The same holds true for processing and other system requirements. What you really need to know is the response time for that system element. A system that takes too long to respond decreases user productivity, which increases the cost of performing any particular task on the system.

Performance means considering the user part of the question as well. For example, it's easy to say that users are more productive if they only need to wait 10 seconds for a download to complete, rather than the 30 seconds it takes right now. A user can respond in 10 seconds with ease. However, what happens when you decrease response time from 1 second to 0.5 second? Is the user going to be any more productive with the higher performance level? The answer is, probably not. Studies of human reaction times show that at the very best, a human commonly responds to any external event, even an emergency, in the 1- to 2-second timeframe. So if you're worried about increasing performance in the 2-second range, it's probably not worth the effort unless the increased performance is there to handle future needs or there's some form of automation to assist the user. As you can see, any capacity planning you do based on performance must take the user's response time into account.

System Losses and Performance

Part of performance monitoring is assessing the amount of loss that various system elements introduce. That's been one of the major topics throughout the book so far. It follows that establishing the performance requirements for your system means adding any losses in to the performance requirements of any applications you run. (You should use the tips and techniques in this book to tune your system to reduce system losses to an acceptable level, but even a fully tuned system has losses of various types.) The one fact you need to remember when assessing the performance requirements for a system is that every system has losses; nothing is 100 percent efficient. The following list details some of the losses you'll encounter in every system.

- **Hardware**   Losses mean that part of the capacity of a system is being used to generate heat or light, rather than process data. You also lose some system capacity because of the way hardware handles data transfers. In some cases, an older piece of hardware may not be able to handle features offered by a new bus, which introduces performance loss in the form of an inability to use existing system capacity.

- **Software**   Every piece of software on your system, including the operating system, has losses. In fact, one of the things Microsoft tried to do during a system update of an existing version of Windows was to rewrite sections of the code to reduce these losses. No matter how well software is written, however, some losses can't be overcome with any ease. Some software introduces inefficiencies by forcing the system to perform tasks that may not be required in a given situation. For example, a piece of software may check for the existence of a file before it attempts to open it. If the file exists, the check introduced a loss into the system as an unnecessary expenditure of time and processing cycles. Yet, the check is required if the application is to operate without error. Every developer includes "safety" code that ensures the application works as anticipated; but since this safety code isn't always required, the processing time is lost. (Safety code, unlike error handling code, often prevents an error from happening, rather than fixing an error once it has occurred.) There are also issues the developer can't overcome at all. For example, the application may introduce losses because of the way the code gets compiled. The conversion of code from human-readable form into machine code isn't always precise.

- **Users**   Even if everything else on your system is perfect, users introduce inefficiencies simply because of the way the creative process works and because of the way training is handled in most companies. Training is important because this is the one area where you can improve user efficiency every time. The less familiar the user is with the system, the higher the losses because the user makes more mistakes in choosing menu options on the application and in entering data. In addition, the creative process involves trial and error. A user may complete a task using the minimum number of steps and still have to redo the work because the end results were less useful than anticipated. In short, the previous steps were wasted and there isn't anything you can do to prevent this type of waste.

This list should tell you something about system performance and future capacity requirements—you always have losses to account for. Depending on your system's design, the user's ability, and the developer's programming prowess, your server may be losing quite a bit of potential processing power to various kinds of losses. Tuning and optimization is a necessary part of keeping losses to a minimum, although performance monitoring is essential to anticipate the level of future losses as part of the capacity-planning process.

Adding capacity to your system to obtain higher performance also means considering the effect of increased system losses. Think for a moment about the reasons most companies add capacity. Adding more users to the network means adding users who may not be familiar with the custom applications your company uses. That's one source of increased system losses. Just the fact that you're adding more users means more of those users will be repeating steps as part of the creative process—again increasing system losses. The more hardware you have, the more heat gets generated, and the higher the losses due to that heat. More connections between nodes also mean the network works less efficiently, which means you have to plan for additional capacity. The list of reasons goes on, but the bottom line is that more capacity means higher losses.

Tip Tuning and optimization goals usually change as the size of your network increases. For example, a tuning tip that normally produces negligible results on a single-server network might produce a significant performance gain on a network with four or five servers, simply because a little change on each server produces a cumulative result. In addition, some goals don't exist on a single-server setup. For example, using a storage area network (SAN) would probably not result in a large performance gain on a single-server network simply because there's only one server to worry about. However, using a SAN on even a two-server network will increase both reliability and performance, making it an important consideration in your tuning strategy.

For the purposes of this chapter, then, determining the extra performance that's required to meet production goals means taking potential losses into account. In fact, in order to predict performance needs accurately, it's best to base your prediction on a worst-case scenario. Make sure you account for the maximum load your site will have after you tune it for maximum performance using current methods. Your company may have additional tuning capability in the future, but you don't want to include it in your calculation since there's no way to predict if the technology will be available or if your company will implement it. For example, some developers counted on Component Load Balancing (CLB) as a performance feature for their COM+ applications running under Windows 2000. Even though this capability will become available later, Microsoft chose not to include it with the initial release of Windows 2000, making it a feature that shouldn't be included in your current or near future planning strategy.

> **More Info**   CLB is going to be a very important feature of Windows 2000 as more developers use COM+ for application. Using CLB will make large applications perform even better than using Network Load Balancing (NLB), which is another performance-enhancing cluster technology. You can find out more about Microsoft's future plans for CLB at *http://support.microsoft.com/support/kb/articles/Q242/0/26.ASP.*

So, if you're adding another server to a single-server network, you'll want to at least double the server-related performance losses, and then add some for potential communication losses. Likewise, when adding users, always add performance losses related to a novice user, rather than the veteran user, since it's unlikely you'll hire a veteran user into the company. If you do manage to reduce losses through additional tuning or gain the services of an experienced user, you can reduce performance requirement estimates later in the process (making management happier than if you were asking for more performance-related capacity).

Considering a Load's Effect on Performance

Unlike the question of performance, which is certainly equal parts science and personal preference, the load on your system can be derived through measurement. A simple way to look at load is this: Load = Task Complexity * Number of Tasks Per Time Interval. The following list describes each of the equation elements.

- **Load**   Understanding the total amount of stress that an application or group of applications place on a server is important because the load affects the overall performance of the server and amount of capacity required to perform the task. For example, a database application places a heavy burden on the disk subsystem. If you're planning on running mainly database applications on a particular server, that server may require a higher proportion of the upgrade monies in the form of disk capacity than in memory or other system elements.

- **Task complexity**   This is a measure of the amount of load a particular application places on the server. This number varies by application and by the kinds of users who need the application. We looked at various application types and their effects on the system in Chapters 7, 8, and 9. However, now you also need to consider the user. An expert typically loads a system more than a novice because an expert uses more of the application's advanced features.

- **Number of tasks per time interval**   We covered the need to look at long-term performance monitoring of a server in the "How Microsoft Windows 2000 Uses Memory" section of Chapter 6, various sections of Chapter 7, and various sections of Chapter 8. The "Histogram Mode" section of Chapter 4 shows you how to use this display. A server's performance varies over time and the instantaneous performance values that you achieve in a quick look hardly reflect the overall performance of the server. You actually need to know three load

levels when working with capacity planning. The first is the average performance of the server over time—this requires a relatively long monitoring interval. The second is the lowest expected load, which requires charting the
instantaneous values over the normal working hours of the system. The third is
the highest expected load, which means finding the peak instantaneous load
level over a period of time. In short, you need to combine both short- and
long-monitoring intervals to obtain the required load information.

Combining task complexity with the amount of tasks done within the monitoring interval gives you the load a particular application places on the server. Task complexity is
measured in a number of ways. For example, when you start a graphics application, you
definitely see a large increase in processor activity. The amount of increase tells you how
much additional load this application is placing on the processor. Although the increase
in disk load is less with a graphics application, there's an increase there as well. In short,
you can use System Monitor, and other utilities, to measure the precise amount of load
that an application places on a system. Once you know the amount of load various tasks
place on a system, you can assign them a task-complexity rating (which is a number that
shows the amount of load the application places on the server). The task-complexity rating
allows you to compare two applications by the amount of load they place on a system.

The number of tasks you perform per second (or other time interval) affects the system
load as well. Double the number of the same task you perform simultaneously, and you
double the kind of load the task places on the system. As the number of tasks increases,
so does the system load. Of course, you have to build a picture of the number of tasks
being performed. Just because your company owns 50 licenses for a database server
doesn't mean all 50 are in use at the same time. A historical view of System Monitor logs
helps you in this case. You need to track the number of application instances running
throughout the day.

The number of tasks running simultaneously varies by the number of people who need
to use the application at any given time. A database application used for order entry is
likely to have a very consistent load, while a graphics application might have an irregu-
lar load without any discernible pattern. E-mail applications are likely to experience a
burst of activity first thing in the morning when people log in to the system, and then
taper off until the end of the day when you see another burst of activity right before people
log off.

The reason you need to know how the number of tasks being performed at any given
time varies during the day is that you need to predict periods of maximum server use by
individual applications. Consider a single server that runs an order entry system and e-
mail. People come in to work, check their e-mail, and then bring up the order entry
system. The two applications can share a certain amount of system capacity because of
the users' usage pattern. The issue of shared capacity brings up another point. Performance isn't a matter of adding up all the requirements of every application that runs on
the server. It's a matter of adding up the overlapping system requirements.

There isn't a single load on a server either. You need to break that server up into subsystems that allow you to measure the load on that subsystem. For example, a database application and a financial application can probably run together and not use much of the other application's resources. There would be two loads on the server: one on the disk subsystem for the database and a second on the processor for the financial application. When you plan server upgrades for such a system, you need to make plans for the processor load and for the disk subsystem load. It's not a matter of saying that all the applications place a given load on the server as a whole, but rather deciding which subsystems need to be upgraded and by how much based on the individual loads.

Adding Reliability to Your Performance Picture

Most network administrators are worried about system reliability today because most systems can't afford any amount of downtime. The Internet and other external forces have made most systems 24-hour-a-day ventures, even if the company itself only runs 8 hours each day. Companies also run mission-critical applications on these servers and rely on the servers to provide access to these applications on a 24/7 basis. Finally, data has become the most valuable commodity on a typical network, which means data integrity is an absolute requirement on today's systems. In short, no matter how large or how small your company is, it's very likely reliability is going to play a major role in future system upgrades, which means reliability must be part of your capacity planning.

Reliability is a two-edged sword when it comes to capacity planning. On the one hand, adding equipment that enhances reliability increases user productivity, reduces downtime, and provides multiple execution paths in many cases. On the other hand, reliability can cost in terms of application efficiency, additional hardware, and processing cycles spent just waiting for a problem to occur. In short, adding reliability to a system changes the performance picture and affects your capacity planning to some degree. The kind of reliability you add to a system affects what kinds of changes you make to your capacity-planning strategy.

Reliability and Windows 2000 Specific Features

Windows 2000 is much more reliable than its predecessors because it includes new features that ensure safe data transfers and storage. Consider the effect of Component Services on reliability. (Component Services is a set of services based on an earlier release of a component-based transaction processing system called Microsoft Transaction Server.) You can rely on transactions to make data transfers safe because Component Services includes so many different recovery modes. Even if the data isn't transferred correctly the first time, it eventually appears at the destination because Windows 2000 tries the transfer again. The only exception to this rule is if you adjust system settings to stop attempting the transfer at some point (at which point you see a log entry regarding the failure) or manually terminate the transaction.

This added reliability comes at a deceptively small cost. The user barely notices any delay at all. In fact, some transactions occur so quickly that there may not be a delay (at least, not one that the user can see) on a moderately loaded server. However, there's still a performance cost and it's a hidden cost in this case. The transaction takes some amount of time that the server can use for some other purpose. The individual user doesn't see the time used, but the system as a whole slows down, especially if multiple users rely on transacted data transfers. You must judge the cumulative effect of using a technology, rather than rely on the individual user experience, to determine the cost of using a reliability feature. In addition, there are hard-drive, memory, and other resource requirements for transactions. If a transaction is taking space on the hard-drive, that space is unavailable for other purposes. You don't get a free ride with any form of reliability. The costs may be difficult to see, but they're present all the same.

The fact that a transaction is going to cost some amount of system resources and server-processing power isn't a problem as long at that transaction is required. There's a fine line between a high-reliability system and a system that's paranoid about reliability to the point that the system wastes resources. Here's an overly simplistic example of a transaction that shouldn't take place. Chris sends Lee a message about the company party. Is that message important enough to waste the system resources required for a transaction? No! Yet, if you set the server up incorrectly, every message, no matter how important, might receive the protection that a transaction provides. It pays to think about what data is important enough to protect, despite the costs of doing so.

> **Tip** Some of the losses incurred by reliability features can't be avoided very easily using an application, security policy, system setting, or other automated technique alone. However, the user who's trained to detect situations that don't require a high-reliability connection can avoid these losses. A user-training program, coupled with company policies, can help you avoid some of the losses incurred by reliability features on the server. For example, you might design a custom application so that high-priority transactions receive Component Services support, while low-priority transactions are sent normally. Although there's still a potential for abuse, the user now has a choice of which transaction type to select. Training, combined with a company policy that dictates what kind of transaction to use for a particular kind of data transfer, can allow a company to retain all the benefits of using Component Services, yet reduce the cost of this reliability feature. Every new user should be aware of the company policy and the method for changing the transaction type. This means training isn't a one-time cost—it's an ongoing concern.

Another Windows 2000 reliability feature is Message Queuing. This feature allows applications to send a transaction to a queue, rather than immediately to the processing application. Using Message Queuing means applications can spread out any required processing over a period of time, 24 hours a day if necessary. The server can maintain a more consistent load, which means you're using the hardware more efficiently. Message

Queuing also allows users to operate an application in disconnected mode, rather than requiring a connection to the network. This means the user's productivity is increased because the server is no longer absolutely necessary to perform certain types of data processing as long as a connection to the server is eventually restored.

You'd think Message Queuing is pure gain from the capacity standpoint because it allows you to use your hardware consistently—maintaining a constant load on the server and ensuring that the server's resources are always fully used. Of course, this viewpoint overlooks some of the details of using Message Queuing. For one thing, Message Queuing requires processor cycles—lots of them. A component has to be set up to listen for user-generated messages that appear in the server's queue. This means there's an application using resources on the server all the time.

As with Component Services, there are hidden costs to using Message Queuing. For example, the queues Message Queuing requires when doing its job take up room on the server. In fact, depending on how the application developer sets the application up, there can be a queue entry for every message on every server the message crosses. Yes, this enhances application reliability in a big way, but it also means the server is now responsible for spending time storing and retrieving messages that it doesn't otherwise need to process.

The actual cost of a message in Message Queuing depends on two factors. The first is whether the developer chooses to send the message using the reliability or express method. The express method transfers the message from server to server using memory and network connections alone. Yes, this still costs some server performance, but not nearly as much as the reliability method that places a copy of the message on every server in the string. The second factor is the kind of data transferred. A Message Queuing message can contain any type of data, including certain types of components. A data transfer includes all this data, plus any data used to wrap the message in a recognizable form. Because every action within the user application is likely to generate a separate message and there might be hundreds of users all relying on Message Queuing at the same time, the cost in hard-drive space can become quite imposing. Of course, this is a transitory loss. As soon as the message is processed, the hard-drive space it consumes can be retrieved. The load on the hard drive varies as a function of the message backlog in Message Queuing.

The simplest way to reduce the load Message Queuing places on your server is not to use it at all. Message Queuing isn't the cure-all for every problem on a network—only certain classes of application actually benefit from the technology. Using Message Queuing means you essentially don't care when a data transaction takes place, which works fine for order entry since the order isn't processed immediately anyway. On the other hand, any kind of two-way data transfer can't be performed using Message Queuing (Message Queuing provides one-way message transfers only) and you don't want to use it for real-time transactions. Message Queuing is a reliability option for very specific situations.

Ensuring that the application is set up correctly is the next best way to avoid problems. For example, it's not necessary to encrypt every message on an application used only for desktop purposes unless someone has access to your network (in which case, you have problems other than reliability and performance to worry about). You can also ensure that the developer uses the right kind of message processing (reliability vs. express) and uses the right level of security.

There's a fixed amount of space Message Queuing can use for messages. However, the setting is a tad difficult to find if you don't know where to look. Open the Active Directory Sites and Services MMC snap-in. Highlight the Default-First-Site-Name (or other) site. Right-click the site, point to View, and then choose Show Services Node. Expand the Services node and you'll see a display similar to the one shown in Figure 11-1. Notice that I've already highlighted the MsmqServices object.

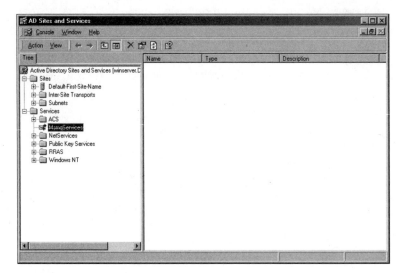

Figure 11-1. *Active Directory Sites and Services is where you find some of the capacity settings for Message Queuing.*

Right-click the MsmqServices object, and then choose Properties. Look at the General tab and you'll see a dialog box like the one shown in Figure 11-2. This is where you choose the amount of time that a message stays in the queue waiting for processing. Normally, server messages are handled right away. However, the server can also send messages to the client. These messages can wait for quite a while for a disconnected application to retrieve them. That's why you need to set a time limit on how long the message waits in the queue and also plan for some amount of storage for them as part of your capacity planning.

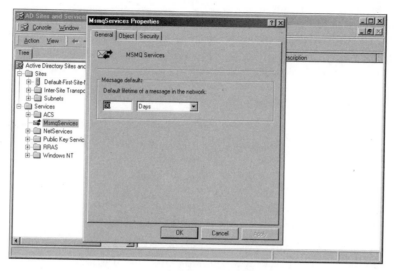

Figure 11-2. *It pays to set a reasonable amount of time for an application to pick up its messages on the server.*

Tip Windows 2000 defaults to a 90-day waiting period for messages. (Remember that a message can convey either user-oriented or application-specific data, so Message Queuing isn't e-mail.) Unless you have users in Outer Mongolia, change this waiting period to something more reasonable. For example, if users normally check in every day, you might want to set the waiting period to seven days and ensure that the users (and their applications) know to pick up messages before they go on vacation. A long waiting period allows the system to retain messages that consume valuable hard-drive space and slow message processing for other applications.

Application Reliability Effects

Some applications provide features that make them more reliable than their counterparts. A common example of such a feature is the automatic save used by many word processing applications. This feature ensures that the user's document is saved at regular intervals. A feature like this is valuable because it keeps users' data safe, even if users get so involved in their work that they forget to save often enough.

As nice as application-supported reliability features are, they do use network resources. The word processor requires some network bandwidth to send a copy of the document to the server, and then some server processing time to store the document. It may seem that this is such an insignificant load, you don't need to think about it. However, multiplying the automatic save feature of something as simple as a word processor by several hundred users does make a big difference. This is another one of those places where you must consider the cumulative load that a particular application feature places on the server in order to add it to your capacity planning. Since the automatic save feature is measurable and occurs on a regular basis (whatever interval is set by the word processor's user or the network administrator), you can predict the amount of capacity required to ensure this feature works as anticipated.

Examples of application-supported reliability features abound. For example, many custom database management systems (DBMS) have an automated archival feature built into them. The application looks for old data in the tables that the company wants to keep, yet no one is using. This old data is placed in offline storage in case someone does need it again. In addition to archiving old data, this feature normally backs up new data and any changes users have made to existing data. In short, this is a form of automatic backup that probably runs in addition to the normal network backup made by the network administrator. This feature offers some form of automated recovery that allows the application to recover when certain common problems occur.

Unlike the word processor example, this feature probably runs once a day, rather than every five minutes. So, the question is whether you need to include this particular feature in your capacity planning. Part of the answer to that question is to determine when the feature runs. If it runs at 1 A.M. when no one is using the server anyway, you need to question whether this reliability feature affects server or network performance at all. Perhaps it's simply using capacity that otherwise gets wasted. Needless to say, this is the kind of feature you need to set up in advance, and then measure its impact on the system. Once the feature is in place and configured, you need to provide a policy that states why the application is set up in this way so future network administrators know to leave it alone or change it with caution.

Tip There are a few things you can do to make applications with reliability features, like automatic save, run more consistently and make capacity planning for them easier as well. Make sure all the applications are set to save at the same interval. For example, it's common to set a word processor to automatically save a document every 10 minutes. This interval is short enough that the user doesn't lose a lot of data, yet long enough that the network isn't overwhelmed with automatic save requests. It also pays to look at the kind of automation used by the application. For example, some word processors allow you to perform a quick save, which includes just the changed information for the document, or a full save, which includes the entire document. Although the quick save is kinder to network resources (it only saves a little information), the full save is more reliable because there isn't any need to reconstruct the document during recovery. In short, you need to know how the application uses a reliability feature and ensure all systems are set up the same so you have a more predictable load to measure.

We already covered the reliability features that Component Services and Message Queuing provide for applications. It's important to understand that some applications already have features that are like those provided by Component Services and Message Queuing, but don't use these operating system features. After all, there was a need for this kind of reliability before Windows 2000 appeared on the scene. In most cases, you use the same strategy to plan for the capacity required by application features that mimic Component Services and Message Queuing as you do for the Windows 2000 version of the feature.

Another type of application reliability feature that's popular today relies on a central repository—essentially a central database. In this case, the changes individual users make are recorded, making it possible to reverse those changes if necessary. In addition, the repository coordinates the actions of the users working on coordinated documents. For example, the application at the center of the repository only allows one user at a time to check out a particular document for editing. Because the repository is so intricately coupled with the data that the users are manipulating, this kind of reliability feature consumes a great deal of network and server resources. In fact, the amount of capacity required can become so great that an application of this type can require a separate server. Any time you install an application that requires some sort of repository (like Visual Source Safe—a team coordination product that comes with Visual Studio), you need to question whether that application should appear on a separate server to prevent it from overwhelming the resources on the main company server. This is one area where capacity planning may mean separating one application from the rest of the network.

Reliability and Hardware

Hardware is one area where PC vendors have concentrated. When a piece of hardware fails, it can take all the applications on one server with it; or, in extreme cases, the entire network. This is especially problematic with devices like hard drives where the effect of a failure can extend past the time when the failure is fixed because the server's data can become inaccessible. The reliability problems with disk drives are compounded by the fact that a disk drive is a mechanical device—a bad bearing can ruin your whole day. Solid state devices are inherently more reliable because they contain no moving parts. Of course, the fact that solid state devices are more reliable doesn't mean they never fail— you find that solid state parts have their share of failures as well.

Because of the nature of server and network hardware and its importance to the overall mission of a company, part of the reliability goal of a hardware setup is to ensure that there's a certain amount of redundancy built into the system. This is especially true of hard-drive subsystems, but has extended to entire servers in the recent past. From a capacity perspective, this means part of your planning revolves around additions that make the system run more reliably. Some hardware capacity upgrades have little, if anything, to do with allowing more users on the system or making the system run faster. Most managers fully understand the need to provide hardware redundancy (or they soon learn after viewing the results of a hardware failure), so this type of capacity planning is both anticipated and expected.

Now that you have a better idea of the two faces of hardware capacity planning, it's time to look at specific pieces of hardware. The following sections help you understand how hardware reliability for specific components (like a hard-drive subsystem) affects capacity planning. We explore some of the things you add with only reliability in mind and the areas where there's some overlap between reliability and performance.

SANs

We previously reviewed SANs in "Working with Storage Area Networks (SANs)" in Chapter 7. Essentially, this device moves hard-drive storage from the inside of the server to a separate external location. Making this move not only makes it easier to repair the hard-drive array without taking the server offline, but it also allows multiple servers to share the same drive subsystem. This means that if a single server fails, you can still access the drive subsystem using another server, making the system failsafe. Read the text in Chapter 7 for additional details.

Once you get past the physical layout of a SAN and the methods used to access it, you have to consider the layout of SAN and how the drives are set up for use. A SAN normally relies on a redundant array of independent disks (RAID) to ensure that a single-drive failure doesn't result in any data loss. The rest of the drives on the system can work together to rebuild the data on the failed drive. A software drive replaces the failed drive until the failed drive is replaced. In most cases, the rebuilding process can take place in the background once the drive is replaced. As far as the user is concerned, nothing has happened.

There are several factors to consider from a capacity perspective. RAID normally relies on having at least one parity drive for recovery purposes. This means that if you have a five-drive RAID setup, you only get four drives worth of disk storage—the fifth drive is used for reliability purposes. If you predict disk drive needs at 4 GB for the next six months, you actually need 5 GB of additional drive space to achieve the required capacity increase. Not only do you need to increase the amount of drive space to account for reliability requirements, but you also need to consider the RAID configuration. A single 5-GB hard drive doesn't work in this case. What you actually need are five 1-GB hard drives. This means the cost of the capacity increase is going to be higher than for a nonRAID setup.

If you remember from our SAN discussion in Chapter 7, they normally use a separate bus. Using a separate bus for SAN means disk requests won't clog up the network normally used by the server for answering client requests. However, using a separate network also muddies the capacity-planning picture. Consider the amount of network traffic normally generated for disk requests on a network without a SAN. At least part of this traffic is now on the SAN's network connection, not the general network connection. So, when working with a disk-bound application, do you increase the capacity of the SAN network or the general network in response to increased user activity? In many cases, you'll come to the conclusion that both networks must increase in capacity to handle the increased number of requests; so then the question becomes one of determining how much of an increase each network needs to achieve the desired result. Unfortunately, the two networks affect each other. An increase of capacity in one network will very likely increase the performance of the other in some degree, but the amount of performance increase is difficult to predict.

Tip   In most cases, the SAN vendor has special hardware that can help you more accurately measure the current performance of your system, at least with regard to the SAN itself. You may need to work in tandem with the SAN vendor to assess any future capacity changes for your system. Of course, you always want to place the recommendations made by the SAN vendor in perspective with the rest of your network. It hardly pays to upgrade the SAN if the rest of the system is already having a hard time using all the capacity the SAN offers.

A final SAN capacity need is the capacity of the box used to house the SAN itself. Remember, the hard drives now sit outside the server's box, which means they require outside support mechanisms, all of which have some level of performance to consider. So, now you also need to consider the performance of the SAN itself as part of the task of determining how much capacity to add to an existing system.

Server Clusters

Server clusters are another modern reliability and performance feature on most networks of any size. A server cluster is a group of servers that all perform the same set of functions. The cluster relies on one or more smart routers to send client requests to one of the servers in the cluster based on that server's current load. In this way, the client always gets the best possible server because the server that's least busy at the moment handles the request. A cluster also makes the servers more reliable because the loss of a single server no longer means the network is nonfunctional. It simply means the network answers client requests slightly slower than before until the failed server is brought back online. We explore the way clusters work and what they mean to you with regard to performance in Chapter 13. For now, all you need to understand is that they help improve both performance and reliability.

There are several capacity-planning issues that are obvious immediately after you realize what a server cluster is and what it can do for you. For example, if the current cluster isn't able to handle the real-time client load, you can try to offload part of the processing into batch processes using technologies like Message Queuing. (We covered the performance-enhancing capabilities of Message Queuing in the "Reliability and Windows 2000 Specific Features" section of the chapter, so I won't discuss them again here.) Of course, offloading the extra processing load doesn't always work, which means adding capacity in the form of a faster router, more network bandwidth, or an additional server. This part of capacity planning is fairly straightforward.

The hidden part of capacity planning is what happens within the server cluster itself. For example, the load-balancing algorithm used to detect the least busy server may not always accurately predict which server to use. This can mean one server ends up with a lighter load than another server in the cluster for some period of time until the load balances out again. The result can be frustrated users who make the request repeatedly, clogging the server cluster and making performance even worse. In short, when relying on network load balancing, it pays to include tuning the load-balancing algorithm or getting improved software as part of your capacity-planning strategy.

Another part of capacity planning for a server cluster is the principle of equalization. If you have five servers in a cluster, those servers should present an equal (or nearly equal) level of capacity. So, when you upgrade one server with additional memory, plan on upgrading all the servers in the cluster to allow all servers to present an equal amount of capacity. Approaching the issue in this way ensures the cluster remains balanced and that you get the anticipated network load-balancing results.

A final hidden issue is the fact that there's a certain amount of cluster-related communication required. The amount of communication required depends on the cluster setup and what tasks you want the servers in the cluster to perform. At the very least, the servers need to communicate with the router to convey current load levels so the router can keep the cluster balanced. This means you'll need to add the load the cluster communication places on the system into your capacity planning. In most cases, the amount of communication is small and is directly proportional to the number of servers within the cluster, not the capacity of each server in that cluster. So adding a new server will increase the amount of communication you need to compensate for, but upgrading the amount of memory in each server won't.

Reserve Hardware

Some networks have a certain amount of hardware that's kept in reserve for either unexpected loads or for system failures. Let's cover the first reason. A Web site is a perfect example of a server setup that requires hardware that isn't normally used until there's an increase in demand. In some cases, the amount of time required to manage the extra hardware doesn't offer any dividends in the form of increased performance, so the hardware is maintained in a ready, but offline state. In other cases, the company doesn't want to receive user complaints based on no-load Web site response times. The idea behind the additional hardware is to maintain some specific level of Web-site performance so users see response time as a constant, no matter how many users are actually visiting the site at a given time. Needless to say, keeping reserve hardware, in this case, is costly but necessary, especially in the case of an e-commerce site.

Capacity planning, in this case, means computing the average level of Web-site activity and using this level to predict future hardware needs for online equipment. An increase in average activity doesn't necessarily affect the amount of peak activity unless both activity levels increase at a consistent rate. A second measurement is taken of the Web site in a peak-usage situation. This value is used to determine the amount of offline equipment required when handling peak loads. In some cases, the second number is far harder to figure out because of the dramatic increase in certain types of activity. For example, many companies were caught off guard this past Christmas season and lost customers due to poor Web site response levels. Even though these companies had reserve hardware for their Web sites, the amount of shopping activity was well beyond expectations. This is one situation when the very best capacity planning can break down because there isn't any way to reliably predict the level of activity that can occur during usage peaks. However, even this type of peak load prediction is improving.

The second form of reserve hardware is used in the case of a failure of a primary piece of hardware. For example, in a mirrored disk setup, the second disk is always kept up-to-date, but isn't necessarily used until a failure of the primary disk becomes evident. Another example might be a tape drive that's only used when the primary drive fails. Again, the secondary tape drive is kept in reserve to ensure that the system gets backed up, despite a failure of the primary tape drive.

Emergency use hardware is easy to plan for. In many cases, one backup system for a cluster of active units is more than sufficient. You only need one spare hard drive whether you're using RAID or disk mirroring for a set of hard drives. A second tape drive is more than sufficient when you only need one tape drive to back up a system normally. You can view the amount of emergency hardware you get as an insurance policy. The more hardware you get, the better you're insured against catastrophic hardware failure, but the additional coverage costs more. Remember that each piece of reserve hardware is essentially waiting for a disaster to happen—it doesn't contribute to the daily performance requirements of the system.

Dependable Networking Technologies

Many network setups provide multiple paths, making it possible for a client to reach a server using more than one path if a primary route fails for some reason. The Internet is the classic example of a network that uses this strategy. One of the things that makes the Internet so reliable is that a server or network link failure only affects the users of that server or network link. The use of multiple paths means the data simply takes a different route to its destination.

Note   Using multiple paths is a reliability strategy for large networks, not something you'd use for a small company network. It allows a large network to continue working even if a partial failure occurs. However, it doesn't prevent problems if the local network fails for some reason. In other words, this is a strategy for a network connected using multiple network segments—usually a WAN, rather than a LAN.

Even though the use of multiple routes is normally considered strictly a reliability and convenience option, it also acts to improve performance. If one network segment is exceptionally busy, the data can always follow another route to its destination. In fact, routers today usually try to determine the best path based on several criteria, including quality of service (QoS).

It might be tempting to say that using a multiple segment setup like the Internet reduces capacity requirements for any individual link because the data always has more than one path to follow. However, this isn't necessarily true. It's true that given multiple segments, there are multiple paths that the data can travel on, but the capacity to handle a given network load still has to be present. The best way to predict future capacity requirements, therefore, is to predict the worst-case scenario data transfer times between remote nodes. By looking at the response time of the weakest links of the network, you can see what happens when the network's capacity is saturated by client requests.

Manual versus Automatic Reliability Features

So far, many of the reliability factors we covered in this chapter are automated. In other words, you set them up and they do something in the background without your interaction. Even the hardware-related reliability factors are automatic. Once you set the hardware up, you have a good idea of how that hardware performs in a given circumstance without any input from you.

One of the factors in favor of automation is that it's predictable. The word processor always saves in the background at specific intervals once you set it up to perform this task. Mean time between failure (MTBF) estimates for hard drives give you some idea of when to expect hard-drive failures. In short, the performance implications of reliability (and therefore the requirements for additional capacity) are relatively easy to measure and predict.

However, what happens when the reliability of a particular network or server is based on the manual input of the network administrator, rather than on some form of automation? For example, Message Queuing provides a lot in the way of automation, but it can't always figure out what to do with errant messages. As a result, those messages end up in a dead letter queue, where they wait for the network administrator to make a decision about their disposition.

The dead letter queue messages consume server resources, which means they affect performance to a certain degree. Because of the resources they use and the way they affect network performance, you need to provide some kind of estimate of dead letter queue messages for capacity planning. Unfortunately, because this part of the system relies on a human interaction, there isn't any consistent value to apply to the effects of the dead letter queue messages. In short, you're left trying to make a guess about the effect of these messages and the amount of capacity you need to add for them.

One of the ways to make this particular element of capacity planning a little more predictable is to put policies in place that enforce some level of network administrator behavior. Something as simple as a system message that appears in the network administrator's e-mail once a week with a reminder to empty the dead letter queue can make a lot of difference. In fact, the system does provide this feature; it just isn't very apparent. The Performance console includes an Alerts feature. You can use this feature to send a message to the network administrator when a message appears in the dead letter queue.

The following procedure shows you a generic method for adding such an alert. Of course, you'll want to modify this procedure to meet your particular needs.

1.   Open the Performance MMC snap-in. This is the snap-in that includes the System Monitor and Performance Logs and Alerts. We've talked about System Monitor quite a bit in the book so far; this is one situation when the Performance Logs and Alerts feature comes in handy.

2.   Right-click Alerts in the Performance Logs and Alerts folder, and then choose New Alert Settings from the Context menu. You'll see a New Alert Settings dialog box like the one shown in Figure 11-3.

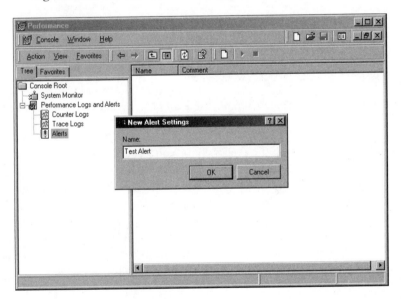

Figure 11-3.   *Creating an alert begins by giving the alert a descriptive name.*

3. Type a descriptive name for the alert. The example uses Test Alert, but you should use something that describes the alert you want to monitor. Click OK and you'll see a Properties dialog box for the alert similar to the one shown in Figure 11-4. As a minimum, you need to define a counter for an alert. It's the counter that's the secret in this case. We'll also want to set up some additional features for this particular alert.

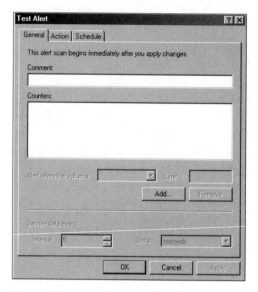

Figure 11-4. *One of the first steps in defining an alert is to add a counter that the alert tracks.*

4. Click the Add button on the General tab. You'll see a Select Counters dialog box.

5. Choose an object in the Performance Object drop-down list, such as MSMQ Queue. We're choosing this particular counter so we can monitor the contents of the queue and alert the network administrator to any errant messages. At this point, you should see the \private$\notify_queue$ queue as one of the entries in the Select Instances From List list box as shown in Figure 11-5. This is the entry that allows us to monitor notifications to the network administrator, like the presence of messages in the dead letter queue.

6. Select the \private$\notify_queue$ entry, and then click Add. Click Close to close the Select Counters dialog box. At this point, some of the other entries on the General tab get enabled.

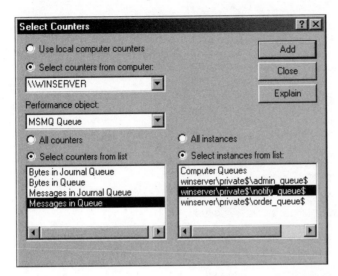

Figure 11-5. *The Select Counters dialog box allows you to choose from any of the counters available on any accessible system.*

7. Choose Over in the Alert When The Value Is drop-down list and type **1** in the Limit box. Of course, you can always set the Limit box higher to allow the network administrator to work with more than one message at a time. Setting these two options tells the Alert to do something when there's a message in the \private$\notify_queue$ queue. Your dialog box should look similar to the one shown in Figure 11-6.

8. Click the Action tab, which will look similar to the one shown in Figure 11-7. This is where we'll choose what the alert will do when there's a message in the queue. The two actions we're interested in are: Log An Entry In The Application Event Log and Send A Network Message To. Notice that you have to add a name to the network message box. I've included the network administrator's name in this case, but you normally include the name of a group of administrators or the single administrator responsible for this server.

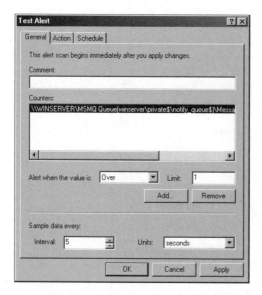

Figure 11-6.   *It's important to set some level of administrator notification.*

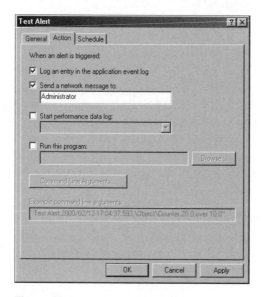

Figure 11-7.   *The final part of the process is to define where you want to send the alert message.*

9.   Click OK to complete the alert.

Although our example is very useful, it points out something more interesting in the big picture. One of the most important elements of capacity planning is getting consistent statistics that you can use to make decisions. This is especially difficult when working with manually maintained elements like the Message Queuing dead letter queue; but consistent statistics are still an essential element if you want to create the best possible predictions of future system requirements.

Understanding Vendor Claims versus Real-World Performance

Capacity planning isn't just based on your current system. Part of your capacity planning is to include new technologies in addition to updates to existing technologies. Figuring out that you'll need another server to handle future employees in an expanding company is hard; figuring out that you want to use a new server with an improved bus and higher-speed processor might be close to impossible.

> **More Info**   One way to ensure that you have the best information possible on new technologies is to visit the vendor's Web site. Most major vendors like IBM (*http://www.ibm.com/*), Dell (*http://www.dell.com/us/en/gen/default.htm*), Cisco (*http://www.cisco.com/*) have major sites online. In fact, many of these Web sites are divided in such a way that they provide very precise information about the product the company feels you need. For example, Dell has separate links for home, small business, medium business, and large business needs.

Part of the problem is figuring out which future technologies will pan out and which won't. We already talked about the problem of differentiating between vendor claims and real-world performance in other areas of the book. For instance, in Chapter 8 we explored the problems of actual vs. theoretical Ethernet performance in "Theoretical versus Real-World Performance." Unfortunately, these problems only get worse when you look at the issue of real-world performance in capacity planning.

When you need to buy a new network interface card (NIC) today, there are statistics, reviews, and other aids to help you differentiate between vendor claims and what you can actually expect. The vendors also revise their literature, in most cases, to at least come closer to the real-world performance of the products they create. However, when you're creating a play for upgrading your system tomorrow so management can set aside the required funds, it's no longer easy or even possible to get any kind of real-world information. Everything you're planning on is still vaporware, or pretty close to it. The vendor can literally predict any set of future capabilities for this equipment or software that sounds in the least plausible. No one can refute the vendor's claims because there isn't any product to test—it may be on the drawing board or just a glint in some engineer's eye.

More Info   It often helps to get reviews of the products you want to buy so that you can compare them. There are many places online to get such reviews at a click of your mouse. One such site is CNET at *http://www.cnet.com/*. This site features both hardware and software reviews, along with price comparisons and other helpful information. The computing magazines associated with Ziff Davis have long been associated with high-quality reviews as well. You'll find the various Ziff Davis magazines, including both *PC Magazine* and *PC Computing,* at *http://www.zdnet.com/*.

There's also a problem of motivation when it comes to discerning the viability of a vendor's claims for some future technology. In some cases, the vendor's claims are honest predictions. Later in the design process the vendor may realize that it just isn't possible to create a new piece of equipment or software that meets or exceeds the expectations created by marketing hype. In other cases, the vendor fully realizes that the claims made about a product can't possibly come true, yet the claims are made to dissuade buyers from getting another product that may be available today. No matter what reason the vendor has for making a particular set of claims, the important fact to realize is that at least some of those claims are unlikely to come true.

So, how do you separate the hype from features that could actually appear in the final product? After all, you need to know where a product line is going in order to predict how that product will affect your system. The following list gives you some ideas on how you separate fact from fiction in the world of future technology.

- **Industry trends**   Despite the furious rate of change in the computer industry, new technologies don't just appear on your doorstep. Those technologies are normally based on an existing idea. So, it pays to look at industry trends with regard to innovation. Ask yourself whether a promised product is within the realm of technologies that everyone is working on.

- **Too good to be true**   A lot of times an idea sounds as though it's going to meet every need you have in a particular area. In fact, it seems like it's custom fit for your needs. Sometimes these future technologies are so good you just can't believe a vendor is going to be putting them together for you. The fact of the matter is, when something sounds too good to be true, it often is.

- **Vendor reputation**   Some vendors have a history of telling you what you want to hear, and then not delivering anything close to what you expect. A vendor's reputation means a lot when it comes to future technology. Those vendors who have a good reputation for delivering at least most of what they promise are the ones you should look at closely for the future direction of technology.

- **Critics**   No one loves a critic—especially if that critic decides that your technology won't work. However, critics do have a place in society and that's to provide some form of an objective evaluation. Although you may not always agree with what they have to say, critics can often point out the potholes in the road to a future technology. So, it at least pays to take a quick look at what they have to say, even if you don't necessarily agree with it.

- **Industry pundits**   A specialist often comes out and says that a new technology won't work for a particular reason. Sometimes the specialist is wrong. However, if you start reading about a whole bunch of specialists who say something won't work and the reasons are similar, you have to begin wondering whether they're correct. In many cases, they are. Specialists get a certain reputation based on the amount of knowledge they demonstrate about industry trends. Trade press papers question these specialists because they've been right in the past. It pays to see what the "experts" are saying with regard to a new technology you want to embrace.

- **Economic factors**   New technologies are expensive. A company spends a great deal of money to develop a new technology in the hopes of gaining back the investment with future sales. However, if a company seems to have economic troubles, investment capital for that company is going to dry up, making it nearly impossible to introduce the new technology on time (or at all).

Creating a Graphical Representation of Your Network

Most network administrators are fairly good with abstract thinking. As a result, a lot of the documentation you find for networks today is in the form of plain text. The problem with a simple text representation is that you can't easily use it for planning purposes because you can't see the big picture. It's hard to envision the effect of a change in a network when you can't physically see the network as a whole. That's why it's important to create a graphical representation of your network.

Of course, the kind of representation you create depends on the size of your network. For example, a company with a single server can probably get by with a single-sheet view of the entire network. It's unlikely that such a company will have more than a few workstations, and those workstations are probably on the same floor of the building. On the other hand, a company with hundreds of servers spread out over several buildings isn't able to get by with a single-sheet representation. A large company normally needs several layers of overview drawings that the network administrator can use to drill down through the hierarchy of machines to a single workstation.

No matter what size your company is, it's likely you want to see how the various machines in a workgroup or other organizational unit are arranged when making capacity-planning decisions. For example, your predictions may show that you'll need an extra server to handle a future increase in employees. It's easy to buy the new server and then find you don't have any room for it in the current server closet if you don't have some form of graphical representation to use. Something as simple as a new printer can become problematic if you don't know where you can place it within the building.

There are other ways a graphical representation of a network can help with capacity planning. Sometimes adding capacity is more a matter of rearranging existing network elements than of buying new equipment or software. For example, a small workgroup may have access to a fairly powerful server that has lots of remaining capacity, while a larger group has completely overrun their current server's capacity. You may decide during the capacity-planning stage that the large group needs a new server. However, instead of buying a new server, you can simply exchange servers between the large and small groups. Not only does this save the company money, but it can also help you with problems of overcrowding. It's not always easy to find a place to put yet another new server.

Finding the Network Graphing Tools You Need

Creating a graphic representation of your network can be a difficult and error-prone task without the right tools. Use the wrong tool and you'll end up spending weekends performing drawing updates as your network configuration changes. On the other hand, using the right tool can make designing and managing a network easier and reduce the time to fix problems. In short, choosing the correct tool is important if you want to keep a network administrator aid from becoming an additional workload.

Designing a network requires different tools than those used to maintain it in some cases. For example, you might want to perform some "what if" analysis to discover whether the design choices you've made are the best possible. Best Fit Computing (*http://www.teleport.com/~bestfit/*) produces a unique product called Columbus that's designed to help you produce the best network design possible. Of course, getting things right in the first place means that you'll spend less time correcting problems and tuning the network later. If you already like products put out by the SAS Institute (*http://www.sas.com/rnd/app/research.html*), you might find netWorks, their new network modeling program, very useful in planning your network. Using netWorks allows you to design very large systems with complex interrelations.

Drawing a picture of your network won't help you keep track of it. Sure, you have a pictorial aid that will help you locate specific machines or peripherals and track their status manually, but larger networks may require more. That's where Harris Network Management (HNM) comes into play (*http://www.commprod.harris.com/network-mgmt/*). It allows you to use the graphic representation of your network as a monitoring tool. As the condition of your network changes, the graphic representation on the network administrator's display changes as well. Another tool that you may want to consider for monitoring your network once you have the initial design and installation completed is Lanware's (*http://www.lanware.net/products/nms/brochure.asp*) Network Monitoring Suite. In addition to condition monitoring, this product provides detailed charting of network performance statistics.

Sometimes you need a suite of tools to get the best view of your network. Intel (*http://www.intel.com/network/products/*) provides several products that you can link together to meet specific needs. Products like Device View allow you to remotely manage individual Intel products. LANDesk Management Suite is an industry leading tool that allows you to manage very large networks using a combination of graphic and text displays. It contains an impressive list of features including client virus protection and integration with remote management products like Device View. The greatest strength of LANDesk is the network device (like routers and hubs) support it provides.

Novell also provides a combination text and graphic management tool in the form of ManageWise (*http://www.novell.com/products/managewise/*). It shares many of the same features of Intel LANDesk, but with a NetWare orientation. As a result, ManageWise provides tight coupling with Novell's ZENworks product, an agent that you can install with Novell's NetWare client for Windows. The greatest strength of ManageWise is analyzing workstation-oriented problems.

Looking for Performance Bottlenecks

Performance has played a very big part in our discussion of capacity planning in this chapter. It's the need for performance that often drives the planning for additional hardware and updated software. It also drives the need for additional user training and, in some cases, the need for new company policies to keep performance problems in check. In Chapters 5, 6, and 7, we looked at three common kinds of performance bottlenecks that affect servers. In these chapters, we talked about the ways you can detect, monitor, and finally eliminate performance bottlenecks. However, looking for and eliminating performance bottlenecks only goes so far in helping you tune your network for maximum performance. Sometimes, you need to use these performance bottlenecks as the criteria for system upgrades.

Capacity planning also requires a look at performance bottlenecks. You can optimize a system, remove every potential cause of a performance bottleneck, and still have problems getting a part of the system to keep up. It's a constant struggle that most network administrators have to fight. Just when the technology for one part of the system comes within range of doing the job, some other part falls behind. For example, in many machines the disk has been a bottleneck. The use of new technologies like SANs, however, has moved the bottleneck from the disk to the peripheral bus. New chip sets from Intel and other companies promise increased front side bus speeds. Although the current standard as of this writing is 100 MHz, there are motherboards on the market that have buses that perform at the 133-MHz level and even higher. About the time that both disk and bus subsystems are up to par, memory falls behind in performance. In fact, poor memory performance is the reason Intel is introducing new memory technologies like Rambus, and other vendors have begun using double data rate (DDR) synchronous dynamic random access memory (SDRAM). It's a never-ending cycle.

Part of your capacity planning needs to revolve around performance bottlenecks. Learning to identify the part of the system that's currently behind the technology curve is every bit as important as figuring out where technology is going in the future and what your company needs in the way of additional performance to manage growth. Performance bottleneck identification is important because it doesn't pay to upgrade the other components in the system if one component causes the others to wait. Of course, you also need to understand how the performance bottleneck fits into the roles your company sees for the network server. A processor bottleneck is far less important to a server that's used for database processing than one that's used for heavy graphics processing.

There's another problem to address when it comes to performance bottlenecks. Some companies try to update their systems continually, rather than buy an entirely new system. In the short run, this strategy does work. It costs less to replace a motherboard than it does to buy an entirely new system—at least in some cases. However, it's doubtful that the company actually gets full use out of the new motherboard. The problem is that there are a lot of old components left in the system that keep the motherboard's performance in check. In essence, the system acts a little faster, but eventually the company has to replace another element, and then another, until it has bought a new machine for three or four times the amount that buying a new system in the first place would have cost. More often than not, it pays to replace an old system with an entirely new system that's balanced for the kinds of applications your company runs.

Another problem you face when looking at performance bottlenecks during capacity planning is the changing company role. Many companies face that problem today because they're getting on the Internet for the first time. Yesterday this company may have had a small network with a relatively small database and some word processing. Today, they have to manage a much larger database, while the amount of word processing has stayed the same. Because of the new Internet site, employees are also using graphics applications, spreadsheets, and other application types that the company may not have used in the past. In short, the role of the server within the company has changed. Unless your capacity-planning strategy changes to meet the new situation, you could find yourself working with a server that isn't tuned to meet the company's current needs.

The bottom line is that performance bottlenecks often determine where a company spends the money it's allocated for a particular system upgrade. I don't know of any companies that have an unlimited supply of cash lying around for system upgrades, so the identification of areas where a company must spend money is very important. Performance bottlenecks that exist in areas where a company needs an exceptional level of performance are also the places where you need to put the greatest time and effort in an upgrade. Capacity planning allows you to determine just how much a particular performance bottleneck requires in the way of remediation.

Summary

By now, you should have a better idea of what you want to do with your own network. As previously mentioned, capacity planning is matter of looking at where you are today, determining where you need to be by tomorrow, and then determining what you need to do to get from one point to the other. You also realize by now that drawing the line isn't as easy as it might seem in many instances. Not only do you have management fighting for every dollar that you spend, users who don't want to learn new techniques, support staff that worries about how they'll accomplish things, but you also have that specter of uncertainty hanging over your head.

You can divide capacity planning into three main areas: software, hardware, and user training. Looking at one area without looking at the others invites disaster because management will see large expenditures for additional capacity, with little to show in the way of improved performance. Adding more hardware doesn't mean the software you own will automatically know how to use that new hardware more efficiently. Sure, the software gobbles up the extra capacity (it always does), but using that hardware efficiently means you'll be able to quantify the improvement in the form of either reduced costs or improved user productivity, or perhaps both.

We also looked at one area in this chapter that most network administrators ignore. The time required to maintain the network is critical. However, you can't just get up one morning and say you're going to reduce network downtime. An improvement of network reliability takes planning, which means you have to perform some type of analysis of network problem areas in advance. Improving the reliability of your system as a whole reduces support staff requirements and system downtime and its associated cost while improving user productivity at the same time. In short, reliability is one of the first capacity areas you should look at because it offers one of the biggest paybacks for most systems today.

Knowing what you own is at least as important as knowing what you want to do tomorrow. Unfortunately, an inventory held in a three-ring binder just doesn't provide what you need for capacity planning. Sure, it's going to tell you that you still have an 80486 in office number 221, but it doesn't tell you how many 80486 machines the company has as a whole and who's using them. Perhaps it doesn't matter that you still own an 80486 if that machine is only used for typing by guests visiting your company. On the other hand, you better plan on replacing it soon if one of your lead programmers is still using that machine. Representing your network graphically pays some pretty big dividends because you can place a piece of equipment in perspective with the rest of the network.

Chapter 12 takes you on a tour of the various Windows 2000 versions. Up until now, we talked about Windows 2000 in generic terms—we've been addressing the requirements for all versions of Windows 2000 Server as a whole. However, the individual server types are designed for special purposes, which means they have individual tuning requirements as well. Chapter 12 explores these special needs and helps you plan for them as you get your network tuned to perfection.

Chapter 12
Microsoft Windows 2000 and Its Versions

One of the problems with many operating systems on the market today is that they come in one flavor. They don't allow you to do things your own way. As a result, there are many situations where the operating system has too many or too few features for a particular situation. In short, you end up with something other than the feature set you wanted and may have paid extra for.

Windows 2000 comes in more than one flavor. Microsoft has provided versions of the product that should appeal to a wide variety of users. Each "flavor" provides a specific set of features that are designed with a specific audience in mind. In many cases, a small-business user is happy with Microsoft Windows 2000 Server. As your company moves up to multiple servers, it might be necessary to move up to Microsoft Windows 2000 Advanced Server as well. Those of you who work in a large corporation with one or more heavy-duty database applications at its center probably need Microsoft Windows 2000 Datacenter Server. As you can see, Windows 2000 Server does go further in allowing you to buy the number of features you actually need to perform a given task.

This is the first chapter that covers the Windows 2000 Server versions from a performance tuning and optimization (PTO) perspective. Most of the other chapters in the book have approached the topic of Windows 2000 Server tuning from a single product perspective. In many cases, you can act as though there's a single version of Windows 2000 Server to work with because each of the versions builds on the other. Windows 2000 Advanced Server is a true superset of Windows 2000 Server. Likewise, Windows 2000 Datacenter Server is a true superset of Windows 2000 Advanced Server. However, the reality is that there are several versions of Windows 2000 Server and that these separate versions require special handling if you want to get the most out of them.

The chapter begins by looking at the differences in the Windows 2000 Server versions. You need to know what each version can do so you understand why specific tuning tips are required with the more complex versions. "Overview of the Windows 2000 Versions" examines version information from three perspectives. We look at the feature set of each product—not in any great detail, but from an overview perspective. Next, we look at the system requirements and capabilities of each version. For example, Server only allows you to use 4 GB of RAM, but the Datacenter version can use a whopping 64 GB. Such a large difference in memory support has a definite effect on performance. Finally, we look at the issue of operating system tasks. It's important to answer the question of why you want to use a particular version of Windows 2000 Server and when it's overkill to use a higher level version of Windows 2000 Server than you really need.

The next section of the chapter, "General Server Tuning Techniques," explores some of the things you can do to tune Windows 2000 Server specifically. We're no longer talking about the server's hardware, the applications that run on the server, the users, or any other factor. Don't look for general tuning techniques that work just as well with Microsoft Windows NT Server as they do with Windows 2000 Server either. This section contains tuning techniques specific to Windows 2000 Server and no other Windows version. In fact, you could go so far as to say that the tuning techniques in this section are unlikely to work with Microsoft Windows 2000 Professional. In short, this is the "meat and potatoes" chapter you've spent the rest of the time reading the book to learn about.

> **Note** It's important to tune your server in a general way using all the techniques discussed in the other chapters of the book before you begin using the techniques in this section. Consider these techniques the fine tuning you need to get every drop of performance from your server. Just as a race car driver doesn't fine tune an engine until everything about the car has been tuned in general, you don't want to use these fine-tuning techniques on your server until you're reasonably sure everything else has been tuned.

Once we get past the general tuning techniques, we look at Windows 2000 Advanced Server-specific techniques in "Special Tuning Concerns for Advanced Server." Windows 2000 Advanced Server provides special features, and those special features require some form of tuning. However, there's a bigger issue here to consider. When you work with Windows 2000 Server, you're more than likely looking at one or two separate servers. Windows 2000 Advanced Server is designed for a different audience, more processors, and servers that work in tandem. Some tuning techniques have to change or get augmented in some way to work properly.

The final section of the chapter, "Special Tuning Concerns for Datacenter Server," explores some techniques for this version of the product. Most of the tips in this section are supposition. Windows 2000 Datacenter Server is a glint in Microsoft's eye, at this point, and not much more. Because this section is written about vaporware, you're going to have to modify some of the ideas to work with the real-world product when it arrives on the scene. In short, the ideas in this section are food for thought and should be approached from that perspective.

Overview of the Windows 2000 Versions

Unless you've been hiding in a cave for the last few years, you understand that the business-computing environment has seen some rather large changes. In fact, the business-computing environment has grown so rapidly that many IT professionals are screaming, "Enough already—I'd just love to get caught up before you give me more new technology to learn about!" Rather than lose your sanity, it's a good idea to reduce the amount of information overload you have to deal with. One way to achieve this goal is to limit the scope of your vision for the company's network by reducing the scope of the technologies you look at.

This isn't a book about dealing with information overload and I wouldn't even pretend to tell you I know more about your business than you do. I do know, however, that you can begin to reduce information overload by determining what's important and what's not when it comes to the server technology you use on your network. That's part of the reason it's so important to understand the Windows 2000 versions. Knowing that your company isn't really large enough to deal with the intricacies of Windows 2000 Datacenter Server reduces the amount of time you have to spend looking at feature sets you'll never use. Of course, the server product you choose determines the type of support hardware and software you need; small systems require less support, which means you can get by with less research if you have some idea of what to look for in the first place. Understanding the Windows 2000 Server feature set eliminates the need to look for hardware you can use, like an eight-processor server setup.

On the other hand, if you do need this product, you also have a support staff that can offload some of the burden from your shoulders. Giving the individual server requirements to an assistant and concentrating on just the high-end features is another way to reduce the effects of information overload that we all suffer from. Even so, you still need to know the capabilities of the server before you can provide any input to subordinates or understand whether the data they've collected helps in your company's efforts to get the right server installed. Table 12-1 contains a list of Windows 2000 features by server types. Although this table provides a mere overview of what we cover in the sections that follow, it's a good place to start. Note that the Windows 2000 Datacenter Server information is incomplete (they're marked "To Be Determined" or TBD) because this product wasn't released as of the time of this writing.

> **Note**   Table 12-1 is oriented toward comparing all three server versions. You should use this as a means for seeing the special features of Windows 2000 Datacenter Server. It helps you to determine if you need the Windows 2000 Datacenter Server in the future based on the information available today. Table 12-2 looks at specific comparisons between the two released versions: Windows 2000 Server and Windows 2000 Advanced Server. This second table is the one to use when determining which product to buy for your network today. It's also the table you should use from a PTO perspective to determine which server provides precisely what you need without being overkill for your networking requirements.

Table 12-1. Windows 2000 Server Platform Feature Differences

Feature	Windows 2000 Server	Windows 2000 Advanced Server	Windows 2000 Datacenter Server
Cluster Support	None	Two Node Failover	Cascading Failover Between Four Nodes
Component Testing Method	Windows Hardware Compatibility List (WHCL)	WHCL	Datacenter Hardware Compatibility List (HCL)
CPU Required	133 MHz Pentium Compatible	133 MHz Pentium Compatible	TBD
CPUs per System	4	8	32
Disk Space Required	2 GB (1 GB Free Space)	2 GB (1 GB Free Space)	TBD
Memory (Minimum and Maximum)	256 MB/4 GB	256 MB/8 GB	TBD/64 GB
Network Load Balancing (NLB)	None	32 Nodes Maximum	32 Nodes Maximum
Server Consolidation Support	No	No	Yes
Symmetric Multiprocessing (SMP) Support	Yes	Yes	Yes

By now, you should have gotten the idea that researching a server is one of the first steps in optimizing your system. Until you understand the capabilities of the server, you really don't have a good idea of what kinds of things you can optimize and the limits of that optimization. Spending all your time fighting the effects of information overload, rather than getting solid information about what Windows 2000 can do for you, doesn't help you or your company get a system put together that's efficient from the outset. With this in mind, you should look at the following sections of the chapter as a means of separating what you need to know from what's nice to know. Hopefully, this chapter does its own small part in reducing information overload at your company.

Windows 2000 Server

Microsoft has targeted Windows 2000 Server to perform four main tasks: file services, print services, intranets, and networking. It's important to realize you can also use Windows 2000 Server as an application server and for other tasks. The point is that this version of the product is designed for the needs of a small- to medium-sized company that relies on individual servers to get the job done. This isn't the high-end product that gets your Web site running—it's more of a product you use to keep a single workgroup or small office running.

From a PTO perspective, Windows 2000 Server is the easiest version to maintain. In most cases, you deal with a single server, so server interaction isn't an issue. Even if you do have to work with multiple servers, the fact that these servers aren't in a cluster or other intensely interactive environment means you could possibly isolate them and work on them singly. Once each server is individually tuned, you work on the network as a whole. In short, this is the easiest platform to tune once you have it up and running. All you need to do to tune Windows 2000 Server as an operating system is look at the information in the "General Server Tuning Techniques" section of this chapter. Of course, you also want to look at the other sections of the book for tips on tuning other areas of the system like the hard disk drives and processor.

Windows 2000 Server is a hands-on system from a network administration perspective. The positive part of this is that the network administrator has full control over every system element and doesn't need to worry about automatic controls overriding decisions for a short-term performance increase. Once the network administrator assigns a user to a specific server, the user continues to use that server and the network administrator can be certain of the user load the server has to bear. This is the optimum way of handling user assignments when the individual user load is likely to remain constant. For example, if your workgroup works on documents all day, the server load is consistent and you can rely on simplified management techniques to handle the situation.

Although Windows 2000 Server definitely provides the simplest tuning environment, tuning isn't the whole picture for most companies. It doesn't matter whether the network is operating at peak efficiency if an individual server can't handle the current processing load or if reliability is a problem. Windows 2000 Server isn't a good platform to choose when user loads change a great deal, especially when you're working with e-commerce sites that also require access to a database. You'll also find that the lack of support for things like Network Load Balancing (NLB) becomes a problem as the size of the network increases.

This brings up another PTO issue. Windows 2000 Server doesn't provide much in the way of scalability. So, although the individual servers are easy to tune, you can't combine them in ways that allow the network to function as a cohesive whole. This means you get individual servers, not servers that are optimized to work together. Individuality is a good thing to look for in creative humans; it's not necessarily a good feature of networks. As a result of a lack of interoperability support, you'll find that Windows 2000 Server becomes a tuning nightmare from an administration perspective once the network achieves a certain size. Consider what happens if you don't balance the server's load between users. A single server might have more than its capacity in user load, while another server is idle. This is a problem Windows 2000 Server can't solve. The ease of tuning individual servers is traded for a lack of ability to handle changing system loads and means you eventually need to move to Advanced Server as your company grows.

Windows 2000 Advanced Server

Microsoft has targeted Windows 2000 Advanced Server as the product of choice for many enterprise-application situations and e-commerce development. The two features that make this product a good choice for these situations are the NLB support and the clustering support. The use of NLB means your servers all share the current processing load, which means all users see similar response times and the response time is the fastest available under the circumstances. The clustering service is important because it allows failover capability. If a server fails, another server in the cluster automatically picks up the load from the failed server. In this case, the cluster size is limited to two servers—sufficient for most business applications, but probably not enough for applications that have to provide 100 percent access 24 hours a day.

Comparison of Windows 2000 Server and Windows 2000 Advanced Server Features

It's important to compare all the features of Windows 2000 Server and Windows 2000 Advanced Server since these are the two versions that are released at the time of this writing. Table 12-2 contains a list of the most important features and tells you which server supports them. You can use this table as a quick buying guide when the determination between server versions is hard to make.

Although Table 12-2 does provide a detailed listing of the features provided by each released server version, you can get more detailed information about each feature, including feature descriptions, on the Microsoft Web site. The best place to look for detailed server feature description information is *http://www.microsoft.com/windows2000/guide/server/features/default.asp*. You can find bits and pieces of information on other areas of the Windows 2000 Server Web site as well.

Table 12-2.   Detailed Comparison of Windows 2000 Server and Windows 2000 Advanced Server Features

Feature	Windows 2000 Server	Windows 2000 Advanced Server
8-GB Memory Support	No	Yes
8-Way Symmetric Multiprocessor (SMP) Support	No	Yes
Active Directory Integration	Yes	Yes
Active Directory-Enabled Applications	Yes	Yes
Active Directory Interoperability	Yes	Yes
Active Directory Synchronization Tools	Yes	Yes
Active Server Pages (ASP) Programming Environment	Yes	Yes
Application Certification and DLL Protection	Yes	Yes
Applications and Directory Interoperability	Yes	Yes

(continued)

Table 12-2.   *(continued)*

Feature	Windows 2000 Server	Windows 2000 Advanced Server
Automatic Restart	Yes	Yes
Backup and Recovery	Yes	Yes
Centralized Desktop Management	Yes	Yes
Cluster Administrator	No	Yes
Cluster Service	No	Yes
Cluster Service Setup	No	Yes
Component Object Model + (COM+)	Yes	Yes
Configuration Wizard	Yes	Yes
Delegated Administration	Yes	Yes
Disk Defragmentation	Yes	Yes
Disk Quotas	Yes	Yes
Distributed File System (DFS)	Yes	Yes
Driver Certification	Yes	Yes
Dynamic Domain Name System (DDNS)	Yes	Yes
Dynamic Volume Management	Yes	Yes
Encrypting File System (EFS)	Yes	Yes
Enhanced ASP Performance	Yes	Yes
eXtensible Markup Language (XML) Parser	Yes	Yes
Group Policy	Yes	Yes
Hierarchical Storage Management	Yes	Yes
High Interoperability with Client Computers	Yes	Yes
High Throughput and Bandwidth Utilization	Yes	Yes
Integrated Directory Services	Yes	Yes
Integrated Network Load Balancing Configuration	No	Yes
Internet Connection Sharing (ICS)	Yes	Yes
Internet Information Services (IIS) 5.0	Yes	Yes
Internet Information Services (IIS) Application Protection	Yes	Yes
Internet Information Services (IIS) CPU Throttling	Yes	Yes
Internet Printing	Yes	Yes
Job Object API	Yes	Yes
Kerberos Authentication	Yes	Yes
Kernel-Mode Write Protection	Yes	Yes
Kill Process Tree	Yes	Yes
Latest Server Hardware Like 8-Way SMP and Intel's Physical Address Extension (PAE)	No	Yes

(continued)

Table 12-2. *(continued)*

Feature	Windows 2000 Server	Windows 2000 Advanced Server
Microsoft Connection Manager Administration Kit and Connection Point Services	Yes	Yes
Microsoft Management Console (MMC)	Yes	Yes
Multimaster Replication	Yes	Yes
Multisite Hosting	Yes	Yes
Network Load Balancing (NLB)	No	Yes
Network Support Includes: Digital Subscriber Line (DSL), Virtual Private Networking (VPN), Routing, Network Address Translation (NAT), Dynamic Host Configuration Protocol (DHCP), Quality of Service (QoS) Hardware, Directory-Enabled Networking Devices, Internet Protocol Security (IPSec), Secure Sockets Layer (SSL), and Asynchronous Transfer Mode (ATM)	Yes	Yes
Peripheral Support Includes: Storage Management Hardware, Universal Serial Bus (USB), Network Interface Cards (NICs), Keyboards and Mouse Devices, Advanced Printer Driver Support, Firewire (IEEE 1394), Personal Computer Memory Card International Association (PCMCIA), Infrared and Digital Devices	Yes	Yes
Plug and Play (PnP)	Yes	Yes
Public Key Infrastructure (PKI) Group Policy Management	Yes	Yes
Public Key Infrastructure Support in the Form of Services Like Certificate Services	Yes	Yes
Remote Management with Terminal Services	Yes	Yes
Rolling Upgrade Support	No	Yes
Routing and Remote Access Service	Yes	Yes
Safe Mode Boot	Yes	Yes
Search for and Connect to Printers from a Desktop	Yes	Yes
Secure Network Communications	Yes	Yes
Security Configuration Tool Set (SCTS)	Yes	Yes
Server and Mainframe Interoperability	Yes	Yes
Service Pack Slipstreaming	Yes	Yes
Smart-Card Support	Yes	Yes
Support for the Latest Security Standards	Yes	Yes
System Preparation Tool	Yes	Yes
Terminal Services	Yes	Yes
Virtual Private Network (VPN)	Yes	Yes
Web Folders	Yes	Yes
Web Telephony Engine	Yes	Yes

(continued)

Table 12-2.   *(continued)*

Feature	Windows 2000 Server	Windows 2000 Advanced Server
Windows 2000 Distributed interNetwork Architecture (DNA)	Yes	Yes
Windows File Protection	Yes	Yes
Windows Installer—Microsoft Installer (MSI) File Support	Yes	Yes
Windows Management Instrumentation (WMI)	Yes	Yes
Windows Media Platform	Yes	Yes
Windows NT 4.0 Domain Migration Tools	Yes	Yes
Windows Script Host (WSH)	Yes	Yes
Windows Telephony Application Programming Interface (TAPI) 3.0	Yes	Yes

Now that we've compared Windows 2000 Server and Windows 2000 Advanced Server, you can see that Advanced Server is designed to handle situations that Windows 2000 Server can't. It's important to realize, however, that this extra performance comes at a price—a price you pay in both actual system performance and the time spent tuning it.

When working with Windows 2000 Advanced Server, you always start by isolating the server and tuning it as an individual. Unfortunately, this isn't very easy to achieve if the server is engaged in NLB or is part of a cluster. The other servers rely on this particular server to handle a specific part of the load and to enhance system reliability. So, removing the server and tuning it probably isn't going to be a choice unless you have a spare server. This means you need to attempt to tune the server in place, which is an error-prone process that doesn't achieve satisfactory results. (Perhaps it's better to say that the individual server tuning results, in this case, don't match those achieved when using Windows 2000 Server.)

The decision of whether to tune the server cluster or the network as a whole comes next. It's not a straightforward decision because both tuning areas are interdependent. When you tune one, you can cause tuning errors in the other. So, it's important to consider what kind of network load you're running. If this load requires additional reliability or if this load varies to any great degree, it's usually a good idea to tune the network first, and then the cluster. Any tuning changes to the cluster that offset changes you made to the network as a whole produce a smaller effect than if you had used the reverse process. The application in question relies on the capabilities of the cluster to a greater degree than the capabilities of the network (which becomes a mere transport mechanism).

Of course, the individual servers within the cluster affect each other's performance as well. For example, there's a certain amount of communication that takes place between the servers and the router. If this communication becomes lengthy, network performance suffers. Part of the tuning process is to ensure that the servers engage in the least amount of communication required to perform a specific task. In addition, you may need to resort to manual tuning, in some cases, to ensure that a particular change doesn't get overridden by the automation that the servers provide—at least not immediately. You want to slowly move the servers into an optimal configuration that's consistent with the type of application you need to run, the number of network users, how often those users log on to the system, and the consistency of the load those users produce.

> **Tip** Servers that interact with each other to a high degree require some special tuning consideration. For example, the tuning you perform has some immediate effect, but also has a delayed effect. Any change you make produces some immediate activity on the part of the servers. However, because the servers are interacting with each other, there is some period of counteractivity and adjustment. As a result, tuning a cluster isn't a one- or two-hour process; it may take days or weeks to perform properly. You must wait for the servers involved to reach some level of equilibrium before you can make another change. You don't see the full effect of a change immediately, so small changes are also recommended. A server cluster begins to take on a life of its own—the servers interact with each other and form an intelligence of sorts. Tuning one server usually isn't enough and making large changes usually produces poor results. Remember, when tuning a cluster, patience is a virtue, but a little stubbornness helps too.

As you can see, when using Windows 2000 Advanced Server, you're trading a great deal of tuning complexity for the flexibility, load balancing, and reliability capabilities that this version of Windows provides. Obviously, this isn't a decision you want to make lightly. Using Windows 2000 Advanced Server means setting aside a great number of additional resources and hiring additional network administrators—even if you're only adding one or two servers to create a cluster. We see in the "Special Tuning Concerns for Advanced Server" section of the chapter how these additional considerations require additional planning on your part. Of course, you want to look at the tips in the "General Server Tuning Techniques" section of the chapter first for tuning tips for the individual server. Remember that you want to tune the individual servers first, and then change the server settings to obtain optimal network and cluster performance.

Windows 2000 Datacenter Server

Microsoft is targeting Windows 2000 Datacenter Server at large enterprise applications that must provide 100 percent access 24 hours a day. In addition, large companies can use this product for online transaction processing (OLTP) and data warehousing. This is the right platform for both application service providers and Internet service providers (ISPs) because it provides a superior level of both reliability and scalability. Reliability enhancements come in the form of advanced clustering that allows for up to four servers in a single cascading cluster. This means all four servers have to fail before the system registers an actual node failure. Scalability comes in the form of enhanced operating system features that allow you to add more memory and processors. A single server case can support a much greater load than other versions of Windows.

It might be hard to grasp the real significance of Windows 2000 Datacenter Server at first. Except for the additional hardware support features, we don't know much about it at this point. However, it's unlikely that Microsoft will add any major features at the operating-system level other than support for the larger quantities of hardware. You don't find any significant additional features like Component Services in Windows 2000 Datacenter Server; you're more likely to find some small incremental change that makes it easier to work with but does not add any additional capability to speak about. Of course, this begs the question of why Windows 2000 Datacenter Server is important from a PTO perspective. If this product contains the same (or just about the same) feature set as Windows 2000, you'd think you'd be able to use the same tuning techniques. Unfortunately, you'd be wrong.

Note   Component Services is based on COM and Microsoft Transaction Server (an earlier release of a component-based transaction processing system).

Consider the size of many large enterprises. Most of them span more than one building; many of them cross state, province, or even country boundaries. In short, these enterprises are very large and require some level of support that allows servers in more than one location to service the needs of individual users. That's the point of using Windows 2000 Datacenter Server. You're dealing with a giant—a network that's larger than most network administrators can easily visualize. Because of the size differential, you need a sledgehammer instead of a tack hammer to make adjustments to the network as a whole.

From a PTO perspective, this version has an even greater problem with interaction than Windows 2000 Advanced Server does. Now you're not only dealing with the problems of crosstalk between servers, but you also have physical time boundaries to consider. You have to contend with both a large distance, which means synchronization occurs over several time zones, and also employees who are literally using the network 24 hours a day, leaving you without any downtime for small tweaks to the network.

There are many companies that need this version of Windows because they require large amounts of processing powers across an even larger physical area. The PTO consideration, in this case, is the sheer size of the network and the number of network administrators required to maintain it. Tuning, in this case, isn't a matter of one person performing a survey on local machines—it's the cooperative effort of more than one network administrator working over a period of weeks to fully tune the system.

General Server Tuning Techniques

General server tuning means looking at the operating system and seeing what you can do to make it work faster, more reliably, and still support a larger load. It's important to differentiate this kind of tuning from the other types of tuning that we've looked at in the book so far. We don't cover bottlenecks in this chapter and we aren't going to spend a lot of time looking at monitoring tools. Other chapters have already covered these issues.

What we need to look at are tried-and-true methods of making the server operating system—the software that controls every action on the server—perform faster. This means looking at both the large and small issues.

Quick Tips for Small Gains

There are a lot of things you can do to tune a server in a general way that have little to do with the hardware or the applications running on it. Many of these changes fall into the tweak category. No, you don't see a big change by implementing them; but yes, they make a difference you can see in the server as a whole. For example, a change in the display settings doesn't make a big difference in performance, but this change could reserve just enough extra performance that one additional user can get on to the system. These small but important tweaks allow you to drain the last ounce of performance from your server. The following list suggests some things you can look at.

- **Keep display settings simple** Some network administrators don't really think about Windows 2000 Server as a server. If you look at other server operating systems, they usually provide a Spartan interface with few, if any, amenities. Windows 2000 Server gives you the opportunity to shoot yourself in the foot by dressing up the display. The point is that if you treat Windows 2000 Server in the same way you treat a desktop operating system, some amount of system resources will be lost generating a pleasant display for the network administrator who's unlikely to use the server console with any regularity. For the most part, you need to keep the display settings as simple as possible. Keep the display settings at the minimum possible and access the server from your workstation. Display settings include items like wallpaper, color depth, and display resolution. All these things use up some small amount of system resources that could be used for other purposes like handling user requests. If possible keep the display at 640 × 480 and at a 16-color resolution. You don't need anything more for most diagnostic purposes. (There are a few dialog boxes in Windows that require an 800 × 600 display resolution.)

- **Log off** You want to log off of the server for security purposes, even if the server is physically locked in a closet. Logging off the server also preserves some amount of resources. This means closing any open dialog boxes before you log off to ensure that all resources used to display data on screen are properly freed. Staying logged on to the server means the screen gets redrawn any time any open applications are updated. If you're using something like System Monitor, the number of screen updates is substantial. A screen update requires processing time that could be used in other areas.

- **Don't install doodads** I put a whole realm of utility programs into the "doodad" category. A lot of servers now come with various sorts of monitoring agents. An example of one of these monitoring agents is the PC Probe utility that comes with ASUS motherboards. For the most part, these agents work fine as long as there's someone at the console to do something about the problem.

However, the agents are practically useless for keeping track of the server's status from a remote station. Even though these utility programs have a useful purpose on a desktop machine or a server that's placed in a centralized location (never a good idea for security reasons), they use up resources on a properly secured server and shouldn't be installed.

Real World

There are a lot of ways to waste server resources, many of which you can't imagine and don't think of until you run into them. One consultant got a call from a customer who was complaining about sluggish server performance. The consultant spent a lot of time with the client trying to figure out what was wrong, to no avail. After he exhausted his usual list of performance-inhibiting problems, the consultant tried a few unusual solutions, none of which worked. Thinking there must be a major hardware failure, the consultant went to the client site to determine the source of the problem.

Imagine the consultant's surprise when he found the server's hard disk drive filled with two kinds of trash. The first was old files that had accumulated in the Recycle Bin. It seems that someone set the maximum size of the Recycle Bin extraordinarily high, which meant that more of the hard disk drive was in use holding what amounted to trash. No one wanted to take responsibility for clearing the Recycle Bin because it might have contained something useful.

The second source of problems was that the server had a modem installed. A bright young star at the company thought the server would make the perfect machine for downloading files from the Internet. After all, the download wouldn't place much of a load on the server and would free up resources on a workstation. Although the files were removed from the server (actually, they had been placed in the Recycle Bin once the person was done with them), the Web pages visited while finding the files weren't. The result was a large amount of space taken up with yet more trash.

Once the consultant took out the garbage, the server returned to its former performance level. It's hard to imagine that you could slow a server by filling it up with garbage, but it can happen. Garbage comes in many forms, many of them bits and pieces left by other applications. We see later in this section of the chapter that you can do quite a few things to keep the garbage level on your system low.

- **Fix leaky applications**   Some programs leak memory. This means any program—everything from utility programs to services to COM+ applications. They allocate memory—indicating to Windows 2000 they need so much space—but never give it back, even after they terminate. After a while, you might find you don't have enough memory to run programs, even though you should. Although this problem could be severe when using custom applications, most developers know how to write applications that don't leak resources. In addition, Windows 2000 does a much better job than Windows NT of looking for errant programs that don't release memory when they're done. Unfortunately, servers tend to handle many small client requests and this tends to accelerate the rate at which memory dissipates. A leaky workstation application is an inconvenience; a leaky server application is a disaster. There are ways of dealing with leaky applications on a workstation. You should never consider keeping a leaky application on your server.

- **Eliminate extra drivers**   Windows 2000 does a fairly good job of cleaning old drivers out of the registry. Even so, you want to take the time to see whether all the drivers got removed from the system after you remove an application. This isn't such a big deal for newer applications that are specifically designed for Windows 2000. The newer installation programs ensure that the program cleans up after itself when you no longer need it. In addition, once a server is set up, there's little reason to change that setup unless your company has a change in direction or the vendor comes out with a new version of the application. The real problems are custom applications. In many cases, these applications don't go through any of the Microsoft logo tests, which means they haven't been fully tested for Windows compliance. Make sure any custom applications you use clean up after themselves.

Tip   Always look for applications that bear the Windows logo when purchasing off-the-shelf applications. This logo assures you that Microsoft has tested the application and that it should perform reasonably well on your machine. The Windows 2000 logo requires the most stringent support of Windows features and is the logo to look for first on an application. Many people complained that the Windows logo program wasn't strict enough in the past. The new program is very stringent and most developers are having problems passing all the requirements. In other words, the Windows logo of today does mean you're getting a high quality product.

- **Don't use MS-DOS/16-bit applications**   Don't even consider running an old application on your Windows 2000 Server. These applications cause nothing but trouble and you definitely run into performance problems. It may seem unreasonable to even think that companies use these old applications, but there are cases when scientific applications still use MS-DOS. For example, data logger applications that grab information about the environment or from attached scientific equipment still exist. You should move any of these nonstandard applications from the main company server to another server set aside for the specific purpose of running an MS-DOS application. Even better, since most of these specialty applications are custom coded for the company, it might be a good idea to simply upgrade your setup to something a little more modern.

- **Use an efficient hard-disk drive format**   It's hard to believe that people use a FAT partition on their server, but it happens. Hard-disk drive format affects system performance in several ways. The most obvious is direct file access; you get the best level of performance using an NTFS partition. (You do, however, give up some flexibility to get this speed boost.) The second area is a little less obvious. Placing your pagefile on an NTFS partition can actually improve performance because NTFS is an optimized disk-formatting technology. I wouldn't count on a large speed improvement, however—moving your pagefile is more in the line of an incremental improvement.

- **Reset your printer for RAW printing**   Windows 2000 automatically installs support for Enhanced Metafile Format (EMF) printing on systems designed to support it. This feature allows Windows 2000 to print faster by translating the output to generic commands in the foreground and then creating printer-specific output in the background. Creating generic commands requires a lot less processing time than writing printer-specific output. Changing the setting of the Spool Data Format field in the Spool Settings dialog box to RAW forces Windows 2000 to create a printer-specific output in the first pass. Using the RAW setting means that less operating system code is maintained in memory during the print process because the data is sent directly to the printer in its current format. Some systems receive a large benefit by using this print mode. Of course, the trade-off is longer foreground print times.

- **Keep your disk defragmented**   Earlier versions of Windows enable you to create a permanent pagefile (swap file). Using a permanent pagefile improves performance by reducing hard-disk head movement to read pagefile data. It doesn't matter how fragmented your hard disk drive gets after you set up the pagefile, because the pagefile is always in the same contiguous disk sectors. Windows 2000 doesn't provide the permanent pagefile option. It always uses a temporary file. Microsoft has improved the access algorithms and reduced the penalty for using a temporary pagefile, however. Of course, the system doesn't work perfectly. You can still get a highly fragmented drive that reduces system performance as Windows moves from area to area in an attempt to read the pagefile. Defragmenting your drive reduces the possibility that the pagefile becomes too fragmented. Most people find that a monthly maintenance session takes care of this requirement.

- **Place your pagefile on the fastest drive**   Windows 2000 usually chooses the NTFS-formatted drive with the largest amount of available space for the pagefile. (There are other occasions when the exact criteria Windows used to select a pagefile location eludes me—it seems to use hit-and-miss tactics from time to time.) In most cases, the drive it uses doesn't make a big difference. If you have a system with one large, slow drive and a second small, fast drive, however, you probably want to change the virtual memory settings to the fastest drive (double-click the System icon in the Control Panel, the Advanced Tab, then the Performance button, and click the Change button).

- **Compress the hard disk drive**   Windows 2000 supports disk compression. A lot of people think this feature's only purpose is to make a single hard disk drive hold more information. Although this is one of the reasons to use this feature, it's not the only reason. Compressing the hard disk drive could also provide a small, but discernible, speed boost. When a client makes a request for information from a compressed hard disk drive, the data is read and then decompressed on the fly. Since the data is compressed, it takes less time to read it from the drive. The drive is a mechanical device, so even a 20 percent compression factor can result in a significant performance gain for reading the file. Of course, part of the performance gain is eaten up decompressing the file. With today's modern server hardware, however, the amount of performance boost gained from reading the file from a compressed drive is always greater than the processing time required to decompress it.

- **Index the hard disk drive**   One of the tasks users perform most often on the server is looking for data. They have some idea of what they need, but a server provides a vast amount of space to look through. It makes sense to reduce the amount of time required to find data and this means creating an index of the data so the user can find it more quickly. Indexing occurs in the background when the server isn't performing any other work. Depending on the speed of your server and the amount of time it spends idle, building the index can take a while but is well worth the effort. You can access the Indexing Service as part of the Computer Management console. This entry appears under the Services and Applications heading. Right-click the Indexing Service entry, and then choose Start from the Context menu to start the indexing process using the predefined entries. There are normally separate entries for your Web site and the system as a whole.

- **Reset application response**   There are few reasons to use a server for running applications on a constant basis. Normally, a server provides some level of support for user requests. This means a server normally runs tasks in the background, not in the foreground, as a workstation does. With this in mind, you should always set the Application Response option on the Performance Options dialog box to Background Services. You can access the Performance Options dialog box by right-clicking My Computer, choosing Properties, clicking the Advanced tab, and then clicking Performance Options.

- **Check environment variables**   Windows 2000 normally sets every user's TEMP and TMP directory settings to their personal folder. This means every user who has server console access is creating temporary files in a separate location on the server. Unlike a workstation, where this might be a feature rather than a hindrance, you want to set the temporary directory used by everyone to the same location on the server hard disk drive. This makes it easier to clean up extraneous files. You also want to look at the number and type of system variables. For example, the length of the PATH statement can increase application search time in some situations. You want to remove path information that the server no longer requires. It also helps to remove any system variables that the server no longer needs. You find all these settings on the Environment Variables dialog box that you can access by right-clicking My Computer, choosing Properties, clicking the Advanced tab, and then clicking Environment Variables.

Taking Out the Trash

We talked earlier about the problem of keeping your server trash-free. A lot of people tend to forget that trash, in the form of unusable files, reduces the amount of disk space available for other needs. A severe trash buildup can cause all kinds of performance problems. For example, the trash buildup could reduce the amount of space available for application temporary files. These temporary files are normally used as performance-boosting buffers. As you can see, taking out the trash is an important issue.

One of the ways to keep trash from building up is to keep it off your hard disk drive in the first place. Right-click the Recycle Bin, and then choose Properties from the Context menu. Click the Global tab and you see a display similar to the one shown in Figure 12-1. This dialog box shows the default settings for a Windows 2000 machine. Notice that 10 percent of the drive is set aside for old files you don't want anymore. Since this particular server has an 18-GB drive, that means 1.8 GB is used for trash collection—an excessively high figure for any machine, much less a server. In most cases, you should set the server to remove the files immediately when deleted. If you feel a safety factor is absolutely essential, try setting the percentage of the hard disk drive used to something more reasonable like 1 percent.

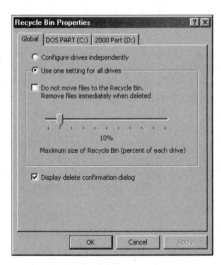

Figure 12-1.   *The Recycle Bin Properties dialog box allows you to choose how much space is devoted to deleted file collection.*

> **Tip** You can always remove files permanently from the hard disk drive by pressing Shift+Delete, rather than Delete alone. You want to keep the Display Delete Confirmation Dialog setting on the Global tab of the Recycle Bin Properties dialog box checked so the network administrator is informed about the permanent nature of such a deletion. It's important that the network administrator realize that Shift+Delete doesn't place the deleted file in the Recycle Bin if you depend on the Recycle Bin as a safety mechanism.

There are other ways to collect trash on a hard disk drive. If there weren't, the Recycle Bin wouldn't be such a problem because it automatically scales itself within certain limits. However, every visit to the Internet collects some files, as do other system activities. In short, the collection of trash is almost unavoidable. So, you need a way of getting rid of it quickly. Fortunately, Windows 2000 provides a disk cleanup mechanism. Right-click any local drive icon, and then choose Properties from the Context menu. Click the General tab. You see a drive Properties dialog box similar to the one shown in Figure 12-2. Notice that the General tab includes a Disk Cleanup button next to the graphic display of current disk capacity.

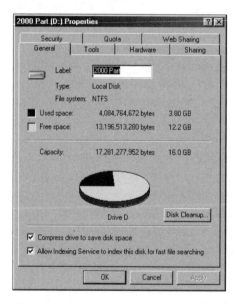

Figure 12-2. *You can check the current capacity of your drive, and then choose to clean it up using features on the General tab of the disk Properties dialog box.*

Click Disk Cleanup and you see a Disk Cleanup dialog box for a few moments as the system calculates the amount of space you save by cleaning up the drive. (Depending on the size of your drive, this can take a relatively long time the first time you use the disk cleanup feature.) Once the calculation is complete, you see a Disk Cleanup dialog box similar to the one shown in Figure 12-3. Notice that this dialog box displays statistics for five main problem areas on the server, including the Recycle Bin and temporary Internet files.

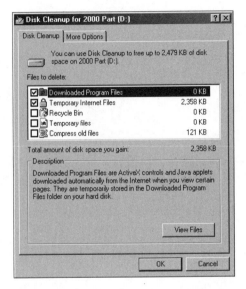

Figure 12-3.   *The Disk Cleanup dialog box allows you to see in a glance how much trash your system has accumulated.*

At this point, all you need to do to clean up your server's hard disk drive is check the items that have wasted space, and then click OK. Windows 2000 automatically removes the files from the hard disk drive for you. You see the Disk Cleanup dialog box again as the system performs the required file deletions and compressions. This frees up space for applications to use for things like storing temporary files and making the system run faster as a whole.

Of course, this action isn't complete until you also defragment the hard disk drive. Defragmenting the drive places all the unused space in one area, allowing the application to make bigger allocations without creating a fragmented file. It also places all the pieces of existing files in one place, making disk access that much faster.

Real World

Some networks crash not from a lack of knowledge on the part of the network administrator, but from a lack of organization. For example, the maintenance action in this section of the chapter is relatively simple. All you need to do is look for old trash files once a month and then defragment the hard disk drive. It should be a simple task and it does provide a boost in server performance, not to mention freeing space for other needs. However, it's almost certain that many of the same network administrators who have a heart attack every time something happens on the network won't complete this task in a timely manner. Completing maintenance tasks is the key to ensuring the network doesn't fail in the first place, which makes your job a lot easier.

In the real world, people get busy with pressing matters and don't always get those lower priority jobs done. The fact is that the squeaky wheel gets the grease, no matter how much we wish things would work otherwise. So, that means you have to make essential tasks like server maintenance a squeaky wheel so someone pays attention.

One way to make server maintenance a squeaky wheel is to set up a maintenance schedule and a maintenance board. Create a calendar that lists all the required maintenance actions, the person responsible for doing them, and the time they should be finished. The person responsible can check off the completed items when finished. This makes it easy for the network administrator to see which tasks are done and which tasks need to be finished for any given month. It also places some amount of peer pressure on every individual on your team to get the maintenance tasks done on time.

Creating Permanent Pagefiles

Many people are under the impression that the dynamic pagefiles used by Windows 2000 are a real boon to server performance. It's true; a dynamic pagefile grows or shrinks as needed (and within the limits you specify). However, there are a couple of problems with dynamic pagefiles, the most important of which is disk fragmentation. A pagefile, unlike other files on the system, is constantly in use. It allows Windows 2000 to simulate additional memory as needed. Because of this constant use, fragmentation of the pagefile is a real problem. You can partially combat this problem by defragmenting your hard disk drive on a regular basis. The fact remains that a dynamic pagefile does introduce some level of performance loss in a system.

Another problem with a dynamic pagefile occurs when your system's load fluctuates to a large extent. The system spends a considerable amount of time growing and shrinking this file to meet demand, or it fails to work with the pagefile in a positive way at all. So, a dynamic pagefile can also waste time on a system with a varying load. It pays to keep this in mind when the system grows the pagefile in the middle of some other task, causing the task at hand to pause for a moment.

What we really have is a situation where there are three possibilities. The server load could remain constant (such as a server used to perform one task all day long), in which case a permanent pagefile is optimal because there isn't any need to grow or shrink it and you gain the benefits of a pagefile that lacks fragmentation. The second possibility is that the server could have a load that varies slowly over time within a given range. Database servers often fall into this category of loading. This is the scenario where a dynamic pagefile works best and you should leave Windows alone to do what it does best. The third possibility is a load that varies a great deal over a short time. Every e-commerce site in the world falls into this category since the user load on them is fickle, to say the least. You still need a dynamic pagefile, in this case, but you want to mitigate some of the performance problems that a dynamic pagefile introduces by reducing the range of pagefile sizes.

Let's forget the second possibility for a moment since Windows 2000 already has it under control with a fully dynamic pagefile. The constant load scenario works best with a permanent pagefile, but we can't create one with Windows 2000—it only allows you to create dynamic pagefiles. There's a method for simulating a permanent pagefile under Windows 2000. Right-click My Computer, and then choose Properties from the Context menu. You see a System Properties dialog box. Click the Advanced tab. Click Performance Options and you see a Performance Options dialog box. Click Change. You see the Virtual Memory dialog box shown in Figure 12-4.

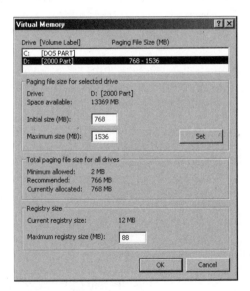

Figure 12-4.   *The Virtual Memory dialog box allows you to change the way Windows 2000 allocates pagefile space on the hard disk drive.*

Tip Windows 2000 normally sets the Maximum Registry Size field to some enormous value when compared to what the server actually has in use at the time of installation. This large size is required to ensure that the registry can grow to the size needed by any applications you install. However, once you have all the applications installed on your server, you can usually recover a lot of the reserved registry space by decreasing the number in the Maximum Registry Size field. A good rule is to wait for about a week after you install the last application on the server, and then reduce the maximum size of the registry to twice the Current Registry Size field value. Always remember to increase the Maximum Registry Size field value again when you want to install more applications.

Simply set the Initial Size and the Maximum Size fields to the same value. In addition, you can incrementally enhance the performance of your system if you have a two-disk system. Just move the pagefile to the first drive while you completely defragment the second. Once you defragment the second drive, move the pagefile from the first drive to the second drive. In short, you create a simulated permanent drive that resides in one contiguous section of the hard disk drive, which improves system performance.

So, what value do you select for your constant load server setup? Monitor the size of the pagefile over a week or two to ensure that you're seeing the full range of values. (You can monitor the size of the pagefile using Windows Explorer—just look for the PAGEFILE.SYS entry in the root directory.) If these values don't vary much, choose the maximum value, plus 5 percent more, as your permanent pagefile size. The additional 5 percent of pagefile space gives your system a little "headroom" when needed for unanticipated surges of activity.

History file monitoring is a key step in creating a pagefile setup for the server with a load that varies a great deal over time as well. However, in this case, you don't want the server to use a lot of resources all the time, especially if the load on the server is small. So, setting the pagefile to use a range of hard-disk drive space is the best path to choose. You want to set the Maximum Size field to a value that's 10 percent higher than the maximum pagefile used by the server over a period of time. This gives the server plenty of room to grow with an increasing load. Set the Initial Size field to half the Maximum Size field value. This ensures that at least most of the pagefile appears within a defragmented area of the hard disk drive at all times.

Let's examine that server that has a load that varies slowly over some period of time, or the second example listed previously. This kind of application load responds favorably to a dynamic pagefile because it changes slowly and varies over time. You don't want the server to keep using resources it doesn't need to use, and the slow change time means the server isn't constantly changing the size of the pagefile either. However, there's still the question of whether the settings Windows 2000 computes for the pagefile are the right ones for your needs. In most cases, you don't want to change the value in the Maximum Size field because the pagefile doesn't grow that large anyway. The setting you might want to change is the Initial Size field. The least amount you can allocate is 2 MB, but that's not very practical. You could monitor the pagefile for an extended time and set the Initial Size field to some median value; but again, that's not making the best use of the dynamic capabilities that Microsoft provides for Windows 2000. Normally, you have to spend some time experimenting to find the best Initial Size in this case. If you find that the server is always near the Initial Size, you may want to reduce it to see if you can gain additional disk resources.

Special Tuning Concerns for Advanced Server

Advanced Server is the next step up from Windows 2000 Server. It's the middle-of-the-road solution that Microsoft recommends for environments like e-commerce and high-reliability applications. This is the server you use for your mission-critical applications and it is the one server setup that most of the users on your network access. In short, this is the server setup for medium to large businesses.

We already looked at the kinds of tuning you can perform on individual Advanced Servers in "General Server Tuning Techniques." These are the kinds of tuning measures you want to explore first. Once you tune the individual servers, you can begin to look at how the servers interact with external devices. For example, if all the servers interface with a storage area network (SAN), you want to ensure that the network connections and other elements of the SAN are tuned before you go any further. Normally, the SAN manufacturer provides the software you need to test connections and ensure that they're working at maximum efficiency.

At this point, you've tuned the individual server and the external peripherals it connects to. It's time to connect the servers. There are actually two connections to consider and separate tuning requirements for each. The first tuning consideration is the cluster. Since each cluster is designed to provide failover support, each server needs to communicate with its partners in the cluster. Any type of communication between the servers reduces the time they spend processing user requests. You want to reduce the amount of data transferred between servers in a cluster and the number of times per day that the data gets transferred.

A second level of tuning is for NLB. There are two levels of tuning in this case. NLB relies on a router (a physical device used to route requests to servers in the cluster) to transfer user requests evenly among servers in the cluster. This means the router has to be tuned to determine which server is the least busy in the smallest amount of time. A user doesn't see a performance gain if the time required to select a server exceeds the performance gained by using the server with the smallest load at the time.

The servers also need to provide information to the router that expresses the amount of load that they're currently carrying and the amount of remaining capacity they can provide. The servers need to provide this information in a concise fashion, yet provide enough detail for the router to calculate which server has the least load in order to direct user requests.

Fortunately, Microsoft has taken most of the guesswork out of both clustering and NLB for Advanced Server. However, Microsoft also allows you to create your own custom schemes. In some cases, it might be better to hire a competent programmer to develop a custom algorithm for balancing the network load.

Special Tuning Concerns for Datacenter Server

One of the main tuning considerations for Windows 2000 Datacenter Server is the size factor. When you look at the statistics in Table 12-1, you notice that we're talking about servers that have the same number of processors as many mainframes do. Memory is no longer in the range required by databases—most of which top out at either 4 GB or 8 GB. Even cluster support speaks of large networks that cross state, province, or even country boundaries. In short, Windows 2000 Datacenter Server is an operating system that's designed for very large networks with heavy processing loads. You shouldn't even consider this product for a network that is in a single building (unless that building is as large as the capabilities of this product). Networks that reside over a large physical area have some unique communication problems that we haven't discussed much in the book.

> **Note** This section is based on current Internet discussions. Since Windows 2000 Datacenter Server won't be released for at least 120 days after the release of the other two Windows 2000 Server products, there isn't any way to determine what features this product will contain or how it may perform in real-world implementations. In sum, you should use the content of this section as a guideline of what may occur, not necessarily as concrete advice on server tuning techniques.

So, how do you tune a network that's so large it defies easy explanation, documentation, or even visualization? Such a network could easily become overwhelming for the management engaged in supporting it. Just the idea of figuring out where to start in the tuning process can be staggering. In fact, given the other concerns for such a network, a network administrator who's in charge of the whole network may not even consider tuning as an option.

The fact remains that this network is made up of individual servers, just like any other network. This means you can at least tune the individual servers—given enough time and opportunity to do so. However, time is the issue here. Unlike the network administrator who has four servers to worry about, you're not going to have time to tune 40 or 50 servers. The fact is that by the time you actually tuned all the servers (after you respond to all the other emergencies during the day), the server would become obsolete and a target for replacement. Tuning the servers after you install them isn't a good idea. You need to tune the individual servers right before you install them on the network, but after you load all the required operating system features and as many of the applications as possible. Is this solution perfect? Probably not; you still find that there are individual server inefficiencies, but these problem areas become less significant when considered in light of the performance of the network as a whole. Generally, you find that tuning the servers this way still yields substantial performance gains for individual network areas and slightly affects the network as a whole.

Once you've added the server to the network, you need to allow it to settle into its new home. Remember that a new server changes the interactions of all the servers within a cluster. You need to wait until the servers reach some point of equilibrium before you attempt to perform additional tuning. The new server also needs time to accept data replicated from other servers on the network. This replication process shouldn't take very long, but it's still important to wait until the process is complete.

Tuning the server within the cluster has already been covered in "Special Tuning Concerns for Advanced Server." However, you still need to tune the server within the network as a whole. Obviously, a server in China will have less of an effect on a server in the United States than on another server within China. Distance does make a difference.

Given the size of the network we're dealing with, some level of coordination is required if you want to tune the entire system. Using a divide-and-conquer approach allows network administrators to work on their specific section of the network and to coordinate their efforts with other network administrators. In other words, you need to define clear boundaries as part of the tuning process.

Scheduling is another important consideration. It might mean that some network administrators have to change their normal working hours so everyone can work at the same time. However, there's an important thing to consider—changes in Thailand don't appear at your offices in Canada right away. There's a latency factor to consider—a delay in the effect of a change once the change has been made. This means you have to schedule short amounts of time over a week or two, depending on the size of your network. When changing settings that modify a connection that crosses boundaries, make small changes and wait for the change to take effect.

Summary

This chapter examined three important facets of the Windows 2000 Server. First, we explored how the server versions differ. Knowing which server version you actually require for your network is important because it allows you to get the maximum level of functionality with the least amount of work. Second, we examined the task orientation of each kind of server. Each server is designed to perform different tasks based on its capabilities. It's important to realize, for example, that Windows 2000 Server isn't well suited for an e-commerce site because it doesn't scale well and doesn't provide the highest level of reliability. Finally, we reviewed server-specific optimization techniques. Using these techniques helps you adjust the server's performance to provide the best possible use of server resources.

Chapter 13 takes a detailed look at Windows 2000 clusters. We explore what you can do with them and how to tune them for best performance. Of course, part of the tuning process for any complex grouping of servers includes some type of capacity planning. This chapter helps you understand the special needs of clusters when it comes to future capacity when viewed from the requirements of today.

Chapter 13
Microsoft Windows 2000 and Clustering

In the past few years we have seen an evolution in Microsoft clustering technology, from the beta product (Wolfpack) to Microsoft Windows NT Server and now Windows 2000 Cluster Service. At one point, clustering was thought to be a solution for only those users in enterprise-wide networks. However, with the emergence of the Internet and Internet-based services such as e-commerce technology, you can find clustering in the smallest Information Services departments to departments responsible for global networks.

Another push for clustering technology has been brought on by the move from traditional mainframe and minicomputer environments to the more interoperable, extensible, and user-friendly enterprise or workgroup servers running Microsoft Windows NT and Windows 2000. This move over the years created a problem for hardware and software vendors alike—how do you recreate the same amount of computing power (if not more) that was available in these colossal mainframes out of server class machines? The answer is clustering. Through a combination of smaller and faster hardware devices and the developments that have occurred with network operating systems enabling them to provide clustering capability, you now have clustered server environments that easily provide double, triple, or quadruple the processing power found in mainframes or mini-computers.

In this chapter we look at how Windows 2000 Cluster Service can help you performance tune Windows 2000 Server and your Windows 2000-networked environment. We review the benefits a cluster has to offer, cluster configurations that lead to increased performance and redundancy of your environment, and the extensibility clustering offers developers when creating ever more scalable applications.

How Cluster Service Can Help You

Through Windows 2000 Cluster Service, organizations can run their business-critical, e-commerce, and line-of-business applications on servers ranging from workgroup to enterprise server class machines. Using Windows 2000 clustering technology, a company no longer has to buy a massively configured server to run its applications. Many organizations are finding that by relying on a single server to run these business-critical applications, they're also creating a single point of failure.

A cluster consists of Windows 2000 Servers (Advanced or Datacenter versions) that are grouped together to run either a single application or a common set of applications. The operating system uses Cluster Service to provide an image of a single system to the client. Even though there are multiple servers in the cluster, the client sees only one server. This means a single server failure no longer leaves the client without a server to use—another server takes the place of the server that failed. In fact, the applications themselves running within a clustered environment also see a single system and not individual servers.

The scalability of Windows 2000 Cluster Service enables network administrators to configure each cluster group to meet their immediate needs. Cluster Service doesn't have to run on enterprise-class servers. For those businesses that simply want to provide redundancy for their Web sites, a clustered solution is perfect. Environments that require a solution that provides increased performance for their applications can create a cluster group to meet those requirements as well. Windows 2000 Cluster Service increases both the redundancy and performance of your network.

Benefits of Clustering Under Windows 2000

In the introduction of this chapter, we highlighted some of the benefits of Windows 2000 clustering technologies. We now go into greater detail regarding these benefits and how each one contributes to the goal of performance tuning and optimizing your Windows 2000 environment.

Scalability

In general, Windows 2000 Server is an even more scalable system than its predecessor, Windows NT. Windows 2000 Server versions can scale up to eight processors for Advanced Server or 32 processors for Datacenter Server. Advanced Server can support up to 8 GB, while Datacenter supports 64 GB of memory—and that's just on a single machine. See the section "Overview of the Windows 2000 Versions" found in Chapter 12 for further information on the differences between the Windows 2000 Server versions.

Note Any statistics stated about Windows 2000 Datacenter Server will more than likely change once the product is released. At the time of writing this book, Windows 2000 Datacenter wasn't available for testing.

Your organization may choose to deploy servers with very large memory and processor configurations in order to throw more computing power at the problem of running resource-intensive applications. However, by placing all your computing power into a single server, you may not allow yourself any room for further growth and redundancy. The operating system may be able to scale, but will your hardware? In this case, the scalability provided through Windows 2000 clustering is unsurpassed. You have the ability to add computing power to a single cluster by adding additional nodes.

Note   Windows 2000 Advanced Server supports two-node failover, while the Datacenter version will support cascading failover between four nodes.

High Availability

High availability of applications is critical in almost every organization—there's at least one application that needs to be available 24/7. This may be a financial package or the Web server running an online store. Network administrators have the responsibility of making these applications available at all times, no excuses. That's why network administrators need to understand the capabilities of the Windows 2000 operating system and to know what services, such as Cluster Service, enable them to gain this level of availability.

If you have an application that fails, not because of a hardware-related problem but because of a fault in the application, a server configured with four or six processors buys you nothing, no matter how redundant the hardware might be. You still need to restart the application. Cluster Service is designed to provide high availability through the distribution of applications across multiple computers. If you have your mission-critical database server running in a clustered environment with a failover policy in place, users are unaware of any downtime because Cluster Service transparently switches users over to the server (node cluster) acting as the failover node. As long as the failover node is configured with the same hardware, users don't even realize a degradation in performance.

Note   Performance of your clustered environment after a failover occurs depends heavily on the cluster configuration you choose. In "Clustered Environment Scenarios" later in the chapter, we review cluster configuration available for deployment. Each configuration offers network administrators a benefit in performance, redundancy, or economy.

Application distribution is one method through which Cluster Service increases application availability. Here are a few additional methods.

- **Rolling upgrades**   This process gives the network administrator the ability to take one node of a cluster offline at a time while the other nodes continue to provide services. The administrator is then free to do routine maintenance such as upgrade the system software or the applications themselves. Network administrators benefit from rolling upgrades through no or very little downtime of services. Secondly, there's no need to reconfigure the clustered configuration. As long as the same applications are part of the failover group you configured, you can upgrade services and walk away.

- **Recovery from network failures**   Windows 2000 Cluster Service, along with application redundancy, also supports network failure recovery. For example, if a network card fails in any node in the clustered environment, Cluster Service determines the cause of the failure and the appropriate action to take.

Cluster Service either utilizes a second or third network card in the server or causes a failover of the resource group. However, there are certain types of network failures that a cluster cannot recover from. For example, a failed router or switch affects direct access to the clustered environment. The only way to create a fully redundant network is to consider the equipment outside the realm of the cluster. Redundant power supplies, T1 lines, and failover devices are all critical components of any mission-critical network.

- **Support for Windows naming and drive-sharing technologies** Organizations that rely heavily on services such as Windows Internet Naming Service (WINS), distributed file system (DFS), and Dynamic Host Configuration Protocol (DHCP) can deploy these services in a clustered environment. Network administrators can configure file sharing for their enterprise environment through the DFS with comfort, knowing they have the processor power and Network Load Balancing (NLB) to support such loads.

Manageability

The potential of having multiple servers in a single cluster provides incredible redundancy and processing power for your environment. However, all this power is nothing without the ability to manage it. Using the Cluster Administrator tool, network administrators are able to manage each node (server) of the cluster from a single point of administration. As soon as Cluster Service is installed on the server, the administration application detects it. Network administrators need not install any additional agents or drivers to manage the newly created node. Below I have a listed some of the features available to administrators managing a Windows 2000 clustered environment.

- **Support for Active Directory services** Cluster Service can now utilize Active Directory services to publish information about available clusters on the network. Users can browse the directory service and, if they have the appropriate permissions, utilize resources available on these clusters.

- **Ability to monitor resource status** Cluster Service monitors the "health" of applications and servers running in the clustered environment (these resources must be configured in a failover group). When Cluster Service detects a problem with the resource, it alerts the Failover Manager to begin the failover process. In most cases, the time from actual detection of the problem to recovery can be less than a minute.

- **Easier management of hardware installation and configuration** One of the enhancements in the Windows 2000 Server family is its improved support for Plug and Play (PnP) technology. Servers that are part of clusters can detect the addition of devices such as network cards and the TCP/IP network stacks the cards will be configured with. Plus, PnP detects shared physical disks, a pivotal piece of hardware for any clustered environment.

- **Cluster API for application developers**   Developers can take advantage of the Cluster API to develop cluster-aware applications. Many organizations invest time and money to develop their own in-house applications with little or no redundancy available for the application. Now developers can create high-availability applications through the Cluster API.

Resource Failover and Network Load Balancing

Clustering isn't unique to the Windows 2000 operating system; most enterprise-class network operating systems offer this service. However, they may be limited to the performance and redundancy they can provide. For example, a certain cluster solution may be able to provide failover support for resources such as file and print services and Web services. However, it may not be capable of providing NLB. NLB enables administrators to load balance incoming TCP/IP traffic across servers. Using NLB, administrators can easily scale their environment according to the traffic they may be experiencing by adding or removing servers from the cluster. You'll find that many operating system vendors offer both resource clustering and NLB; however, they are sold as separate cluster solutions. In the case of Windows 2000, you get both for the price of one.

Through Windows 2000 Cluster Service, your Advanced or Datacenter Servers are able to provide your customers with failover support for their databases, file and print services, messaging services such as Microsoft Exchange 2000, and NLB.

Understanding Resource Failover and Failback

When a service or application in a server cluster fails, Cluster Service attempts a two-step process to recover from this failure. First, Cluster Service tries to restart the service or application. If after this, the resource is still down, Cluster Service moves the resource (after taking it offline) and restarts it on another node previously configured as a failover node. This process of moving and restarting the resource on a second node is called "failover."

There are three criteria that determine when Cluster Service attempts to fail over a group. A group, in the terms of Cluster Service, is a collection of resources needed to run an application or service. Failover criteria are as follows:

- **The node on which the group is configured and running is no longer functioning**   This can occur if the server experiences a failure (hardware or software) that the operating system can't recover from.
- **The network administrators forces a failover**   There are several reasons a network administrator would want to force a failover, including the need to take the node where the resource is currently running offline for extended maintenance.

- **A resource within the group fails, causing a failover**   Network administrators can configure the failover policy so Cluster Service detects when individual resources within a group fail, which causes the service to initiate a failover. You need to do this if applications rely on the individual resources to be functioning correctly; otherwise the application itself could stop functioning.

During a failover, all groups hosted on the node that failed are moved over to a second node. For example, if you're hosting your Web services on Node 1 and the power supply fails on the server, Cluster Service moves the Web services to Node 2 as part of the failover policy you set up. After you replace the damaged power supply on Node 1 and the server is up and running again, Cluster Service detects this. At this point, a failback occurs—Cluster Service moves the Web services back so the services are running on Node 1 once again. Cluster Service goes through the same steps to fail back a resource as it does during a failover. When a failure occurs in a cluster implementing NLB, traffic will be diverted from a failed node to nodes that are part of the same cluster. When the node that failed is online again, it can begin to participate in the load balancing immediately. We discuss NLB in more detail in the section that follows.

Understanding Network Load Balancing

Many times, NLB is the only reason Internet service providers turn to clustering as a method to performance tune their environments. NLB involves load balancing incoming IP traffic across clusters consisting of up to 32 nodes. If you're hosting an e-commerce site, NLB can help split the load among your Web servers. Your customers don't experience the delays experienced by users attempting to access Web sites overwhelmed by user IP traffic.

NLB also benefits your site by allowing you to scale more efficiently. Rather than rushing to an expensive hardware-based solution for a quick remedy to handling IP traffic, you can deploy a single NLB cluster to take care of the immediate need of handling network traffic. You can then concentrate on addressing what your true needs are. Should you be hosting the Web service or should it be outsourced to an application service provider? You make better decisions under less pressure.

Web services aren't the only applications that can benefit from NLB; any IP-based service, such as Microsoft Terminal Services or Windows Media Services, can also take advantage of NLB. When designing your environment, don't forget you can combine the powers of both clustering technologies (Cluster Service and NLB) to provide a highly scalable, redundant, and well-performing environment.

Guidelines for Creating a Cluster

The purpose of this section is to review guidelines you need to follow to install, configure, and maintain your server cluster. By following these guidelines, you not only save yourself valuable time but you also understand limitations that exist when installing Cluster Service.

- When you install Cluster Service, you must be logged in to the domain with administrative-level permissions to each server that is either a node in the cluster or one you plan on adding to the cluster.

- You can't configure a cluster node to be part of two different clusters. A node can be part of only one cluster at a time, no matter if the clusters are within the same domain.

- The shared drive for the cluster must be formatted NTFS (NT file system). The drive or drives must also be SCSI (Small Computer System Interface). If you have IDE (Integrated Device Electronics), EIDE (Enhanced Integrated Device Electronics), or Ultra-IDE drives, you aren't able to install Cluster Service because it isn't able to detect a set of configured, shared SCSI drives.

- To prevent data corruption, only one node can have access to the shared SCSI disk.

- Always verify that each cluster node can detect one another. Try either the ping command, or type **net view** to see a list of network resources.

Additional Information Needed Before Installation Begins

In this section, we outline some additional information you need before installation begins. You are asked to provide the following information during installation of Cluster Service.

- **IP addresses for each node**   You need to configure each server that will be a node in the cluster with a TCP/IP address. You have the option of either assigning the IP addresses via DHCP or configuring the server with a static address. Keep in mind that by using DHCP for addressing purposes, you create a single point of failure. If the DHCP server isn't available, the servers are unable to communicate with each other or communicate on the network. You should configure each server with a static IP address to avoid DHCP-related failures.

- **An IP address for the cluster itself**   To help paint the picture of a single server providing services to your clients, you need to assign the cluster itself a TCP/IP address. This address can't be assigned by a DHCP server; it must be a static IP address.

- **Cluster name**   You should come up with a nomenclature to help organize and manage the domain. For example, you can name the cluster according to its geographical location (CLUSTER_PHILLY) or its role (CLUSTER_DATABASE). The name for the cluster *must* be different from the actual domain name or the name of any computer on the network.

- **Domain accounts for cluster nodes**   Each node in the cluster requires a computer account be created for that node in the domain in which the cluster resides. *All* nodes of a cluster must be members of the same domain.

- **Cluster hardware and drivers**   All hardware including the computers themselves, network cards, and disk drives should be on the Windows 2000 Hardware Compatibility List (HCL). You should also verify with hardware vendors that you have the latest drivers for hardware you're installing.

- **Create a user account for Cluster Service**   You can configure Cluster Service, like many of the services under Windows 2000, to be run under a specific user account. Before installation begins, you should create this account with local administrative privileges for each node on the cluster.

- **Disk space for configuration information**   You need to create a separate partition on the clustered disks where configuration information for the actual cluster is stored. Cluster Service uses this information to recover from a node failure. This configuration information is known as the quorum resource.

Installing Cluster Service

You have the choice of installing Cluster Service either during or after the installation of Windows 2000 Server (Advanced or Datacenter versions). If you plan on attaching to a shared disk, you should boot only one of the Windows 2000 Servers that will be a node in the cluster into Windows 2000 Server. This is to prevent both servers from trying to attach to the shared disk and causing data corruption.

Note   Before you proceed to the actual installation steps, there's one basic system requirement to be aware of. Windows 2000 Cluster Service can only be installed and configured on an Advanced or Datacenter version of Windows 2000 Server. Some network administrators may have existing installations of Windows 2000 Server Standard Edition on which they want to install Cluster Service. These servers need to have a new installation of Advanced Server or Datacenter Server installed on them; however, you can't upgrade a Standard Edition Server to Advanced or Datacenter. In the case of the following installation, we review the steps to install Cluster Service on a server that already has Windows 2000 Advanced Server installed.

1. When you're ready to begin the installation, launch the Add/Remove Programs tool from the Control Panel. Click Add/Remove Windows Component and then click Components to launch the Windows Components Wizard.

2. You are presented with a list of possible components you can add or remove, including Cluster Service (see Figure 13-1). Select Cluster Service and then click Next.

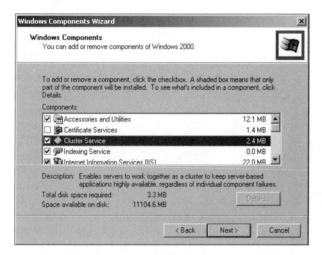

Figure 13-1. *The first step to creating a clustered environment begins with the installation of Cluster Service.*

Note   If your server isn't a member of a domain, an error message box appears. You have no choice but to click OK and quit the installation of Cluster Service. Your server must be either a domain controller or a member server of a domain. Please see the previous section "Guidelines for Creating a Cluster" for further requirement details.

3. The installation program begins configuring the component. You are prompted to insert the Windows 2000 Advanced Server CD-ROM; do so, and click OK.

4. After the component has been configured and files copied, the Cluster Service Configuration Wizard launches. Click Next.

5. The screen that now appears is so important for you to understand that the installation wizard has dimmed the Next button. The only way you can proceed is if you click the I Understand button, signifying that you understand the need for *all* hardware used as part of the cluster group to be on the Microsoft HCL. After you have read the requirements, click I Understand and click Next.

More Info If your server is on the Windows HCL, this doesn't mean its components, such as the drive controller, are fit for Cluster Service. The server must be under the Cluster category of the HCL. You can view the most up-to-date HCL at the following Web address: *http://www.microsoft.com/hcl/default.asp.* From the main page, you can select to view hardware by product category, or you can search by keywords such as Windows 2000. You should always check back to view updates made to the HCL. Also, check with hardware vendors, in case their hardware isn't listed.

6. In the next screen, you are asked if the server you're configuring will be the first node in the cluster, or the second or next node in the cluster. A node is a server running Cluster Service and is part of a cluster. In this example, we're creating a new cluster, so click The First Node In The Cluster (see Figure 13-2). Click Next.

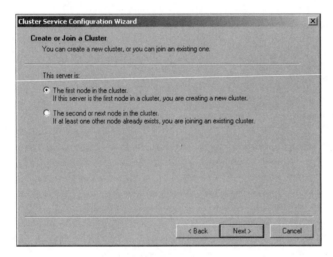

Figure 13-2. *At this point, you can choose to either create a new cluster or join an existing cluster.*

Note After clicking Next, you may run into one more error. This is generated by the installation program if it detects that you don't have shared SCSI device attached to the server. The error message box also appears if no disks on a SCSI bus are formatted as NTFS or the disks on the bus are Dynamic. (A dynamic disk is a partitionless disk that contains dynamic volumes created by Disk Management.) Disks can't be of the Dynamic type—they must be of the Basic type. You have no choice but to quit and install a SCSI drive(s), format them NTFS, and select them to be of the Basic type (see Figure 13-3).

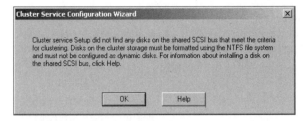

Figure 13-3.   *An error message box appears if you don't have the right set of disks or if they aren't formatted correctly.*

7.   In this next screen, you are prompted to enter the name for the newly created cluster. When naming a cluster, keep in mind that for easy management you may not want to have spaces within the name—you run into small nuances such as having to put quotation marks around the name each time you use the cluster command line tool. Click Next.

8.   You now have to specify an account for Cluster Service to use. It's always a good idea to create a separate account to manage Cluster Service. Enter the account information and click Next.

9.   In this next screen, you must select what disks will be managed by Cluster Service. Add or remove disks as you see fit and click Next.

10.   The installation program now asks for the location of the Checkpoint and Log files for Cluster Service. The service depends on these files to help manage the cluster. These files must be stored on a shared, clustered disk. The installation points out two suggestions to keep in mind. First, the disk partition should have a recommended disk size of 100MB. Second, you should keep the Checkpoint and Log files stored on a separate disk drive from where your user applications are stored. If possible, you should also consider storing the files on disks managed by a separate disk controller. This increases the overall performance of read and writes for the server because Cluster Service doesn't have to compete with disk traffic from user applications. Select the disk, and click Next.

11.   You should be careful not to click Next quickly at this screen; there's some important information you should be aware of. It recommends that you don't use a single network for your clustered environment, because this causes the network to be a single point of failure. All you need is a switch or a hub to go out and your servers are at a standstill. Overall redundancy of your environment is greatly diminished as soon as a piece of network hardware fails. This screen also refers to private and public networks and when you should use one over the other or when you should use both.

- **Private network** All cluster communication should be done through a private network. When you create a clustered environment, the nodes (servers that make up the clustered environment) are constantly communicating with each other. Each node must be able to determine what the other's status is—for example, whether the node is available.

- **Public network** When clients access the clustered environment, they do so over a public network. For example, if you have Microsoft SQL Server 7.0 Enterprise Edition available via a clustered environment, a client executing a query against a node in that cluster does so through the public network.

- **Mixed network** When you combine the functionality of a public and private network, you create a mixed network. Creating a mixed network provides failover for network traffic in case either the public or private networks experiences a failure.

12. After clicking Next, you can configure the network environment. The screen displays the configuration information for each network adapter in your servers. Remember, if you have two network cards, you should configure one for public traffic and the other as a private network. However, if the server is configured with more than two network cards, you will be able to create a configuration where you have both redundancy and efficiency. Cluster communication is restricted to the private network, public traffic to cluster resources remains on the public network, and the mixed network can serve as a backup for either public or private network in case of failure. Click Next.

13. You have to specify which one of your network cards you want to be dedicated for cluster communications. Click Next.

14. In this screen, you have to specify the cluster IP Address. The cluster IP address enables clients to point to a single address and not individual addresses for each node in the cluster. For example, let's say you have a clustered environment with two nodes A and B configured to run SQL Server 7.0 Enterprise Edition. If you have a client looking to run a query against the server, the client has to specify either Node A or Node B's IP address. However, this becomes a problem when a failure occurs with either one of these nodes. It can be a real project having to change the client configuration for each user in your network. Windows 2000 Cluster Service eliminates this confusion by enabling all nodes of the clustered environment to share the cluster IP address. This way, clients need to point only to a single IP address no matter if a failure occurs with the node they are currently attached to. After specifying the IP address for the cluster, select the network card that will be used for client traffic. You can either select the public or mixed network. Click Next.

15. This is the last screen for the installation. Click Finish to complete the installation.

Network Failure Detection

Network failure detection, a new feature available in Windows 2000, enables the clustered environment to detect network failures caused by failed network cards, bad cables, or a cable being unplugged. Windows 2000 Cluster Service switches to the next available network card in the server. Network failure detection is of no use to you if you have only a single network card in the server.

Clustered Environment Scenarios

The first step in designing a Windows 2000 Server clustered environment is determining what the purpose of the cluster will be. Creating a clustered environment can enhance performance by making additional resources available to applications. A clustered environment can also offer high availability by creating a hot-spare solution. In this section of the chapter, we go through the most common scenarios of deploying the Windows 2000 clustered environment, and the purpose of each.

Hot Spare

The hot-spare solution is designed to provide the highest performance and availability in times of failover, and is comprised of a primary node and a hot-spare node (see Figure 13-4). The primary node is active at all times, servicing clients who are accessing defined resources on the server. The hot-spare server is idle during normal operations, simply waiting for the moment of failure.

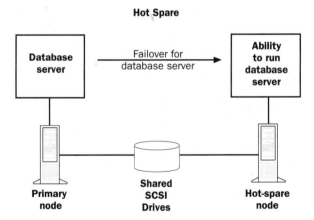

Figure 13-4.   *The hot-spare configuration is costly but worth it if you want maximum availability.*

If and when a failure does occur with the primary node, the hot-spare node takes over the services of the primary node. Clients who were accessing an application resource on the primary node are switched over unbeknownst to the users. For organizations that have mission-critical applications, such as e-commerce Web sites, the hot-spare configuration is ideal. Businesses need not worry about lost time, effort and, most important of all, lost income in a time of failure. Even though the cost of the hot-spare configuration is high (because organizations are required to keep an entire duplicate server on standby), businesses find that a single failure pays for this added expense.

Benefits of Hot-Spare Configuration
- Very high availability
- Maximum performance after a failover
- No performance degradation during failover

Negatives of Hot-Spare Configuration
- High-cost solution

Note Performance of the hot-spare solution is heavily dependent on the hardware configuration of the hot-spare node. If the hot-spare node isn't configured with an equal or higher level of hardware, users experience performance degradation.

Static Load Balancing

Static load balancing involves configuring your clustered environment with two nodes (see Figure 13-5). The network administrator configures each node with a set of resources that run as virtual servers. (For more information on virtual servers, see the section that follows.) At a time of failure, either node is capable of picking up for the other. For example, you could configure Node 1 to run file and print services as a group resource, and Node 2 to run file and print services as a separate group resource. If Node 2 experiences a failure, users on Node 2 are switched to Node 1 and are serviced by its group resource. This switchover puts a burden on the Node 1 server, because it now has to service twice the user load. However, as soon as Node 2 is up and running, its users are automatically switched back over.

Static Load Balancing

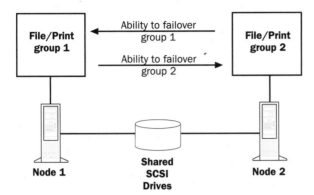

Figure 13-5.   *Static load balancing provides a redundant solution for resources without having hardware idle.*

Static load balancing is optimal if access to additional hardware resources is difficult and you can't configure a full hot-spare solution. As long as both nodes are active, the static load configuration also provides a high level of availability, and, unlike the hot-spare solution, the hardware isn't idle. Both servers are constantly accessed, providing services to your user environment.

Benefits of Static Load Balancing
- High availability
- Maximum performance (with both nodes active)
- Maximum utilization of hardware resources

Negatives of Static Load Balancing
- Performance degrades with only single node active

Virtual Server (No Failover)

The virtual server configuration offers zero redundancy and zero performance gains, yet, it can be worthwhile for administrators to deploy. Configuring a server as a virtual server enables you to configure resources such as file and print services, Web services, or database services into groups. These groups not only ease the actual administration of applications defined in the groups, but they also provide a greater convenience for users accessing the server.

For instance, you could group file and print services according to individual departments (see Figure 13-6). Now when your users need access to these resources, they no longer have to deal with cumbersome navigation through various servers' shares. They can go straight to virtual servers, which you can provide user-friendly names for such as Marketing Files.

If you ever decide to add a second node to your clustered environment to provide redundancy, performance, or high availability to the server, all you need to do is configure failover policies, because the groups already are defined. Virtual servers also have the added advantage of being able to restart the services they provide automatically in times of failure. When the server restarts and the particular resource doesn't have a method of restarting itself, Cluster Service can do that for you.

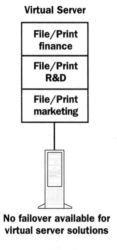

Virtual Server

| File/Print finance |
| File/Print R&D |
| File/Print marketing |

No failover available for virtual server solutions

Figure 13-6.   *The virtual server configuration can be an excellent method of administrating application services.*

Benefits of Virtual Servers
- Provide an easier method for resource management

Negatives of Virtual Servers
- No failover for individual groups
- No failover for entire node
- Performance level stagnant

Hybrid Cluster

Not all organizations require high availability for all their application resources. In fact, some organizations are comfortable with a nightly backup and are willing to put up with the time it would take to restore lost data from tape. However, there may be applications or services running on the same server that do require redundancy. A business may want to have a failover solution in place just for those applications. For times such as these, the hybrid cluster configuration can serve a network administrator's needs (see Figure 13-7).

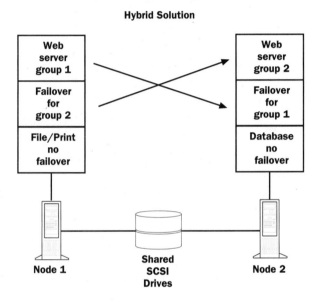

Figure 13-7.   *The hybrid configuration allows you to take advantage of other cluster configurations.*

The hybrid-clustered solution enables network administrators to configure multiple failover scenarios. For instance, you could have static load balancing for your Web services to help increase performance and provide redundancy. On the other hand, you could configure your file and print services as virtual servers for the sake of easier management. The hybrid cluster configuration is an extremely flexible solution, allowing you to configure your services according to your company's needs.

Benefits of the Hybrid Configuration
- Applications and services can have high availability according to the failover policies you set in place
- Allows you to take advantage of other cluster configuration models to meet your organization's specific needs and requirements

Negatives of the Hybrid Configuration
- Can be difficult to keep track of and manage multiple failover policies

Partial Server Cluster

This particular configuration shows the flexibility you have when deploying your applications in a Microsoft Windows 2000 clustered environment. It's not necessary for only those applications that are cluster-aware and have failover capabilities to run on a clustered server. You have the ability to run noncluster-aware applications, applications that can't fail over, and applications that don't require high availability, on clustered servers (see Figure 13-8).

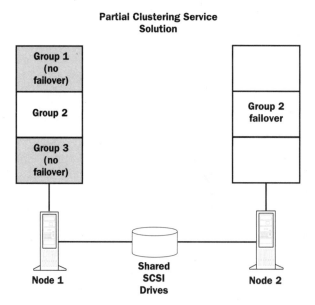

Figure 13-8. *The partial server configuration illustrates the flexibility in deploying applications in a clustered environment.*

When you deploy an application on a clustered server to offer your users high availability for that application through clustering, there are several configuration steps you must go through. You can deploy a server that's running several services such as Web, file and print, and database services. Out of all these services, you may be concerned only about uptime of the database services. So, rather than configure failover groups for each service, using a partial server configuration, you only have to configure a failover group on the second node for those applications that require high availability.

There are certain limitations you must note when deploying applications that aren't placed into a group failover. Applications that aren't cluster-aware must store their data on local disks. Also, these applications can't take advantage of any redundancy or performance gains made available through the clustered environment. Lastly, when a failover does occur, these applications aren't available at all since their clients were accessing them through the cluster's virtual IP address. They only become available once more when the node on which they are located is restarted and the actual services for the applications are restarted manually or automatically via the Windows 2000 Server services (or some other form of automation, such as scripting).

In the case of cluster-aware applications that have been placed into a group failover, during a node failure these applications are available through the failover group, which was configured on the second node (see Figure 13-8). The partial server cluster solution is optimal for those administrators who can't afford to run applications on individual servers and therefore must place all services on a single server. The configuration allows the administrator to deploy these applications along with applications requiring high availability on the same server.

Benefits of Partial Cluster Server Configuration
- High availability for only applications that require such redundancy

Negatives of Partial Cluster Server Configuration
- No performance gain during normal node operation

Managing a Windows 2000 Server Cluster

Network administrators have two primary methods for creating and managing clusters in their network environment. One is the graphical user interface (GUI) Cluster Administrator tool and the other is the command line tool, CLUSTER.EXE. In this section, we review some basic tasks you can accomplish through the Cluster Administrator Tool and review the command line tool in detail.

Cluster Administrator Tool

In this section, we review the functionality of the Cluster Administrator tool. If you're at the console for a node in a cluster, you find the tool in the Administrative Tools folder. Otherwise, you can install the tool on a Windows 2000 machine using the Windows 2000 Administration Tools Setup Wizard. You find the Administration Tools Setup Wizard (ADMINPAK.MSI) program on your Windows 2000 Server CD in the I386 directory.

Using the Cluster Administrator tool, you can connect to a specific cluster by specifying the cluster's IP address or name as part of the command line to launch the administration tool. You also have the option to view all the clusters within the domain by clicking Browse once you are in the administration tool. You can only manage those clusters that are in the same domain as the computer running Cluster Administrator tool. To manage a cluster within a different domain, you must make the management computer part of that domain.

An important task for any network administrator managing a clustered environment is to continuously check the status of all clusters. Keeping track of all failover activities allows the network administrator to configure better failover policies, determine cluster needs, and take a more proactive approach to capacity planning. By monitoring failover activity the network administrator can help avoid performance degradation caused by continuous failovers. You can view the failover status for nodes within a cluster by launching the Cluster Administrator tool. Each node and its current status is listed.

Another task you find yourself turning to the Cluster Administrator tool for is configuration of your applications. Using the Cluster Application Wizard, you can configure applications to run on a cluster. The Cluster Application Wizard walks you through all the necessary steps, including creating the virtual server to host the application, creating failover and failback policies, and creating dependencies between cluster resources.

Note Applications that developers intend to create as cluster-aware applications can have extensions written to them, allowing the Cluster Administrator tool to manage these applications as it does any other resource in the cluster.

Note For easier management of your cluster, you can always install the Cluster Administrator tool on a remote computer. The workstation or server where you install the tool can be a Windows NT machine running server pack 3 or later, or a Windows 2000 machine. Windows NT 4.0 machines can't have the Cluster Administrator tool installed through Windows 2000 Server; you need to use the Cluster Administrator tool that came with Microsoft Windows NT Server Enterprise Edition 4.0. You are still able to manage the cluster running on Windows 2000 Advanced Server; however, certain features aren't available to manage.

Command Line Administration

There are many network administrators, including myself, who'd rather execute commands from the command line than use a GUI. Whether it's a longing for the "good old days" of MS-DOS, or the flexibility the command line interface has to offer, many of the administrative tools in Windows 2000 have an alternative to the GUI in the form of a command line .exe. In this section, we review what options you have available to you when using the command line tool for Cluster Service.

The cluster command is available for execution from any Windows 2000 machine. This allows flexibility in creating and executing scripts to help manage your clustered environment. To use the CLUSTER.EXE command, get to a Windows 2000 command prompt and type **cluster**. All the command options are displayed for the tool. The two major command options used with the CLUSTER.EXE administration tool are:

```
CLUSTER /LIST[:domain-name]
CLUSTER [[/CLUSTER:]cluster-name] <options>
```

The CLUSTER /LIST[:domain-name] command displays all clusters that exist within the computer's domain (if no domain is specified) or all clusters in the specified domain. Otherwise, you can execute the CLUSTER.EXE command along with the options in the following list.

- **/PROP[ERTIES] [<prop-list>]**   Specifying this option enables you to set or view the common cluster properties. Used in conjunction with the /PROP[ERTIES][:propname[,propname …] /USEDEFAULT] option.

- **/PRIV [PROPERTIES] [<prop-list>]**   Used to set the cluster private properties. Used in conjunction with the /PRIV[PROPERTIES][:propname[,propname …] /USEDEFAULT] option.

- **/PROP[ERTIES][:propname[,propname …] /USEDEFAULT]**   You can execute this option against property lists to set property options such as Dword, MultiString, or Security values.

- **/PRIV[PROPERTIES][:propname[,propname …] /USEDEFAULT]**   You can use this option against property lists to set property options such as Dword, MultiString, or Security values.

- **/REN[AME]:cluster-name**   Used to rename the cluster. Before using this option, it's a good idea to view the currently configured clusters using the CLUSTER /LIST[:domain-name] command.

- **VER[SION]**   Displays Cluster Service version. Use this option to confirm what version of software you are running before applying patches or upgrading software.

- **QUORUM[RESOURCE][:resource-name] [/PATH:path] [/MAXLOGSIZE:max-size-kbytes]**   Used to change the size of the quorum log or the actual path for the log.

- **/SETFAIL[UREACTIONS][:node-name[,node-name …]]**

- **/REG[ADMIN]EXT:admin-extension-dll[,admin-extension-dll …]**   Using this option registers a Cluster Administrator extension DLL with the cluster. A Cluster Administrator extension enables the Cluster Administrator to configure a new resource type.

- **/UNREG[ADMIN]EXT:admin-extension-dll[,admin-extension-dll …]**   Used to unregister a Cluster Administrator extension.

- **NODE [node-name] node-command**   Allows you to execute a command against a specific node in the cluster. For example, to view the status of the FS1 node, type

```
cluster node FS1 / status
```

- **GROUP [group-name] group-command**   Similar to the NODE command only this is used against specific groups defined within a cluster. If you want to move a group named WEB GROUP 1 from the WEB1 node to the WEB2 node you do so by typing:

```
cluster webcluster group "WEB GROUP 1" /moveto:WEB2
```
where "webcluster" is the name of the cluster in which the nodes are located.

- **RES[OURCE] [resource-name] resource-command**   Used to administer resources defined within a cluster. For example, you can delete a resource named "webresource" in the cluster "webcluster" by typing:

```
cluster /cluster:webcluster resource webresource /delete
```

- **{RESOURCETYPE | RESTYPE} [resourcetype-name] resourcetype-command**   Print spooler, file share, or physical disk are all classes of resources. Using the resource type command option, you can delete, list, or create a resource type.

- **NET[WORK] [network-name] network-command**   Used to view the status, view the properties (common and private), rename the network, or list the network interfaces for the cluster's network.

- **NETINT[ERFACE] [interface-name] interface-command**   Used against a specific interface of the network. For example, typing:

```
Cluster /cluster:webcluster network primarynetwork /listinterfaces
```
lists the interfaces for the network called "primarynetwork" for the cluster named "webcluster."

- **<prop-list> = name=value[value, ...][:<format>] [name=value[,value ...][:<format>] ...]**   How to specify the property in the command line. For example, typing:

```
cluster webcluster node web1 /priv prop1=string1,string2:multistring
```
sets the string1 and string2 values for the private properties of the node Web1 on the cluster named "webcluster."

- **<format> =BINARY | DWORD | STR[ING] | EXPANDSTR[ING] | MULTISTR[ING] | SECURITY | ULARGE**   The format types for common or private cluster properties.

- **CLUSTER /?** and **CLUSTER / HELP**   Displays the previous command options.

When administrating your clusters from the command line, you must be careful of a few things.

- By specifying a PERIOD (.) in the command for cluster name, you're specifying the local cluster.

- You have the ability to specify multiple options in a single command line. The CLUSTER.EXE command executes from left to right; in case one of the options fails, the command stops executing at the point of failure.

- When writing a script for the CLUSTER.EXE command, you can specify a properties value to be True with a 1 (one) or 0 (zero) for False.

- If a command line string has two consecutive double quotes, use double quotation marks in that string.

- If a name, such as the cluster name or domain name within the command line, has a space or a special character such as a comma (,) you must use quotation marks around it.

Third-Party Support for Cluster Service

We covered the various enhancements to your environment that Windows 2000 Cluster Service offers. When you use Cluster Service, your applications experience increased performance, redundancy, and, in some cases, increased capabilities. The amount of performance increase you see depends on whether these applications are written to take advantage of the Windows 2000 Cluster Service. When looking for applications for your cluster server, you need to ask, "Is the application *cluster-aware?*" An application certified by the vendor as being cluster-aware must meet two basic criteria defined by Microsoft:

- The vendor's application uses the Cluster Service API to exploit Cluster Service in some way.

- The vendor supports customers if they install the listed application on a cluster according to the vendor's instructions.

The satisfaction you get from knowing that the application can recognize Cluster Service features such as network failover and Network Load Balancing isn't the only thing you gain. You also get the added satisfaction of knowing you can call the vendor in your time of need without worrying that you'll be turned away because you're running the application within a clustered environment. If you plan on deploying applications such as messaging servers, database servers, or Web servers, be sure to verify with the vendor whether the product meets the cluster-aware criteria. Table 13-1 displays a list of vendors, the category their product fits in, a description of each application, and the name of the application.

Note   Table 13-1 is meant only to give you an idea of what cluster-aware products offer you. You should always check with the vendor for additional cluster-aware capabilities the product may have.

More Info   This is only a partial list of vendors and products. To see the complete list of products currently certified by each vendor, visit: *http://www.microsoft.com/ntserver/ntserverenterprise/exec/overview/clustering/partnerlist.asp*. Also note that this list is always growing. If you don't see your application's vendor there, it always helps to check with the vendor.

Table 13-1.   A List of Vendors and Products Certified to Support Windows 2000 Cluster Service

Company/Web site	Product	Category	Description
Microsoft *http://www.microsoft.com*	SQL Server 7.0 Enterprise Edition	Database Server	SQL Server 7.0 is Microsoft's powerful relational database management system (RDBMS) that is scalable up to 32 processors and 64 GB of memory. SQL Server 7.0 also delivers failover clustering and more.
NSI Software *http://www.nsisw.com*	Double-Take for Windows NT	Disaster Recovery and Storage	Double-Take enables you to replicate data between Microsoft Cluster Server (MSCS) over your LAN or WAN. One possible advantage is for offsite data storage, providing enhanced redundancy for your environment.
NetIQ Corporation *http://www.netiq.com*	NetIQ AppManager Suite	Cluster Service Management	Use NetIQ to manage your actual cluster services running on either Advanced or Datacenter Server versions of Windows 2000. With NetIQ you have a wealth of management options, including the ability to monitor your Windows 2000 Server performance from a single point of administration.
Veritas *http://www.veritas.com*	Cluster X	Cluster Service Management	Cluster X, among other benefits, provides a statistical view of your clustered environment including server uptimes.
BEA Systems Inc. *http://www.bea.com*	BEA Extensions for Microsoft Cluster Server	Messaging/Collaboration	Integrate BEA's TUXEDO and WebLogic into your clustered environment.

(continued)

Table 13-1.   *(continued)*

Company/Web site	Product	Category	Description
Microsoft *http://www.microsoft.com*	Exchange 5.5 Enterprise Edition	Messaging/ Collaboration	For enterprise-wide messaging needs, you can run Exchange Server within a Windows 2000 clustered environment to meet the hardware needs of an enterprise-wide messaging and collaboration solution.
Legato Systems Inc. *http://www.legato.com*	Legato Networker Power Edition	Storage	Other than enhanced backup and recovery times, Networker Power Edition enables failover of backup and restore services through cluster-aware extensions.
Ultrabac.com *http://www.ultrabac.com*	Ultrabac	Disaster Recovery	Enables you to back up and restore your clustered environment with speed and efficiency.

What is a cluster-aware application anyway? We just went over what you need to look for in your applications to determine whether they are cluster-aware. In the examples of applications listed previously, you're looking for vendors to certify that their application meets the criteria specified by Microsoft. Microsoft has another set of criteria that can help determine whether an application is capable of being cluster-aware. An application that is capable of being cluster-aware:

- Uses TCP/IP
- Maintains a configurable location
- Supports transaction processing

These applications can then be placed into two categories: applications that are cluster resources or applications that interact with the cluster. We look at both of these categories next.

Cluster Resources

Applications such as database servers, Web servers, or services like file and print services all fit into the category of cluster resources as long as they:

- **Can be brought online and offline**   During the failover and failback process, Cluster Service needs to take resources offline to move them to a resource group located on a secondary node. After the resource has been moved, Cluster Service then brings the resource back online. If you're developing applications to be cluster-aware, you must add this ability into the application amongst other cluster-aware criteria covered earlier.

- **Can be hosted by only one node at a time** The resource you're installing must not require that it run on more than one node at a single time for proper operation. Cluster Service isn't capable of failover if the resource requires a second server to function.

- **Can be managed in a server cluster** If the application can't be managed within a cluster, you aren't able to create failover policies for that application. Without failover policies, application redundancy is nonexistent.

Cluster Application

Any application that provides information regarding a cluster and its components is considered to interact with the cluster. A prime example of an application that interacts with the cluster is the Cluster Administrator tool. Earlier in the chapter, we reviewed some of the tasks the tool allows you to accomplish, including viewing the status of each node and adding cluster-aware applications to the cluster. Another example of a cluster-interactive application is Cluster X by Veritas (listed in Table 13-1). This particular application provides statistical information regarding the cluster. It's important for network administrators to know what tools they have to manage their clusters, particularly if they want to gain the most performance out of their clustered environments. For example, viewing the statistical trends of the cluster helps in capacity planning. You know from the statistics whether you need additional servers to accommodate the amount of user load currently on a particular cluster.

Summary

It's only been in the last five years that we've seen a real improvement in the clustering options available to network administrators of Windows NT systems. Clustering was something Microsoft couldn't pass over lightly. By adding clustering, Microsoft showed it understood the needs of network administrators, particularly those in enterprise environments. Today, we're seeing organizations that may not necessarily fit the description of being an enterprise network turn to clustering. These smaller environments are doing so to help deal with the heavy Internet traffic their e-commerce site may be experiencing. Clustering is also the mainstay for many ISPs and now application service providers.

When you decide to turn to clustering as an option to increase the overall performance of your network and the applications that run on that network, there are some things to keep in mind. Understand your current needs—don't design a clustered environment that can't or doesn't meet those needs. If redundancy is imperative, don't create a partial clustered configuration in place of a hot-spare configuration. You should also keep your goals in mind. Clustering should be part of your capacity planning. Know how many and what type of servers you need to handle your organization's growth. Often administrators simply throw server cases into a cluster. A cluster consisting of 10 workgroup class servers, when the same amount of processing power can be generated by four departmental servers, only increases the number of nodes you must manage within that cluster and prevents you from scaling your clustered environment efficiently. You reach the maximum node number per cluster quicker when you have 10 nodes per cluster instead of four.

In this chapter, we also reviewed the benefits of Network Load Balancing (NLB). When you combine Cluster Service with NLB, you give yourself and your environment additional options in meeting redundancy requirements, improving application availability, and increasing application performance. We also saw how clustering combined with NLB isn't only a method for providing more processor power to your network; it's also a capacity planning tool. These two services provide you with avenues when planning for your future needs and requirements.

Chapter 14
Microsoft Windows 2000 and the Internet

In the last few years, the Internet has become integral to an organization's future. Many businesses are scrambling to create a presence on the Web—however, it's not a simple Web site they're looking for. They want to conduct their entire business online, which means they're searching for the right e-commerce solution and a platform to run that solution on.

Those organizations that choose to create their e-commerce sites with Microsoft applications will have a plethora of applications and solutions to select from, such as Microsoft Site Server, Microsoft Exchange Server, and Microsoft SQL Server 7.0. These applications—when combined with Microsoft Windows 2000 Server and Microsoft's Web server Internet Information Services (IIS) 5.0—enable a network administrator to create a solution that's interoperable, robust, and efficient. In this chapter, we concentrate on what can be considered the foundation for the Web site, Internet Information Services 5.0, and specifically the performance enhancements found in this latest version of Microsoft's Web server.

Internet Information Services 5.0

Windows 2000 Server includes the latest update to Microsoft's Internet Information Services (IIS) 5.0. IIS is a full-featured application enabling network administrators to provide full scalable Web services. This increased scalability enables a single IIS server to host multiple Web sites, providing ISPs the scalability to host thousands of Web sites. This feature can also benefit individual organizations by enabling them to use one server to host Web sites for different departments, such as a dedicated Web site for the accounting group.

IIS is also fully integrated with the suite of applications and development tools Microsoft has to offer. For example, a Visual Basic developer can easily port applications created to run on a Microsoft Windows desktop to run within Microsoft Internet Explorer. Developers can take advantage of powerful development and scripting languages such as VBScript and JScript and, using features built within IIS, they can control how these applications utilize server resources such as the CPU.

In this chapter, we cover performance-enhancing features such as processor throttling, process accounting, and network bandwidth control. We also explore performance tuning that can be done at an even greater level of detail by editing the IIS 5.0 metabase. The metabase serves the same purpose as the Windows 2000 registry, only it stores configuration information for IIS.

Another aspect of IIS that we cover in this chapter is how you can test the performance of the various applications running on the server. If you test the application before you deploy it, you can determine ahead of time the needs of the application, allowing you to plan for its deployment. For example, an application running under IIS might be designed to accommodate large user loads; however, your Web server's hardware configuration might fall short. By testing the configuration using various performance-testing tools, you realize and are able to deal with performance deficiency in a test environment rather than in full production, allowing you to make changes to hardware and software configurations before affecting user uptime. Before we proceed to performance tuning, we first review the steps to install IIS.

Installing IIS 5.0

In this section, we review the steps to install IIS 5.0; however, we don't go into the actual configuration of the services. For example, we don't cover how to create a Web site, FTP site, or virtual directory. For that, you need to consult the online help.

1. You install all Microsoft applications and services that are integrated within Windows 2000 Server through the Add/Remove Programs application in Control Panel. Launch the application by double-clicking its Control Panel icon.

2. Click Add/Remove Windows Components located in the left-hand pane of the Add/Remove Programs dialog box. Click Components to open the Windows Components Wizard (see Figure 14-1).

3. Locate Internet Information Services (IIS) in the Components list. If it is not checked, continue with Step 4; otherwise you must verify that the server is actually installed. Click Details to open the Internet Information Services (IIS) dialog box and then locate World Wide Web Server in the Subcomponents Of Internet Information Services (IIS) list. If it is checked, the server is already installed on your computer and you can click Cancel twice to exit the installation. Otherwise, check the server and Click OK to close the Internet Information Services (IIS) dialog box.

4. If Internet Information Services (IIS) isn't checked, select to install IIS by placing a check mark in the box and clicking Next.

5. You need to specify the location of your Windows 2000 Server setup files. The Windows Component Wizard installs the required system and application files. Click Finish to complete the install.

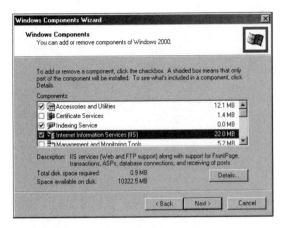

Figure 14-1.   *Installing Internet Information Services by using the Windows Components Wizard.*

Performance and Reliability

In IIS 5.0, administrators now have a faster and more reliable Web server than ever before. Internal improvements—such as a more refined and improved coding engine—and performance parameters—such as processor throttling that the network administrator can tune—all contribute to a more responsive and faster Web server. Performance features such as processor throttling contribute not only to the performance of the server but also its reliability. You can now specify the maximum amount of CPU usage by Web-application. Application faults such as runaway processes no longer have the ability to "take over" the processor, which eventually could cause the system and all Web sites running on the system to crash.

Developers will find that reliability of their applications running under IIS 5.0 has also improved through the support for pooled out-of-process applications. In this section, we review in detail these performance enhancements and where you can configure them at the server level. We also cover performance-enhancing features in Windows 2000 Server, such as clustering that enables IIS 5.0 to be the robust and scalable Web solution required by network administrators in this new e-commerce driven economy.

Clustering and IIS

As organizations begin to have more and more successes on the Internet, and e-commerce becomes a larger portion of their revenue, the organizations' Web sites eventually become the economic lifeline for that business. Network administrators have increased demands placed on them to improve the reliability, availability, and overall performance of the business's Web servers. Downtime for a Web site providing e-commerce services, or for that matter any company-specific information for any time period, can mean the loss of hundreds of thousands (if not millions) of dollars.

Real World

The Internet affects our lives in many ways. It was only a few years ago that people were amazed by the fact that they could have access to entire dictionaries and encyclopedias online. Today, you can buy, sell, and trade practically anything with a few clicks of your mouse button. In March of 2000, Stephen King, who's most famous for his horror stories, wanted to try something new when it came to selling books. Rather than publishing his latest novella using the traditional methods and then placing it on sale at bookstores and online, he decided to have the entire book available for download. Readers no longer had to wait the 24 hours or even longer for shipping; they could download the file and begin reading his latest work of art. This sounded as though it would be an extremely efficient method of selling books. However, there was one part of the process many overlooked and that was whether the network infrastructure was in place to handle the load. It turned out that the servers at the online stores weren't designed to handle the millions of users attempting to download the book. It didn't help the situation that certain sites were giving it away for free on the first day. In this case, users attempting to access the sites were being denied, not because of Denial of Service attacks by teenage hackers, but rather by degradation of the network caused by the user load alone. This example helps to illustrate the importance of anticipating traffic loads when designing Web applications. If you feel that a product is going to be a hot commodity or a service will be in heavy demand, think of contingency plans well ahead of when it goes online. Consider options that will increase performance and redundancy such as clustering, secondary dedicated lines, or entire sites that function as redundant datacenters.

One approach to the problem of improving reliability, availability, and overall performance is to link more than one computer together. Linking computers together is called *clustering* (for more information on clustering, see Chapter 13, "Microsoft Windows 2000 and Clustering").

This solution not only provides performance enhancements but also redundancy. Servers could be designated with the role of acting as a backup machine ready to pick up the load should the primary server fail. Also, clustered computers can help alleviate workload by distributing it across the clustered computers.

Cluster Service itself is only available in Microsoft Windows 2000 Advanced and Datacenter Servers. When you configure your IIS 5.0 servers to run on servers running Cluster Service, Web servers such as FTP and WWW seem as though a single computer is providing them. Another benefit of clustering is the redundancy it provides through the failover feature of Windows 2000 Cluster Service.

Failover enables one server to pick up the work of a failed server. For example, if you're running a Web site on Node 1 (nodes are any servers running Cluster Service) and a poorly written ASP application causes the Web services to fail, as long as you've configured another node such as Node 2 as the failover point, your users see little or no interruption in their work. Data loss is nonexistent during this transition as Node 1 and Node 2 point to a set of shared drives where information for the site is stored (see Figure 14-2 for an example of IIS running in a clustered environment).

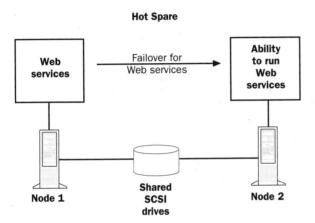

Figure 14-2.   *In this example, Node 2 can fully take over the Web services for Node 1.*

Another issue facing network administrators is the user load that occurs on a server when hosting single or multiple Web sites. Through clustering, you can load-balance incoming traffic between two or more servers. This way, not a single one-server node is overloaded or underutilized in the cluster.

Processor Throttling

Network administrators running multiple Web sites on a single IIS computer, or running other applications in addition to the Web sites on the same computer, have tended to experience problems with processor usage. For example, many companies allow their employees to create personal Web sites on the same server where company Web sites are running. When processor usage by one of these noncritical employee Web sites begins to increase and the performance of the more critical company Web sites diminishes, it becomes a problem for the network administrator. With the new feature of processor throttling, the network administrator can limit how much processor usage each Web site can have, rather than removing the Web site or application altogether.

Processor throttling isn't enabled by default; each Web site can have access to as much of the processor as it can possibly get. To turn processor throttling on, take the following steps:

1. Launch the Internet Information Services administration tool by clicking Start, pointing to Programs, pointing to Administrative Tools and clicking Internet Services Manager.

2. All computers running IIS within the network are listed in the console tree located in the left pane of the window. Expand the computer's icon on which the Web site is located.

3. Right-click the Web site and click Properties.

4. Click the Performance tab and check the Enable Process Throttling check box. This enables the Maximum CPU Use box. Enter the maximum percentage of CPU usage the selected Web site can get (see Figure 14-3).

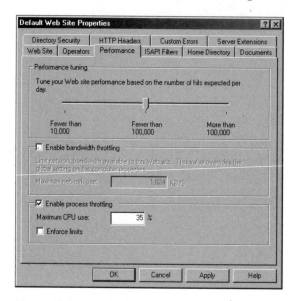

Figure 14-3. *In this example, I've limited the percentage of CPU processing time—however, it's not being enforced. Therefore, the Web site can continue to consume processor time over the set limit.*

Note The Web site isn't limited to the amount of CPU processing time you enter unless you check the Enforce Limits check box. If this check box isn't checked, the only consequence of a Web site going over the limit is that an event is written to Event Log.

5. Click OK to save your changes.

Bandwidth Throttling

If we continue with the example about the employees' Web sites mentioned in the previous section, CPU utilization isn't the only resource the Web site could overutilize. Network bandwidth is another precious commodity that can be overutilized by a Web site. To limit the bandwidth used by a particular Web site, open the Web Site Properties dialog box for the Web site and click the Performance tab (see the previous section on how to get to the Web Site Properties dialog box). Enable throttling by checking the Enable Bandwidth Throttling check box. Enter a value in the Maximum Network Use box to specify the amount of data in KB/s that can be transferred by the selected Web site. This setting overrides the value set at the computer level, even if it's greater (see Figure 14-4).

Note   Understanding that a single computer could potentially host multiple Web sites, Microsoft has enabled network administrators to configure settings at both the Web site and computer levels. Certain configuration settings made at the computer level will be propagated down to the Web site level, while others, such as at the bandwidth level, are Web site independent. The next time you config-ure a setting at the Web site level but don't understand why the setting is not working, verify that it hasn't already been configured at the computer level.

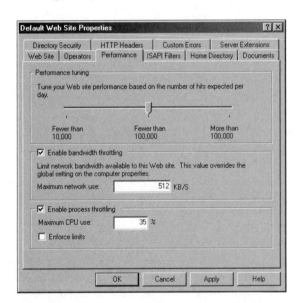

Figure 14-4.   *On the Performance tab, you can limit Web sites that aren't mission-critical to the amount of network bandwidth they utilize.*

Process Accounting

Process accounting is an essential feature if you want to use processor throttling. Process accounting enables network administrators to monitor and log the use of the CPU per Web site. This way, network administrators have an accurate log of what sites might be overutilizing CPU resources and what percentage the processor throttle should be set at.

You shouldn't think of process accounting just as a method of keeping tabs on CPU usage per Web site—it's also a method of troubleshooting Web sites and the scripts or applications running on them. For example, if you track high CPU utilization by one particular site, you might find that a script running on the Web site is executing incorrectly and using up CPU time. If you select to record Web site use to a log file, process accounting adds fields to it. However, you are only able to log process accounting information to a W3C Extended log file. You must also have chosen to log process accounting information by selecting the Process Accounting option found under the Extended Logging Options. To change Extended Logging Options, take the following steps:

1. Open the Extended Logging Properties dialog box by clicking the Web Site tab on the Web Site Properties dialog box, selecting W3C Extended Log File Format from the Active Log Format drop-down list and then clicking Properties.

2. Click the Extended Properties tab to view the logging options.

3. You can now scroll down the list of Extended Logging Options configuring the logging options you prefer.

Real World

After hearing complaints about the response time for Web sites running on a particular computer, the network administrator began investigating the issue by running Performance and looking at System Monitor. He selected some general counters including processor utilization. After a short period of monitoring, the network administrator was able to determine that processor time was abnormally high. He decided to further investigate by utilizing IIS 5.0's process accounting feature. After some time monitoring the Web sites and viewing the log file, he found one site had continuous high levels of CPU usage. After a more detailed look into the Web site, he found that a company employee created the Web site. Even though the policy for this organization was to allow employees to use space on the server to build their own Web sites, the organization always had the right to limit traffic to the Web site or shut it down altogether. When the network administrator looked into what was attracting so many users to the site, he discovered that the employee had actually created an e-commerce site selling questionable products. Not only did the network administrator save the company from public scrutiny, but also possible lawsuits.

Another useful function of process accounting is the ability for ISPs to charge by CPU usage. Most ISPs charge users by the amount of hits to their Web site or amount of downloads taking place at the server. They can now charge a customer by processor usage. This can also serve as a good indication for the ISP if the customer is ready to move to a dedicated Web server instead of a server running multiple Web sites.

Application Protection

Through constant improvements to IIS and new releases of the product including IIS 5.0, Microsoft has made it easier for developers to create applications that run more reliably and are even more robust. For example, under IIS 3.0, developers were limited to how their applications shared resources and memory. All Internet Server API (ISAPI) applications (including Active Server Pages (ASP) technology) had to share resources and memory of the server process. The server process is the memory area where the operating system runs applications. This was a weak point in Microsoft Windows NT and IIS 3.0, because a Web site application could corrupt the process space because they were sharing the same process area or, worse yet, destabilize the operating system. The main reason for doing this in the first place was to provide faster performance of the applications. With the release of IIS 4.0, developers could either select to run applications in the same process as the Web server (INETINFO.EXE) or in a separate area known as DLLHOST.EXE.

IIS 5.0 has further improved on this by enabling you to run applications within a third process area called the pooled process area. Each process area offers a level varying in stability by the level of isolation. If you run applications within the main process area (INETINFO.EXE), you run a greater risk of the application bringing down your entire Web server because that area isn't isolated from the Web server services. While running an application in the isolated process area (DLLHOST.EXE), the operating system, Web server, and other applications are protected from each other.

However, stability does come at a performance cost—the level of isolation also affects the performance of the computer. Running an application in the main process area makes the server run more responsively, as compared to an application running in the new pooled process area.

You need to specify what level of protection you want your applications to run under. The protection level can be specified at either the Web site or virtual directory level. To specify protection level for the entire Web site, open the Properties dialog box for the Web site, and click the Home Directory tab. You can select one of the three levels of protection contained in the Application Protection drop-down list (see Figure 14-5):

- **High (Isolated)**   Applications running within this area run at a higher performance cost than others. However, if the application malfunctions it can't affect the Web server or other Web sites. Mission-critical Web sites should be configured to run under this level of protection.
- **Medium (Pooled)**   This level of protection offers a medium level of protection for the Web server. However, the protection of the Web server comes at the cost of the other applications running within the same isolated process. If one application misbehaves, all of the other applications are affected.
- **Low (IIS Process)**   This last level should only have noncritical Web sites configured to run under it because any unstable application could easily bring down the server.

Figure 14-5. *By setting the Web site to run under a Medium level of protection, I can be assured that applications running under this Web site won't cause the Web server to crash.*

Note By specifying the protection level at the Web site level, you leave yourself little room if you want to further isolate applications that may be running within a virtual directory. For example, you could have an application whose stability is in question. To protect other applications, you would want to isolate that process by running it at a higher protection level.

Socket Pooling

A socket is an identifier for a particular node on a network. The socket itself consists of two numbers, one for the node and the other the port number. Port numbers help identify the particular service or services running on the Web server. For example, port 21 on an Internet node represents an FTP server, while port 80 represents a Web server. Under Web servers such as IIS 4.0, a socket is created for each Web site because individual sites created on IIS 4.0 servers require their own IP addresses. Because of this inability to share IP addresses among individual Web sites, sockets couldn't be shared across Web sites. This is a performance barrier, because each socket you create on your Web server takes up a certain amount of system resources and keeps hold of those resources until the server or individual Web site is shut down.

Under IIS 5.0, the process of creating sockets and binding them to Web site IP addresses has changed. IIS 5.0 allows Web sites that share the same port number but are bound to different IP addresses to share the same set of sockets. This enhancement reduces the number of sockets needed, which effectively reduces resource consumption.

> **Note** Sharing socket sets across Web sites isn't recommended for mission-critical Web sites. Any time a Web site is sharing socket information, you run the risk of one Web site taking down the other because of possible errors that might occur at the socket level. You might also compromise the security of your Web site that is running in a secured domain with multiple networks.

HTTP Compression

The ability to provide HTTP compression is yet another new feature provided by IIS 5.0. Environments that either have low bandwidth connections, or clients accessing the Web site using low bandwidth such as dialup, can provide content to their users faster through HTTP compression. HTTP clients must be running compression-enabled browsers to take advantage of HTTP compression (Internet Explorer 5.0 is compression-enabled). One important fact to note is the overhead that comes with compressing Web content. Compression is extremely costly in terms of processor usage. It's always a good idea to monitor your processor usage before turning on HTTP compression.

Real World

A company that was maintaining an extranet site wanted to gain a better understanding of how their users were accessing its Web site. So, along with the customer relations department, the IS director conducted a quick telephone survey with each client. To the company's surprise, a majority of the customers (80 percent) were accessing the Web site through ISP dialup connections with a bandwidth no greater than 56Kb/s. After seeing the results of this survey, the network administrator enabled HTTP compression at the server, and ran some benchmark tests to provide performance data to the end users as to the benefits of HTTP compression. With more educated end users, convincing users to upgrade their browsers to compression-enabled browsers wasn't the uphill battle the network administrator expected.

HTTP compression isn't enabled by default. To turn the compression on, you need to launch the Internet Services Manager and take the following steps:

1. Right-click the computer's icon in the console pane and click Properties to display the computer's Properties dialog box.

2. Under Master Properties, click Edit to open the WWW Service Master Properties dialog box for the selected server. Click the Service tab.

3. Under HTTP Compression, you can select to compress application or static files or both by checking the appropriate check boxes (see Figure 14-6).

If you want to compress application files, you need to select to compress both static and application files. The location where you select to store temporary files can't be a compressed directory or remote drive, and neither can it be shared such as in a cluster drive. Temporary files must also reside on an NTFS partition. Because space will be a critical issue, be sure you have enough space on your local drive if you select Unlimited for The Maximum Temporary Folder Size.

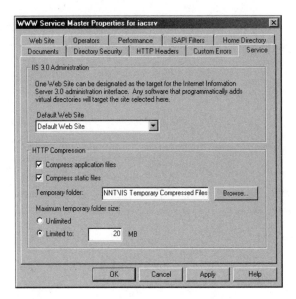

Figure 14-6. *In this example, I have limited the size of the temporary folder to 20 MBs.*

Tuning IIS 5.0

In this section, we cover some configuration settings you can change on your IIS server for increased performance. These changes require that you already be familiar with the IIS management tools and various settings. If you aren't familiar with these settings, consult the online help for more information. For increased performance configuration, changes need to take place both at the server and operating system levels.

If you're wondering how these changes differ from those discussed earlier, these features or configuration settings aren't new to IIS 5.0. In fact, you find many of these configuration settings are in the same place under IIS 4.0. However, registry settings might be in a different location.

Performance Bar

Web sites experiencing a high volume of traffic should have the performance bar set to more than 100,000 hits per day. Likewise, sites experiencing low levels of traffic shouldn't have performance bar levels increased.

If the performance bar is set to a high number, IIS retains additional system resources such as memory. The more resources the server has available to it, the less it must call on the operating system. However, this can also hurt performance if server load levels fall below the anticipated mark for extended periods. To set the performance bar, take the following steps.

1. Launch the Internet Information Services administration tool found in the Administrative Tools folder.

2. Expand the server and right-click the Web site to bring up its Properties dialog box.

3. Click the Performance tab to view the current settings for the performance bar.

4. If you expect heavy traffic, move the slider to the right so it's set to More Than 100,000. If traffic is expected to be light, move the slider to the left to Fewer Than 10,000 (see Figure 14-7).

5. Click OK to save your settings.

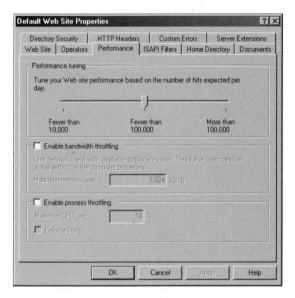

Figure 14-7.   *Changing the performance bar settings can result in immediate performance gains.*

Application Response

Set application response for the server to be optimized for applications. It's good practice to run Web services only on servers hosting Web sites and Web-enabled applications. This decreases the chance of other applications interfering with the performance of the Web services running on the server by using precious system resources. Also, a malfunctioning Web service or other non-Internet service is capable of crashing the other.

However, there are times you could justify running multiple application services on the same server—times such as when you anticipate low usage of the server and feel the server is capable of handling both application and Web server loads, or if neither service is capable of crashing the other. If applications are to be run on the server, you should *not* run them in the foreground. IIS requires as much of the system resources as the system is able to give it.

To change the performance of foreground and background programs, take the following steps.

1. Open Control Panel and double-click the System icon to open the System Properties dialog box.

2. Click the Advanced tab and click Performance Options to open the Performance Options dialog box.

3. Under Application Response, click Background Services so its performance is optimized for background programs (see Figure 14-8).

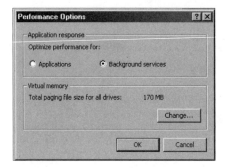

Figure 14-8. *According to your server's role, you want to adjust how processor resources are assigned to foreground and background services.*

Logging Only When Needed

Log Web server activity only when you truly need to. Running the logging service takes up additional system resources, resources that once freed up could be used by the Web server or other applications running on the server. For example, if you're administrating an IIS 5.0 development server, there should be no reason for logging unless it's part of your debugging strategy.

Note Later in the chapter, we review the benefit of testing Web applications against real-world scenarios. During your benchmarking and system testing, you should always configure the server exactly as it will be during production. If logging is a requirement in the production environment, turn it on when performance testing the server.

Note   If you do decide to enable logging, then log files should be written to a striped partition configured on a controller that enables write-back caching. Web sites, particularly those experiencing heavy traffic, find the log disk becoming a bottleneck if the location of the log file isn't optimized.

Network Configuration and Settings

When performance tuning, IIS network administrators tend to overlook a critical aspect of their environment, which has a direct effect on the performance of IIS—the network architecture and network settings. A poorly designed network topology leads to poor response from Web sites and Web-enabled applications running within these sites.

In Chapter 8, "Network Problems," problems related to network settings, configuration, and design are explored, along with methods to avoid such problems both at the operating system and network infrastructure level. For example, the chapter reviews obscure problems such as vibrations in a building causing poor network throughput. In this section, we don't go into such details regarding network issues. However, we do cover network-specific settings you can implement at the operating system level, which lead to a better-performing Web server. We also explore network topology considerations that allow you to maximize performance through elements outside the server.

Network Topology Considerations

Many times, the issue behind a poorly performing Web site isn't the server configuration, application design, or operating system. Rather, it can be attributed to inadequate network bandwidth. Inadequate bandwidth is usually the cause of poor planning and poor Web site design. For example, a company creates a simple Web site just for the purpose of being able to say it has a presence on the Internet. Soon it finds itself adding features to the Web site to satisfy the needs of its users visiting the site, features such as a document depot where users can download the latest manuals for the widgets the company makes. These additional features only increase the demand for bandwidth, and inevitably the current bandwidth becomes inadequate. If the company had planned appropriately, adding bandwidth as it added features to the Web site, it wouldn't be experiencing such performance issues.

Monitoring your Web site's incoming network traffic goes a long way in helping to plan ahead. There are many tools you can turn to for the purpose of monitoring Web site network traffic, including Microsoft's Network Monitor. Certain firewalls and routers also have the capability of monitoring and logging network traffic to hosts on their network. Another option for network administrators for extracting network traffic information about their Web site is to turn to the ISP providing the dedicated line to the Internet.

Most good ISPs provide network statistics mapped over a daily, weekly, monthly, or annual period. Viewing this data allows network administrators to draw decisive conclusions as to when a peak season might exist for traffic to their Web site. For example, many online merchants expect to be hit heavily during Christmas. However, there might be other periods during the year, such as right before Christmas, when their Web sites could be getting large amounts of hits per day but sales figures don't show it, mainly because customers are browsing the site to see what to buy but not actually buying until Christmas rolls around. Depending on the data you retrieve from activity logs, you might want to:

- **Increase bandwidth**   Upgrading the dedicated lines from your data centers to the outside world helps to increase the response of Web sites and Web-enabled applications. Moving from a T1 to a T3 has an immediate impact on user experience with your Web site, particularly if the T1 was being saturated by the amount of traffic at your site.

Note   Upgrading the bandwidth for your Web site only has an effect on how well your network is able to handle traffic. You find a dramatic decrease in the amount of collisions occurring on the network and faster response time by Web sites to users' requests. However, the time it takes for a user to get the response from the server heavily depends on the bandwidth the user is operating under. If the user has 28.8 Kb/s mode, the T3 on your end doesn't have the impact you hope it does. On the other hand, if users have access to a T1, Digital Subscriber Line (DSL), or cable modem, they are able to take advantage of the increase in network efficiency on your end.

- **Upgrade to Fast Ethernet**   If there are devices such as servers, hubs, or switches still operating under 10 Mb/s, you should seriously consider upgrading these devices to 100 Mb/s. Slower devices can turn into bottlenecks, eventually affecting the performance of the entire Web site. As an example, let's take the case of the very common three-tiered Web site design. In a three-tiered network, you have a Web server, database server, and some form of connection management service running between the two. If the network traffic speed running between the Web server and database is 100 Mb/s, however, the speed drops at the connection management piece. The advantage of running 100 Mb/s at either the Web server or database server is for naught if parts of the network run at a slower speed.

- **Consider turning to an application service provider**   In the last two performance tips, it's been suggested that you upgrade your current network environment to meet the performance demands of your Web site. This is easier said than done, especially when you need to approach the bean counters in accounting with that suggestion. It can be particularly difficult if the size of your organization makes it difficult to not only justify the cost of upgrading, but also hire the staff to continuously administer the site. In today's world of Web and Internet application hosting, a few good solutions are popping up, including application service providers. Application service providers host and maintain not only your Web site, but also the applications running on those servers. The advantage of hosting your Web site through an application service provider is that you don't need to concern yourself with hardware issues such as dedicated lines, server configuration, and maintenance issues. The application service provider monitors the site for you on a 24/7 basis, correcting and informing you of any problems that might occur with the site. Your developers simply have to update the site with new content and applications hosted on the site and you can concentrate on other mission-critical network services.

TCP Parameter

Protocol parameter settings are essential to a well-tuned server. If connections are being left open longer than need be, or timing out too quickly, users experience connection problems such as server time-out, connection reset by server, or Web pages loading halfway. By creating a MaxUserPort value, you can make sure you don't run out of user ports. Also, a TcpWindowSize with a large value increases the window size, which optimizes server performance, particularly for high-speed networks (TCP stops when the window fills up). You create or edit the two values, MaxUserPort and TcpWindowSize, from the registry by taking the following steps.

1. Using Regedt32, navigate to HKEY_LOCAL_MACHINE\SYSTEM\ CurrentControlSet\Services\Tcpip\Parameters.

2. Add the value MaxUserPort if it's not already there, and set to 0xfffe.

3. Add the value TcpWindowSize if it's not already there, and set to 0x4470.

Receive Buffers

The receive buffers help to minimize the number of dropped packets on the receiving end of a network transmission. Each time a packet is dropped on the receiving end, it causes TCP to retransmit that packet. With fewer dropped packets, you have more successful transmissions, thus increased performance.

Tip   Many times, you can test the usefulness of configuration settings, such as the receive buffers setting, by adjusting the setting in a controlled test environment. You can set up a server and client machine, making sure to change the receive buffers setting on both computers. Next, you can use benchmarking tools, which we explore in the section "Performance Testing Your Web Site," to place a load on both server and client machine. Adjusting the setting gradually enables you to tell if it's making an impact on the performance of your Web site. If not, the performance issues might lie elsewhere.

You should set the receive buffers for the network interface card (NIC) to its maximum value. How you do this depends on the NIC installed in the server. Many manufacturers allow you to adjust this value from the Local Area Connection Properties for the server; others might require you to run configuration software for that card or edit the registry entries. Consult your network card's documentation for information on how to change this setting.

Additional Performance Tuning Tips

A few versions ago, network administrators tended to think of IIS as a service that ran under Windows NT and that's all. However, with the release of IIS 3.0, then 4.0, and now 5.0, IIS has developed into a true application server and thus it should be treated as such. In this section, we cover additional tips that make your Web server and the applications running on it perform better and become even more stable.

Many of the changes are ones you can make to your Web applications. For that reason, we don't go in depth with the suggestions, because this book isn't meant for programmers. However, as the person responsible for the performance of the server, you can always run these suggestions by the developers to help them produce more efficient running applications.

- **Use real-world tests** When you test your Web site applications for performance, create activity that mirrors what you expect once the application goes into production. Many times, developers and network administrators test their Web site and Web site applications by having someone at the help desk hit the server continuously for a few hours. These results don't allow you to draw an accurate picture of how capable your server and applications are in handling real-world user load. In the section "Performance Testing Your Web Site," we cover various methods and tools available to you for testing Web server capacity and Web server application capacity.

- **Don't use blocking calls disparagingly** When writing applications that run on IIS, or, for that matter, Windows 2000 Server in general, developers should avoid using blocking calls when writing for server class machines. Blocking calls are a poor method of manipulating CPUs on a server, because the I/O takes millions of cycles to complete.

- **When you cache data, do so wisely** Caching comes at a cost to resources, mainly memory. If you cache too much at a time, you negatively affect the performance of applications and system operations running on the server. On the other hand, if you cache too little at a time, applications need to recalculate the data missed by the cache.

- **Carefully monitor active threads** The number of active threads on a server has a direct impact on the performance of that server and its applications. Creating additional threads, in most cases, helps with the throughput of the application. However, if you have too many threads, performance of the server suffers.

Performance Tuning Active Server Pages

Since the inception of HTML (Hypertext Markup Language), the flock of software developers to the Internet seems to have grown exponentially. However, HTML alone has shown it lacks the flexibility and extensibility developers require to create dynamic, secure, and robust Web sites.

Dropping HTML altogether is really out of the question; HTML is still essential for the development of any Web site, static or dynamic. What developers have done is to turn to alternative programming languages designed for the Internet and to write the core aspects of their Internet-based applications or Web sites using HTML when necessary, or when it's not feasible to use these alternative development languages.

One such development language that developers have turned to in great numbers has been Active Server Pages (ASP). Active Server Pages isn't a development language the way Java or C++ are; rather, it's a server-side scripting environment that's been designed to run on IIS, Windows NT, and Windows 2000. Because ASP pages execute server-side scripts, they enable developers to program for a known Web server and operating system platform rather than being concerned about unknown factors such as what browser the client is using. However, server-side scripting can also be a negative in that all processing is done at the server, which in turn adds to the load experienced by the Web server. In this section of the chapter, we configure settings that can be made through the IIS administration tool, or made by configuring the IIS metabase.

The metabase is a hierarchical database used to store configuration values for IIS. In the past, network administrators had to modify IIS configuration properties through the registry. Now, through the metabase, they gain more granularity. There are several methods to configure the metabase. You can configure values through the use of administration tools such as the IIS snap-in, or programmatically through the use of IIS Admin Objects and MetaEdit 2.0 (the Microsoft Metabase Editor), a utility that comes with the Windows 2000 Resource Kit.

Note   As with the Windows 2000 registry, any changes made directly to the metabase could lead to failures with Web services if made incorrectly. It's a good idea to back up the metabase before you decide to make configuration changes.

Because MetaEdit 2.0 doesn't allow you to connect to remote computers, each IIS server requires its own copy of MetaEdit installed on it. After installation, launch the program to begin editing the local metabase. For those of you already familiar with the Windows 2000 registry, you find a similar hierarchy that you can navigate when implementing changes to the metabase. You can add, modify, and delete key information by selecting the key you want to edit and selecting the appropriate command from the Edit menu. Whenever you select to modify information in the metabase, an Edit Metabase Data dialog box appears with possible settings you can modify and values you can choose from. For more information on how to configure changes in the metabase, or where specific metabase keys are located, see the online help for MetaEdit 2.0.

Note   Later in this section, we review settings you can modify in the metabase. One quick and easy way to find these settings is to click Find on the Edit menu. Simply type the Key, Name, or Data values you want to find.

Session Timeout

Each time a user connects to a Web site running on IIS 5.0, the Web server must allocate system resources to maintain that session's state. When you have several hundred or thousands of users connected at the same time, it begins to have a negative effect on the server's performance because the server has to allocate enough resources to maintain each connection. Minimizing the Session Timeout value frees up system resources for the server, thus increasing performance.

To set the Session Timeout value, take the following steps:

1. Open the Web site Properties dialog box, and click the Home Directory tab.
2. Click Configuration under Application Settings. Click the App Options tab in the Application Configuration dialog box.
3. Enter a Session Timeout value just large enough to maintain a normal user's connection.

Enable Buffering

When output generated by an ASP page is sent to the browser, it's done by sending data as the server generates it. By choosing to buffer output, you instruct the Web server to first collect all output from an ASP page and then present it to the client's browser. With buffering enabled, you are able to set HTTP headers anywhere within your ASP scripts. To enable buffering, take the following steps:

1. Open the Internet Services Manager and right-click the site or application and click Properties.
2. Click the Home Directory or Virtual Directory tab and click Configuration under Application Settings.
3. Click the App Options tab and check mark the Enable Buffering check box.

ASP Threads and Script Engines

You can decrease the execution time of an ASP page running on your Web site by adjusting the ASPScriptEngineCacheMax property. When you adjust this property, each ASP thread is capable of caching a script engine.

You set the ASPScriptEngineCacheMax property setting according to the number of processors you have in your system multiplied by the ProcessorThreadMax value. For example, if your enterprise server is configured with four Pentium III processors and the current ProcessorThreadMax value is set to the default value of 25, you set the ASPScriptEngineCacheMax value to 100.

You should also consider increasing the AspProcessorThreadMax value if you're running ASP applications that are making long running calls to external components. When you increase the AspProcessorThreadMax value, the server is able to create more threads to handle more concurrent requests.

Performance Testing Your Web Site

Many times, network administrators don't realize that their Web sites and Web servers require some form of performance tuning until it's too late. For months, they might have tested the various functions of their Web site against multiple types of Web browsers, operating system platforms, and even Internet connection methods. However, they failed to actually test the configuration against some form of user load; and then, when it's showtime, everything comes to a screeching halt.

In this section, we cover a few Web performance and Web capacity monitoring tools. Running one of these performance applications against your Web site produces the necessary data required for any network administrator to determine whether the current hardware or Web server configuration is capable of handling certain types and amounts of load on the Web site. Each tool allows you to test one particular aspect of your Web site. For example, Windows Application Stress (WAS) is designed to monitor applications running on your Web site, while the Windows Media Load Simulator is designed to test whether your Web site is capable of handling the load associated with running a particular media stream.

More Info   You can find many of these applications at Microsoft's Web site; however, you can easily install them from the Windows 2000 Resource Kit CD-ROM.

Windows Media Load Simulator

Increased bandwidth, faster client machines, and powerful servers allow Web site developers to create even more elaborate Web sites and Web-enabled applications than ever before. Many times, you can browse to a Web site and the first thing you are hit with is an intense animation sequence. In many cases, enabling access to media (mainly audio/video presentations) over the Internet is the primary service of up-and-coming dot com ventures. Customers visit these sites to either download or view prerecorded or live presentations.

Windows media or, for that matter, any audio/video played back or recorded through the computer, requires a robust hardware configuration. In fact, these media files can be extremely taxing to the operating system—that's why you find professionals who create computerized animations, edit feature-length films, or do any form of audio/video editing turning to the Windows NT or Windows 2000 operating system rather than consumer-level Microsoft Windows 95 or Microsoft Windows 98. Windows 2000 enables users to run their applications on a platform that can handle the complex instructions generated by editing software. It also allows users to scale their desktops so they can run a desktop environment with up to 512 MBs of RAM.

This ability of Windows 2000 at the desktop is also apparent in its server versions, but on a much grander level.

More Info For detailed information on the versions of Windows 2000 Server and how each one differs from the other, see Chapter 12, "Microsoft Windows 2000 and Its Versions."

As covered earlier, there's a trend occurring in today's Internet market of creating a Web site that not only offers a slew of services online, but also has a very aesthetic feel to it. However, some developers find themselves having to tone down the features of their Web sites because of limitations either at the client or server level. With the introduction of Windows 2000 Server, developers and network administrators now have a platform that can support many of the complex features and media-hosting abilities that they want to make available through their Web sites.

The problem that occurs for the network administrator is of scaling the server to accommodate the needs of the application or Web site. You need the ability to test the limitations not of the application or Web site, but rather the hardware configuration. When designing the right hardware solution for a server expected to host Web sites running Windows media files, network administrators should ask themselves the following questions:

- Will the current server hardware specifications be able to handle the loads that will be placed on it by the users running media presentations?
- What is or will be the real cause of performance degradation—the streams or user load?
- What's the user limit for the server with the current hardware configuration?

If network administrators can answer those three questions, they have enough information to design an optimal hardware solution to run their Web sites. There's always the possibility that these questions will also cause a network administrator to turn back to the developers of the Web site and say they need to tone down the number of features, particularly Windows Media-related features.

Windows Media Load Simulator enables you test the capacity of the Windows Media Unicast service running on a server configured with the Windows Media Services.

More Info For more information on the Windows Media Services service and Windows Media Unicast service, see the Windows 2000 Server online help documentation.

By installing the load simulator on the server hosting the Windows Media Unicast service, you can run tests to determine how application and client requests for that application affect server and network performance. In the three questions for network administrators, one issue was whether the cause of performance degradation was the streams or user load—running the simulator could very easily determine that for you. If you see that performance degradation is occurring with only a user load of three for a particular stream, while other streams running on the server can easily handle 200 users, performance degradation is caused by the stream and not user load.

To gain a better understanding on how to test actual streams and how to analyze the results, we now review the features of Windows Media Load Simulator. If you haven't already installed the tool, you can find it on the Windows 2000 Server Resource Kit.

Note   Those of you hosting Web sites in a clustered environment can't run simulations against a clustered environment with a single installation of Windows Media Load Simulator. You need to install individual copies on each node in the cluster (see Chapter 13, "Microsoft Windows 2000 and Clustering" for more information on clustering under Windows 2000).

When you launch Windows Media Load Simulator, the Windows Media Load Simulator Configuration Wizard launches. To successfully specify a stream to test, you are walked through seven easy steps.

1. Enter the name of the server you want to test and click Next.

2. Next, you have to specify the location of the stream and the specific protocol that will be used when clients access the stream. This is important, because each protocol can have an effect on the performance between client and server. Click Next.

3. The next screen asks specifics about the client, including the rate at which each client connects to the stream and more detailed questions such as the fixed bit rate. Click Next.

4. If users need to be authenticated before accessing the stream, check the Test Server Authentication check box. Specify this option only if you plan on requiring authentication; otherwise, unnecessary load is placed on the server. Click Next.

5. You have to specify the duration for the simulation. Most administrators run the test for 12 to 24 hours to gain a thorough understanding of the effects on server performance. Click Next.

6. You should definitely check both the Enable Logging and Enable Performance Logging check boxes; otherwise, the simulation is for naught since you couldn't review any type of performance information. Click Next.

Note   As with any logging you do at the server, always be aware of available drive space on the server. If you have to, specify a different location than the default location if you feel you will run out of space on the server, particularly if you plan on running the simulation for an extended period.

7. Click Finish to complete the simulation configuration.

After you complete the configuration you can begin the test by clicking the Start button on the toolbar. To pause or stop the test use the Pause or Stop buttons on the toolbar. If you want to change any of the settings for the simulation, you do so by clicking the Tool Settings button on the toolbar. The Settings dialog box (see Figure 14-9) allows you to change any of the choices you made using the wizard, including the bandwidth at which clients are streaming content from the server.

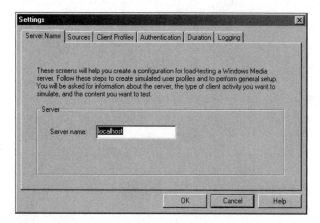

Figure 14-9. *You can change simulation settings from the Settings dialog box.*

From the simulator's main window, you can view real-time statistics as the simulator is running. These statistics are also being written to the log files you specified during the settings configuration. For an explanation on the statistics displayed by the simulator, see Table 14-1.

Table 14-1. Statistics Displayed by Windows Media Load Simulator

Actual Statistic	Description of Statistic
Open Streams	The total number of stream files opened at the server.
Clients Playing	The total number of clients the program is simulating as playing back streams on the server.
Clients Seeking	The total number of Seek clients streaming content.
Total Bandwidth (Kb/s)	The bandwidth at which clients are accessing streams located on the server.
Bytes Received	Total number of bytes received by all clients.
Packets Received	Total number of packets received by all clients.
Packets Lost	Total number of packets lost as reported by the clients. This number is a reflection of all clients being simulated.
Test Errors	Total number of test errors recorded in the Test Transactions window.
Test Duration	The elapsed time for the simulation.

Using common scripting or programming languages such as Perl, Visual Basic, or C++, you can create alerts to trigger for specific types of activity that might occur during the simulation. So, if you're looking for particular activity such as packet loss, you have the flexibility of either being alerted or, using Windows Script Host 2.0, you can have information recorded to Event Log for future reference.

Windows Media Load Simulator is a very useful capacity and performance-planning tool. Even though its usefulness is only apparent for those of us running stream files, it serves as a good example of what performance-testing tools can do for us when we attempt to determine server or network environment capacities.

Web Capacity Analysis Tool

The Microsoft Web Capacity Analysis Tool (WCAT) has been designed to run various simulations against client/server configurations to help network administrators determine how their server and network respond to requests sent to the Web site. Unlike Windows Media Load Simulator, which tests for stream files running on a server, WCAT tests for requests made for content, data, and HTML pages.

If you're deploying a newly created site or are simply adding additional features to your current site, running WCAT simulations provides you with the critical capacity planning and performance analysis data you need to design the right environment for the Web site.

Subsystems of WCAT

WCAT consists of four distinct subsystems: the server, client, controller, and network. You have the option of running three of these subsystems—server, client, and controller—on a single machine. However, it's strongly recommended that you run each subsystem on individual systems.

Server Subsystem

The server subsystem is the one component of WCAT that resides on a server configured with Internet Information Services (IIS). IIS typically runs on a Windows NT, or a Windows 2000 Server, Advanced Server, or Datacenter Server. One flexibility WCAT offers network administrators is the ability to test Web servers other than IIS as long as they run on Windows NT or Windows 2000 Server.

Client Subsystem

The client subsystem is, in fact, a client application that creates up to 200 virtual clients. Each virtual client is built to create one connection and page request to the WCAT server. You have the ability to create 200 virtual clients on a single client computer. The WCAT tests enable you to specify client details such as the number of browsers in the test, duration of the test, and the rate at which client requests are sent. If you know the typical client configuration (for example, all clients are connecting via 56-Kb/s dialup connections), you can simulate a more accurate test.

Controller Subsystem

The controller subsystem keeps track of tests, collects test results, and creates output files for users to analyze. Because of the overhead placed on the server running the controller subsystem, it's strongly recommended that you run the controller service on a separate computer. Otherwise, test results are convoluted because loads placed on the system resources by the controller subsystem are taken as loads generated by the tests being executed.

Network Subsystem

The network subsystem is simply the backbone that links the above three subsystems together. When conducting tests, you have the ability to adjust network environment specifics, such as bandwidth, to closely simulate production client/server environments.

Available Tests

The Web Capacity Analysis Tool allows you to run either prebuilt tests (more than 40 in all) or tests you create. Either way, you have the option of testing various aspects of Web server performance both at the application and network level. In this section, we cover some types of tests you can run, including custom ones to help simulate various forms of loads on the server. You can find predefined tests in the Control\Scripts directory located in the WCAT installation directory.

- **Server responsiveness against Secure Sockets Layer (SSL)** You should test sites, particularly e-commerce sites, for their response to SSL. Additional encryption to any data transmission taxes the system—you need to determine to what extent the system will be taxed and what possible bottlenecks might arise from it. Versions 2.0 and 3.0 of SSL are supported by WCAT, along with version 1.0 of Private Communications Technology (PCT). WCAT provides network administrators with prebuilt simulations of SSL activity on a Web server.

- **Server responsiveness to HTTP Keep-Alives** HTTP Keep-Alives have been created as part of the HTTP version 1.1 specification. HTTP Keep-Alives enable client connections to be maintained even after the initial request is satisfied. By running this prebuilt simulation, you can determine the effects Keep-Alives could have on the overall network performance of your server and server performance in general. Remember that allowing client connections to remain open can cause performance issues when any new connections need to be created.

- **Server responsiveness to ASP** WCAT has prebuilt workload simulations that test a server for its responsiveness to ASP running on the server. Those of you without ASP can still run the test. This way, you can gain a good understanding of whether your server configuration would be capable of running ASP with little performance degradation.

- **User-defined client-server simulations** If none of the default simulations provide you with the performance data you need for proper analysis, you have to create custom simulations. These simulations tend to test aspects of the Web server that reflect the role your Web server plays in your environment. For example, you could create a simulation that mixes and matches many of the features of the default simulations.

The tests you conduct using WCAT heavily depend on the role the server plays in your environment. However, running these tests alone doesn't do anything for you unless you monitor the effects on the server through tools such as System Monitor. Only then can you determine how various types of loads placed on the server are taxing the system.

Installing and Configuring WCAT

You find the installation files for WCAT on the Windows 2000 Resource Kit. The installation directory also includes a WCAT User's Guide that you can reference for further information on installing the product. To install WCAT, do the following:

1. Place the CD-ROM in your server; the autorun feature of the CD-ROM should open the resource kit's main window. Select Additional Components and then select Microsoft Applications.

2. Click the Web Capacity Analysis Tool link in the left frame of the window.

3. Select to install the application by clicking the link Click Here To Open Program Folder. You are presented with the contents of the \Apps\WCAT folder.

4. Double-click the Setupex icon and follow the instructions to install the application. Part of the installation procedure is the ability to install one or more of the subsystems on the same system. If you plan on installing subsystems to run on separate machines, make sure you select Custom install. For example, select the Client subsystem from the list of components if you only plan on running the Client subsystem on the destination machine.

Part of the proper installation of WCAT is configuring the controller and client subsystem correctly. If the subsystems aren't configured with the right information, the client subsystem fails to connect and you are unable to run the tests.

Configuring a WCAT Controller

The configuration of the controller simply involves specifying the name or IP address of the server to be tested. From a command prompt, change directories to the Control directory located in the WCAT installation directory. From here, type **config 10.1.0.101** where 10.1.0.101 is the IP address for the server. This can also be the name of the server.

Configuring a WCAT Client

You need to configure the client so it connects to the correct controller. To configure the client, open a command window and this time change directories to the Client directory located in the WCAT installation directory. At the command prompt, type **config machine1 10.1.0.102** where machine1 is the name of the controller and 10.1.0.102 is the IP address for the controller. You can also specify a name in place of the IP address. At this point, we can move on to actually launching these subsystems in preparation for running tests.

Preparing for a Test

After installing the subsystems and in preparation for running actual tests, you need to start the IIS server, client, and controller WCAT subsystems. If you're running IIS 5.0, you can verify whether the server service is running from Control Panel/Services. You can access Services from Administrative Tools in the Control Panel. With the Services windows open, scroll down and look to make sure the World Wide Web Publishing Service has been started.

Launching the WCAT Client

Before running any tests, you need to launch the WCAT client program. To do so, open a command window on the client machine and change directories to the Client directory located in the WCAT installation directory. You can launch the client by type **client** at the command prompt. The client attempts to connect to the computer running the controller. You get an error message stating *Controller is either not running a test or the name or ip address is incorrect.* Once the controller is launched, the test starts to run.

Launching the WCAT Controller

For WCAT clients to know what tests to run and how to run them, the controller must be started. To start the WCAT controller, open a command window and change directories to the control directory of the WCAT install directory. You can now type **run** followed by the name of a test. See the next section on how to actually execute tests.

Performing WCAT Simulations

At this point, it's assumed you've installed the WCAT program and determined where each subsystem is to run. In addition, each subsystem has been started. As mentioned earlier, WCAT comes with 40 predefined tests that enable you to immediately begin testing without having to go through the process of creating your own tests. In fact, running the tests is quite straightforward. For example, the filemix test tests for server responsiveness when clients are requesting 12 files ranging from the size of 256 bytes to 256KB. To execute this test, you open a command window at the machine running the controller subsystem and change directories to Control located in the WCAT install directory. You then type **Run filemix.**

Because the default location for all tests is the Scripts directory and filemix is a predefined test, you don't have to specify a path for the test file. If you want to specify a test you had written and saved in a location other than the Scripts directory, you have to specify the entire path by typing **Run d:\mytests\asp1.**

Viewing WCAT Results

After you execute the WCAT tests, test results are stored in the computer running the controller subsystem. All statistical information collected during the test is stored in a log file named after the test that was executed. For example, if you execute the filemix test, a log file named FILEMIX.LOG contains the results for test. All log files for tests executed by default are in the Scripts directory.

The first part of the log file displays configuration information for the test, information such as the server being tested and the number of virtual clients being simulated. The actual meat of the results is in the section labeled Results. Here you find data reflecting client activity and server response to that activity. To understand what each datum means, reference the WCAT User's Guide. Here are the contents of the filemix log file.

```
WCAT Version          = 4.35
ConfigFile            = scripts\filemix.cfg
ScriptFile            = scripts\filemix.scr
DistribFile           = scripts\filemix.dst
PerfCounterFile       =
LogFile               = scripts\filemix.log
Author                =
Creation Date         =
Test Run Date         = Tue Mar 28 00:30:23 2000

Comment               = Configuration For File Size Mix
Server [IpAddr]       = 10.1.0.101 [10.1.0.101]
Clients               = 1
Threads               = 5
Buffer Size           = 131072 bytes
Duration              = 300 seconds (Warmup 30 seconds, Cooldown 30 seconds)

Results:


                  Data, Summary,   Rate,  10.1.0.101,

           Client Id,       0,     0.00,      1,
           Duration,      302,     1.00,    302,
     Pages Requested,  143022,   473.58, 143022,
         Pages Read,   143022,   473.58, 143022,
      Total Responses, 143022,   473.58, 143022,
   Redirect Responses,      0,     0.00,      0,
    Avg Response Time,     10,     0.03,     10,
    Min Response Time,      0,     0.00,      0,
    Max Response Time,  23083,    76.43,  23083,
 StdDev Response Time,    145,     0.48,    145,
       Total Connects, 143022,   473.58, 143022,
     Avg Connect Time,      2,     0.01,      2,
     Min Connect Time,      0,     0.00,      0,
     Max Connect Time,   1462,     4.84,   1462,
  StdDev Connect Time,     14,     0.05,     14,
       Connect Errors,      0,     0.00,      0,
       Receive Errors,      0,     0.00,      0,
```

```
               Send Errors,        0,     0.00,     0,
     Internal Memory Errors,        0,     0.00,     0,
          No Headers Errors,        0,     0.00,     0,
      No Status Code Errors,        0,     0.00,     0,
          Bad Status Errors,        0,     0.00,     0,
  Bad Response Header Errors,       0,     0.00,     0,
    Bad Response Data Errors,       0,     0.00,     0,
  No Redirect Location Errors,      0,     0.00,     0,
 Bad Redirect Location Errors,      0,     0.00,     0,
              Data Read, 2376250880, 7868380.40, 2376250880,
           Header Bytes,  32623047,  108023.34,  32623047,
          Total Bytes, 2408873927, 7976403.73, 2408873927,
      Avg Header per Page,      228,      0.76,      228,
       Avg Bytes per Page,    16842,     55.77,    16842,

           Files Requested,     143022,  473.58, 143022,
               Files Read,     143022,  473.58, 143022,


Per Class Statistics:

              1 Fetched,    13014,    43.09,  13014,
              1 Errored,        0,     0.00,      0,
              1 distrib,      909,     3.01,    909,

              2 Fetched,    11301,    37.42,  11301,
              2 Errored,        0,     0.00,      0,
              2 distrib,      790,     2.62,    790,

              3 Fetched,    24197,    80.12,  24197,
              3 Errored,        0,     0.00,      0,
              3 distrib,     1691,     5.60,   1691,

              4 Fetched,     9965,    33.00,   9965,
              4 Errored,        0,     0.00,      0,
              4 distrib,      696,     2.31,    696,

              5 Fetched,     7266,    24.06,   7266,
              5 Errored,        0,     0.00,      0,
              5 distrib,      508,     1.68,    508,

              6 Fetched,    14335,    47.47,  14335,
              6 Errored,        0,     0.00,      0,
              6 distrib,     1002,     3.32,   1002,
```

```
 7 Fetched,      9950,      32.95,    9950,
 7 Errored,         0,       0.00,       0,
 7 distrib,       695,       2.30,     695,

 8 Fetched,      5640,      18.68,    5640,
 8 Errored,         0,       0.00,       0,
 8 distrib,       394,       1.31,     394,

10 Fetched,      4325,      14.32,    4325,
10 Errored,         0,       0.00,       0,
10 distrib,       302,       1.00,     302,

11 Fetched,     11530,      38.18,   11530,
11 Errored,         0,       0.00,       0,
11 distrib,       806,       2.67,     806,

15 Fetched,     17143,      56.77,   17143,
15 Errored,         0,       0.00,       0,
15 distrib,      1198,       3.97,    1198,

16 Fetched,     14356,      47.54,   14356,
16 Errored,         0,       0.00,       0,
16 distrib,      1003,       3.32,    1003,
```

For those of you who want additional information from these tests, you have the option of showing a Performance Counters section as part of the results. Performance counters display information about critical resources on the server including memory cache, disk subsystem, and processors. To user performance counters you need to:

- **Create a .pfc file** This file must have the same name as the test you want to conduct and an extension of .pfc. Save the file to Scripts directory so it can be read when the test executes. Here are the contents of the default performance counter file.

```
#    Counters for NT server
#
#  For Microsoft Internet Information Server, the process name is:
_inetinfo.exe
#
#

###
#NT4
#System\% Total Processor Time
```

```
##
#Windows 2000
Processor(_Total)\% Processor Time

Processor(0)\DPC Rate
Processor(0)\Interrupts/sec
Processor(0)\DPCs Queued/sec
Process(inetinfo)\% Processor Time
Process(inetinfo)\% Privileged Time
Process(inetinfo)\% User Time
System\Context Switches/sec
System\System Calls/sec
Process(inetinfo)\Thread Count
```

- **Specify the –p option**   Again, using the filemix test as an example, type **run –p filemix.pfc filemix** to start collecting information on the performance counters listed in the FILEMIX.PFC file while running the filemix test.

Windows Application Stress Tool

The Windows Application Stress (WAS) tool is yet another application that enables you to run simulations against a server configured with IIS. However, WAS offers additional features missing in WCAT, and has an easy-to-use graphical user interface, rather than the cumbersome command line interface. Many of the features WAS has are geared toward running more powerful and useful tests. These additional features include the ability to run simulations against ports other than 80, support for C++ and ASP, and bandwidth throttling. Table 14-2 lists some of the major functional differences between WAS and WCAT. You realize by these differences alone the increased support for testing you gain by using WAS.

Table 14-2.   Functional Differences Between WAS and WCAT

Feature	Supported in WAS	Supported in WCAT
Graphical User Interface	Yes	No
Secure Socket Layer	Yes	Yes
All Forms of Authentication	Yes	No
Support for Ports Other Than 80	Yes	Yes
Bandwidth Throttling	Yes	No

WAS works by simulating client connections to the Web server and executing set instructions specified in script files. You can choose from sample script files, scripts you can manually create within the WAS client application, or scripts extracted from IIS log files.

Installing WAS

The files for the WAS tool are on the Windows 2000 Resource Kit CD-ROM. To begin the installation, take the following steps:

1. Select the option to install Additional Components from the Windows 2000 Server Kit's main window.

2. Select Microsoft Applications and browse down the left pane of the window to find Web Application Stress Tool.

3. Click the link to open the \Apps\WebStress folder on the CD-ROM and double-click the Setup icon and follow the setup wizard to complete the install.

4. Install WAS on each client machine that will be used during the test. Don't install and run WAS on the Web server because this skews results.

Executing Simulations Using WAS

The WAS tool retrieves test instructions from script files you specify. By selecting the appropriate scripts, you can create a test environment that's close to your production environment. The results then reflect what could possibly occur in a real-world situation. If the results show possible performance or stability problems, you can address them before going into full production.

When you first launch WAS at the client computer, a dialog box appears requesting the source of the script file to be tested against. Your choices are:

- **Manual**   You can specify what scripts should be called and additional test attributes such as the delay between each script by selecting the Manual option.

- **Record**   If the Web site is functional, you can navigate the Web site as a user would and record activities such as GET or POST. This feature is particularly useful if you want to test the performance of a particular feature of your Web site.

- **Log File**   You can have WAS read an IIS log file and test the server for application-specific activities that have occurred within that log file.

- **Content**   If you have content available to test from, you can test against that content by specifying its location and selecting items to be included in the script file.

The main window of the WAS application contains two panes that allow you to quickly adjust the configuration of your test script. The left-hand pane contains the Script View window, which allows you to quickly navigate to various test script attributes. The Script View window contains a tree that exposes the following attributes:

- **Defaults** Settings that new scripts will be configured with when first created. You can edit settings for individual scripts once the script is created. You can change the default settings so new scripts take on these settings when they are created.

  The next set of values is for the Sample script and any new scripts you've created. These values are:

- **Content Tree** If you specified that the script should retrieve test parameters from pre-existing content, you can specify the location for that content and items that should be tested from that content.

- **Settings** The Settings option allows you to change the parameters such as the duration of the test for the script. All new scripts are created with the settings specified under Default.

- **Perf Counters** You can specify performance counters that should be measured while the simulation is taking place. However, the GUI interface for WAS makes selecting these counters easier. In this case, there's no need to create and specify a separate file listing performance counters as is the case with WCAT (see Figure 14-10).

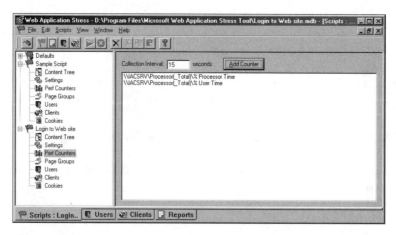

Figure 14-10. *As part of the results generated by WAS, you can choose to view specific performance counter activity.*

- **Page Groups** You can view and edit page group values, including group names, distribution, and distribution values.

- **Users**   Configuring this setting allows you to specify users so authentication and data storage features of the Web site can be tested.

- **Clients**   Select client machines or groups of client machines that will be part of the test. Specifying client machines enables you to spread the load that's created by testing across several client machines.

- **Cookies**   You can specify whether cookies are used as part of the stress tests. WAS supports two forms of cookies: static and dynamic. Many Web sites, particularly those requiring authentication to the Web site, utilize cookies. By including cookies in your test, you portray real-world use of the Web site more accurately.

After specifying the test script you want to use and making any changes to the configuration of the script file, click Run on the toolbar. The test runs and begins recording data to be viewed later from the Report views. You can view reports by clicking Reports on the toolbar. If you selected the right script to run and configured the settings for the script correctly, the report generated by WAS should be sufficient information for you to draw conclusions about the server's performance and its ability to handle application load.

We've just reviewed three very useful tools for measuring Web server performance. These tools only serve your purposes if you configure them. In fact, you should treat them very much like System Monitor. As is the case with System Monitor, if you don't select the correct objects to monitor, you aren't provided with the information you need to make an educated determination as to possible performance issues with the server.

Server capacity tools such as those we just reviewed are particularly useful for determining the stability of your system. They can let you know at what thresholds system stability can be questioned, for example, a specific user load.

This section was meant to serve as an overview of some very useful analysis tools for IIS. You can find detailed information about the use, features, and capabilities of each tool in the online help or documentation for each application.

Summary

The Internet has grown from simply chat rooms, Web pages, and e-mail messages, to a lifeline for organizations worth billions of dollars. Without the Internet, organizations such as the many dot coms would be out of business and their customers would no longer have access to the efficiency of the services provided by the Internet.

The metamorphosis that has occurred with the Internet has also added complexity to the applications and services you plan on providing access to via the Internet. When you wrote an application that would be used within your organization, you had the comfort of knowing you were working within a controlled environment, with user load that could be easily accounted for. On the other hand, estimating user load for an e-commerce site open to the public is extremely difficult. There have been many companies that have suffered not because the services or products they offered were poorly accepted by the public, but due to their popularity. Basically, the Web sites for these organizations experienced traffic that went well beyond the capabilities of their Web sites.

When designing an e-commerce solution for your organization, there are many factors you must take into account including the type and amount of traffic you expect to experience. You should also take into account the Web server on which these services and applications will be hosted. The Web server is the foundation of your Internet site, extranet site, and e-commerce business services. Like any structure, the foundation is the most critical part of that building. If the foundation is weak or has cracks in it, you're already on the path toward failure. However, by utilizing many of the useful testing tools available to you, such as those discussed in this chapter, you can detect these possible weaknesses and resolve issues before it becomes critical.

Overall, IIS is now an even more robust Web server. IIS 5.0 adds the performance and reliability improvements you need to run a various range of applications on the Web server. Through its enhanced restart features, Web sites can be up and running faster after a failure. IIS also improves application protection and reliability. In the past, to protect the server from a malfunctioning application, you had to run each application in a separate process, which could reduce performance. Now, to better balance the tradeoff between performance and protection, you can pool less-essential applications in one process, and run only essential applications in isolation. You can achieve even greater reliability by using the clustering services available in Windows 2000 Advanced and Datacenter Servers. Scalability is improved by support for multisite hosting, which allows more Web sites to run on the same server.

With the slew of performance-enhancing features in Windows 2000 Server and in IIS 5.0, you have a marriage between operating system and Web server that not only increases the reliability of your Web-enabled applications, but also their performance.

Part V
Special Tuning Tools

Chapter 15
Microsoft Windows 2000
Resource Kit Performance Tools

The Microsoft Windows 2000 Resource Kit is an add-on product for Windows 2000. It contains a wealth of information about the operating system and, more importantly, tools you can use to manage and tune the operating system. You might have noticed that there were many areas in the previous chapters where we could have perhaps done more in the way of tuning, yet the operating system itself lacked the tools required to do so. The Windows 2000 Resource Kit offers the additional tools you need to perform a variety of tuning tasks.

The first section of this chapter provides an overview of what you must do to install the Windows 2000 Resource Kit. The installation itself is very easy; deciding what to install might take a little more time since the Windows 2000 Resource Kit is packed with utilities and management aids. Obviously, you need to choose tools based on the requirements for your network. Some systems don't require all the tools because they might not provide the services the tool is designed to work with. For example, not every server requires the Web server tools because not every server is involved with servicing the Internet or an intranet in some way.

Note A typical installation of the Windows 2000 Resource Kit requires 65 MB of free hard drive space (which includes more than the performance tools covered in this chapter). These space requirements are only for the resource kit executable and Help files—data files created by the various tools require additional space. Make sure you have at least this much room free for a typical installation. A custom installation requires less space for the executable and Help files, but the amount of reduction depends on the resource kit features you install on your system. In most cases, you'll find that you want to try all the resource kit features for the initial installation, and then remove features you don't need later. In addition to the initial installation requirements, some Windows 2000 Resource Kit tools require additional setup. These tools require additional space for the separate installation.

"A Look at the Additional Components Option" section of the chapter takes a very brief look at some of the additional components you can use with Windows 2000. These are components that are either designed by Microsoft or third parties. They appear on the Windows 2000 Resource Kit CD-ROM, but require separate installation. Fortunately, the CD-ROM does contain a description of each tool and a link to a place on the Internet where you can learn more or perhaps download the tool for free. We take a much more detailed look at third-party tools in Chapter 16, "Third-Party Tuning Tools." The whole intent of this section is to familiarize you with some of the details of this part of the CD-ROM. It's an important addition, so you should spend some time exploring it.

More Info Microsoft constantly updates the Windows 2000 Resource Kit and tools to reflect the addition of new Windows 2000 features or to reflect changes in the way you need to accomplish certain tasks. Since the operating system gets updated to help users work with it better, the resource kit needs to change as well. With this in mind, visit the Windows 2000 Resource Kit Web site at *http:// www.microsoft.com/windows2000/library/resources/reskit/default.asp* on a regular basis to learn about product updates and changes.

Once we've looked at installation, we begin to look at the various tools within the resource kit. This chapter isn't meant as a complete source of documentation for any tool. At best, we can provide an overview of a particular tool within the confines of a single chapter. In addition, we don't even look at all the tools the Windows 2000 Resource Kit has to offer. That's because the Windows 2000 Resource Kit provides a vast array of tools for you to use. It would take a very thick book (or perhaps a series of books) to do this add-on justice. Consider this chapter a taste of what you find if you get the Windows 2000 Resource Kit.

Installation Overview

Installation of the Windows 2000 Resource Kit couldn't be easier. All you need to do is stick the CD-ROM in the drive. If you have Autoplay enabled (the default setting), the installation program starts automatically and you see an initial dialog box like the one shown in Figure 15-1. Notice that this dialog box contains an option to install the resource kit, as well as an option to read through the release notes. It's usually a good idea to read the release notes first, and then move on to the installation. You can also explore the CD-ROM, which is essentially the same as viewing it with a single pane view of Microsoft Windows Explorer, or look at some links for Additional Components. We explore this particular option in more detail in "A Look at the Additional Components Option."

Click Install Resource Kit if you see the initial dialog box shown in Figure 15-1 when you insert the CD-ROM into the drive. Otherwise, you need to double-click the Setup icon in the root directory of the CD-ROM. (A third alternative is to right-click the W2000RK.MSI file, and then click Install from the Context menu.) In all three cases, you see a Welcome to the Microsoft Windows 2000 Resource Kit Setup Wizard screen. The following procedure helps you complete the installation.

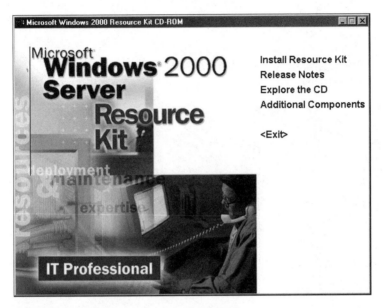

Figure 15-1.   *The initial Windows 2000 Resource Kit installation dialog box contains options for looking at the release notes or learning about other tools.*

Caution   The Windows 2000 Resource Kit is designed for use with a Windows 2000 system and might produce unpredictable results when used with other versions of the operating system. This restriction also means you can't use this version of the resource kit to update your Microsoft Windows NT installation. You also want to use the Windows 2000 Resource Kit within the confines of any Microsoft restrictions. For example, as of this writing, you need to use the English language version of the Windows 2000 Resource Kit with the English language version of Windows 2000. Finally, make sure you uninstall any previous versions of the resource kit before you install this one. Otherwise, you might find that that installation is corrupted by the presence of old files.

1. Click Next to get past the welcome screen. Read and accept the licensing agreement, and then click Next again. The Setup wizard asks for your name and organization information.

2. Fill out the required identification fields, and then click Next. You see a Select An Installation Type screen like the one shown in Figure 15-2. Unless you're

absolutely certain that you never want to remove parts of the Windows 2000 Resource Kit, select the Custom option. The Typical option installs all the Windows 2000 Resource Kit features and requires 65 MB of hard drive space to store the Help and executable files. I'm going to assume you're like most network administrators who need some of, but not all of, the tools the Windows 2000 Resource Kit provides.

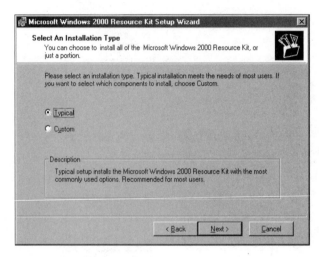

Figure 15-2. *The Select An Installation Type screen allows you to choose between a typical and custom installation.*

3. Click Custom, and then click Next. You see a Custom Installation screen like the one shown in Figure 15-3. Notice that this screen uses the new Windows Installer interface. You have the option of installing a single feature, all the features within a group of features, or not installing a particular feature on the hard drive. This chapter assumes you're installing the Performance Tools feature as a bare minimum. We might discuss other tools, but this chapter concentrates on the Performance Tools.

4. Select all the tools you want to install, and then click Next. You see a Begin Installation screen.

5. Click Next. You see a Progress screen. The progress indicator changes as the Setup wizard completes the installation. Once the installation is complete, you see a Completing the Microsoft Windows 2000 Resource Kit Setup Wizard screen.

6. Click Finish. The installation is complete.

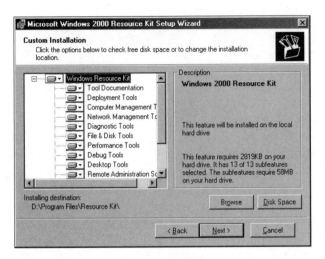

Figure 15-3. *The Custom Installation screen allows you to determine which tools you want to install.*

At this point, the Windows 2000 Resource Kit is installed on your machine. You can view the tools, explore the CD-ROM, spend some time looking at the additional components, or check out the release notes again. The Additional Components option of the initial installation dialog box (Figure 15-1) provides you with some ideas of where you can get additional tools. We look at this important feature in the next section of the chapter.

A Look at the Additional Components Option

Microsoft wants to ensure that you have all the tools required to work with Windows 2000. Clicking the Additional Components option on the initial installation dialog box (Figure 15-1) opens a copy of Microsoft Internet Explorer with a file that looks like the one shown in Figure 15-4. Notice that this page allows you to choose between Microsoft and third-party applications.

Note   Any specific content we talk about in this section of the chapter is subject to change. Microsoft might decide to include additional tools with the resource kit (reducing the number of Microsoft tools shown here), if it becomes aware of additional tools produced internally or by third-party developers, or finds that some tools need to be removed because they no longer serve a useful purpose. This section of the chapter provides a quick look at some of the tools that might be available at the time you read this.

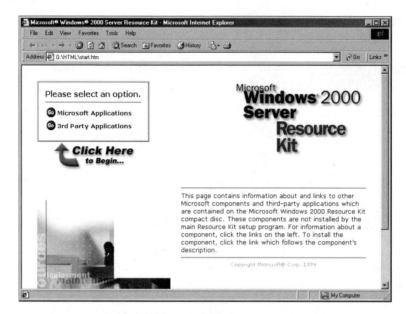

Figure 15-4. *The additional components are divided into those provided by Microsoft and those provided by third-party developers.*

Microsoft Applications Option

Click the Go icon next to the Microsoft Applications option and you see a listing similar to the one shown in Figure 15-5. On the left side of the display is a list of tools and tool types. These links take you to an area of the additional component listing that deals specifically with that kind of tool. However, if you're looking for performance tools in particular, the best method of looking through this information is to scroll through the full documentation on the right side of the display.

When you look at the full text description for any of these products, you see the application name, the Windows 2000 product version it works with, a short product summary, and (in some cases) a bulleted list of product features. In most cases, this short overview is enough to tell you whether you want to install the product. However, it's usually not enough to tell you about the product's functionality. You have to install interesting products to try them out. To do that, just click the link next to the yellow folder at the bottom of the display.

There are quite a few interesting tools available on this part of the CD-ROM at the time of this writing. For example, if you're interested in determining the capacity of your Web server, you can use the Web Capacity Analysis Tool (WCAT), which is discussed in detail in Chapter 14 in the section entitled "Web Capacity Analysis Tool." This particular tool only runs on Microsoft Windows 2000 Server (any version), so you can't use it to test the Personal Web Server (PWS) that comes with Microsoft Windows 2000 Professional.

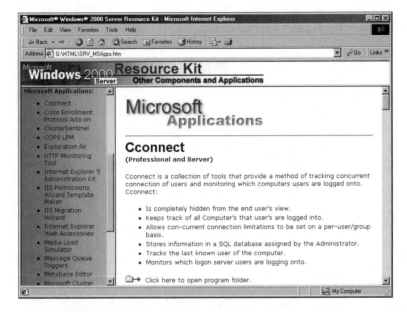

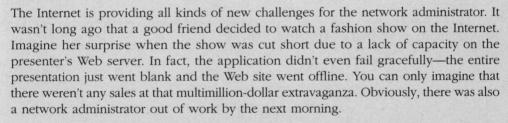

Figure 15-5.   *The left side of the display contains a list of products, while the right side contains a full description of individual products.*

Real World

The Internet is providing all kinds of new challenges for the network administrator. It wasn't long ago that a good friend decided to watch a fashion show on the Internet. Imagine her surprise when the show was cut short due to a lack of capacity on the presenter's Web server. In fact, the application didn't even fail gracefully—the entire presentation just went blank and the Web site went offline. You can only imagine that there weren't any sales at that multimillion-dollar extravaganza. Obviously, there was also a network administrator out of work by the next morning.

The problem, in this case, wasn't one of technology. In fact, the application used for the multimedia presentation could have easily supported a lot more users without any problem. The problem wasn't the hardware either. The server itself was just fine after the crash. In this case, the problem was a simple lack of capacity that the network administrator would have had a hard time predicting, and an even harder time testing for, given the tools at the time.

If your company is interested in serving media content for either your local intranet or on an Internet site, the Microsoft Windows Media Load Simulator (covered in Chapter 14 in the section entitled "Windows Media Load Simulator") can help you determine in advance whether your server will crash at a given load level. This can prevent those awkward crashes when more than a few extra people decide to crash the multimedia party to see what's going on in your company.

3rd Party Applications Option

The 3rd Party Applications option works much like the Microsoft Applications option we just covered. You see a product name and description, and have a chance to install that product on your server if you want. Some of these products might be fully functional demos or restricted-use versions of a full-featured product offered by the vendor. In many cases, it pays to ask the vendor about other product versions if you see something you like.

One of the more interesting tools (at least as of this writing) is Log Analyst by CyberSafe. You might wonder how a tool that's designed to analyze your security logs helps with performance tuning and optimization (PTO). The fact of the matter is that most networks have some type of security hole that allows people to use resources that they might not otherwise have access to. In some cases, that use is completely innocent; the person discovered the hole by mistake and simply used the resource without knowing that any usage of the resource was wrong. Log Analyst allows you to better organize your log information so you can detect a wide range of security breaches, including the innocent type where system resources get used, rather than where data get damaged. If you're looking for more generic event logs reports, check out Crystal Reports from Seagate.

The third-party tool that definitely falls into the PTO category is Tru-Access Manager Lite by Telco Research. This product allows you to track network usage by both individuals and workgroups. Tracking who uses what resources is one of the first steps to capacity planning, as mentioned in Chapter 11, "Capacity Planning." This particular tool allows you to track all kinds of user statistics, including how long the user remains logged into the system and the amount of bandwidth used while connected.

An Overview of Performance Tools

The Windows 2000 Resource Install Setup wizard creates several new startup menu entries for you under the Windows 2000 Resource Kit folder. These include tools help, and the tools themselves. Most people find it interesting that clicking the Tools entry brings up a Windows Explorer listing like the one shown in Figure 15-6 instead of another menu entry (like Administrative Tools would). Figure 15-6 shows all the entries you see for a full Windows 2000 Resource Kit installation. You might or might not see all these folders if you perform a custom installation with only a few of the features installed.

When you double-click the Performance Tools icon, you see another group of icons. This time they're for Help and application files. In some cases, you don't see an application file for a particular Help file. The Windows 2000 Resource Kit includes a lot of command line utilities that you run from the MS-DOS command prompt or using the Run command on the Start menu. These Help files allow you to learn about the utility so you can use it better.

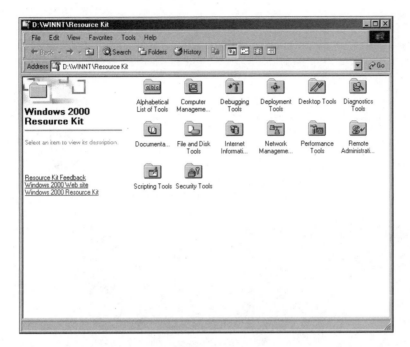

Figure 15-6. *You access the Windows 2000 Resource Kit tools through a set of folders displayed on a Windows Explorer page, rather than through a standard menu.*

Now that we've gotten the folder overview out of the way, let's spend some time examining the tools. The following sections provide you with an overview of the performance-related tools in the Windows 2000 Resource Kit. As you saw from Figure 15-6, the Performance Tool category only makes up a subset of what the resource kit has to offer.

Clear Memory

This is a command line utility that allows you to clear system memory. It accomplishes this task by allocating more memory than the machine physically possesses. Of course, the question is, *Why would you want to do this?* This utility creates a short-term processor and memory bottleneck that actually slows system performance for some time.

Clear Memory is actually designed to force the file cache and other working sets in Windows to flush the contents of their memory. Windows often allows the file cache and other working sets to grow unhindered, which could make it appear that the server has less memory installed than it actually does. (A working set is the set of virtual memory pages that belong to a single process. These virtual memory pages are a subset of all the virtual memory in use by the system.) The long-term effect of using Clear Memory is to improve system performance by making more system memory available for applications and other uses. In short, clearing the various caches is a good way to recover resources that aren't necessarily lost, but aren't needed either.

Tip Clear Memory is designed to clear the memory used by all working sets on the system. If you want to clear a single working set, look at the "Empty Working Set" section later in this chapter. This utility allows you to clear memory on a process-by-process basis.

The command line name of Clear Memory is CLEARMEM.EXE. You have to run this utility several times to get the desired effect since Windows generally reduces the size of the various caches slowly, rather than all at once. Running Clear Memory by itself produces a display similar to the one shown in Figure 15-7. Notice that the time required to flush memory the second time is a lot less than the first time. This is an indicator that the cache files on this machine were fairly dirty. You know the cache files are clean when the elapsed flushing time between runs is about the same.

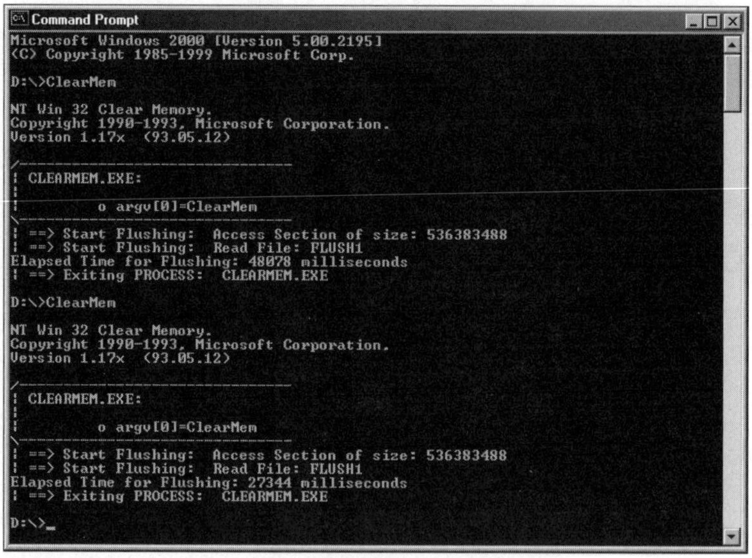

Figure 15-7. *Clear Memory allows you to flush the contents of memory and free up precious system resources.*

ClusterSentinel

You might remember from Chapter 12 that Microsoft Windows Advanced Server provides features like network load balancing (NLB). This feature allows you to use a cluster of servers to respond to user needs without configuring an explicit server for a list of users. In short, NLB offers the ability to make your network setup more flexible and scalable. The use of clusters also provides failover capability in case a particular server fails. This means the user can continue to work without any loss of server availability—another server takes over the failed server's load.

ClusterSentinel is a utility that monitors the application layer health of the servers in a cluster. Although NLB can check whether a server is physically able to participate in the cluster, it can't establish the server's availability. For example, a server might not have any hardware problems now, but a failed component later could cause problems until the system detects and terminates it. Failure detection by the system could take quite some time (at least from the computer's perspective). Since ClusterSentinel's whole purpose is to monitor the server's availability, detection of the problem by ClusterSentinel is much faster.

The way ClusterSentinel works is fairly easy to understand. It performs background tests to determine the availability of the servers within a cluster. When a server fails the tests, it's removed from the cluster. This means your network can respond before a server becomes completely nonoperational. ClusterSentinel continues to test the failed server. Theoretically, the server either clears the problem itself, or notifies the network administrator (in which case, the network administrator fixes the problem). When the server successfully passes the tests again, ClusterSentinel automatically adds it back into the cluster. This means a server's recovery period from a failed application need not affect network performance in such a way that user requests get lost. Yes, another server has to take on the failed server's load, but there isn't any loss of router performance when the application attempts to work with a nonresponsive server.

Counter List

Counter List is a command line utility that allows you to list all the objects and counters installed on the server. You could use this list to check for certain server performance-monitoring capabilities or simply as a means for determining whether you can monitor a particular application or system value. Using redirection allows you to place the output from the application in a text file for further analysis. Counter List only examines one language at a time (English is the default) and you can use a universal naming convention (UNC) machine name to monitor something other than the local machine. Of course, it takes a while to create a complete list of all the counters Windows 2000 is capable of monitoring; but once completed, the list can come in quite handy for research purposes.

Note   The output file for this application is quite large. Even on a newly installed server with a minimum number of applications installed, plan on setting aside 1 MB of disk space for each data file you create. If your system supports more than one language, you need 1 MB of disk space for each language you want to track.

Figure 15-8 shows some typical output from this utility. In this case, I used the Web-Based Enterprise Management (WBEM) Managed Object Format (MOF) format with performance data instances defined and the English language for the local machine. (MOF refers to the file format used by Windows Management Instrumentation.) As you can see, the output from this utility is very detailed and something an application developer is more likely to appreciate than a typical network administrator. However, there's still a lot of good information you can get from this output. It allows you to see precisely how various objects are set up, what kinds of data they monitor, and how they monitor the data. Figure 15-9 shows how this same performance object and associated counters appear within System Monitor.

Figure 15-8. *The Counter List (CtrList) utility allows you to print a complete list of performance objects and counters.*

CPU Stress

The CPU Stress utility does just what its name implies—it places a load on a CPU to see just how well it works in a given situation. Figure 15-10 shows the initial CPU Stress display. As you can see, the program is designed to create from one to four threads at specific priority levels. You can also choose how busy each thread should be during the testing process.

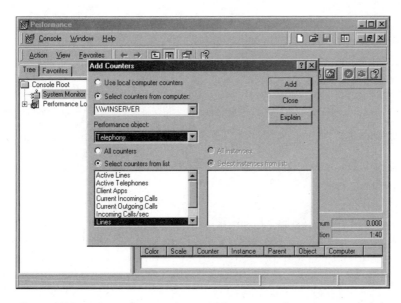

Figure 15-9.   *The association between the output of Counter List and the System Monitor MMC snap-in is unmistakable.*

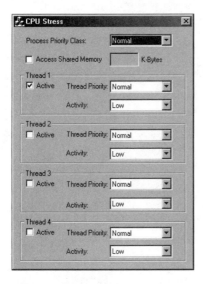

Figure 15-10.   *The CPU Stress utility is designed to test a workstation's ability to handle a given load.*

Other than set the number of threads, the thread and process priority, and the level of activity, you don't have to do anything else with the CPU Stress utility. This program is already doing the work you need it to do as soon as you start it. You can use this utility to measure the ability of your server to handle specific system loads and can use it to measure server degradation over time. It also comes in handy for placing a load on your system so you can simulate the performance characteristics of a less capable system. Stressing the processors and then placing a test application on the machine allows you to see what happens when specific levels of processor resources are removed from the server environment.

CPU Usage in Processes

Sometimes the System Monitor displays can get too cumbersome when measuring something as simple as the amount of CPU time each application on the server is using. On the other hand, Task Manager displays the individual process data as text, making it difficult to perform quick comparisons. The Windows 2000 Resource Kit comes with an icon marked CPU Usage in Processes, which is the plain language version of the QuickSlice utility shown in Figure 15-11.

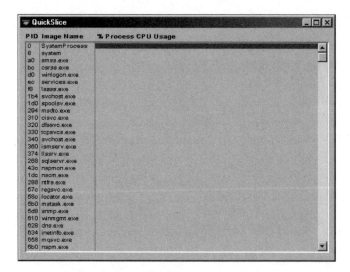

Figure 15-11. *The QuickSlice utility allows you to view the amount of CPU processing time each process is using with relative ease.*

As you can see, QuickSlice provides you with a display of the process identifier (PID), the name of the executable program, and a histogram bar that shows the current percentage of CPU usage. The bar can appear in one of two colors. Red indicates a process that's operating in privileged (kernel) mode, while blue indicates that the process is operating in user mode. The larger you make this display, the easier it is to determine just how much processor time each process is using. Unfortunately, you can't sort the data, making it more difficult to find a particular process. The only command line switch for this utility allows you to set the interval between samples.

Disk Alignment Tool

The Disk Alignment Tool, also known as DiskPar, is a command line utility that allows you to query and optionally set the partition information for a drive. The query feature is nice because you can see how the drive is configured. This is a feature you only want to use on a new drive. Figure 15-12 shows the output from this utility.

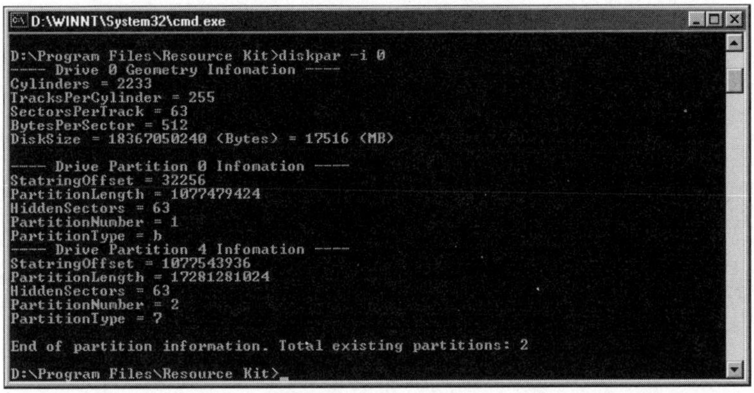

```
D:\WINNT\System32\cmd.exe

D:\Program Files\Resource Kit>diskpar -i 0
----- Drive 0 Geometry Infomation -----
Cylinders = 2233
TracksPerCylinder = 255
SectorsPerTrack = 63
BytesPerSector = 512
DiskSize = 18367050240 (Bytes) = 17516 (MB)

----- Drive Partition 0 Infomation -----
StatringOffset = 32256
PartitionLength = 1077479424
HiddenSectors = 63
PartitionNumber = 1
PartitionType = b
----- Drive Partition 4 Infomation -----
StatringOffset = 1077543936
PartitionLength = 17281281024
HiddenSectors = 63
PartitionNumber = 2
PartitionType = 7

End of partition information. Total existing partitions: 2

D:\Program Files\Resource Kit>
```

Figure 15-12.   *The Disk Alignment Tool allows you to check the geometry of any drive on your system.*

Caution   The partition information setting feature of the DiskPar utility (enabled with the -s command line switch) is incredibly dangerous. Never use it on a drive with data. Since the drive geometry is predetermined for the first Windows 2000 drive, never use this utility on a single-drive system—this utility is only useful on multiple-drive systems.

As you can see, the sample drive has 2233 cylinders, 255 tracks per cylinder, 63 sectors per track, and 512 bytes per sector for a total drive size of 18 GB. There are two partitions on this drive. Each of these partitions uses 63 hidden sectors per track. There's a starting offset and partition length recorded for each partition. In addition, the PartitionType value identifies the first partition as a DOS partition and the second as a NTFS5 partition.

So, why would you even want to look at this drive information, much less modify it? Some drives ship with a geometry where there are more than 63 sectors per track. Unfortunately, the maximum number of hidden sectors per track that Windows 2000 allows is 63. This means the 64th sector is treated as the beginning of another track. At this point, you should hear alarms going off in your head because the cause of the drive alignment problem should be clear. If the second track is offset by one sector (to make up for the remaining sector from the first track), the third track is offset by two sectors. The result is that the logical drive organization that Windows recognizes doesn't match the physical organization of the drive.

Windows is designed to write data to a single track if possible to minimize drive head movement. However, if Windows and the drive are using different drive organizations, head movement can become an issue anyway because what Windows considers a single track might actually be two on the drive. It doesn't take long to figure out that drive misalignment can be a major performance problem and one that you should fix—preferably before you place any data on the drive.

Empty Working Set

Empty Working Set, also known as EMPTY.EXE, is a command line utility that performs about the same task as Clear Memory does. However, instead of clearing all the memory used by the system, it allows you to clear memory on a process-by-process basis.

Unlike Clear Memory, you must provide some input data to get Empty to work. Empty allows you to provide either a PID or program name for the process whose memory you want to clear. Either of these values is available with Task Manager.

You want to use Empty when an application has run for a week or more. It allows you to clear the memory that the application has used and not freed right away, making more memory available to the system in general. Since Empty is less invasive than Clear Memory, the momentary performance penalty for using it is minimal. Like Clear Memory, you must run the Empty utility several times to completely clear the memory used by an application. However, unlike Clear Memory, Empty doesn't provide any output display, so you can't judge the amount of memory cleared by the time required to run the utility.

Extensible Performance Counter List

The Extensible Performance Counter List utility allows you to see a list of all the performance counters that applications have added to the operating system. Figure 15-13 shows the initial Extensible Counter List dialog box. Notice that the Machine Name field appears at the top of the dialog box in UNC format. You can enter a new machine name and click Refresh to monitor another machine.

The Sort Order group allows you to determine which way the counters get sorted. The default setting of the Service option is the most useful if you have some idea of what you're looking for in human-readable form. This list is also good if you want to associate a set of counters with a specific DLL on the system. One DLL can provide services for more than one counter, however, so you need to be careful about removing or updating any

DLLs using this utility as your sole source of information. The Library File sort order is useful if you know what the DLL name is and you want to discover what set of performance counters it's associated with. The Counter ID sort order is really only useful if you have detailed knowledge of the counter values from the registry or another utility.

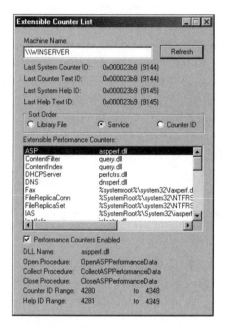

Figure 15-13.   *The Extensible Counter List dialog box allows you to view and optionally disable counters.*

Notice the Performance Counters Enabled check box at the bottom of the dialog box. Highlighting a counter, and then clearing this option, disables the counters and makes them unusable. Why would you want to do this? First, a counter might cause system problems—it might have some kind of a bug. If you're a system administrator, you might not want others who are working with you to use the errant counter by mistake and cause the server to malfunction. Another good reason is that collecting data takes system resources. Disabling counters that you don't need ensures that those DLLs don't get loaded into memory and waste resources.

Leaky Application

We explored the effects of leaky applications on system resources in Chapter 6, "Diagnosing Memory Bottlenecks." Some of the problems you experience are a slow degradation of server performance and the inability to service the required number of users after a while. Of course, the hard part is identifying the leaky application before it becomes a problem you need to fix by getting service packs, or even a new application. The Leaky Application that ships with the Windows 2000 Resource Kit is designed to help network administrators learn to identify the problems associated with leaky applications. Figure 15-14 shows the very simple interface for this application.

Figure 15-14. *My Leaky App is one way to learn about the effects of leaky applications on your server.*

Essentially, the Leaky Application simulates the effects of a leaky application in a controlled way. You click Start Leaking, and the application slowly eats up all the available system memory. It's a good idea to run a few applications to see how they degrade as this process takes place. You might find that some of your applications don't work well in low-memory conditions. Recording the effect of the leaky application can help you better locate the true source of a problem in a real-world situation by monitoring the effects of a leaky application on the various applications you normally run.

It's also a good idea to run System Monitor. You can use System Monitor's output to track the performance of applications as system resources degrade. This information not only helps you track the source of a problem later, but it also helps you understand how other applications react. You can use this information for capacity planning and as a method for determining what course of emergency action to pursue when you discover a leaky application on the server.

List Loaded Drivers

The List Loaded Drivers utility, also known as Drivers, allows you to obtain some detailed information about the drivers loaded on your server in a text format that's suitable for a variety of purposes. For example, you could translate the fixed length records into something a database could use; or cut and paste the information into an e-mail as part of a diagnostic procedure with a third-party vendor. Figure 15-15 shows what the output from this utility looks like.

ModuleName	Code	Data	Bss	Paged	Init	LinkDate
ntoskrnl.exe	434624	98880	0	733568	138752	Tue Dec 07 13:05:26 1999
hal.dll	32416	8544	0	25184	18880	Sat Oct 30 17:48:21 1999
BOOTVID.dll	5664	2464	0	0	320	Wed Nov 03 19:24:33 1999
pci.sys	12704	1536	0	31264	4608	Wed Oct 27 18:11:08 1999
isapnp.sys	14368	832	0	22944	2048	Sat Oct 02 15:00:35 1999
intelide.sys	1760	32	0	0	128	Thu Oct 28 18:20:03 1999
PCIIDEX.SYS	4544	480	0	22496	2176	Fri Oct 22 17:48:06 1999
MountMgr.sys	1088	0	0	95072	3392	Mon Nov 22 13:36:23 1999
ftdisk.sys	4640	32	0	2016	1088	Thu Sep 30 19:30:40 1999
Diskperf.sys	1728	32	0	1152	192	Sat Sep 25 13:36:47 1999
WMILIB.SYS	512	0	0	0	608	Tue Nov 30 13:47:49 1999
dmload.sys	2848	64	0	0	2720	Tue Nov 30 13:47:49 1999
dmio.sys	104672	15168	0	0	1376	Thu Oct 14 19:59:16 1999
PartMgr.sys	576	0	0	6656	8128	Sat Dec 04 14:19:32 1999
atapi.sys	42656	3392	0	21792	672	Sat Sep 25 14:11:39 1999
amsint.sys	8704	0	0	0	4672	Tue Oct 26 18:28:46 1999
SCSIPORT.SYS	21728	384	0	35424	832	Mon Oct 18 17:35:12 1999
aic78u2.sys	54528	6752	0	0	4384	Fri Oct 22 17:27:46 1999
disk.sys	8128	160	0	10240	2368	Wed Oct 06 18:55:45 1999
CLASSPNP.SYS	14432	64	0	11136	3104	Tue Nov 30 18:23:01 1999
Dfs.sys	14016	9536	0	40480	1632	Fri Oct 22 18:38:14 1999
KSecDD.sys	22080	6432	0	31616	12480	Tue Nov 30 01:37:55 1999
Ntfs.sys	73792	5888	0	417120	5472	Tue Nov 30 01:37:30 1999
NDIS.sys	12192	1344	0	129472	3104	Fri Nov 05 16:31:58 1999
Mup.sys	6592	6688	0	61952	960	Tue Sep 28 18:37:32 1999
agp440.sys	4416	32	0	12000	320	Sat Sep 25 13:35:33 1999
audstub.sys	0	0	0	416	2432	Tue Nov 30 01:09:07 1999
ras12tp.sys	44288	416	0	0	1344	Tue Oct 12 18:54:43 1999
ndistapi.sys	4544	96	0	0	7712	Tue Nov 30 01:09:01 1999
ndiswan.sys	71136	2208	0	288	1344	Tue Nov 30 01:19:49 1999
TDI.SYS	9920	320	0	0	1952	Tue Nov 30 01:09:13 1999
raspptp.sys	40576	800	0	0	3744	Tue Nov 30 01:38:11 1999
psched.sys	49280	1696	0	448	1024	Tue Nov 30 01:37:21 1999
msgpc.sys	28224	1280	0	384	2688	Sat Oct 09 15:59:21 1999
EFS.SYS	15456	4960	0	0	1248	Wed Oct 13 18:29:00 1999
ptilink.sys	4896	160	0	0	2144	Fri Oct 08 15:45:10 1999
raspti.sys	11136	608	0	30944	4192	Sat Nov 06 15:55:20 1999
VIDEOPRT.SYS	6272	96	0	39136	1440	Fri Nov 05 17:43:11 1999
atiragem.sys	10880	9504	0	31488	9408	Mon Oct 25 14:27:55 1999
serial.sys	8768	256	0	19616	2464	Sat Sep 25 13:34:55 1999
Modem.SYS	1248	64	0	6976	1312	Sat Oct 09 15:41:58 1999
USBD.SYS	7488	544	0	3232	1728	Tue Oct 05 15:45:47 1999
uhcd.sys	23872	128	0	3904	2336	Wed Oct 27 18:46:36 1999
cdrom.sys	17568	64				

Figure 15-15. *The List Loaded Drivers utility allows you to see which drivers are loaded on your system, along with other helpful information.*

Although most of the information presented by this utility is easy to figure out, a few of the columns are cryptic. The following list provides a quick definition of each of the columns. You can use this information to decipher the output of the List Loaded Drivers utility.

- **ModuleName**   The driver's filename. Unfortunately, there isn't any path information provided. Normally, this isn't a problem because most drivers are located within either the System or System32 folders.

- **Code**   The amount of executable code within the driver file.

- **Data**   The amount of nonblock storage space (BSS) data within the driver file. This data is part of the executable image—that is, it appears within the driver file and the value of the data is known.

- **Bss**   The amount of BSS data within the driver file. BSS data isn't good to have on a server for several reasons. For one thing, the .bss data section only appears in 16-bit drivers. If you have a 16-bit driver loaded on your machine, it's high time to get it replaced. Even if a 32-bit application were to somehow emulate this section, it means the data is uninitialized and therefore prone to causing errors during loading. As you can see from Figure 15-15, your chances of seeing anything in the Bss column are relatively small.

- **Paged** The amount of nonBSS data within the driver file that's loaded into paged memory.

- **Init** The size of the driver file on disk. Since most executables are stored in compressed format, this value might or might not match the combination of the Code and Data fields.

- **LinkDate** The date and time the file was linked. The combination of the driver filename and the link date are usually enough to tell a vendor what version of a DLL you're using. Sending this information to the vendor provides it with version information for all the critical drivers loaded on your server and makes the process of finding driver-specific problems easier.

Page Fault Monitor

Page Fault Monitor, also known as PFMon, allows you to monitor the page faults an application creates as it runs. There's a wealth of command line options you can use with this tool, most of which don't help you much when it comes to PTO. This is really a developer's tool that has been adapted to PTO use.

So, what good is this tool? We explored memory bottlenecks in Chapter 6, and I provided you with a variety of ways to detect this very serious problem. The Page Fault Monitor provides another way to look for memory bottlenecks, at least if you use it correctly. Figure 15-16 shows the output from a test application. Notice that there are a lot of soft page faults (indicated as SOFT in the figure), but there aren't any hard page faults. If you were to see a high number of hard page faults, the application in question is requesting a lot of memory and Windows 2000 is spending a lot of time shuffling things around on disk to accommodate it. An application that produces a lot of hard page faults isn't necessarily poorly written or full of bugs, but it definitely isn't running efficiently on the host machine. This is an example of an application that produces a memory bottleneck.

Next to the type of page fault is the Windows API call that the application made at the time of the page fault. There are times when this information might help a third-party vendor locate errant code or at least help you tune the application to run more efficiently under Windows. The usefulness of this information depends on the complexity of the application, the capabilities of the vendor, and the way you're using the application. In short, although the API call readout might be useful in some situations, it's not so useful that you need to spend a lot of time worrying about it.

Figure 15-16. *Page Fault Monitor allows you to detect memory bottlenecks produced by a specific application.*

Immediately after you finish working with the application (in other words, you terminate the test application), Page Fault Monitor prints out a summary of the soft and hard page faults by module. Figure 15-17 shows a listing for one of my test applications. Notice that the left side of the display contains a list of module names. If you don't see a module name, it's safe to assume the module was application-specific. The module name information is followed by the total number of page faults created by the module, and then the total number of soft and hard faults. The test application has a very high percentage of soft page faults compared to hard page faults. This is another way to measure the memory burden of an application. The higher the percentage of soft to hard page faults, the lower the memory burden.

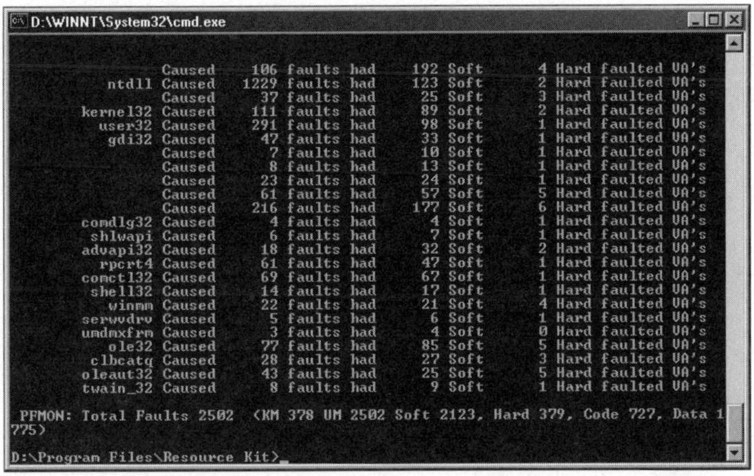

Figure 15-17. *Always check the application statistics once you finish running; a high soft page fault percentage indicates a low memory burden.*

There are a few things you need to consider when using this application. The first is the problem of other applications running on the server. On the one hand, you don't want to create an environment that doesn't reflect reality during testing. Only a real-world environment helps you see the performance of the application as it really is. On the other hand, you need to know that this particular application is causing the problem. Running a lot of other applications on the system at the same time you perform memory bottleneck testing makes it harder to determine with absolute certainty that you have the right application. In most cases, you're going to have to do a lot of detective work to ensure that you know the true source of a memory bottleneck. The Page Fault Monitor utility is only one step along the way, albeit a very useful one.

PerfMon Chart Setting Editor

We've used System Monitor quite a bit throughout the book, so you already know how valuable this tool is in creating a performance picture of your system. Performance Monitor is a non-MMC version of the same tool and it's included with the Windows 2000 Resource Kit for those who don't particularly like using the MMC version. This tool absolutely doesn't work with System Monitor (MMC); you must use it with Performance Monitor instead. However, except for the MMC interface, you'll find that both of these tools are essentially the same.

The PerfMon Chart Setting Editor, also known as SetEdit, is a tool that makes repetitive use of Performance Monitor easier. When you open this tool, you see a strangely familiar display like the one shown in Figure 15-18. As you can see, the display looks similar to part of the Performance Monitor display; but this utility is used to edit the Performance Monitor chart settings, not display performance data. Saving the settings you create in this utility to a file, and then reading them in Performance Monitor, allows you to set up Performance Monitor faster and repeat monitoring scenarios with great accuracy.

Adding counters to the PerfMon Chart Setting Editor is just like adding them to Performance Monitor. However, you have a little more freedom in the way you enter some of the data. Figure 15-19 shows the Add To Chart dialog box you use when adding counters. Notice that you can change the value in the Instance field to select instances that don't appear on the current machine. In addition, note that you can provide a value in the Parent field. The ability to edit these fields means you can create Performance Monitor chart setting files on one machine and use them on another.

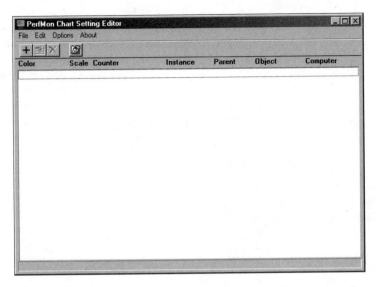

Figure 15-18.   *The PerfMon Chart Setting Editor allows you to edit or create System Monitor setting files.*

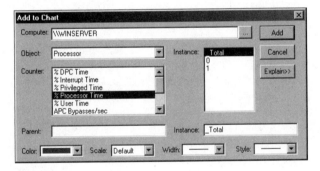

Figure 15-19.   *Adding counters to your chart setting file is just like using Performance Monitor.*

Performance Data Block Dump Utility

Have you ever wondered if you're seeing all the possible counters Windows has to offer in System Monitor? I used to wonder about it, as well, because it always seemed like there must be more ways to check my system than System Monitor had to offer, at least in certain areas. The Performance Data Block Dump Utility, also known as ShowPerf, is a developer tool you can use to accomplish two PTO tasks. The first is to verify that all the counters supported by Windows 2000 are returning current and correct data. Nothing defeats your PTO efforts more than having utilities that provide you with less than accurate information. The second is to see all the counters available on your server, even those that don't appear in System Monitor. Figure 15-20 shows a typical Performance Data Block Dump Utility display.

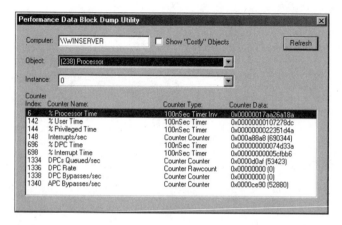

Figure 15-20. *The Performance Data Block Dump Utility can help you locate new counters as well as check existing counters for errors.*

Using the Performance Data Block Dump Utility is fairly straightforward. If you want to monitor a different machine, type the UNC name in the Computer field, and then click Refresh. You can select objects and instances of those objects, just as you do within System Monitor. The only option that might be a mystery is Show "Costly" Objects. Checking this option displays additional counters that perform detailed monitoring of areas like the operating system kernel, but are relatively costly in terms of performance. In other words, you don't use these counters unless they are absolutely required to monitor specific areas of the operating system, and only after you perform some preliminary research to expose other potential causes of performance problems.

Tip You can combine the Performance Data Block Dump Utility with the Extensible Performance Counter List utility we covered earlier to find the precise source of counter errors. Simply disable all the counters using the Extensible Performance Counter List utility, except those that begin with Perf like PerfProc. Run the Performance Data Block Dump Utility. You should see a list of the core performance counters that weren't disabled. Start enabling the counters you disabled. Every time you enable a new counter, click the Refresh button in the Performance Data Block Dump Utility. When an error appears, you've found the faulty counter. Although this method takes a little while to do, it beats using hit-and-miss methods that might not find the problem counter in the first place.

Performance Data in the Command Window

You don't have to use the GUI methods that we looked at so far in the book to gain access to performance data. The Performance Data in the Command Window utility, better known as TypePerf, allows you to display performance data in a DOS window in comma-separated variable (CSV) format. In fact, you can redirect this output to a text file if you want to make it available for entry into a database or as an inclusion with an e-mail message to a third-party vendor. Figure 15-21 shows some typical output from this utility. In this case, I told TypePerf I wanted to monitor the Processes instance of the Objects object once every second, as you can see from the command line. The output includes the date and time of the reading, along with the performance data. There are 49 processes running on the target machine. If you want to add more counters, just add them to the command line separated by commas.

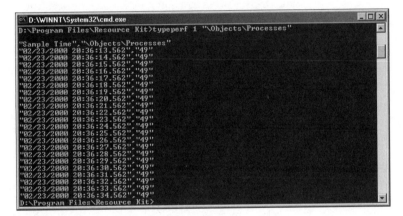

Figure 15-21.   *TypePerf allows you to send a specific set of counter data to the command window or a text file for later processing.*

Performance Meter

Performance Meter, also known as PerfMtr, allows you to monitor various system statistics from the command prompt. You can change the statistic shown by typing single character commands at the command prompt. Table 15-1 shows the list of keystrokes you can use with this utility and describes their purpose. Figure 15-22 shows some typical output from this application.

Table 15-1. Performance Meter Command Summary

Key	Data	Description
c	CPU Usage	The amount of processor capacity in use. This includes statistics like the current number of page faults, the thread count, and other important processor activity.
f	File Cache Usage	The amount of file cache capacity in use. This includes the number of page faults, the current size of the file cache, peak size, total number of faults, and the current fault count.
h	Header	Displays the heading for the currently monitored statistic. This is the same heading that appears when you change the statistics being monitored using one of the statistic monitoring commands like "s".
i	I/O Usage	Provides specific I/O information including the read, write, and other I/O's read, write, and transfers, file objects, and file handles.
p	POOL usage	Displays pooled memory usage including the amount of memory allocated and freed, paged memory, and committed memory.
q	Quit	Allows you to leave the application.
r	Cache Manager Read and Write Operations	Includes a lot of statistical information about cache manager performance including the number of read ahead I/Os, read ahead calls, fast reads, lazy writes, and other useful statistics.
s	Server Statistics	Tallies the amount of activity the server has had with regard to client file server requests. This includes the number of bytes sent or received, the amount of memory used for server needs, the number of client sessions, and other server statistics.
v	Virtual Memory Usage	The amount of virtual memory capacity in use. This includes the number of page faults, reads, writes, and types of memory activity.
x	x86-based Processor Virtual Device Manager (VDM) Statistics	This series of statistics is generated for DOS applications. Normally, you won't see any activity here at all. The statistics include the number of interrupt returns, stack pushes and pops, halt instructions, and interrupt statistics.

Figure 15-22. *PerfMtr allows you to monitor specific server statistics in a command window.*

Performance Monitor 4

Performance Monitor is the predecessor to System Monitor in terms of performance. We've already reviewed the operation of this utility in depth in Chapter 4, so I don't cover it again here. The main difference between this utility and System Monitor is the interface—Performance Monitor is System Monitor without the MMC interface.

Even though System Monitor and Performance Monitor work essentially the same and provide the same results, they aren't interchangeable. There are differences between the two utilities, so you should consider choosing one or the other for all your PTO needs. One of the bigger differences between the two products is that they use different file formats for storing views. We examined this issue earlier in the PerfMon Chart Setting Editor section.

Perf Monitor

It would probably be easy to consider Perf Monitor (WPERF.EXE) as a miniature version of Performance Monitor or System Monitor. After all, it does monitor system performance in a smaller way than either program. You still see a chart with the performance data you selected to display. One of the advantages of using Perf Monitor is that it has a much smaller memory footprint than either System Monitor or Performance Monitor, making it less likely that your readings will get offset by the resource requirements of the monitoring application.

Perf Monitor does have a few extra features you don't find in the other monitoring utilities we looked at so far. Open the Perf Monitor utility, double-click the window if you don't see the File menu, then click Select, and you see a Wperf Option Selection dialog box like the one shown in Figure 15-23. Notice that this dialog box has many of the same entries we've seen before, but in check box format, which might make things easier for some people. The items of interest, however, are the 1st Level TB Fills / Sec and 2nd Level TB Fills / Sec check boxes. These two statistics aren't included in the other monitoring programs because they're typically used only by RISC processors. Of course, it's kind of odd that Microsoft would worry about these statistics at all, considering there aren't any RISC platforms for Windows 2000. Perhaps this is a leftover from some other development effort.

Perf Monitor has another special feature that you should know about. If you have more than one processor, try checking all the processors, plus the CPU Total check boxes. What you see is a display like the one in Figure 15-24. This separate display might seem like a nuisance at first, but it actually makes the statistics a bit easier to see once you get used to it. The usefulness of this display is a factor of the number of processors on your server and the size of the server display.

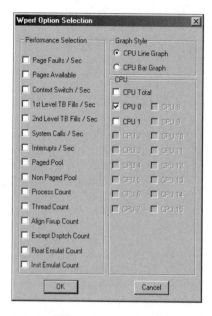

Figure 15-23. *The Wperf Option Selection dialog box allows you to choose the counters you want to monitor.*

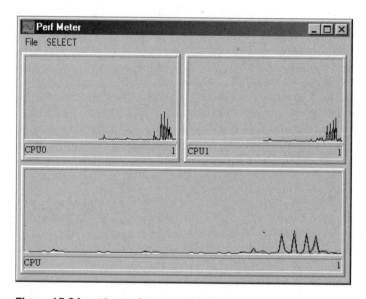

Figure 15-24. *The Perf Monitor display can provide a clearer view of CPU usage statistics in some situations.*

Program Timer

There's almost always a need to time how long something takes, especially on a server. You might want to find out how long it takes to execute a script, for example. In addition, it's often helpful to find out how the application used the execution time. Program Timer (NTIMER.EXE) might not provide all the statistics you're looking for, but it does give you the total application execution time, the amount of time it spent in user mode, and the amount of time spent in kernel mode.

Using this utility is easy. All you need to do is type **NTIMER** at the command prompt, along with the name and path of the application you want to test. The -l argument displays all the output statistics on one line. You can use the -f argument to display additional statistics like the process page faults, total system interrupts, context switches, and system calls. Finally, you need to use the -s argument with server processes, and then press Ctrl+C to get the results. Figure 15-25 shows some typical output from this application.

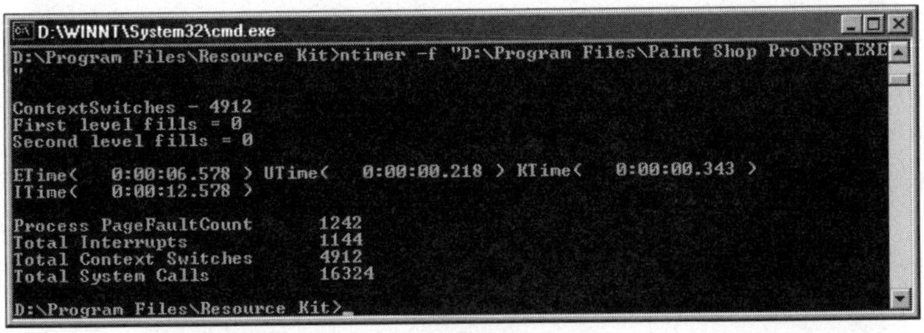

Figure 15-25.   *The Program Timer utility allows you to track the amount of time required to execute an application.*

Time Ordered Processes

The Time Ordered Processes (TOP.EXE) utility is a quick way to see which server processes are using the most CPU time. The display is constantly updated with a list of processes currently using CPU time, with the most CPU-intensive tasks listed at the top. Figure 15-26 shows an example of this utility in action. As you can see, the display provides all the information needed to track the process. Typing **Q** at the command prompt allows you to exit the utility.

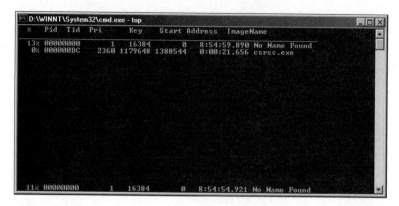

Figure 15-26.   *The Time Ordered Processes utility is a very fast way to see which processes are using the most CPU time.*

Total Processors

This utility allows you to measure the amount of memory in use by all installed processors. Total Processors is a new utility designed to allow you to measure the processor time on applications launched by the system interrupt. Using this utility requires some work on your part, and because it's a new utility, there are some rough edges you have to work around as well.

The first task you need to do is install the counter required for this utility. A counter is usually a DLL that is located in the System32 directory. We saw examples of these DLLs in the "Extensible Performance Counter List" section of the chapter (see Figure 15-13). Windows accesses the DLL through a registry entry. With this in mind, use the following six-step procedure to register and install the PerfTP.DLL used as a counter for Total Processors.

1. Open a command window. You can't use the Run command of the Start menu to perform the steps in this procedure.

2. Change directories to the \Program Files\Resource Kit directory. This is where the files you need are located.

3. Type **REGEDIT TP.REG** at the command prompt. RegEdit asks if you want to add the required registry entries to the registry. Click Yes. Click OK.

4. Type **LODCTR PERFTP.INI** at the command prompt. You should see the cursor change to an hourglass for a few moments, but you don't get any other confirmation that this step worked as anticipated.

5. Type **COPY PERFTP.DLL** %SYSTEMROOT%/**SYSTEM32/PERFTP.DLL** at the command prompt. Windows 2000 informs you that it successfully copied the file for you.

6.   Open the Extensible Performance Counter List utility by typing EXCTRLST and pressing Enter. Verify the TotalProcessor counter appears in the Extensible Performance Counter List as shown in Figure 15-27. If it does, you successfully installed the counter.

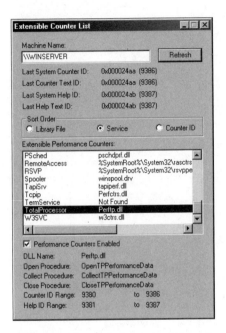

Figure 15-27.   *Verify that the Extensible Performance Counter List utility displays the TotalProcessor counter.*

At this point, there should be several different ways to display the counter. However, there's a chance you'll run into problems trying the load the counter directly in System Monitor or Performance Monitor. What you can do instead is use the PerfMon Chart Setting Editor to create a Performance Monitor view that features the Total Processor object and Total Processor Time counter. You can then load this view in the Performance Monitor. Make sure you can see the counter at the bottom of the utility.

It's time to start the Total Processors utility. You see a Total Processor Usage dialog box like the one shown in Figure 15-28. Notice that it displays total processor memory usage as a percentage. You can minimize this utility if you like, but it has to remain running for the counter to work. In addition, you find that none of the other processor counters work right when this utility is running. They should all measure 100 percent usage.

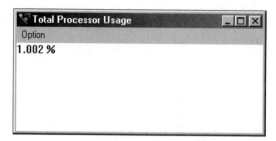

Figure 15-28. *The Total Processor Usage dialog box displays total processor memory usage as a percentage.*

As soon as you start the Total Processors utility, Performance Monitor should begin showing some activity. Figure 15-29 shows a typical example of the output from this particular counter. Remember to close both Performance Monitor and the Total Processors utility once you finish taking readings on your system.

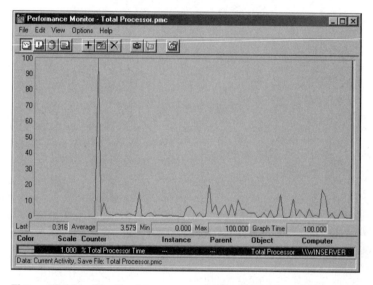

Figure 15-29. *The Total Processors utility makes it possible to display total processor memory usage on a Performance Monitor graph.*

Virtual Address Dump

You use the Virtual Address Dump utility (VADUMP.EXE) to look at the contents of virtual memory. This means looking at the size and state of each virtual address space segment. The purpose of this exercise is to ensure that the virtual address space isn't overallocated.

You find that the Virtual Address Dump utility lists the address of each segment, the total amount of committed memory for the image, .exe files, DLLs, and system DLLs, the total mapped committed memory, total private committed memory, total reserved memory, and information about the working set. There are several different levels at which you can look for information; these include the entire address space, the current working set, and any additions to the current working set. If you decide to use the third option of dumping changes to the current working set, Virtual Address Dump continues running until you tell it to stop using Ctrl+C. There's also a wealth of command line options you can use to augment the Virtual Address Dump output.

Figure 15-30 shows typical output from this utility. In this case, I chose to display the current working set for an application running on the server. This display represents only the summary information. Virtual Address Dump can provide a lot of other information as well, including precise memory range allocations. If you choose to display a large data set of information, you need to redirect the output to a file since the display overruns the command window's display buffer.

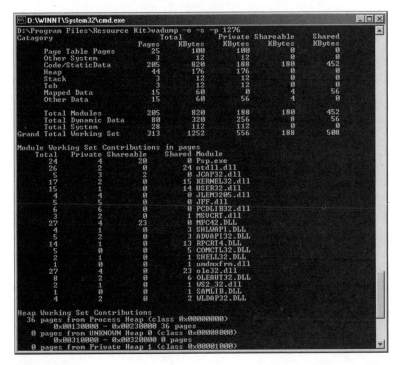

Figure 15-30.   *The Virtual Address Dump utility allows you to look at the virtual address space in a variety of ways.*

Summary

The purpose of this chapter is to show you the add-on tools for Windows 2000 that Microsoft provides in the form of the Windows 2000 Resource Kit. The kit itself is a collection of utility programs created by Microsoft and third-party developers. These utilities allow you to perform a variety of tasks, some of which are performance-oriented. This chapter concentrated on the performance-oriented tools since those tools coincide with the purpose of this book—to tune your system for optimum efficiency. However, it's very important that you consider looking at other tools in the Windows 2000 Resource Kit. They can help you perform a variety of tasks like improving the security of your server or finding problems with the hardware that supports server tasks.

We also looked at some other tools you can use with Windows 2000. You find links for these tools in the Additional Components portion of the Windows 2000 Resource Kit setup program. Although these tools aren't automatically installed, they are contained on the CD-ROM and you will find that they come in quite handy for managing and maintaining your system. Although we didn't cover any third-party tools in this chapter, we do so in Chapter 16.

Chapter 16
Third-Party Tuning Tools

Performance is a concept everyone understands. The perceived need to tune a server is about as old as servers are. In fact, many of the innovations we now enjoy as part of a standard server are the result of tuning sometime in the past. In some cases, an innovation occurs because someone couldn't find a tool to perform some type of tuning; in others, it's simply in response to the request for better tools to work with. No matter what kind of server you use, the need for high performance is a constant. Microsoft Windows 2000 Server is no different from any other server product out there in this regard. The fact that Microsoft recognizes this need and encourages a strong third-party tool market to answer specific kinds of tuning tool needs is beneficial to both Microsoft and the user.

This chapter examines the subject of third-party tuning tools. Yes, the tools Microsoft provides are a good place to start working with your system because they provide a standardized basis for beginning the tuning process. As your system increases in complexity, however, generic tuning methods become less and less successful in getting every ounce of performance out of your system. At some point, the generic tools Microsoft's engineers can think to provide don't meet all the requirements for your server and you need to turn to third-party tools for help.

We review several different classes of tools in this chapter. I chose to include a separate "Shareware Tools" section because you can usually get some good deals going this route. Even if a shareware tool doesn't fully meet your needs, it at least allows you to see what's possible. Often, a view of what's possible and what's unreasonable can keep you from making mistakes when it comes time to buy off-the-shelf software or contract a developer to build a custom tool for you.

The remaining sections of the chapter explore software you pay for before you use it. "General Administration Tools" examines some of the products on the market that help you work with users or system resources in some way. "Hardware-Oriented Tools" deals with tools that help you locate and troubleshoot PTO problems with your hardware. This section doesn't go over anything too esoteric, but this hardware isn't run-of-the-mill either. Finally, we examine networks in the "Network-Specific Tools" section of the chapter. It's important to understand that networks are a separate, yet integrated, part of your server. In many cases, you need to buy tools that help you tune this part of the network as a separate entity, in order to find the precise cause of a PTO problem.

> **Note** This chapter doesn't review custom tuning tools or the type of tools that come with the hardware. A developer usually writes custom tuning tools with a specific network in mind. There isn't any way we can anticipate the custom tool needs you might have, except to say that a custom tool might be the only choice when shareware or off-the-shelf tools can't meet your needs. More and more pieces of hardware are shipping with a combination of diagnostic and tuning tools. These tools represent the best way to tune that individual piece of hardware and you should use them as a first step to getting your system in shape. These tools don't test the piece of hardware's interactions with other hardware within the system or on the network, so you need more tools than what you get with the hardware. Make sure you take time to read the hardware vendor's documentation and learn the capabilities of the tuning tools that come with your hardware. Equally important, learn the problem areas of the hardware-specific tuning tools and document them for network administrators who follow in your footsteps.

Shareware Tools

There are many network administrators who look at shareware as the cheap, shiny trinket of the PC world. They view every piece of shareware with skepticism and have no doubt that the software will fail to perform as advertised. The facts are rather different than folklore indicates. Yes, some shareware is poorly written, poorly supported, and a danger to your network, but this shareware usually doesn't stick around for very long. No one is willing to take a chance on such software, so it gets removed from Web sites and is gone before very long.

Shareware that stays around for a while is normally well written (at least as well as shrink-wrapped software), very well supported as long as the vendor stays in business, and relatively low cost because of the way the software is distributed to the public. In fact, the support issue is one you should think about because a shareware developer relies on word of mouth for advertising. It doesn't take too much in the way of bad support for the developer to gain a bad reputation and to lose sales. For the most part, shareware developers are strongly motivated to provide a superior level of support (at least, in some ways) for their products and are usually more willing to consider feature requests than a shrink-wrap vendor would ever think about.

So, why would someone use the shareware method of marketing their product when shrink-wrap and custom software both sell for a great deal more? The answer is simple. Most of these developers begin very small and don't have the marketing dollars to do the job right. They need grassroots support for their product and word-of-mouth recommendations from users to gain sales. In short, this is a small fish that's swimming in a world of sharks. This doesn't mean shareware vendors remain small—some have grown to the point where their company is on par with many shrink-wrap vendors in size. The only real difference is the starting size of the company and the amount of capital it has to begin with.

Real World

You might expect that every software vendor would provide only the best products and that the limitations of those products would be clearly explained on the product label. The reality is that some software is buggy when you get it and remains so because the vendor doesn't have the resources required to support it. In addition, all tuning aids have limitations, some of which are obvious at the time of purchase. The problem is that the vendor can't anticipate the unique features of your network and therefore has no way of knowing what limitations the tuning software has in that environment. In short, you need to inquire about a return policy for every piece of software, no matter how good it looks when you buy it. The combination of bugs and limitations often keeps a good piece of tuning software from doing the work you need it to do on your system, which means your system doesn't work any better after you're finished using the tuning software.

There are some real-world examples of the limits of testing software that are easy to understand. In one case, a consultant bought a piece of diagnostic software that tested the limits of the processing speed of an individual PC using standardized tests. These tests helped the consultant quickly locate machines that were configured for less-than-optimal performance. At first, the software worked precisely as anticipated. However, as the hardware improved and the software remained the same, the software became unable to fully test the capabilities of the machine it was supposed to support. In short, the software wasn't poorly written or nonfunctional—the only problem was an unanticipated increase in hardware potential and a lack of upgrade support on the part of the tuning software vendor.

In some cases, a lack of capability can also place limits on what you can expect out of a piece of tuning software. One piece of software that I tested used very simple TCP/IP commands to determine the configuration of a network. It simply tried a range of addresses until it figured out the network's configuration based on the responses to simple questions to each machine. This software worked fine on a small 10-node (or fewer) network. However, I had to stop the software after it ran for eight hours on a 15-node network. The software was still capable of doing the job, but the limitations of the software's design prevented it from doing so in a realistic amount of time.

As a network administrator who depends on tuning software to keep your network running, these facts tell you several things about shareware. The first problem with shareware is that you don't know if the vendor will be around tomorrow to support its product. You might buy the product today, only to find tomorrow that the vendor has closed shop and moved to Bermuda. In short, don't rely on shareware vendors to provide the tuning tools you need for mission-critical applications. When working with mission-critical tuning needs, always go with a shrink-wrap vendor with lots of experience and a good reputation.

Shareware vendors have one other problem when it comes to tuning software. A shareware vendor often disregards the mainstream tuning needs of a company to secure a good position in a niche market. This means some shareware might seem feature-rich as long as you need the tuning equivalent of a left-handed monkey wrench, but fails when it comes to the right-handed version of the very same product. Again, it pays to look at shareware as a means of experimenting with different kinds of software; but, in some cases, that's about all you can do because the software lacks some important feature you must have to make your network run properly.

More Info This chapter provides a very quick overview of shareware. It pays to spend more time looking at this subject if you plan on buying shareware on a regular basis. Like many other groups of people in the world, those who produce shareware have formed an organization known as the Association of Shareware Professionals (ASP). You can find out more about this group at *http://www.asp-shareware.org/tableof.asp*. In many cases, shareware vendors also belong to a much larger organization known as the Software and Information Industry Association (SIIA). This is the same group that used to be known as the Software Publishers Association (SPA). You find this group at *http://www.siia.net.*

Now that you have some idea of what shareware is all about, let's look at some of the products you'll find. All these products are available on the Internet, so we provide URLs for all of them. You can download any of these products and try them for the amount of time specified in the software agreement for free. If you decide to use the shareware for an extended trial, make sure you support the shareware vendor's efforts by buying your shareware.

Caution Some of the software in the following sections still shows its Microsoft Windows NT origins. As of this writing, absolutely none of this software is certified for use with Microsoft Windows 2000, which means Microsoft hasn't checked it for compatibility and conformance with the Windows 2000 logo requirements. Only one product is specifically designed for Windows 2000. All the software was tested on two different Microsoft Windows 2000 Servers and two Microsoft Windows 2000 Professional Workstations. Even though this is hardly a conclusive set of tests, it does indicate the software will run on Windows 2000 given the right circumstances. As with any piece of software you load on your server, working with the shareware in this section is a try-at-your-own-risk proposition. There aren't any guarantees, either expressed or implied, by anyone. If you try this software, use it on a test machine first and then move it to a production machine with great caution. Otherwise, you might get unanticipated results.

Fundelete

Fundelete is one of those utilities that becomes an obvious addition to your toolbox once you see it in action. This program replaces the standard Recycle Bin with an enhanced version that operates within the graphical user interface (GUI) and the command prompt. In other words, deleting something at the command prompt no longer means it can't be undeleted. I've included Fundelete because Windows 2000 Server administration can occur at the command prompt just as easily as within Microsoft Windows itself. There have probably been times when you deleted something at the command prompt, only to find that you needed it later. Fundelete can make this problem a thing of the past.

Note   This is the first of several freeware sections in this chapter. Unlike shareware, which you need to register and pay for after a given amount of review time, freeware is just that—free. You don't have to register or pay for it. In some cases, the author even makes the source code for the freeware available to those who want to make their own version of the product.

Installing Fundelete is relatively easy, but it does require a reboot for full implementation. Considering the fact that you're replacing the Recycle Bin with another product, the need to reboot isn't too far out of line. However, it would be nice if the product could install itself without rebooting once the vendor completes any Windows 2000 upgrade. Theoretically, you could change the Fundelete setup to get around the need to reboot since the source code for this product is available online.

More Info   You can get more information about Fundelete, including an explanation of internal operation and source code, at *http://www.sysinternals.com/ fundelete.htm*. Since this is freeware, there's no charge for using it within the confines that the authors of the product have set. The Web site contains the e-mail addresses of both authors. If you plan to distribute this product in any way, contact the authors first.

A quick test of Fundelete reveals that it does indeed work at the MS-DOS command prompt. Opening the Fundelete Bin icon displays a very simplified dialog box like the one shown in Figure 16-1. Notice that just about every menu entry and toolbar button has something to do with deleted files. Sometimes the standard Recycle Bin menu and toolbar seem a bit crowded.

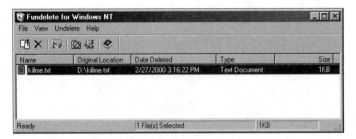

Figure 16-1.   *The Fundelete window contains a very simplified set of controls for working with deleted files on your server.*

There's one control here that doesn't appear within the standard Recycle Bin. You can click either the Exclude button or use the Undelete \ Exclusion List command to display the Fundelete Exclusion List dialog box shown in Figure 16-2. This dialog box allows you to exclude files by file extension or by directory. Excluded files don't get placed in the Fundelete Bin. This means you no longer have to sort through a list of .bak files to find the one file you really need to restore. It's a small feature, but one that also reduces clutter on the server, something we talked about earlier as a performance inhibitor.

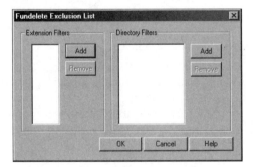

Figure 16-2.   *You can use the Fundelete Exclusion List dialog box to keep certain types of files out of the Fundelete Bin.*

PsKill

How many of you sit at your server just waiting to kill errant processes all day? That's what I thought. Even if your server isn't locked away in some closet, you have more important things to do than sit around and wait for something to go wrong with the server. Yet, the need to kill processes does arise and there are times when an errant process can quickly gobble up system resources, so you can't wait around to do it—you have to kill it quickly. That's where PsKill can help. This freeware utility allows you to kill processes on your server from a remote location.

> **More Info**   You can get an overview of PsKill and the command line parameters at *http://www.sysinternals.com/pskill.htm*. This particular piece of freeware doesn't offer any source code. The author's contact information does appear on the download page.

PsKill uses a command line interface. All you need to do to use it is type the proper command line parameters. Here's what the command line looks like, along with an explanation of the command line parameters.

```
pskill [-?] [\\<computer> [-u <username>] [-p <password>]]
 <process name | process id>
```

- **-?**   Displays the supported options.
- **\\<computer>**   Specifies the name of a remote computer. The remote computer must be accessible via the Windows NT network neighborhood. You don't have to specify this option when killing a process on the local machine.
- **-u <username>**   Specifies a username for the remote system. You use this option to log on to a remote system using a specific username. The username you choose must have administrative privileges. If the account you're currently using on the local machine has administrative privileges on the remote machine, you don't need to use this option.
- **-p <password>**   Specifies the password associated with the username on the remote machine. If you don't provide a password, PsKill prompts you to provide one interactively. The password you type doesn't show up on the local machine's display. Using this option comes in handy for batch files, but also introduces a security breach if someone gains access to the batch file contents.
- **<process name>**   Specifies the process name of the process or processes you want to kill.
- **<process id>**   Specifies the process identification number (PID) of the process you want to kill.

Portmon

If you ever wanted to keep track of what your server ports are doing, Portmon is the tool for the job. This utility takes a very close view of port activity and can even help you read the data as it gets transferred to and from the server. In fact, it works sort of like the sniffer you probably use to monitor network traffic, but for the various ports on your machine instead.

More Info You can get an overview of Portmon features and a list of related utilities at *http://www.sysinternals.com/portmon.htm*. This Web site also includes the author's contact information. Most important of all, this Web site gives you a brief overview of how the utility works under different versions of Windows, which should give you a better idea of how Windows works with ports.

One of the advantages of using Portmon is that you can look at remote machines. In fact, you can monitor more than one machine at a time. Each machine is located in a different Window. Figure 16-3 shows a typical Portmon display. In this case, I'm monitoring the serial port on the server. The display provides similar information for other port types. You can also choose which ports to monitor, and can filter the kinds of data you want to see from that port.

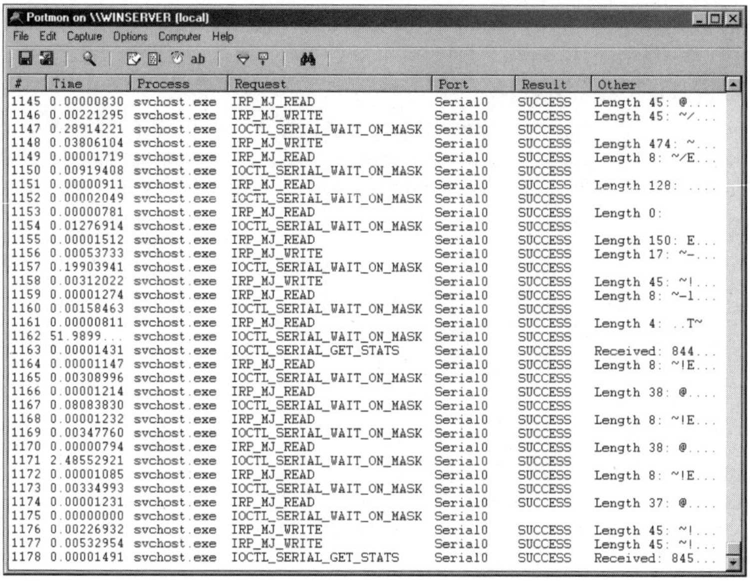

#	Time	Process	Request	Port	Result	Other
1145	0.00000830	svchost.exe	IRP_MJ_READ	Serial0	SUCCESS	Length 45: @....
1146	0.00221295	svchost.exe	IRP_MJ_WRITE	Serial0	SUCCESS	Length 45: ~/...
1147	0.28914221	svchost.exe	IOCTL_SERIAL_WAIT_ON_MASK	Serial0	SUCCESS	
1148	0.03806104	svchost.exe	IRP_MJ_WRITE	Serial0	SUCCESS	Length 474: ~...
1149	0.00001719	svchost.exe	IRP_MJ_READ	Serial0	SUCCESS	Length 8: ~/E...
1150	0.00919408	svchost.exe	IOCTL_SERIAL_WAIT_ON_MASK	Serial0	SUCCESS	
1151	0.00000911	svchost.exe	IRP_MJ_READ	Serial0	SUCCESS	Length 128: ....
1152	0.00002049	svchost.exe	IOCTL_SERIAL_WAIT_ON_MASK	Serial0	SUCCESS	
1153	0.00000781	svchost.exe	IRP_MJ_READ	Serial0	SUCCESS	Length 0:
1154	0.01276914	svchost.exe	IOCTL_SERIAL_WAIT_ON_MASK	Serial0	SUCCESS	
1155	0.00001512	svchost.exe	IRP_MJ_READ	Serial0	SUCCESS	Length 150: E...
1156	0.00053733	svchost.exe	IRP_MJ_WRITE	Serial0	SUCCESS	Length 17: ~-...
1157	0.19903941	svchost.exe	IOCTL_SERIAL_WAIT_ON_MASK	Serial0	SUCCESS	
1158	0.00312022	svchost.exe	IRP_MJ_WRITE	Serial0	SUCCESS	Length 45: ~!...
1159	0.00001274	svchost.exe	IRP_MJ_READ	Serial0	SUCCESS	Length 8: ~-1...
1160	0.00158463	svchost.exe	IOCTL_SERIAL_WAIT_ON_MASK	Serial0	SUCCESS	
1161	0.00000811	svchost.exe	IRP_MJ_READ	Serial0	SUCCESS	Length 4: ..T~
1162	51.9899...	svchost.exe	IOCTL_SERIAL_WAIT_ON_MASK	Serial0	SUCCESS	
1163	0.00001431	svchost.exe	IOCTL_SERIAL_GET_STATS	Serial0	SUCCESS	Received: 844...
1164	0.00001147	svchost.exe	IRP_MJ_READ	Serial0	SUCCESS	Length 8: ~!E...
1165	0.00308996	svchost.exe	IOCTL_SERIAL_WAIT_ON_MASK	Serial0	SUCCESS	
1166	0.00001214	svchost.exe	IRP_MJ_READ	Serial0	SUCCESS	Length 38: @....
1167	0.08083830	svchost.exe	IOCTL_SERIAL_WAIT_ON_MASK	Serial0	SUCCESS	
1168	0.00001232	svchost.exe	IRP_MJ_READ	Serial0	SUCCESS	Length 8: ~!E...
1169	0.00347760	svchost.exe	IOCTL_SERIAL_WAIT_ON_MASK	Serial0	SUCCESS	
1170	0.00000794	svchost.exe	IRP_MJ_READ	Serial0	SUCCESS	Length 38: @....
1171	2.48552921	svchost.exe	IOCTL_SERIAL_WAIT_ON_MASK	Serial0	SUCCESS	
1172	0.00001085	svchost.exe	IRP_MJ_READ	Serial0	SUCCESS	Length 8: ~!E...
1173	0.00334993	svchost.exe	IOCTL_SERIAL_WAIT_ON_MASK	Serial0	SUCCESS	
1174	0.00001231	svchost.exe	IRP_MJ_READ	Serial0	SUCCESS	Length 37: @....
1175	0.00000000	svchost.exe	IOCTL_SERIAL_WAIT_ON_MASK	Serial0		
1176	0.00226932	svchost.exe	IRP_MJ_WRITE	Serial0	SUCCESS	Length 45: ~!...
1177	0.00532954	svchost.exe	IRP_MJ_WRITE	Serial0	SUCCESS	Length 45: ~!...
1178	0.00001491	svchost.exe	IOCTL_SERIAL_GET_STATS	Serial0	SUCCESS	Received: 845...

Figure 16-3. *Portmon provides a great deal of flexibility in monitoring ports on your server, even from a remote location.*

As you can see, the port data includes the name of the process making the request, the kind of request made, the port the request was made from, whether the call was successful, and the data associated with the call. All this information can help you diagnose performance problems with your server setup. You can also use it for troubleshooting the system and to see what kinds of data the user is transferring to the server. Portmon also allows you to save the data in a log file for future analysis.

There are a number of display options with this product. You can choose the display clock option and whether the data is displayed in hexadecimal or ASCII format. Another option allows you to change the method used to highlight information. A history depth setting allows you to reduce the amount of data Portmon retains between sessions (or you can retain all the data collected).

Smartline DeviceLock

Managing system resources is one of the best ways to optimize performance. In this case, tuning occurs by denying access to those who don't need to use the resource and providing access to those who do. Windows 2000 provides a number of methods of managing security. For the most part, the Microsoft Management Console (MMC) snap-ins and utilities (like Microsoft Windows Explorer) used to perform this service are user-oriented. In other words, your main concern is ensuring that users gain the right level of access to a particular resource.

DeviceLock provides extensions to the normal Windows 2000 capabilities in several ways that allow you to better tune security for your server. For one thing, this utility is device-oriented, not user-oriented. It allows you a full view of the device, its capabilities, and the users who can access the device. In short, this product allows you to work with the device at several levels. Here's a short list of product features.

- Control which users or groups can access devices. This particular service can be performed at the access control list (ACL) level.
- Flush unsaved file buffers. This is an especially important feature for removable media. It ensures that you can gain the full benefits of using the Windows 2000 lazy write (cached) feature, yet maintain data integrity.
- Get extended information about devices like the file system used, number and type of partitions, and other physical and logical device characteristics.
- Get extended information about NTFS partitions like the master file table (MFT) and position of the partition on the hard drive.
- Control all functions from a remote computer, which means you can access complete information about the server from your desk.
- Full multilingual support, which means this product works in corporations that have a worldwide presence.
- There are native code versions for both the Intel *x86* and Compaq Alpha platforms. This means the utility has a minimal impact on server performance.

> **More Info** You can get more information about DeviceLock at *http://www.protect-me.com/dl*. This same company has other products you might want to look at. In this chapter, we're only looking at the one product that helps you with PTO issues. You can get a free download of this product at *http://protect-me.com/dl/download.html*.

One of the more important considerations for this product is that it works in a mixed operating system environment. As long as there's a connection between machines, you can lock the devices on those machines. Figure 16-4 shows an example of what you might see using this utility. This environment contains a mix of NetWare, Windows 2000, and Windows 9*x* machines. Each machine is represented as part of a particular network.

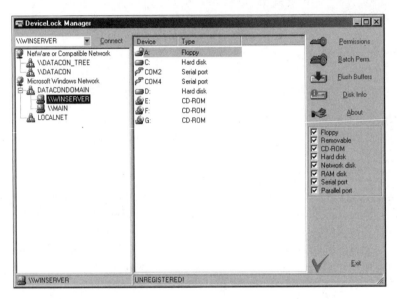

Figure 16-4. *DeviceLock Manager allows you to see all the machines on the network, even if you're running in a mixed environment.*

Notice that Figure 16-4 shows the Windows server for DataConDomain highlighted. This machine includes a floppy drive, hard drive, serial ports, and several CD-ROM drives. The single hard drive is split into two partitions, which is why the hard disk type appears twice on the display.

All the major controls for this application appear on the right side of the DeviceLock Manager dialog box. The two top buttons handle security. Although this feature is interesting, it's not the PTO main event. Right below these two security buttons is a Flush Buffers button. Click this button and you see a message box stating that all the buffers were flushed. If the selected device is a removable media, you can remove the current media from the drive and replace it with something else.

The Disk Info button displays information about the device dialog box shown in Figure 16-5. This is where you find detailed information about the device in question. In this case, we're looking at a FAT 32-formatted DOS partition. At the top of the display, you find all the drive's physical characteristics. The middle section shows the partition information for the drive. The bottom section shows the information for this logical drive. You have to select each partition on a drive separately to see information for that partition.

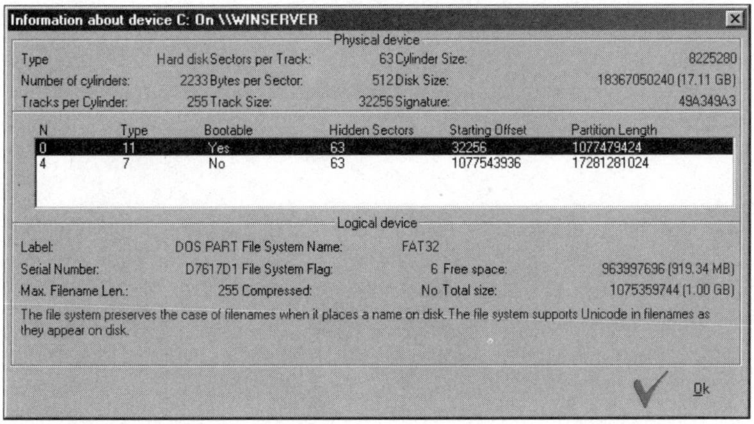

Figure 16-5.   *This dialog box lists the specifics about the partition you selected.*

DeviceLock Manager provides additional information for NTFS drives as shown in Figure 16-6. Notice the dialog box now includes additional MFT information. You can find out the MFT size, current usage level, location on the hard drive, and other factors. In short, this display tells you about the drive's health from a capacity perspective. You can learn some information about the drive that isn't available directly using the Windows 2000 utilities.

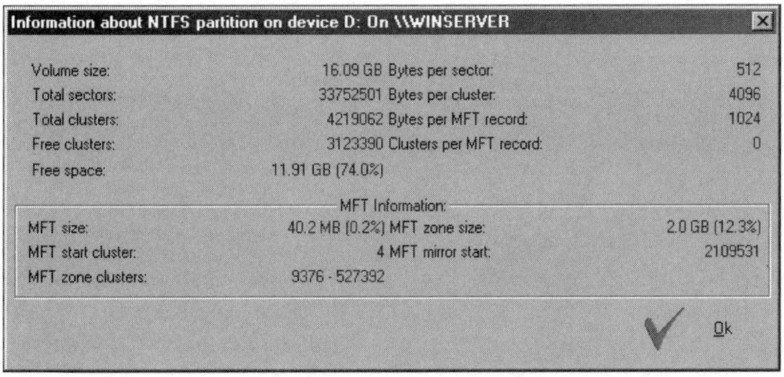

Figure 16-6.   *DeviceLock Manager even provides information about the MFT for an NTFS-formatted drive partition.*

TOTALidea WinRAM Booster

Memory is one of the scarcest resources on any server. Every year, network administrators fortify their servers with yet more memory to meet new user demands and ever-increasing application requirements (along with requirements for additional server uptime and performance). Unfortunately, there's a problem in all versions of Windows in the form of memory fragmentation. Like hard drive fragmentation, this problem increases the amount of time required to find all the pieces of an application. Of course, given the speed of RAM, this is hardly the performance problem of hard drive fragmentation. Memory fragmentation does present another sort of problem, however. It means your system spends more time moving data from RAM onto the pagefile on the hard drive. Any data moved from RAM to the hard drive must be moved back at some time, which means you're paying for a two-way trip. All this movement costs a lot in the way of performance.

More Info   WinRAM Booster provides much of the same functionality as any commercial product—even the Web site looks more like a commercial Web site than other shareware sites you might visit. You find complete product information at *http://www.totalidea.de/frameset-wrbp2k.htm*. This includes a relatively long list of product features, a link to a page where you can download a sample copy of the product, and screenshots of what you can expect to see when using the product. Note that there's also a freeware version of this product (albeit with very reduced functionality) that you can get from *http://www.totalidea.de/frameset-opti.htm*. Essentially, this is just another kind of test version of the WinRAM product and shouldn't be viewed as the end-all product for production systems.

WinRAM Booster provides the means to defragment your memory. It works by adding several memory monitors to your system and providing a utility for managing the contents of your pagefile. You use this program to reorganize the physical RAM on your system, which means you should have better control over how applications load. Less time spent moving data to and from the hard drive means more time spent processing user requests. Theoretically, reduced memory problems should also mean fewer application crashes. Although application crashes are less of a problem with Windows 2000, users still pay a penalty because they have to make any failed requests again.

Installation of this product is very straightforward. There's the usual warning about closing any open applications first. Like many utilities on the market, WinRAM Booster requires a reboot of your server, something I hope changes as time goes on. Once you install WinRAM Booster, you see a new icon on the Windows desktop that you use to start the application. Start the application and you see a display like the one shown in Figure 16-7. Notice that this display shows you the current level of memory and swapfile usage. This is just one of several displays that show how memory is used on the server, but it's probably the one you use most often. I've also expanded the Settings area for the application, so you can see some of the settings this utility has to offer. As you can see, you have full control over product features such as when WinRAM Booster starts and how the optimization process is handled.

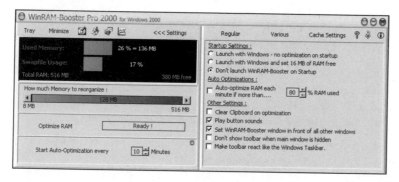

Figure 16-7. *WinRAM Booster allows you to see current memory usage on your system.*

Optimization occurs automatically in some circumstances. Precisely when this happens is up to you. You can also click the Starts The Optimization toolbar button to manually optimize server memory. The Optimize RAM indicator changes to show the current memory optimization status. Once the memory is optimized, the memory displays get updated and the Optimize RAM indicator shows Ready! again.

One of the more interesting features WinRAM boost provides is the ability to monitor and set your cache settings. This program monitors the IoPageLockLimit registry setting and makes recommendations about changing the setting based on memory usage and installed memory on your server. A simple test of this feature shows that it's fairly accurate in predicting the optimal cache size. My system saw a 15 percent boost in file system performance by adjusting the size of the cache—a significant amount if your applications are disk-bound. Predicting how the system uses memory isn't an exact science and you want to monitor the benefits of any changes you make. The fact that this feature appears to work is a real plus, however, and you should at least look at it once you have WinRAM Boost installed on your server.

General Administration Tools

Administering a network can require vast amounts of time, especially if you don't have the right tools. Anyone can manage a network with 20 or 30 users without much help. On a network this size, you probably know all the users on a first-name basis and there isn't any doubt as to what resources the user needs. Windows provides tools that help you manage networks of any size; but what happens when a network grows to 100 users, or 1,000 users? Do you think the MMC snap-ins provided with the default Windows 2000 setup can keep up with that many users? Sure, you see all the users and you might even be able to organize them; but how do you answer the questions such as how many users require access to the company's customer list and at what level and at what time? As networks get larger, the questions get more difficult, and the complexity of wading through all the information becomes even greater.

Of course, users are only part of the question of administrating a network. As a company gets larger, the need to keep track of every resource gets harder. You might find yourself dealing with such esoteric issues as the requirements for logging access to company vehicles. Although you won't be responsible for the day-to-day operation of such a database, you are involved in creating the database and performing certain administrative tasks like backing up the data and keeping the database clear of old data. Resource management can become a real nightmare in a relatively short time.

Obviously, there are a number of administrative tasks you need to perform, no matter what size network you have. The following sections examine some third-party tools that fall into the general administration task category. The descriptions don't include prices, since the price of software changes relatively quickly and depends on where you're located. The version numbers are current as of this writing, but are subject to change.

Real World

No matter how well any set of third-party utilities work, there's always a chance a common DLL used by one utility will conflict with another version of the same DLL used by another utility. Every time Microsoft provides upgrades for the DLLs used within Windows, that's one more version of the DLL that vendors have to think about supporting. The problem is that developers often program around bugs they see in the common DLLs. In other words, the utility depends on a certain DLL feature or function (something Microsoft doesn't recommend). When Microsoft either corrects bugs in the DLL or enhances the DLL in some way, the utility is broken. It needs the old version of the DLL to function properly. Yet, a new utility might need Microsoft's latest version of the DLL to operate because it relies on the fixed or enhanced feature Microsoft has provided. Since one version only of the DLL can appear in the System32 folder, you get a conflict situation that some network administrators refer to as "DLL hell."

Microsoft is aware of the DLL hell-related problems, and is taking steps to fix them. In some cases, this means coming up with unique solutions because network administrators require the functionality of both DLL versions to make the network run as anticipated. The best solution, however, is to upgrade your utilities to use the same DLL version whenever possible, or at least test the utility with the latest DLL version to see if it works.

One solution is to make registry changes and run an application called DUPS.EXE. DUPS is short for DLL Universal Problem Solver. The DUPS tool is actually a set of utilities that allow you to monitor the version numbers of DLLs stored on multiple Windows machines, making it possible to look for incompatibilities across your entire network instead of one machine at a time. This tool is based on a Microsoft Developer Network (MSDN) article entitled "An End to DLL Hell" by Rick Anderson. The MSDN article appears at *http://msdn.microsoft.com/isapi/msdnlib.idc?theURL=/library/techart/DLLdanger1.htm.* You can find out more about this solution and the problems of DLL hell at *http://support.microsoft.com/support/kb/articles/q247/9/57.asp.*

CyberSafe Log Analyst

Log Analyst is specifically designed to work with the security event log on your server. It helps you analyze various kinds of security problems on your system using an MMC snap-in. For example, you can determine how many times a particular user logged in to the system. Of course, you need to enable various forms of Windows 2000 auditing before you get enough data to actually analyze with this product. In short, you have to take a short-term performance hit to get a long-term performance gain.

From a PTO perspective, ensuring that your server has the fewest possible security problems is a big concern for several reasons. First, true security breaches mean someone other than an authorized user is using system resources, which means, from a company perspective, those resources are wasted. Second, application setup problems can show up in the form of security breaches. Yes, users are authorized to use the application, but they don't get to access it on the first pass for some reason. (If the user couldn't access the application at all, you can be sure you'd hear about it.)

Using Log Analyst is fairly straightforward. You save the data you want to analyze using the Event Viewer MMC snap-in. Remember, Log Analyst only works with the security data on your system—it isn't designed to analyze other types of event logs (even though it definitely tries without complaining). Once you save the event log, add it to the Logs To Be Analyzed folder of Log Analyst. You analyze the file, which automatically places it in the Analyzed Logs folder. Finally, you choose one of the predefined reports, or create one of your own, to output the analyzed data. Figure 16-8 shows the kinds of reports you can create with this product.

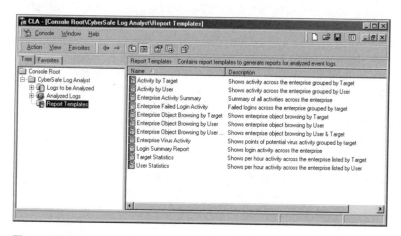

Figure 16-8.   *Log Analyst provides a few of the more common reports you need as predefined templates.*

Seagate Crystal Reports 6

Trying to do Crystal Reports justice in the space of a chapter section is like trying to tell someone all about *War and Peace* in a sentence. This product is huge, it's feature-complete, and it's going to take a long time to learn. (The version of the product I used for this chapter was notably easier than previous versions because it includes more automation in the form of wizards, but learning Crystal Reports still isn't something you do in a day.) The fact of the matter is that with this product you can create every kind of report imaginable from just about any data source on your server, and Seagate just keeps improving it with every release. In short, Crystal Reports is a product you use for more than simple PTO purposes; you use it for a wide range of network administration needs and might even find use for it in collaboration with the database administrator.

Note Although the Windows 2000 Resource Kit ships with a sample version of Crystal Reports 6 at the time of this writing, Seagate is currently working on Crystal Reports 8. This upgrade of a product that has long been used to create reports includes an updated engine that support multiple threads of execution, which means you can run multiple print jobs at the same time. The new version also generates reports in both HTML and RTF, which means you can view report output over a Web page. Besides static output, Crystal Reports 8 allows you to create DHTML output. This report format, when coupled with Java or ActiveX controls, allows you to provide fully interactive, presentation-quality reports through a Web site, allowing administrators to review current server status no matter where they're at. You find new graphic formats in this version of the product like Joint Photographic Experts Group (JPEG) and Portable Network Graphics (PNG) files. Crystal Report 8 users are able to create reports using products like Microsoft Office 97 through Office 2000 by clicking a button, rather than using the native Crystal Reports tools. Developers find that the Report Designer Component has been expanded to include multithreading, which means transacted data that relies on Microsoft Transaction Server (MTS) should move faster. Seagate plans to release three versions of Crystal Report 8 including Standard (targeted at business users), Professional (offers complex report handling), and Developer (the version best suited for enterprise tasks).

To give you an idea of just how complex this product is, the first page dialog box you see is the Report Gallery. You can choose from a standard, form letter, form, cross-tab, subreport, mailing label, top N, or drill-down report. If none of these reports provide the format you need, there's also an option to create your own custom report format. There really isn't any limit to the number of formats you can use—all it takes is a bit of imagination to come up with something new.

Once you finish selecting a report format, you have to choose a data source. Don't get the idea that you're going to be limited to what you find in an event log somewhere. You can choose a data file, a query, an SQL/ODBC connection, a data dictionary, Microsoft Exchange, Microsoft SQL Server, a Web log, or an event log. About the only Windows 2000-specific entity that's missing is Active Directory services (I have no doubt Seagate will add support for Active Directory in the future).

Of all the data sources we covered, it's likely the data you need appears in one of the event logs, or in a custom database designed to hold the output from various performance counters. No matter what data source you use, you need to choose specific fields within that data source as your next step in creating a report. This means determining a sort order for your data and the fields you want to use to create totals. Finally, you choose the style of output you want for graphs and reports. Crystal Reports gives you all the standard options here and probably a few more. For example, instead of giving you just one pie chart, Crystal Reports allows you to create a standard pie, multiple pie, or weighted pie chart. Just figuring out which of the literally thousands of options you want to use to achieve a specific result with the data you've collected could take some time and experimentation.

Hardware-Oriented Tools

A lot of the hardware currently on the market comes with its own diagnostic and tuning aids. This is a welcome change from years past when you'd get a barely usable diagnostic utility, or nothing at all. If you do have a piece of hardware that doesn't come with both diagnostic and tuning aids, this is the first area you need to cover. Most generic diagnostic packages in use today also come with some form of tuning software. In some cases, you also find that the packages help you develop an inventory of the system in question.

Tuning individual pieces of hardware usually isn't enough to ensure that the hardware works to its full capacity. Likewise, diagnosing hardware errors on a component-by-component basis doesn't help much when an interaction between two pieces is the real cause of a problem. As a result, you need diagnostic and tuning software that can evaluate the system as whole, rather than at a component level. You always need third-party software to accomplish this second goal—none of the software that comes with the piece of hardware tests the hardware's interaction with other hardware on your server or helps you tune the system as a whole. The reason is simple: Most hardware vendors are only interested in allowing you to perform intense examinations of their hardware.

Tip   Generic third-party diagnostic programs allow you to test your system as a whole and perform generic testing of individual components. However, hardware vendors make money by differentiating their product from similar products on the market through the use of additional features. A display adapter might support some standard set of resolution and color depth, but it might also support resolutions and color depths that exceed the normal display as an added feature. Of course, your generic diagnostic software doesn't support these "extra" hardware features. That's why the vendor-supplied software is so important. Although this software doesn't do much for the server as a whole, it tests the special features of any hardware that it does support. In short, your hardware strategy should include a combination of generic diagnostic and tuning software, and custom software provided by the hardware vendor.

Now that you have a better idea of what kinds of hardware-oriented tuning software we're going to examine, it's time to review products. The following sections cover some third-party tools that fall into the hardware diagnostic and tuning category. The descriptions don't include prices, since the price of software changes relatively quickly and depends on where you're located. The version numbers are current as of this writing, but are subject to change.

More Info   A lot of the new tools in this chapter use the Microsoft Installer (MSI) file, which is also known as a package. In fact, use of the Microsoft Installer is one of the logo requirements for Windows 2000. Sometimes, the way you install a product plays a role in the way the product operates later. Certainly, the installation options you use control what the user sees as the product gets installed. Finally, when installing a product on the server from a remote location, you don't want dialog boxes to pop up on the display. For all these reasons and more, it pays to know the MSI file command line options. You can find a complete list of all the command line switches at *http://support.microsoft.com/support/kb/articles/q227/0/91.asp?LNG=ENG&SA=TECH*. If you're also a developer and need additional information about MSI, look at the software development kit (SDK) site at *http://msdn.microsoft.com/downloads/sdks/platform/wininst.asp*. Finally, there are some helpful hints about creating installation programs at *http://www.installsite.org/*. Even though this last site concentrates on information about past Windows installation techniques, there's an entirely new section on Windows 2000 that you should view.

Executive Software Diskeeper

Most users usually treat maintenance of any kind along the same lines as leprosy. It doesn't take a rocket scientist to figure out that you're probably losing a lot of potential performance because the hard drives on your system aren't optimized. Of course, many network administrators are at a loss about this problem. Going to each machine individually isn't an option, so the hard drives on every workstation on the network slowly clog to the point that you never get the full performance out of your system. Tuning isn't a matter of making a single machine work efficiently; it's a matter of making every machine on the network work efficiently. Diskeeper is one answer to this problem and it even works in the background for you.

Diskeeper works in the background monitoring the hard drives on the network for fragmentation. When it spots a drive that has exceeded a specific level of fragmentation, the drive is automatically defragmented for you in the background. In addition, this product works in mixed environments, so it doesn't matter if you're using a mix of Windows 2000, Windows NT, and Windows 9x machines on the network.

More Info   You can find out about Executive Software products in general at *http://www.diskeeper.com/execsoft.asp*. Executive Software offers a free trial version of Diskeeper. You can find out more about this product and download the trial version at *http://www.execsoft.com/downloads/menu.asp*.

It's important to note that Diskeeper is one of the few certified tools for Windows 2000 at the time of this writing. This means Diskeeper has met all the Microsoft logo requirements, which is no small undertaking. Diskeeper is also designed to work with all Windows support partition types and even works with encrypted files.

Using Diskeeper is much like using the Windows Disk Defragmenter utility. The main difference is the level of detail you get from this utility. It also does a better job of defragmenting drives for you. Figure 16-9 shows a typical example of the output you see from the manual defragmenting portion of this product. Notice that you get a much greater level of detail and that the product provides more in the way of hard drive usage information.

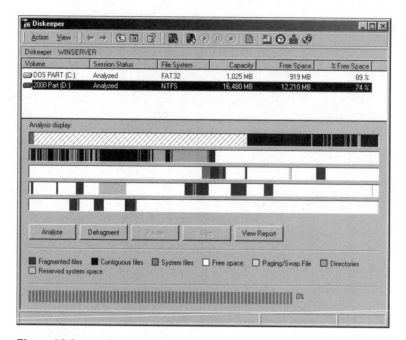

Figure 16-9. *Diskeeper provides you with detailed information about the way your hard drive is used, along with the more common fragmented file information.*

Of course, creating a manual defragmenter that provides a little more information than what you get with Windows 2000 already isn't much of an accomplishment. The real reason you want to get this product is the background defragmenter. This part of the product monitors all participating workstations and the server for fragmentation and removes any fragmentation in the background. In other words, your system gets defragmented manually one time, and then stays defragmented in the background. All you really need to do at the server is perform a quick check of the system from time to time to ensure that everything is working as anticipated. Diskeeper takes care of the rest for you.

Norton CleanSweep

It doesn't matter which version of Windows you talk about, the hard drive eventually gets loaded with crud you don't want to keep around. The Internet has made the problem a lot worse because every Web site has its own special cookies, downloaded files, ActiveX controls, and other files to place on your hard drive. Although most people don't use the Internet features on their server regularly (unless the server is also used as a proxy, in which case, they have lots of opportunities to worry about extraneous files), they do use it on occasion to find new drivers and perform updates on Windows itself.

The problem, especially with servers, is figuring out what to keep and what to get rid of. After all, you can't simply remove files without knowing what they do. In addition, reformatting a server's drive and starting from scratch to ensure the hard drive is clean is usually out of the question. No one in their right mind would do this unless absolutely required. That's where Norton CleanSweep comes into play. It allows you to look for unused or unneeded files on your hard drive. Many people associate this product with something you use on a workstation, but the fact is it also works just fine on your server.

More Info   Have you ever been frustrated by a lack of ability to look at the preboot screens for a machine from a remote location? Anyone who has had to administrate a network has faced this problem. Unfortunately, tuning a network begins with the BIOS settings, which means you need some way to access the machine before it boots Windows 2000. Although there isn't a solution (at least, not one that I know of) available today, the future looks bright for this technology. Phoenix Technologies has a solution available for network vendors. You can read about it at *http://www.phoenix.com/platform/preboot-manager.html*. Although this solution isn't available to end users, you can plan on seeing it sometime in the future.

The latest version of CleanSweep is designed to rid your hard drive of extra Internet files without causing problems for other applications. It uses the same interface as the other Norton products, which means you don't spend a lot of time learning how to use CleanSweep. In fact, Symantec has totally integrated the various Norton products so you can launch them using a single front end. The most important feature, however, is that CleanSweep creates a backup of the files when it first cleans your system. This ensures that absolutely nothing gets deleted that you need to run your system. The file backups get deleted permanently later when you're absolutely sure you no longer need them.

Now that you have some idea of what CleanSweep does for your server's performance, let's talk about system requirements. Any server is going to be able to run this product—at least if that server is modern enough to run Windows 2000. Here are the specifics.

- IBM PC or 100 percent compatible computer
- 80486 or higher processor
- Windows 95, Windows 98, or Windows NT (workstation or server)
- 13 MB of available hard drive space
- 8 MB of RAM for Windows 95 or Windows 98
- 16 MB RAM for Windows NT
- CD-ROM drive
- Minimum 256-color VGA video

More Info   At the time of this writing, the Symantec public Web site contains the list of system requirements shown here. However, independent sources have indicated that they're working on Windows 2000 versions of their product that should be available by the time you read this. Many Windows 2000 products were held up due to new logo requirements. Browse to *http://www.symantec.com/sabu/ qdeck/ncs/* for additional information.

Norton Utilities

The Norton Utilities (or an equivalent product) rank high on the list of must-have software for network administrators. Not only has the software been around since the early days of the PC, but it also contains a veritable Swiss army knife of tools designed to keep track of various system resources. Here's a short list of product features that most network administrators are concerned about.

- Defragment disk drives
- Recover deleted files
- Monitor system resources automatically
- Obtain system information
- Receive free online updates using LiveUpdate

More Info   You can find out about all the Norton products (which are actually sold by Symantec) at *http://www.symantec.com/*. In fact, you find that Symantec markets a wide range of Windows products, most of which help improve performance or security in some way.

It's true Windows 2000 does include defragmentation features now, but some people want a little more in the way of functionality. The Norton Utilities are designed to get the very last bit of fragmentation out of your system for optimum server performance. Some people might consider this overkill, and for some systems it might be. Given that some systems can't spare any performance benefit, total drive defragmentation might not be a bad idea.

Some of the other features are true add-ons to Windows 2000. For example, Windows 2000 still doesn't protect you from deleting files at the command prompt. In many cases, the network administrator needs to perform work at the command prompt, making protection at this level a very good idea. Since the network administrator is about the only one who uses the server console on a regular basis, the Norton Utilities can provide a very real benefit on a server.

System information, at least good system information, is also fairly difficult to get on any system. Windows 2000 does a very good job of identifying new and common hardware, but it could experience problems getting all the details for older or unusual hardware. When you try to troubleshoot this hardware, you find the lack of information difficult to deal with and it definitely hampers your troubleshooting efforts. The server is one place where you don't want to take a lot of time troubleshooting errant hardware, so complete identification is a must.

As with CleanSweep, any server capable of running Windows 2000 is also capable of running Norton Utilities. Here is a list of the system requirements for this product.

- IBM PC or 100 percent compatible
- Windows NT 4.0 (this product doesn't run under DOS, Windows 3.*x*, Windows 95, or Windows NT 3.51)
- 80486 processor minimum
- 16 MB RAM
- 25 MB hard disk space required
- Double-speed CD-ROM drive minimum
- 256 color VGA video minimum

Note   At the time of this writing, the Symantec public Web site contains the list of system requirements shown here. However, independent sources have indicated that they're working on Windows 2000 versions of their product that should be available by the time you read this. Many Windows 2000 products were held up due to new logo requirements.

PowerQuest ServerMagic and DriveCopy

PowerQuest has made a reputation with its disk management products. Many network managers are probably familiar with the PartitionMagic product used to create multiple boot partitions on a single drive. ServerMagic is another in a list of disk management products. It allows a network manager to resize and change the partitions on a server without much effort. You can also use it to copy the entire contents of one drive to another (the kind of copy required when you upgrade a drive on the server and want to move the data without having to reinstall the operating system). In addition, the ability to perform this work isn't limited to the local drive; ServerMagic also works with redundant array of independent disks (RAID) setups and other complex server systems.

You might find that you don't need the full capabilities of ServerMagic for your setup. DriveCopy is another drive management utility. It allows you to copy the contents of one drive to another so you can perform painless server and workstation upgrades. Although you might not need this product every day, it makes life a lot easier when you do. Anyone who's performed a disk upgrade knows the hassles that normally occur when you perform this task.

More Info   You can find out more about PowerQuest's full line of products at *http:// www.powerquest.com/products/l*. The ServerMagic-specific information appears at *http://www.powerquest.com/servermagic/index.html*, while the DriveCopy-specific information appears at *http://www.powerquest.com/drivecopy/index.html*.

TouchStone CheckIt

One of the PTO tasks that network administrators hate to perform is inventorying their machines. There's an easy way to perform this task—allow a program designed for the task to do it for you. CheckIt is more than a hardware inventory program, however. It also includes a variety of diagnostics, a virus scanner, a hard disk formatter, CD-ROM drive diagnostic, and a floppy disk alignment checker. The fact that CheckIt runs from floppies if you need it to is a real plus if you don't want to maintain a DOS partition on your server. (You need three floppies: one boot, one for CheckIt, and a third for SysTest.)

More Info   TouchStone updates CheckIt regularly to keep up with current hardware technology. The latest version offers expanded test features that the original product doesn't include. The most important update is the ability to test advanced Intel Pentium II/III features. The amount of memory you can test has also increased, along with the capabilities of just about every other test. Of course, this version also includes updates for the CD-ROM test that was one of the new features in the 4.0 product. TouchStone doesn't recommend the use of WinCheckIt with Windows NT or Windows 2000. This means you need to use the DOS version of the product only. Be sure to contact TouchStone for the updated version at *http://www.touchstonesoftware.com/products/products.htm*.

Network-Specific Tools

In some ways, a network could be looked at as the living element of your system. After all, it grows and shrinks as the result of outside stimulus and two networks are unlikely to be the same, even if they do have similar attributes. This makes the network the hardest part of your system to tune. It's difficult to create a single or even a suite of tools that works with the vast majority of networks out there. Network tuning often lags behind other areas of your system simply because the right tool to do the job isn't available.

There are, however, those attributes that allow one network to communicate with another network. You can even say such attributes make your network part of a family of networks with similar attributes. It's this family resemblance that we focus on in the chapter. Generic third-party tools need to concentrate on the similarities between network hardware and software to provide some level of generic tuning.

Of course, at some point, you get the network tuned in a generic way and look for ways to provide further performance benefits through additional tuning. This is where custom software comes into play. Although we don't look at custom software in this chapter, it's important to understand the need for this kind of software in some circumstances. If you're running a very large network and need every last ounce of performance from it, custom software might be a viable option. Using custom software could help you derive additional tuning benefits.

As you can see, networks are usually unique and hard to categorize. They do, however, have certain attributes that are the same for a given network type, no matter how you look at other network elements. The following sections cover some third-party tools that fall into the network administration and diagnostic category. We don't look at software that performs some special task on a particular network. These sections concentrate on software that's generic and could work across several network types. The descriptions don't include prices, since the price of software changes relatively quickly and depends on where you're located. The version numbers are current as of this writing, but are subject to change.

Intergraph SmartSketch LE

Intergraph has been making various kinds of drawing software and other products for longer than most users can remember. Of course, the big question is why you need this product in the first place. The answer is simple: Part of our capacity-planning chapter revolved around the need for a graphical representation of the network. Since this is a very good drawing package and you get a sample with the Windows 2000 Resource Kit, it's also a very good choice for seeing what you need to maintain the graphical record of your network. (Anyone who thinks they can do an adequate job with Microsoft Paint, at this point, is either working with a very small network or just hasn't tried drawing something large with Paint recently.)

Interestingly enough, SmartSketch includes all the symbols you need to diagram your network—they just aren't readily apparent when you first start the program. Look in the Symbols\Diagramming\Network directory and you see a lot of subdirectories containing predrawn network components. Figure 16-10 shows a typical view of SmartSketch. Notice the Symbol Explorer on the right side. It contains three windows. The top window allows you to find the symbol location on a hard drive or other storage resource. The middle window shows the symbols in that location. In this case, we're looking at bridges and routers. Finally, the bottom window shows the attributes for the selected symbol on the drawing. (It doesn't show the attributes until you actually place a copy of the symbols on the drawing area.)

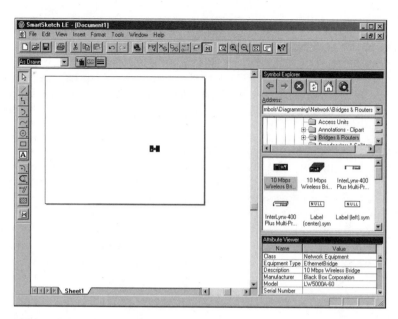

Figure 16-10. *SmartSketch provides a full set of network symbols, which is all you need to diagram your network for capacity-planning purposes.*

More Info SmartSketch is a relatively complex product that allows you to draw more than just network diagrams. You can use this product to design new products as well as document an existing network configuration. Intergraph offers training, a gallery of symbols, and even a few free downloads of their product at *http://www.intergraph.com/smartsketch*. The gallery is impressive and includes a variety of drawing types. You can even choose whether you want to see the drawing in bitmap format or download the CAD file. Even more impressive is that you can download an evaluation copy of their current product (at least as of this writing).

Along with the symbols, SmartSketch contains all the tools you normally associate with a basic CAD program (or any high-end drawing program for that matter). You can create lines of various types, dimension those lines, and place objects on different layers to keep them separated. A full tour of a drawing package is outside the realm of what we can cover here, but learning to use this product is well worth the effort.

Summary

This chapter has reviewed a variety of third-party tools. Each of these tools can help you tune your system to get the very most out of the resources your server can provide. In many cases, tuning is a matter of perception—it's based on what you expect to get out of the server. With this in mind, not every tool listed here works on every network. In some cases, the goals for your network conflict with the end results that the tool can provide. This means you need to buy tools wisely. Keep your goals in mind as you test the tool rather than getting distracted by the "gee whiz" factor that some tools produce.

The chapter began with a look of shareware tools. It's important to understand that the "try before you buy" concept of buying software is relatively old in the PC arena. It allows a small vendor with few marketing resources to compete with larger tool vendors. In many cases, the quality of the tools you get from a shareware vendor exceeds those of other vendors on the market—that's how some shareware vendors grow up to become industry leaders. Obviously, not every piece of shareware is high quality; but, at the very least, shareware can help you learn about the kind of software that you actually need to tune your system.

Off-the-shelf shrink-wrapped tools provide you with a sense of security about the tuning tools you're using to maintain your network. There are many different categories of off-the-shelf tools, many of which test very esoteric areas of the server. This chapter concentrated on three main areas of tuning: general administration, hardware, and network. You should have a much better idea of the kinds of software available now for tuning, but never assume a particular category of software isn't available because I haven't listed it here. Make sure you check vendor catalogs and online; you might be surprised at what you find.

At this point, you've read about all the tuning topics in this book. It's important to realize that your network is unique and that you probably need to add to the information you learned here. The next section of the book contains the Glossary, which contains a list of every new or unfamiliar acronym used throughout the book and a list of terms you might need help with.

Glossary

This glossary has several important features you need to be aware of. First, every relatively new or unfamiliar acronym in the entire book is listed here—even if there's a better-than-even chance you already know what the acronym means. This way there isn't any doubt that you'll always find everything you need to use the book properly. The second thing you need to know is that these definitions are specific to the book. In other words, when you look through this glossary, you're seeing the words defined in the context in which they're used. This might or might not always coincide with current industry usage since the computer industry changes the meaning of words so often. Finally, the definitions here use a conversational tone in most cases. This means they might sacrifice a bit of puritanical accuracy for the sake of better understanding.

More Info   What happens if you can't find the acronym you need in the computer dictionary you just bought? Fortunately, there are at least two sites on the Internet that you can go to for help. The first is the University of Texas site at *http://www-hep.uta.edu/~variable/e_comm/pages/r_dic-en.htm*. This site is updated fairly often and provides only acronyms (another page at the same site includes a glossary). The second site is Acronym Finder. You find it at *http://www.acronymfinder.com/*. Although this site isn't updated as often as the first one, it does have the advantage of providing an extremely large list of acronyms to choose from. At the time of this writing, the Acronym Finder sported 141,000 acronyms. If neither of these sites provides what you need, you might want to look at A Web of Online Dictionaries at *http://www.yourdictionary.com/*. One of the interesting features of this Web site is that it provides access to more than one dictionary and in more than one language.

There are always other online solutions, many of which are free. For example, Webopedia has become one of my favorite places to visit because it provides encyclopedic coverage of many computer terms and includes links to other Web sites. You can find Webopedia at *http://webopedia.internet.com*. In some cases, such as Microsoft's Encarta (*http://encarta.msn.com*), you have to pay for the support provided, but it's still worth the effort to seek out these locations to ensure that you always understand the terms used in our jargon-filled trade.

A

Accelerated Graphics Port (AGP) A special PC bus used specifically for display adapters. An AGP-based display adapter can operate at much higher speeds than the normal ISA or PCI bus allows. What this means to the user is that display speeds are much higher. In addition to making the display adapter faster, AGP also allows the adapter to directly access main memory as if it were part of the adapter's private memory storage. This in turn allows the display adapter to store more complex objects like textures, which are used to improve display appearance.

access token A definition of the rights a service or resource requester has to the operating system. This is the data structure that tells the security system what rights a user has to access a particular object. The object's access requirements are contained in a security descriptor. In short, the security descriptor is the lock and the access token is the key.

ACPI *See* Advanced Configuration and Power Interface.

Active Directory Service Interfaces (ADSI) Enables Windows 95, Windows 98, Windows NT, and Windows 2000 applications to access and interact with various directory services, including Active Directory services, NetWare Directory Services, and LDAP.

Active Directory services The directory service of the Windows 2000 operating system. Active Directory services offers network administrators a more scalable, flexible, and interoperable directory service than its predecessor (Windows NT directory services). Active Directory services offers a single point of administration for all network objects, which are organized using a hierarchical display. Through its transitive domain proper-

ties, users can have access to any resource on the network through a single login.

Active Server Pages (ASP) A special type of scripting environment used by Windows 2000 and Windows NT Server equipped with IIS. This specialized scripting environment allows the programmer to create very flexible Web server scripts using a scripting language like VBScript. The use of variables and other features, such as access to server variables, allows a programmer to create scripts that can compensate for user and environmental needs as well as security concerns. Active Server Pages use HTML to display content to the user.

ActiveX Control *See* OLE Custom eXtension.

ADSI *See* Active Directory Service Interfaces.

Advanced Configuration and Power Interface (ACPI) A specification that defines specific behaviors for the way PCs manage power and configure devices. This includes tasks like enumerating the boards installed on the motherboard and providing a power management timer. The specification also provides for optional features like supporting fan control and a number of CPU power states.

AGP *See* Accelerated Graphics Port.

American Standard Code for Information Interchange (ASCII) A standard method of equating the numeric representations available in a computer to human-readable form. The number 32 represents a space, for example. The standard ASCII code contains 128 characters (7 bits). The extended ASCII code uses 8 bits for 256 characters. Display adapters from the same machine type usually use the same upper 128 characters. Printers, however, might reserve these upper

128 characters for nonstandard characters. Many Epson printers use them for the italic representations of the lower 128 characters, however.

API *See* application programming interface.

application programming interface (API) A standard set of function calls and other interface elements. It usually defines the interface between a high-level language and the lower level elements used by a device driver or operating system. The ultimate goal is to provide some type of service to an application that requires access to the operating system or device feature set.

ASCII *See* American Standard Code for Information Interchange.

ASP *See* Active Server Pages.

B

basic input/output system (BIOS) A set of low-level computer interface functions stored in a chip on a computer's motherboard. BIOS performs basic tasks like booting the computer during startup and performing the power-on startup tests (POST). DOS relied heavily on BIOS to perform all types of low-level device interface tasks. In most cases, Windows 95 relies on BIOS a lot less and Windows NT not at all (except for the act of booting the computer system initially).

BIOS *See* basic input/output system.

bottleneck The perceptible slowing of a system due to excess resource requirements by an application or user. A bottleneck might also appear when there's a disparity in the performance potential between two system components. Bottlenecks are normally classified by type. For example, a disk bottleneck could be caused by an application that uses disk resources excessively, or by hardware that's incapable of keeping up with other machine elements like the processor.

C

cache buffers A term that refers to the smallest storage elements in a cache (an area of RAM devoted to storing commonly used pieces of information normally stored on the hard drive). Think of each buffer as a box that can store a single piece of information. The more buffers (boxes) you have, the greater the storage capacity of the cache.

CAD *See* computer-aided design.

CDFS *See* Compact Disc File System.

CGI *See* Common Gateway Interface.

child domain A domain located directly beneath its parent domain. For example, "marketing.microsoft.com" is the child domain of the parent domain "microsoft.com."

CLB *See* Component Load Balancing.

client The recipient of data, services, or resources from a file or other server. This term can refer to a workstation or an application. The server can be another PC or an application.

cluster administrator The graphical user interface (GUI) administration tool for the Windows 2000 Cluster Service. Cluster administrator allows you to manage and configure cluster nodes, groups, and resources.

Cluster-Aware Application An application written so it runs on a cluster node and can be managed as a cluster resource. The application must be written to use the Cluster API; otherwise it cannot communicate with other resources and nodes in the cluster.

Cluster Service The service running on Windows 2000 Advanced or Datacenter servers that controls all aspects of server cluster operation. Each node in the cluster runs an instance of Cluster Service.

CMOS *See* complementary metal-oxide semiconductor.

COM *See* Component Object Model.

Common Gateway Interface (CGI) One of the more common methods of transferring data from a client machine to a Web server on the Internet. CGI is a specification that defines how a Web server can launch EXEs and communicate with them. A GCI application is normally written with a low-level language like C and is designed to receive input through the standard input device and output data through the standard output device. There are two basic data transfer types. The user can send new information to the server or can query data already existing on the server. A data entry form asking for the user's name and address is an example of the first type of transaction. A search engine page on the Internet (a page that helps the user find information on other sites) is an example of the second type of transaction. The Web server normally provides some type of feedback for the user by transmitting a new page of information once the CGI application is complete. This could be as simple as an acknowledgment for data entry or a list of Internet sites for a data query.

Compact Disc File System (CDFS) The portion of the file subsystem specifically designed to interact with compact disc drives. It also provides the user with interface elements required to tune this part of the subsystem. CDFS takes the place of an FSD for CD-ROM drives.

complementary metal-oxide semiconductor (CMOS) Normally refers to a construction method for low-power, battery-backed memory. When used in the context of a PC, this term usually refers to the memory used to store system configuration information and the real-time clock status. The configuration information normally includes the amount of system memory, the type and size of floppy drives, the hard drive parameters, and the video display type. Some vendors include other configurations as part of this chip as well.

Component Load Balancing (CLB) A specialized form of load balancing that deals with the ability of COM+ applications to balance the processing load across multiple servers at the component level. CLB allows the application to perform load balancing at a finer level, which means the processing load is better distributed across the processing elements. This also allows multiple servers to handle requests from a single client, potentially increasing data throughput by an order of magnitude.

Component Object Model (COM) A Microsoft specification for an object-oriented code and data encapsulation method and transference technique. It's the replacement for technologies such as OLE and implemented by ActiveX (the replacement name for OCXs—an object-oriented code library technology). COM is limited to local connections. DCOM (distributed component object model) is the technology used to allow data transfers and the use of objects within the distributed environment. (DCOM, however, will eventually be replaced by SOAP (Simple Object Access Protocol).)

Component Services A set of services in Windows 2000 that are based on Microsoft Transaction Server (MTS) and extensions of the Component Object Model (COM). Component Services is a transaction processing system for developing, deploying, and managing distributed server applications. Component Services is also the name of a snap-in for Microsoft Management Console (MMC) where administrators and developers can administer COM+ applications and distributed transactions.

computer-aided design (CAD) A special type of graphics program used for creating, printing, storing, and editing architectural, electrical, mechanical, or other forms of engineering drawings. CAD programs normally provide precise measuring capabilities and libraries of predefined objects, such as sinks, desks, resistors, and gears.

cooked data Data that has been processed in some way before transmission to another location. For example, output from a computer to a printer is often changed to bitmap format so that the printer can output it directly. Contrast this to raw data, which isn't processed in any way.

D

data spike The point at which the value recorded by a performance counter reaches its maximum potential. Data spikes are normally short in duration and look very much like an inverted spike when displayed on a graph.

database management system (DBMS) A method for storing and retrieving data based on tables, forms, queries, reports, fields, and other data elements. Each field represents a specific piece of data, such as an employee's last name. Records are made up of one or more fields. Each record is one complete entry in a table. A table contains one type of data, such as the names and ad-

dresses of all the employees in a company. It's composed of records (rows) and fields (columns), just like the tables you see in books. A database might contain one or more related tables. It might include a list of employees in one table, for example, and the pay records for each of those employees in a second table.

DBMS *See* database management system.

DDK *See* driver development kit.

DDR SDRAM *See* Double Data Rate Synchronous Dynamic Random Access Memory.

delegation Rather than assigning responsibilities to the entire namespace, network administrators can delegate permission to certain portions of the namespace.

dense wavelength, division multiplexed (DWDM) One of several methods used to enhance the performance characteristics of fiber-optic networks. This method multiplexes several signals together prior to transmission, and then demultiplexes them after transmission. The use of more than one signal path ensures that the entire bandwidth of the cable is used. These systems include high-quality components like splitters, couplers, and optical amplifiers.

DHCP A method for automatically determining the IP address on a TCP/IP connection. A server provides this address to the client as part of the setup communications. Using DHCP means a server can use fewer addresses to communicate with clients and that clients don't need to provide a hard-coded address to the server. You must configure your server to provide these services.

DIP *See* dual inline package.

direct memory access (DMA) A method addressing technique in which the processor doesn't perform the actual data transfer. This method of memory access is faster than any other technique.

Direct Rambus Dynamic Random Access Memory (DRDRAM) A memory technology that partially builds on the techniques used by SDRAM. It uses a special bus known as the Direct Rambus Channel, a 400 MHz 16-bit bus. It might seem counterproductive at first to reduce the width of the data bus (current machine architectures are at 64 bits and moving toward 128 bits), but the reduction in width allows the higher bus clock speed. DRDRAM transfers data on both the up and down stroke of the clock, effectively doubling the transfer rate. Theoretically, DRDRAM should be able to move data at 1.6 GB/s. DRDRAM also uses a different construction method. In this case, we're talking about the same methods used to create CMOS chips. These are the same chips used to store computer configuration information. The use of this low component count construction technique allows DRDRAM to provide higher performance than SDRAM at a lower level of power consumption.

disk duplexing The process of running two hard disk drive subsystems in parallel. The drives are paired from one subsystem to the other and contain the same information. The drive subsystems are totally separate, which means one drive can take over for the other in the event of any drive or controller failure.

disk mirroring The process of running two hard disk drives in parallel. The two drives share the same controller. They also contain the same information. One drive can take over for the other in the event of a drive failure. This redundant method of data storage doesn't provide any backup for the drive controller.

disk operating system *See* DOS.

dispatcher objects One of a group of kernel-defined objects like timers, events, mutexes, and semaphores used by the operating system to manage the system state. Even thread objects created by the kernel are considered dispatch objects. Every dispatch object has two states: signaled and nonsignaled. Normally, a thread waits for a nonsignaled dispatcher object to register a state change. As soon as the state change does occur, the state of the object is signaled and the waiting thread continues execution.

distinguished name (DN) The name that helps identify not only the object within Active Directory services but also the container objects and domains that contain that object. For example, CN=Naila, CN=Users, DC=Microsoft, DC=com. This identifies Naila as a user in the Microsoft.com domain.

Distributed interNet Architecture A term used to describe Microsoft's vision of a three-tier development architecture. The three tiers include the user's desktop, business logic processing on a middle-tier server, and database processing on a back-end server. DNA is used to help emphasize various features of Microsoft products like Visual Studio and to help the developer modularize large-scale applications.

DLL *See* dynamic-link library.

DMA *See* direct memory access.

DN *See* distinguished name.

DNA *See* Distributed interNet Architecture.

DNS (Domain Name System) The naming service used by Windows 2000 Server when deploying Active Directory services. Environments that do not choose to use Active Directory services and instead stay with the Windows NT directory service can continue to use Windows Internet Naming Service (WINS) or a host table (such as LMHOSTS) as the naming service of choice.

domain forest A collection of domain trees or noncontiguous domains that share a common schema, global catalog, or configuration.

Domain Name System *See* DNS.

domain tree The result of two or more Windows 2000 domains forming a contiguous namespace through a set of hierarchical relationships. For example, when a bidirectional trust relationship is created between two domains, they form a domain tree. Multiple domain trees form a domain forest. *See also* domain forest.

DOS The underlying software used by many PCs to provide basic system services and to allow the user to run application software. The operating system performs many low-level tasks through BIOS. The specifics of the services it offers are defined by the current revision number of the software; check your user manual for details.

Double Data Rate Synchronous Dynamic Random Access Memory (DDR DRAM) A memory technology built on the data storage techniques used by SDRAM. The only difference is that this type of RAM transfers data on both the up and the down clock. In essence, it transfers data at twice the speed because it transfers data twice per clock cycle.

DRDRAM *See* Direct Rambus Dynamic Random Access Memory.

driver A special operating system file that allows some presentation graphic programs to send data to an output device.

driver development kit (DDK) A special set of libraries—including files, source code, and utility programs—designed to augment the native capabilities of a programming language product. A programmer normally writes driver software to allow applications or the operating system to communicate with the underlying hardware in some way. A DDK is designed to make the development of such software easier. Most drivers are written to run at the operating system level, so the associated DDK provides utility programs that also operate at that level.

dual inline package (DIP) A method of encasing computer chip circuitry that relies on two rows of parallel pins to make contact between the chip circuitry and the circuit board.

DWDM *See* dense wavelength, division multiplexed.

Dynamic Host Configuration Protocol *See* DHCP.

dynamic-link library (DDL) A specific form of application code loaded into memory by request. It's not executable by itself. A DLL does contain one or more discrete routines that an application might use to provide specific features. For example, a DLL could provide a common set of file dialog boxes used to access information on the hard drive. More than one application can use the functions provided by a DLL, reducing overall memory requirements when more than one application is running.

E

ECC *See* error-correcting code.

EDO DRAM *See* Extended Data Out Dynamic Random Access Memory.

EMF *See* Enhanced Metafile Format.

Enhanced Metafile Format (EMF) Used as an alternative storage format by some graphics applications. This is a vector graphic format, so it provides a certain level of device independence and other features that a vector graphic normally provides.

error-correcting code (ECC) Originally meant a self-diagnostic technique used to correct errors in RAM. The term now includes the same type of diagnostics provided with tape, hard disk, and floppy disk drives. In all cases, the device uses some type of microcode contained in a peripheral chip to detect and correct soft errors in the data stream.

Extended Data Out Dynamic Random Access Memory (EDO DRAM) A type of DRAM that buffers the address data and the output data. This change represents a major reduction in circuitry and still enhances performance. EDO DRAM works by loading the column address data in a buffer. The entire page of RAM is read into a buffer, the correct column selected, and the data is then output while the next incoming address is buffered.

F

FC-AL *See* Fibre Channel Arbitrated Loop.

Fibre Channel Arbitrated Loop (FC-AL) One method of connecting devices in a SAN to a special server-only network. This is normally considered part of the SAN interface component of a SAS system.

file system driver (FSD) A file subsystem component responsible for defining the interface between Windows and long-term storage. The FSD also defines features such as long filenames and what types of interaction the device supports. For example, the CD-ROM FSD wouldn't support file writes

unless you provided a device that could perform that sort of task.

File Transfer Protocol *See* FTP.

FSD *See* file system driver.

FTP (File Transfer Protocol) One of several common data transfer protocols for the Internet. This particular protocol specializes in data transfer in the form of a file download. The user is presented with a list of available files in a directory list format. An FTP site might choose DOS or UNIX formatting for the file listing, although the DOS format is extremely rare. Unlike HTTP sites, an FTP site provides a definite information hierarchy through the use of directories and subdirectories, much like the file directory structure used on most workstation hard drives.

G

GC *See* Global Catalog.

General Protection Fault (GPF) A processor or memory error that occurs when an application makes a request that the system can't honor. This type of error results in some kind of severe action on the part of the operating system. Normally, the operating system terminates the offending application.

Global Catalog (GC) Stores a partial replica of every domain in Active Directory services. GC is used to increase performance in searches performed against Active Directory services by only storing those attributes of Active Directory objects most frequently used in search operations. For example, GC stores a user object's first name and last name but not a custom attribute such as a user's date of hire (network administrators have the choice of adding additional attributes to be stored in GC after the catalog has been installed and configured).

Gopher One of several common Internet data transfer protocols. Like FTP, Gopher specializes in file transfers. However, the two protocols differ in that Gopher always uses the UNIX file-naming convention and it provides a friendlier interface than FTP. Even though Gopher transfers tend to be more reliable than those provided by FTP, FTP sites are far more common.

GPF *See* General Protection Fault.

H

HAL *See* hardware abstraction layer.

hardware abstraction layer (HAL) A conceptual element of the Windows NT architecture. Microsoft wrote the drivers and other software elements in such a way that it could easily move Windows NT to other platforms. That's how it moved Windows NT to the MIPS and Alpha machines. The basic architecture of Windows NT is the same, but the low-level drivers—the ones that directly interface with the hardware—are different. The important fact to remember is that as far as your application is concerned, it's still running on an Intel machine. The only time you run into trouble is if your application bypasses the Windows API and goes directly to the hardware.

histogram A special variation of the bar graph that shows the frequency with which a data point appears within a specific range.

HTML *See* Hypertext Markup Language.

HTTP *See* Hypertext Transfer Protocol.

Hypertext Markup Language (HTML)
1. A scripting language for the Internet that depends on the use of tags (keywords within angle brackets <>) to display formatted information onscreen in a nonplatform-specific manner. The nonplatform-specific nature of this scripting language makes it difficult to perform some basic tasks such as placement of a screen element at a specific location. However, the language does provide for the use of fonts, color, and various other enhancements onscreen. There are also tags for displaying graphic images. Scripting tags for using more complex scripting languages such as VBScript and JavaScript were recently added, although not all browsers support this addition. The latest tag addition allows the use of ActiveX controls. **2.** One method of displaying text, graphics, and sound on the Internet. HTML provides an ASCII-formatted page of information read by a special application called a browser. Depending on the browser's capabilities, some keywords are translated into graphics elements, sounds, or text with special characteristics, such as color, font, or other attributes. Most browsers discard any keywords they don't recognize, allowing browsers of various capabilities to explore the same page without problem. If a browser doesn't support a specific keyword, there's a loss of capability.

Hypertext Transfer Protocol (HTTP) One of several common data transfer protocols for the Internet. This particular protocol specializes in the display of onscreen information such as data entry forms or information displays. HTTP relies on HTML as a scripting language for describing special screen display elements, although you can also use HTTP to display nonformatted text.

I

IDE *See* Integrated Development Environment.

IIS *See* Internet Information Services.

input The process of entering information into a program. Input takes many forms, the most common of which is through the keyboard, mouse, communications port, and other programs.

input/output request packet (IRP) The messaging and data transfer vehicle used by Windows device drivers. It allows the device driver to define the work that needs to be performed and acts as a container for the associated data.

integral subsystem An operating system component that's part of a larger element like the managers that are part of a service. An integral subsystem is normally a specialized component that acts as a server for a specific purpose like security.

Integrated Development Environment (IDE) A programming language front end that provides all the tools you need to write an application through a single editor. Older DOS programming language products provided several utilities—one for each of the main programming tasks. Most (if not all) Windows programming languages provide some kind of IDE support.

Internet Information Services (IIS) Microsoft's full-fledged Web server that normally runs under the Windows NT Server operating system. IIS includes all the features you normally expect with a Web server: FTP, HTTP, and Gopher protocols along with both mail and news services. Both Windows NT Workstation and Windows 95 can run PWS, which is a scaled-down version of IIS.

IRP *See* input/output request packet.

K

kernel The set of drivers, low-level functions, executables, and other constructs required to create the core of an operating system. The kernel is responsible for honoring application requests for device and data access. It also provides security and system-level functionality.

L

LAN *See* local area network.

LDAP *See* Lightweight Directory Access Protocol.

Lightweight Directory Access Protocol (LDAP) A set of protocols used to access directories that is based on a simplified version of the X.500 standard. Unlike X.500, LDAP provides support for TCP/IP, a requirement for Internet communication. LDAP makes it possible for a client to request directory information like e-mail addresses and public keys from any server. In addition, since LDAP is an open protocol, applications need not worry about the type of server used to host the directory.

local area network (LAN) Two or more devices connected using a combination of hardware and software. The devices, normally computers and peripheral equipment such as printers, are called nodes. A NIC provides the hardware communication between nodes through an appropriate medium (cable or microwave transmission.)

There are two common types of LANs (also called networks). Peer-to-peer networks allow each node to connect to any other node on the network with shareable resources. This is a distributed method of files and peripheral devices. A client-server network uses one or more servers to share resources. This is a centralized method of sharing files and peripheral devices. A server provides resources to clients (usually workstations). The most common server is the file server, which provides file-sharing resources. Other server types include print servers and communication servers.

local procedure call (LPC) A method of accessing a function that is located outside the application's current process but within a process found on the same machine.

LPC *See* local procedure call.

M

mean time between failures (MTBF) A reliability statistic that predicts the average life of a device based on the component structure of that device and real-world testing. This number represents the amount of time the average device runs before it requires replacement. Some devices run longer and others shorter than the number of hours specified using MTBF. MTBF is designed to allow companies to plan a component replacement strategy.

memory fragmentation A type of memory bottleneck that occurs when an operating system is left running for extended periods. The allocation and deallocation of memory by applications can leave pockets of memory too small to handle typical application requests, even though there's more than enough

memory to handle the request. The result of memory fragmentation is a loss of performance due to increased disk thrashing as the operating system moves data from physical memory to the hard drive and back again.

Message Queuing A messaging infrastructure in Windows 2000. In previous versions, Message Queuing was called Microsoft Message Queue Server or MSMQ 1.0. Developers can use Message Queuing to build large-scale distributed systems with reliable communications. Message Queuing uses temporary storage locations, called queues, to ensure that messages reach their destination, even when networked systems are unavailable.

message transfer agent (MTA) An X.400 standard term that refers to the part of a message transfer system (MTS) responsible for interacting with the client. For example, in an e-mail system, MTA delivers e-mail to the individual users of that system.

message transfer system (MTS) A method of transferring mail from one location to another. In most cases, this requires some form of encryption along with other transport-specific issues. Most NOSs provide some types of MTS as part of their base services. However, the Internet requires special transport mechanisms. Several standards are available on the Internet for providing MTS as part of a Web site. The two most notable specifications are the IETF RFC1421 from the IETF and X.400 from the ITU (formerly CCITT). (This term may also be known as a message transfer service in some operating systems.)

Microsoft Distributed Transaction Coordinator (MS DTC) The Windows service that manages transactions. MS DTC was originally sold as a separate product designed to ensure that database entries were processed at least once, but only once. The product is provided as part of Windows 2000 COM+. It now allows the transactional processing of both objects and data.

Microsoft Management Console (MMC)
A special application that acts as an object container for Windows management objects like Component Services and Computer Management. The management objects are actually special components that provide interfaces that allow them to be used within MMC to maintain and control the operation of Windows. A developer can create special versions of these objects for application management or other tasks. Using a single application like MMC helps maintain the same user interface across all management applications.

MMC *See* Microsoft Management Console.

MS DTC *See* Microsoft Distributed Transaction Coordinator.

MTA *See* message transfer agent.

MTBF *See* mean time between failures.

MTS *See* message transfer system.

multimaster replication The replication method used by Active Directory services to synchronize domain data between domain controllers within a given domain. Multimaster replication differs from master/slave replication, the replication method used with Windows NT directory service. Multimaster replication allows updates to be applied to any domain controller in the domain; master/slave replication required that all updates be applied against the PDC of the domain.

multitasking The ability of some processor and operating environment/system combina-

tions to perform more than one task at a time. The applications appear to run simultaneously. For example, you could download messages from an online service, print from a word processor, and recalculate a spreadsheet at the same time. Each application receives a slice of time before the processor moves on to the next application. Because the time slices are fairly small, it appears to the user as if these actions occur simultaneously.

mutex One of several synchronization methodologies supported by Windows. This particular form provides mutually exclusive access to a resource, which means no other application can access the resource while another application has a lock on it. Mutexes are normally used by high-level drivers like the FSDs.

N

network interface card (NIC) The device responsible for allowing a workstation to communicate with the file server and other workstations. It provides the physical means for creating the connection. The card plugs into an expansion slot in the computer. A cable that attaches to the back of the card completes the communication path.

NIC *See* network interface card.

NTFS *See* Windows NT file system.

O

object When used in the OLE sense of the word, a representation of all or part of a graphic, text, sound, or other data file within a compound document. An object retains its original format and properties. The client application must call on the server application to change or manipulate the object.

When used in the COM sense of the word, the encapsulation of data and code into one file. COM objects don't allow direct manipulation of the data they contain. Data is manipulated through the use of methods that the object contains. In most cases, data manipulation is limited to a list of properties exposed by the object that define the object's operation and other characteristics. Some objects generate events in response to certain types of stimulus by either the system or user. Objects can also receive event notifications through the use of sinks. *See also* Component Object Model.

object linking and embedding (OLE) The process of packaging a filename, application name, and any required parameters into an object, then pasting this object into the file created by another application. For example, you could place a graphic object within a word processing document or spreadsheet. When you look at the object, it appears as if you simply pasted the data from the originating application into the current application (similar to Dynamic Data Exchange). The data provided by the object automatically changes as you change the data in the original object. Often you can start the originating application and automatically load the required data by double-clicking on the object.

OCX *See* OLE Custom eXtension.

OLE *See* object linking and embedding.

OLE Custom eXtension (OCX) A special form of Visual Basic eXtension (VBX) designed to make adding OLE capabilities to an application easier for the programmer. Essentially, an OCX is a DLL with an added program design and OLE interface. As the OCX has evolved, its name has changed to reflect added capability. The most common name for an OCX now is an ActiveX Control.

This name reflects the ability of controls to add capabilities to a wide range of applications, including the Web pages used by browsers.

optical return loss (ORL) A measurement of the amount of light degradation within a fiber-optic cable due to the reflectivity of the glass. The light is bounced back to the source and is therefore unavailable for data transmission.

ORL *See* optical return loss.

P

PCI *See* Peripheral Component Interconnect.

PDC *See* Primary Domain Controller.

Peripheral Component Interconnect (PCI) A type of computer system bus that has relatively high access speeds and a minimum of 32-bit access to the system's memory and processor. Older forms of the bus provided a 33 MHz bus speed. A newer form of the PCI bus allows 64-bit data access and a 66 MHz bus speed, although the older 32-bit data path is normally used for compatibility purposes.

Personal Web Server (PWS) A less capable version of IIS that is designed to provided limited Web access on an intranet. PWS isn't designed to provide the same level of services as IIS, but it does provide enough capability for a small company intranet or for a developer's test setup.

PID *See* process identification number.

PMD *See* polarization modal dispersion.

Point-to-Point Tunneling Protocol (PPTP) A technology jointly created by Microsoft, US Robotics, and other members for the PPTP forum used to create VPNs. A VPN is a private network of computers that uses the

Internet to connect some nodes. PPTP incorporates various forms of security to ensure the data transmitted across the Internet (essentially an open network) remains secure. A VPN would allow a user to dial into the corporate network from home.

pointer 1. An arrow-shaped object used to show the currently selected menu item. **2.** An arrow-shaped graphic used to show the viewer which object a label identifies.

polarization modal dispersion (PMD) The amount of light dispersed from a light stream within a fiber-optic cable due to the effects of polarization. (Polarization is the same glare-reducing effect you get from sunglasses.)

POSIX A government-specified form of UNIX that's supposed to be portable across a variety of platforms. It appeared in 1988 as IEEE Standard 1003.1-1988.

PPTP *See* Point-to-Point Tunneling Protocol.

Primary Domain Controller (PDC) The Windows NT server responsible for tracking changes made to the domain accounts and storing them in the directory database. A domain has one PDC.

process identification number (PID) A numeric value associated with a process running on a specific machine. Every process has a unique PID, making it possible to locate a specific process, even if there are multiple copies of a single application running on the machine. PID is used by a wide variety of monitoring applications. It's also used to access an application or as a means of identification when terminating an errant application.

protection ring The Intel *x*86 series of processors use what's known as rings of protection to provide secure access to certain

processor activities. There are four rings, or levels, of protection supported by the processor. Two of these rings are used by Windows. The innermost ring, or ring 0, is known as kernel mode. This is the ring used by the operating system. The outermost ring, or ring 3, is known as user mode. This is where application code normally executes.

PWS *See* Personal Web Server.

Q

QoS *See* quality of service.

quality of service (QoS) A network bandwidth reservation policy that ensures an application receives a minimum level of network resources. In other words, the application might not receive anything more than it absolutely needs to run, but it receives at least this minimal amount of support. If the network can't reserve the requested amount of bandwidth, it denies the reservation and the application has to wait until more bandwidth becomes available or it lowers the amount of bandwidth requested.

queue Commonly, a programming construct used to hold data while it awaits processing. A queue uses a FIFO (first in/first out) storage technique. The first data element in is also the first data element that gets processed. Think of a queue as a line at the bank or grocery store and you have the right idea. There are also hardware queues, which emulate the processing capability of their software counterparts.

quorum log The log where the quorum resource stores configuration data. This log must be at least 5 MB in size; however, 500 MB is recommended. *See also* quorum resource.

quorum resource The resource that stores all cluster configuration information data.

This data enables network administrators to restore the cluster configuration in times of a disaster. *See also* quorum log.

R

RAID *See* redundant array of independent disks.

RAS *See* remote access server.

raw data Unprocessed data that's sent directly to an input/output device like a printer. Contrast this with cooked data, which is processed in some way before it's transferred. There are usually efficiency and quality tradeoffs when considering raw versus cooked data. Raw data requires fewer host machine resources and is therefore more efficient for the host machine; cooked data is more efficient for the input/output device to work with. The quality of cooked versus raw data depends a great deal on the capabilities of the host machine versus the input/output device.

redundant array of independent (or inexpensive) disks (RAID) A set of interconnected drives located outside the file server in most cases. There are several levels of RAID. Each level defines precisely how the data is placed on each of the drives. In every case, all the drives in a group share responsibility for storing the data. They act in parallel to both read and write the data. In addition, there's a special drive in most of these systems devoted to helping the network recover when one drive fails. In most cases, the user never even knows anything happened; the "spare drive" takes over for the failed drive without any noticeable degradation in network operation. RAID systems increase network reliability and throughput.

remote access server (RAS) An optional Windows service that allows users to call into the server from a remote location to access server resources. There are a variety of ways this service can be used, including as a callback mechanism.

remote procedure call (RPC) One of several methods for accessing data within another application. RPC is designed to look for the application first on the local workstation, and then across the network at the applications stored on other workstations. This is an advanced capability that will eventually pave the way for decentralized applications.

reparse points The method NTFS5 uses to associate file paths with an actual location. Each step of the directory path is individually parsed and, if necessary, redirected to another location. For example, if you had a path of C:\Windows\README.TXT, the path gets parsed once for C: and again for Windows. This capability will eventually allow for multiple drive links into one. You could connect to any drive on your machine using a single drive letter. This feature is also extensible. A developer can create customized reparse filters that adjust the way the file path gets parsed.

replication The process of copying Active Directory data between domain controllers. Active Directory services uses multimaster replication to replicate information within the domain; this is compared to Windows NT directory services, which uses master/slave replication. *See also* multimaster replication.

Resource Reservation Protocol (RSVP) A set of network rules that allows an application to request the resources it needs to run from the server in advance, which ensures that the network administrator can manage resource usage and that the operating system can plan for application needs. This is an especially important feature for resource-hungry applications like multimedia or voice over LAN.

router A device used to connect two LANs. The router moves signals from one LAN to the other.

RPC *See* remote procedure call.

RSVP *See* Resource Reservation Protocol.

S

SAN *See* storage area network.

SAS *See* storage area network attached storage.

SCSI *See* Small Computer System Interface.

SDRAM *See* Synchronous Dynamic Random Access Memory.

security identifier (SID) The part of a user's access token that identifies the user throughout the network—it's like having an account number. The user token the SID identifies tells what groups the user belongs to and what privileges the user has. Each group also has a SID so the user's SID contains references to the various group SIDs that he or she belongs to, not a complete set of group access rights. You normally use the User Manager utility under Windows NT to change the contents of this access token. You'll use the Active Directory Users and Computers console when working with Windows 2000.

semaphore The technique (actually a signaling device) used for controlling access to critical areas of code. A semaphore is a synchronization technique typically used to ensure that only one thread accesses critical code in a multithreaded environment. Semaphores are also commonly used to protect data. For example, a database manager might use a semaphore to protect the contents of a data structure.

Serial Presence Detect (SPD) This chip tells the motherboard what type of memory you have installed on your system and how to configure itself to use that memory. SPD always provides the system with the vendor's suggested memory configuration, rather than the maximum performance configuration that you might be able to use. Most BIOS configuration programs in use today provide an SPD position in the memory configuration area so you don't need to worry about the vagaries of memory-timing parameters. The SPD setting represents the safest way to configure your system's memory if the motherboard and memory you purchase both support this feature.

SID *See* security identifier.

site In terms of Active Directory services, a site is a well-connected (highly reliable and fast) TCP/IP subnet. Sites enable a network administrator to configure Active Directory access and replication for faster performance and increased reliability.

site link The network connection created between two sites for the purposes of replicating Active Directory information. This connection determines the performance of replication between the sites. The site link network administrators choose to go with depends on the "cost" value they are willing to handle as part of using that link. For example, a continental site link has a higher cost value than a LAN site link running within the same building.

Small Computer System Interface (SCSI) A computer interface that allows you to connect up to seven devices to the computer system. The current SCSI standard is SCSI-2.

Typical SCSI devices include tape drives, hard disk drives, and CD-ROM drives. SCSI devices typically provide high-transfer rates (10-15 MB/s) and access times (device type-dependent).

solid state drive (SSD) A hard drive created from memory instead of the more traditional mechanical method. SSDs use battery backup to ensure the data remains intact when the machine is turned off, but the data still can't be considered permanent in the same way data on a mechanical drive is permanent. The main reason to use an SSD is for high-speed data access and mechanical reliability. The lack of moving parts means SSDs have greater longevity than their mechanical counterpart.

SPD *See* Serial Presence Detect.

spinlock A methodology used by device drivers and other low-level operating system components to protect data from inadvertent change during a critical operation like an input from or output to a device. Using a spinlock requires special coding, and the developer needs to use them with care to avoid specific problems with the operating system.

SRAM *See* Static Random Access Memory.

SSD *See* solid state drive.

Static Random Access Memory (SRAM) One of several types of basic memory. SRAM uses transistors in place of capacitors to record data. The transistors don't need to be refreshed, making SRAM much faster than its DRAM counterpart. Because of the higher component count, however, SRAM tends to be bulkier and more expensive than DRAM.

storage area network (SAN) One of several methods used for network-specific storage because it offers several distinct advantages over the normal methods of storing data locally within the server. A SAN is a special form of LAN. It's a high-speed subnetwork that consists exclusively of storage devices. The goal is to take the hard drive out of the individual server, create a new entity out of the existing peripheral device, and make it accessible to multiple servers on the same network. The concept of a SAN has been around in mainframe systems for quite some time. The original mainframe version relies on a bus technology known as Enterprise System Connection (ESCON). ESCON allows the mainframe to dynamically connect to a variety of peripheral devices, including drive arrays and clusters. In fact, the DEC VMS network environment is based on a combination of SANs and clustered servers.

storage area network attached storage (SAS) One of several methods used to attach a SAN to the servers it supplies with disk resources. The SAN is directly attached to all the servers through a special bus. This bus is totally separate from the Ethernet or other common network bus used by the clients. A SAS consists of three major components: SAN interfaces, SAN interconnects, and SAN fabric. These three components might appear as separate elements, but are normally combined in some way. In all cases, data travels from the interface, to the interconnect, to the fabric, to the interconnect, and finally to the interface.

synchronization object There are two considerations for this term. Objects are simply instantiated components within the Windows environment. Each object has a life of its own. However, there are times when you want to allow the data within a group of objects to interact in such a way that the end result is a composite of the data contained within all the objects. For example, you might want to synchronize the data within the appointment, contact, e-mail, and task objects of a groupware package. In this case, you need to create a synchronization object in place of a standard object. The synchronization object differs from the standard object in one important way—it maintains a database of changes since the last synchronization. In this way, a synchronization object can compare the updates from a group of objects quickly, find conflicts, and then do something about those conflicts. There are also examples of operating system-specific synchronization objects like semaphores. A semaphore restricts access to shared resources to a predetermined number of threads. In short, it synchronizes data access within an application.

Synchronous Dynamic Random Access Memory (SDRAM) A type of memory that improves on the access speed of standard DRAM using specialized access methods. The assumption behind this technology is that applications seldom need to access a single bit of data. SDRAM is designed to deliver a minimum of 4 bits or 8 bits of data at a time. The secret to the speed of this DRAM is that RAM itself provides the address of the next bit of data to retrieve. In other words, RAM delivers data in bursts. The processor programs a burst length and burst type into SDRAM, and then allows RAM itself to deliver the requested data as quickly as possible. In most cases, the new memory architecture allows a burst mode operation of 100 MHz.

T

TAPI *See* Telephony Application Programming Interface.

TCP/IP (Transmission Control Protocol/Internet Protocol) A standard communication line protocol developed by the United States Department of Defense. The protocol defines how two devices communicate with each other. Think of the protocol as a type of language used by the two devices.

Telephony Application Programming Interface (TAPI) An interface used by applications to interface with various types of communication equipment. This currently includes both modems and fax devices.

thread One executable unit within an application. Running an application creates a main thread. One of the tasks the main thread normally does is display a window with a menu. The main thread can also create other threads. Background printing might appear as a thread, for example. Only 32-bit applications support multiple threads.

threshold A predetermined point within the range of operation for a device or piece of software. The threshold normally indicates the point at which the device is overwhelmed and requires correction. Of course, thresholds can indicate anything the person setting the threshold wants. For example, it could indicate the point at which the network administrator needs to add another server to a cluster to process user requests.

timer The Windows object responsible for coordinating events that rely on a time base. For example, an application could use a timer to keep a clock updated on the application's interface. There are a number of reasons to use timers, most of which have something to do with measuring time or performing tasks at a specific time or time interval.

Transmission Control Protocol/Internet Protocol *See* TCP/IP.

U

UDF *See* Universal Disk Format.

UMA *See* Unified Memory Architecture.

UNC *See* universal naming convention.

Unified Memory Architecture (UMA) The specifications that define a movement from the special memory setups previously used for the hard drive, display adapter, and processor to a combined memory setup. AGP is actually a form of UMA because it allows the display adapter to use main system memory to store certain graphics features like textures. A complete UMA solution most definitely decreases system costs because you're using main memory for everything. However, many analysts say UMA also decreases system performance by an order of magnitude because current memory architectures depend on sequential memory access to overcome the problems of DRAM latency. A UMA system completely randomizes memory access because main memory is now used for a variety of purposes.

Universal Disk Format (UDF) A method of accessing CD-ROM and DVD drives based on the International Standards Organization (ISO) 13346 standard. This file system replaces the older CDFS, which is based on ISO 9660. There are a lot of low-level differences between these two standards. However, from a user perspective, the difference is very easy to understand. UDF supports both CD-ROM drives and DVD-ROM drives. This additional support allows you to gain the advantages DVDs provide when it comes to choice of media and density of data storage.

universal naming convention (UNC) A method for identifying network resources without using specific locations. In most cases, this convention is used with drives and printers, but it can also be used with other types of resources. A UNC normally uses a device name in place of an identifier. For example, a disk drive on a remote machine might be referred to as \\AUX\DRIVE-C. The advantage of using UNC is that the resource name doesn't change, even if the user's drive mappings do.

user interface The portion of an expert system that lets the user and the expert system communicate with one another.

V

VDM *See* virtual DOS machine.

virtual DOS machine (VDM) Essentially a single copy of a DOS machine created in memory. This machine provides all the access features of the real thing, but it doesn't physically exist. Windows NT places each DOS application in its own VDM. The reason is simple. To provide the higher level of system reliability that Windows NT users demand, Microsoft had to make sure each application had its own environment completely separate from that used by every other application. It's also important to remember that 16-bit Windows applications share one VDM. You need to remember that Windows NT always starts a VDM, and then runs a copy of 16-bit Windows in it to service the needs of 16-bit Windows applications. This effectively adds two layers to every interaction—one for the VDM and another for the Win32 subsystem. As with everything else, this additional layering is transparent to the programmer. You still use the same interfaces as before.

virtual memory manager (VMM) The part responsible for creating and maintaining the swap file on disk. The swap file contains data that can no longer fit in memory and makes it appear you have more memory than physical memory supports. VMM also handles the actual task of swapping data between disk and physical memory as applications request specific data.

Virtual Private Network (VPN) A special setup that Windows 2000 and Windows 98 SE provide for allowing someone on the road to use the server at work. This is where the virtual part comes in; the connection isn't permanent—you're using it for a short time. The reason this connection has to be private is that you don't want anyone else to have access to your company's network. What you do is call into your ISP using dial-up networking. Now that you have access to the Internet, you can use dial-up networking to make a second connection to the server using PPTP. The setup is very secure because it actually uses two levels of data encryption: digital signing of packets and encrypted passwords.

VMM *See* virtual memory manager.

voice over Internet protocol (VOIP) A method of transmitting voice patterns over the Internet. This technique involves converting the
analog voice input into a digital signal, transferring it over the Internet, and then converting it back to an analog signal.
The quality of the transfer depends on the amount of bandwidth available to the transmitting applications.

VOIP *See* voice over Internet protocol.

VPN *See* Virtual Private Network.

W

WAN *See* wide area network.

WDM *See* Windows Driver Model.

wide area network (WAN) An extension of the LAN, a WAN connects two or more LANs using a variety of methods. A WAN usually encompasses more than one physical site, such as a building. Most WANs rely on microwave communications, fiber-optic connections, or leased telephone lines to provide the internetwork connections required to keep all nodes in the network communicating with each other.

Windows Driver Model (WDM) A new method of creating software interfaces to system hardware for Windows. In the past, Windows NT and Windows 9*x* used separate driver systems. WDM unites the two operating systems and allows both of them to use the same drivers.

Windows NT file system (NTFS) The method of formatting a hard disk drive used by Windows 2000 and Windows NT. While it provides significant speed advantages over other formatting techniques, only the Windows 2000 and Windows NT operating systems and applications designed to work with those operating systems can access a drive formatted using this technique. Windows 2000 uses NTFS5, a version of this file system designed to provide additional features, like enhanced security.

Index

Note to reader: *Italicized* page references refer to illustrations.

Z

John Mueller   John Mueller is a freelance author and technical editor who has produced 47 books and over 200 articles to date. The topics range from networking to artificial intelligence and from database management to heads-down programming. Some of his current books include a COM+ programmer's guide and a Windows user's guide. His technical editing skills have helped over 23 authors refine the content of their manuscripts. John has provided technical editing services to *Data Based Advisor* and *Coast Compute* magazines. A recognized authority on computer industry certifications, he's also contributed certification-related articles to magazines such as *Certified Professional Magazine*. When John isn't working at the computer, he's likely spending time in his workshop. He's an avid woodworker and candlemaker. One of his newest craft projects is glycerin soapmaking, which comes in pretty handy for gift baskets. You can reach John on the Internet at JMueller@mwt.net. John is also setting up a new Web site at *http://www.mwt.net/~jmueller/*; feel free to take a look and make suggestions on how he can improve it. One of his current projects is creating book FAQ sheets that will help readers find the book information they need much faster.

Irfan Chaudhry   For several years, Irfan Chaudhry has acted as a consultant for various sized businesses, including Fortune 500 companies and nationally recognized legal firms. He has worked on projects that include designing LAN/WAN environments as well as other migration projects involving NT, UNIX, and NetWare. He has worked on several Internet-based projects that include implementing e-Commerce Web sites and designing environments to run Web-based applications. Irfan has authored books and articles on Windows NT, NetWare, Internet Information Services, SQL Server 7.0, SQL Server 7.0 Programming, and Windows 2000. He works as a Windows NT platform architect for Dataloom, a Seattle-based company. If Irfan's not in front of a computer, he's probably at the Dojang training for his second degree black belt. He is always thankful to his loving wife, Noreen, for her consistent support.

The manuscript for this book was prepared and submitted to Microsoft Press in electronic form. Text files were prepared using Microsoft Word 2000 for Windows. Pages were composed by nSight, Inc., using Adobe Pagemaker 6.5 for Windows, with text in Garamond Light and display type in ITC Franklin Gothic. Composed pages were delivered to the printer as electronic prepress files.

Cover Designer:	Girvin|Branding & Design
Cover Illustrator:	Tom Draper
Interior Graphic Designer:	James D. Kramer
Layout Artist:	Joanna Zito
Project Manager:	Lisa A. Wehrle
Technical Editors:	Jack Beaudry, Robert Lyon, and Lynn Lunik
Copy Editor:	Bernadette Murphy Bentley
Proofreaders:	Renee Cote and Rebecca Merz
Indexer:	Jack Lewis

Ready solutions *for the* IT administrator

Keep your IT systems up and running with the ADMINISTRATOR'S COMPANION series from Microsoft. These expert guides serve as both tutorials and references for critical deployment and maintenance of Microsoft products and technologies. Packed with real-world expertise, hands-on numbered procedures, and handy workarounds, ADMINISTRATOR'S COMPANIONS deliver ready answers for on-the-job results.

Microsoft® Resource Kits— powerhouse resources to minimize costs while maximizing performance

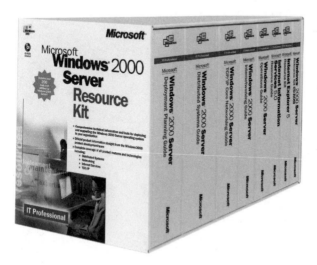

Microsoft® Windows® 2000 Server Resource Kit
ISBN 1-57231-805-8
U.S.A. $299.99
U.K. £189.99 [V.A.T. included]
Canada $460.99

Microsoft Windows 2000 Professional Resource Kit
ISBN 1-57231-808-2
U.S.A. $69.99
U.K. £45.99 [V.A.T. included]
Canada $107.99

Microsoft BackOffice® 4.5 Resource Kit
ISBN 0-7356-0583-1
U.S.A. $249.99
U.K. £161.99 [V.A.T. included]
Canada $374.99

Microsoft Internet Explorer 5 Resource Kit
ISBN 0-7356-0587-4
U.S.A. $59.99
U.K. £38.99 [V.A.T. included]
Canada $89.99

Microsoft Office 2000 Resource Kit
ISBN 0-7356-0555-6
U.S.A. $59.99
U.K. £38.99 [V.A.T. included]
Canada $89.99

Microsoft Windows NT® Server 4.0 Resource Kit
ISBN 1-57231-344-7
U.S.A. $149.95
U.K. £96.99 [V.A.T. included]
Canada $199.95

Microsoft Windows NT Workstation 4.0 Resource Kit
ISBN 1-57231-343-9
U.S.A. $69.95
U.K. £45.99 [V.A.T. included]
Canada $94.95

Deploy and support your enterprise business systems using the expertise and tools of those who know the technology best—the Microsoft product groups. Each RESOURCE KIT packs precise technical reference, installation and rollout tactics, planning guides, upgrade strategies, and essential utilities on CD-ROM. They're everything you need to help maximize system performance as you reduce ownership and support costs!

Microsoft Press® products are available worldwide wherever quality computer books are sold. For more information, contact your book or computer retailer, software reseller, or local Microsoft Sales Office, or visit our Web site at mspress.microsoft.com. To locate your nearest source for Microsoft Press products, or to order directly, call 1-800-MSPRESS in the U.S. (in Canada, call 1-800-268-2222).

Prices and availability dates are subject to change.

Microsoft®
mspress.microsoft.com

*For information about Microsoft Press®
products, visit our Web site at*
mspress.microsoft.com